✳

Philosophical and Religious Issues

Philosophical and Religious Issues

CLASSICAL AND CONTEMPORARY STATEMENTS

Ed. L. Miller

University of Colorado

Dickenson Publishing Company, Inc.
Encino, California and Belmont, California

FOR TERRY, TIM, AND TAD

❋ CONTENTS

�֍ PREFACE

It is sometimes observed these days that God is dead but theology is very much alive. I doubt very much that the former is true though I am certain the latter is.

It is difficult to say what accounts for the growing interest, among college students especially, in matters religious, theological, and philosophical. Perhaps the scientific outlook has come full circle, and the inevitable reaction has begun to take shape. No doubt it has something to do also with a growing disillusionment with the "establishment" religion and a turning to a more private, existential, and active form of belief and worship. It may be a product of the Bomb, the gloomy prospect of a world catastrophe. Certainly the moral ambiguities and crises among men and nations have suggested a reconsideration of ultimate values and meaning. All of these, plus a growing consciousness of the sufferings of man, seem to be calling our society to suspend its technological pursuits and to return to the pursuit of wisdom. The present volume has been designed for a concerned and cosmopolitan generation. It reflects traditional and contemporary approaches. The selections have been drawn not only from analytic philosophy but also existential philosophy. The reader will confront spokesmen not only for traditional theology but also radical theology. It is hoped, then, that the spectrum of positions contained in these pages is commensurate with the full spectrum of issues and alternatives confronted by a serious course in the philosophy of religion.

It is true that in some philosophical circles the existence of God, as a philosophical problem, is "out." On the other hand, we may wonder whether this question is as obsolete for most teachers and students as some professional philosophers would lead us to believe. Be that as it may, a whole section devoted to the theistic arguments and religious experience can be justified, I think, on the grounds that this problem remains one of the (if not *the*) most useful instruments for the introduction of important philosophical concepts, distinctions, and theories.

The three-part organization of the book provides for various possibilities, depending on the needs and the imagination of the teacher. The last part might be entirely deleted by the not so theologically inclined, though it is included because those approaches are becoming increasingly popular among students, and the distinction at that point between philosophy and theology is becoming harder to defend. Certain central figures (for example, Aquinas, Kant, Hume, and Tillich) will be found to recur in different contexts, thus establishing some measure of continuity and development. Further, it is often possible to "cross reference" whole sections as well as particular selections: The traditional speculative approaches to God may be seen as constituting the very thing that Barth rejects; both the existential and analytic selections provide backdrops for certain strains in the new theologies; one may want to consider, say, Hamilton's treatment of the death of God or Bultmann's demythologizing program in light of certain philosophical angles on religious language; the Stoic doctrine of the "goodness of the whole" may be used as a good historical example of the sort of position that Flew challenges as being vacuous; one might raise the question of how Bonhoeffer would respond to Otto's doctrine of an *a priori* religious "sense"; and so on. Though the selections have been chosen with a view toward representing the most important approaches, it is sometimes the case that an important document does not always "teach" well (professors will know what I mean) and thus the selections have been made in light of this criterion also.

The introductory notes at the beginning of each section pretend to be neither critical nor exhaustive, because I have operated on the principle that a teacher who opts for a book of readings is thereby evincing his interest in primary sources, as well as his ability to provide his own explanation and interpretation. Second, I have restated and considered most of these positions in my *God and Reason: A Historical Approach to Philosophical Theology* (New York: Macmillan, 1972) to which the reader may be referred for further discussion. The introductory comments aim only to draw a few important distinctions, to anticipate in outline what is fully disclosed in the selections, and to suggest an occasional question or problem. The selected bibliographies appended to the sections suggest ample material for further reading and research. These have been designed for a wide range of students and thus it may be necessary for the teacher to assist the student in the interpretation of the lists. Mention should be made of two standard secondary sources which may be consulted for discussion of most of the thinkers and positions represented in the present volume: F. C. Copleston, *A History of Philosophy* (Multi-volume) (Westminster, Md.: Newman Press, 1946–) and *The Encyclopedia of Philosophy* (eight vols.), ed. Paul Edwards (New York: Macmillan, 1967); each of the articles in the latter work also provides bibliographical information on the subject.

At the risk of intruding too presumptuously into the selections, I have added in brackets an occasional scripture reference (following the King James Version numbering of the Psalms), explanatory note, or documentation, when it seemed appropriate.

Ed. L. Miller
University of Colorado
Boulder, Colorado

✻ PART ONE

APPROACHES TO GOD

God and the Idea of God

✳ INTRODUCTION

According to St. Thomas Aquinas, the whole edifice of philosophical theology (knowledge of divine things arrived at philosophically, through natural reason) is built upon the question of God's existence, since theology has nothing to talk about—no subject matter—if there is no God: "If we do not demonstrate that God exists, all investigation of divine matters is impossible."[1] This, then, is the traditional starting place.

We must, however, distinguish between two very different approaches: the argumentative and the experiential, the approach that seeks to establish the existence of God on rational evidence and the approach that grounds the knowledge of God in religious experience of some kind or other. We will return later to the question of religious experience; for the moment let us focus our attention on what we may call the rational approach, that is, the approach of the traditional arguments.

Some of these arguments attempt to demonstrate the existence of God without any appeal to the world of nature. These are usually called the *a priori* arguments because they are thought to deduce God's existence independently of, or prior to, experience. No doubt the best example of this kind of theistic argument is the Ontological Argument which claims to prove through a consideration of the mere idea of God that God himself actually exists. This argument was first formulated by St. Anselm, an eleventh-century Christian Platonist, and later restated by the French thinker René Descartes.

In both Anselm and Descartes, the main trust of the argument is the same. All of us—even the atheist—understand the idea of God, otherwise we could never say (at least not with any meaning), "God this," or "God that," or even "God does not exist." But what do we mean by the concept or idea or word "God"? Most of us mean, according to Anselm's formula, "that than which no greater can be conceived," or, to use Descartes' formula, "the most perfect being." (Of course, it is this idea or concept that is important, not the word "God.") Having settled that we do possess the idea of God and that it is not a meaningless one, the problem is whether God, or "that than which no greater can be conceived," or "the most perfect being," exists only in our minds or in reality as well. Anselm answers that the greatest conceivable being must exist outside our minds, that is, in reality, otherwise one could conceive of something still greater. Descartes say that if God does not exist in reality, then the most perfect being would be lacking the perfection of existence and would therefore not be the most perfect being. From either

---

[1]St. Thomas Aquinas, *Summa Contra Gentiles*, I, 9 (my translation).

expression it is supposed to follow that it is self-contradictory to deny the existence of God. It is clear, says Anselm, why the Scriptures call the atheist "a fool" (Ps. 14:1): When the atheist says "God does not exist," he is saying something absurd, that is, something that implies a contradiction.

Some readers will not be able to resist the temptation of accusing Anselm and Decartes either of playing a verbal game or being very naive. It is, however, easier to engage in such accusations than it is to identify precisely what, if anything, is fallacious about their reasoning. Indeed, this argument has been debated for centuries, beginning with the monk Gaunilon (Anselm's contemporary) who first raised what is surely the most obvious objection: If we can move immediately from the mere idea of God to his actual existence, we should be able also to move from the idea of a lost desert island to its real existence, which is fantastic. But Anselm's rebuttal was ready at hand: Only in the one case of God can we make the move from the idea of the thing to the necessity of its real existence; it is true only of the greatest conceivable being or sum of all perfections (which is hardly what we mean by "lost desert island," even a perfect one) that it *must* possess the attribute of existence.

It might be, then, that Gaunilon is an example of a critic whose understanding of the argument is exceeded by his rush to attack it. Or is he? In some ways even contemporary critiques continue to bear the stamp of Gaunilon's original. Be that as it may, in the next section we will see St. Thomas Aquinas shifting the ground entirely and challenging the very conception of knowledge and reality that the argument assumes, suggesting that arguments such as Anselm's raise, in turn, the most fundamental issues in philosophy.

With the selection from Immanuel Kant we are led to the objection that has been posed by most modern critics. Descartes (and possibly Anselm) had construed existence as an attribute, defining property, or predicate of God; his argument is successful only if one is willing to agree that God possesses existence in the same way as he possesses omnipotence, benevolence, justice, and so forth. But Kant observed that though existence functions grammatically as a predicate, it does not function logically as a predicate, an insight that has generated a great deal of continuing philosophical interest. To see that Kant's point is a worthy one, we have only to see that nothing is altered in the concept of a thing when the "attribute" of existence is added. As Kant says, a hundred existing dollars involves not a cent more than a hundred imaginary dollars, and, we might add, an existing unicorn does not look any different from a non-existing one. To state this in a more recent way: In the statement "x exists," "exists" looks indeed like a predicate but in fact predicates nothing of x; its functions is, rather, to assert that there are instantiations—existing instances—of x; that is, that there are things in the world that possess the attributes entailed by the concept x. Similarly, in the statement "God exists," nothing is being affirmed about the *nature* of God. What is affirmed is the *instantiation* of that nature, something that could (at least logically) be denied as well.

There is another, related side to Kant's critique. Descartes, for example,

had said that God's existence follows from his nature in the same way that
the equality of its three angles to two right angles follows necessarily from
the nature or essence of a triangle. But Kant observes that the necessity of
the statement "A triangle's three angles are equal to two right angles" lies
in its *analyticity*, that is, in the fact that the predicate of the statement ("equal
to two right angles") is already contained in the subject ("a triangle's three
angles"). Such statements (called analytic statements or tautologies) cannot
be denied without self-contradiction. But while their truth is logically necessary, it is also purely hypothetical: No statement of the form "*A* is *A*" can
ever affirm that *A* exists, but only that if *A* exists then it is *A*. Likewise
in the case of "God exists." If God's existence is analytically contained in
the concept of God, then it is a logically necessary truth but of no interest
to those who want to know about his actual existence.

Norman Malcolm at once returns us to Anselm and provides us with
a contemporary restatement of the Ontological Argument. It is largely to
Malcolm's credit that two different arguments in Anselm have been distinguished and brought to light. And though he rejects the argument presented
by Anselm in *Proslogium*, Chapter 2, he finds the argument of *Proslogium*,
Chapter 3 (which contains the same reasoning as in Anselm's reply to Gaunilon) to be valid. The essential difference between the two arguments is the
difference between arguing that God must exist because existence is better
than non-existence, and arguing that God must exist because by his very
conception he cannot not-exist. In the former reasoning, existence is construed
as a perfection or predicate to be attributed to God, and this construction
Malcolm rejects for the same reasons that Kant did, namely, because existence
is not a predicate. But in Anselm's second argument, what is predicated of
God is not existence but *necessary* existence, and Malcolm believes that necessary existence may indeed be taken as an attribute of God in a way that
escapes the Kantian-type criticisms, and he proceeds to formulate his own
version of the Ontological Argument after the example of *Proslogium*, Chapter
3. Malcolm's argument is succinctly summarized near the end of Part II, and
the reader will do well to understand the concepts and movement of that
passage, and to identify the mistake in the reasoning—if there is one.

Aside from the intrinsic interest of Malcolm's article, it serves to
illuminate further the Kantian criticisms and other moves pertaining to the
Ontological Argument. It also reflects certain contemporary and recurring ideas
concerning philosophical language, for example the distinction between "necessary" and "contingent" propositions, and the thesis (which Malcolm does
not share) that no "existential proposition" (a proposition that affirms the
existence of something) can be necessary. Also of interest is Malcolm's review
and rejection of J. N. Findlay's ontological *dis*proof of God.

Malcolm's restatement of the Ontological Argument should be, perhaps, an example to those who may tend to bury rational theism before it
is dead. Not that Malcolm's has been the last word on the subject. His article
generated a whole new discussion (as he himself indicates in his closing foot-

note), making the Ontological Argument a continuing object of philosophical fascination.

✳ ST. ANSELM

1. Why the Atheist Is a Fool

St. Anselm (1033–1109) was a Benedictine monk and later the Archbishop of Canterbury. He was the first to formulate the Ontological Argument and had to defend his new argument against his fellow monk and critic Gaunilon. Anselm's works include the *Monologium* and *Cur Deus Homo* ("Why God became Man"), in which he attempted to demonstrate philosophically the Trinity and the Incarnation and Atonement of Christ.

From St. Anselm's *Proslogium*

CHAPTER 1: EXHORTATION OF THE MIND TO THE CONTEMPLATION OF GOD

. . . Be it mine to look up to thy light, even from afar, even from the depths. Teach me to seek thee, and reveal thyself to me, when I seek thee, for I cannot seek thee, except thou teach me, nor find thee, except thou reveal thyself. Let me seek thee in longing, let me long for thee in seeking; let me find thee in love, and love thee in finding. Lord, I acknowledge and I thank thee that thou has created me in this thine image, in order that I may be mindful of thee, may conceive of thee, and love thee; but that image has been so consumed and wasted away by vices, and obscured by the smoke of wrong-doing, that it cannot achieve that for which it was made, except thou renew it, and create it anew. I do not endeavor, O Lord, to penetrate thy sublimity, for in no wise do I compare my understanding with that; but I long to understand in some degree thy truth, which my heart believes and loves. For I do not seek to understand that I may believe, but I believe in order to understand. For this also I believe, —that unless I believed, I shall not understand.

CHAPTER 2: TRULY THERE IS A GOD, ALTHOUGH THE FOOL HATH SAID IN HIS HEART, THERE IS NO GOD

And so, Lord, do thou, who dost give understanding to faith, give me, so far as thou knowest it to be profitable, to understand that thou art as we believe; and that thou art that which we believe. And, indeed, we

St. Anselm, *Proslogium*, in *St. Anselm: Basic Writings*, tr. S. N. Deane, second ed. (La Salle, Ill.: Open Court, 1966). Reprinted by permission of The Open Court Publishing Company, La Salle, Illinois.

believe that thou art a being than which nothing greater can be conceived. Or is there no such nature, since the fool hath said in his heart, there is no God? [Ps. 14:1]. But, at any rate, this very fool, when he hears of this being of which I speak—a being than which nothing greater can be conceived—understands what he hears, and what he understands is in his understanding; although he does not understand it to exist.

For, it is one thing for an object to be in the understanding, and another to understand that the object exists. When a painter first conceives of what he will afterwards perform, he has it in his understanding, but he does not yet understand it to be, because he has not yet performed it. But after he has made the painting, he both has it in his understanding, and he understand that it exists, because he has made it.

Hence, even the fool is convinced that something exists in the understanding, at least, than which nothing greater can be conceived. For, when he hears of this, he understands it. And whatever is understood, exists in the understanding. And assuredly that, than which nothing greater can be conceived, cannot exist in the understanding alone. For, suppose it exists in the understanding alone: then it can be conceived to exist in reality; which is greater.

Therefore, if that, than which nothing greater can be conceived, exists in the understanding alone, the very being, than which nothing greater can be conceived, is one, than which a greater can be conceived. But obviously this is impossible. Hence, there is no doubt that there exists a being, than which nothing greater can be conceived, and it exists both in the understanding and in reality.

Chapter 3: God Cannot Be Conceived Not to Exist

And it assuredly exists so truly, that it cannot be conceived not to exist. For, it is possible to conceive of a being which cannot be conceived not to exist; and this is greater than one which can be conceived not to exist. Hence, if that, than which nothing greater can be conceived, can be conceived not to exist, it is not that, than which nothing greater can be conceived. But this in an irreconcilable contradiction. There is, then, so truly a being than which nothing greater can be conceived to exist, that it cannot even be conceived not to exist; and this being thou art, O Lord, our God.

So truly, therefore, dost thou exist, O Lord, my God, that thou canst not be conceived not to exist; and rightly. For, if a mind could conceive of a being better than thee, the creature would rise above the Creator; and this is most absurd. And, indeed, whatever else there is, except thee alone, can be conceived not to exist. To thee alone, therefore, it belongs to exist more truly than all other beings, and hence in a higher degree than all others. For, whatever else exists does not exist so truly, and hence in a less degree it belongs to it to exist. Why, then, has the fool said in his heart, there is no God, since it is so evident, to a rational mind, that thou dost exist in the highest degree of all? Why, except that he is dull and a fool?

Chapter 4: How the Fool Has Said in His Heart What Cannot Be Conceived

But how has the fool said in his heart what he could not conceive; or how is it that he could not conceive what he said in his heart? since it is the same to say in the heart, and to conceive.

But, if really, nay, since really, he both conceived, because he said in his heart; and did not say in his heart, because he could not conceive; there is more than one way in which a thing is said in the heart or conceived. For, in one sense, an object is conceived, when the word signifying it is conceived; and in another, when the very entity, which the object is, is understood.

In the former sense, then, God can be conceived not to exist; but in the latter, not at all. For no one who understands what fire and water are can conceive fire to be water, in accordance with the nature of the facts themselves, although this is possible according to the words. So, then, no one who understands what God is can conceive that God does not exist; although he says these words in his heart, either without any, or with some foreign, signification. For, God is that than which a greater cannot be conceived. And he who thoroughly understands this, assuredly understands that this being so truly exists, that not even in concept can it be non-existent. Therefore, he who understands that God so exists, cannot conceive that he does not exist.

I thank thee, gracious Lord, I thank thee; because what I formerly believed by thy bounty, I now so understand by thine illumination, that if I were unwilling to believe that thou dost exist, I should not be able to understand this to be true.

From Gaunilon's *In Behalf of the Fool*

5. . . . if it should be said that a being which cannot be even conceived in terms of any fact, is in the understanding, I do not deny that this being is, accordingly, in my understanding. But since through this fact it can in no wise attain to real existence also, I do not yet concede to it that existence at all, until some certain proof of it shall be given.

For he who says that this being exists, because otherwise the being which is greater than all will not be greater than all, does not attend strictly enough to what he is saying. For I do not yet say, no, I even deny or doubt that this being is greater than any real object. Nor do I concede to it any other existence than this (if it should be called existence) which it has when the mind, according to a word merely heard, tries to form the image of an object absolutely unknown to it.

Gaunilon, *In Behalf of the Fool*, in *St. Anselm: Basic Writings*, tr. S. N. Deane, second ed. (La Salle, Ill.: Open Court, 1966). Reprinted by permission of The Open Court Publishing Company, La Salle, Illinois.

How, then, is the veritable existence of that being proved to me from the assumption, by hypothesis, that it is greater than all other things? For I should still deny this, or doubt your demonstration of it, to this extent, that I should not admit that this being is in my understanding and concept even in the way in which many objects whose real existence is uncertain and doubtful, are in my understanding and concept. For it should be proved first that this being itself really exists somewhere; and then, from the fact that it is greater than all, we shall not hesitate to infer that it also subsists in itself.

6. For example: it is said that somewhere in the ocean is an island, which, because of the difficulty, or rather the impossibility, of discovering what does not exist, is called the lost island. And they say that this island has an inestimable wealth of all manner of riches and delicacies in greater abundance than is told of the Islands of the Blest; and that having no owner or inhabitant, it is more excellent than all other countries, which are inhabited by mankind, in the abundance with which it is stored.

Now if some one should tell me that there is such an island, I should easily understand his words, in which there is no difficulty. But suppose that he went on to say, as if by a logical inference: "You can no longer doubt that this island which is more excellent than all lands exists somewhere, since you have no doubt that it is in your understanding. And since it is more excellent not to be in the understanding alone, but to exist both in the understanding and in reality, for this reason it must exist. For if it does not exist, any land which really exists will be more excellent than it; and so the island already understood by you to be more excellent will not be more excellent."

If a man should try to prove to me by such reasoning that this island truly exists, and that its existence should no longer be doubted, either I should believe that he was jesting, or I know not which I ought to regard as the greater fool: myself, supposing that I should allow this proof; or him, if he should suppose that he had established with any certainty the existence of this island. For he ought to show first that the hypothetical excellence of this island exists as a real and indubitable fact, and in no wise as any unreal object, or one whose existence is uncertain, in my understanding.

From St. Anselm's *Apologetic*

CHAPTER 2: IT IS SHOWN THAT A BEING THAN WHICH A GREATER IS INCONCEIVABLE CAN BE CONCEIVED, AND ALSO, IN SO FAR EXISTS

I have said, then, in the argument which you dispute, that when the fool hears mentioned a being than which a greater is inconceivable, he understands what he hears. Certainly a man who does not understand when a familiar language is spoken, has no understanding at all, or a very dull one.

St. Anselm, *Apologetic*, in *St. Anselm: Basic Writings*, tr. S. N. Deane, second ed. (La Salle, Ill.: Open Court, 1966). Reprinted by permission of The Open Court Publishing Company, La Salle, Illinois.

Moreover, I have said that if this being is understood, it is in the understanding. Is that in no understanding which has been proved necessarily to exist in the reality of fact?

But you will say that although it is in the understanding, it does not follow that it is understood. But observe that the fact of its being understood does necessitate its being in the understanding. For as what is conceived, is conceived by conception, and what is conceived by conception, as it is conceived, so is in conception; so what is understood, is understood by understanding, and what is understood by understanding, as it is understood, so is in the understanding. What can be more clear than this?

After this, I have said that if it is even in the understanding alone, it can be conceived also to exist in reality, which is greater. If, then, it is in the understanding alone, obviously the very being than which a greater cannot be conceived is one than which a greater can be conceived. What is more logical? For if it exists even in the understanding alone, can it not be conceived also to exist in reality? And if it can be so conceived, does not he who conceives of this conceive of a thing greater than that being, if it exists in the understanding alone? What more consistent inference, then, can be made than this: that if a being than which a greater cannot be conceived is in the understanding alone, it is not that than which a greater cannot be conceived?

But, assuredly, in no understanding is a being than which a greater is conceivable a being than which a greater is inconceivable. Does it not follow, then, that if a being than which a greater cannot be conceived is in any understanding, it does not exist in the understanding alone? For if it is in the understanding alone, it is a being than which a greater can be conceived, which is inconsistent with the hypothesis.

CHAPTER 3: A CRITICISM OF GAUNILON'S EXAMPLE, IN WHICH HE TRIES TO SHOW THAT IN THIS WAY THE REAL EXISTENCE OF A LOST ISLAND MIGHT BE INFERRED FROM THE FACT OF ITS BEING CONCEIVED

But, you say, it is as if one should suppose an island in the ocean, which surpasses all islands in its fertility, and which, because of the difficulty, or rather the impossibility, of discovering what does not exist, is called a lost island; and should say that there can be no doubt that this island truly exists in reality, for this reason, that one who hears it described easily understands what he hears.

Now I promise confidently that if any man shall devise anything existing either in reality or in concept alone (except that than which a greater cannot be conceived) to which he can adapt the sequence of my reasoning, I will discover that thing, and will give him his lost island, not to be lost again.

But it now appears that this being than which a greater is inconceivable cannot be conceived not to be, because it exists on so assured a ground of truth; for otherwise it would not exist at all.

Hence, if any one says that he conceives this being not to exist, I say that at the time when he conceives of this either he conceives of a being than which a greater is inconceivable, or he does not conceive at all. If he does not conceive, he does not conceive of the non-existence of that of which he does not conceive. But if he does conceive, he certainly conceives of a being which cannot be even conceived not to exist. For if it could be conceived not to exist, it could be conceived to have a beginning and an end. But this is impossible.

He, then, who conceives of this being conceives of a being which cannot be even conceived not to exist; but he who conceives of this being does not conceive that it does not exist; else he conceives what is inconceivable. The non-existence, then, of that than which a greater cannot be conceived is inconceivable.

❋ RENÉ DESCARTES

2. *The Cartesian Version*

Though René Descartes (1596–1650) was educated at a Jesuit college, he renounced traditional philosophy and developed a new one, a "geometrical" one, deducing every truth, ultimately, from his fundamental certainty: *Cogito ergo sum*, "I think, therefore I am." The Cartesian mind-matter dualism proved to be the point of departure for many modern thinkers, making Descartes, as he is often called, the father of modern philosophy. His philosophical works include *Discourse on Method, Meditations*, and *Rules for the Direction of the Mind*.

From *Meditations*

FIFTH MEDIATION: OF THE ESSENCE OF MATERIAL THINGS AND, ONCE MORE, OF GOD: THAT HE EXISTS

There are many other questions for me to inquire into concerning the attributes of God and concerning my own nature, or the nature of my mind. I may, perhaps, pursue this investigation some other time; for the present, having noticed what must be done or avoided in order to arrive at the knowledge of the truth, my principal task is to attempt to escape from and relieve myself of all the doubts into which I have fallen in these last few days, and to see if we cannot know anything certain about material objects. But before examining whether such objects exist outside of myself, I must consider the concepts of these objects, in so far as they occur in my thought, and see which of them are distinct and which of them are confused.

René Descartes, *Discourse on Method and Meditations*, tr. Laurence J. Lafleur (Indianapolis, Ind.: Library of Liberal Arts, 1960). Copyright © 1960 by The Liberal Arts Press, Inc., reprinted by permission of the Liberal Arts Press Division of the Bobbs-Merrill Company, Inc.

In the first place, I picture distinctly that quality which philosophers commonly call the "continuum," or extension in length, width, and depth which exists in this quantity, or rather in the body to which we attribute it. Furthermore, I can distinguish in it various different parts and attribute to each of these parts all sorts of sizes, shapes, positions, and movements; and, finally, I can assign to each of these movements all degrees of duration.

And I not only know these things distinctly when I consider them thus in general, but also, however little I am applying my attention to it, I come to recognize an infinity of details concerning numbers, shapes, movements, and other similar things, the truth of which makes itself so apparent and accords so well with my nature that when I discover them for the first time it does not seem to me as though I were learning anything new, but rather as though I were remembering what I had previously known—that is, that I am perceiving things which were already in my mind, even though I had not yet focussed any attention upon them.

And what I believe to be more important here is that I find in myself an infinity of ideas of certain things which cannot be assumed to be pure nothingness, even though they may perhaps have no existence outside of my thought. These things are no figments of my imagination, even though it is within my power to think of them or not to think of them; on the contrary, they have their own true and immutable natures. Thus, for example, when I imagine a triangle, even though there may perhaps be no such figure anywhere in the world outside of my thought, nor ever have been, nevertheless the figure cannot help having a certain determinate nature, or form, or essence, which is immutable and eternal, which I have not invented and which does not in any way depend upon my mind. This is evidenced by the fact that we can demonstrate various properties of this triangle, namely, that its three angles are equal to two right angles, that the greatest angle subtends the longest side, and other similar properties. Whether I wish it or not, I now recognize very clearly and evidently that these are properties of the triangle, even though I had never previously thought of them in any way when I first imagined one. And therefore it cannot be said that I have imagined or invented them.

Nor can I raise the objection here that possibly this idea of the triangle came to my mind from external things through the medium of my senses, since I have sometimes seen triangularly shaped objects; for I can picture in my mind an infinity of other shapes such that I cannot have the least suspicion that they have ever been present to my senses, and I am still no less able to demonstrate various properties about their nature than I am about that of the triangle. These properties, certainly, must be wholly true, since I conceive them clearly. And thus they are something, and not pure negation, since it is quite evident that everything which is true is something, as truth is the same as being. I have already amply demonstrated that everything that I recognize clearly and distinctly is true; and even if I had not demonstrated this, the nature of my mind is such that I can nevertheless not help believing things to be true while I am conceiving them clearly and distinctly.

And I recollect that even when I was still strongly attached to the objects of sense, I numbered among the most constant truths that which I conceived clearly and distinctly about the shapes, numbers, and other properties which belong to the fields of arithmetic and geometry or, in general, to pure and abstract mathematics.

Now, if from the very fact that I can derive from my thoughts the idea of something, it follows that all that I clearly and distinctly recognize as characteristic of this thing does in reality characterize it, can I not derive from this an argument which will demonstratively prove the existence of God? It is certain that I find in my mind the idea of God, of a supremely perfect Being, no less than that of any shape or number whatsoever; and I recognize that an actual and eternal existence belongs to his nature no less clearly and distinctly than I recognize that all I can demonstrate about some figure or number actually belongs to the nature of that figure or number. Thus, even if everything that I concluded in the preceding Meditations were by chance not true, the existence of God should pass in my mind as at least as certain as I have hitherto considered all the truths of mathematics, which deal only with numbers and figures.

And this is true even though I must admit that it does not at first appear entirely obvious, but seems to have some appearance of sophistry. For since in all other matters I have become accustomed to make a distinction between existence and essence, I am easily convinced that the existence of God can be separated from his essence, and that thus I can conceive of God as not actually existing. Nevertheless, when I consider this with more attention, I feel it manifest that we can no more separate the existence of God from his essence than we can separate from the essence of a rectilinear triangle the fact that the size of its three angles equals two right angles, or from the idea of a mountain the idea of a valley. Thus it is no less self-contradictory to conceive of a God, a supremely perfect Being, who lacks existence—that is, who lacks some perfection—than it is to conceive of a mountain for which there is no valley.

But even though in fact I cannot conceive of a God without existence, any more than of a mountain without a valley, nevertheless, just as from the mere fact that I conceive a mountain with a valley, it does not follow that any mountain exists in the world, so likewise, though I conceive of God as existing, it does not seem to follow for this reason that God exists. For my thought does not impose any necessity upon things; and just as I can at my pleasure imagine a winged horse, even though no horse has wings, so I could perhaps attribute existence to God, even though no God existed.

This is far from the truth; it is here that there is sophistry hidden under the guise of a valid objection. For from the fact that I cannot conceive a mountain without a valley it does not follow that there is a mountain or a valley anywhere in the world, but only that the mountain and the valley, whether they exist or not, are inseparable from each other. From the fact alone that I cannot conceive God except as existing, it follows that existence is inseparable from him, and consequently that he does, in truth, exist. Not that my thought can bring about this result or that it imposes any necessity upon things; on the contrary, the necessity which is in the thing itself—that is, the necessity of the existence of God—determines me to have this thought. For it is not in my power to conceive of a God without existence—that is to say, of a supremely perfect Being without a supreme prefection—as it is in my power to imagine a horse either with or without wings.

And it must not be said here that it is only necessary that I admit that God exists after I have supposed that he possesses all sorts of perfections, since existence is one of them, but that my first supposition was not really necessary. Thus it is not necessary to think that all four-sided figures can be inscribed in a circle; but if we suppose that I do have this idea, I am forced to admit that a rhombus can be inscribed in one, since it is a four-sided figure, and by this I will be forced to admit what is clearly false. We must not, I say, argue thus; for even though it is not necessary that I should ever have any thought about God, nevertheless, whenever I do choose to think of a first and supreme being and to derive, so to speak, the idea of God from the treasure house of my mind, it is necessary that I attribute to him all kinds of perfections, even though it does not occur to me to mention them all and to pay attention to each one of them severally. And this necessity is enough to bring it about that afterward, as soon as I come to recognize that existence is a perfection, I conclude very properly that this first and supreme Being truly exists; just as it is not necessary that I should ever imagine any triangle, but every time that I wish to consider a rectilinear figure containing three angles only, it is absolutely necessary that I attribute to it everything that leads to the conclusion that these three angles are not greater than two right angles, even if perhaps I do not then consider this matter in particular. But when I wish to determine what figures can be inscribed in a circle, it is in no way necessary that I think that all four-sided figures are of this number; on the contrary, I cannot even pretend that this is the case as long as I do not wish to accept anything but what I can conceive clearly and distinctly. Consequently, there is a vast difference between false suppositions, such as this one, and the true ideas which are inborn in me, of which the first and chief one is that of God. For actually I have several reasons for recognizing that this idea is not something imaginary or fictitious, depending only on my thought, but that it is the image of a true and immutable nature. The first reason is that I cannot conceive anything but God alone, to whose essence existence belongs with necessity. Another reason is that it is not possible for me to conceive in the same way two or more gods such as he. Again, assuming that there is now a God who exists, I see clearly that he must have existed before from all eternity and that he should be eternally in the future. And a final reason is that I conceive various other qualities in God, of which I can neither diminish nor change a particle.

For the rest, whatever proof or argument I use, I must always come back to this conclusion: that it is only the things that I conceive clearly and distinctly which have the power to convince me completely. And although among the things which I conceive in this way there are, in truth, some which are obviously known to everyone, while others of them only become known to those who consider them more closely and examine them more carefully, nevertheless, after they have once been discovered, none of them can be esteemed less certain than the rest. Thus, for example, in every right-angled triangle, even though it is not so readily apparent that the square of the hypotenuse is equal to the squares of the other two sides as it is that this hypotenuse is opposite the greatest angle, nevertheless, after this fact has once been recognized, we are as much convinced of the truth of the one proposition as of the other. And as for the question of God, certainly, if my mind were not prejudiced and if my thought were not distracted by the constant presence on all sides of images of sensible objects, there would be nothing that I would recognize sooner or more easily than God. For is there anything clearer and more obvious in itself than to think that there is a God, that is to say, a supreme and perfect Being, in whom uniquely necessary or eternal existence is included in essence and who consequently exists? . . .

�֍ IMMANUEL KANT

3. *Is Existence a Predicate?*

The German thinker Immanuel Kant (1724–1804) rejected the theoretical approach of speculative philosophy and sought, rather, to ground our knowledge of God, freedom, and immortality in the practical evidence of moral experience. Kant's *Critique of Pure Reason* marks a turning point in the history of philosophy, and his *Critique of Practical Reason* and *Religion Within the Bounds of Reason Alone* make a positive contribution to theology.

From *Critique of Pure Reason*

Transcendental Dialectic, Chapter 3

Section 4: The Impossibility of an Ontological Proof of the Existence of God

It is evident, from what has been said, that the concept of an absolutely necessary being is a concept of pure reason, that is, a mere idea the objective reality of which is very far from being proved by the fact that reason requires it. For the idea instructs us only in regard to a certain unattainable completeness, and so serves rather to limit the understanding than to extend it to new objects. But we are here faced by what is indeed strange and perplexing, namely, that while the inference from a given existence in general to some absolutely necessary being seems to be both imperative and legitimate, all those conditions under which alone the understanding can form a concept of such a necessity are so many obstacles in the way of our doing so.

Immanuel Kant, *Critique of Pure Reason*, tr. Norman Kemp Smith (London: Macmillan, 1929). Reprinted by permission of St. Martin's Press, The Macmillan Company of Canada, and Macmillan & Company, Ltd.

In all ages men have spoken of an *absolutely necessary* being, and in so doing have endeavoured, not so much to understand whether and how a thing of this kind allows even of being thought, but rather to prove its existence. There is, of course, no difficulty in giving a verbal definition of the concept, namely, that it is something the non-existence of which is impossible. But this yields no insight into the conditions which make it necessary to regard the non-existence of a thing as absolutely unthinkable. It is precisely these conditions that we desire to know, in order that we may determine whether or not, in resorting to this concept, we are thinking anything at all. The expedient of removing all those conditions which the understanding indispensably requires in order to regard something as necessary, simply through the introduction of the word *unconditioned*, is very far from sufficing to show whether I am still thinking anything in the concept of the unconditionally necessary, or perhaps rather nothing at all.

Nay more, this concept, at first ventured upon blindly, and now become so completely familiar, has been supposed to have its meaning exhibited in a number of examples; and on this account all further enquiry into its intelligibility has seemed to be quite needless. Thus the fact that every geometrical proposition, as, for instance, that a triangle has three angles, is absolutely necessary, has been taken as justifying us in speaking of an object which lies entirely outside the sphere of our understanding as if we understood perfectly what it is that we intend to convey by the concept of that object.

All the alleged examples are, without exception, taken from *judgments*, not from *things* and their existence. But the unconditioned necessity of judgments is not the same as an absolute necessity of things. The absolute necessity of the judgment is only a conditioned necessity of the thing, or of the predicate in the judgment. The above proposition does not declare that three angles are absolutely necessary, but that, under the condition that there is a triangle (that is, that a triangle is given), three angles will necessarily be found in it. So great, indeed, is the deluding influence exercised by this logical necessity that, by the simple device of forming an *a priori* concept of a thing in such a manner as to include existence within the scope of its meaning, we have supposed ourselves to have justified the conclusion that because existence necessarily belongs to the object of this concept—always under the condition that we posit the thing as given (as existing)—we are also of necessity, in accordance with the law of identity, required to posit the existence of its object, and that this being is therefore itself absolutely necessary—and this, to repeat, for the reason that the existence of this being has already been thought in a concept which is assumed arbitrarily and on condition that we posit its object.

If, in an identical proposition, I reject the predicate while retaining the subject, contradiction results; and I therefore say that the former belongs necessarily to the latter. But if we reject subject and predicate alike, there is no contradiction; for nothing is then left that can be contradicted. To posit a triangle, and yet to reject its three angles, is self-contradictory; but there is no contradiction in rejecting the triangle together with its three angles.

The same holds true of the concept of an absolutely necessary being. If its existence is rejected, we reject the thing itself with all its predicates; and no question of contradiction can then arise. There is nothing outside it that would then be contradicted, since the necessity of the thing is not supposed to be derived from anything external; nor is there anything internal that would be contradicted, since in rejecting the thing itself we have at the same time rejected all its internal properties. 'God is omnipotent' is a necessary judgment. The omnipotence cannot be rejected if we posit a Deity, that is, an infinite being; for the two concepts are identical. But if we say, 'There is no God,' neither the omnipotence nor any other of its predicates is given; they are one and all rejected together with the subject, and there is therefore not the least contradiction in such a judgment.

We have thus seen that if the predicate of a judgment is rejected together with the subject, no internal contradiction can result, and that this holds no matter what the predicate may be. The only way of evading this conclusion is to argue that there are subjects which cannot be removed, and must always remain. That, however, would only be another way of saying that there are absolutely necessary subjects; and that is the very assumption which I have called in question, and the possibility of which the above argument professes to establish. For I cannot form the least concept of a thing which, should it be rejected with all its predicates, leaves behind a contradiction; and in the absence of contradiction I have, through pure *a priori* concepts alone, no criterion of impossibility.

Notwithstanding all these general considerations, in which every one must concur, we may be challenged with a case which is brought forward as proof that in actual fact the contrary holds, namely, that there is one concept, and indeed only one, in reference to which the not-being or rejection of its object is in itself contradictory, namely, the concept of the *ens realissimum*.[1] It is declared that it possesses all reality, and that we are justified in assuming that such a being is possible (the fact that a concept does not contradict itself by no means proves the possibility of its object: but the contrary assertion I am for the moment willing to allow).[2] Now [the argument proceeds][3] 'all reality' includes existence; existence is therefore contained in the concept of a thing that is possible. If, then, this thing is rejected, the internal possibility of the thing is rejected—which is self-contradictory.

My answer is as follows. There is already a contradiction in introducing the concept of existence—no matter under what title it may be disguised—into the concept of a thing which we profess to be thinking solely in reference

[1] ["most real being."]

[2] A concept is always possible if it is not self-contradictory. This is the logical criterion of possibility, and by it the object of the concept is distinguishable from the *nihil negativum* ["nothing of negation"]. But it may none the less be an empty concept, unless the objective reality of the synthesis through which the concept is generated has been specifically proved; and such proof, as we have shown above, rests on principles of possible experience, and not on the principle of analysis (the law of contradiction). This is a warning against arguing directly from the logical possibility of concepts to the real possibility of things.

[3] [Translator's bracketing here and following.]

to its possibility. If that be allowed as legitimate, a seeming victory has been won; but in actual fact nothing at all is said: the assertion is a mere tautology. We must ask: Is the proposition that *this or that thing* (which, whatever it may be, is allowed as possible) *exists*, an analytic or a synthetic proposition? If it is analytic, the assertion of the existence of the thing adds nothing to the thought of the thing; but in that case either the thought, which is in us, is the thing itself, or we have presupposed an existence as belonging to the realm of the possible, and have then, on that pretext, inferred its existence from its internal possibility—which is nothing but a miserable tautology. The word 'reality,' which in the concept of the thing sounds other than the word 'existence' in the concept of the predicate, is of no avail in meeting this objection. For if all positing (no matter what it may be that is posited) is entitled reality, the thing with all its predicates is already posited in the concept of the subject, and is assumed as actual; and in the predicate this is merely repeated. But if, on the other hand, we admit, as every reasonable person must, that all existential propositions are synthetic, how can we profess to maintain that the predicate of existence cannot be rejected without contradiction? This is a feature which is found only in analytic propositions, and is indeed precisely what constitutes their analytic character.

I should have hoped to put an end to these idle and fruitless disputations in a direct manner, by an accurate determination of the concept of existence, had I not found that the illusion which is caused by the confusion of a logical with a real predicate (that is, with a predicate which determines a thing) is almost beyond correction. Anything we please can be made to serve as a logical predicate; the subject can even be predicted of itself; for logic abstracts from all content. But a *determining* predicate is a predicate which is added to the concept of the subject and enlarges it. Consequently, it must not be already contained in the concept.

'*Being*' is obviously not a real predicate; that is, it is not a concept of something which could be added to the concept of a thing. It is merely the positing of a thing, or of certain determinations, as existing in themselves. Logically, it is merely the copula of a judgment. The proposition, 'God is omnipotent,' contains two concepts, each of which has its object—God and omnipotence. The small word 'is' adds no new predicate, but only serves to posit the predicate *in its relation* to the subject. If, now, we take the subject (God) with all its predicates (among which is omnipotence), and say 'God is,' or 'There is a God,' we attach no new predicate to the concept of God, but only posit the subject in itself with all its predicates, and indeed posit it as being an *object* that stands in relation to my *concept*. The content of both must be one and the same; nothing can have been added to the concept, which expresses merely what is possible, by my thinking its object (through the expression 'it is') as given absolutely. Otherwise stated, the real contains no more than the merely possible. A hundred real thalers do not contain the least coin more than a hundred possible thalers. For as the latter signify the concept, and the former the object and the positing of the object, should the former contain more than the latter, my concept would not, in that case, express the whole object, and would not therefore be an adequate concept of it. My financial position is, however, affected very differently by a hundred real thalers than it is by the mere concept of them (that is, of their possibility). For the object, as it actually exists, is not analytically contained in my concept, but is added to my concept (which is a determination of my state) synthetically; and yet the conceived hundred thalers are not themselves in the least increased through thus acquiring existence outside my concept.

By whatever and by however many predicates we may think a thing—even if we completely determine it—we do not make the least addition to the thing when we further declare that this thing *is*. Otherwise, it would not be exactly the same thing that exists, but something more than we had thought in the concept; and we could not, therefore, say that the exact object of my concept exists. If we think in a thing every feature of reality except one, the missing reality is not added by my saying that this defective thing exists. On the contrary, it exists with the same defect with which I have thought it, since otherwise what exists would be something different from what I thought. When, therefore, I think a being as the supreme reality, without any defect, the question still remains whether it exists or not. For though, in my concept, nothing may be lacking of the possible real content of a thing in general, something is still lacking in its relation to my whole state of thought, namely, [in so far as I am unable to assert] that knowledge of this object is also possible *a posteriori*. And here we find the source of our present difficulty. Were we dealing with an object of the senses, we could not confound the existence of the thing with the mere concept of it. For through the concept the object is thought only as conforming to the *universal conditions* of possible empirical knowledge in general, whereas through its existence it is thought as belonging to the context of experience as a whole. In being thus connected with the *content* of experience as a whole, the concept of the object is not, however, in the least enlarged; all that has happened is that our thought has thereby obtained an additional possible perception. It is not, therefore, surprising that, if we attempt to think existence through the pure category alone, we cannot specify a single mark distinguishing it from mere possibility.

Whatever, therefore, and however much, our concept of an object may contain, we must go inside it, if we are to ascribe existence to the object. In the case of objects of the senses, this takes place through their connection with some one of our perceptions, in accordance with empirical laws. But in dealing with objects of pure thought, we have no means whatsoever of knowing their existence, since it would have to be known in a completely *a priori* manner. Our consciousness of all existence (whether immediately through perception, or mediately through inferences which connect something with perception) belongs exclusively to the unity of experience; any [alleged] existence outside this field, while not indeed such as we can declare to be absolutely impossible, is of the nature of an assumption which we can never be in a position to justify.

The concept of a supreme being is in many respects a very useful idea; but just because it is a mere idea, it is altogether incapable, by itself alone, of enlarging our knowledge in regard to what exists. It is not even competent to enlighten us as to the *possibility* of any existence beyond that which is known in and through experience. The analytic criterion of possibility, as consisting in the principle that bare positives (realities) give rise to no contradiction, cannot be denied to it. But since the realities are not given to us in their specific characters; since even if they were, we should still not be in a position to pass judgment; since the criterion of the possibility of synthetic knowledge is never to be looked for save in experience, to which the object of an idea cannot belong, the connection of all real properties in a thing is a synthesis, the possibility of which we are unable to determine *a priori*. And thus the celebrated Leibniz is far from having succeeded in what he plumed himself on achieving—the comprehension *a priori* of the possibility of this sublime ideal being.[4]

This attempt to establish the existence of a supreme being by means of the famous ontological argument of Descartes is therefore merely so much labour and effort lost; we can no more extend our stock of [theoretical] insight by mere ideas, than a merchant can better his position by adding a few noughts to his cash account.

[4][Cf. G. W. Leibniz, *Monadology*, 44 f.; *New Essays Concerning the Human Understanding*, Book IV, Ch. 10.]

And if it can be so conceived does not he who conceives of this conceive of a thing greater than it, if it does exist merely in the understanding? Can anything follow better than this: that if a being a greater than which cannot be conceived exists merely in the understanding, it is something a greater than which can be conceived? What could be plainer?[7]

He is implying, in the first sentence, that if I conceive of something which does not exist then it is possible for it to exist, and *it will be greater if it exists than if it does not exist.*

The doctrine that existence is a perfection is remarkably queer. It makes sense and is true to say that my future house will be a better one if it is insulated than if it is not insulated; but what could it mean to say that it will be a better house if it exists than if it does not? My future child will be a better man if he is honest than if he is not; but who would understand the saying that he will be a better man if he exists than if he does not? Or who understands the saying that if God exists He is more perfect than if He does not exist? One might say, with some intelligibility, that it would be better (for oneself or for mankind) if God exists than if He does not—but that is a different matter.

A king might desire that his next chancellor should have knowledge, wit, and resolution; but it is ludicrous to add that the king's desire is to have a chancellor who exists. Suppose that two royal councilors, A and B, were asked to draw up separately descriptions of the most perfect chancellor they could conceive, and that the descriptions they produced were identical except that A included existence in his list of attributes of a perfect chancellor and B did not. (I do not mean that B put non-existence in his list.) One and the same person could satisfy both descriptions. More to the point, any person who satisfied A's description would *necessarily* satify B's description and *vice versa!* This is to say that A and B did not produce descriptions of necessary and desirable qualities in a chancellor. A only made a show of putting down a desirable quality that B had failed to include.

I believe I am merely restating an observation that Kant made in attacking the notion that "existence" or "being" is a "real predicate." He says:

By whatever and by however many predicates we may think a thing—even if we completely determine it—we do not make the least addition to the thing when we further declare that this thing *is.* Otherwise, it would not be exactly the same thing that exists, but something more than we had thought in the concept; and we could not, therefore, say that the exact object of my concept exists.[8]

Anselm's ontological proof of *Proslogion* 2 is fallacious because it rests on the false doctrine that existence is a perfection (and therefore that "existence" is a "real predicate"). It would be desirable to have a rigorous refutation of the doctrine but I have not been able to provide one. I am compelled to leave the matter at the more or less intuitive level of Kant's observation.

[7]*Responsio* 2; Deane, *St. Anselm*, pp. 157–158.

[8]*The Critique of Pure Reason*, tr. by Norman Kemp Smith (New York: The Macmillan Company, 1929), p. 505.

In any case, I believe that the doctrine does not belong to Anselm's other formulation of the ontological argument. It is worth noting that Gassendi anticipated Kant's criticism when he said, against Descartes:

Existence is a perfection neither in God nor in anything else; it is rather that in the absence of which there is no perfection. . . . Hence neither is existence held to exist in a thing in the way that perfections do, nor if the thing lacks existence is it said to be imperfect (or deprived of a perfection), so much as to be nothing.[9]

II

I take up now the consideration of the second ontological proof, which Anselm presents in the very next chapter of the *Proslogion*. (There is no evidence that he thought of himself as offering two different proofs.) Speaking of the being a greater than which cannot be conceived, he says:

And it so truly exists that it cannot be conceived not to exist. For it is possible to conceive of a being which cannot be conceived not to exist; and this is greater than one which can be conceived not to exist. Hence, if that, than which nothing greater can be conceived, can be conceived not to exist, it is not that than which nothing greater can be conceived. But this is a contradiction. So truly, therefore, is there something than which nothing greater can be conceived, that it cannot even be conceived not to exist. And this being thou art, O Lord, our God.[10]

Anselm is saying two things: first, that a being whose nonexistence is logically impossible is "greater" than a being whose nonexistence is logically possible (and therefore that a being a greater than which cannot be conceived must be one whose nonexistence is logically impossible); second, that *God* is a being than which a greater cannot be conceived.

In regard to the second of these assertions, there certainly is *a* use of the word "God," and I think far the more common use, in accordance with which the statements "God is the greatest of all beings," "God is the most perfect thing," "God is the supreme being," are *logically* necessary truths, in the same sense that the statement "A square has four sides" is a logically necessary truth. If there is a man named "Jones" who is the tallest man in the world, the statement "Jones is the tallest man in the world" is merely true and is not a logically necessary truth. It is a virtue of Anselm's unusual phrase, "a being a greater than which cannot be conceived,"[11] to make it explicit that the sentence "God is the greatest of all beings" expresses a logically necessary truth and not a mere matter of fact such as the one we imagined about Jones.

With regard to Anselm's first assertion (namely, that a being whose nonexistence is logically impossible is greater than a being whose nonexistence is logically possible) perhaps the most puzzling thing about it is the use of

---

[9]Haldane and Ross, *The Philosophical Works of Descartes*, II, 186.

[10]*Proslogion* 3; Deane, *St. Anselm*, pp. 8–9.

[11]Professor Robert Calhoun has pointed out to me that a similar locution had been used by Augustine. In *De moribus Manichaeorum* (Bk. II, ch. 11, sec. 24), he says that God is being *quo esse aut cogitari melius nihil possit* (*Patrologiae Patrum Latinorum*, J. P. Migne, ed. [Paris, 1841–1845], Vol. 32; *Augustinus*, Vol. 1).

the word "greater." It appears to mean exactly the same as "superior," "more excellent," "more perfect." This equivalent by itself is of no help to us, however, since the latter expressions would be equally puzzling here. What is required is some explanation of their use.

We do think of *knowledge*, say, as an excellence, a good thing. If A has more knowledge of algebra than B we express this in common language by saying that A has a *better* knowledge of algebra than B, or that A's knowledge of algebra is *superior* to B's, whereas we should not say that B has a better or superior *ignorance* of algebra than A. We do say "greater ignorance," but here the word "greater" is used purely quantitatively.

Previously I rejected *existence* as a perfection. Anselm is maintaining in the remarks last quoted, not that existence is a perfection, but that *the logical impossibility of nonexistence is a perfection*. In other words, *necessary existence is a perfection*. His first ontological proof uses the principle that a thing is greater if it exists than if it does not exist. His second proof employs the different principle that a thing is greater if it necessarily exists than if it does not necessarily exist.

Some remarks about the notion of *dependence* may help to make this latter principle intelligible. Many things depend for their existence on other things and events. My house was built by a carpenter: its coming into existence was dependent on a certain creative activity. Its continued existence is dependent on many things: that a tree does not crush it, that it is not consumed by fire, and so on. If we reflect on the common meaning of the word "God" (no matter how vague and confused this is), we realize that it is incompatible with this meaning that God's existence should *depend* on anything. Whether we believe in Him or not we must admit that the "almighty and everlasting God" (as several ancient prayers begin), the "Maker of heaven and earth, and of all things visible and invisible" (as is said in the Nicene Creed), cannot be thought of as being brought into existence by anything or as depending for His continued existence on anything. To conceive of anything as dependent upon something else for its existence is to conceive of it as a lesser being than God.

If a housewife has a set of extremely fragile dishes, then as dishes they are *inferior* to those of another set like them in all respects except that they are *not* fragile. Those of the first set are *dependent* for their continued existence on gentle handling; those of the second set are not. There is a definite connection in common language between the notions of dependency and inferiority, and independence and superiority. To say that something which was dependent on nothing whatever was superior to ("greater than") anything that was dependent in any way upon anything is quite in keeping with the everyday use of the terms "superior" and "greater." Correlative with the notions of dependence and independence are the notions of *limited* and *unlimited*. An engine requires fuel and this is a limitation. It is the same thing to say that an engine's operation is *dependent* on as that it is *limited* by its fuel supply. An engine that could accomplish the same work in the same time and was in other respects satisfactory, but did not require fuel, would be a *superior* engine.

God is usually conceived of as an *unlimited* being. He is conceived of as a being who *could not* be limited, that is, as an absolutely unlimited being. This is no less than to conceive of Him as *something a greater than which cannot be conceived.* If God is conceived to be an absolutely unlimited being He must be conceived to be unlimited in regard to His existence as well as His operation. In this conception it will not make sense to say that He depends on anything for coming into or continuing in existence. Nor, as Spinoza observed, will it make sense to say that something could *prevent* Him from existing.[12] Lack of moisture can prevent trees from existing in a certain region of the earth. But it would be contrary to the concept of God as an unlimited being to suppose that anything other than God Himself could prevent Him from existing, and it would be self-contradictory to suppose that He Himself could do it.

Some may be inclined to object that although nothing could prevent God's existence, still it might just *happen* that He did not exist. And if He did exist that too would be by chance. I think, however, that from the supposition that it could happen that God did not exist it would follow that, if He existed, He would have mere duration and not eternity. It would make sense to ask, "How long has He existed?," "Will He still exist next week?," "He was in existence yesterday but how about today?," and so on. It seems absurd to make God the subject of such questions. According to our ordinary conception of Him, He is an eternal being. And eternity does not mean endless duration, as Spinoza noted. To ascribe eternity to something is to exclude as senseless all sentences that imply that it has duration. If a thing has duration then it would be merely a *contingent* fact, if it was a fact, that its duration was endless. The moon could have endless duration but not eternity. If something has endless duration it will *make sense* (although it will be false) to say that it will cease to exist, and it will make sense (although it will be false) to say that something will *cause* it to cease to exist. A being with endless duration is not, therefore, an absolutely unlimited being. That God is conceived to be eternal follows from the fact that He is conceived to be an absolutely unlimited being.

I have been trying to expand the argument of *Proslogion* 3. In *Responsio* 1 Anselm adds the following acute point: if you can conceive of a certain thing and this thing does not exist then if it *were* to exist its nonexistence would be *possible.* It follows, I believe, that if the thing were to exist it would depend on other things both for coming into and continuing in existence, and also that it would have duration and not eternity. Therefore it would not be, either in reality or in conception, an unlimited being, *aliquid quo nihil maius cogitari possit.*

Anselm states his argument as follows:

If it [the thing a greater than which cannot be conceived] can be conceived at all it must exist. For no one who denies or doubts the existence of a being a greater than which is inconceivable, denies or doubts that if it did exist its non-existence, either in reality or in the understanding, would be impossible. For otherwise it

---

[12]*Ethics*, Part I, prop. 11.

would not be a being a greater than which cannot be conceived. But as to whatever can be conceived but does not exist: if it were to exist its non-existence either in reality or in the understanding would be possible. Therefore, if a being a greater than which cannot be conceived, can even be conceived, it must exist.[13]

What Anselm has proved is that the notion of contingent existence or of contingent nonexistence cannot have any application to God. His existence must either be logically necessary or logically impossible. The only intelligible way of rejecting Anselm's claim that God's existence is necessary is to maintain that the concept of God, as a being a greater than which cannot be conceived, is self-contradictory or nonsensical.[14] Supposing that this is false, Anselm is right to deduce God's necessary existence from his characterization of Him as a being a greater than which cannot be conceived.

Let me summarize the proof. If God, a being a greater than which cannot be conceived, does not exist then He cannot *come* into existence. For if He did He would either have been *caused* to come into existence or have *happened* to come into existence, and in either case He would be a limited being, which by our conception of Him He is not. Since He cannot come into existence, if He does not exist His existence is impossible. If He does exist He cannot have come into existence (for the reasons given), nor can He cease to exist, for nothing could cause Him to cease to exist nor could it just happen that He ceased to exist. So if God exists His existence is necessary. Thus God's existence is either impossible or necessary. It can be the former only if the concept of such a being is self-contradictory or in some way logically absurd. Assuming that this is not so, it follows that He necessarily exists.[15]

It may be helpful to express ourselves in the following way: to say, not that *omnipotence* is a property of God, but rather that *necessary omnipotence* is; and to say, not that omniscience is a property of God, but rather that *necessary omniscience* is. We have criteria for determining that a man knows this and that and can do this and that, and for determining that one man

---

[13]*Responsio* 1; Deane, *St. Anselm*, pp. 154–155 [Malcolm's bracketing].

[14]Gaunilo attacked Anselm's argument on this very point. He would not concede that a being a greater than which cannot be conceived existed in his understanding (*Gaunilonis Pro Insipiente*, secs. 4 and 5; Deane, *St. Anselm*, pp. 148–150). Anselm's reply is: "I call on your faith and conscience to attest that this is most false" (*Responsio* 1; Deane, *St. Anselm*, p. 154). Gaunilo's faith and conscience will attest that it is false that "God is not a being a greater than which is inconceivable," and false that "He is not understood (*intelligitur*) or conceived (*cogitatur*)" (*ibid.*). Descartes remarks that one would go to "strange extremes" who denied that we understand the words "*that thing which is the most perfect that we can conceive*; for that is what all men call God" (Haldane and Ross, *The Philosophical Works of Descartes*, II, 129).

[15]The following elegant argument occurs in *Responsio* 1: "That than which a greater cannot be conceived cannot be conceived to begin to exist. Whatever can be conceived to exist and does not exist, can be conceived to begin to exist. Therefore, that than which a greater cannot be conceived, cannot be conceived to exist and yet not exist. So if it can be conceived to exist it exists from necessity." (*Nam quo maius cogitari nequit non potest cogitari esse nisi sine initio. Quidquid autem potest cogitari esse et non est, per initium potest cigitari esse. Non ergo quo maius cogitari nequit cogitari potest esse et non est. Si ergo cogitari potest esse, ex necessitate est.*) (Schmitt, *Opera Omnia*, p. 131; Deane, *St. Anselm*, p. 154.)

has greater knowledge and abilities in a certain subject than another. We could think of various tests to give them. But there is nothing we should wish to describe, seriously and literally, as "testing" God's knowledge and powers. That God is omniscient and omnipotent has not been determined by the application of criteria: rather these are requirements of our conception of Him. They are internal properties of the concept, although they are also rightly said to be properties of God. *Necessary existence* is a property of God in the *same sense* that *necessary omnipotence* and *necessary omniscience* are His properties. And we are not to think that "God necessarily exists" means that it follows necessarily from something that God exists *contingently.* The a priori proposition "God necessarily exists" entails the proposition "God exists," if and only if the latter also is understood as an a priori proposition: in which case the two propositions are equivalent. In this sense Anselm's proof is a proof of God's existence.

Descartes was somewhat hazy on the question of whether existence is a property of things that exist, but at the same time he saw clearly enough that *necessary existence* is a property of God. Both points are illustrated in his reply to Gassendi's remark, which I quoted above:

I do not see to what class of reality you wish to assign existence, nor do I see why it may not be said to be a property as well as omnipotence, taking the word property as equivalent to any attribute or anything which can be predicated of a thing, as in the present case it should be by all means regarded. Nay, necessary existence in the case of God is also a true property in the strictest sense of the word, because it belongs to Him and forms part of His essence alone.[16]

Elsewhere he speaks of "the necessity of existence" as being "that crown of perfections without which we cannot comprehend God."[17] He is emphatic on the point that necessary existence applies solely to "an absolutely perfect Being."[18]

III

I wish to consider now a part of Kant's criticism of the ontological argument which I believe to be wrong. He says:

If, in an identical proposition, I reject the predicate while retaining the subject, contradiction results; and I therefore say that the former belongs necessarily to the latter. But if we reject subject and predicate alike, there is no contradiction; for nothing is then left that can be contradicted. To posit a triangle, and yet to reject its three angles, is self-contradictory; but there is no contradiction in rejecting the triangle together with its three angles. The same holds true of the concept of an absolutely necessary being. If its existence is rejected, we reject the thing itself with all its predicates; and no question of contradiction can then arise. There is nothing outside it that would then be contradicted, since the necessity of the thing

---

[16]Haldane and Ross, *The Philosophical Works of Descartes,* II, 228.

[17]*Ibid.,* I, 445.

[18]E.g., *ibid.,* Principle 15, p. 225.

is not supposed to be derived from anything external; nor is there anything internal that would be contradicted, since in rejecting the thing itself we have at the same time rejected all its internal properties. "God is omnipotent" is a necessary judgment. The omnipotence cannot be rejected if we posit a Deity, that is, an infinite being; for the two concepts are identical. But if we say "There is no God" neither the omnipotence nor any other of its predicates is given; they are one and all rejected together with the subject, and there is therefore not the least contradiction in such a judgment.[19]

To these remarks the reply is that when the concept of God is correctly understood one sees that one cannot "reject the subject." "There is no God" is seen to be a necessarily false statement. Anselm's demonstration proves that the proposition "God exists" has the same a priori footing as the proposition "God is omnipotent."

Many present-day philosophers, in agreement with Kant, declare that existence is not a property and think that this overthrows the ontological argument. Although it is an error to regard existence as a property of things that have contingent existence, it does not follow that it is an error to regard necessary existence as a property of God. A recent writer says, against Anselm, that a proof of God's existence "based on the necessities of thought" is "universally regarded as fallacious: it is not thought possible to build bridges between mere abstractions and concrete existence."[20] But this way of putting the matter obscures the distinction we need to make. Does "concrete existence" mean contingent existence? Then to build bridges between concrete existence and mere abstractions would be like inferring the existence of an island from the concept of a perfect island, which both Anselm and Descartes regarded as absurd. What Anselm did was to give a demonstration that the proposition "God necessarily exists" is entailed by the proposition "God is a being a greater than which cannot be conceived" (which is equivalent to "God is an absolutely unlimited being"). Kant declares that when "I think a being as the supreme reality, without any defect, the question still remains whether it exists or not."[21] But once one has grasped Anselm's proof of the necessary existence of a being a greater than which cannot be conceived, no question remains as to whether it exists or not, just as Euclid's demonstration of the existence of an infinity of prime numbers leaves no question on that issue.

Kant says that "every reasonable person" must admit that "all existential propositions are synthetic."[22] Part of the perplexity one has about the ontological argument is in deciding whether or not the proposition "God necessarily exists" is or is not an "existential proposition." But let us look around. Is the Euclidean theorem in number theory, "There exists an infinite number of prime numbers," an "existential proposition"? Do we not want to say that *in some sense* it asserts the existence of something? Cannot we

[19]*Op. cit.*, p. 502.
[20]J. N. Findlay, "Can God's Existence Be Disproved?" *New Essays in Philosophical Theology*, A. N. Flew and A. MacIntyre, eds. (New York: The Macmillan Company, 1955), p. 47.
[21]*Op. cit.*, pp. 505–506.
[22]*Ibid.*, p. 504.

say, with equal justification, that the proposition "God necessarily exists" asserts the existence of something, *in some sense*? What we need to understand, in each case, is the particular sense of the assertion. Neither proposition has the same sort of sense as do the propositions "A low pressure area exists over the Great Lakes," "There still exists some possibility that he will survive," "The pain continues to exist in his abdomen." One good way of seeing the difference in sense of these various propositions is to see the variously different ways in which they are proved or supported. It is wrong to think that all assertions of existence have the same kind of meaning. There are as many kinds of existential propositions as there are kinds of subjects of discourse.

Closely related to Kant's view that all existential propositions are "synthetic" is the contemporary dogma that all existential propositions are contingent. Professor Gilbert Ryle tells us that "Any assertion of the existence of something, like any assertion of the occurrence of something, can be denied without logical absurdity."[23] "All existential statements are contingent," says Mr. I. M. Crombie.[24] Professor J. J. C. Smart remarks that "Existence is not a property" and then goes on to assert that "There can never be any *logical contradiction* in denying that God exists."[25] He declares that "The concept of a logically necessary being is a self-contradictory concept, like the concept of a round square. . . . No existential proposition can be logically necessary," he maintains, for "the truth of a logically necessary proposition depends only on our symbolism, or to put the same thing in another way, on the relationship of concepts (p. 38). Professor K. E. M. Baier says, "It is no longer seriously in dispute that the notion of a logically necessary being is self-contradictory. Whatever can be conceived of as existing can equally be conceived of as not existing."[26] This is a repetition of Hume's assertion, "Whatever we conceive as existent, we can also conceive as non-existent. There is no being, therefore, whose non-existence implies a contradiction."[27]

Professor J. N. Findlay ingeniously constructs an ontological *dis*proof of God's existence, based on a "modern" view of the nature of "necessity in propositions": the view, namely, that necessity in propositions "merely reflects our use of words, the arbitrary conventions of our language."[28] Findlay undertakes to characterize what he calls "religious attitude," and here there is a striking agreement between his observations and some of the things I have said in expounding Anselm's proof. Religious attitude, he says, presumes *superiority* in its object and superiority so great that the worshiper is in comparison as nothing. Religious attitude finds it "anomalous to worship anything *limited* in any thinkable manner. . . . And hence we are led on irresistibly

---

[23]*The Nature of Metaphysics*, D. F. Pears, ed. (New York: St. Martin's Press, Inc., 1957), p. 150.

[24]*New Essays in Philosophical Theology*, p. 114.

[25]*Ibid.*, p. 34.

[26]*The Meaning of Life*, Inaugural Lecture, Canberra University College (Canberra, 1957), p. 8.

[27]*Dialogues Concerning Natural Religion*, Part IX.

[28]Findlay, *op. cit.*, p. 54.

to demand that our religious object should have an *unsurpassable* supremacy along all avenues, that it should tower *infinitely* above all other objects" (p. 51). We cannot help feeling that "the worthy object of our worship can never be a thing that merely *happens* to exist, nor one on which all other objects merely *happen* to depend. The true object of religious reverence must not be one, merely, to which no *actual* independent realities stand opposed: it must be one to which such opposition is totally *inconceivable*. . . . And not only must the existence of *other* things be unthinkable without him, but his own non-existence must be wholly unthinkable in any circumstances" (p. 52). And now, says Findlay, when we add up these various requirements, what they entail is "not only that there isn't a God, but that the Divine Existence is either senseless or impossible" (p. 54). For on the one hand, "if God is to satisfy religious claims and needs, He must be a being in every way inescapable, One whose existence and whose possession of certain excellences we cannot possibly conceive away." On the other hand, "modern views make it self-evidently absurd (if they don't make it ungrammatical) to speak of such a Being and attribute existence to Him. It was indeed an ill day for Anselm when he hit upon his famous proof. For on that day he not only laid bare something that is of the essence of an adequate religious object, but also something that entails its necessary non-existence" (p. 55).

Now I am inclined to hold the "modern" view that logically necessary truth "merely reflects our use of words" (although I do not believe that the conventions of language are always *arbitrary*). But I confess that I am unable to see how that view is supposed to lead to the conclusion that "the Divine existence is either senseless or impossible." Findlay does not explain how this result comes about. Surely he cannot mean that this view entails that nothing can have necessary properties: for this would imply that mathematics is "senseless or impossible," which no one wants to hold. Trying to fill in the argument that is missing from his article, the most plausible conjecture I can make is the following: Findlay thinks that the view that logical necessity "reflects the use of words" implies, not that nothing has necessary properties, but that *existence* cannot be a necessary property of anything. That is to say, every proposition of the form "*x exists,*" including the proposition "God exists," must be *contingent.*[29] At the same time, our concept of God requires that His existence be *necessary,* that is, that "God exists" be a necessary truth. Therefore, the modern view of necessity proves that what the concept of God requires *cannot* be fulfilled. It proves that God *cannot* exist.

The correct reply is that the view that logical necessity merely reflects the use of words cannot possibly have the implication that every existential proposition must be contingent. That view requires us to *look at* the use of words and not manufacture a priori theses about it. In the Ninetieth Psalm it is said: "Before the mountains were brought forth, or ever thou hadst formed

[29]The other philosophers I have just cited may be led to this opinion by the same thinking. Smart, for example, says that "the truth of a logically necessary proposition depends only on our symbolism, or to put the same thing in another way, on the relationship of concepts" (*supra*). This is very similar to saying that it "reflects our use of words."

the earth and the world, even from everlasting to everlasting, thou art God."
Here is expressed the idea of the necessary existence and eternity of God,
an idea that is essential to the Jewish and Christian religions. In those complex
systems of thought, those "languages-games," God has the status of a necessary being. Who can doubt that? Here we must say with Wittgenstein, "This
language-game is played!"[30] I believe we may rightly take the existence of
those religious systems of thought in which God figures as a necessary being
to be a disproof of the dogma, affirmed by Hume and others, that no existential
proposition can be necessary.

Another way of criticizing the ontological argument is the following:
"Granted that the concept of necessary existence follows from the concept
of a being a greater than which cannot be conceived, this amounts to no
more than granting the *a priori* truth of the *conditional* proposition, 'If such
a being exists then it necessarily exists.' This proposition, however, does not
entail the *existence of anything*, and one can deny its antecedent without contradiction." Kant, for example, compares the proposition (or "judgment," as he
calls it) "A triangle has three angles" with the proposition "God is a necessary
being." He allows that the former is "absolutely necessary" and goes on to
say:

The absolute necessity of the judgment is only a conditional necessity of the thing,
or of the predicate in the judgment. The above proposition does not declare that
three angles are absolutely necessary, but that, under the condition that there is a
triangle (that is, that a triangle is given), three angles will necessarily be found in
it.[31]

He is saying, quite correctly, that the proposition about triangles is equivalent
to the conditional proposition. "If a triangle exists, it has three angles." He
then makes the comment that there is no contradiction "in rejecting the triangle
together with its three angles." He proceeds to draw the alleged parallel: "The
same holds true of the concept of an absolutely necessary being. If its existence
is rejected, we reject the thing itself with all its predicates; and no question
of contradiction can then arise."[32] The priest, Caterus, made the same objection
to Descartes when he said:

Though it be conceded that an entity of the highest perfection implies its existence
by its very name, yet it does not follow that that very existence is anything actual
in the real world, but merely that the concept of existence is inseparably united
with the concept of highest being. Hence you cannot infer that the existence of
God is anything actual, unless you assume that that highest being actually exists;
for then it will actually contain all its perfections, together with this perfection of
real existence.[33]

I think that Caterus, Kant, and numerous other philosophers have been mistaken in supposing that the proposition "God is a necessary being" (or "God
necessarily exists") is equivalent to the conditional proposition "If God exists

[30]*Philosophical Investigations* (New York: The Macmillan Company, 1953), sec. 654.
[31]*Op. cit.*, pp. 501–502.
[32]*Ibid.*, p. 502.
[33]Haldane and Ross, *The Philosophical Works of Descartes*, II, 7.

then He necessarily exists."[34] For how do they want the antecedent clause "If God exists" to be understood? Clearly they want it to imply that it is *possible* that God does *not* exist.[35] The whole point of Kant's analysis is to try to show that it is possible to "reject the subject." Let us make this implication explicit in the conditional proposition, so that it reads: "If God exists (and it is possible that He does not) then He necessarily exists." But now it is apparent, I think, that these philosophers have arrived at a self-contradictory position. I do not mean that this conditional proposition, taken alone, is self-contradictory. Their position is self-contradictory in the following way. On the one hand, they agree that the proposition "God necessarily exists" is an a priori truth; Kant implies that it is "absolutely necessary," and Caterus says that God's existence is implied by His very name. On the other hand, they think that it is correct to analyze this proposition in such a way that it will entail the proposition "It is possible that God does not exist." But so far from its being the case that the proposition "God necessarily exists" entails the proposition "It is possible that God does not exist," it is rather the case that they are *incompatible* with one another! Can anything be clearer than the conjunction "God necessarily exists but it is possible that He does not exist" is self-contradictory? Is it not just as plainly self-contradictory as the conjunction "A square necessarily has four sides but it is possible for a square not to have four sides"? In short, this familiar criticism of the ontological argument is self-contradictory, because it accepts *both* of two incompatible propositions.[36]

[34]I have heard it said by more than one person in discussion that Kant's view was that it is really a misuse of language to speak of a "necessary being," on the grounds that necessity is properly predicated only of propositions (judgments) not of *things*. This is not a correct account of Kant. (See his discussion of "The Postulates of Empirical Thought in General," *op. cit.*, pp. 239–256, esp. p. 239 and pp. 247–248.) But if he had held this, as perhaps the above philosophers think he should have, then presumably his view would not have been that the pseudo-proposition "God is a necessary being" is equivalent to the conditional "If God exists then He necessarily exists." Rather his view would have been that the genuine proposition " 'God exists' is necessarily true" is equivalent to the conditional "If God exists then He exists" (*not* "If God exists then He necessarily exists," which would be an illegitimate formulation, on the view imaginatively attributed to Kant).

"If God exists then He exists" is a foolish tautology which says nothing different from the tautology "If a new earth satellite exists then it exists." If "If God exists then He exists" were a correct analysis of " 'God exists' is necessarily true," then "If a new earth satellite exists then it exists" would be a correct analysis of " 'A new earth satellite exists' is necessarily true." If the *analysans* is necessarily true then the *analysandum* must be necessarily true, provided the analysis is correct. If this proposed Kantian analysis of " 'God exists' is necessarily true" were correct, we should be presented with the consequence that not only is it necessarily true that God exists, but also it is necessarily true that a new earth satellite exists, which is absurd.

[35]When summarizing Anselm's proof (in Part II, *supra*) I said: "If God exists He necessarily exists." But there I was merely stating an entailment. "If God exists" did not have the implication that it is possible He does not exist. And of course I was not regarding the conditional as *equivalent* to "God necessarily exists."

[36]This fallacious criticism of Anselm is implied in the following remarks by Gilson: "To show that the affirmation of necessary existence is analytically implied in the idea of God, would be . . . to show that God is necessary if He exists, but would not prove that He does exist" (E. Gilson, *The Spirit of Medieval Philosophy* [New York: Charles Scribner's Sons, 1940], p. 62).

One conclusion we may draw from our examination of this criticism is that (contrary to Kant) there is a lack of symmetry, in an important respect, between the propositions "A triangle has three angles" and "God has necessary existence," although both are a priori. The former can be expressed in the conditional assertion "If a triangle exists (and it is possible that none does) it has three angles." The latter cannot be expressed in the corresponding conditional assertion without contradiction.

IV

I turn to the question of whether the idea of a being a greater than which cannot be conceived is self-contradictory. Here Leibniz made a contribution to the discussion of the ontological argument. He remarked that the argument of Anselm and Descartes

is not a paralogism, but it is an imperfect demonstration, which assumes something that must still be proved in order to render it mathematically evident; that is, it is tacitly assumed that this idea of the all-great or all-perfect being is possible, and implies no contradiction. And it is already something that by this remark it is proved that, assuming that God is possible, he exists, which is the privilege of divinity alone.[37]

Leibniz undertook to give a proof that God is possible. He defined a *perfection* as a simple, positive quality in the highest degree.[38] He argued that since perfections are *simple* qualities they must be compatible with one another. Therefore the concept of a being possessing all perfections is consistent.

I will not review his argument because I do not find his definition of a perfection intelligible. For one thing, it assumes that certain qualities or attributes are "positive" in their intrinsic nature, and others "negative" or "privative," and I have not been able to clearly understand that. For another thing, it assumes that some qualities are intrinsically simple. I believe that Wittgenstein has shown in the *Investigations* that nothing is *intrinsically* simple, but that whatever has the status of a simple, an indefinable, in one system of concepts, may have the status, of a complex thing, a definable thing, in another system of concepts.

I do not know how to demonstrate that the concept of God—that is, of a being a greater than which cannot be conceived—is not self-contradictory. But I do not think that it is legitimate to demand such a demonstration. I also do not know how to demonstrate that either the concept of a material thing or the concept of *seeing* a material thing is not self-contradictory, and philosophers have argued that both of them are. With respect to any particular reasoning that is offered for holding that the concept of seeing a material thing, for example, is self-contradictory, one may try to show the invalidity of the reasoning and thus free the concept from the charge of being self-contradictory *on that ground*. But I do not understand what it would mean to demonstrate *in general*, and not in respect to any particular reasoning, that the concept is not self-contradictory. So it is with the concept of God: I should

[37]*New Essays Concerning the Human Understanding*, Bk. IV, ch. 10; A. G. Langley, ed. (La Salle, Ill.: Open Court Publishing Company, 1949), p. 504.
[38]See *ibid.*, Appendix X, p. 714.

think there is no more of a presumption that it is self-contradictory than is the concept of seeing a material thing. Both concepts have a place in the thinking and the lives of human beings.

But even if one allows that Anselm's phrase may be free of self-contradiction, one wants to know how it can have any *meaning* for anyone. Why is it that human beings have even *formed* the concept of an infinite being, a being a greater than which cannot be conceived? This is a legitimate and important question. I am sure there cannot be a deep understanding of that concept without an understanding of the phenomena of human life that give rise to it. To give an account of the latter is beyond my ability. I wish, however, to make one suggestion (which should not be understood as autobiographical).

There is the phenomenon of feeling guilt for something that one has done or thought or felt or for a disposition that one has. One wants to be free of this guilt. But sometimes the guilt is felt to be so great that one is sure that nothing one could do oneself, nor any forgiveness by another human being, would remove it. One feels a guilt that is beyond all measure, a guilt "a greater than which cannot be conceived." Paradoxically, it would seem, one nevertheless has an intense desire to have this incomparable guilt removed. One requires a forgiveness that is beyond all measure, a forgiveness "a greater than which cannot be conceived." Out of such a storm in the soul, I am suggesting, there arises the conception of a forgiving mercy that is limitless, beyond all measure.[39] This is one important feature of the Jewish and Christian conception of God.

I wish to relate this thought to a remark made by Kierkegaard, who was speaking about belief in Christianity but whose remark may have a wider application. He says:

There is only one proof of the truth of Christianity and that, quite rightly, is from the emotions, when the dread of sin and a heavy conscience torture a man into crossing the narrow line between despair bordering upon madness—and Christendom.[40]

One may think it absurd for a human being to feel a guilt of such magnitude, and even more absurd that, if he feels it, he should *desire* its removal. I have nothing to say about that. It may also be absurd for people to fall in love, but they do it. I wish only to say that there *is* that human phenomenon of an unbearably heavy conscience and that it is importantly connected with the genesis of the concept of God, that is, with the formation of the "grammar" of the word "God." I am sure that this concept is related to human experience in other ways. If one had the acuteness and depth to perceive these connections one could grasp the *sense* of the concept. When we encounter this concept as a problem in philosophy, we do not consider the human phenomena that lie behind it. It is not surprising that many philosophers believe that the idea of a necessary being is an arbitrary and absurd construction.

[39]*Psalm* 116: "The sorrows of death compassed me, and the pains of hell gat hold upon me: I found trouble and sorrow. Then called I upon the name of the Lord; O Lord, I beseech thee, deliver my soul." *Psalm* 130: "Out of the depths have I cried unto thee, O Lord."
[40]*The Journals,* tr. by A. Dru (New York: Oxford University Press, 1938), sec. 926.

What is the relation of Ansel'm ontological argument to religious belief? This is a difficult question. I can imagine an atheist going through the argument, becoming convinced of its validity, acutely defending it against objections, yet remaining an atheist. The only effect it could have on the fool of the Psalm would be that he stopped saying in his heart "There is no God," because he would now realize that this is something he cannot meaningfully say or think. It is hardly to be expected that a demonstrative argument should, in addition, produce in him a living faith. Surely there is a level at which one can view the argument as a piece of logic, following the deductive moves but not being touched religiously? I think so. But even at this level the argument may not be without religious value, for it may help to remove some philosophical scruples that stand in the way of faith. At a deeper level, I suspect that the argument can be thoroughly understood only by one who has a view of that human "form of life" that gives rise to the idea of an infinitely great being, who views it from the *inside* not just from the outside and who has, therefore, at least some inclination to *partake* in that religious form of life. This inclination, in Kierkegaard's words, is "from the emotions." This inclination can hardly be an *effect* of Anselm's argument, but is rather presupposed in the fullest understanding of it. It would be unreasonable to require that the recognition of Anselm's demonstration as valid must produce a conversion.[41]

[41]Since the appearance of this essay [first published in The Philosophical Review, LXIX (January, 1960)] many acute criticisms of it have been published or communicated to me in private correspondence. In The Philosophical Review, LXX, No. 1, January 1961, there are the following articles: Raziel Abelson, "Not Necessarily"; R. E. Allen, "The Ontological Argument"; Paul Henle, "Uses of the Ontological Argument"; Gareth B. Matthews, "On Conceivability in Anselm and Malcolm"; Alvin Plantinga, "A Valid Ontological Argument?"; Terence Penelhum, "On the Second Ontological Argument." Some other published articles are: Jan Berg, "An Examination of the Ontological Proof," Theoria, XXVII, No. 3 (1961); T. P. Brown, "Professor Malcolm on 'Anselm's Ontological Arguments,' " Analysis, October 1961; W. J. Huggett, "The Nonexistence of Ontological Arguments," The Philosophical Review, LXXI, No. 3, July 1962; Jerome Shaffer, "Existence, Predication, and the Ontological Argument," Mind, LXXI, No. 283, July 1962. It would be a major undertaking to attempt to reply to all of the criticisms, and I hope that my not doing so will not be construed as a failure to appreciate them. I do not know that it is possible to meet all of the objections; on the other hand, I do not know that it is impossible.

✳ SELECTED BIBLIOGRAPHY
FOR SECTION 1

Relevant selections and articles on the Ontological Argument are collected in two anthologies: Alvin Plantinga (ed.), *The Ontological Argument* (Garden City, N.Y.: Anchor Books, 1965) and John Hick and Arthur C. McGill (eds.), *The Many-faced Argument* (New York: Macmillan, 1967). The former includes additional classical sources of the argument such as Leibniz's, and the latter concludes with an exhaustive and annotated bibliography. Both contain good discussions of the existence-as-a-predicate question and responses to Malcolm's article.

Worthy material, in addition to that contained in the above anthologies, includes Cyril Richardson, "The Strange Fascination of the Ontological Argument," *Union Seminary Quarterly Review*, XVIII (November, 1962); Gilbert Ryle, "Systematically Misleading Expressions," *Proceedings of the Aristotelian Society*, XXXII (1931-32); Paul J. W. Miller's treatment of the metaphysics of Anselm's Argument, "The Ontological Argument for God," *The Personalist*, XLII (July, 1961); Alvin Plantinga, "Kant's Objection to the Ontological Argument," *Journal of Philosophy*, LXIII (October, 1966); and the several articles in *The Monist*, LIV (April, 1970). For a brief statement of Bertrand Russell's influential analysis of the logic of "exists," see his *History of Philosophy* (New York: Simon & Schuster, 1945), pp. 830 f.

Good general discussions of Anselm may be found in Étienne Gilson, *History of Christian Philosophy in the Middle Ages*, Part VI, Ch. 2 (New York: Random House, 1955) and John McIntyre, *St. Anselm and His Critics* (Edinburgh; Oliver & Boyd, 1954). Special attention should be called to M. J. Charlesworth, *St. Anselm's Proslogion* (Oxford, England: Clarendon Press, 1965), with Latin text, new translation, philosophical commentary, and introductory essays on Anselm's life and times, Anselm's relation to Augustine, his position on faith and reason, and so forth. A treatment of Anselm's logic and its relevance for contemporary philosophical issues may be found in Desmond Paul Henry, *The Logic of Saint Anselm* (Oxford, England: Clarendon Press, 1967). A discussion of Descartes' proofs for the existence of God may be found in Norman Kemp Smith, *New Studies in the Philosophy of Descartes* (New York: Russell & Russell, 1963). For a brief commentary on Kant's criticism, see Norman Kemp Smith, *A Commentary to Kant's Critique of Pure Reason*, revised ed. (New York: Macmillan, 1923), pp. 527 ff.

Several critiques of Malcolm's argument are collected in the *Philosophical Review*, LXX (January, 1961); and one should note also A. C. Ewing's criticism, "Further Thoughts on the Ontological Argument," *Religious Studies*, V (October, 1969). For a general (though at times technical) discussion of the positions of Anselm, Kant, and Malcolm, see Alvin Plantinga, *God and Other Minds*, Chs. 2 and 3 (Ithaca, N. Y.: Cornell University Press, 1967). Another contemporary reformulation of the Ontological Argument is that of Charles Hartshorne, who develops the argument with the aid of modal logic. Hartshorne's statement of the argument may be found in *Anselm's Discovery* (La Salle, Ill.: Open Court, 1962). Hartshorne's position is further illuminated in the following interchange: Charles Hartshorne, "Necessity," R. L. Purtell, "Ontological Modalities," and Hartshorne's "Rejoinder to Purtell," all in *Review of Metaphysics*, XXI (December, 1967); and R. L. Purtell, "Hartshorne's Modal Proof," *Journal of Philosophy*, LXVII (July, 1966).

Two different attempts to elucidate the broader significance of the Ontological Argument within a theological context may be found in Karl Barth, *Anselm: Fides Quaerens Intellectum*, tr. Ian Robertson (London: Student Christian Movement Press, 1960) and Paul Tillich, "Two Types of Philosophy of Religion," in *Theology of Culture*, ed. Robert C. Kimball (New York: Oxford University Press, 1959). For a further, and brief, treatment of the argument by Tillich, see his *Systematic Theology*, Vol. I, Part II, I, 11 (Chicago: University of Chicago Press, 1951-63).

SECTION 2

God and the Cosmos

❋ INTRODUCTION

Very different from the Ontological Argument are the *a posteriori* (or empirical) arguments which, drawing their evidence from sense-experience, attempt to establish a knowledge of God from nature. The Cosmological Argument (often called the First-Cause Argument) attempts to prove the existence of God as the ultimate cause of some empirical reality or other, usually the world or universe itself. The Teleological Argument (the Design Argument) proves the existence of God as the cause of something *about* reality or the world, namely, its apparent design or order.

The most famous statement of the Cosmological Argument is contained in the celebrated "Five Ways" of St. Thomas Aquinas. In the course of a few pages near the beginning of his *Summa Theologica,* Thomas both rejects Anselm's Ontological Argument and presents his own fivefold proof on the basis of his empiricist principle, *Nihil est in intellectu quod non prius fuerit in sensu,* "Nothing is in the intellect which was not first in the senses." Thomas derived his empirical outlook from Aristotle ("The Philosopher") and it is reflected in almost every aspect of Thomistic philosophy, and certainly in this one.

It follows, for example, that we can have no knowledge of God's full essence since we can know him only indirectly through his effects in nature, and therefore it is not possible to deduce his existence *a priori* from his essence as Anselm attempted to do. On the other hand, Thomas believed that we *are* able to construct arguments for God's existence based upon the natural world, specifically from the (1) moved, (2) caused, (3) non-necessary, (4) graduated, and (5) ordered character of creation. Though the relation between Thomas' five proofs is sometimes debated, clearly the first three are versions of the Cosmological Argument. The crux of Thomas' reasoning in these proofs is this. The world (which could not come from nothing, nor be the cause of itself) is *contingent*, that is, it is not self-explanatory, it depends for its existence upon something else; and since an infinite chain of causes and effects is impossible, we are led inevitably to a transcendent first cause of the world. Thomas' argument, then, seeks to establish God not as a *logical* necessity (as the Ontological Argument is often thought to do) but a *metaphysical* necessity: God's necessity follows from the very nature of all other things as contingent.

It is extremely important, however, to understand exactly what Thomas means—and does not mean—by "first" cause. Though Thomas believed as a Christian that God created the world in time, he argues throughout his Five Ways on the assumption (exhibited best in the Third Way) that the universe has existed from eternity. He is therefore willing to grant at the very beginning what his opponent will surely demand sooner or later:

The most efficacious way to prove that God exists is on the supposition that the world is eternal. Granted this supposition, that God exists is less manifest. For, if the world and motion have a first beginning, some cause must clearly be posited to account for this origin of the world and of motion.[1]

The God that Thomas attempts to prove, then, is not a first cause standing at the beginning of the temporal series, but rather, like Aristotle's Unmoved Mover, an *ultimate* being upon whom the world at every moment depends for its existence, even its eternal existence. As Copleston states it, "We have to imagine, not a lineal or horizontal series, so to speak, but a vertical hierarchy in which a lower member depends here and now on the present causal activity of the member above it. It is the latter type of series, if prolonged to infinity, which Aquinas rejects."[2] There is, of course, a form of the Cosmological Argument that does reason to the existence of a first cause in time (that is, a cause of all things standing at the beginning of the temporal series) on the grounds that the world could not have always existed, a point that has often been argued both ways. That is not, however, the more classical form of the argument, nor is it St. Thomas'.

Most readers will recognize Thomas' Fifth Way as an expression of the Teleological Argument, the argument from design, though some interpreters emphasize that it should be read, rather, as a variation on Thomas' *one* argument. Be that as it may, William Paley's is surely the best-known statement of the Design Argument. Paley, who wrote prior to Darwin, attempts to prove the existence of God from instances of "special design," products immediately assignable to intelligence. It would never occur to any reasonable person that pieces and particles of matter should, through sheer chance, assume the shapes and relations so as to produce a ticking watch. Now, says Paley, how much more incredible would be the suggestion that the contrivance and mechanism of this vast universe (infinitely more complicated than a watch) should have occurred through chance and coincidence. Indeed, if the only evidence were that of the human eye, it would be sufficient to establish belief in "special creation" and therefore the existence of a Divine Being, an Architect and Contriver.

With the selections from Hume and Kant we come, no doubt, to the most devastating critiques ever leveled against the traditional arguments for God. Both the Cosmological and Teleological Arguments are, obviously, *causal* arguments; they move to the existence of God as the cause of something, namely, the world and its apparent design. Hume and Kant both attack this theistic employment of the causal principle—"Every event must have a cause"—though in very different ways.

[1]St. Thomas Aquinas, *Summa Contra Gentiles*, I, 13, tr. Anton C. Pegis (Garden City, N.Y.: Image Books, 1955).

[2]F. C. Copleston, *Aquinas* (Baltimore, Md.: Penguin Books, 1955), p. 118.

David Hume, a radical empiricist, insists that we have no rational justification for extending the causal principle to God's creation or design of the world, since the knowledge of all causal relations is founded upon sense-experience. The only reason we have for positing A as the cause of B is our past and repeated *observation* of A giving rise to B; the "constant conjunction" between carpenters and houses leads to the establishment, in our minds, of a causal relation, that is, the purely psychological expectation of like effects from like causes. But who has ever made repeated observations (or even a single observation) of God creating or designing worlds? In fact, is there anything in experience to which the divine being and his omnipotent activity could ever be likened? Hume presents several criticisms of the *a posteriori* arguments for God, but most of them reduce, essentially, to the thesis that experience provides no knowledge, no analogies, no clues as to the divine causality. The Cosmological and Teleological Arguments represent both illegitimate extensions of our empirically derived concepts and illegitimate inferences beyond the evidence.

For Immanuel Kant, too, these arguments involve an illegitimate extension of causality, but not because the concept of causality, as a philosophical principle, has a purely empirical origin. Rather, according to Kant, causality is one of the concepts or fundamental "categories" which are part of the mind's very structure and which themselves help make experience possible. On this understanding, every event must have a cause (Hume denied that even that was certain as a rational principle) because the causal relation is one of the ways in which the "theoretical reason" necessarily organizes or, better, *represents* reality. But if that is so, causality can have no bearing except on objects of possible experience, and thus God (and every other supra-empirical or metaphysical concept) lies forever beyond the reach of theoretical reason. Furthermore, and aside from the question of causality, the Teleological Argument (which Kant calls the "Physico-theological Argument") proves at best only an Architect of the universe, not necessarily a Supreme Being. This argument, therefore, is powerless apart from the Cosmological Argument, and the Cosmological Argument, Kant argues, reduces to the Ontological Argument which, as we have seen, he has already rejected.

Hume and Kant lead us, therefore, to a series of very important questions concerning the concept of causality as it applies to theistic arguments: Is the principle of causality (considered as a rational principle) a mere generalization based on experience? If so, can we ever be *certain* that every event has a cause? And does such a concept have any application beyond experience? Or is it the case that causality and order do not exist "out there" at all but are, rather, products of our own minds? Is there *anything* in our experience that does not reflect merely the working of our own minds? And how does one know the difference?

With F. R. Tennant we come to what many would call the strongest theistic argument that could be provided for modern man, schooled as he is in the empirical sciences. Tennant, disenchanted with traditional speculative proofs, thought it possible to develop a scientific-type argument for God's existence, an empirical argument that would possess the same degree of plausibility and command as much respect as any well-established scientific hypothesis, one that would provide, as he says, "grounds for reasonable belief." The evidence for Tennant's Teleological Argument is not the special designs seized upon by Paley (the idea of special design and special creation went out when Darwin came in) but the "wider teleology," the universal cooperation of the many strands of nature bent upon the production of higher and higher levels of intelligibility, beauty, unity, and coming to fruition ultimately in man, the moral creature. Though evolution meant the downfall of Paley's argument, it thus becomes one of the most obvious evidences in support of Tennant's argument as well as a whole new style of philosophical theology. Whether Tennant is successful in developing a theistic application of empirical concepts and probabilities in a way that escapes, say, Hume's criticisms of earlier arguments may be a profitable question.

ST. THOMAS AQUINAS

5. *The Five Ways*

St. Thomas Aquinas (1225–1274) was a Dominican friar and the most influential thinker of the scholastic period. His most important works, the *Summa Theologica* and the *Summa Contra Gentiles,* were intended to demonstrate that belief in revelation is not incompatible with a philosophical theology that proceeds by the light of natural reason and draws its concepts from the created order. Thomism continues to be the dominating philosophy of the Roman Catholic Church.

From *Summa Theologica*

Part I, Question II

First Article: Whether the Existence of God is Self-Evident?

Objection 1. It seems that the existence of God is self-evident. For those things are said to be self-evident to us the knowledge of which exists naturally in us, as we can see in regard to first principles. But as Damascene says, *the knowledge of God is naturally implanted in all.*[1] Therefore the existence of God is self-evident.

Obj. 2. Further, those things are said to be self-evident which are known as soon as the terms are known, which the Philosopher says is true of the first principles of demonstration.[2] Thus, when the nature of a

St. Thomas Aquinas, *Summa Theologica,* in *Basic Writings of St. Thomas Aquinas,* ed. Anton C. Pegis (New York: Random House, 1945), I. Reprinted by permission of Random House, Inc. and Burnes & Oates, Ltd.

[1][Cf. St. John Damascene, *On the Orthodox Faith,* I, 1, 3.]

[2][Cf. Aristotle, *Posterior Analytics,* I, 3 (72b 18) .]

whole and of a part is known, it is at once recognized that every whole is greater than its part. But as soon as the signification of the name *God* is understood, it is at once seen that God exists. For by this name is signified that thing than which nothing greater can be conceived. But that which exists actually and mentally is greater than that which exists only mentally. Therefore, since as soon as the name *God* is understood it exists mentally, it also follows that it exists actually. Therefore the proposition *God exists* is self-evident.

Obj. 3. Further, the existence of truth is self-evident. For whoever denies the existence of truth grants that truth does not exist: and, if truth does not exist, then the proposition *Truth does not exist* is true: and if there is anything true, there must be truth. But God is truth itself: *I am the way, the truth, and the life* [John 14:6]. Therefore *God exists* is self-evident.

On the contrary, No one can mentally admit the opposite of what is self-evident as the Philosopher states concerning the first principles of demonstration.[3] But the opposite of the proposition *God is* can be mentally admitted: *The fool said in his heart, There is no God* [Ps. 14:1]. Therefore, that God exists is not self-evident.

I answer that, A thing can be self-evident in either of two ways: on the one hand, self-evident in itself, though not to us; on the other, self-evident in itself, and to us. A proposition is self-evident because the predicate is included in the essence of the subject: *e.g., Man is an animal,* for animal is contained in the essence of man. If, therefore, the essence of the predicate and subject be known to all, the proposition will be self-evident to all; as is clear with regard to the first principles of demonstration, the terms of which are certain common notions that no one is ignorant of, such as being and non-being, whole and part, and the like. If, however, there are some to whom the essence of the predicate and subject is unknown, the proposition will be self-evident in itself, but not to those who do not know the meaning of the predicate and subject of the proposition. Therefore, it happens, as Boethius says, that there are some notions of the mind which are common and self-evident only to the learned, as that incorporeal substances are not in space.[4] Therefore I say that this proposition, *God exists,* of itself is self-evident, for the predicate is the same as the subject, because God is His own existence as will be hereafter shown. Now because we do not know the essence of God, the proposition is not self-evident to us, but needs to be demonstrated by things that are more known to us, though less known in their nature—namely, by His effects.

Reply Obj. 1. To know that God exists in a general and confused way is implanted in us by nature, inasmuch as God is man's beatitude. For man naturally desires happiness, and what is naturally desired by man is naturally known by him. This, however, is not to know absolutely that God exists; just as to know that someone is approaching is not the same as to know that Peter is approaching, even though it is Peter who is approaching;

[3][Cf. Aristotle, *Metaphysics,* III, 3 (1005b 11) .]
[4][Cf. St. Boethius, *On The Seven Days* (in J. P. Migne, *Patrologia Latina,* 64, 1311).]

for there are many who imagine that man's perfect good, which is happiness, consists in riches, and others in pleasures, and others in something else.

Reply Obj. 2.   Perhaps not everyone who hears this name *God* understands it to signify something than which nothing greater can be thought, seeing that some have believed God to be a body. Yet, granted that everyone understands that by this name *God* is signified something than which nothing greater can be thought, nevertheless, it does not therefore follow that he understands that what the name signifies exists actually, but only that it exists mentally. Nor can it be argued that it actually exists, unless it be admitted that there actually exists something than which nothing greater can be thought; and this precisely is not admitted by those who hold that God does not exist.

Reply Obj. 3.   The existence of truth is self-evident, but the existence of a Primal Truth is not self-evident to us.

Second Article: Whether It Can Be Demonstrated that God Exists?

Objection 1.   It seems that the existence of God cannot be demonstrated. For it is an article of faith that God exists. But what is of faith cannot be demonstrated, because a demonstration produces scientific knowledge, whereas faith is of the unseen, as is clear from the Apostle [cf. Heb. 11:1]. Therefore it cannot be demonstrated that God exists.

Obj. 2.   Further, essence is the middle term of demonstration. But we cannot know in what God's essence consists, but solely in what it does not consist, as Damascene says.[5] Therefore we cannot demonstrate that God exists.

Obj. 3.   Further, if the existence of God were demonstrated, this could only be from His effects. But His effects are not proportioned to Him, since He is infinite and His effects are finite, and between the finite and infinite there is no proportion. Therefore, since a cause cannot be demonstrated by an effect not proportioned to it, it seems that the existence of God cannot be demonstrated.

On the contrary, The Apostle says: *The invisible things of Him are clearly seen, being understood by the things that are made* [Rom. 1:20]. But this would not be unless the existence of God could be demonstrated through the things that are made; for the first thing we must know of anything is, whether it exists.

I answer that, Demonstration can be made in two ways: One is through the cause, and is called *propter quid,* and this is to argue from what is prior absolutely. The other is through the effect, and is called a demonstration *quia;* this is to argue from what is prior relatively only to us. When an effect is better known to us than its cause, from the effect we proceed to the knowledge of the cause. And from every effect the existence of its proper cause can be demonstrated, so long as its effects are better known to us; because, since every effect depends upon its cause, if the effect exists, the cause must preexist. Hence the existence of God, in so far as it is not self-evident to us, can be demonstrated from those of His effects which are known to us.

[5][Cf. St. John Damascene, *On the Orthodox Faith,* I, 4.]

Reply Obj. 1.   The existence of God and other like truths about God, which can be known by natural reason, are not articles of faith, but are preambles to the articles; for faith presupposes natural knowledge, even as grace presupposes nature and perfection the perfectible. Nevertheless, there is nothing to prevent a man, who cannot grasp a proof, from accepting, as a matter of faith, something which in itself is capable of being scientifically known and demonstrated.

Reply Obj. 2.   When the existence of a cause is demonstrated from an effect, this effect takes the place of the definition of the cause in proving the cause's existence. This is especially the case in regard to God, because, in order to prove the existence of anything, it is necessary to accept as a middle term the meaning of the name, and not its essence, for the question of its essence follows on the question of its existence. Now the names given to God are derived from His effects, as will be later shown. Consequently, in demonstrating the existence of God from His effects, we may take for the middle term the meaning of the name *God*.

Reply Obj. 3.   From effects not proportioned to the cause no perfect knowledge of that cause can be obtained. Yet from every effect the existence of the cause can be clearly demonstrated, and so we can demonstrate the existence of God from His effects; though from them we cannot know God perfectly as He is in His essence.

Third Article: Whether God Exists?

Objection 1.   It seems that God does not exist; because if one of two contraries be infinite, the other would be altogether destroyed. But the name *God* means that He is infinite goodness. If, therefore, God existed, there would be no evil discoverable; but there is evil in the world. Therefore God does not exist.

Obj. 2.   Further, it is superfluous to suppose that what can be accounted for by few principles has been produced by many. But it seems that everything we see in the world can be accounted for by other principles, supposing God did not exist. For all natural things can be reduced to one principle, which is nature; and all voluntary things can be reduced to one principle, which is human reason, or will. Therefore there is no need to suppose God's existence.

On the contrary, It is said in the person of God: *I am Who am* [Ex. 3:14].

I answer that, The existence of God can be proved in five ways.

The first and more manifest way is the argument from motion. It is certain, and evident to our senses, that in the world some things are in motion. Now whatever is moved is moved by another, for nothing can be moved except it is in potentiality to that towards which it is moved; whereas a thing moves inasmuch as it is in act. For motion is nothing else than the reduction of something from potentiality to actuality. But nothing can be reduced from potentiality to actuality, except by something in a state of actuality. Thus that which is actually hot, as fire, makes wood, which is potentially hot, to be actually hot, and thereby moves and changes it. Now it is not possible that the same thing should be at once in actuality and potentiality in the same respect, but only in different respects. For what is actually hot cannot simultaneously be potentially hot; but it is simultaneously potentially cold. It is therefore impossible that in the same respect and in the same way a thing should be both mover and moved, *i.e.,* that it should move itself. Therefore, whatever is moved must be moved by another. If that by which it is moved be itself moved, then this also must needs be moved by another, and that by another again. But this cannot go on to infinity, because then there would be no first mover, and, consequently, no other mover, seeing that subsequent movers move only inasmuch as they are moved by the first mover; as the staff moves only because it is moved by the hand. Therefore it is necessary to arrive at a first mover, moved by no other; and this everyone understands to be God.

The second way is from the nature of efficient cause. In the world of sensible things we find there is an order of efficient causes. There is no case known (neither is it, indeed, possible) in which a thing is found to be the efficient cause of itself; for so it would be prior to itself, which is impossible. Now in efficient causes it is not possible to go on to infinity, because in all efficient causes following in order, the first is the cause of the intermediate cause, and the intermediate is the cause of the ultimate cause, whether the intermediate cause be several, or one only. Now to take away the cause is to take away the effect. Therefore, if there be no first cause among efficient causes, there will be no ultimate, nor any intermediate, cause. But if in efficient causes it is possible to go on to infinity, there will be no first efficient cause, neither will there be an ultimate effect, nor any intermediate efficient causes; all of which is plainly false. Therefore it is necessary to admit a first efficient cause, to which everyone gives the name of God.

The third way is taken from possibility and necessity, and runs thus. We find in nature things that are possible to be and not to be, since they are found to be generated, and to be corrupted, and consequently, it is possible for them to be and not to be. But is is impossible for these always to exist, for that which can not-be at some time is not. Therefore, if everything can not-be, then at one time there was nothing in existence. Now if this were true, even now there would be nothing in existence, because that which does not exist begins to exist only through something already existing. Therefore, if at one time nothing was in existence, it would have been impossible for anything to have begun to exist; and thus even now nothing would be in existence—which is absurd. Therefore, not all beings are merely possible, but there must exist something the existence of which is necessary. But every necessary thing either has its necessity caused by another, or not. Now it is impossible to go on to infinity in necessary things which have their necessity caused by another, as has been already proved in regard to efficient causes. Therefore we cannot but admit the existence of some being having of itself its own necessity, and not receiving it from another, but rather causing in others their necessity. This all men speak of as God.

The fourth way is taken from the gradation to be found in things. Among beings there are some more and some less good, true, noble, and the like. But *more* and *less* are predicated of different things according as they resemble in their different ways something which is the maximum, as a thing is said to be hotter according as it more nearly resembles that which is hottest; so that there is something which is truest, something best, something noblest, and, consequently, something which is most being, for those things that are greatest in truth are greatest in being, as it is written in *Metaph.* ii. Now the maximum in any genus is the cause of all in that genus, as fire, which is the maximum of heat, is the cause of all hot things, as is said in the same book.[6] Therefore there must also be something which is to all beings the cause of their being, goodness, and every other perfection; and this we call God.

The fifth way is taken from the governance of the world. We see that things which lack knowledge, such as natural bodies, act for an end, and this is evident from their acting always, or nearly always, in the same way, so as to obtain the best result. Hence it is plain that they achieve their end, not fortuitously, but designedly. Now whatever lacks knowledge cannot move towards an end, unless it be directed by some being endowed with knowledge and intelligence; as the arrow is directed by the archer. Therefore some intelligent being exists by whom all natural things are directed to their end; and this being we call God.

Reply Obj. 1. As Augustine says: *Since God is the highest good, He would not allow any evil to exist in His works, unless His omnipotence and goodness were such as to bring good even out of evil.*[7] This is part of the infinite goodness of God, that He should allow evil to exist, and out of it produce good.

Reply Obj. 2. Since nature works for a determinate end under the direction of a higher agent, whatever is done by nature must be traced back to God as to its first cause. So likewise whatever is done voluntarily must be traced back to some higher cause other than human reason and will, since these can change and fail; for all things that are changeable and capable of defect must be traced back to an immovable and self-necessary first principle, as has been shown.

[6][Cf. Aristotle, *Metaphysics*, II, 1 (993b 25 ff.).]

[7][Cf. St. Augustine, *Enchiridion*, 11.]

✳ WILLIAM PALEY

6. The Analogy of the Watch

William Paley (1743–1805) was Archdeacon of Carlisle and a defender of
Christian orthodoxy. His work was intended, as is reflected in his
Evidences for Christianity, as a buttress for the faithful at a time when
geology and biology were threatening the faith, and his *Natural Theology*
provides, no doubt, the most familiar statement of the kind of argument
that tries to establish an intelligent Creator from instances of special
design in the world.

From *Natural Theology*

Chapter 1: State of the Argument

In crossing a heath, suppose I pitched my foot against a *stone* and
were asked how the stone came to be there, I might possibly answer that
for anything I knew to the contrary it had lain there forever; nor would it,
perhaps, be very easy to show the absurdity of this answer. But suppose
I had found a *watch* upon the ground, and it should be inquired how the
watch happened to be in that place, I should hardly think of the answer
which I had before given, that for anything I knew the watch might have
always been there. Yet why should not this answer serve for the watch as
well as for the stone; why is it not as admissible in the second case as in
the first? For this reason, and for no other, namely, that when we come to
inspect the watch, we perceive—what we could not discover in the stone—that
its several parts are framed and put together for a purpose, e.g., that they
are so formed and adjusted as to produce motion, and that motion so regulated
as to point out the hour of the day; that if the different parts had been
differently shaped from what they are, or placed after any other manner or
in any other order than that in which they are placed, either no motion at
all would have been carried on in the machine, or none which would have
answered the use that is now served by it. To reckon up a few of the plainest
of these parts and of their offices, all tending to one result: we see a cylindrical
box containing a coiled elastic spring, which, by its endeavor to relax itself,
turns round the box. We next observe a flexible chain—artificially wrought
for the sake of flexure—communicating the action of the spring from the
box to the fusee. We then find a series of wheels, the teeth of which catch
in and apply to each other, conducting the motion from the fusee to the
balance and from the balance to the pointer, and at the same time, by the

size and shape of those wheels, so regulating that motion as to terminate in causing an index, by an equable and measured progression, to pass over a given space in a given time. We take notice that the wheels are made of brass, in order to keep them from rust; the springs of steel, no other metal being so elastic; that over the face of the watch there is placed a glass, a material employed in no other part of the work, but in the room of which, if there had been any other than a transparent substance, the hour could not be seen without opening the case. This mechanism being observed—it requires indeed an examination of the instrument, and perhaps some previous knowledge of the subject, to perceive and understand it; but being once, as we have said, observed and understood—the inference we think is inevitable, that the watch must have had a maker—that there must have existed, at some time and at some place or other, an artificer or artificers who formed it for the purpose which we find it actually to answer, who completely comprehended its construction and designed its use.

I. Nor would it, I apprehend, weaken the conclusion, that we had never seen a watch made—that we had never known an artist capable of making one—that we were altogether incapable of executing such a piece of workmanship ourselves, or of understanding in what manner it was performed; all this being no more than what is true of some exquisite remains of ancient art, of some lost arts, and, to the generality of mankind, of the more curious productions of modern manufacture. Does one man in a million know how oval frames are turned? Ignorance of this kind exalts our opinion of the unseen and unknown artist's skill, if he be unseen and unknown, but raises no doubt in our minds of the existence and agency of such an artist, at some former time and in some place or other. Nor can I perceive that it varies at all the inference, whether the question arise concerning a human agent or concerning an agent of a different species, or an agent possessing in some respects a different nature.

II. Neither, secondly, would it invalidate our conclusion, that the watch sometimes went wrong or that it seldom went exactly right. The purpose of the machinery, the design, and the designer might be evident, and in the case supposed, would be evident, in whatever way we accounted for the irregularity of the movement, or whether we could account for it or not. It is not necessary that a machine be perfect in order to show with what design it was made: still less necessary, where the only question is whether it were made with any design at all.

III. Nor, thirdly, would it bring any uncertainty into the argument, if there were a few parts of the watch, concerning which we could not discover or had not yet discovered in what manner they conduced to the general effect; or even some parts, concerning which we could not ascertain whether they conduced to that effect in any manner whatever. For, as to the first branch of the case, if by the loss, or disorder, or decay of the parts in question, the movement of the watch were found in fact to be stopped, or disturbed, or retarded, no doubt would remain in our minds as to the utility or intention of these parts, although we should be unable to investigate the manner according to which, or the connection by which, the ultimate effect depended upon their action or assistance; and the more complex the machine, the more likely is this obscurity to arise. Then, as to the second thing supposed, namely, that there were parts which might be spared without prejudice to the movement of the watch, and that we had proved this by experiment, these superfluous parts, even if we were completely assured that they were such, would not vacate the reasoning which we had instituted concerning other parts. The indication of contrivance remained, with respect to them, nearly as it was before.

IV. Nor, fourthly, would any man in his senses think the existence of the watch with its various machinery accounted for, by being told that it was one out of possible combinations of material forms; that whatever he had found in the place where he found the watch, must have contained some internal configuration or other; and that this configuration might be the structure now exhibited, namely, of the works of a watch, as well as a different structure.

V. Nor, fifthly, would it yield his inquiry more satisfaction, to be answered that there existed in things a principle of order, which had disposed the parts of the watch into their present form and situation. He never knew a watch made by the principle of order; nor can he even form to himself an idea of what is meant by a principle of order distinct from the intelligence of the watchmaker.

VI. Sixthly, he would be surprised to hear that the mechanism of the watch was no proof of contrivance, only a motive to induce the mind to think so:

VII. And not less surprised to be informed that the watch in his hand was nothing more than the result of the laws of *metallic* nature. It is a perversion of language to assign any law as the efficient, operative cause of any thing. A law presupposes an agent, for it is only the mode according to which an agent proceeds: it implies a power, for it is the order according to which that power acts. Without this agent, without this power, which are both distinct from itself, the *law* does nothing, is nothing. The expression, "the law of metallic nature," may sound strange and harsh to a philosophic ear; but it seems quite as justifiable as some others which are more familiar to him, such as "the law of vegetable nature," "the law of animal nature," or, indeed, as "the law of nature" in general, when assigned as the cause of phenomena, in exclusion of agency and power, or when it is substituted into the place of these.

VIII. Neither, lastly, would our observer be driven out of his conclusion or from his confidence in its truth by being told that he knew nothing at all about the matter. He knows enough for his argument; he knows the utility of the end; he knows the subserviency and adaptation of the means to the end. These points being known, his ignorance of other points, his doubts concerning other points affect not the certainty of his reasoning. The consciousness of knowing little need not beget a distrust of that which he does know.

CHAPTER 2: STATE OF THE ARGUMENT CONTINUED

Suppose, in the next place, that the person who found the watch should after some time discover that, in addition to all the properties which he had hitherto observed in it, it possessed the unexpected property of producing in the course of its movement another watch like itself—the thing is conceivable; that it contained within it a mechanism, a system of parts—a mold, for instance, or a complex adjustment of lathes, files, and other tools—evidently and separately calculated for this purpose; let us inquire what effect ought such a discovery to have upon his former conclusion.

I. The first effect would be to increase his admiration of the contrivance, and his conviction of the consummate skill of the contriver. Whether he regarded the object of the contrivance, the distinct apparatus, the intricate, yet in many parts intelligible mechanism by which it was carried on, he would perceive in this new observation nothing but an additional reason for doing what he had already done—for referring the construction of the watch to design and to supreme art. If that construction *without* this property, or, which is the same thing, before this property had been noticed, proved intention and art to have been employed about it, still more strong would the proof appear when he came to the knowledge of this further property, the crown and perfection of all the rest.

II. He would reflect that, though the watch before him were *in some sense* the maker of the watch which was fabricated in the course of its movements, yet it was in a very different sense from that in which a carpenter, for instance, is the maker of a chair—the author of its contrivance, the cause of the relation of its parts to their use. With respect to these, the first watch was no cause at all to the second; in no such sense as this was it the author of the constitution and order, either of the parts which the new watch contained, or of the parts by the aid and instrumentality of which it was produced. We might possibly say, but with great latitude of expression, that a stream of water ground corn; but no latitude of expression would allow us to say, no stretch of conjecture could lead us to think that the stream of water built the mill, though it were too ancient for us to know who the builder was. What the stream of water does in the affair is neither more nor less than this: by the application of an unintelligent impulse to a mechanism previously arranged, arranged independently of it and arranged by intelligence, an effect is produced, namely, the corn is ground. But the effect results from the arrangement. The force of the stream cannot be said to be the cause or the author of the effect, still less of the arrangement. Understanding and plan in the formation of the mill were not the less necessary for any share which the water has in grinding the corn; yet is this share the same as that which the watch would have contributed to the production of the new watch, upon the supposition assumed in the last section. Therefore,

III. Though it be now no longer probable that the individual watch which our observer had found was made immediately by the hand of an artificer, yet this alteration does not in anywise affect the inference that an artificer had been originally employed and concerned in the production. The argument from design remains as it was. Marks of design and contrivance are no more accounted for now than they were before. In the same thing, we may ask for the cause of different properties. We may ask for the cause of the color of a body, of its hardness, of its heat; and these causes may be all different. We are now asking for the cause of that subserviency to a use, that relation to an end, which we have remarked in the watch before us. No answer is given to this question by telling us that a preceding watch produced it. There cannot be design without a designer; contrivance without a contriver; order without choice; arrangement without anything capable of arranging; subserviency and relation to a purpose without that which could intend a purpose; means suitable to an end, and executing their office in accomplishing that end, without the end ever having been contemplated or the means accommodated to it. Arrangement, disposition of parts, subserviency of means to an end, relation of instruments to a use imply the presence of intelligence and mind. No one, therefore, can rationally believe that the insensible, inanimate watch, from which the watch before us issued, was the proper cause of the mechanism we so much admire in it—could be truly said to have constructed the instrument, disposed its parts, assigned their office, determined their order, action, and mutual dependency, combined their several motions into one result, and that also a result connected with the utilities of other beings. All these properties, therefore, are as much unaccounted for as they were before.

IV. Nor is anything gained by running the difficulty farther back, that is, by supposing the watch before us to have been produced from another watch, that from a former, and so on indefinitely. Our going back ever so far brings us no nearer to the least degree of satisfaction upon the subject. Contrivance is still unaccounted for. We still want a contriver. A designing mind is neither supplied by this supposition nor dispensed with. If the difficulty were diminished the farther we went back, by going back indefinitely we might exhaust it. And this is the only case to which this sort of reasoning applies. Where there is a tendency, or, as we increase the number of terms, a continual approach toward a limit, *there*, by supposing the number of terms to be what is called infinite, we may conceive the limit to be attained; but where there is no such tendency or approach, nothing is effected by lengthening the series. There is no difference as to the point in question, whatever there may be as to many points, between one series and another—between a series which is finite and a series which is infinite. A chain composed of an infinite number of links can no more support itself than a chain composed of a finite number of links. And of this we are assured, though we never *can* have tried the experiment; because, by increasing the number of links, from ten, for instance, to a hundred, from a hundred to a thousand, etc., we make not the smallest approach, we observe not the smallest tendency toward self-support. There is no difference in this respect—yet there may be a great difference in several respects—between a chain of a greater or less length, between one chain and another, between one that is finite and one that is infinite. This very much resembles the case before us. The machine which we are inspecting demonstrates, by its construction, contrivance and design. Contrivance must have had a contriver, design a designer, whether the machine immediately proceeded from another machine or not. That circumstance alters not the case. That other machine may, in like manner, have proceeded from a former machine: nor does that alter the case; the contrivance must have had a contriver. That former one from one preceding it: no alteration still; a contriver is still necessary. No tendency is perceived, no approach toward a diminution of this necessity. It is the same with any and every succession of these machines—a succession of ten, of a hundred, of a thousand; with one series, as with another—a series which is finite, as with a series which is infinite. In whatever other respects they may differ, in this they do not. In all equally, contrivance and design are unaccounted for.

The question is not simply, how came the first watch into existence?—which question, it may be pretended, is done away by supposing the series of watches thus produced from one another to have been infinite, and consequently to have had no such *first* for which it was necessary to provide a cause. This, perhaps, would have been nearly the state of the question, if nothing had been before us but an unorganized, unmechanized substance, without mark or indication of contrivance. It might be difficult to show that such substance could not have existed from eternity, either in succession—if it were possible, which I think it is not, for unorganized bodies to spring from one another—or by individual perpetuity. But that is not the question now. To suppose it to be so is to suppose that it made no difference whether he had found a watch or a stone. As it is, the metaphysics of that question have no place; for, in the watch which we are examining are seen contrivance, design, an end, a purpose, means for the end, adaptation to the purpose. And the question which irresistibly presses upon our thoughts is, whence this contrivance and design? The thing required is the intending mind, the adapted hand, the intelligence by which that hand was directed. This question, this demand is not shaken off by increasing a number or succession of substances destitute of these properties; not the more, by increasing that number to infinity. If it be said that, upon the supposition of one watch being produced from another in the course of that other's movements and by means of the mechanism within it, we have a cause for the watch in my hand, namely, the watch from which it proceeded; I deny that for the design, the contrivance, the suitableness of means to an end, the adaptation of instruments to a use, all of which we discover in the watch, we have any cause whatever. It is in vain, therefore, to assign a series of such causes or to allege that a series may be carried back to infinity; for I do not admit that we have yet any cause at all for the phenomena, still less any series of causes either finite or infinite. Here is contrivance but no contriver; proofs of design, but no designer.

V. Our observer would further also reflect that the maker of the watch before him was in truth and reality the maker of every watch produced from it; there being no difference, except that the latter manifests a more exquisite skill, between the making of another watch with his own hands, by the mediation of files, lathes, chisels, etc., and the disposing, fixing, and inserting of these instruments, or of others equivalent to them, in the body of the watch already made, in such a manner as to form a new watch in the course of the movements which he had given to the old one. It is only working by one set of tools instead of another.

The conclusion which the *first* examination of the watch, of its works, construction, and movement, suggested, was that it must have had, for cause and author of that construction, an artificer who understood its mechanism and designed its use. This conclusion is invincible. A *second* examination presents us with a new discovery. The watch is found, in the course of its movement, to produce another watch similar to itself; and not only so, but we perceive in it a system or organization separately calculated for that purpose. What effect would this discovery have or ought it to have upon our former inference? What, as has already been said, but to increase beyond measure our admiration of the skill which had been employed in the formation of such a machine? Or shall it, instead of this, all at once turn us round to an opposite conclusion, namely, that no art or skill whatever has been concerned in the business, although all other evidences of art and skill remain as they were, and this last and supreme piece of art be now added to the rest? Can this be maintained without absurdity? Yet this is atheism.

CHAPTER 3: APPLICATION OF THE ARGUMENT

This is atheism; for every indication of contrivance, every manifestation of design which existed in the watch, exists in the works of nature, with the difference on the side of nature of being greater and more, and that in a degree which exceeds all computation. I mean that the contrivances of nature surpass the contrivances of art in the complexity, subtlety, and curiosity of the mechanism; and still more, if possible, do they go beyond them in number and variety; yet, in a multitude of cases, are not less evidently mechanical, not less evidently contrivances, not less evidently accommodated to their end or suited to their office than are the most perfect productions of human ingenuity.

I know no better method of introducing so large a subject than that of comparing a single thing with a single thing: an eye, for example, with a telescope. As far as the examination of the instrument goes, there is precisely the same proof that the eye was made for vision as there is that the telescope was made for assisting it. They are made upon the same principles, both being adjusted to the laws by which the transmission and refraction of rays of light are regulated. I speak not of the origin of the laws themselves; but such laws being fixed, the construction in both cases is adapted to them. For instance, these laws require, in order to produce the same effect, that rays of light in passing from water into the eye should be refracted by a more convex surface than when it passes out of air into the eye. Accordingly, we find that the eye of a fish, in that part of it called the crystalline lens, is much rounder than the eye of terrestrial animals. What plainer manifestation of design can there be than this difference? What could a mathematical instrument maker have done more to show his knowledge of his principle, his application of that knowledge, his suiting of his means to his end—I will not say to display the compass or excellence of his skill and art, for in these all comparison is indecorous, but to testify counsel, choice, consideration, purpose?

To some it may appear a difference sufficient to destroy all similitude between the eye and the telescope, that the one is a perceiving organ, the other an unperceiving instrument. The fact is that they are both instruments. And as to the mechanism, at least to the mechanism being employed, and even as to the kind of it, this circumstance varies not the analogy at all. For observe what the constitution of the eye is. It is necessary, in order to produce distinct vision, that an image or picture of the object be formed at the bottom of the eye. Whence this necessity arises, or how the picture is connected with the sensation or contributes to it, it may be difficult, nay, we will confess, if you please, impossible for us to search out. But the present question is not concerned in the inquiry. It may be true that in this and in other instances we trace mechanical contrivance a certain way, and that then we come to something which is not mechanical, or which is inscrutable. But this affects not the certainty of our investigation, as far as we have gone. The difference between an animal and an automatic statue consists in this, that in the animal we trace the mechanism to a certain point, and then we are stopped, either the mechanism being too subtle for our discernment, or something else beside the known laws of mechanism taking place; whereas, in the automaton, for the comparatively few motions of which it is capable, we trace the mechanism throughout. But, up to the limit, the reasoning is as clear and certain in the one case as in the other. In the example before us it is a matter of certainty, because it is a matter which experience and observation demonstrate, that the formation of an image at the bottom of the eye is necessary to perfect vision. The formation then of such an image being necessary—no matter how—to the sense of sight and to the exercise of that sense, the apparatus by which it is formed is constructed and put together not only with infinitely more art, but upon the selfsame principles of art as in the telescope or the camera obscura. The perception arising from the image may be laid out of the question; for the production of the image, these are instruments of the same kind. The end is the same, the means are the same. The purpose in both is alike, the contrivance for accomplishing that purpose is in both alike. The lenses of the telescopes and humors of the eye bear a complete resemblance to one another, in their figure, their position, and in their power over the rays of light, namely, in bringing each pencil to a point at the right distance from the lens; namely, in the eye, at the exact place where the membrane is spread to receive it. How is it possible, under circumstances of such close affinity, and under the operation of equal evidence, to exclude contrivance from the one, yet to acknowledge the proof of contrivance having been employed, as the plainest and clearest of all propositions, in the other?

The resemblance between the two cases is still more accurate, and obtains in more points than we have yet represented, or than we are, on the first view of the subject, aware of. In dioptric telescopes there is an imperfection of this nature. Pencils of light in passing through glass lenses are separated into different colors, thereby tinging the object, especially the edges of it, as if it were viewed through a prism. To correct this inconvenience had been long a desideratum in the art. At last it came into the mind of a sagacious optician to inquire how this matter was managed in the eye, in which there was exactly the same difficulty to contend with as in the telescope. His observation taught him that in the eye the evil was cured by combining lenses composed of different substances, that is, of substances which possesssed different refracting powers. Our artist borrowed thence his hint and produced a correction of the defect by imitating, in glasses made from different materials, the effects of the different humors through which the rays of light pass before they reach the bottom of the eye. Could this be in the eye without purpose, which suggested to the optician the only effectual means of attaining that purpose?

But further, there are other points not so much perhaps of strict resemblance between the two as of superiority of the eye over the telescope, yet of a superiority which, being founded in the laws that regulate both, may furnish topics of fair and just comparison. Two things were wanted to the eye, which were not wanted, at least in the same degree, to the telescope; and these were the adaptation of the organ, first, to different degrees of light, and secondly, to the vast diversity of distance at which objects are viewed by the naked eye, namely, from a few inches to as many miles. These difficulties present not themselves to the maker of the telescope. He wants all the light he can get; and he never directs his instrument to objects near at hand. In the eye, both these cases were to be provided for; and for the purpose of providing for them, a subtle and appropriate mechanism is introduced.
. . .

Chapter 6: The Argument Cumulative

Were there no example in the world of contrivance except that of the *eye*, it would be alone sufficient to support the conclusion which we draw from it, as to the necessity of an intelligent Creator. It could never be got rid of, because it could not be accounted for by any other supposition which did not contradict all the principles we possess of knowledge—the principles according to which things do, as often as they can be brought to the test of experience, turn out to be true or false. Its coats and humors, constructed as the lenses of a telescope are constructed, for the refraction of rays of light to a point, which forms the proper action of the organ; the provision in its muscular tendons for turning its pupil to the object, similar to that which is given to the telescope by screws, and upon which power of direction in the eye the exercise of its office as an optical instrument depends; the further provision for its defense, for its constant lubricity and moisture, which we see in its socket and its lids, in its glands for the secretion of the matter of tears, its outlet or communication with the nose for carrying off the liquid after the eye is washed with it; these provisions compose altogether an apparatus, a system of parts, a preparation of means, so manifest in their design, so exquisite in their contrivance, so successful in their issue, so precious, and so infinitely beneficial in their use, as, in my opinion, to bear down all doubt that can be raised upon the subject. And what I wish, under the title of the present chapter, to observe is that, if other parts of nature were inaccessible to our inquiries, or even if other parts of nature presented nothing to our examination but disorder and confusion, the validity of this example would remain the same. If there were but one watch in the world, it would not be less certain that it had a maker. If we had never in our lives seen any but one single kind of hydraulic machine, yet if of that one kind we understood the mechanism and use, we should be as perfectly assured that it proceeded from the hand and thought and skill of a workman, as if we visited a museum of the arts and saw collected there twenty different kinds of machines for drawing water, or a thousand different kinds for other purposes. Of this point each machine is a proof independently of all the rest. So it is with the evidences of a divine agency. The proof is not a conclusion which lies at the end of a chain of reasoning, of which chain each instance of contrivance is only a link, and of which, if one link fail, the whole fails; but it is an argument separately supplied by every separate example. An error in stating an example affects only that example. The argument is cumulative in the fullest sense of that term. The eye proves it without the ear; the ear without the eye. The proof in each example is complete; for when the design of the part and the conduciveness of its structure to that design is shown, the mind may set itself at rest; no future consideration can detract anything from the force of the example.

✤ DAVID HUME

7. The Failure of Analogies

David Hume (1711–1776) is often regarded as the greatest thinker of the British empiricist tradition. His skeptical philosophy is worked out in *A Treatise of Human Nature*, and his critiques of religion and theology are contained in his *Dialogues Concerning Natural Religion* (a classic indictment of the attempt to demonstrate God's attributes from his so-called effects in nature), *Natural History of Religion*, and his essay "On Miracles."

From *Dialogues Concerning Natural Religion*

Part II

I must own, Cleanthes, said Demea, that nothing can more surprise me than the light in which you have all along put this argument. By the whole tenor of your discourse, one would imagine that you were maintaining the Being of a God against the cavils of atheists and infidels, and were necessitated to become a champion for that fundamental principle of all religion. But this, I hope, is not by any means a question among us. No man, no man at least of common sense, I am persuaded, ever entertained a serious doubt with regard to a truth so certain and self-evident. The question is not concerning the *being* but the *nature* of God. This I affirm, from the infirmities of human understanding, to be altogether incomprehensible and unknown to us. The essence of that supreme Mind, his attributes, the manner of his existence, the very nature of his duration—these and every particular which regards so divine a Being are mysterious to men. Finite, weak, and blind creatures, we ought to humble ourselves in his august presence, and, conscious of our frailties, adore in silence his infinite perfections which eye hath not seen, ear hath not heard, neither hath it entered into the heart of man to conceive. They are covered in a deep cloud from human curiosity; it is profaneness to attempt penetrating through these sacred obscurities, and, next to the impiety of denying his existence, is the temerity of prying into his nature and essence, decrees and attributes.

But lest you should think that my *piety* has here got the better of my *philosophy*, I shall support my opinion, if it needs any support, by a very great authority. I might cite all the divines, almost from the foundation of Christianity, who have ever treated of this or any other theological subject; but I shall confine myself, at present, to one equally celebrated for piety and philosophy. It is Father Malebranche who, I remember, thus expresses himself.[1] "One ought not so much," says he, "to call God a spirit in order to express positively what he is, as in order to signify that he is not matter.

David Hume, *Dialogues Concerning Natural Religion*, ed. Henry D. Aiken (New York: Hafner, 1948). Reprinted by permission of the publisher.

[1]*Recherche de la Vérité*, liv. 3, cap. 9.

He is a Being infinitely perfect—of this we cannot doubt. But in the same manner as we ought not to imagine, even supposing him corporeal, that he is clothed with a human body, as the anthropomorphites asserted, under colour that that figure was the most perfect of any, so neither ought we to imagine that the spirit of God has human ideas or bears any resemblance to our spirit, under colour that we know nothing more perfect than a human mind. We ought rather to believe that as he comprehends the perfections of matter without being material . . . he comprehends also the perfections of created spirits without being spirit, in the manner we conceive spirit: that his true name is *He that is* [cf. Ex. 3:14], or, in other words, Being without restriction, All Being, the Being infinite and universal."

After so great an authority, Demea, replied Philo, as that which you have produced, and a thousand more which you might produce, it would appear ridiculous in me to add my sentiment or express my approbation of your doctrine. But surely, where reasonable men treat these subjects, the question can never be concerning the *being* but only the *nature* of the Deity. The former truth, as you well observe, is unquestionable and self-evident. Nothing exists without a cause; and the original cause of this universe (whatever it be) we call God, and piously ascribe to him every species of perfection. Whoever scruples this fundamental truth deserves every punishment which can be inflicted among philosophers, to wit, the greatest ridicule, contempt, and disapprobation. But as all perfection is entirely relative, we ought never to imagine that we comprehend the attributes of this divine Being, or to suppose that his perfections have any analogy or likeness to the perfections of a human creature. Wisdom, thought, design, knowledge—these we justly ascribe to him because these words are honourable among men, and we have no other language or other conceptions by which we can express our adoration of him. But let us beware lest we think that our ideas anywise correspond to his perfections, or that his attributes have any resemblance to these qualities among men. He is infinitely superior to our limited view and comprehension, and is more the object of worship in the temple than of disputation in the schools.

In reality, Cleanthes, continued he, there is no need of having recourse to that affected scepticism so displeasing to you in order to come at this determination. Our ideas reach no farther than our experience. We have no experience of divine attributes and operations. I need not conclude my syllogism, you can draw the inference yourself. And it is a pleasure to me (and I hope to you, too) that just reasoning and sound piety here concur in the same conclusion, and both of them establish the adorably mysterious and incomprehensible nature of the Supreme Being.

Not to lose any time in circumlocutions, said Cleanthes, addressing himself to Demea, much less in replying to the pious declamations of Philo, I shall briefly explain how I conceive this matter. Look round the world, contemplate the whole and every part of it: you will find it to be nothing but one great machine, subdivided into an infinite number of lesser machines, which again admit of subdivisions to a degree beyond what human senses and faculties can trace and explain. All these various machines, and even their most minute parts, are adjusted to each other with an accuracy which ravishes into admiration all men who have ever contemplated them. The curious adapting of means to ends, throughout all nature, resembles exactly, though it much exceeds, the productions of human contrivance—of human design, thought, wisdom, and intelligence. Since therefore the effects resemble each other, we are led to infer, by all the rules of analogy, that the causes also resemble, and that the Author of nature is somewhat similar to the mind of man, though possessed of much larger faculties, proportioned to the grandeur of the work which he has executed. By this argument *a posteriori*, and by this argument alone, do we prove at once the existence of a Deity and his similarity to human mind and intelligence.

I shall be so free, Cleanthes, said Demea, as to tell you that from the beginning I could not approve of your conclusion concerning the similarity of the Deity to men, still less can I approve of the mediums by which you endeavour to establish it. What! No demonstration of the Being of God! No abstract arguments! No proofs *a priori*! Are these which have hitherto been so much insisted on by philosophers all fallacy, all sophism? Can we reach no farther in this subject than experience and probability? I will not say that this is betraying the cause of a Deity; but surely, by this affected candour, you give advantages to atheists which they never could obtain by the mere dint of argument and reasoning.

What I chiefly scruple in this subject, said Philo, is not so much that all religious arguments are by Cleanthes reduced to experience, as that they appear not to be even the most certain and irrefragable of that inferior kind. That a stone will fall, that fire will burn, that the earth has solidity, we have observed a thousand and a thousand times; and when any new instance of this nature is presented, we draw without hesitation the accustomed inference. The exact similarity of the cases gives us a perfect assurance of a similar event, and a stronger evidence is never desired nor sought after. But wherever you depart, in the least, from the similarity of the cases, you diminish proportionably the evidence, and may at last bring it to a very weak *analogy*, which is confessedly liable to error and uncertainty. After having experienced the circulation of the blood in human creatures, we make no doubt that it takes place in Titius and Maevius; but from its circulation in frogs and fishes it is only a presumption, though a strong one, from analogy that it takes place in men and other animals. The analogical reasoning is much weaker when we infer the circulation of the sap in vegetables from our experience that the blood circulates in animals; and those who hastily followed that imperfect analogy are found, by more accurate experiments, to have been mistaken.

If we see a house, Cleanthes, we conclude, with the greatest certainty, that it had an architect or builder because this is precisely that species of effect which we have experienced to proceed from that species of cause. But surely you will not affirm that the universe bears such a resemblance to a house that we can with the same certainty infer a similar cause, or that the analogy is here entire and perfect. The dissimilitude is so striking that the utmost you can here pretend to is a guess, a conjecture, a presumption concerning a similar cause; and how that pretension will be received in the world, I leave you to consider.

It would surely be very ill received, replied Cleanthes; and I should be deservedly blamed and detested did I allow that the proofs of a Deity amounted to no more than a guess or conjecture. But is the whole adjustment of means to ends in a house and in the universe so slight a resemblance? the economy of final causes? the order, proportion, and arrangement of every part? Steps of a stair are plainly contrived that human legs may use them in mounting; and this inference is certain and infallible. Human legs are also contrived for walking and mounting; and this inference, I allow, is not altogether so certain because of the dissimilarity which you remark; but does it, therefore, deserve the name only of presumption or conjecture?

Good God! cried Demea, interrupting him, where are we? Zealous defenders of religion allow that the proofs of a Deity fall short of perfect evidence! And you, Philo, on whose assistance I depended in proving the adorable mysteriousness of the Divine Nature, do you assent to all these extravagant opinions of Cleanthes? For what other name can I give them? or, why spare my censure when such principles are advanced, supported by such an authority, before so young a man as Pamphilus?

You seem not to apprehend, replied Philo, that I argue with Cleanthes in his own way, and, by showing him the dangerous consequences of his tenets, hope at last to reduce him to our opinion. But what sticks most with you, I observe, is the representation which Cleanthes has made of the argument *a posteriori*; and, finding that that argument is likely to escape your hold and vanish into air, you think it so disguised that you can scarcely believe it to be set in its true light. Now, however much I may dissent, in other respects, from the dangerous principle of Cleanthes, I must allow that he has fairly represented that argument, and I shall endeavour so to state the matter to you that you will entertain no further scruples with regard to it.

Were a man to abstract from everything which he knows or has seen, he would be altogether incapable, merely from his own ideas, to determine what kind of scene the universe must be, or to give the preference to one state or situation of things above another. For as nothing which he clearly conceives could be esteemed impossible or implying a contradiction, every chimera of his fancy would be upon an equal footing; nor could he assign any just reason why he adheres to one idea or system, and rejects the others which are equally possible.

Again, after he opens his eyes and contemplates the world as it really is, it would be impossible for him at first to assign the cause of any one event, much less of the whole of things, or of the universe. He might set his fancy a rambling, and she might bring him in an infinite variety of reports and representations. These would all be possible, but, being all equally possible, he would never of himself give a satisfactory account for his preferring one of them to the rest. Experience alone can point out to him the true cause of any phenomenon.

Now, according to this method of reasoning, Demea, it follows (and is, indeed, tacitly allowed by Cleanthes himself) that order, arrangement, or the adjustment of final causes, is not of itself any proof of design, but only so far as it has been experienced to proceed from that principle. For aught we can know *a priori*, matter may contain the source or spring of order originally within himself, as well as mind does; and there is no more difficulty in conceiving that the several elements, from an internal unknown cause, may fall into the most exquisite arrangement, than to conceive that their ideas, in the great universal mind, from a like internal unknown cause, fall into that arrangement. The equal possibility of both these suppositions is allowed. But, by the experience, we find (according to Cleanthes) that there is a difference between them. Throw several pieces of steel together, without shape or form, they will never arrange themselves so as to compose a watch. Stone and mortar and wood, without an architect, never erect a house. But the ideas in a human mind, we see, by an unknown, inexplicable economy, arrange themselves so as to form the plan of a watch or house. Experience, therefore, proves that there is an original principle of order in mind, not in matter. From similar effects we infer similar causes. The adjustment of means to ends is alike in the universe, as in a machine of human contrivance. The causes, therefore, must be resembling.

I was from the beginning scandalized, I must own, with this resemblance which is asserted between the Deity and human creatures, and must conceive it to imply such a degradation of the Supreme Being as no sound theist could endure. With your assistance, therefore, Demea, I shall endeavour to defend what you justly call the adorable mysteriousness of the Divine Nature, and shall refute this reasoning of Cleanthes, provided he allows that I have made a fair representation of it.

When Cleanthes had assented, Philo, after a short pause, proceeded in the following manner.

That all inferences, Cleanthes, concerning fact are founded on experience, and that all experimental reasonings are founded on the supposition that similar causes prove similar effects, and similar effects similar causes, I shall not at present much dispute with you. But observe, I entreat you, with what extreme caution all just reasoners proceed in the transferring of experiments to similar cases. Unless the cases be exactly similar, they repose no perfect confidence in applying their past observation to any particular phenomenon. Every alteration of circumstances occasions a doubt concerning the event; and it requires new experiments to prove certainly that the new circumstances are of no moment or importance. A change in bulk, situation, arrangement, age, disposition of the air, or surrounding bodies—any of these particulars may be attended with the most unexpected consequences. And unless the objects be quite familiar to us, it is the highest temerity to expect with assurance, after any of these changes, an event similar to that which before fell under our observation. The slow and deliberate steps of philosophers here, if anywhere, are distinguished from the precipitate march of the vulgar, who, hurried on by the smallest similitude, are incapable of all discernment or consideration.

But can you think, Cleanthes, that your usual phlegm and philosophy have been preserved in so wide a step as you have taken when you compared to the universe houses, ships, furniture, machines, and, from their similarity in some circumstances, inferred a similarity in their causes? Thought, design, intelligence, such as we discover in men and other animals, is no more than one of the springs and principles of the universe, as well as heat or cold, attraction or repulsion, and a hundred others which fall under daily observation. It is an active cause by which some particular parts of nature, we find, produce alterations on other parts. But can a conclusion, with any propriety, be transferred from parts to the whole? Does not the great disproportion bar all comparison and inference? From observing the growth of a hair, can we learn anything concerning the generation of a man? Would the manner of a leaf's blowing, even though perfectly known, afford us any instruction concerning the vegetation of a tree?

But allowing that we were to take the *operations* of one part of nature upon another for the foundation of our judgment concerning the *origin* of the whole (which never can be admitted), yet why select so minute, so weak, so bounded a principle as the reason and design of animals is found to be upon this planet? What peculiar privilege has this little agitation of the brain which we call *thought*, that we must thus make it the model of the whole universe? Our partiality in our own favour does indeed present it on all occasions, but sound philosophy ought carefully to guard against so natural an illusion.

So far from admitting, continued Philo, that the operations of a part can afford us any just conclusion concerning the origin of the whole, I will not allow any one part to form a rule for another part if the latter be very remote from the former. Is there any reasonable ground to conclude that the inhabitants of other planets possess thought, intelligence, reason, or anything similar to these faculties in men? When nature has so extremely diversified her manner of operation in this small globe, can we imagine that she incessantly copies herself throughout so immense a universe? And if thought, as we may well suppose, be confined merely to this narrow corner and has even there so limited a sphere of action, with what propriety can we assign it for the original cause of all things? The narrow views of a peasant who makes his domestic economy the rule for the government of kingdoms is in comparison a pardonable sophism.

But were we ever so much assured that a thought and reason resembling the human were to be found throughout the whole universe, and were its activity elsewhere vastly greater and more commanding than it appears in this globe, yet I cannot see why the operations of a world constituted, arranged, adjusted, can with any propriety be extended to a world which is in its embryo state, and is advancing towards that constitution and arrangement. By observation we know somewhat of the economy, action, and nourishment of a finished animal, but we must transfer with great caution that observation to the growth of a foetus in the womb, and still more to the formation of an animalcule in the loins of its male parent. Nature, we find, even from our limited experience, possesses an infinite number of springs and principles which incessantly discover themselves on every change of her position and situation. And what new and unknown principles would actuate her in so new and unknown a situation as that of the formation of a universe, we cannot, without the utmost temerity, pretend to determine.

A very small part of this great system, during a very short time, is very imperfectly discovered to us; and do we thence pronounce decisively concerning the origin of the whole?

Admirable conclusion! Stone, wood, brick, iron, brass, have not, at this time, in this minute globe of earth, an order or arrangement without human art and contrivance; therefore, the universe could not originally attain its order and arrangement without something similar to human art. But is a part of nature a rule for another part very wide of the former? Is it a rule for the whole? Is a very small part a rule for the universe? Is nature in one situation a certain rule for nature in another situation vastly different from the former?

And can you blame me, Cleanthes, if I here imitate the prudent reserve of Simonides, who, according to the noted story, being asked by Hiero, *What God was?* desired a day to think of it, and then two days more; and after that manner continually prolonged the term, without every bringing his defini- tion or description? Could you even blame me if I had answered, at first, *that I did not know*, and was sensible that this subject lay vastly beyond the reach of my faculties? You might cry out sceptic and rallier, as much as you pleased; but, having found in so many other subjects much more familiar the imperfections and even contradictions of human reason, I never should expect any success from its feeble conjectures in a subject so sublime and so remote from the sphere of our observation. When two *species* of objects have always been observed to be conjoined together, I can *infer*, by custom, the existence of one wherever I *see* the existence of the other; and this I call an argument from experience. But how this argument can have place where the objects, as in the present case, are single, individual, without parallel or specific resemblance, may be difficult to explain. And will any man tell me with a serious countenance that an orderly universe must arise from some thought and art like the human because we have experience of it? To ascertain this reasoning it were requisite that we had experience of the origin of worlds; and it is not sufficient, surely, that we have seen ships and cities arise from human art and contrivance.

Philo was proceeding in this vehement manner, somewhat between jest and earnest, as it appeared to me, when he observed some signs of impa- tience in Cleanthes, and then immediately stopped short. What I had to sug- gest, said Cleanthes, is only that you would not abuse terms, or make use of popular expressions to subvert philosophical reasonings. You know that the vulgar often distinguish reason from experience, even where the question relates only to matter of fact and existence, though it is found, where that *reason* is properly analyzed, that it is nothing but a species of experience. To prove by experience the origin of the universe from mind is not more contrary to common speech than to prove the motion of the earth from the same principle. And a caviller might raise all the same objections to the Copernican system which you have urged against my reasonings. Have you other earths, might he say, which you have seen to move? Have . . .

Yes! cried Philo, interrupting him, we have other earths. Is not the moon another earth, which we see to turn round its centre? Is not Venus another earth, where we observe the same phenomenon? Are not the revolutions of the sun also a confirmation, from analogy, of the same theory? All the planets, are they not earths which revolve about the sun? Are not the satellites moons which move round Jupiter and Saturn, and along with these primary planets round the sun? These analogies and resemblances, with others which I have not mentioned, are the sole proofs of the Copernican system; and to you it belongs to consider whether you have any analogies of the same kind to support your theory.

In reality, Cleanthes, continued he, the modern system of astronomy is now so much received by all inquirers, and has become so essential a part even of our earliest education, that we are not commonly very scrupulous in examining the reasons upon which it is founded. It is now become a matter of mere curiosity to study the first writers on that subject who had the full force of prejudice to encounter, and were obliged to turn their arguments on every side in order to render them popular and convincing. But if we peruse Galileo's famous *Dialogues* concerning the system of the world, we shall find that that great genius, one of the sublimest that ever existed, first bent all his endeavours to prove that there was no foundation for the distinction commonly made between elementary and celestial substances. The schools, proceeding from the illusions of sense, had carried this distinction very far; and had established the latter substances to be ingenerable, incorruptible, unalterable, impassible; and has assigned all the opposite qualities to the former. But Galileo, beginning with the moon, proved its similarity in every particular to the earth: its convex figure, its natural darkness when not illuminated, its density, its distinction into solid and liquid, the variations of its phases, the mutual illuminations of the earth and moon, their mutual eclipses, the inequalities of the lunar surface, etc. After many instances of this kind, with regard to all the planets, men plainly saw that these bodies became proper objects of experience, and that the similarity of their nature enabled us to extend the same arguments and phenomena from one to the other.

In this cautious proceeding of the astronomers you may read your own condemnation, Cleanthes, or rather may see that the subject in which you are engaged exceeds all human reason and inquiry. Can you pretend to show any such similarity between the fabric of a house and the generation of a universe? Have you ever seen nature in any such situation as resembles the first arrangement of the elements? Have worlds ever been formed under your eye, and have you had leisure to observe the whole progress of the phenomenon, from the first appearance of order to its final consummation? If you have, then cite your experience and deliver your theory.

Part VII

But here, continued Philo, in examining the ancient system of the soul of the world there strikes me, all of a sudden, a new idea which, if just, must go near to subvert all your reasoning, and destroy even your first inferences on which you repose such confidence. If the universe bears a greater likeness to animal bodies and to vegetables than to the works of human art, it is more probable that its cause resembles the cause of the former than that of the latter, and its origin ought rather to be ascribed to generation or vegetation than to reason or design. Your conclusion, even according to your own principles, is therefore lame and defective.

Pray open up this argument a little further, said Demea, for I do not rightly apprehend it in that concise manner in which you have expressed it.

Our friend Cleanthes, replied Philo, as you have heard, asserts that, since no question of fact can be proved otherwise than by experience, the existence of a Deity admits not of proof from any other medium. The world, says he, resembles the works of human contrivance; therefore its cause must also resemble that of the other. Here we may remark that the operation of one very small part of nature, to wit, man, upon another very small part, to wit, that inanimate matter lying within his reach, is the rule by which Cleanthes judges of the origin of the whole; and he measures objects, so widely disproportioned, by the same individual standard. But to waive all objections drawn from this topic, I affirm that there are other parts of the universe (besides the machines of human invention) which bear still a greater resemblance to the fabric of the world, and which, therefore, afford a better conjecture concerning the universal origin of this system. These parts are animals and vegetables. The world plainly resembles more an animal or a vegetable than it does a watch or knitting-loom. Its cause, therefore, it is more probable, resembles the cause of the former. The cause of the former is generation or vegetation. The cause, therefore, of the world we may infer to be somthing similar or analogous to generation or vegetation.

But how is it conceivable, said Demea, that the world can arise from anything similar to vegetation or generation?

Very easily, replied Philo. In like manner as a tree sheds its seed into the neighboring fields and produces other trees, so the great vegetable, the world, or this planetary system, produces within itself certain seeds which, being scattered into the surrounding chaos, vegetate into new worlds. A comet, for instance, is the seed of a world; and after it has been fully ripened, by passing from sun to sun, and star to star, it is, at last, tossed into the unformed elements which everywhere surround this universe, and immediately sprouts up into a new system.

Or if, for the sake of variety (for I see no other advantage), we should suppose this world to be an animal: a comet is the egg of this animal; and in like manner as an ostrich lays its egg in the sand, which, without any further care, hatches the egg and produces a new animal, so . . . I understand you, says Demea. But what wild, arbitrary suppositions are these! What *data* have you for such extraordinary conclusions? And is the slight, imaginary resemblance of the world to a vegetable or an animal sufficient to establish the same inference with regard to both? Objects which are in general so widely different ought they to be a standard for each other?

Right, cries Philo: This is the topic on which I have all along insisted. I have still asserted that we have no *data* to establish any system of cosmogony. Our experience, so imperfect in itself and so limited both in extent and duration, can afford us no probable conjecture concerning the whole of things. But if we must need fix on some hypothesis, by what rule, pray, ought we to determine our choice? Is there any other rule than the greater similarity of the objects compared? And does not a plant or an animal, which springs from vegetation or generation, bear a stronger resemblance to the world than does any artificial machine, which arises from reason and design?

But what is this vegetation and generation of which you talk? said Demea. Can you explain their operations, and anatomize that fine internal structure on which they depend?

As much, at least, replied Philo, as Cleanthes can explain the operation of reason, or anatomize that internal structure on which it depends. But without any such elaborate disquisitions, when I see an animal, I infer that it sprang from generation; and that with as great certainty as you conclude a house to have been reared by design. These words *generation, reason* mark only certain powers and energies in nature whose effects are known, but whose essence is incomprehensible; and one of these principles, more than the other, has no privilege for being made a standard to the whole of nature.

In reality, Demea, it may reasonably be expected that the larger the views are which we take of things, the better will they conduct us in our conclusions concerning such extraordinary and such magnificent subjects. In this little corner of the world alone, there are four principles, *reason, instinct, generation, vegetation*, which are similar to each other, and are the cause of similar effects. What a number of other principles may we naturally suppose in the immense extent and variety of the universe could we travel from planet to planet, and from system to system, in order to examine each part of this mighty fabric? Any one of these four principles above mentioned (and a hundred others which lie open to our conjecture) may afford us a theory by which to judge of the origin of the world; and it is a palpable and egregious partiality to confine our view entirely to that principle by which our own minds operate. Were this principle more intelligible on that account, such a partiality might be somewhat excusable; but reason, in its internal fabric and structure, is really as little known to us as instinct or vegetation; and, perhaps, even that vague, undeterminate word *nature* to which the vulgar refer everything is not at the bottom more inexplicable. The effects of these principles are all known to us from experience; but the principles themselves and their manner of operation are totally unknown; nor is it less intelligible or less comfortable to experience to say that the world arose by vegetation, from a seed shed by another world, than to say that it arose from a divine reason or contrivance, according to the sense in which Cleanthes understands it.

But methinks, said Demea, if the world had a vegetative quality and could sow the seeds of new worlds into the infinite chaos, this power would be still an additional argument for design in its author. For whence could arise so wonderful a faculty but from design? Or how can order spring from anything which perceives not that order which it bestows.

You need only look around you, replied Philo, to satisfy yourself with regard to this question. A tree bestows order and organization on that tree which springs from it, without knowing the order; an animal in the same manner on its offspring; a bird on its nest; and instances of this kind are even more frequent in the world than those of order which arise from reason and contrivance. To say that all this order in animals and vegetables proceeds ultimately from design is begging the question; nor can that great point be ascertained otherwise than by proving, *a priori*, both that order is, from its nature, inseparably attached to thought and that it can never of itself or from original unknown principles belong to matter.

But further, Demea, this objection which you urge can never be made use of by Cleanthes, without renouncing a defence which he has already made against one of my objections. When I inquired concerning the cause of that supreme reason and intelligence into which he resolves everything, he told me that the impossibility of satisfying such inquiries could never be admitted as an objection in any species of philosophy. *We must stop somewhere*, says he; *nor is it ever within the reach of human capacity to explain ultimate causes or show the last connections of any objects. It is sufficient if any steps, so far as we go, are supported by experience and observation.* Now that vegetation and generation, as well as reason, are experienced to be principles of order in nature is undeniable. If I rest my system of cosmogony on the former, preferably to the latter, it is at my choice. The matter seems entirely arbitrary. And when Cleanthes asks me what is the cause of my great vegetative or generative principle, I am equally entitled to ask him the cause of his great reasoning principle. These questions we have agreed to forbear on both sides; and it is chiefly his interest on the present occasion to stick to this agreement. Judging by our limited and imperfect experience, generation has some privileges above reason; for we see every day the latter arise from the former, never the former from the latter.

Compare, I beseech you, the consequences on both sides. The world, say I, resembles an animal; therefore it is an animal, therefore it arose from generation. The steps, I confess, are wide, yet there is some small appearance of analogy in each step. The world, says Cleanthes, resembles a machine; therefore it is a machine, therefore it arose from design. The steps are here equally wide, and the analogy less striking. And if he pretends to carry on *my* hypothesis a step further, and to infer design or reason from the great principle of generation on which I insist, I may, with better authority, use the same freedom to push further *his* hypothesis, and infer a divine generation or theogony from his principle of reason. I have at least some faint shadow of experience, which is the utmost that can ever be attained in the present subject. Reason, in innumerable instances, is observed to arise from the principle of generation, and never to arise from any other principle.

Hesiod and all the ancient mythologists were so struck with this analogy that they universally explained the origin of nature from an animal birth, and copulation. Plato, too, so far as he is intelligible, seems to have adopted some such notion in his *Timæus*.

The Brahmins assert that the world arose from an infinite spider, who spun this whole complicated mass from his bowels, and annihilates afterwards the whole or any part of it, by absorbing it again and resolving it into his own essence. Here is a species of cosmogony which appears to us ridiculous because a spider is a little contemptible animal whose operations we are never likely to take for a model of the whole universe. But still here is a new species of analogy, even in our globe. And were there a planet wholly inhabited by spiders (which is very possible), this inference would there appear as natural and irrefragable as that which in our planet ascribes the origin of all things to design and intelligence, as explained by Cleanthes. Why an orderly system may not be spun from the belly as well as from the brain, it will be difficult for him to give a satisfactory reason.

I must confess, Philo, replied Cleanthes, that, of all men living, the task which you have undertaken, of raising doubts and objections, suits you best and seems, in a manner, natural and unavoidable to you. So great is your fertility of invention that I am not ashamed to acknowledge myself unable, on a sudden, to solve regularly such out-of-the-way difficulties as you incessantly start upon me, though I clearly see, in general, their fallacy and error. And I question not, but you are yourself, at present, in the same case, and have not the solution so ready as the objection, while you must be sensible that common sense and reason are entirely against you, and that such whimsies as you have delivered may puzzle but never can convince us.

Part VIII

What you ascribe to the fertility of my invention, replied Philo, is entirely owing to the nature of the subject. In subjects adapted to the narrow compass of human reason there is commonly but one determination which carries probability or conviction with it; and to a man of sound judgment all other suppositions but that one appear entirely absurd and chimerical. But in such questions as the present, a hundred contradictory views may preserve a kind of imperfect analogy, and invention has here full scope to exert itself. Without any great effort of thought, I believe that I could, in an instant, propose other systems of cosmogony which would have some faint appearance of truth, though it is a thousand, a million to one if either yours or any one of mine be the true system.

For instance, what if I should revive the old Epicurean hypothesis? This is commonly, and I believe justly, esteemed the most absurd system that has yet been proposed; yet I know not whether, with a few alterations, it might not be brought to bear a faint appearance of probability. Instead of supposing matter infinite, as Epicurus did, let us suppose it finite. A finite number of particles is only susceptible of finite transpositions; and it must happen, in an eternal duration, that every possible order or position must be tried an infinite number of times. This world, therefore, with all its events, even the most minute, has before been produced and destroyed, and will again be produced and destroyed, without any bounds and limitations. No one who has a conception of the powers of infinite, in comparison of finite, will ever scruple this determination.

But this supposes, said Demea, that matter can acquire motion without any voluntary agent or first mover.

And where is the difficulty, replied Philo, of that supposition? Every event, before experience, is equally difficult and incomprehensible; and every event, after experience, is equally easy and intelligible. Motion, in many instances, from gravity, from elasticity, from electricity, begins in matter, without any known voluntary agent; and to suppose always, in these cases, an unknown voluntary agent is mere hypothesis and hypothesis attended with no advantages. The beginning of motion in matter itself is as conceivable *a priori* as its communication from mind and intelligence.

Besides, why may not motion have been propagated by impulse through all eternity, and the same stock of it, or nearly the same, be still upheld in the universe? As much is lost by the composition of motion, as much is gained by its resolution. And whatever the causes are, the fact is certain that matter is and always has been in continual agitation, as far as human experience or tradition reaches. There is not probably, at present, in the whole universe, one particle of matter at absolute rest.

And this very consideration, too, continued Philo, which we have stumbled on in the course of the argument suggests a new hypothesis of cosmogony that is not absolutely absurd and improbable. Is there a system, an order, an economy of things, by which matter can preserve that perpetual agitation which seems essential to it, and yet maintain a constancy in the forms which it produces? There certainly is such an economy, for this is actually the case with the present world. The continual motion of matter, therfore, in less than infinite transpositions, must produce this economy or order, and, by its very nature, that order, when once established, supports itself for many ages if not to eternity. But whatever matter is so poised, arranged, and adjusted, as to continue in perpetual motion, and yet preserve a constancy in the forms, its situation must, of necessity, have all the same appearance of art and contrivance which we observe at present. All the parts of each form must have a relation to each other and to the whole; and the whole itself must have a relation to the other parts of the universe, to the element in which the form subsists, to the materials with which it repairs its waste and decay, and to every form which is hostile or friendly. A defect in any of these particulars destroys the form, and the matter of which it is composed is again set loose, and is thrown into irregular motions and fermentation till it unite itself to some other regular form. If no such form be prepared to receive it, and if there be a great quantity of this corrupted matter in the universe, the universe itself is entirely disordered, whether it be the feeble embryo of a world in its first beginnings that is thus destroyed or the rotten carcase of one languishing in old age and infirmity. In either case, a chaos ensues till finite though innumerable revolutions produce, at last, some forms whose parts and organs are so adjusted as to support the forms amidst a continued succession of matter.

Suppose (for we shall endeavour to vary the expression) that matter were thrown into any position by a blind, unguided force; it is evident that this first position must, in all probability, be the most confused and most disorderly imaginable, without any resemblance to those works of human contrivance which, along with a symmetry of parts, discover an adjustment of means to ends and a tendency to self-preservation. If the actuating force cease after this operation, matter must remain for ever in disorder and continue an immense chaos, without any proportion or activity. But suppose that the actuating force, whatever it be, still continues in matter, this first position will immediately give place to a second which will likewise, in all probability, be as disorderly as the first, and so on through many successions of changes and revolutions. No particular order or position ever continues a moment unaltered. The original force, still remaining in activity, gives a perpetual restlessness to matter. Every possible situation is produced, and instantly destroyed. If a glimpse or dawn of order appears for a moment, it is instantly hurried away and confounded by that never-ceasing force which actuates every part of matter.

Thus the universe goes on for many ages in a continued succession of chaos and disorder. But is it not possible that it may settle at last, so as not to lose its motion and active force (for that we have supposed inherent in it), yet so as to preserve an uniformity of appearance, amidst the continual motion and fluctuation of its parts? This we find to be the case with the universe at present. Every individual is perpetually changing, and every part of every individual; and yet the whole remains, in appearance, the same. May we not hope for such a position or rather be assured of it from the eternal revolutions of unguided matter; and may not this account for all the appearing wisdom and contrivance which is in the universe? Let us contemplate the subject a little, and we shall find that this adjustment if attained by matter of a seeming stability in the forms, with a real and perpetual revolution or motion of parts, affords a plausible, if not a true, solution of the difficulty.

It is in vain, therefore, to insist upon the uses of the parts in animals or vegetables, and their curious adjustment to each other. I would fain know how an animal could subsist unless its parts were so adjusted? Do we not find that it immediately perishes whenever this adjustment ceases, and that its matter, corrupting, tries some new form? It happens indeed that the parts of the world are so well adjusted that some regular form immediately lays claim to this corrupted matter; and if it were not so, could the world subsist? Must it not dissolve, as well as the animal, and pass through new positions and situations till in great but finite succession it fall, at last, into the present or some such order?

It is well, replied Cleanthes, you told us that this hypothesis was suggested on a sudden, in the course of the argument. Had you had leisure to examine it, you would soon have perceived the insuperable objections to which it is exposed. No form, you say, can subsist unless it possesses those powers and organs requisite for its subsistence; some new order or economy must be tried, and so on, without intermission, till at last some matter which can support and maintain itself is fallen upon. But according to this hypothesis, whence arise the many conveniences and advantages which men and all animals possess? Two eyes, two ears are not absolutely necessary for the subsistence of the species. Human race might have been propagated and preserved without horses, dogs, cows, sheep, and those innumerable fruits and products which serve to our satisfaction and enjoyment. If no camels had been created for the use of man in the sandy deserts of Africa and Arabia, would the world have been dissolved? If no loadstone had been framed to give that wonderful and useful direction to the needle, would human society and the human kind have been immediately extinguished? Though the maxims of nature be in general very frugal, yet instances of this kind are far from being rare; and any one of them is a sufficient proof of design—and of a benevolent design—which gave rise to the order and arrangement of the universe.

At least, you may safely infer, said Philo, that the foregoing hypothesis is so far incomplete and imperfect, which I shall not scruple to allow. But can we ever reasonably expect greater success in any attempts of this nature? Or can we ever hope to erect a system of cosmogony that will be liable to no exceptions, and will contain no circumstance repugnant to our limited and imperfect experience of the analogy of nature? Your theory itself cannot surely pretend to any such advantage, even though you have run into *anthropomorphism*, the better to preserve a conformity to common experience. Let us once more put it to trial. In all instances which we have ever seen, ideas are copied from real objects, and are ectypal, not archetypal, to express myself in learned terms. You reverse this order and give thought the precedence. In all instances which we have ever seen, thought has no influence upon matter except where that matter is so conjoined with it as to have an equal reciprocal influence upon it. No animal can move immediately anything but the members of its own body; and, indeed, the equality of action and reaction seems to be an universal law of nature; but your theory implies a contradiction to this experience. These instances, with many more which it were easy to collect (particularly the supposition of a mind or system of thought that is eternal or, in other words, an animal ingenerable and immortal) —these instances, I say, may teach all of us sobriety in condemning each other, and let us see that as no system of this kind ought ever to be received from a slight analogy, so neither ought any to be rejected on account of a small incongruity. For that is an inconvenience from which we can justly pronounce no one to be exempted.

All religious systems, it is confessed, are subject to great and insuperable difficulties. Each disputant triumphs in his turn, while he carries on an offensive war, and exposes the absurdities, barbarities, and pernicious tenets of his antagonist. But all of them, on the whole, prepare a complete triumph for the *sceptic*, who tells them that no system ought ever to be embraced with regard to such subjects: for this plain reason that no absurdity ought ever to be assented to with regard to any subject. A total suspense of judgment is here our only reasonable resource. And if every attack, as is commonly observed, and no defense among theologians is successful, how complete must be *his* victory who remains always, with all mankind, on the offensive, and has himself no fixed station or abiding city which he is ever, on any occasion, obliged to defend?

IMMANUEL KANT

8. *The Limits of Causality*

The German thinker Immanuel Kant (1724–1804) rejected the theoretical approach of speculative philosophy and sought to ground our knowledge of God, freedom, and immortality in the practical evidence of moral experience. Kant's *Critique of Pure Reason* marks a turning point in the history of philosophy, and his *Critique of Practical Reason* and *Religion Within the Bounds of Reason Alone* make a positive contribution to theology.

From *Critique of Pure Reason*

Transcendental Dialectic, Chapter 3

Section 5: The Impossibility of a Cosmological Proof of the Existence of God

To attempt to extract from a purely arbitrary idea the existence of an object corresponding to it is a quite unnatural procedure and a mere innovation of scholastic subtlety. Such an attempt would never have been made if there had not been antecedently, on the part of our reason, the need to assume as a basis of existence in general something necessary (in which our regress may terminate); and if, since this necessity must be unconditioned and certain *a priori*, reason had not, in consequence, been forced to seek a concept which would satisfy, if possible, such a demand, and enable us to know an existence in a completely *a priori* manner. Such a concept was supposed to have been found in the idea of an *ens realissimum*[1]; and that idea was therefore used only for the more definite knowledge of that necessary

Immanuel Kant, *Critique of Pure Reason*, tr. Norman Kemp Smith (London: Macmillan, 1929). Reprinted by permission of St. Martin's Press, The Macmillan Company of Canada, and Macmillan & Company, Ltd.

[1]["most real being."]

being, of the necessary existence of which we were already convinced, or persuaded, on other grounds. This natural procedure of reason was, however, concealed from view, and instead of ending with this concept, the attempt was made to begin with it, and so to deduce from it that necessity of existence which it was only fitted to supplement. Thus arose the unfortunate ontological proof, which yields satisfaction neither to the natural and healthy understanding nor to the more academic demands of strict proof.

The *cosmological proof*, which we are now about to examine, retains the connection of absolute necessity with the highest reality, but instead of reasoning, like the former proof, from the highest reality to necessity of existence, it reasons from the previously given unconditioned necessity of some being to the unlimited reality of that being. It thus enters upon a course of reasoning which, whether rational or only pseudo-rational, is at any rate natural, and the most convincing not only for common sense but even for speculative understanding. It also sketches the first outline of all the proofs in natural theology, an outline which has always been and always will be followed, however much embellished and disguised by superfluous additions. This proof, termed by Leibniz the proof *a contingentia mundi*,[2] we shall now proceed to expound and examine.

It runs thus: If anything exists, an absolutely necessary being must also exist. Now I, at least, exist. Therefore an absolutely necessary being exists. The minor premiss contains an experience, the major premiss the inference from there being any experience at all to the existence of the necessary.[3] The proof therefore really begins with experience, and is not wholly *a priori* or ontological. For this reason, and because the object of all possible experience is called the world, it is entitled the *cosmological* proof. Since, in dealing with the objects of experience, the proof abstracts from all special properties through which this world may differ from any other possible world, the title also serves to distinguish it from the physico-theological proof, which is based upon observations of the particular properties of the world disclosed to us by our senses.

The proof then proceeds as follows: The necessary being can be determined in one way only, that is, by one out of each possible pair of opposed predicates. It must therefore be *completely* determined through its own concept. Now there is only one possible concept which determines a thing completely *a priori*, namely, the concept of the *ens realissimum*. The concept of the *ens realissimum* is therefore the only concept through which a necessary being can be thought. In other words, a supreme being necessarily exists.

In this cosmological argument there are combined so many pseudo-rational principles that speculative reason seems in this case to have brought to bear all the resources of its dialectical skill to produce the greatest possible

---

[2]["from the contingency of the world."]

[3]This inference is too well known to require detailed statement. It depends on the supposedly transcendental law of natural causality: that everything contingent has a cause, which, if itself contingent, must likewise have a cause, till the series of subordinate causes ends with an absolutely necessary cause, without which it would have no completeness.

transcendental illusion. The testing of the argument may meantime be postponed while we detail in order the various devices whereby an old argument is diguised as a new one, and by which appeal is made to the agreement of two witnesses, the one with credentials of pure reason and the other with those of experience. In reality the only witness is that which speaks in the name of pure reason; in the endeavour to pass as a second witness it merely changes its dress and voice. In order to lay a secure foundation for itself, this proof takes its stand on experience, and thereby makes profession of being distinct from the ontological proof, which puts its entire trust in pure *a priori* concepts. But the cosmological proof uses this experience only for a single step in the argument, namely, to conclude the existence of a necessary being. What properties this being may have, the empirical premiss cannot tell us. Reason therefore abandons experience altogether, and endeavours to discover from mere concepts what properties an absolutely necessary being must have, that is, which among all possible things contains in itself the conditions (*requisita*) essential to absolute necessity. Now these, it is supposed, are nowhere to be found save in the concept of an *ens realissimum*; and the conclusion is therefore drawn, that the *ens realissimum* is the absolutely necessary being. But it is evident that we are here presupposing that the concept of the highest reality is completely adequate to the concept of absolute necessity of existence; that is, that the latter can be inferred from the former. Now this is the proposition maintained by the ontological proof; it is here being assumed in the cosmological proof, and indeed made the basis of the proof; and yet it is an assumption with which this latter proof has professed to dispense. For absolute necessity is an existence determined from mere concepts. If I say, the concept of the *ens realissimum* is a concept, and indeed the only concept, which is appropriate and adequate to necessary existence, I must also admit that necessary existence can be inferred from this concept. Thus the so-called cosmological proof really owes any cogency which it may have to the ontological proof from mere concepts. The appeal to experience is quite superfluous; experience may perhaps lead us to the concept of absolute necessity, but is unable to demonstrate this necessity as belonging to any determinate thing. For immediately we endeavour to do so, we must abandon all experience and search among pure concepts to discover whether any one of them contains the conditions of the possibility of an absolutely necessary being. If in this way we can determine the possibility of a necessary being, we likewise establish its existence. For what we are then saying is this: that of all possible beings there is one which carries with it absolute necessity, that is, that this being exists with absolute necessity. . . .

Thus the second path upon which speculative reason enters in its attempt to prove the existence of a supreme being is not only as deceptive as the first, but has this additional defect, that it is guilty of an *ignoratio elenchi*. It professes to lead us by a new path, but after a short circuit brings us back to the very path which we had deserted at its bidding.

I have stated that in this cosmological argument there lies hidden a whole nest of dialectical assumptions, which the transcendental critique can easily detect and destroy. These deceptive principles I shall merely enumerate, leaving to the reader, who by this time will be sufficiently expert in these matters, the task of investigating them further, and of refuting them.

We find, for instance, (1) the transcendental principle whereby from the contingent we infer a cause. This principle is applicable only in the sensible world; outside that world it has no meaning whatsoever. For the mere intellectual concept of the contingent cannot give rise to any synthetic proposition, such as that of causality. The principle of causality has no meaning and no criterion for its application save only in the sensible world. But in the cosmological proof it is precisely in order to enable us to advance beyond the sensible world that it is employed. (2) The inference to a first cause, from the impossibility of an infinite series of causes, given one after the other, in the sensible world. The principles of the employment of reason do not justify this conclusion even within the world of experience, still less beyond this world in a realm into which this series can never be extended. (3) The unjustified self-satisfaction of reason in respect of the completion of this series. The removal of all the conditions without which no concept of necessity is possible is taken by reason to be a completion of the concept of the series, on the ground that we can then conceive nothing further. (4) The confusion between the logical possibility of a concept of all reality united into one (without inner contradiction) and the transcendental possibility of such a reality. In the case of the latter there is needed a principle to establish the practicability of such a synthesis, a principle which itself, however, can apply only to the field of possible experiences—etc.

The procedure of the cosmological proof is artfully designed to enable us to escape having to prove the existence of a necessary being *a priori* through mere concepts. Such proof would require to be carried out in the ontological manner, and that is an enterprise for which we feel ourselves to be altogether incompetent. Accordingly, we take as the starting-point of our inference an actual existence (an experience in general), and advance, in such manner as we can, to some absolutely necessary condition of this existence. We have then no need to show the possibility of this condition. For if it has been proved to exist, the question as to its possibility is entirely superfluous. If now we want to determine more fully the nature of this necessary being, we do not endeavour to do so in the manner that would be really adequate, namely, by discovering from its concept the necessity of its existence. For could we do that, we should be in no need of an empirical starting-point. No, all we seek is the negative condition (*conditio sine qua non*), without which a being would not be absolutely necessary. And in all other kinds of reasoning from a given consequence to its ground this would be legitimate; but in the present case it unfortunately happens that the condition which is needed for absolute necessity is only to be found in one single being. This being must therefore contain in its concept all that is required for absolute necessity, and consequently it enables me to infer this absolute necessity *a priori*. I must therefore be able also to reverse the inference, and to say: Anything to which this concept (of supreme reality) applies is absolutely necessary.

If I cannot make this inference (as I must concede, if I am to avoid admitting the ontological proof), I have come to grief in the new way that I have been following, and am back again at any starting-point. The concept of the supreme being satisfies all questions *a priori* which can be raised regarding the inner determinations of a thing, and is therefore an ideal that is quite unique, in that the concept, while universal, also at the same time designates an individual as being among the things that are possible. But it does not give satisfaction concerning the question of its own existence—though this is the real purpose of our enquiries—and if anyone admitted the existence of a necessary being but wanted to know which among all [existing][4] things is to be identified with that being, we could not answer: 'This, not that, is the necessary being.'

We may indeed be allowed to *postulate* the existence of an all-sufficient being, as the cause of all possible effects, with a view to lightening the task of reason in its search for the unity of the grounds of explanation. But in presuming so far as to say that such a being *necessarily exists*, we are no longer giving modest expression to an admissible hypothesis, but are confidently laying claim to apodeictic certainty. For the knowledge of what we profess to know as absolutely necessary must itself carry with it absolute necessity.

The whole problem of the transcendental ideal amounts to this: either, given absolute necessity, to find a concept which possesses it, or, given the concept of something, to find that something to be absolutely necessary. If either task be possible, so must the other; for reason recognizes that only as absolutely necessary which follows of necessity from its concept. But both tasks are quite beyond our utmost efforts to *satisfy* our understanding in this matter; and equally unavailing are all attempts to induce it to acquiesce in its incapacity.

Unconditioned necessity, which we so indispensably require as the last bearer of all things, is for human reason the veritable abyss. Eternity itself, in all its terrible sublimity, as depicted by a Haller, is far from making the same overwhelming impression on the mind; for it only *measures* the duration of things, it does not *support* them. We cannot put aside, and yet also cannot endure the thought, that a being, which we represent to ourselves as supreme amongst all possible beings, should, as it were, say to itself: 'I am from eternity to eternity, and outside me there is nothing save what is through my will, *but whence then am I?*' All support here fails us; and the *greatest* perfection, no less than the *least* perfection, is unsubstantial and baseless for the merely speculative reason, which makes not the least effort to retain either the one or the other, and feels indeed no loss in allowing them to vanish entirely.

Many forces in nature, which manifest their existence through certain effects, remain for us inscrutable; for we cannot track them sufficiently far by observation. Also, the transcendental object lying at the basis of appearances (and with it the reason why our sensibility is subject to certain supreme conditions rather than to others) is and remains for us inscrutable. The thing itself is indeed given, but we can have no insight into its nature. But it is

[4][Translator's bracketing here and following.]

quite otherwise with an ideal of pure reason; it can never be said to be inscrutable. For since it is not required to give any credentials of its reality save only the need on the part of reason to complete all synthetic unity by means of it; and since, therefore, it is in no wise given as thinkable *object*, it cannot be inscrutable in the manner in which an object is. On the contrary it must, as a mere idea, find its place and its solution in the nature of reason, and must therefore allow of investigation. For it is of the very essence of reason that we should be able to give an account of all our concepts, opinions, and assertions, either upon objective or, in the case of mere illusion, upon subjective grounds.

Section 6: The Impossibility of the Physico-Theological Proof

If, then, neither the concept of things in general nor the experience of any *existence in general* can supply what is required, it remains only to try whether a *determinate experience*, the experience of the things of the present world, and the constitution and order of these, does not provide the basis of a proof which may help us to attain to an assured conviction of a supreme being. Such proof we propose to entitle the *physico-theological.* Should this attempt also fail, it must follow that no satisfactory proof of the existence of a being corresponding to our transcendental idea can be possible by pure speculative reason.

In view of what has already been said, it is evident that we can count upon a quite easy and conclusive answer to this enquiry. For how can any experience ever be adequate to an idea? The peculiar nature of the latter consists just in the fact that no experience can ever be equal to it. The transcendental idea of a necessary and all-sufficient original being is so overwhelmingly great, so high above everything empirical, the latter being always conditioned, that it leaves us at a loss, partly because we can never find in experience material sufficient to satisfy such a concept, and partly because it is always in the sphere of the conditioned that we carry out our search, seeking there ever vainly for the unconditioned—no law of any empirical synthesis giving us an example of any such unconditioned or providing the least guidance in its pursuit.

If the supreme being should itself stand in this chain of conditions, it would be a member of the series, and like the lower members which it precedes, would call for further enquiry as to the still higher ground from which it follows. If, on the other hand, we propose to separate it from the chain, and to conceive it as a purely intelligible being, existing apart from the series of natural causes, by what bridge can reason contrive to pass over to it? For all laws governing the transition from effects to causes, all synthesis and extension of our knowledge, refer to nothing but possible experience, and therefore solely to objects of the sensible world, and apart from them can have no meaning whatsoever.

This world presents to us so immeasurable a stage of variety, order, purposiveness, and beauty, as displayed alike in its infinite extent and in the unlimited divisibility of its parts, that even with such knowledge as our weak understanding can acquire of it, we are brought face to face with so many marvels immeasurably great, that all speech loses its force, all numbers their power to measure, our thoughts themselves all definiteness, and that our judgment of the whole resolves itself into an amazement which is speechless, and only the more eloquent on that account. Everywhere we see a chain of effects and causes, of ends and means, a regularity in origination and dissolution. Nothing has of itself come into the condition in which we find it to exist, but always points to something else as its cause, while this in turn commits us to repetition of the same enquiry. The whole universe must thus sink into the abyss of nothingness, unless, over and above this infinite chain of contingencies, we assume something to support it—something which is original and independently self-subsistent, and which as the cause of the origin of the universe secures also at the same time its continuance. What magnitude are we to ascribe to this supreme cause—admitting that it is supreme in respect of all things in the world? We are not acquainted with the whole content of the world, still less do we know how to estimate its magnitude by comparison with all that is possible. But since we cannot, as regards causality, dispense with an ultimate and supreme being, what is there to prevent us ascribing to it a degree of perfection that sets it *above everything else that is possible*? This we can easily do—though only through the slender outline of an abstract concept—by representing this being to ourselves as combining in itself all possible perfection, as in a single substance. This concept is in conformity with the demand of our reason for parsimony of principles; it is free from self-contradiction, and is never decisively contradicted by any experience; and it is likewise of such a character that it contributes to the extension of the employment of reason within experience, through the guidance which it yields in the discovery of order and purposiveness.

This proof always deserves to be mentioned with respect. It is the oldest, the clearest, and the most accordant with the common reason of mankind. It enlivens the study of nature, just as it itself derives its existence and gains ever new vigour from that source. It suggests ends and purposes, where our observation would not have detected them by itself, and extends our knowledge of nature by means of the guiding-concept of a special unity, the principle of which is outside nature. This knowledge again reacts on its cause, namely, upon the idea which has led to it, and so strengthens the belief in a supreme Author [of nature] that the belief acquires the force of an irresistible conviction.

It would therefore not only be uncomforting but utterly vain to attempt to diminish in any way the authority of this argument. Reason, constantly upheld by this ever-increasing evidence, which, though empirical, is yet so powerful, cannot be so depressed through doubts suggested by subtle and abstruse speculation, that it is not at once aroused from the indecision of all melancholy reflection, as from a dream, by one glance at the wonders of nature and the majesty of the universe—ascending from height to height up to the all-highest, from the conditioned to its conditions, up to the supreme and unconditioned Author [of all conditioned being].

But although we have nothing to bring against the rationality and utility of this procedure, but have rather to commend and to further it, we still cannot approve the claims, which this mode of argument would fain advance, to apodeictic certainty and to an assent founded on no special favour or support from other quarters. It cannot hurt the good cause, if the dogmatic language of the overweening sophist be toned down to the more moderate and humble requirements of a belief adequate to quieten our doubts, though not to command unconditional submission. I therefore maintain that the physico-theological proof can never by itself establish the existence of a supreme being, but must always fall back upon the ontological argument to make good its deficiency. It only serves as an introduction to the ontological argument; and the latter therefore contains (in so far as a speculative proof is possible at all) *the one possible ground of proof* with which human reason can never dispense.

The chief points of the physico-theological proof are as follows: (1) In the world we everywhere find clear signs of an order in accordance with a determinate purpose, carried out with great wisdom; and this in a universe which is indescribably varied in content and unlimited in extent. (2) This purposive order is quite alien to the things of the world, and only belongs to them contingently; that is to say, the diverse things could not of themselves have co-operated, by so great a combination of diverse means, to the fulfilment of determinate final purposes, had they not been chosen and designed for these purposes by an ordering rational principle in conformity with underlying ideas. (3) There exists, therefore, a sublime and wise cause (or more than one), which must be the cause of the world not merely as a blindly working all-powerful nature, by *fecundity*, but as intelligence, through *freedom*. (4) The unity of this cause may be inferred from the unity of the reciprocal relations existing between the parts of the world, as members of an artfully arranged structure—inferred with certainty in so far as our observation suffices for its verification, and beyond these limits with probability, in accordance with the principles of analogy.

We need not here criticise natural reason too strictly in regard to its conclusion from the analogy between certain natural products and what our human art produces when we do violence to nature, and constrain it to proceed not according to its own ends but in conformity with ours—appealing to the similarity of these particular natural products with houses, ships, watches. Nor need we here question its conclusion that there lies at the basis of nature a causality similar to that responsible for artificial products, namely, an understanding and a will; and that the inner possibility of a self-acting nature (which is what makes all art, and even, it may be, reason itself, possible) is therefore derived from another, though superhuman, art—a mode of reasoning which could not perhaps withstand a searching transcendental criticism. But at any rate we must admit that, if we are to specify a cause at all, we cannot here proceed more securely than by analogy with those purposive productions of which alone the cause and mode of action are fully known to us. Reason could never be justified in abandoning the causality which it knows for grounds of explanation which are obscure, of which it does not have any knowledge, and which are incapable of proof.

On this method of argument, the purposiveness and harmonious adaptation of so much in nature can suffice to prove the contingency of the form merely, not of the matter, that is, not of the substance in the world. To prove the latter we should have to demonstrate that the things in the world would not of themselves be capable of such order and harmony, in accordance with universal laws, if they were not *in their substance* the product of supreme wisdom. But to prove this we should require quite other grounds of proof than those which are derived from the analogy with human art. The utmost, therefore, that the argument can prove is an *architect* of the world who is always very much hampered by the adaptability of the material in which he works, not a *creator* of the world to whose idea everything is subject. This, however, is altogether inadequate to the lofty purpose which we have before our eyes, namely, the proof of an all-sufficient primordial being. To prove the contingency of matter itself, we should have to resort to a transcendental argument, and this is precisely what we have here set out to avoid.

The inference, therefore, is that the order and purposiveness everywhere observable throughout the world may be regarded as a completely contingent arrangement, and that we may argue to the existence of a cause *proportioned* to it. But the concept of this cause must enable us to know something quite *determinate* about it, and can therefore be no other than the concept of a being who possesses all might, wisdom, etc., in a word, all the perfection which is proper to an all-sufficient being. For the predicates—'very great,' 'astounding,' 'immeasurable' in power and excellence—give no determinate concept at all, and do not really tell us what the thing is in itself. They are only relative representations of the magnitude of the object, which the observer, in contemplating the world, compares with himself and with his capacity of comprehension, and which are equally terms of eulogy whether we be magnifying the object or be depreciating the observing subject in relation to that object. Where we are concerned with the magnitude (of the perfection) of a thing, there is no determinate concept except that which comprehends all possible perfection; and in that concept only the allness (*omnitudo*) of the reality is completely determined.

Now no one, I trust, will be so bold as to profess that he comprehends the relation of the magnitude of the world as he has observed it (alike as regards both extent and content) to omnipotence, of the world order to supreme wisdom, of the world unity to the absolute unity of its Author, etc. Physico-theology is therefore unable to give any determinate concept of the supreme cause of the world, and cannot therefore serve as the foundation of a theology which is itself in turn to form the basis of religion.

To advance to absolute totality by the empirical road is utterly impossible. None the less this is what is attempted in the physico-theological proof. What, then, are the means which have been adopted to bridge this wide abyss?

The physico-theological argument can indeed lead us to the point of admiring the greatness, wisdom, power, etc., of the Author of the world, but can take us no further. Accordingly, we then abandon the argument from empirical grounds of proof, and fall back upon the contingency which, in the first steps of the argument, we had inferred from the order and purposiveness of the world. With this contingency as our sole premiss, we then advance, by means of transcendental concepts alone, to the existence of an absolutely necessary being, and [as a final step] from the concept of the absolute necessity of the first cause to the completely determinate or determinable concept of that necessary being, namely, to the concept of an all-embracing reality. Thus the physico-theological proof, failing in its undertaking, has in face of this difficulty suddenly fallen back upon the cosmological proof; and since the latter is only a disguised ontological proof, it has really achieved its purpose by pure reason alone—although at the start it disclaimed all kinship with pure reason and professed to establish its conclusions on convincing evidence derived from experience.

Those who propound the physico-theological argument have therefore no ground for being so contemptuous in their attitude to the transcendental mode of proof, posing as clear-sighted students of nature, and complacently looking down upon that proof as the artificial product of obscure speculative refinements. For were they willing to scrutinise their own procedure, they would find that, after advancing some considerable way on the solid ground of nature and experience, and finding themselves just as far distant as ever from the object which discloses itself to their reason, they suddenly leave this ground, and pass over into the realm of mere possibilities, where they hope upon the wings of ideas to draw near to the object—the object that has refused itself to all their *empirical* enquiries. For after this tremendous leap, when they have, as they think, found firm ground, they extend their concept—the *determinate* concept, into the possession of which they have now come, they know not how—over the whole sphere of creation. And the ideal [which this reasoning thus involves, and], which is entirely a product of pure reason, they then elucidate by reference to experience, though inadequately enough, and in a manner far below the dignity of its object; and throughout they persist in refusing to admit that they have arrived at this knowledge or hypothesis by a road quite other than that of experience.

Thus the physico-theological proof of the existence of an original or supreme being rests upon the cosmological proof, and the cosmological upon the ontological. And since, besides these three, there is no other path open to speculative reason, the ontological proof from pure concepts of reason is the only possible one, if indeed any proof of a proposition so far exalted above all empirical employment of the understanding is possible at all.

✽ F. R. TENNANT

9. *The Wider Teleology*

Though F. R. Tennant (1866–1957) was a trained chemist and physicist he is known primarily for his contributions to philosophical theology. He rejected religious experience as a valid foundation for religious belief and, in his two volume *Philosophical Theology*, attempted to provide a scientific and inductive basis for theism. Tennant's other theological and philosophical works include *Miracle and Its Philosophical Presuppositions* and several studies on sin and the Fall.

From *Philosophical Theology*, Volume II

Chapter 4: The Empirical Approach to Theism: Cosmic Teleology

The classical proofs of the being of God sought to demonstrate that there is a Real counterpart to a preconceived idea of God, such as was moulded in the course of the development of religion, or constructed by speculative philosophy aloof from religious experience and from avowedly anthropic interpretation, or obtained by both these methods combined. The empirically-minded theologian adopts a different procedure. He asks how the world, inclusive of man, is to be explained. He would let the Actual world tell its own story and offer its own suggestions: not silence it while abstractive speculation, setting out with presuppositions possibly irrelevant to Actuality, weaves a system of thought which may prove to conflict with facts. The *explicanda* which he investigates, and the results of his investigation, alone will determine the content or essence of the explicative idea of God to which he is led, as well as the grounds for belief that such an essence exists. He will thus entertain, at the outset, no such presuppositions as that the Supreme Being, to which the world may point as its principle of explanation, is infinite, perfect, immutable, suprapersonal, unqualifiedly omnipotent or omniscient. The attributes to be ascribed to God will be such as empirical facts and their sufficient explanation indicate or require. And if the empiricist deems the alleged religious 'instinct' and the *lumen naturale*[1] proved to be non-existent, and, previously to the inferential establishment of theism, he must consider the mystic's claims to be untrustworthy, all that he can expect to emerge from his inquiry is grounds for reasonable belief rather than rational and coercive demonstration. Should this seem a mean ambition for the theologian, we need but recall that other selves, as to whose existence each of us has an unshakable conviction, and whose works we can understand or explain only by using

F. R. Tennant, *Philosophical Theology* (Cambridge, England: Cambridge University Press, 1928–30), II. Reprinted by permission of the publisher.
[1]["natural light (of reason)."]

teleological categories, are neither directly apprehended nor provable otherwise than by cumulative pragmatic verification.

It has already been submitted that revealed religion, such as the Christian Faith, logically presupposes natural religion, in so far as a distinction between the two is to be drawn, and that religion presupposes some theological notion, crude or refined according to stage of development, suggested by observation of man and the world. And now it may further be remarked that natural theology is not to be identified with rational theology, though one name has often covered both of them. Rational and *a priori* theology stands or falls with the ontological argument; and if that argument—or some substitute for it, alleged to express its intent—still seems self-evidently cogent to a philosopher here and there, its fallaciousness is self-evident to all the rest. Natural theology, on the other hand, sets out from facts and inductions; its premises are as firmly established and as universally acknowledged as any of the stable generalisations of science. Here there is at least common ground, as distinct from private certitude, from which argumentation may proceed. Coercive demonstration being confessedly unattainable, it is to be inquired what kind of justification for reasonable belief natural theology can afford. And the first step is to set forth the facts and generalisations which collectively constitute our data or premises.

The forcibleness of Nature's suggestion that she is the outcome of intelligent design lies not in particular cases of adaptedness in the world, nor even in the multiplicity of them. It is conceivable that every such instance may individually admit of explanation in terms of proximate causes or, in the first instance, of explanation other than in terms of cosmic or 'external' teleology. And if it also admits of teleological interpretation, that fact will not of itself constitute a rigorous certification of external design. The forcibleness of the world's appeal consists rather in the conspiration of innumerable causes to produce, by their united and reciprocal action, and to maintain, a general order of Nature. Narrower kinds of teleological argument, based on surveys of restricted spheres of fact, are much more precarious than that for which the name of 'the wider teleology' may be appropriated in that the comprehensive design-argument is the outcome of synopsis or conspection of the knowable world.

The knowable world, however, is not identical with the universe as to which, as a whole, we have no knowledge. It may be objected, therefore, that to use the phrase 'the world' to denote both of these things seems to beg a vital question. Of course, if trustworthy evidence of design in the limited portion of the universe that we know were forthcoming, a world-designer would be 'proved,' and our ignorance as to other parts would be irrelevant. But it is a graver objection—perhaps the gravest that the teleologist has to encounter—that rich suggestions of design in the known world yielded no proof of design in the universe, since our ordered fragment may be but a temporary and casual episode in the history of the universe, an oasis in a desert of 'chaos,' a chance product of mindless agency in a universe which has had opportunity to produce all sorts of local and ephemeral worlds within

A World. To this objection it may be replied teleology does not profess to base itself on the principle of 'the inconceivability of the opposite,' while interpretations of the known cannot be refuted, even if they can be made to appear more precarious, by considerations as to possibilities within the unknowable. Certainly a mechanical theory of the universe must not be tacitly assumed to which our known world gives the lie. More specifically it may be said that the ordered oasis is not an isolable fragment. It and the supposed desert or 'chaos' are interdependent. It is because the desert is what it is that the oasis is what it is; and the one has orderedness only by permission, so to say, of the other. The force of the objection, indeed, seems to be derived from the assumption that our ordered world is due to some evolutionary process within the whole universe analogous to that secured within organic Nature by a natural selection out of random variations. This is but conjecture or appeal to the unknown, and, confronted with the second law of thermodynamics, is overwhelmingly improbable. And if it includes the supposition that even unlimited re-shufflings of matter by mechanical forces can produce minds and personalities in a corner of the universe, it conflicts with knowledge. Further, if the nerve of the teleological argument be that design issues in the realisation of ethical values, the spatio-temporal immensities of the universe become less significant than the petty oasis. Teleology, after all, is a value-concept; and magnitude and worth are incommensurable.

Nevertheless the inquiry that is here first to be undertaken, whether the knowable world, or Nature, has been devised by intelligence, is to be distinguished, though it cannot be separated, from the further inquiry, what the ultimate purpose or goal of the world-process is. The latter question may admit of no complete answer by man: reasonable belief as to the former involves but the application of mother-wit to forthcoming facts. A machine can evince intelligent contrivance or design to a man ignorant of engineering and unable to tell precisely what the machine is for. Once more, by way of making relevant distinctions, a teleological interpretation of Nature does not require that every detail in Nature was purposed or fore-ordained. Processes may inevitably produce by-products which, as such, were not purposed, but are the necessary outcome of processes by which a purpose is fulfilled.

The main fields of fact in which adaptation is conspicuous, and which have severally afforded data for particular arguments of the teleological kind and of restricted scope, are those of the knowability or intelligibility of the world (or the adaptation of thought to things), the internal adaptedness of organic beings, the fitness of the inorganic to minister to life, the aesthetic value of Nature, the world's instrumentality in the realisation of moral ends, and the progressiveness in the evolutionary process culminating in the emergence of man with his rational and moral status. A brief examination of these fields in turn will not only enable us to estimate the respective strengths of the more or less independent arguments derived from them severally, but also to appreciate the interconnexions within the world, and the comprehensive teleology which such interconnectedness suggests.

(i) We may begin with the mutual adaptation of thought and things,

Nature and Knowledge. The correspondence between human thought and the external world, rendering science possible, has evoked what may be called epistemological arguments for the being of God. Descartes accounted for the marvel, as it seemed to him, of this correspondence by invoking, as its necessary cause, the veracious Deity, whose existence he sought to prove—almost superfluously, on his own presuppositions—by other lines of reasoning. If a subject's 'ideas' were as disparate from percepts and from external Objects as Descartes supposed, each class forming a closed system independent of the other, there might be something to be said for the invocation of divine agency to explain the elaborate correspondence between the two systems. But if our primary ideas of objects are but images of such objects defecated to pure transparency, or are but elements of the objective matter of perceptual experience isolated for thought by selective and restricted attention, then that they apply to the objects from which they have but been abstracted is no wonder to be supernaturally accounted for. And if, as in science, general ideas and the constituents of developed thought are determined and controlled by things external to thought, and so enjoy validity, there is no cause for amazement even at the predictiveness of theoretical physics. The mysterious element in knowledge does not lie where Descartes would place it: it lies deeper. Similarly, Shelly's apostrophe,

> O thou immortal Deity
> Whose throne is in the depths of human thought,

supposing it to have any relevance to the present context, errs as to the location of the "throne." It is in the world, as allowing itself to be thought about, rather than in our thinking, if anywhere, that considerations as to the penetrability of things by thought may lead teleology to enthrone its Deity. Reason might soliloquize: world or no world, I must think thus and thus, in order to think at all. Pure reason may have power to decree *how* thoughts must be linked in order to yield Thought, and certainly can without limit form ideas—as in the pure sciences—to which there is no knowable counterpart in Actuality; but it is powerless to prescribe to things *what* they shall be, and that they shall satisfy the demands of any pure science. The world might answer: you must think me thus and thus, as to my 'what,' and not otherwise, if you would know me. Nature will open to the right pass-word; but she has chosen it, not we. To revert to plain speech: the primary epistemological contribution to teleological reasoning consists in the fact that the world is more or less intelligible, in that it happens to be more or less a cosmos, when conceivably it might have been a self-subsistent and determinate 'chaos' in which similar events never occurred, none recurred, universals had no place, relations no fixity, things no nexus of determination, and 'real' categories no foothold. But whether such logico-mathematical order as has been found to obtain in our world bespeaks 'chance'[2] in self-subsistent entities, or pur-

---

[2] By 'chance' is here meant absence of a sufficient ground. The word, as commonly used, carries several meanings; and which of them is to the fore in any context where the term subsequently appears will perhaps not need to be stated. Among its senses the following may be mentioned. It may signify an event not as yet included by known law, or one which, in

posiveness in a designer or a creator, there is of course no logical method of deciding: the probability-calculus can gain no purchase. We know that similar ordering is sometimes due to human design; that it always is due to design we have no means of knowing. Again, the amenability of things to the more interpretative kind of knowledge, constituted by the 'real' or the anthropic categories, shews that things, or their ontal counterparts, have so much of affinity with us as to be assimilable and to be understood, or alogically interpreted, as well as to be ordered by number, etc.: it does not of itself testify that the adaptedness is teleological.

It is in that Nature evokes thought of richer kind than is involved in scientific knowledge, and responds to thinking such as is neither logically necessary nor biologically needful, thus suggesting a Beyond, that considerations as to the relation between thought and things assume their chief significance for the teleologist. These considerations, however, belong to another context; and those, the logical coerciveness of which has been denied, will later be discussed again when criticism of demonstrative proofs will give place to construction of a cumulative argument for a reasonable, if indemonstrable, teleological interpretation.

(ii) The adaptiveness that is so abundantly evinced in the organic world has already been discussed from the point of view of science and proximate causation. We have seen that if the behaviour of matter be regarded as completely descibable in terms of least action, shortest path, dissipation of kinetic energy, and so forth, matter must be regarded also as unable, of itself, to fall into such systems as organisms. There is indeed some tendency to-day in scientific circles to seek an organic conception of the physical atom, etc., rather than a mechanical conception of the organism. But as for the organic at the molar and phenomenal level of description, its formative principle, irreducible to rigid mechanism, is provided by mentality wherever we have reason to infer psychic behaviour; there we can account for the facts of function and structure, heredity and progressive adaptation. Where, as in plants, there is no macroscopic evidence of psychic behaviour, the formative principle, as yet mysterious to science, is further to seek. It may be that only in metaphysics such as spiritualistic monadism, or hylozoism of the microscopic order, is a natural explanation to be found. But in proportion as psychological or other explanation is forthcoming in the organic realm as a whole, resort to external or cosmic teleology, in order to account for adaptations within the organism, becomes superfluous for the special sciences. So long as organisms were believed to have originated, in their present forms and with all their specialised organs 'ready made,' the argument that adaptation of part to whole, of whole to environment, and of organ to function, implied design, was forcible. But its premiss became untenable when Darwin shewed that every organic structure had come to be what it now is through a long series of successive and

that it is unique, is absolutely non-subsumable under a general law; or one that is determined by causes as to which we have but imperfect, or perhaps no relevant, knowledge. It may simply exclude final causation, and then denote the non-purposed. It may even suggest the supposed indeterminateness, which can never actually subsist, *e.g.* of a configuration.

gradual modifications. Gradualness of construction is in itself no proof of the absence of external design: it is not at this point that Darwinism delivered its alleged death-blow to teleology. The sting of Darwinism rather lay in the suggestion that proximate and 'mechanical' causes were sufficient to produce the adaptations from which the teleology of the eighteenth century had argued to God. Assignable proximate causes, whether mechanical or not, are sufficient to dispose of the particular kind of teleological proof supplied by Paley. But the fact of organic evolution, even when the maximum of instrumentality is accredited to what is figuratively called natural selection, is not incompatible with teleology on a grander scale: as exponents of Darwinism were perhaps the first to recognise and to proclaim. Subversive of Paley's argument, it does not invalidate his theistic conclusion, nor even his view that every organism and organ is an end as well as a means. Indeed the science of evolution was the primary source of the wider teleology current for the last half century, as well as the main incentive to the recovery of the closely connected doctrine of divine immanence. This kind of teleology does not set out from the particular adaptations in individual organisms or species so much as from considerations as to the progressiveness of the evolutionary process and as to the organic realm as a whole; but its connexion with the former class of facts belongs to the subject-matter of the present section.

The survival of the fittest presupposes the arrival of the fit, and throws no light thereupon. Darwin did not account for the origin of variations; their forthcomingness was simply a datum for him. It is of no great significance for the wider teleology that variations are not in all cases so indefinite or random, nor so infinitesimal and gradual, as was generally assumed in *The Origin of Species*. But it may be observed that, in the absence either of a mechanical or of an 'internal' explanation of variation, room is left for the possibility that variation is externally predetermined or guided, so that not only the general trend of the organic process, but also its every detail, may be pre-ordained or divinely controlled. Even this observation is pointless save for those who regard a nexus of traceable proximate causes and a theistic interpretation as incompatibilities. Theism such as has over-emphasised the idea of God's immanence denies proximate causes as distinct from acts of God; and advocates of anti-theistic mechanism sometimes appear to think that the traceability of proximate causes bespeaks the superfluity, to philosophy as well as to science, of the idea of God. Thus, in connexion with the topic now before us, Weismann wrote: "It is certainly the absence of a theoretical definition of variability which leaves open the door for smuggling in a teleological power. A mechanical explanation of variability must form the basis of this side of natural selection." But theism, such as is sufficiently leavened with deism to distinguish itself from pantheism, and the world from a deified mechanism, is indifferent to the banishment of the Paleyan type of teleology which relied on particular organic adaptations, any one of which was deemed sufficient to prove a divine artificer; and at the same time it has no need of going to the extreme of asserting that God is "either everywhere or nowhere," or that He is nothing if not all. The discovery of organic evolution has caused the teleologist to shift his ground from special design in the products to directivity in the process, and plan in the primary collocations. It has also served to suggest that the organic realm supplies no better basis for teleological argument of the narrower type than does inorganic Nature. Indeed it suggests that, since the adaptiveness of an organism is non-teleological, the adaptiveness of the whole world may perhaps similarly be *Zweckmässigkeit ohne Zweck*.[3] But this suggestion calls for examination later.

(iii) Although teleologists in the past have generally set out from adaptations in organisms, it has occurred now and again to a theistic apologist, *e.g.* to Aquinas, that adaptation in inorganic Nature, where there cannot be a formative principle such as non-intelligent organisms evince, should more unequivocally bespeak external design. The teleologist of to-day, however, would rather call attention to the continuity of apparent purposiveness between the two realms, or to the dependence of adaptation in the one on adaptiveness in the other. Since Darwin, we have realised that organisms can only be understood in connexion with their environment. And more recently it has been argued, as by Mr. Henderson, that the inorganic environment is as plainly adapted to life as living creatures are to their environment. The vast complexity of the physico-chemical conditions of life on the earth suggests to common sense that the inorganic world may retrospectively receive a biocentric explanation, which, if 'unconscious purpose' do but restate the facts rather than account for them, and ungrounded coincidence be as humanly incredible as it is logically unassailable, becomes a teleological explanation. Waiving, as here irrelevant, the metaphysical possibility that what we call inorganic matter is an appearance of relatively unorganised spirit, we may say that if science is to be trusted when it regards the organic realm as later in time than the inorganic world, and when it asserts that the processes, which made the emergence and persistence of life possible, would have been precisely the same had life not emerged at all, then there would seem to be a developement of this fitness for life, involving convergence of innumerable events towards a result, as if that result were an end to which the inorganic processes were means. The fitness of our world to be the home of living beings depends upon certain primary conditions, astronomical, thermal, chemical, etc., and on the coincidence of qualities apparently not causally connected with one another, the number of which would doubtless surprise anyone wholly unlearned in the sciences; and these primary conditions, in their turn, involve many of secondary order. Unique assemblages of unique properties on so vast a scale being thus essential to the maintenance of life, their forthcomingness makes the inorganic world seem in some respects comparable with an organism. It is suggestive of a formative principle. But, if there be such a principle, it is not conceivable after analogy with the life and mind of organisms, and cannot be said to be intrinsic or internal; because the inorganic—at the molar and phenomenal level of explanation—is devoid of life, and—at any level of explanation—is devoid of intelligence and foresight. Un-

---

[3]["adaptiveness without purpose."]

less cosmic teleology is invoked, the intricate adaptations that have been mentioned must be referred by the dualist to a mechanically controlled concourse of atoms, and by the pluralistic spiritualist to conative monads that are no more capable of conspiration than are inert particles.

Such is the teleological appeal of this field of facts to common-sense reasonableness, or mother-wit, which regards the 'probability,' that the apparent preparedness of the world to be a theatre of life is due to 'chance,' as infinitesimally small. It remains to ask whether either science or logic is able to abate the forcibleness of this appeal.

Science does not seem to lessen the convincingness of the argument now before us when it suggests that (as if organic chemistry were irrelevant), had the conditions upon which life, as we know it, depends been wholly or partly different, other forms of organism might equally well have emerged, adapted to the altered environment: silicon perhaps replacing carbon in another kind of protoplasm, and iron replacing calcium phosphate in skeletons. For the point is that, for the existence of any forms of life that we may conceive, the necessary environment, whatever its nature, must be complex and dependent on a multiplicity of coincident conditions, such as are not reasonably attributable to blind forces or to pure mechanism. Nor, again, can science explain the adaptation of the inorganic environment to life after the manner in which Darwinism, its sufficiency being assumed, explains progressive adaptations in organisms without resort to design. Of a struggle for existence between rival worlds, out of which ours has survived as the fittest, we have no knowledge upon which to draw. Natural selection cannot here be invoked; and if the term 'evolution' be applicable at all to the whole world-process, it must have a different meaning from that which it bears in Darwinian biology. Presumably the world is comparable with a single throw of dice. And common sense is not foolish in suspecting the dice to have been loaded.

But here the logician intervenes. He will first point out that the remarkableness, or surprisingness, of manifold coincidences, evoking our teleological explanation of them, is but a fact pertaining to human psychology, unless 'remarkable' means what he calls antecedently improbable. He will then remind us that a remarkable world might result from 'one throw' in spite of there being indefinitely large chances against it, just as double sixes may be cast in one's first toss of two unloaded dice, although the adverse odds are 35 to 1. But his most harmful observation will be that, if the world be the sole instance of its kind, or be analogous to a single throw, there can be no talk of chances or of antecedent probability in connexion with our question. Sound as this caution is, it does not affect the teleologist; for, when he calls coincidence on the vast scale improbable, he has in mind not mathematical probability, or a logical relation, but the alogical probability which is the guide of life and which has been found to be the ultimate basis of all scientific induction. If teleology here strays from the path of logical rectitude into one marked by logicians with a warning-post, it does so in the light-hearted company of common sense and inductive science. Science has been so continuously successful in its venturesomeness that the wise-head, logic, now lets it pass without remonstrance; but theology, though arm in arm with science, receives a reprimand. The teleologist is told that there is no antecedent probability, as to the existence of the intelligent Being invoked to explain adaptation suggestive of intelligent activity, after observation of the facts in question, unless there was an appreciable probability, before observation of them, that such a Being exists. Robinson Crusoe can be said to have inferred Friday from footprints legitimately, because he already knew that men existed and that they could reach his island; but the teleologist does not know beforehand that any superhuman being exists, and therefore cannot legitimately reason from what apparently are Mind-prints to their divine causation. But some favouritism would seem to be shewn to science in this illustration; for when we inquire how Crusoe originally got his knowledge as to the existence of fellow-men who can not only make footprints but also supply service and friendship, we find that it seems to have been mediated in much the same way as is the teleologist's belief in God. It is true that in the former case there is a psychologically stronger compulsion, a nearer analogy, and a more immediate and constantly reiterated verification-process than in the latter; but the origination of our belief in fellow-subjects, like remarkableness of coincidences, is ultimately an affair of human psychology and life, of teleology and not of logic or of direct apprehension of soul-substance. Moreover, though we have no 'knowledge' of a spirit above man in the hierarchy of spirits that we 'know,' neither have we knowledge that there is no such being. Knowledge leaves room for the faith which teleology involves; and the faith-venture is similar *in kind* to that on which all scientific knowledge relies. Previously to verification of his faith the teleologist need ask of science no further recognition than this. He would but insist that, in so far as relations with logic are concerned, it is not true that science rests on reason while, in a corresponding sense, teleology rests on unreason.

(iv) Besides possessing a structure that happens to render it habitable by living creatures and intelligible to some of them, the world is a bearer of values, thus evincing affinity with beings such as can appreciate as well as understand. The beauty and sublimity of Nature have been made the basis of a special teleological argument; and if, as standing by itself, this argument falls short of cogency, the facts from which it sets out may be said to form a link in the chain of evidence which comprehensive teleology presents. The few considerations that lend themselves to either of these uses do not call for lengthy or subtle disputation; and fortunately it is not necessary to enter the scientifically trackless domain of aesthetics in order to ascertain their bearing on theism. Whether the adaptation to our faculties, involved in aesthetic estimation, be, as Kant thought, formal and the same for all, though subjective; whether it be subjectively constituted and not the same for all; whether beauty be wholly Objective and literally intrinsic to Nature: these controversial questions are here immaterial. For the doctrine that aesthetic value is constituted by feeling does not imply that the feeling is not objectively evoked, as if we could see beauty when and where we chose. It has a parallel in the phenomenalist theory of knowledge: that is to say, beauty is not created by minds out of nothing, but is subjectively made out of *rapport* with the ontal. Thus diverse theories as to the constitution of beauty may be said to have in common the implication that the ontal world is ultimately responsible for the evocation of aesthetic thrills and sentiments, though the value-judgments evoked by the same 'perceptual' Objects are different in different percipients. Theories differ but as to what exactly is intrinsic, whether that is intrinsic to Nature as ontal or as phenomenal, and how much is subjectively contributed. And whatever be our proportioning of the shares of the human mind and external Reality in constituting aesthetic value, the dependence or non-dependence of beauty on design will not be affected by it. There is a point in Toby Veck's remark as to the chimes: "If I hear 'em, what does it matter whether they speak it or not?" Yet "We receive but what we give,"[4] in this connexion, is a partial truth because it suppresses the fact that our giving is solicited by a prior and different gift to us. If we minimise phenomenal Nature's gift by denying that her beauty is intrinsic, as is form or colour, we must allow to ontal Nature an intrinsic constitution such that minds can make beauty as well as nomic order out of it. And the more we magnify man's part in this making, phenomenalising, and appreciating, the more motivation have we to believe that Nature comes to herself in man, has a significance for man that exists not for herself, and without man is a broken circle. Theologically expressed, this is the belief that Nature is meaningless and valueless without God behind it and man in front; and that is what teleology in its comprehensiveness, and the aesthetic argument in its particularity, endeavour to establish.

The latter argument, at least in its more popular forms, treats the beauty of Nature as Paley treated organic adaptations. That it discusses the beauty of the world, as we now contemplate it, as if it were a 'special creation' with no past history or developement, may not signify. The weak spot in what purports to be a special proof of theism lies rather in the assumption that, since in human art a beautiful or sublime production is the outcome of human design, similar effects must everywhere be due to design. This generalisation is all too precarious; it can hardly be maintained that arrangements of matter, accounted beautiful, humanly caused but not contrived or selectively constructed with a view to exciting aesthetic admiration, *never* occur. Prescience or purpose is involved in art; but art is not necessarily the sole source of beauty. We may deem some of Kant's criticisms of the teleological explanation of the beautiful and the sublime to be captious, and such explanation to be natural and reasonable; but it is hardly necessitated by the considerations on which this would-be coercive argument relies.

The aesthetic argument for theism becomes more persuasive when it renounces all claim to proof and appeals to alogical probability. And it becomes stronger when it takes as the most significant fact not the forth-

---

4   ". . . We receive but what we give,
             And in our life alone does Nature live:
             Ours is her wedding-garment, ours her shroud!"
                                        S. T. Coleridge, *Dejection: An Ode.*

comingness of beautiful phenomena but what may be called, with almost negligible need of qualification, the saturation of Nature with beauty. On the telescopic and on the microscopic scale, from the starry heaven to the siliceous skeleton of the diatom, in her inward parts (if scientific imagination be veridical) as well as on the surface, in flowers that "blush unseen" and gems that the "unfathomed caves of ocean bear," Nature is sublime or beautiful, and the exceptions do but prove the rule. However various be the taste for beauty, and however diverse the levels of its education or the degrees of its refinement, Nature elicits aesthetic sentiment from men severally and collectively; and the more fastidious becomes this taste, the more poignantly and the more lavishly does she gratify it. Indeed, from contemplation of Nature, whose "every prospect pleases," the atheist might be led to conclude that processes only need *not* to be fraught with aesthetic design in order to excite, almost without fail, aesthetic admiration. But his generalisation would become untenable as soon as he bethought himself of similar causal *nexa* into which human agency, seeking any end save beauty, enters. In general, man's productions (other than professed works of art), and almost only they, are aesthetically vile. An automobile, with its noises, stench, etc., can disgust all our senses simultaneously, and is not wholly untypical; while human output of larger scale is often not only unsightly and otherwise offensive in itself, but mars the fair face of Nature. Here, then, are two kinds of agency, *ex hypothesi* proceeding with indifference to the realisation of aesthetic values: we might almost say the one never achieves, while the other never misses, the beautiful. And the same contrast subsists between their processes as between their products. Compare, *e.g.*, "the rattling looms and the hammering noise of human workshops" with Nature's silent or musical constructiveness; or the devastating stinks of chemical works with Nature's fragrant distillations. "In the very act of labouring as a machine [Nature] also sleeps as a picture."[5]

If "God made the country" whereas man made the town—and the black country—we have a possible explanation of these things; but if the theism contained in this saying be rejected, explanation does not seem to be forthcoming. The universality of Nature's beauty,—to speak as if beauty were the same for all and were intrinsic—is a generalisation roughly comparable with the uniformity of natural law. That natural Objects evoke aesthetic sentiment is as much a fact about them as that they obey the laws of motion or that they have such and such chemical composition. And this potency is not coextensive with "mechanicalness," or absence of aesthetic design, as man's utilitarian productions shew. Nor can Nature's mechanism be regarded as a sufficient cause of the adaptiveness to our subjectivity in which beauty consists; for we may still ask why *Nature's* mechanism affects us in such wise that we deem her sublime and beautiful, since mere mechanism, as such, is under no universal necessity to do so, and what we may call human mechanisms usually fail to do so. Yet this potency, describable as the Objective factor in beauty, belongs to Nature's very texture. And our scientific knowledge that the world-elements are ordered by number brings us no nearer to under-

[5] J. B. Mozley, *University Sermons*, 6th ed., p. 123 [Tennant's bracketing].

standing why Nature is comparable with elaborately polyphonic music, or a harmony of many combined melodies.

It may further be observed that, in so far as the mechanical stability and the analytic intelligibility of the inorganic world are concerned, beauty is a superfluity. Also that in the organic world aesthetic pleasingness of colour, etc., seems to possess survival-value on but a limited scale, and then is not to be identified with the complex and intellectualised aesthetic sentiments of humanity, which apparently have no survival-value. From the point of view of science, beauty proper is, in both its subjective and its objective factors, but a by-product, an epiphenomenon, a biologically superfluous accompaniment of the cosmic process. Once more then lucky accidents and coincidences bewilderingly accumulate until the idea of purposiveness, already lying to hand as indispensable within the sphere of human conduct, is applied to effect the substitution of reasonable, if alogical, probability for groundless contingency. If we do apply this category of design to the whole time-process, the beauty of Nature may not only be assigned a cause but also a meaning, or a revelational function. It may then be regarded as no mere by-product, like physical evil, in a teleologically ordered world whose *raison d'être* is the realisation of other values—the moral and the religious. Indeed Nature's potency to evoke aesthetic sentiment, however otiose in the cosmic process studied by science, is efficient in the world's *rapport* with man. From its very origination religious experience seems to have been conditioned by the impressiveness or the awesomeness of natural phenomena, suggestive of an invisible and mysterious presence. Aesthetic values are closely associated, and often are inextricably interwoven, with ethico-religious values. God reveals Himself, to such as have differentiated these valuations, in many ways; and some men enter His Temple by the Gate Beautiful. Values alone can provide guidance as to the world's meaning, structure being unable to suggest more than intelligent power. And beauty may well be *a* meaning. That is the element of sense contained in the romanticist's paradox, beauty is truth, or truth is beauty.

It may be remarked by the way that if sensuous beauty be accounted a world-meaning, so far will the anthropocentric factor in interpretation of the world become accentuated. For as to the ontal counterpart to sensory beauty, or what Nature's beauty is for the Creator Himself, we cannot speculate. If Nature's beauty embody a purpose *of* God, it would seem to be a purpose *for* man, and to bespeak that God is "mindful of him." Theistically regarded, Nature's beauty is of a piece with the world's intelligibility and with its being a theatre for moral life; and thus far the case for theism is strengthened by aesthetic considerations.

(v) . . . In an exposition of the significance of the moral order for theistic philosophy, the first step is to point out that man belongs to Nature, and is an essential part of it, in such a sense that the world cannot be described or explained as a whole without taking him and his moral values into account. Prof. Pringle-Pattison, especially, has elaborated the doctrine that, as he expresses it, "man is organic to the world." What precisely this, or the similar phrase "man is the child of Nature," should mean, if either is to be more than a half-truth, needs to be made clear. In so far as man's soul, *i.e.* man as *noümenon*, or (in the language of spiritualistic pluralism) the dominant monad in the empirical self, is concerned, we are not authorised by known facts to regard man as organic to Nature, or as the child of Nature, in the sense that he is an emergent product of cosmic evolution. We are rather forbidden by psychology to entertain any such notion. But, this proviso being observed—it must qualify all that is further said in the present connexion—we can affirm that man's body, with all its conditioning of his mentality, his sociality, knowledge and morality, is 'of a piece' with Nature; and that, in so far as he is a phenomenal being, man is organic to Nature, or a product of the world. And this fact is as significant for our estimation of Nature as for our anthropology. If man is Nature's child, Nature is the wonderful mother of such a child. Any account of her which ignores the fact of her maternity is scientifically partial and philosophically insignificant. Her capacity to produce man must be reckoned among her potencies, explain it how we may. And man is no monstrous birth out of due time, no freak or sport. In respect of his body and the bodily conditioning of his mentality, man is like, and has genetic continuity with, Nature's humbler and earlier-born children. In the fulness of time Nature found self-utterance in a son possessed of the intelligent and moral status. Maybe she was pregnant with him from the beginning, and the world-ages are the period of her gestation. As to this anthropocentric view of the world-process, and its co-extensiveness with teleological interpretation, more will presently be said. But in the light of man's continuity with the rest of the world we can at once dismiss the view that Nature suddenly "stumbled" or "darkly blundered" on man, while "churning the universe with mindless motion." The world-process is a *praeparatio anthropologica*,[6] whether designedly or not, and man is the culmination, up to the present stage of the knowable history of Nature, of a gradual ascent. We cannot explain man in terms of physical Nature; conceivably Nature may be found explicable—in another sense of the word—in terms of man, and can be called 'the threshold of spirit.' Judging the genealogical tree by its roots, naturalism once preached that Darwin had put an end to the assumption that man occupies an exceptional position on our planet; apparently implying that there is no difference of status between man and the primordial slime because stages between the two are traceable. But if we judge the tree by its fruits, Darwin may rather be said to have restored man to the position from which Copernicus seemed to have ousted him, in making it possible to read the humanising of Nature in the naturalising of man, and to regard man as not only the last term and the crown of Nature's long upward effort, but also as its end or goal.[7]

The phrase 'organic to Nature,' as applied to man, may serve to sum up other relations between humanity and the world besides that of parentage or blood-affinity. It implies also a denial of the assertion that man is

[6]["preparation for man."]

[7]A. Seth Pringle-Pattison, *The Idea of God*, 1917, pp. 82 f.

an excrescence upon Nature in the sense of being an alien in a world that is indifferent to his moral aims, or hostile to his ideals. The most forcible presentation of this view, that the cosmic process and human morality are antithetical, is perhaps that contained in Huxley's *Romanes Lecture*. It is therefore here selected for examination. Huxley's first point was that the world, as involving struggle for existence and extermination of the less fit, is no "school of virtue." If that statement merely meant that it is not from Nature that we are to imbibe our ethical maxims, no one would wish to dispute it. But it would then overlook the fact that in other senses Nature may fairly be called a school of virtue. In the first place, Nature is largely a cosmos ruled by uniformity or law; and if Nature's uniformity and impartiality are a main source of the trouble to which man is born, they are also a precondition of all intelligent, and therefore of all moral, life. In this respect Nature is the power that makes it possible for noümenal man to be, as phenomenal man, a moral being. Further, it is partly through his being "the plaything of hazard and the prey of hardship" that man's moral virtues are acquired. The world is thus instrumental to the emergence, maintenance, and progressiveness, of morality. The second charge which Huxley preferred against the cosmos is that the physical world works upon man solely through his lower nature, his ingrained appetites, etc., and against his higher ethical interests. Nature is thus the cause of his 'original sin,' and is diabolically provocative of his diverse immoralities. This also is true; but again it presents but one aspect of the facts. For, apart from man's bodily appetites and impulses it is inconceivable that ethical principles should gain purchase on him. Hunger and sex are the bed-rock of human morality; and the self-determination which human morality presupposes is hardly possible without the conflict between moral reason and non-moral impulse. Morality cannot be made without raw material; and in providing this raw material Nature is once more instrumental to man's acquisition of the moral status. Morality thus has its roots in Nature, however indispensable be the innate and non-inherited potentialities of the pure ego or soul. The non-moral cosmos, personified into a morally evil world by pessimistic poets for the purpose of giving it, as Mr Chesterton has said of one of them, a piece of their mind, has nevertheless subserved the moralisation of human souls, even when soliciting to carnality. And it is an exaggeration to say that Nature fosters only tendencies that issue in vice. We have seen before that there is such a thing as 'natural virtue,' or 'original rectitude,' as 'instinctive' as is self-seeking; and Nature plainly appraises health and vigour, thus inciting to temperance and self-control. Lastly, Huxley maintained that the world is indifferent to man's moral aspirations, in that they along with him are destined to be extinguished before the break-up of the solar system. Here he became unwarrantably dogmatical: for, apart from the fact that science's predictions are not unconditional, speculations as to the ruin of a fragment of the universe, based on partial knowledge of a larger fragment of what, for all we know, may be possessed of a power to make all things new, are too precarious to be considered exhaustive of the possibilities even as to our terrestrial home, let alone those as to a future life.

Nature, then, has produced moral beings, is instrumental to moral life and therefore amenable to 'instrumental' moral valuation, and is relatively modifiable by operative moral ideas—or, rather, by moral agents pursuing ideals. Nature and moral man are not at strife, but are organically one. The whole process of Nature is capable of being regarded as instrumental to the developement of intelligent and moral creatures. Acquisition of the moral status is in line with the other stages of the long 'ascent of man,' and is its climax—unless we reserve that name for the morality which, tinged with sentiment transcending reverence for duty, passes into religion.

(vi) The more or less separable fields of fact which have now been surveyed may each be said to admit of teleological explanation even if explanation of the causal or the descriptive type be forthcoming in every case. None of them calls for resort to final causes merely because other kinds of causality, or linkage according to law, are not assignable. Theism no longer plants its God in the gaps between the explanatory achievements of natural science, which are apt to get scientifically closed up. Causal explanation and teleological explanation are not mutually exclusive alternatives; and neither can perform the function of the other. It is rather when these several fields of fact are no longer considered one by one, but as parts of a whole or terms of a continuous series, and when for their dovetailing and interconnectedness a sufficient ground is sought, such as mechanical and proximate causation no longer seems to supply, that divine design is forcibly suggested. Paley's watch is no analogue of the human eye; but it may none the less be an approximate analogue of Nature as a whole. Thus the wider teleological argument is not comparable with a chain whose strength is precisely that of its weakest link; it is comparable rather with a piece of chain-armour. And this can the better be seen if the relevant facts be presented again so as to display especially their connexions and their gradually increasing suggestiveness. . . .

❊ SELECTED BIBLIOGRAPHY
FOR SECTION 2

Many of the classical and contemporary statements of the Cosmological and Teleological Arguments may be found in a useful anthology edited by Donald Burrill, *The Cosmological Arguments* (Garden City, N. Y.: Anchor Books, 1967); included are the early formulations of Plato and Aristotle as well as recent influential analyses.

General discussions of Aquinas' argument may be found in Étienne Gilson, *The Christian Philosophy of St. Thomas Aquinas*, Part I, tr. L. K. Shook (New York: Random House, 1956) and F. C. Copleston, *Aquinas*, Ch. 3 (London: Penguin Books, 1955). One should note also the articles in *Aquinas: A Collection of Critical Essays*, Part II, ed. Anthony Kenny (Garden City, N. Y.: Anchor Books, 1969). The following contain important restatements and discussions of the Thomist approach by contemporary Thomists: Étienne Gilson, *God and Philosophy*, Ch. 4 (New Haven, Conn.: Yale University Press, 1941); Jacques Maritain, *Approaches to God*, tr. Peter O'Reilly (New York: Harper and Row, 1954); E. L. Mascall, *He Who Is, passim*, revised ed. (London: Libra Books, 1966); D. J. B. Hawkins, *The Essentials of Theism*, Ch. 4 (New York: Sheed & Ward, 1949) ; and W. E. Kennick, "A New Way with the Five Ways," *Australasian Journal of Philosophy*, XXXVIII (May, 1960). An attempt to illuminate the Thomistic position by means of analytic techniques is contained in James F. Ross, *Philosophical*

Theology, Chs. 4 and 7, and *passim* (Indianapolis, Ind.: Bobbs-Merrill, 1967). For a complete, up-to-date, and sometimes technical study, see Anthony Kenny, *The Five Ways* (London: Routledge & Kegan Paul, 1969).

For analytic-type and critical treatments of the argument, see J. J. C. Smart, "The Existence of God," in Burrill, *op. cit.*, also reprinted in *New Essays in Philosophical Theology*, ed. Antony Flew and Alasdair MacIntyre (London: Student Christian Movement Press, 1955), and Ronald Hepburn, *Christianity and Paradox*, Chs. 9 and 10 (London: Watts, 1958). These two thinkers, along with J. N. Findlay, "Can God's Existence be Disproved?," also in *New Essays in Philosophical Theology*, charge that among other things, St. Thomas' notion of God as a necessary being (as in his Third Way) involves him in the contradiction of ascribing logical necessity to an existential proposition. Three attempts to exonerate the Cosmological Argument from this charge and to construe God as involving factual or metaphysical necessity may be found in John Hick, "God as Necessary Being," *Journal of Philosophy*, LVII (October 27 and November 10, 1960); Patterson Brown, "St. Thomas' Doctrine of Necessary Being," reprinted in Anthony Kenny (ed.), *Aquinas: A Collection of Critical Essays*, and A. C. Ewing, "Two 'Proofs' of God's Existence," *Religious Studies*, I (October, 1965). Note also Alvin Plantinga's rebuttal to Findlay in *God and Other Minds*, Ch. 7, Part 3 (Ithaca, N.Y.: Cornell University Press, 1967) .

A. E. Taylor's old but still important defense of the argument is contained in his *Essays Catholic and Critical*, Sec. I, ed. E. G. Selwyn (Saffron Walden, England: Society for Promoting Christian Knowledge, 1926). Paul Tillich's "existential" treatment of the argument may be found in two places: "Two Types of Philosophy of Religion," in *Theology of Culture*, ed. Robert C. Kimball (New York: Oxford University Press, 1959) and *Systematic Theology*, Vol I, Part II, I, 12 (Chicago: University of Chicago Press, 1951–63).

Some of the important concepts, distinctions, and angles that must be considered in relation to the question of God and creation are reflected in Erich Frank, *Philosophical Understanding and Religious Truth*, Ch. 3 (New York: Oxford University Press, 1945); Milton K. Munitz, *The Mystery of Existence*, Part III (New York: Appleton-Century-Crofts, 1965); and Antony Flew and D. M. MacKinnon, "Creation," in Antony Flew and Alasdair MacIntyre, *op. cit.*; Langdon Gilkey, in *Maker of Heaven and Earth* (Garden City, N. Y.: Anchor Books, 1959), provides an exhaustive treatment of the concept of creation from a Christian standpoint, relating it to the whole of Christian thought.

Perhaps the best-known of the modern versions of the Teleological Argument is Lecomte du Noüy's *Human Destiny* (New York: Longmans, Green & Co., 1947) in which he argues to cosmic purpose from, for example, the infinitesimal odds against the chance-occurrences required for the production of life. Evidence of a more cosmological sort has been embraced by certain physicists and mathematicians including Arthur Eddington, *The Nature of the Physical World*, Ch. 4 and *passim* (New York: Macmillan, 1928), and James Jeans, *The Mysterious Universe*, Ch. 5, revised ed., (New York: Macmillan, 1932). One should consult also the general treatment in E. L. Mascall, *Christian Theology and Natural Science* (London: Longmans, Green & Co., 1956). Criticisms of this approach may be found in Bertrand Russell, *The Scientific Outlook*, Ch. 5 (London: George Allen & Unwin, 1931); L. Susan Stebbing, *Philosophy and the Physicists*, Chs. 1 and 2 (London: Methuen, 1937); John Laird, *Theism and Cosmology* (London: George Allen & Unwin, 1940); W. R. Inge, *God and the Astronomers* (London: Longmans, Green & Co., 1937); and Ernest Nagel, *Logic Without Metaphysics*, Ch. 19 (Glencoe, Ill.: Free Press, 1957). For a brief and mildly critical consideration of the cosmological-astronomical evidence for God, see Jagjit Singh, *Great Ideas and Theories of Modern Cosmology*, Ch. 16 (New York: Dover, 1961).

Among those who argue to God, or at least to real teleology in nature, on the evidence of evolution are Henri Bergson in *Creative Evolution*, tr. Arthur Mitchell (New York: Henry Holt, 1911) and, more recently, Teilhard de Chardin in *The Phenome-*

non of Man, tr. Bernard Wall (New York: Harper & Row, 1959). A complete survey of the Christian view of evolution is provided by Ernst Benz, *Evolution and Christian Hope*, tr. Heinz G. Frank (Garden City, N.Y.: Anchor Books, 1966). General discussions of teleology may be found in John V. Canfield (ed.), *Purpose in Nature* (Englewood Cliffs, N. J.: Prentice-Hall, 1963).

For a logical (and critical) analysis of both arguments, see Alvin Plantinga, *God and Other Minds*, Chs. 1 and 4. A forceful and positive statement of the arguments (and a good piece of reading) may be found in Richard Taylor, *Metaphysics*, Ch. 7 (Englewood Cliffs, N. J.: Prentice-Hall, 1963). A variety of relevant issues are considered in the several articles in *The Monist*, LIV (July, 1970).

Hume's criticisms from the *Dialogues* should be read alongside Section X of his *Enquiry Concerning Human Understanding*, ed. L. A. Selby-Bigge (Oxford, England: Clarendon Press, 1902). A thorough discussion of Hume's critical position on religion is provided in Antony Flew, *Hume's Philosophy of Belief* (London: Routledge & Kegan Paul, 1961). For an exposition of Kant's criticisms, see Norman Kemp Smith, *A Commentary to Kant's Critique of Pure Reason*, revised ed. (New York: Macmillan, 1923), pp. 531 ff. and H. W. Cassirer, *Kant's First Critique*, Ch. 13 (London: George Allen & Unwin, 1954).

God and the Moral Law

✳ INTRODUCTION

Few thinkers in the history of philosophy did more than Immanuel Kant to divest the traditional theistic arguments of their long-standing authority. It would be a mistake, however, to conclude from this that Kant was an atheist. He was, in fact, raised in a Pietist home and his interest in religious and theological issues characterized his whole intellectual career. In fact, after destroying to his own satisfaction all possibility of philosophical knowledge of God through the "theoretical reason," he immediately formulated a new argument for God: the Moral Argument.

In the concluding paragraphs of the *Critique of Practical Reason*, Kant wrote no doubt his most famous lines: "Two things fill the mind with ever new and increasing admiration and awe, the oftener and more steadily we reflect on them: the starry heavens above me and moral law within me."[1] It is important to notice that the "moral law within" does not mean for Kant an awareness of specific moral codes but, rather, the moral consciousness or sense of duty, the feeling of being morally conditioned from without. Some have, indeed, attempted to make a case for a Divine Lawgiver on the basis of the (more or less) universality of certain moral principles. This may be an interesting possibility, but it has nothing to do with the direction of Kant's argument. The Moral Law presents itself, according to Kant, just as inexorably and undeniably as the wondrous world of nature itself, and provides the point of departure for a new knowledge of God, this time a practical rather than a theoretical knowledge. As Kant expresses it, God is required by the "practical reason" as a "postulate" of morality: He must exist if there is to be any meaning to the concept of moral law and obligation. Kant's reasoning is not easily reproduced in a few words, but the central idea is that in a truly moral universe virtuous conduct must be rewarded by a due proportion of happiness and wrongdoing must be punished, and that a supreme power must therefore exist to insure that such justice is recompensed.

There have been many variations and versions of the argument first expounded by Kant, one of the simplest and most interesting being that of Hastings Rashdall. Rashdall too begins with the reality of value, "absolute" and "objective" value, by which he (and most others) mean values or ideals that exist in themselves, independently of our thoughts and desires. He then reasons that if we take values seriously, that is, not as being merely conventional or relative, but rather as objectively given and unconditioned, then

---

[1]Immanuel Kant, *Critique of Practical Reason*, tr. Lewis White Beck (Indianapolis: Library of Liberal Arts, 1956), p. 166.

we must also believe in God. Stated succinctly the argument is that ideals are the kind of things that exist only in minds, and where could absolute and unchanging ideals exist except in a mind that is adequate to them, an Absolute or Divine Mind?

It is clear that both Kant's and Rashdall's versions of this argument depend for their force on the acceptance of value as real and objective. But this is the Achilles' heel of the argument, for it is precisely at this starting point that many balk. Jean-Paul Sartre, in his well-known lecture "Existentialism," rejects the suggestion that there is given any objective value in the first place. In this respect the existentialist position of Sartre must be contrasted with all those traditional philosophies stemming in one way or another from Plato and believing more or less that there is a rational structure or order of things, that history and the cosmos unfold in terms of some purpose, that there is a fixed and abiding essence of things. For Sartre, however, the world is devoid of any objective meaning or value, and we are, in this unhappy situation, "condemned to be free." Now, says Sartre, if there were objective values then we would have to believe in God from whose mind they spring; but since there are no such values we are hardly compelled to accept the Moral Argument. For Sartre, all that is given is existence, and any meaning or value or essence for man must be evolved along the way through men's choices and commitments: "Existence precedes essence."

The existentialist denial of objective value is not, however, the only one. In the debate between Bertrand Russell and Father F. C. Copleston, we find Russell arguing from the standpoint of a purely naturalistic ethics (admittedly the position here taken by Russell is an extreme one and would be rejected even by many naturalists) that value-judgments such as "x is good" or "x is bad" are reducible to statement of fact, that is, statements about nature, about physics and chemistry, about perception, disposition, desire, and so on. The statement "x is good" has, then, no more claim to objectivity or universality than the statement "I like cherry pie." Moral perception like sense-perception is an individual, subjective, and relative state of affairs. The color-blind man may be in the minority, but his judgment about colors cannot be called *wrong*; it is simply a matter of the way most people perceive colors.

But can we really believe that the moral issue involved in the Nazi extermination of Jews, for example, may be resolved by an appeal to mere convention or the ethical wisdom of a few leaders or even the feeelings of the majority? Can we believe that moral judgments are mere expressions of subjective delight or disgust, that they have no truth-falsity status and are therefore cognitively meaningless? Or, against the Sartrean position, can we believe that morality is grounded *in vacuo*, that it is the (arbitrary?) product of the existential freedom that Sartre propounds as the "baseless basis of value"? These are suggestive of the questions raised by Father Copleston as well as by most critics of the various forms of ethical subjectivism and ethical nihilism.

No value-judgment, according to Copleston, can be made except on the assumption of an objective moral order. Of course we may be mistaken in our moral judgments and we may change our minds from time to time; but whenever we say "*x* is good" we believe (whether or not we admit it) that there is something *in terms of which* the truth of that judgment can, at least in theory, be confirmed. How can one live for a cause, and perhaps even die for it, unless he believes that there is a real and objective truth involved? Would he not otherwise be a fool? At the very least, he would appear to be involved in a kind of practical self-contradiction, saying one thing and living another. Furthermore, there is the matter of the "naturalistic fallacy," an alleged mistake in moral reasoning that Copleston attributes (at least implicitly) to Russell. The naturalistic fallacy is the mistake of deriving "ought" from "is," the mistake of thinking that because things *are* a certain way that is the way they *ought* to be, the reduction of moral judgments to factual judgments. It does not take a great deal of imagination to see that an uncritical identification of *is* with *ought* could legitimize all sorts of unseemly conduct. Most reflective people, whether right or wrong, would probably distinguish the realm of moral experience from the world of nature, insisting that moral experience and duty somehow stand over against the world of physics and chemistry, evolutionary processes, and the casual determinism that are part and parcel of nature. Of course, it will be noted that Sartre himself (in the latter parts of his essay) defends his position against the arbitrary-charge, and others will reject as ill-conceived the either/or bifurcations involved in talk about absolute vs. relative, natural vs. non-natural, objective vs. subjective, and so forth.

In any event, it would appear that the Moral Argument for God can have no force for someone who denies the objective reality and truth of moral ideals. Whether that latter position can be maintained consistently is, as should be clear by now, a good question.

✻ IMMANUEL KANT

10. *God: A Postulate of Morality*

The German thinker Immanuel Kant (1724–1804) rejected the theoretical approach of speculative philosophy and sought to ground our knowledge of God, freedom, and immortality in the practical evidence of moral experience. Kant's *Critique of Pure Reason* marks a turning point in the history of philosophy, and his *Critique of Practical Reason* and *Religion Within the Bounds of Reason Alone* make a positive contribution to theology.

Immanual Kant, *Critique of Practical Reason*, tr. Lewis White Beck (Indianapolis, Ind.: Library of Liberal Arts, 1956). Copyright © 1956 by The Liberal Arts Press, Inc., reprinted by permission of the Liberal Arts Press Division of The Bobbs-Merrill Company, Inc.

From *Critique of Practical Reason*

Part I, Book II

Chapter 2: The Dialectic of Pure Reason in Defining the Concept of the Highest Good

The concept of the "highest" contains as ambiguity which, if not attended to, can occasion unnecessary disputes. The "highest" can mean the "supreme" (*supremum*) or the "perfect" (*consummatum*). The former is the unconditional condition, *i.e.*, the condition which is subordinate to no other (*originarium*); the latter is that whole which is no part of a yet larger whole of the same kind (*perfectissimum*). That virtue (as the worthiness to be happy) is the supreme condition of whatever appears to us to be desirable and thus of all our pursuit of happiness and, consequently, that it is the supreme good have been proved in the Analytic. But these truths do not imply that virtue is the entire and perfect good as the object of the faculty of desire of rational finite beings. For this, happiness is also required, and indeed not merely in the partial eyes of a person who makes himself his end but even in the judgment of an impartial reason, which impartially regards persons in the world as ends-in-themselves. For to be in need of happiness and also worthy of it and yet not to partake of it could not be in accordance with the complete volition of an omnipotent rational being, if we assume such only for the sake of the argument. Inasmuch as virtue and happiness together constitute the possession of the highest good for one person, and happiness in exact proportion to morality (as the worth of a person and his worthiness to be happy) constitutes that of a possible world, the highest good means the whole, the perfect good, wherein virtue is always the supreme good, being the condition having no condition superior to it, while happiness, though something always pleasant to him who possess it, is not of itself absolutely good in every respect but always presupposes conduct in accordance with the moral law as its condition. . . .

IV: The Immortality of the Soul as a Postulate of Pure Practical Reason

The achievement of the highest good in the world is the necessary object of a will determinable by the moral law. In such a will, however, the complete fitness of intentions to the moral law is the supreme condition of the highest good. This fitness, therefore, must be just as possible as its object, because it is contained in the command that requires us to promote the latter. But complete fitness of the will to the moral law is holiness, which is a perfection of which no rational being in the world of sense is at any time capable. But since it is required as practically necessary. It can be found only in an endless progress to that complete fitness; on principles of pure practical reason, it is necessary to assume such a practical progress as the real object of our will.

This infinite progress is possible, however, only under the presuppsition of an infinitely enduring existence and personality of the same rational being; this is called the immortality of the soul. Thus the highest good is practically possible only on the supposition of the immortality of the soul, and the latter, as inseparably bound to the moral law, is a postulate of pure practical reason. By a postulate of pure practical reason, I understand a theoretical proposition which is not as such demonstrable, but which is an inseparable corollary of an a priori unconditionally valid practical law.

The thesis of the moral destiny of our nature, viz, that it is able only in an infinte progress toward complete fitness to the moral law, is of great use, not merely for the present purpose of supplementing the impotence of speculative reason, but also with respect to religion. Without it, either the moral law is completely degraded from its holiness, by being made out as lenient (indulgent) and thus compliant to our convenience, or its call and its demands are strained to an unattainable destination, i.e., a hoped-for complete attainment of holiness of will, and are lost in fanatical theosophical dreams which completely contradict our knowledge of ourselves. In either case, we are only hindered in the unceasing striving toward the precise and persistent obedience to a command of reason which is stern, unindulgent, truly commanding, really and not just ideally possible.

Only endless progress from lower to higher stages of moral perfection is possible to a rational but finite being. The Infinite Being, to whom the temporal condition is nothing, sees in this series, which is for us without end, a whole conformable to the moral law; holiness, which His law inexorably commands in order to be true to His justice in the share He assigns to each in the highest good, is to be found in a single intellectual intuition of the existence of rational beings. All that can be granted to a creature with respect to hope for this share is consciousness of his tried character. And on the basis of his previous progress from the worse to the morally better, and of the immutability of intention which thus becomes known to him, he may hope for a further uninterrupted continuance of this progress, however long his existence may last, even beyond his life.[1] But he cannot hope here or at any foreseeable point of his future existence to be fully adequate to God's will, without indulgence or remission which would not harmonize with justice. This he can do only in the infinity of his duration which God alone can survey.

[1] The conviction of the immutability of character in progress toward the good may appear to be impossible for a creature. For this reason, Christian doctrine lets it derive from the same Spirit which works sanctification, i.e., this firm intention and therewith the consciousness of steadfastness in moral progress. But naturally one who is conscious of having persisted, from legitimate moral motives, to the end of a long life in a progress to the better may very well have the comforting hope, though not the certainty, that he will be steadfast in these principles in an existence continuing beyond this life. Though he can never be justified in his own eyes either here or in the hoped-for increase of natural perfection together with an increase of his duties, nevertheless in this progress toward a goal infinitely remote (a progress which in God's sight is regarded as equivalent to possession) he can have prospect of a blessed future. For "blessed" is the word which reason uses to designate a perfect well-being independent of all contingent causes in the world. Like holiness, it is an idea which can be contained only in an infinite progress and its totality and thus is never fully reached by any creature.

V: The Existence of God as a Postulate of Pure Practical Reason

The moral law led, in the foregoing analysis, to a practical problem which is assigned solely by pure reason and without any concurrence of sensuous incentives. It is the problem of the completeness of the first and principal part of the highest good, viz., morality; since this problem can be solved only in eternity, it led to the postulate of immortality. The same law must also lead us to affirm the possibility of the second element of the highest good, i.e., happiness proportional to that morality; it must do so just as disinterestedly as heretofore, by a purely impartial reason. This it can do on the supposition of the existence of a cause adequate to this effect, i.e., it must postulate the existence of God as necessarily belonging to the possibility of the highest good (the object of our will which is necessarily connected with the moral legislation of pure reason). We proceed to exhibit this connection in a convincing manner.

Happiness is the condition of a rational being in the world, in whose whole existence everything goes according to wish and will. It thus rests on the harmony of nature with his entire end and with the essential determining ground of his will. But the moral law commands as a law of freedom through motives wholly independent of nature and of its harmony with our faculty of desire (as incentives). Still, the acting rational being in the world is not at the same time the cause of the world and of nature itself. Hence there is not the slightest ground in the moral law for a necessary connection between the morality and proportionate happiness of a being which belongs to the world as one of its parts and as thus dependent on it. Not being nature's cause, his will cannot by its own strength bring nature, as it touches on his happiness, into complete harmony with his practical principles. Nevertheless, in the practical task of pure reason, i.e., in the necessary endeavor after the highest good, such a connection is postulated as necessary: we *should* seek to further the highest good (which therefore must be at least possible). Therefore also the existence is postulated of a cause of the whole of nature, itself distinct from nature, which contains the ground of the exact coincidence of happiness with morality. This supreme cause, however, must contain the ground of the agreement of nature not merely with a law of the will of rational beings but with the idea of this law so far as they make it the supreme ground of determination of the will. Thus it contains the ground of the agreement of nature not merely with actions moral in their form but also with their morality as the motives to such actions, i.e., with their moral intention. Therefore, the highest good is possible in the world only on the supposition of a supreme cause of nature which has a casuality corresponding to the moral intention. Now a being which is capable of actions by the idea of laws is an intelligence (a rational being), and the casuality of such a being according to this idea of laws is his will. Therefore, the supreme cause of nature, in so far as it must be presupposed for the highest good, is a being which is the cause (and consequently the author) of nature through understanding and will, i.e., God. As a consequence, the postulate of the possibility of a highest derived good (the best world) is at the same time the postulate of the reality of a highest original good, namely, the existence of God. Now it was our duty to promote the highest good; and it is not merely our privilege but a necessity connected with duty as a requisite to presuppose the possibility of this highest good. The presupposition is made only under the condition of the existence of God, and this condition inseparably connects this supposition with duty. Therefore, it is morally necessary to assume the existence of God.

It is well to notice here that this moral necessity is subjective, i.e., a need, and not objective, i.e., duty itself. For there cannot be any duty to assume the existence of a thing, because such a supposition concerns only the theoretical use of reason. It is also not to be understood that the assumption of the existence of God is necessary as a ground of all obligation in general (for this rests, as has been fully shown, solely on the autonomy of reason itself). All that here belongs to duty is the endeavor to produce and to further the highest good in the world, the existence of which may thus be postulated though our reason cannot conceive it except by presupposing a highest intelligence. To assume its existence is thus connected with the consciousness of our duty, though this assumption itself belongs to the realm of theoretical reason. Considered only in reference to the latter, it is a hypothesis, i.e., a ground of explanation. But in reference to the comprehensibility of an object (the highest good) placed before us by the moral law, and thus as a practical need, it can be called *faith* and even pure *rational faith*, because pure reason alone (by its theoretical as well as practical employment) is the source from which it springs. . . .

VI: On the Postulates of Pure Practical Reason in General

The postulates of pure practical reason all proceed from the principle of morality, which is not a posulate but a law by which reason directly determines the will. This will, by the fact that it is so determined, as a pure will requires these necessary conditions for obedience to its precept. These postulates are not theoretical dogmas but presuppositions of necessarily practical import; thus, while they do not extend speculative knowledge, they give objective reality to the ideas of speculative reason in general (by means of their relation to the practical sphere), and they justify it in holding to concepts even the possibility of which it could not otherwise venture to affirm.

These postulates are those of immortality, of freedom affirmatively regarded (as the causality of a being so far as he belongs to the intelligible world), and of the existence of God. The first derives from the practically necessary condition of a duration adequate to the perfect fulfilment of the moral law. The second comes from the necessary presupposition of independence from the world of sense and of the capacity of determining man's will by the law of an intelligible world, i.e., the law of freedom itself; the third arises from the necessary condition of such an intelligible world by which it may be the highest good, through the presupposition of the highest independent good, i.e., the existence of God.

The prospect of the highest good, necessary through respect for the moral law and the consequent supposition of its objective reality, thus leads through postulates of practical reason to concepts which the speculative reason only exhibited as problems which it could not solve. It leads first to the problem of immortality, in the solution of which speculative reason could only commit paralogisms, because the marks of permanence, by which the psychological concept of an ultimate subject necessarily ascribed to the soul in self-consciousness, were lacking though they were needed to complete the real conception of a substance. Practical reason, through the postulates of fitness to the moral law in the highest good as the whole end of practical reason, consigns to this subject the requisite duration. Secondly, it leads to the concept which speculative reason contained only as an antinomy, and the solution of which it could base only on a problematical, though thinkable, concept whose objective reality was not provable or determinable by speculative reason. This is the cosmological idea of an intelligible world and the consciousness of our existence in it. It leads to this by means of the postulate of freedom (the reality of which practical reason exhibits in the moral law, at the same time exhibiting the law of an intelligible world, which the speculative reason could only indicate but whose concept it could not define). Thirdly, it gives significance to what speculative reason could indeed think but had to leave indeterminate as a mere transcendental ideal, i.e., to the theological concept of a First Being. This significance is given in a practical point of view, i.e., as a condition of the possibility of the object of a will determined by that law. It is that of a supreme principle of the highest good in an intelligible world having sovereign power in it by means of a moral legislation.

Is our knowledge really widened in such a way by pure practical reason, and is that which was transcendent for speculative reason immanent in practical reason? Certainly, but only from a practical point of view. For we thereby know neither the nature of our soul, nor the intelligible world, nor the Supreme Being as they are in themselves, but have only united the concepts of them in a practical concept of the highest good as the object of our will and have done so entirely a priori through pure reason. We have so united them only by means of the moral law and merely in relation to it, with respect to the object which it commands. But how freedom is possible, and how we should think theoretically and positively of this type of causality, is not thereby discovered. All that is comprehended is that such a causality is postulated through the moral law and for its sake. It is the same with the remaining ideas, whose possibility cannot be fathomed by human understanding, though no sophistry will ever wrest from the conviction of even the most ordinary man an admission that they are not true.

✵ HASTINGS RASHDALL

11. *From Moral Ideals to God*

Hastings Rashdall (1858–1924) was an English theologian, philosopher, and historian. Philosophically, Rashdall is especially noted for his contribution to ethical theory as contained in his *The Theory of Good and Evil*. Theologically, Rashdall was active in the liberalization of the Anglican Church, describing himself as "on the left wing of the Church and the right wing of philosophy."

From *The Theory of Good and Evil*, Volume II

Book III

Chapter 1: Metaphysics and Morality

IV. We have seen that certain metaphysical presuppositions as to the nature of knowledge and the nature of the self are necessary to the very existence of an ethical system which can be regarded as representing and justifying the deliverances of the moral consciousness. When we have admitted that knowledge is not mere subjective feeling or passive experience, that the self is as real as or more real than any 'thing' of which Physical Science can tell us, and that the self causes certain events which are commonly spoken of as its actions, then we are able to recognize the reality of duty, of ideals, of a good which includes right conduct. And *prima facie* it might appear that the truth and validity of these ideals are independent of any particular conclusions as to the ultimate nature of things which go beyond these simple presuppositions. The man who wishes to see any meaning in the deliverances of his own moral consciousness and to represent to himself the attempt to live up to the ideal which they set before him as an intelligible and rational aim, must assume this much about knowledge and about the self; but it may possibly be contended that he need assume nothing further about the ultimate nature of things, except that it is a Universe, part of whose nature is to produce this moral consciousness of his. And it is no doubt true that the Agnostic (in Metaphysic or Theology) cannot be convicted of any positive inconsistency, if he simply accepts the dictates of his moral consciousness as final, and says: 'I know nothing as to the ultimate source of these moral ideas, except that they come to me in the same way as the rest of my knowledge, or anything as to the ultimate outcome of this moral life which I feel to be incumbent upon me. I simply know the meaning of the good, and that it is right for me to aim at it, and that I can, to some extent, bring it into existence by my voluntary action.' Psychologically this attitude is a possible one. The term

Hastings Rashdall, *The Theory of Good and Evil* (Oxford, England: Clarendon Press, 1907), II.

'good' or 'right' does not contain any *explicit* reference to any theological or metaphysical theory of the Universe. The proposition that some things are right, others wrong, is not in any sense an inference or deduction from any such theory; it is an immediate datum or deliverance of consciousness. The truth is assented to, and acted upon, by men of all religions or of none, by persons who hold most dissimilar views as to the ultimate nature of the Universe, and by men who profess to have no theory of the Universe at all. And it is impossible to say that the words 'good' and 'right' have no meaning for such persons or an entirely different meaning from what they have for the Metaphysician who refuses to acquiesce in Agnosticism. In this sense it is of the highest possible importance to recognize what is sometimes spoken of as the 'independence of Morality.' But it remains a further question whether the true meaning of Morality is capable of being made explicit, and of being reconciled or harmonized with other facts of our knowledge or experience without necessitating the adoption of certain views concerning the ultimate nature of things and the rejection of certain other views. If this should turn out to be the case, Morality will be in exactly the same position as any other part of our knowledge. So long as we refuse to bring any piece of our knowledge or experience into connexion with any other part of it, the particular piece of knowledge cannot be shown to be either consistent or inconsistent with such other parts of our knowledge. So long as that is the case, it may no doubt from a high metaphysical attitude be maintained that this knowledge may not be altogether true, since it may require to be corrected and limited in order to bring it into harmony with other parts of our knowledge: for the only test that we have of the validity of any part of our knowledge is its capacity for being harmonized or co-ordinated with the rest of it. But, from a rough practical point of view, it is possible to be certain of the truth of Science without holding any metaphysical position at all: and in that sense it is equally possible to combine a strong conviction of the reality or objective validity of moral distinctions with complete Agnosticism as to the general nature of the Universe, though in practice Agnosticism is very apt to involve negative assumptions the irreconcilability of which with what is implied in the idea of moral obligation, can with difficulty remain unrecognized. But after all the question remains whether this refusal to bring one part of our knowledge into connexion with the rest is a reasonable attitude of mind. It is always easy to escape inconsistency by resolutely shutting our eyes to a portion of the facts, by refusing to think or by arbitrarily stopping the process of thought at some particular point.[1] When we ask whether a

---

[1]The strongest assertion of the validity of the idea of duty that has ever been made from an agnostic point of view is perhaps to be found in Huxley's brilliant Romanes Lecture on *Evolution and Ethics* (Collected Essays, Vol. IX). It is interesting to see how near the contention that Natural and Moral Law have equal validity brings him to the admission that they have ultimately a common source. What Huxley refuses to ask is whether the validity of the Moral Law does not throw some light upon the nature of that Reality which is revealed both by Physical Law and by Moral Law—whether the belief that we ought to resist the 'cosmic process' and the impulse to act upon that belief are not as much a product of the Cosmos, and a revelation of its ultimate nature, as those physical and psychological tendencies which Morality bids us resist.

certain intellectual attitude is ultimately reasonable, we presuppose that we are making up our minds to look at the whole of the facts. Agnosticism is not a reasonable attitude of mind when it is possible to know. And the question arises whether, when the attempt to harmonize and so to justify our beliefs is honestly made, the man who wishes to defend and rationalize his practical recognition of moral obligation may not be forced into the alternative of giving up his ethical creed or of giving up certain views of the Universe which reflection has shown to be inconsistent with that creed.

Are there then any metaphysical positions about the ultimate nature of things which logically exclude the idea of an objective Moral Law? Let us suppose, for instance, that, without giving up that bare minimum of metaphysical belief about the self which we have found to be absolutely presupposed in the very idea of Morality, a man has nevertheless adopted a materialistic or naturalistic view of the world to this extent—that he believes that the origin of the self, and of the knowledge which resides in the self, may actually be traced to certain material processes of a Reality in which previously no mind resided except as a 'promise and potency' of the future. Such a man is not, indeed, technically in the most thorough-going sense of the word a Materialist if he admits that after all a true view of the Universe must include a recognition of the spiritual nature which the Universe has ultimately, by whatever process, evolved. And it is quite right to emphasize the difference between a position of this kind and the old confused puzzle-headed Materialism which was inclined to look on matter and motion as real things and on thought, feeling (with perhaps some not very logical exception in favour of pleasure and pain), emotion, aspiration, ideals as mere arbitrary inventions or hallucinations. But, putting aside for the present the purely metaphysical difficulties of such a position, we have to ask how it must affect our attitude towards Morality.

So long as the ultimate reality of things is regarded as purely material, so long as material process is regarded as the sole cause or source or ground of mind and all its contents, there is always the possibility of scepticism as to the knowledge of which this material world has somehow delivered itself. Our knowledge may be conceived of as representing, not the real truth of things, but the way in which it is most conducive to the survival of the race that we should think of them. Error and delusion may be valuable elements in Evolution; to a certain extent it is undeniable, from any metaphysical standpoint, that they have actually been so. But on the naturalistic view of things the doubt arises not merely whether this or that particular belief of ours is a delusion, but whether human thought in general may not wholly fail to correspond with Reality, whether thought *qua* thought may not be a delusion, whether (to put it still more paradoxically) the more rational a man's thought becomes, the more faithfully the individual adheres to the canons of human Reason, the wider may be the gulf between his thinking and the facts. Arguments might no doubt be found for putting away such an 'unmotived' doubt as to the trustworthiness of our knowledge about ordinary matters of fact—its self-consistency, the constant correspondence of the predictions which it makes with subsequent experience, the practical serviceableness for the purposes of life of its assumed validity, and the uselessness of entertaining doubts as to the trustworthiness of our faculties which from the nature of the case can be neither confirmed nor refuted; though after all such arguments at bottom assume the validity of thought. But these considerations do not apply in the same degree to moral knowledge. It is often possible to explain in a sense this or that particular ethical belief by the history of the race, the environment of the individual, and the like. Such considerations do not shake belief in the ultimate validity of moral distinctions for an Idealist who believes that the Universe owes its very existence to the Mind which assures him of these distinctions (though he is aware that the evolution of his individual mind has been conditioned by physical processes and social environment); but they wear a totally different aspect for one who has no general *a priori* reason for assuming a correspondence of thought with things.[2] The Idealist has every reason for believing the ultimate moral ideas to be true that he has for believing any other ideas to be true, though he realizes that he does not know the whole truth, and that his knowledge of this or ignorance of that element in the moral ideal (like his knowledge or ignorance of ordinary scientific truth) is in part explicable by the accident of antecedents or environment. But to the man who regards all spiritual life as a mere inexplicable incident in the career of a world which is essentially material (were it not for the human and animal minds which it is known to have produced) and as a whole essentially purposeless, there is no conclusive reason why all moral ideas—the very conception of 'value,' the very notion that one thing is intrinsically better than another, the very conviction that there is something which a man ought to do—may not be merely some strange illusion due to the unaccountable freaks of a mindless process or to the exigencies of natural selection. It cannot be said that a man who allowed such doubts to shake or modify his allegiance to the dictates of Morality, where they do not happen to coincide with his actual desires or inclinations, would be doing anything essentially unreasonable. Reasonable conduct would for him mean merely 'conduct comformable to his own private reason': intrinsically or absolutely reasonable or unreasonable conduct could not exist in a world which was not itself the product of Reason or governed by its dictates.

Another way of putting much the same difficulty is this. We say that the Moral Law has a real existence, that there is such a thing as an absolute Morality, that there is something absolutely true or false in ethical judgements, whether we or any number of human beings at any given time actually think so or not. Such a belief is distinctly implied in what we mean by Morality. The idea of such an unconditional, objectively valid, Moral Law or ideal

---

[2]I am quite alive to the difficulties involved in the 'correspondence theory' as to the nature of Truth, which have been brilliantly developed by Mr. Joachim in his recent Essay on *The Nature of Truth*, and it is one which no Idealist can well regard as the final and ultimate account of the matter, but any discussion of such a question would be quite out of place in an ethical treatise. Mr. Joachim would no doubt admit that we cannot help employing such language in such a connexion as the present.

undoubtedly exists as a psychological fact. The question before us is whether it is capable of theoretical justification. We must then face the question *where* such an ideal exists, and what manner of existence we are to attribute to it. Certainly it is to be found, wholly and completely, in no individual human consciousness. Men actually think differently about moral questions, and there is no empirical reason for supposing that they will ever do otherwise. Where then and how does the moral ideal really exist? As regards matters of fact or physical law, we have no difficulty in satisfying ourselves that there is an objective reality which is what it is irrespectively of our beliefs or disbeliefs about it. For the man who supposes that objective reality resides in the things themselves, our ideas about them are objectively true or false so far as they correspond or fail to correspond with this real and independent archetype, though he might be puzzled to give a metaphysical account of the nature of this 'correspondence' between experience and a Reality whose *esse*[3] is something other than to be experienced. In the physical region the existence of divergent ideas does not throw doubt upon the existence of a reality independent of our ideas. But in the case of moral ideals it is otherwise. On materialistic or naturalistic assumptions the moral ideal can hardly be regarded as a real thing. Nor could it well be regarded as a property of any real thing: it can be no more than an aspiration, a product of the imagination, which may be useful to stimulate effort in directions in which we happen to want to move, but which cannot compel respect when we feel no desire to act in conformity with it. An absolute Moral Law or moral ideal cannot exist *in* material things. And it does not (we have seen) exist in the mind of this or that individual. Only if we believe in the existence of a Mind for which the true moral ideal is already in some sense real, a Mind which is the source of whatever is true in our own moral judgements, can we rationally think of the moral ideal as no less real than the world itself. Only so can we believe in an absolute standard of right and wrong, which is as independent of this or that man's actual ideas and actual desires as the facts of material nature. The belief in God, though not (like the belief in a real and an active self) a postulate of there being any such thing as Morality at all, is the logical presupposition of an 'objective' or absolute Morality. A moral ideal can exist nowhere and nohow but in a mind; an absolute moral ideal can exist only in a Mind from which all Reality is derived.[4] Our moral ideal can only claim objective validity in so far as it can rationally be regarded as the revelation of a moral ideal eternally existing in the mind of God.

We may be able, perhaps, to give some meaning to Morality without the postulate of God, but not its true or full meaning. If the existence of God is not a postulate of all Morality, it is a postulate of a sound Morality; for it is essential to that belief which vaguely and implicitly underlies all moral beliefs, and which forms the very heart of Morality in its highest, more devel-

---

[3]["being."]

[4]Or at least a mind by which all Reality is controlled. Want of space forbids my discussing the ethical aspect of Pluralism or of a theory which regards spirits other than God as having no beginning.

oped, more explicit forms. The truth that the moral ideal is what it is whether we like it or not is the most essential element in what the popular consciousness understands by 'moral obligation.' Moral obligation means moral objectivity. That *at least* seems to be implied in any legitimate use of the term: at least it implies the existence of an absolute, objective moral ideal. And such a belief we have seen imperatively to demand an explanation of the Universe which shall be idealistic or at least spiritualistic, which shall recognize the existence of a Mind whose thoughts are the standard of truth and falsehood alike in Morality and in respect of all other existence. In other words, objective Morality implies the belief in God. The belief in God, if not so obviously and primarily a postulate of Morality as the belief in a permanent spiritual and active self, is still a postulate of a Morality which shall be able fully to satisfy the demands of the moral consciousness. It may conveniently be called the secondary postulate of Morality.

✸ JEAN-PAUL SARTRE

12. *An Existentialist Rejection*

Jean-Paul Sartre, a French thinker and writer, was born in 1905. His novels, dramas, and philosophical writings have made him the leading thinker of contemporary atheistic (or humanistic) existentialism, a philosophy that subordinates all essence and value to human existence. Sartre was a member of the French underground during World War II and has been a champion of various political and social causes, including Marxism. In 1964 he was awarded the Nobel prize for literature, which he declined. Sartre's philosophical magnum opus is *Being and Nothingness*.

From "Existentialism"

. . . What is meant by the term *existentialism?*

Most people who use the word would be rather embarrassed if they had to explain it, since, now that the word is all the rage, even the work of a musician or painter is being called existentialist. A gossip columnist in *Clartés* signs himself *The Existentialist*, so that by this time the word has been so stretched and has taken on so broad a meaning, that it no longer means anything at all. It seems that for want of an advance-guard doctrine analogous to surrealism, the kind of people who are eager for scandal and flurry turn to this philosophy which in other respects does not at all serve their purposes in this sphere.

Jean-Paul Sartre, "Existentialism," tr. Bernard Frechtman, in *Existentialism and Human Emotions* (New York: Philosophical Library, 1947). Reprinted by permission of Philosophical Library, Associated Book Publishers International Ltd., and Les Editions Nagel. Copyright Les Editions Nagel 1948.

Actually, it is the least scandalous, the most austere of doctrines. It is intended strictly for specialists and philosophers. Yet it can be defined easily. What complicates matters is that there are two kinds of existentialist; first, those who are Christian, among whom I would include Jaspers and Gabriel Marcel, both Catholic; and on the other hand the atheistic existentialists, among whom I class Heidegger, and then the French existentialists and myself. What they have in common is that they think that existence precedes essence, or, if you prefer, that subjectivity must be the starting point.

Just what does that mean? Let us consider some object that is manufactured, for example, a book or a paper-cutter: here is an object which has been made by an artisan whose inspiration came from a concept. He referred to the concept of what a paper-cutter is and likewise to a known method of production, which is part of the concept, something which is, by and large, a routine. Thus, the paper-cutter is at once an object produced in a certain way and, on the other hand, one having a specific use; and one can not postulate a man who produces a paper-cutter but does not know what it is used for. Therefore, let us say that, for the paper-cutter, essence—that is, the ensemble of both the production routines and the properties which enable it to be both produced and defined—precedes existence. Thus, the presence of the paper-cutter or book in front of me is determined. Therefore, we have here a technical view of the world whereby it can be said that production precedes existence.

When we conceive God as the Creator, He is generally thought of as a superior sort of artisan. Whatever doctrine we may be considering, whether one like that of Descartes or that of Leibnitz, we always grant that will more or less follows understanding or, at the very least, accompanies it, and that when God creates He knows exactly what He is creating. Thus, the concept of man in the mind of God is comparable to the concept of paper-cutter in the mind of the manufacturer, and, following certain techniques and a conception, God produces man, just as the artisan, following a definition and a technique, makes a paper-cutter. Thus, the individual man is the realization of a certain concept in the divine intelligence.

In the eighteeenth century, the atheism of the *philosophes* discarded the idea of God, but not so much for the notion that essence precedes existence. To a certain extent, this idea is found everywhere; we find it in Diderot, in Voltaire, and even in Kant. Man has a human nature; this human nature, which is the concept of the human, is found in all men, which means that each man is a particular example of a universal concept, man. In Kant the result of this universality is that the wild-man, the natural man, as well as the bourgeois, are circumscribed by the same definition and have the same basic qualities. Thus, here too the essence of man precedes the historical existence that we find in nature.

Atheistic existentialism, which I represent, is more coherent. It states that if God does not exist, there is at least one being in whom existence precedes essence, a being who exists before he can be defined by any concept, and that this being is man, or, as Heidegger says, human reality. What is meant here by saying that existence precedes essence? It means that, first of all, man exists, turns up, appears on the scene, and, only afterwards, defines himself. If man, as the existentialist conceives him, is indefinable, it is because at first he is nothing. Only afterward will he be something, and he himself will have made what he will be. Thus, there is no human nature, since there is no God to conceive it. Not only is man what he conceives himself to be, but he is also only what he wills himself to be after this thrust toward existence.

Man is nothing else but what he makes of himself. Such is the first principle of existentialism. It is also what is called subjectivity, the name we are labeled with when charges are brought against us. But what do we mean by this, if not that man has a greater dignity than a stone or table? For we mean that man first exists, that is, that man first of all is the being who hurls himself toward a future and who is conscious of imagining himself as being in the future. Man is at the start a plan which is aware of itself, rather than a patch of moss, a piece of garbage, or a cauliflower; nothing exists prior to this plan; there is nothing in heaven; man will be what he will have planned to be. Not what he will want to be. Because by the word "will" we generally mean a conscious decision, which is subsequent to what we have already made of ourselves. I may want to belong to a political party, write a book, get married; but all that is only a manifestation of an earlier, more spontaneous choice that is called "will." But if existence really does precede essence, man is responsible for what he is. Thus, existentialism's first move is to make every man aware of what he is and to make the full responsibility of his existence rest on him. And when we say that a man is responsible for himself, we do not only mean that he is responsible for his own individuality, but that he is responsible for all men.

The word subjectivism has two meanings, and our opponents play on the two. Subjectivism means, on the one hand, that an individual chooses and makes himself; and, on the other, that it is impossible for man to transcend human subjectivity. The second of these is the essential meaning of existentialism. When we say that man chooses his own self, we mean that every one of us does likewise; but we also mean by that that in making this choice he also chooses all men. In fact, in creating the man that we want to be, there is not a single one of our acts which does not at the same time create an image of man as we think he ought to be. To choose to be this or that is to affirm at the same time the value of what we choose, because we can never choose evil. We always choose the good, and nothing can be good for us without being good for all.

If, on the other hand, existence precedes essence, and if we grant that we exist and fashion our image at one and the same time, the image is valid for everybody and for our whole age. Thus, our responsibility is much greater than we might have supposed, because it involves all mankind. If I am a workingman and choose to join a Christian trade-union rather than be a communist, and if by being a member I want to show that the best thing, for man is resignation, that the kingdom of man is not of this world, I am not only involving my own case—I want to be resigned for everyone.

As a result, my action has involved all humanity. To take a more individual matter, if I want to marry, to have children; even if this marriage depends solely on my own circumstances or passion or wish, I am involving all humanity in monogamy and not merely myself. Therefore, I am responsible for myself and for everyone else. I am creating a certain image of man of my own choosing. In choosing myself, I choose man.

This helps us understand what the actual content is of such rather grandiloquent words as anguish, forlornness, despair. As you will see, it's all quite simple.

First, what is meant by anguish? The existentialists say at once that man is anguish. What that means is this: the man who involves himself and who realizes that he is not only the person he chooses to be, but also a lawmaker who is, at the same time, choosing all mankind as well as himself, can not help escape the feeling of his total and deep responsibility. Of course, there are many people who are not anxious; but we claim that they are hiding their anxiety, that they are fleeing from it. Certainly, many people believe that when they do something, they themselves are the only ones involved, and when someone says to them, "What if everyone acted that way?" they shrug their shoulders and answer, "Everyone doesn't act that way." But really, one should always ask himself, "What would happen if everybody looked at things that way?" There is no escaping this disturbing thought except by a kind of double-dealing. A man who lies and makes excuses for himself by saying "not everybody does that," is someone with an uneasy conscience, because the act of lying implies that a universal value is conferred upon the lie.

Anguish is evident even when it conceals itself. This is the anguish that Kierkegaard called the anguish of Abraham. You know the story: an angel has ordered Abraham to sacrifice his son; if it really were an angel who has come and said, "You are Abraham, you shall sacrifice your son," everything would be all right. But everyone might first wonder, "Is it really an angel, and am I really Abraham? What proof do I have?"

There was a madwoman who had hallucinations; someone used to speak to her on the telephone and give her orders. Her doctor asked her, "Who is it who talks to you?" She answered, "He says it's God." What proof did she really have that it was God? If an angel comes to me, what proof is there that it's an angel? And if I hear voices, what proof is there that they come from heaven and not from hell, or from the subconscious, or a pathological condition? What proves that they are addressed to me? What proof is there that I have been appointed to impose my choice and my conception of man on humanity? I'll never find any proof or sign to convince me of that. If a voice addresses me, it is always for me to decide that this is the angel's voice; if I consider that such an act is a good one, it is I who will choose to say that it is good rather than bad.

Now, I'm not being singled out as an Abraham, and yet at every moment I'm obliged to perform exemplary acts. For every man, everything happens as if all mankind had its eyes fixed on him and were guiding itself by what he does. And every man ought to say to himself, "Am I really the kind of man who has the right to act in such a way that humanity might guide itself by my actions?" And if he does not say that to himself, he is masking his anguish.

There is no question here of the kind of anguish which would lead to quietism, to inaction. It is a matter of a simple sort of anguish that anybody who has had responsibilities is familiar with. For example, when a military officer takes the responsibility for an attack and sends a certain number of men to death, he chooses to do so, and in the main he alone makes the choice. Doubtless, orders come from above, but they are too broad; he interprets them, and on this interpretation depend the lives of ten or fourteen or twenty men. In making a decision he can not help having a certain anguish. All leaders know this anguish. That doesn't keep them from acting; on the contrary, it is the very condition of their action. For it implies that they envisage a number of possibilities, and when they choose one, they realize that it has value only because it is chosen. We shall see that this kind of anguish, which is the kind that existentialism describes, is explained, in addition, by a direct responsibility to the other men whom it involves. It is not a curtain separating us from action, but is part of action itself.

When we speak of forlornness, a term Heidegger was fond of, we mean only that God does not exist and that we have to face all the consequences of this. The existentialist is strongly opposed to a certain kind of secular ethics which would like to abolish God with the least possible expense. About 1880, some French teachers tried to set up a secular ethics which went something like this: God is a useless and costly hypothesis; we are discarding it; but, meanwhile, in order for there to be an ethics, a society, a civilization, it is essential that certain values be taken seriously and that they be considered as having an *a priori* existence. It must be obligatory, *a priori*, to be honest, not to lie, not to beat your wife, to have children, etc., etc. So we're going to try a little device which will make it possible to show that values exist all the same, inscribed in a heaven of ideas, though otherwise God does not exist. In other words—and this, I believe, is the tendency of everything called reformism in France—nothing will be changed if God does not exist. We shall find ourselves with the same norms of honesty, progress, and humanism, and we shall have made of God an outdated hypothesis which will peacefully die off by itself.

The existentialist, on the contrary, thinks it very distressing that God does not exist, because all possibility of finding values in a heaven of ideas disappears along with Him; there can no longer be an *a priori* Good, since there is no infinite and perfect consciousness to think it. Nowhere is it written that the Good exists, that we must be honest, that we must not lie; because the fact is we are on a plane where there are only men. Dostoievsky said, "If God didn't exist, everything would be possible." That is the very starting point of existentialism. Indeed, everything is permissible if God does not exist, and as a result man is forlorn, because neither within him nor without does he find anything to cling to. He can't start making excuses for himself.

If existence really does precede essence, there is no explaining things away by reference to a fixed and given human nature. In other words, there is no determinism, man is free, man is freedom. On the other hand, if God does not exist, we find no values or commands to turn to which legitimize our conduct. So, in the bright realm of values, we have no excuse behind us, nor justification before us. We are alone, with no excuses.

That is the idea I shall try to convey when I say that man is condemned to be free. Condemned, because he did not create himself, yet, in other respects is free; because, once thrown into the world, he is responsible for everything he does. The existentialist does not believe in the power of passion. He will never agree that a sweeping passion is a ravaging torrent which fatally leads a man to certain acts and is therefore an excuse. He thinks that man is responsible for his passion.

The existentialist does not think that man is going to help himself by finding in the world some omen by which to orient himself. Because he thinks that man will interpret the omen to suit himself. Therefore, he thinks that man, with no support and no aid, is condemned every moment to invent man. Ponge, in a very fine article, has said, "Man is the future of man." That's exactly it. But if it is taken to mean that this future is recorded in heaven, that God sees it, then it is false, because it would really no longer be a future. If it is taken to mean that, whatever a man may be, there is a future to be forged, a virgin future before him, then this remark is sound. But then we are forlorn.

. . . Subjectivity of the individual is indeed our point of departure, and this for strictly philosophic reasons. Not because we are bourgeois, but because we want a doctrine based on truth and not a lot of fine theories, full of hope but with no real basis. There can be no other truth to take off from than this: *I think; therefore, I exist.* There we have the absolute truth of consciousness becoming aware of itself. Every theory which takes man out of the moment in which he becomes aware of himself is, at its very beginning, a theory which confounds truth, for outside the Cartesian *cogito,* all views are only probable, and a doctrine of probability which is not bound to a truth dissolves into thin air. In order to describe the probable, you must have a firm hold on the true. Therefore, before there can be any truth whatsoever, there must be an absolute truth; and this one is simple and easily arrived at; it's on everyone's doorstep; it's a matter of grasping it directly.

Secondly, this theory is the only one which gives man dignity, the only one which does not reduce him to an object. The effect of all materialism is to treat all men, including the one philosophizing, as objects, that is, as an ensemble of determined reactions in no way distinguished from the ensemble of qualities and phenomena which constitute a table or a chair or a stone. We definitely wish to establish the human realm as an ensemble of values distinct from the material realm. But the subjectivity that we have thus arrived at, and which we have claimed to be truth, is not a strictly individual subjectivity, for we have demonstrated that one discovers in the *cogito* not only himself, but others as well.

The philosophies of Descartes and Kant to the contrary, through the *I think* we reach our own self in the presence of others, and the others are just as real to us as our own self. Thus, the man who becomes aware of himself through the *cogito* also perceives all others, and he perceives them as the condition of his own existence. He realizes that he can not be anything (in the sense that we say that someone is witty or nasty or jealous) unless others recognize it as such. In order to get any truth about myself, I must have contact with another person. The other is indispensable to my own existence, as well as to my knowledge about myself. This being so, in discovering my inner being I discover the other person at the same time, like a freedom placed in front of me which thinks and wills only for or against me. Hence, let us at once announce the discovery of a world which we shall call intersubjectivity; this is the world in which man decides what he is and what others are.

Besides, if it is impossible to find in every man some universal essence which would be human nature, yet there does exist a universal human condition. It's not by chance that today's thinkers speak more readily of man's condition than of his nature. By condition they mean, more or less definitely, the *a priori* limits which outline man's fundamental situation in the universe. Historical situations vary; a man may be born a slave in a pagan society or a feudal lord or a proletarian. What does not vary is the necessity for him to exist in the world, to be at work there, to be there in the midst of other people, and to be mortal there. The limits are neither subjective nor objective, or, rather, they have an objective and a subjective side. Objective because they are to be found everywhere and are recognizable everywhere; subjective because they are *lived* and are nothing if man does not live them, that is, freely determine his existence with reference to them. And though the configurations may differ, at least none of them are completely strange to me, because they all appear as attempts either to pass beyond these limits or recede from them or deny them or adapt to them. Consequently, every configuration, however individual it may be, has a universal value.

Every configuration, even the Chinese, the Indian, or the Negro, can be understood by a Westerner. "Can be understood" means that by virtue of a situation that he can imagine, a European of 1945 can, in like manner, push himself to his limits and reconstitute within himself the configuration of the Chinese, the Indian, or the African. Every configuration has universality in the sense that every configuration can be understood by every man. This does not at all mean that this configuration defines man forever, but that it can be met with again. There is always a way to understand the idiot, the child, the savage, the foreigner, provided one has the necessary information.

In this sense we may say that there is a universality of man; but it is not given, it is perpetually being made. I build the universal in choosing myself; I build it in understanding the configuration of every other man, whatever age he might have lived in. This absoluteness of choice does not do away with the relativeness of each epoch. At heart, what existentialism shows is the connection between the absolute character of free involvement, by virtue of which every man realizes himself in realizing a type of mankind, an involvement always comprehensible in any age whatsoever and by any person whosoever, and the relativeness of the cultural ensemble which may result from such a choice; it must be stressed that the relativity of Cartesianism and the absolute character of Cartesian involvement go together. In this sense, you may, if you like, say that each of us performs an absolute act in breathing, eating, sleeping, or behaving in any way whatever. There is no difference between being free, like a configuration, like an existence which chooses its essence, and being absolute. There is no difference between being an absolute temporarily localized, that is, localized in history, and being universally comprehensible.

This does not entirely settle the objection to subjectivism. In fact, the objection still takes several forms. First, there is the following: we are told, "So you're able to do anything, no matter what!" This is expressed in various ways. First we are accused of anarchy; then they say, "You're unable to pass judgment on others, because there's no reason to prefer one configuration to another"; finally they tell us, "Everything is arbitrary in this choosing of yours. You take something from one pocket and pretend you're putting it into the other."

These three objections aren't very serious. Take the first objection. "You're able to do anything, no matter what" is not to the point. In one sense choice is possible, but what is not possible is not to choose. I can always choose, but I ought to know that if I do not choose, I am still choosing. Though this may seem purely formal, it is highly important for keeping fantasy and caprice within bounds. If it is true that in facing a situation, for example, one in which, as a person capable of having sexual relations, of having children, I am obliged to choose an attitude, and if I in any way assume responsibility for a choice which, in involving myself, also involves all mankind, this has nothing to do with caprice, even if no *a priori* value determines my choice.

If anybody thinks that he recognizes here Gide's theory of the arbitrary act, he fails to see the enormous difference between this doctrine and Gide's. Gide does not know what a situation is. He acts out of pure caprice. For us, on the contrary, man is in an organized situation in which he himself is involved. Through his choice, he involves all mankind, and he can not avoid making a choice: either he will remain chaste, or he will marry without having children, or he will marry and have children; anyhow, whatever he may do, it is impossible for him not to take full responsibility for the way he handles this problem. Doubtless, he chooses without referring to pre-established values, but it is unfair to accuse him of caprice. Instead, let us say that moral choice is to be compared to the making of a work of art. And before going any further, let it be said at once that we are not dealing here with an aesthetic ethics, because our opponents are so dishonest that they even accuse us of that. The example I've chosen is a comparison only.

Having said that, may I ask whether anyone has ever accused an artist who has painted a picture of not having drawn his inspiration from rules set up *a priori?* Has anyone ever asked, "What painting ought he to make?" It is clearly understood that there is no definite painting to be made, that the artist is engaged in the making of his painting, and that the painting to be made is precisely the painting he will have made. It is clearly understood that there are no *a priori* aesthetic values, but that there are values which appear subsequently in the coherence of the painting, in the correspondence between what the artist intended and the result. Nobody can tell what the painting of tomorrow will be like. Painting can be judged only after it has once been made. What connection does that have with ethics? We are in the same creative situation. We never say that a work of art is arbitrary. When we speak of a canvas of Picasso, we never say that it is arbitrary; we understand quite well that he was making himself what he is at the very time he was painting, that the ensemble of his work is embodied in his life.

The same holds on the ethical plane. What art and ethics have in common is that we have creation and invention in both cases. We can not decide *a priori* what there is to be done. I think that I pointed that out quite sufficiently when I mentioned the case of the student who came to see me, and who might have applied to all the ethical systems, Kantian or otherwise, without getting any sort of guidance. He was obliged to devise his law himself. Never let it be said by us that this man—who, taking affection, individual action, and kind-heartedness toward a specific person as his ethical first principle, chooses to remain with his mother, or who, preferring to make a sacrifice, chooses to go to England—has made an arbitrary choice. Man makes himself. He isn't ready made at the start. In choosing his ethics, he makes himself, and force of circumstances is such that he can not abstain from choosing one. We define man only in relationship to involvement. It is therefore absurd to charge us with arbitrariness of choice.

In the second place, it is said that we are unable to pass judgment on others. In a way this is true, and in another way, false. It is true in this sense, that, whenever a man sanely and sincerely involves himself and chooses his configuration, it is impossible for him to prefer another configuration, regardless of what his own may be in other respects. It is true in this sense, that we do not believe in progress. Progress is betterment. Man is always the same. The situation confronting him varies. Choice always remains a choice in a situation. The problem has not changed since the time one could choose between those for and those against slavery, for example, at the time of the Civil War, and the present time, when one can side with the Maquis Resistance Party, or with the Communists.

But, nevertheless, one can still pass judgment, for, as I have said, one makes a choice in relationship to others. First, one can judge (and this is perhaps not a judgment of value, but a logical judgment) that certain choices are based on error and others on truth. If we have defined man's situation as a free choice, with no excuses and no recourse, every man who takes refuge behind the excuse of his passions, every man who sets up a determinism, is a dishonest man.

The objection may be raised, "But why mayn't he choose himself dishonestly?" I reply that I am not obliged to pass moral judgment on him, but that I do define his dishonesty as an error. One cannot help considering the truth of the matter. Dishonesty is obviously a falsehood because it belies the complete freedom of involvement. On the same grounds, I maintain that there is also dishonesty if I choose to state that certain values exist prior to me; it is self-contradictory for me to want them and at the same state that they are imposed on me. Suppose someone says to me, "What if I want to be dishonest?" I'll answer, "There's no reason for you not to be, but I'm saying that that's what you are, and that the strictly coherent attitude is that of honesty."

Besides, I can bring moral judgment to bear. When I declare that freedom in every concrete circumstance can have no other aim than to want itself, if man has once become aware that in his forlornness he imposes values, he can no longer want but one thing, and that is freedom, as the basis of all values. That doesn't mean that he wants it in the abstract. It means simply that the ultimate meaning of the acts of honest men is the quest for freedom as such. A man who belongs to a communist or revolutionary union wants concrete goals; these goals imply an abstract desire for freedom; but this freedom is wanted in something concrete. We want freedom for freedom's sake and in every particular circumstance. And in wanting freedom we discover that it depends entirely on the freedom of others, and that the freedom of others depends on ours. Of course, freedom as the definition of man does not depend on others, but as soon as there is involvement, I am obliged to want others to have freedom at the same time that I want my own freedom. I can take freedom as my goal only if I take that of others as a goal as well. Consequently, when, in all honesty, I've recognized that man is a being in whom existence precedes essence, that he is a free being who, in various circumstances, can want only his freedom, I have at the same time recognized that I can want only the freedom of others.

Therefore, in the name of this will for freedom, which freedom itself implies, I may pass judgment on those who seek to hide from themselves the complete arbitrariness and the complete freedom of their existence. Those who hide their complete freedom from themselves out of a spirit of seriousness or by means of deterministic excuses, I shall call cowards; those who try to show that their existence was necessary, when it is the very contingency of man's appearance on earth, I shall call stinkers. But cowards or stinkers can be judged only from a strictly unbiased point of view.

Therefore though the content of ethics is variable, a certain form of it is universal. Kant says that freedom desires both itself and the freedom of others. Granted. But he believes that the formal and the universal are enough to constitute an ethics. We, on the other hand, think that principles which are too abstract run aground in trying to decide action. Once again, take the case of the student. In the name of what, in the name of what great moral maxim do you think he could have decided, in perfect peace of mind, to abandon his mother or to stay with her? There is no way of judging. The content is always concrete and thereby unforeseeable; there is always the element of invention. The one thing that counts is knowing whether the inventing that has been done, has been done in the name of freedom.

For example, let us look at the following two cases. You will see to what extent they correspond, yet differ. Take *The Mill on the Floss.* We find a certain young girl, Maggie Tulliver, who is an embodiment of the value of passion and who is aware of it. She is in love with a young man, Stephen, who is engaged to an insignificant young girl. This Maggie Tulliver, instead of heedlessly preferring her own happiness, chooses, in the name of human solidarity, to sacrifice herself and give up the man she loves. On the other hand, Sanseverina, in *The Charterhouse of Parma*, believing that passion is man's true value, would say that a great love deserves sacrifices; that it is to be preferred to the banality of the conjugal love that would tie Stephen to the young ninny he had to marry. She would choose to sacrifice the girl and fulfill her happiness; and, as Stendhal shows, she is even ready to sacrifice herself for the sake of passion, if this life demands it. Here we are in the presence of two strictly opposed moralities. I claim that they are much the same thing; in both cases what has been set up as the goal is freedom.

You can imagine two highly similar attitudes: one girl prefers to renounce her love out of resignation; another prefers to disregard the prior attachment of the man she loves out of sexual desire. On the surface these two actions resemble those we've just described. However, they are completely different. Sanseverina's attitude is much nearer that of Maggie Tulliver, one of heedless rapacity.

Thus, you see that the second charge is true and, at the same time, false. One may choose anything if it is on the grounds of free involvement.

The third objection is the following: "You take something from one pocket and put it into the other. That is, fundamentally, values aren't serious, since you choose them." My answer to this is that I'm quite vexed that that's the way it is; but if I've discarded God the Father, there has to be someone to invent values. You've got to take things as they are. Moreover, to say that we invent values means nothing else but this: life has no meaning *a priori.* Before you come alive, life is nothing; it's up to you to give it a meaning, and value is nothing else but the meaning that you choose. In that way, you see, there is a possibility of creating a human community.

I've been reproached for asking whether existentialism is humanistic. It's been said, "But you said in *Nausea* that the humanists were all wrong. You made fun of a certain kind of humanist. Why come back to it now?" Actually, the word humanism has two very different meanings. By humanism one can mean a theory which takes man as an end and as a higher value. Humanism in this sense can be found in Cocteau's tale *Around the World in Eighty Hours* when a character, because he is flying over some mountains in an airplane, declares, "Man is simply amazing." That means that I, who did not build the airplanes, shall personally benefit from these particular inventions, and that I, as man, shall personally consider myself responsible for, and honored by, acts of a few particular men. This would imply that we ascribe a value to man on the basis of the highest deeds of certain men.

This humanism is absurd, because only the dog or the horse would be able to make such an over-all judgment about man, which they are careful not to do, at least to my knowledge.

But it cannot be granted that a man may make a judgment about man. Existentialism spares him from any such judgment. The existentialist will never consider man as an end because he is always in the making. Nor should we believe that there is a mankind to which we might set up a cult in the manner of Auguste Comte. The cult of mankind ends in the self-enclosed humanism of Comte, and, let it be said, of fascism. This kind of humanism we can do without.

But there is another meaning of humanism. Fundamentally it is this: man is constantly outside of himself; in projecting himself, in losing himself outside of himself, he makes for man's existing; and, on the other hand, it is by pursuing transcendent goals that he is able to exist; man, being this state of passing-beyond, and seizing upon things only as they bear upon this passing-beyond, is at the heart, at the center of this passing-beyond. There is no universe other than a human universe, the universe of human subjectivity. This connection between transcendency, as a constituent element of man—not in the sense that God is transcendent, but in the sense of passing beyond—and subjectivity, in the sense that man is not closed in on himself but is always present in a human universe, is what we call existentialism humanism. Humanism, because we remind man that there is no law-maker other than himself, and that in his forlornness he will decide by himself; because we point out that man will fulfill himself as man, not in turning toward himself, but in seeking outside of himself a goal which is just this liberation, just this particular fulfillment.

From these few reflections it is evident that nothing is more unjust than the objections that have been raised against us. Existentialism is nothing else than an attempt to draw all the consequences of a coherent atheistic position. It isn't trying to plunge man into despair at all. But if one calls every attitude of unbelief despair, like the Christians, then the word is not being used in its original sense. Existentialism isn't so atheistic that it wears itself out showing that God doesn't exist. Rather, it declares that even if God did exist, that would change nothing. There you've got out point of view. Not that we believe that God exists, but we think that the problem of His existence is not the issue. In this sense existentialism is optimistic, a doctrine of action, and it is plain dishonesty for Christians to make no distinction between their own despair and ours and then to call us despairing.

✳ BERTRAND RUSSELL AND FREDERICK C. COPLESTON

13. *The Moral Argument Pro and Con*

Bertrand Russell (1872-1970) was a leading figure of contemporary British philosophy. His contributions to modern thought lie in a number of areas ranging from scientific and logical treatises to critical analyses of religion, morals, and politics. Russell's many indictments against theology and organized religion are summarized in his volume of popular essay *Why I Am Not a Christian.*

Frederick C. Copleston (born 1907), a Jesuit priest, is an outspoken and articulate defender of traditional theism. His scholarly works include volumes on Aquinas, Nietzsche, and Schopenhauer, and his multi-volume *A History of Philosophy* has become a standard work.

From "The Existence of God: A Debate"

THE MORAL ARGUMENT

COPLESTON: I don't say, of course, that God is the sum-total or system of what is good in the pantheistic sense; I'm not a pantheist, but I do think that all goodness reflects God in some way and proceeds from Him, so that in a sense the man who loves what is truly good, loves God even if he doesn't advert to God. But still I agree that the validity of such an interpretation of a man's conduct depends on the recognition of God's existence, obviously.

RUSSEL: Yes, but that's a point to be proved.

COPLESTON: Quite so, but I regard the metaphysical argument as probative, but there we differ.

RUSSELL: You see, I feel that some things are good and that some things are bad. I love the things that are good, that I think are good, and I hate the things that I think are bad. I don't say that these things are good because they participate in the Divine goodness.

COPLESTON: Yes, but what's your justification for distinguishing between good and bad or how do you view the distinction between them?

RUSSELL: I don't have any justification any more than I have when I distinguish between blue and yellow. What is my justification for distinguishing between blue and yellow? I can see they are different.

Bertrand Russell and F. C. Copleston, "The Existence of God: A Debate between Bertrand Russell and Father F. C. Copleston," in Bertrand Russell, *Why I Am Not a Christian* (London: George Allen & Unwin, 1957) . Reprinted by permission of the publisher and F. C. Copleston.

COPLESTON: Well, that is an excellent justification, I agree. You distinguish blue and yellow by seeing them, so you distinguish good and bad by what faculty?

RUSSELL: By my feelings.

COPLESTON: By your feelings. Well, that's what I was asking. You think that good and evil have reference simply to feeling?

RUSSELL: Well, why does one type of object look yellow and another look blue? I can more or less give an answer to that thanks to the physicists, and as to why I think one sort of thing good and another evil, probably there is an answer of the same sort, but it hasn't been gone into in the same way and I couldn't give it you.

COPLESTON: Well, let's take the behavior of the Commandant of Belsen. That appears to you as undesirable and evil and to me too. To Adolf Hitler we suppose it appeared as something good and desirable. I suppose you'd have to admit that for Hitler it was good and for you it is evil.

RUSSELL: No, I shouldn't quite go so far as that. I mean, I think people can make mistakes in that as they can in other things. If you have jaundice you see things yellow that are not yellow. You're making a mistake.

COPLESTON: Yes, one can make mistakes, but can you make a mistake if it's simply a question of reference to a feeling or emotion? Surely Hitler would be the only possible judge of what appealed to his emotions.

RUSSELL: It would be quite right to say that it appealed to his emotions, but you can say various things about that among others, that if that sort of thing makes that sort of appeal to Hitler's emotions, then Hitler makes quite a different appeal to my emotions.

COPLESTON: Granted. But there's no objective criterion outside feeling then for condemning the conduct of the Commandant of Belsen, in your view?

RUSSELL: No more than there is for the color-blinded person who's in exactly the same state. Why do we intellectually condemn the color-blinded man? Isn't it because he's in the minority?

COPLESTON: I would say because he is lacking in a thing which normally belongs to human nature.

RUSSELL: Yes, but if he were in the majority, we shouldn't say that.

COPLESTON: Then you'd say that there's no criterion outside feeling that will enable one to distinguish between the behavior of the Commandant of Belsen and the behavior, say, of Sir Stafford Cripps or the Archbishop of Canterbury.

RUSSELL: The feeling is a little too simplified. You've got to take account of the effects of actions and your feelings towards those effects. You see, you can have an argument about it if you say that certain sorts of occurrences are the sort you like and certain others the sort you don't like. Then you have to take account of the effects of actions. You can very well say that the effects of the actions of the Commandant of Belsen were painful and unpleasant.

COPLESTON: They certainly were, I agree, very painful and unpleasant to all the people in the camp.

RUSSELL: Yes, but not only to the people in the camp, but to outsiders contemplating them also.

COPLESTON: Yes, quite true in imagination. But that's my point. I don't approve of them, and I know you don't approve of them, but I don't see what ground you have for not approving of them, because after all, to the Commandant of Belsen himself, they're pleasant, those actions.

RUSSELL: Yes, but you see I don't need any more ground in that case than I do in the case of color perception. There are some people who think everything is yellow, there are people suffering from jaundice, and I don't agree with these people. I can't prove that the things are not yellow, there isn't any proof, but most people agree with me that they're not yellow, and most people agree with me that the Commandant of Belsen was making mistakes.

COPLESTON: Well, do you accept any moral obligation?

RUSSELL: Well, I should have to answer at considerable length to answer that. Practically speaking—yes. Theoretically speaking I should have to define moral obligation rather carefully.

COPLESTON: Well, do you think that the word "ought" simply has an emotional connotation?

RUSSELL: No, I don't think that, because you see, as I was saying a moment ago, one has to take account of the effects, and I think right conduct is that which would probably produce the greatest possible balance in intrinsic value of all the acts possible in the circumstances, and you've got to take account of the probable effects of your action in considering what is right.

COPLESTON: Well, I brought in moral obligation because I think that one can approach the question of God's existence in that way. The vast majority of the human race will make, and always have made, some distinction between right and wrong. The vast majority I think has some consciousness of an obligation in the moral sphere. It's my opinion that the perception of values and the consciousness of moral law and obligation are best explained through the hypothesis of a transcendent ground of value and of an author of the moral law. I do mean by "author of the moral law" an arbitrary author of the moral law. I think, in fact, that those modern atheists who have argued in the converse way "there is no God; therefore, there are no absolute values and no absolute law," are quite logical.

RUSSELL: I don't like the word "absolute." I don't think there is anything absolute whatever. The moral law, for example, is always changing. At one period in the development of the human race, almost everybody thought cannibalism was a duty.

COPLESTON: Well, I don't see that differences in particular moral judgments are any conclusive argument against the universality of the moral law. Let's assume for the moment that there are absolute moral values, even on that hypothesis it's only to be expected that different individuals and different groups should enjoy varying degrees of insight into those values.

RUSSELL: I'm inclined to think that "ought," the feeling that one has about "ought" is an echo of what has been told one by one's parents or one's nurses.

COPLESTON: Well, I wonder if you can explain away the idea of the "ought" merely in terms of nurses and parents. I really don't see how it can be conveyed to anybody in other terms than itself. It seems to me that if there is a moral order bearing upon the human conscience, that that moral order is unintelligible apart from the existence of God.

RUSSELL: Then you have to say one or other of two things. Either God only speaks to a very small percentage of mankind—which happens to include yourself—or He deliberately says things that are not true in talking to the consciences of savages.

COPLESTON: Well, you see, I'm not suggesting that God actually dictates moral precepts to the conscience. The human being's ideas of the content of the moral law depends certainly to a large extent on education and environment, and a man has to use his reason in assessing the validity of the actual moral ideas of his social group. But the possibility of criticizing the accepted moral code presupposes that there is an objective standard, that there is an ideal moral order, which imposes itself (I mean the obligatory character of which can be recognized). I think that the recognition of this ideal moral order is part of the recognition of contingency. It implies the existence of a real foundation of God.

RUSSELL: But the law-giver has always been, it seems to me, one's parents or someone like. There are plenty of terrestrial law-givers to account for it, and that would explain why people's consciences are so amazingly different in different times and places.

COPLESTON: It helps to explain differences in the perception of particular moral values, which otherwise are inexplicable. It will help to explain changes in the matter of the moral law in the content of the precepts as accepted by this or that nation, or this or that individual. But the form of it, what Kant calls the categorical imperative, the "ought," I really don't see how that can possibly be conveyed to anybody by nurse or parent because there aren't any possible terms, so far as I can see, with which it can be explained. It can't be defined in other terms than itself, because once you've defined it in other terms than itself you've explained it away. It's no longer a moral "ought." It's something else.

RUSSELL: Well, I think the sense of "ought" is the effect of somebody's imagined disapproval, it may be God's imagined disapproval, but it's somebody's imagined disapproval. And I think that is what is meant by "ought."

COPLESTON: It seems to me to be external customs and taboos and things of that sort which can most easily be explained simply through environment and education, but all that seems to me to belong to what I call the matter of the law, the content. The idea of the "ought" as such can never be conveyed to a man by the trival chief or by anybody else, because there

are no other terms in which it could be conveyed. It seems to me entirely—
[Russell breaks in].

RUSSELL: But I don't see any reason to say that—I mean we all know
about conditioned reflexes. We know that an animal, if punished habitually
for a certain sort of act, after a time will refrain. I don't think the animal
refrains from arguing within himself, "Master will be angry if I do this."
He has a feeling that that's not the thing to do. That's what we can do with
ourselves and nothing more.

COPLESTON: I see no reason to suppose that an animal has a consciousness of moral obligation; and we certainly don't regard an animal as
morally responsible for his acts of disobedience. But a man has a consciousness
of obligation and of moral values. I see no reason to suppose that one could
condition all men as one can "condition" an animal, and I don't suppose
you'd really want to do so even if one could. If "behaviorism" were true,
there would be no objective moral distinction between the emperor Nero
and St. Francis of Assisi. I can't help feeling, Lord Russell, you know, that
you regard the conduct of the Commandant at Belsen as morally reprehensible,
and that you yourself would never under any circumstances act in that way,
even if you thought, or had reason to think, that possibly the balance of
the happiness of the human race might be increased through some people
being treated in that abominable manner.

RUSSELL: No. I wouldn't imitate the conduct of a mad dog. The fact
that I wouldn't do it doesn't really bear on this question we're discussing.

COPLESTON: No, but if you were making a utilitarian explanation of
right and wrong in terms of consequences, it might be held, and I suppose
some of the Nazis of the better type would have held that although it's lamen-
table to have to act in this way, yet the balance in the long run leads to
greater happiness. I don't think you'd say that, would you? I think you'd
say that that sort of action is wrong—and in itself, quite apart from whether
the general balance of happiness is increased or not. Then, if you're prepared
to say that, then I think you must have some criterion of right and wrong,
that is outside the criterion of feeling, at any rate. To me, that admission
would ultimately result in the admission of an ultimate ground of value in
God. . . .

❋ SELECTED BIBLIOGRAPHY
FOR SECTION 3

Additional and rather standard statements and versions of the Moral Argument may be found in W. R. Sorley, *Moral Values and the Idea of God*, Ch. 13 (Cambridge, England: Cambridge University Press, 1918); John Baillie, *The Interpretation of Religion*, Chs. 5 and 6 (Edinburgh: T. & T. Clark, 1929); D. M. Baillie, *Faith in God*, Ch. 5 (Edinbursh: T. & T. Clark, 1927); and A. E. Taylor, *Does God Exist?* (New York: Macmillan, 1947).

Josiah Royce provides a kind of Moral Argument in *The Religious Aspect of Philosophy* (New York: Houghton, Mifflin and Co., 1885) based upon the possibility of error in intellectual judgment. C. S. Lewis argues (in a popular style) to the existence of a Law-Giver from the universality of certain moral codes in *Mere Christianity*, Book I (New York: Macmillan, 1943). H. P. Owen's small volume, *The Moral Argument for Christian Theism* (London: George Allen & Urwin, 1965), is given wholly to a defense of the argument as leading to belief in the Christian God, beginning with a critical discussion of naturalist and subjectivist interpretations of value. A possible analytic point of departure is suggested by Austin Farrer's "A Starting-Point for the Philosophical Examination of Theological Belief," in *Faith and Logic*, ed. Basil Mitchell (London: George Allen & Unwin, 1957).

For an exposition of the Kantian argument, see Lewis White Beck, *A Commentary on Kant's Critique of Practical Reason*, Ch. 14 (Chicago: University of Chicago Press, 1960) and C. D. Broad, *Five Types of Ethical Theory*, Ch. 5 (London: Routledge & Kegan Paul, 1930). On Kant's theological position one should consult also his *Religion Within the Bounds of Reason Alone*, tr. Theodore M. Greene and Hoyt H. Hudson (New York: Harper & Row, 1960), along with the worthy introductory essays by Theodore M. Greene and John R. Silber.

The naturalistic interpretation of ethical value is defended, in different ways, by John Stuart Mill, *Utilitarianism*, ed. Oskar Piest (Indianapolis, Ind,: Liberal Arts Press, 1957) and John Dewey, *Human Nature and Conduct* (New York: Holt, 1922). On Russell's subjectivism, see Justus Buchler's essay, "Russell and the Principles of Ethics," and Russell's rejoinder (pp. 719 ff.), in *The Philosophy of Bertrand Russell*, ed. Paul Arthur Schilpp (Evanston, Ill.: Northwestern University Press, 1944). The two best-known expressions of "emotivism" may be found in A. J. Ayer, *Language, Truth and Logic*, Ch. 7 and Introduction, second ed. (London: Gollancz, 1946) and C. L. Stevenson, *Ethics and Language* (New Haven, Conn.: Yale University Press, 1943). Related approaches are suggested by S. E. Toulmin, *The Place of Reason in Ethics* (Cambridge, England: Cambridge University Press, 1950) and R. M. Hare, *The Language of Morals* (Oxford, England: Clarendon Press, 1952).

A defense of non-naturalistic ethics is provided by A. C. Ewing, *The Definition of Good* (London: Routledge & Kegan Paul, 1947) and Chs. 6 and 7 of his *Ethics* (New York: Free Press, 1953); W. D. Ross, *The Right and the Good* (London: Oxford University Press, 1931); and G. E. Moore's abiding work *Principia Ethica* (Cambridge, England: Cambridge University Press, 1903). Moore's important contribution is further stated and evaluated in *The Philosophy of G. E. Moore, passim*, ed. Paul Arthur Schilpp (Evanston, Ill.: Northwestern University Press, 1942). For a critical response to emotivism, see A. Stroll, *The Emotive Theory of Meaning* (Berkeley, Calif.: University of California Press, 1954).

Moore's work provoked a long and involved debate over the "naturalistic fallacy." On this subject, one should consult the several selections (especially W. K. Frankena's important article, "The Naturalistic Fallacy") in *Readings in Ethical Theory*, ed. Wilfrid Sellars and John Hospers (New York: Appleton-Century-Crofts, 1952). A more recent contribution to the discussion is John R. Searles' "How to Derive 'Ought' from 'Is,' " *Philosophical Review*, LXXIII (January, 1964). A complete analysis of the naturalistic fallacy *vis à vis* God is provided by Burton F. Porter, *Deity and Morality* (New York: Humanities Press, 1968).

General discussions of the above issues and still others (including the problem of ethical relativism vs. objective morality) may be found in Charles L. Stevenson, *Facts and Values*, Chs. 4–7 (New Haven, Conn.: Yale University Press, 1963); Philip Blair Rice, *On the Knowledge of Good and Evil*, Chs. 1–5 (New York: Random House, 1955); and in the several contemporary selections represented in Paul W. Taylor's sourcebook *The Moral Judgment* (Englewood Cliffs, N. J.: Prentice-Hall, 1963). An excellent introduction to moral philosophy (and specific treatment of the issues mentioned above) is W. K. Frankena's *Ethics* (Englewood Cliffs, N. J.: Prentice-Hall, 1963).

Selections from many of the existentialist thinkers, along with an instructive introduction, are provided in Walter Kaufmann (ed.), *Existentialism from Dostoevsky to Sartre* (New York: Meridian Books, 1956). For general discussions of Sartre and other existentialists, see William Barrett, *Irrational Man* (Garden City, N. Y.: Doubleday, 1958); James Collins, *The Existentialists* (Chicago: Henry Regnery, 1952) (see especially Ch. 2, "Sartre's Postulatory Atheism"); Frederick Copleston, *Contemporary Philosophy*, Chs. 8–12 (Westminster, Md.: Newman Press, 1956); and David E. Roberts, *Existentialism and Religious Belief* (New York: Oxford University Press, 1957). Sympathetic treatments of Sartre may be found in Iris Murdoch, *Sartre: Romantic and Rationalist* (New Haven, Conn.: Yale University Press, 1953); Philip Thody, *Sartre: A Literary and Political Study* (London: Hamish Hamilton, 1960); Hazel E. Barnes, *Humanistic Existentialism* (Lincoln, Neb.: University of Nebraska Press, 1962); and the translator's introduction to Sartre's *Being and Nothingness*, tr. Hazel E. Barnes (New York: Philosophical Library, 1956). Also of interest is Robert Cumming's comparison of the Kierkegaardian and Sartrean approaches in his essay "The Literature of Extreme Situations," in *Aesthetics Today*, ed. Morris Philipson (Cleveland, Ohio: Meridian Books, 1961).

The Sartrean position on ethics and values is further represented by Simone de Beauvoir in *The Ethics of Ambiguity* (New York: Philosophical Library, 1948) and by Hazel E. Barnes, *An Existentialist Ethics* (New York: Knopf, 1967). Criticisms of this position are suggested by Copleston in Ch. 12 of the work cited above; by Gabriel Marcel, "Existence and Human Freedom," in *The Philosophy of Existentialism*, tr. Manya Harari (New York: Citadel Press, 1956); and by Parul Roubiczek, *Existentialism: For and Against*, Ch. 5 (Cambridge, England: Cambridge University Press, 1964).

God and Religious Experience

❊ INTRODUCTION

As was suggested earlier, the traditional approaches to God take two quite different routes. One, as we have seen, is the approach through discursive reason; it attempts to infer or deduce the existence of God through evidence *a priori* or *a posteriori*. This is the rational approach. There is, however, an approach that is said to transcend reason: the non-rational way of religious experience. Such a knowledge of God is direct, immediate, and self-authenticating. It should not be surprising that many of those who claim to have experienced God first-hand look sometimes with mild amusement upon philosophers haggling through the centuries over the applicability of causality to God or whether existence is a predicate. What could be more superfluous for a man who claims to have experienced God for himself?

There are, to be sure, "varieties of religious experience" as William James has suitably emphasized in the title of his classic work. What comes to mind may be anything from a revelling in Bacchic frenzy, to absorption in the divine disclosure of a tree leaf, to seeing visions and hearing voices, to Christian conversion, to mystical transports, to eerie feelings of the supernatural, and so on. It is impossible to represent all such versions of religious experience in the course of a few selections. On the other hand, it does seem possible to provide statements that witness to at least some of its more classical or consequential forms.

One such experience is considered by Rudolf Otto. Otto, disenchanted with the prevailing and one-sided intellectualist interpretation of religion, sought to recover what he took to be the non-rational essence of religion: the feeling or sense of the divine, or, as Otto calls it, the feeling of the "numinous," experienced by almost everyone at one time or another. Though variously manifested, this universal feeling of *mysterium tremendum* (which includes the elements of Awefulness, Overpoweringness, Urgency, Wholly Other, and Fascination), this revelatory sense of the divine presence engulfing all things is, according to Otto, the real stuff of all religions worthy of the name. The reader who rejects this latter claim might feel suitably challenged to substitute a better one.

Though Martin Buber also seeks the knowledge of God outside dogmatic and intellectual structures, his analysis differs from Otto's in at least two important respects. First, whereas Otto is preoccupied with the Wholly-Other-ness of God, a majestic and aweful Something "out there," Buber stresses, rather, the Wholly-Same-ness of God; there is nothing in which he is not present. More specifically, and this is the second difference, Buber believes that God, the Supreme Person, is most adequately grasped in a *particular* experience: the "I-Thou" relation. If we would know God, we must cultivate the "thou" in other people and even things, we must engage them, we must stand in relation with them; we must transcend "its" and allow the eternal Thou to be unlocked and disclosed through particular "thous."

One does not find in Buber (at least not in *I and Thou*) a closely reasoned and unfolded argument. Buber's aphoristic and poetic style suggests that such experiences may only be considered obliquely, pointed to and hinted at. They are, after all, non-rational (or better, supra-rational) ways of grasping God. When we come to mysticism, however, we are in the presence of an experience that claims to be completely ineffable. Ineffability, in fact, is one of the truly distinctive features of the kind of mysticism exemplified in the poems of St. John of the Cross.

"Mysticism" suggests many things to many people including, unfortunately, such things as astrology and palm-reading. The sooner one rids his mind of these associations the better. Classical Western mysticism, like that of Plotinus, St. Augustine, St. Francis, Meister Eckhart, St. Teresa, and St. John of the Cross, is a historical phenomenon that should not be taken lightly. Such mystics claim to apprehend God in a direct way, through a transcendent and ecstatic experience. More specifically, as is evident in the selection from St. John of the Cross, we must withdraw from the multiplicity and mutability of sense-experience, blotting out all sensible images; we must empty our souls of all ideas and passions (St. John's "dark night of the soul"); and transcending even our own selves we may ascend to a union with the divine in which even the duality between ourselves and God is overcome—at least in the sense that the soul is completely conformed to the divine will, as St. John makes clear in his windowpane simile. Mysticism assumes many shapes, but the "introverted" mysticism reflected by St. John is the more classical and influential version.

One might reasonably be struck by the claimed ineffability of mysticism on the one hand, and the prolixity of some mystics (for example, St. John) on the other. At the very least, it may be assumed that mystic language is indeed a strange one inasmuch as it talks about things that it says cannot be talked about, though one may wonder whether there is not some instruction in the fact that St. John saw in poetry an appropriate medium of mystic expression. This whole problem is raised recurringly in the selections.

The passages from the *Bhagavad-Gita* represent an Eastern variation on the mystical theme and thus emphasize the mystical point of contact between the East and West. In the *Bhagavad-Gita*, Arjuna (who represents everyman) has been enlisted by his father Pandu to fight against the Kurus led by Dhritarashtra, Pandu's brother and enemy. Faced with this moral dilemma (his fated duty to kill his own kinsman), Arjuna is counseled by the god Krishna, an incarnate manifestation of Vishnu, the divine Preserver. Krishna first provides both philosophical and practical appeals in an attempt to persuade Arjuna to fulfill his *dharma* ("duty") as a member of the warrior caste, and thus to advance toward enlightenment. Krishna then begins to instruct

Arjuna in the several Yogas or "Ways" (literally, "yokings") in which self-realization may be attained. The various Yogas converge on a detached renunciation of the world of sense and desire, a withdrawal into one's own consciousness, and an illumination of one's essential relation to Brahman, the divine principle of all things. It is not surprising that much of the *Bhagavad-Gita* focuses on Karma Yoga ("Way of Action") as preparatory to Bakhti Yoga ("Way of Devotion"), inasmuch as Arjuna's caste-status as a warrior requires of him active involvement. That such action may be performed without detachment is the message of the *Gita*. It might be mentioned, incidentally, that Otto takes the eleventh chapter of the *Bhagavad-Gita*, wherein Krishna reveals himself in all his glory to Arjuna (providing a transition to Bakhti Yoga), to be one of the most magnificent witnesses to the "numinous" to be found anywhere—though not as magnificent as Isaiah's vision of the Lord recorded in the first verses of Isaiah 6.[1]

We mentioned above that the *Gita* selection may be helpful as a reminder of the mystic bond between East and West. It would be simplistic, however, to think that in St. John and the *Gita* we have but one and the same position spelled out in differing cultural and linguistic attire. It would, in fact, be a useful exercise not only to align the similarities, but also to search out the important differences in the world-views, assumptions about human nature, conceptions of mystic union, and methods embodied in the two approaches.

Of course the mystics and others who claim to have had direct experience of the divine do not escape attack by the skeptics. C. D. Broad, in his analysis, considers a whole series of issues involved in the notion of religious experience, including the inevitable neuropathic and Freudian critiques which reduce mystical experience to either abnormal psychology or sublimated sexual desires. Such criticisms are weighed by Broad and found wanting. Psychology aside, the single biggest problem concerning the truth of religious experience has surely to do with its verification. How does one argue with a man who claims to have experienced God directly? If the claim of religious experience is, as it would appear, wholly subjective, non-verifiable, and non-falsifiable, then does it possess any truth-value at all? Is there *any* way in which the experience of such people constitute an evidence for a divine reality? Do we exclude as irrelevant the testimony of countless witnesses? It depends, of course.

[1] Rudolf Otto, *The Idea of the Holy*, tr. John W. Harvey, second ed. (London: Oxford University Press, 1950), p. 62 and n. 1.

✳ RUDOLF OTTO

14. *The Sense of the Numinous*

Rudolf Otto (1869–1937), who held chairs in theology at several German universities, was more of a religious philosopher than a systematic theologian. Though deeply committed to Christianity, Otto was a student of the living religions of the world, and *Das Heilige*, published in 1917 and later translated as *The Idea of the Holy*, contributed much to the interpretation of the universal religious consciousness.

From *The Idea of the Holy*

Chapter 1: The Rational and the Non-Rational

It is essential to every theistic conception of God, and most of all to the Christian, that it designates and precisely characterizes deity by the attributes spirit, reason, purpose, good will, supreme power, unity, selfhood. The nature of God is thus thought of by analogy with our human nature of reason and personality; only, whereas in ourselves we are aware of this as qualified by restriction and limitation, as applied to God the attributes we use are 'completed,' i.e. thought as absolute and unqualified. Now all these attributes constitute clear and definite *concepts*: they can be grasped by the intellect; they can be analysed by thought; they even admit of definition. An object that can thus be thought conceptually may be termed *rational*. The nature of deity described in the attributes above mentioned is, then, a rational nature; and a religion which recognizes and maintains such a view of God is in so far a 'rational' religion. Only on such terms is *belief* possible in contrast to mere *feeling*. And of Christianity at least it is false that 'feeling is all, the name but sound and smoke,'[1]—where 'name' stands for conception or thought. Rather we count this the very mark and criterion of a religion's high rank and superior value—that it should have no lack of *conceptions* about God; that it should admit knowledge—the knowledge that comes by faith—of the transcendent in terms of conceptual thought, whether those already mentioned or others which continue and develop them. Christianity not only possesses such conceptions but possesses them in unique clarity and abundance, and this is, though not the sole or even the chief, yet a very real sign of its superiority over religions of other forms and at other levels. This must be asserted at the outset and with the most positive emphasis.

But, when this is granted, we have to be on our guard against an error which would lead to a wrong and one-sided interpretation of religion.

Rudolf Otto, *The Idea of the Holy*, tr. John W. Harvey, second ed. (New York: Oxford University Press, 1950). Oxford University Press, 1923, 1950. Reprinted by permission.
[1]Goethe, *Faust*.

This is the view that the essence of deity can be given completely and exhaustively in such 'rational' attributions as have been referred to above and in others like them. It is not an unnatural misconception. We are prompted to it by the traditional language of edification, with its characteristic phraseology and ideas; by the learned treatment of religious themes in sermon and theological instruction; and further even by our Holy Scriptures themselves. In all these cases the 'rational' element occupies the foreground, and often nothing else seems to be present at all. But this is after all to be expected. All language, in so far as it consists of words, purports to convey ideas or concepts;—that is what language means;—and the more clearly and unequivocally it does so, the better the language. And hence expositions of religious truth in language inevitably tend to stress the 'rational' attributes of God.

But though the above mistake is thus a natural one enough, it is none the less seriously misleading. For so far are these 'rational' attributes from exhausting the idea of deity, that they in fact imply a non-rational or supra-rational Subject of which they are predicates. They are 'essential' (and not merely 'accidental') attributes of that subject, but they are also, it is important to notice, *synthetic* essential attributes. That is to say, we have to predicate them of a subject which they qualify, but which in its deeper essence is not, nor indeed can be, comprehended in them; which rather requires comprehension of a quite different kind. Yet, though it eludes the conceptual way of understanding, it must be in some way or other within our grasp, else absolutely nothing could be asserted of it. And even mysticism, in speaking of it as τὸ ἄρρητον, the ineffable, does not really mean to imply that absolutely nothing can be asserted of the object of the religious consciousness; otherwise, mysticism could exist only in unbroken silence, whereas what has generally been a characteristic of the mystics is their copious eloquence.

Here for the first time we come up against the contrast between rationalism and profounder religion, and with this contrast and its signs we shall be repeatedly concerned in what follows. We have here in fact the first and most distinctive mark of rationalism, with which all the rest are bound up. It is not that which is commonly asserted, that rationalism is the denial, and its opposite the affirmation, of the miraculous. That is manifestly a wrong or at least a very superficial distinction. For the traditional theory of the miraculous as the occasional breach in the causal nexus in nature by a Being who himself instituted and must therefore be master of it—this theory is itself as massively 'rational' as it is possible to be. Rationalists have often enough acquiesced in the possibility of the miraculous in this sense; they have even themselves contributed to frame a theory of it;—whereas anti-rationalists have been often indifferent to the whole controversy about miracles. The difference between rationalism and its opposite is to be found elsewhere. It resolves itself rather into a peculiar difference of *quality* in the mental attitude and emotional content of the religious life itself. All depends upon this: in our idea of God is the non-rational overborne, even perhaps wholly excluded, by the rational? Or conversely, does the non-rational itself preponderate over the rational? Looking at the matter thus, we see that the common dictum, that orthodoxy itself has been the mother of rationalism, is in some measure well founded. It is not simply that orthodoxy was preoccupied with doctrine and the framing of dogma, for these have been no less a concern of the wildest mystics. It is rather that orthodoxy found in the construction of dogma and doctrine no way to do justice to the non-rational aspect of its subject. So far from keeping the non-rational element in religion alive in the heart of the religious experience, orthodox Christianity manifestly failed to recognize its value, and by this failure gave to the idea of God a one-sidedly intellectualistic and rationalistic interpretation.

This bias to rationalization still prevails, not only in theology but in the science of comparative religion in general, and from top to bottom of it. The modern students of mythology, and those who pursue research into the religion of 'primitive man' and attempt to reconstruct the 'bases' or 'sources' of religion, are all victims to it. Men do not, of course, in these cases employ those lofty 'rational' concepts which we took as our point of departure; but they tend to take these concepts and their gradual 'evolution' as setting the main problem of their inquiry, and fashion ideas and notions of lower value, which they regard as paving the way for them. It is always in terms of concepts and ideas that the subject is pursued, 'natural' ones, moreover, such as have a place in the general sphere of man's ideational life, and are not specifically 'religious.' And then with a resolution and cunning which one can hardly help admiring, men shut their eyes to that which is quite unique in the religious experience, even in its most primitive manifestations. But it is rather a matter for astonishment than for admiration! For if there be any single domain of human experience that presents us with something unmistakably specific and unique, peculiar to itself, assuredly it is that of the religious life. In truth the enemy has often a keener vision in this matter than either the champion of religion or the neutral and professedly impartial theorist. For the adversaries on their side know very well that the entire 'pother about mysticism' has nothing to do with 'reason' and 'rationality.'

And so it is salutary that we should be incited to notice that religion is not exclusively contained and exhaustively comprised in any series of 'rational' assertions; and it is well worth while to attempt to bring the relation of the different 'moments' of religion to one another clearly before the mind, so that its nature may become more manifest.

This attempt we are now to make with respect to the quite distinctive category of the holy or sacred.

Chapter 2: 'Numen' and the 'Numinous'

'Holiness'—'the holy'—is a category of interpretation and valuation peculiar to the sphere of religion. It is, indeed, applied by transference to another sphere—that of ethics—but it is not itself derived from this. While it is complex, it contains a quite specific element or 'moment,' which sets it apart from 'the rational' in the meaning we gave to that word above, and which remains inexpressible—an ἄρρητον or *ineffabile*—in the sense that it completely eludes apprehension in terms of concepts. The same thing is true (to take a quite different region of experience) of the category of the beautiful.

Now these statements would be untrue from the outset if 'the holy' were merely what is meant by the word, not only in common parlance, but in philosophical, and generally even in theological usage. The fact is we have come to use the words 'holy,' 'sacred' (*heilig*) in an entirely derivative sense, quite different from that which they originally bore. We generally take 'holy' as meaning 'completely good'; it is the absolute moral attribute, denoting the consummation of moral goodness. In this sense Kant calls the will which remains unwaveringly obedient to the moral law from the motive of duty a 'holy' will; here clearly we have simply the *perfectly moral* will. In the same way we may speak of the holiness or sanctity of duty or law, meaning merely that they are imperative upon conduct and universally obligatory.

But this common usage of the term is inaccurate. It is true that all this moral significance is contained in the word 'holy,' but it includes in addition—as even we cannot but feel—a clear overplus of meaning, and this it is now our task to isolate. Nor is this merely a later or acquired meaning; rather, 'holy,' or at least the equivalent words in Latin and Greek, in Semitic and other ancient languages, denoted first and foremost *only* this overplus: if the ethical element was present at all, at any rate it was not original and never constituted the whole meaning of the word. Any one who uses it to-day does undoubtedly always feel 'the morally good' to be implied in 'holy'; and accordingly in our inquiry into that element which is separate and peculiar to the idea of the holy it will be useful, at least for the temporary purpose of the investigation, to invent a special term to stand for 'the holy' *minus* its moral factor or 'moment,' and, as we can now add, minus its 'rational' aspect altogether.

It will be our endeavour to suggest this unnamed Something to the reader as far as we may, so that he may himself feel it. There is no religion in which it does not live as the real innermost core, and without it no religion would be worthy of the name. It is pre-eminently a living force in the Semitic religions, and of these again in none has it such vigour as in that of the Bible. Here, too, it has a name of its own, viz. the Hebrew *qādôsh*, to which the Greek ἅγιος and the Latin *sanctus*, and, more accurately still, *sacer*, are the corresponding terms. It is not, of course, disputed that these terms in all three languages connote, as part of their meaning, *good, absolute goodness*, when, that is, the notion has ripened and reached the highest stage in its development. And we then use the word 'holy' to translate them. But this 'holy' then represents the gradual shaping and filling in with ethical meaning, or what we shall call the 'schematization,' of what was a unique original feeling-response, which can be in itself ethically neutral and claims consideration in its own right. And when this moment or element first emerges and begins its long development, all those expressions (*qādôsh*, ἅγιος, &c.) mean beyond all question something quite other than 'the good.' This is universally agreed by contemporary criticism, which rightly explains the rendering of *qādôsh* by 'good' as a mistranslation and unwarranted 'rationalization' or 'moralization' of the term.

Accordingly, it is worth while, as we have said, to find a word to stand for this element in isolation, this 'extra' in the meaning of 'holy' above and beyond the meaning of goodness. By means of a special term we shall the better be able, first, to keep the meaning clearly apart and distinct, and second, to apprehend and classify connectedly whatever subordinate forms or stages of development it may show. For this purpose I adopt a word coined from the Latin *numen*.[2] *Omen* has given us 'ominous,' and there is no reason why from *numen* we should not similarly form a word 'numinous.' I shall speak, then, of a unique 'numinous' category of value and of a definitely 'numinous' state of mind, which is always found wherever the category is applied. This mental state is perfectly *sui generis* and irreducible to any other; and therefore, like every absolutely primary and elementary datum, while it admits of being discussed, it cannot be strictly defined. There is only one way to help another to an understanding of it. He must be guided and led on by consideration and discussion of the matter through the ways of his own mind, until he reach the point at which 'the numinous' in him perforce begins to stir, to start into life and into consciousness. We can co-operate in this process by bringing before his notice all that can be found in other regions of the mind, already known and familiar, to resemble, or again to afford some special contrast to, the particular experience we wish to elucidate. Then we must add: 'This X of ours is not precisely *this* experience, but akin to this one and the opposite of that other. Cannot you now realize for yourself what it is?' In other words our X cannot, strictly speaking, be taught, it can only be evoked, awakened in the mind; as everything that comes 'of the spirit' must be awakened.

Chapter 3: The Elements In The 'Numinous'

The reader is invited to direct his mind to a moment of deeply-felt religious experience, as little as possible qualified by other forms of consciousness. Whoever cannot do this, whoever knows no such moments in his experience, is requested to read no farther; for it is not easy to discuss questions of religious psychology with one who can recollect the emotions of his adolescence, the discomforts of indigestion, or, say, social feelings, but cannot recall any intrinsically religious feelings. We do not blame such an one, when he tries for himself to advance as far as he can with the help of such principles of explanation as he knows, interpreting 'aesthetics' in terms of sensuous pleasure, and 'religion' as a function of gregarious instinct and social standards, or as something more primitive still. But the artist, who for his part has an intimate personal knowledge of the distinctive element in the aesthetic experience, will decline his theories with thanks, and the religious man will reject them even more uncompromisingly.

---

[2]["divine will" or "divine power," and by extension "divine presence."]

Next, in the probing and analysis of such states of the soul as that of solemn worship, it will be well if regard be paid to what is unique in them rather than to what they have in common with other similar states. To be *rapt* in worship is one thing; to be morally *uplifted* by the contemplation of a good deed is another; and it is not to their common features, but to those elements of emotional content peculiar to the first that we would have attention directed as precisely as possible. As Christians we undoubtedly here first meet with feelings familiar enough in a weaker form in other departments of experience, such as feelings of gratitude, trust, love, reliance, humble submission, and dedication. But this does not by any means exhaust the content of religious worship. Not in any of these have we got the special features of the quite unique and incomparable experience of solemn worship. In what does this consist?

Schleiermacher has the credit of isolating a very important element in such an experience. This is the 'feeling of dependence.'[3] But this important discovery of Schleiermacher is open to criticism in more than one respect.

In the first place, the feeling or emotion which he really has in mind in this phrase is in its specific quality not a 'feeling of dependence' in the 'natural' sense of the word. As such, other domains of life and other regions of experience than the religious occasion the feeling, as a sense of personal insufficiency and impotence, a consciousness of being determined by circumstances and environment. The feeling of which Schleiermacher wrote has an undeniable analogy with these states of mind; they serve as an indication to it, and its nature may be elucidated by them, so that, by following the direction in which they point, the feeling itself may be spontaneously felt. But the feeling is at the same time also qualitatively different from such analogous states of mind. Schleiermacher himself, in a way, recognizes this by distinguishing the feelings of dependence. His mistake is in making the distinction merely that between 'absolute' and 'relative' dependence, and therefore a difference of degree and not of intrinsic quality. What he overlooks is that, in giving the feeling the name 'feeling of dependence' at all, we are really employing what is no more than a very close analogy. Anyone who compares and contrasts the two states of mind introspectively will find out, I think, what I mean. It cannot be expressed by means of anything else, just because it is so primary and elementary a datum in our psychical life, and therefore only definable through itself. It may perhaps help him if I cite a well-known example, in which the precise 'moment' or element of religious feeling of which we are speaking is most actively present. When Abraham ventures to plead with God for the men of Sodom, he says (Gen. xviii. 27): 'Behold now, I have taken upon me to speak unto the Lord, which am but dust and ashes.' There you have a self-confessed 'feeling of dependence,' which is yet at the same time far more than, and something other than, *merely* a feeling of dependence. Desiring to give it a name of its own, I propose

---

[3][Cf. Friedrich Schleiermacher, *The Christian Faith*, I, Ch. 1, sect. 4.]

to call it 'creature-consciousness' or creature-feeling. It is the emotion of a creature, submerged and overwhelmed by its own nothingness in contrast to that which is supreme above all creatures.

It is easily seen that, once again, this phrase, whatever it is, is not a *conceptual* explanation of the matter. All that this new term, 'creature-feeling,' can express, is the note of submergence into nothingness before an overpowering, absolute might of some kind; whereas everything turns upon the *character* of this overpowering might, a character which cannot be expressed verbally, and can only be suggested indirectly through the tone and content of a man's feeling-response to it. And this response must be directly experienced in oneself to be understood.

We have now to note a second defect in the formulation of Schleiermacher's principle. The religious category discovered by him, by whose means he professes to determine the real content of the religious emotion, is merely a category of *self*-valuation, in the sense of self-depreciation. According to him the religious emotion would be directly and primarily a sort of *self*-consciousness, a feeling concerning oneself in a special, determined relation, viz. one's dependence. Thus, according to Schleiermacher, I can only come upon the very fact of God as the result of an inference, that is, by reasoning to a cause beyond myself to account for my 'feeling of dependence.' But this is entirely opposed to the psychological facts of the case. Rather, the 'creature-feeling' is itself a first subjective concomitant and effect of another feeling-element, which casts it like a shadow, but which in itself indubitably has immediate and primary reference to an object outside the self.[4]

CHAPTER 4: 'MYSTERIUM TREMENDUM'

We said above that the nature of the numinous can only be suggested by means of the special way in which it is reflected in the mind in terms of feeling. 'It's nature is such that it grips or stirs the human mind with this and that determinate affective state.' We have now to attempt to give

---

[4]This is so manifestly borne out by experience that it must be about the first thing to force itself upon the notice of psychologists analyzing the facts of religion. There is a certain naïveté in the following passage from William James's *Varieties of Religious Experience* (p. 58), where, alluding to the origin of the Grecian representations of the gods, he says: 'As regards the origin of the Greek gods, we need not at present seek an opinion. But the whole array of our instances leads to a conclusion something like this: It is as if there were in the human consciousness *a sense of reality, a feeling of objective presence*, a *perception* of what we may call "*something there*," more deep and more general than any of the special and particular "senses" by which the current psychology supposes existent realities to be originally revealed.' (The italics are James's own.) James is debarred by his empiricist and pragmatist standpoint from coming to a recognition of faculties of knowledge and potentialities of thought in the spirit itself, and he is therefore obliged to have recourse to somewhat singular and mysterious hypotheses to explain this fact. But he grasps the fact itself clearly enough and is sufficient of a realist not to explain it away. But this 'feeling of reality,' the feeling of a 'numinous' *object* objectively given, must be posited as a primary immediate datum of consciousness, and the 'feeling of dependence' is then a consequence, following very closely upon it, viz. a depreciation of the *subject* in his own eyes. The latter presupposes the former.

a further indication of these determinate states. We must once again endeavour, by adducing feelings akin to them for the purpose of analogy or contrast, and by the use of metaphor and symbolic expressions, to make the states of mind we are investigating ring out, as it were, of themselves.

Let us consider the deepest and most fundamental element in all strong and sincerely felt religious emotion. Faith unto salvation, trust, love—all these are there. But over and above these is an element which may also on occasion, quite apart from them, profoundly affect us and occupy the mind with a wellnigh bewildering strength. Let us follow it up with every effort of sympathy and imaginative intuition wherever it is to be found, in the lives of those around us, in sudden, strong ebullitions of personal piety and the frames of mind such ebullitions evince, in the fixed and ordered solemnities of rites and liturgies, and again in the atmosphere that clings to old religious monuments and buildings, to temples and to churches. If we do so we shall find we are dealing with something for which there is only one appropriate expression, 'mysterium tremendum.' The feeling of it may at times come sweeping like a gentle tide, prevading the mind with a tranquil mood of deepest worship. It may pass over into a more set and lasting attitude of the soul, continuing, as it were, thrillingly vibrant and resonant, until at last it dies away and the soul resumes its 'profane,' non-religious mood of everyday experience. It may burst in sudden eruption up from the depths of the soul with spasms and convulsions, or lead to the strangest excitements, to intoxicated frenzy, to transport, and to estasy. It has its wild and demonic forms and can sink to an almost grisly horror and shuddering. It has its crude, barbaric antecedents and early manifestations, and again it may be developed into something beautiful and pure and glorious. It may become the hushed, trembling, and speechless humility of the creature in the presence of—whom or what? In the presence of that which is a *mystery* inexpressible and above all creatures.

It is again evident at once that here too our attempted formulation by means of a concept is once more a merely negative one. Conceptually *mysterium* denotes merely that which is hidden and esoteric, that which is beyond conception or understanding, extraordinary and unfamiliar. The term does not define the object more positively in its qualitative character. But though what is enunciated in the word is negative, what is meant is something absolutely and intensely positive. This pure positive we can experience in feelings, feelings which our discussion can help to make clear to us, in so far as it arouses them actually in our hearts. . . .

✳ MARTIN BUBER

15. *The Eternal Thou*

Martin Buber (1878–1965) was a renowned Jewish philosopher. During his early years he was actively involved in Zionism and later played a role in the revival of Hasidism, a Jewish mystical movement. From 1938 to 1951 Buber taught at the Hebrew University in Jerusalem. *I and Thou*, first published in 1937, is a classic statement of one form of man's revelatory encounter with God.

From *I and Thou*

Part Three

The extended lines of relations meet in the eternal *Thou*.

Every particular *Thou* is a glimpse through to the eternal *Thou*; by means of every particular *Thou* the primary word addresses the eternal *Thou*. Through this mediation of the *Thou* of all beings fulfilment, and non-fulfilment, of relations comes to them: the inborn *Thou* is realised in each relation and consummated in none. It is consummated only in the direct relation with the *Thou* that by its nature cannot become *It*.

Men have addressed their eternal *Thou* with many names. In singing of Him who was thus named they always had the *Thou* in mind: the first myths were hymns of praise. Then the names took refuge in the language of *It*; men were more and more strongly moved to think of and to address their eternal *Thou* as an *It*. But all God's names are hallowed, for in them He is not merely spoken about, but also spoken to.

Many men wish to reject the word God as a legitimate usage, because it is so misused. It is indeed the most heavily laden of all the words used by men. For that very reason it is the most imperishable and most indispensable. What does all mistaken talk about God's being and works (though there has been, and can be, no other talk about these) matter in comparison with the one truth that all men who have addressed God had God Himself in mind? For he who speaks the word God and really has *Thou* in mind (whatever the illusion by which he is held), addresses the true *Thou* of his life, which cannot be limited by another *Thou*, and to which he stands in a relation that gathers up and includes all others.

But when he, too, who abhors the name, and believes himself to be godless, gives his whole being to addressing the *Thou* of his life, as a *Thou* that cannot be limited by another, he addresses God.

Martin Buber, *I and Thou*, tr. Ronald Gregor Smith, second ed. (New York: Scribner, 1958). Reprinted from pp. 75–83 by permission of Charles Scribner's Sons. Also reprinted by permission of T. & T. Clark, Edinburgh, Scotland.

If we go on our way and meet a man who has advanced towards us and has also gone on *his* way, we know only our part of the way, not his—his we experience only in the meeting.

Of the complete relational event we know, with the knowledge of life lived, our going out to the relation, our part of the way. The other part only comes upon us, we do not know it; it comes upon us in the meeting. But we strain ourselves on it if we speak of it as though it were some thing beyond the meeting.

We have to be concerned, to be troubled, not about the other side but about our side, not about grace but about will. Grace concerns us in so far as we go out to it and persist in its presence; but it is not our object.

The *Thou* confronts me. But I step into direct relation with it. Hence the relation means being chosen and choosing, suffering and action in one; just as any action of the whole being which means the suspension of all partial actions, and consequently of all sensations of actions grounded only in their particular limitation, is bound to resemble suffering.

This is the activity of the man who has become a whole being, an activity that has been termed doing nothing: nothing separate or partial stirs in the man any more, thus he makes no intervention in the world; it is the whole man, enclosed and at rest in his wholeness, that is effective—he has become an effective whole. To have won stability in this state is to be able to go out to the supreme meeting.

To this end the world of sense does not need to be laid aside as though it were illusory. There is no illusory world, there is only the world—which appears to us as twofold in accordance with our twofold attitude. Only the barrier of separation has to be destroyed. Further, no "going beyond sense-experience" is necessary; for every experience, even the most spiritual, could yield us only an *It*. Nor is any recourse necessary to a world of ideas and values; for they cannot become presentness for us. None of these things is necessary. Can it be said what really is necessary?—Not in the sense of a precept. For everything that has ever been devised and contrived in the time of the human spirit as precept, alleged preparation, practice, or meditation, has nothing to do with the primal, simple fact of the meeting. Whatever the advantages in knowledge or the wielding of power for which we have to thank this or that practice, none of this affects the meeting of which we are speaking; it all has its place in the world of *It* and does not lead one step, does not take *the* step, out of it. Going out to the relation cannot be taught in the sense of precepts being given. It can only be indicated by the drawing of a circle which excludes everything that is not going out. Then the one thing that matters is visible, full acceptance of the present.

To be sure, this acceptance presupposes that the further a man has wandered in separated being the more difficult is the venture and the more elemental the turning. This does not mean a giving up of, say, the *I*, as mystical writings usually suppose: the *I* is as indispensable to this, the supreme, as to every relation, since relation is only possible between *I* and *Thou*. It is not the *I*, then, that is given up, but that false self-asserting instinct that makes a man flee to the possessing of things before the unreliable, perilous world of relation which has neither density nor duration and cannot be surveyed.

Every real relation with a being or life in the world is exclusive. Its *Thou* is freed, steps forth, is single, and confronts you. It fills the heavens. This does not mean that nothing else exists; but all else lives in *its* light. As long as the presence of the relation continues, this its cosmic range is inviolable. But as soon as a *Thou* becomes *It*, the cosmic range of the relation appears as an offence to the world, its exclusiveness as an exclusion of the universe.

In the relation with God unconditional exclusiveness and unconditional inclusiveness are one. He who enters on the absolute relation is concerned with nothing isolated any more, neither things nor beings, neither earth nor heaven; but everything is gathered up in the relation. For to step into pure relation is not to disregard everything but to see everything in the *Thou*, not to renounce the world but to establish it on its true basis. To look away from the world, or to stare at it, does not help a man to reach God; but he who sees the world in Him stands in His presence. "Here world, there God" is the language of *It*; "God in the world" is another language of *It*; but to eliminate or leave behind nothing at all, to include the whole world in the *Thou*, to give the world its due and its truth, to include nothing beside God but everything in him—this is full and complete relation.

Men do not find God if they stay in the world. They do not find Him if they leave the world. He who goes out with his whole being to meet his *Thou* and carries to it all being that is in the world, finds Him who cannot be sought.

Of course God is the "wholly Other"; but He is also the wholly Same, the wholly Present. Of course He is the *Mysterium Tremendum* that appears and overthrows; but He is also the mystery of the self-evident, nearer to me than my *I*.

If you explore the life of things and of conditioned being you come to the unfathomable, if you deny the life of things and of conditioned being you stand before nothingness, if you hallow this life you meet the living God.

Man's sense of *Thou*, which experiences in the relations with every particular *Thou* the disappointment of the change to *It*, strives out but not away from them all to its eternal *Thou*; but not as something is sought: actually there is no such thing as seeking God, for there is nothing in which He could not be found. How foolish and hopeless would be the man who turned aside from the course of his life in order to seek God; even though he won all the wisdom of solitude and all the power of concentrated being he would miss God. Rather is it as when a man goes his way and simply wishes that it might be the way: in the strength of his wish his striving is expressed. Every relational event is a stage that affords him a glimpse into the consummating event. So in each event he does not partake, but also (for he is waiting) does partake, of the one event. Waiting, not seeking, he goes his way; hence he is composed before all things, and makes contact with them which helps them. But when he has *found*, his heart is not turned from them, though everything now meets him in the one event. He blesses every cell that sheltered him, and every cell into which he will yet turn. For this finding is not the end, but only the eternal middle, of the way.

It is a finding without seeking, a discovering of the primal, of origin. His sense of *Thou*, which cannot be satiated till he finds the endless *Thou*, had the *Thou* present to it from the beginning; the presence had only to become wholly real to him in the reality of the hallowed life of the world.

God cannot be inferred in anything—in nature, say, as its author, or in history as its master, or in the subject as the self that is thought in it. Something else is not "given" and God then elicited from it; but God is the Being that is directly, most nearly, and lastingly, over against us, that may properly only be addressed, not expressed.

Men wish to regard a feeling (called feeling of dependence, and re- cently, more precisely, creaturely feeling) as the real element in the relation with God. In proportion as the isolation and definition of this element is accurate, its unbalanced emphasis only makes the character of complete rela- tion the more misunderstood.

What has already been said of love is even more unshakably valid here. Feelings are a mere accompaniment to the metaphysical and meta- psychical fact of the relation, which is fulfilled not in the soul but between *I* and *Thou*. A feeling may be considered ever so essential, it remains never- theless subject to the dynamic of the soul, where one feeling is outstripped, outdone, and abolished by another. In distinction from relation a feeling has its place in a scale. But above all, every feeling has its place within a polar tension, obtaining its colour and significance not from itself alone, but also from the opposite pole: every feeling is conditioned by its opposite. Thus the absolute relation (which gathers up into reality all those that are relative, and is no more a part, as these are, but is the whole that completes and unifies them all), in being reduced to the status of an isolated and limited feeling, is made into a relative psychological matter.

If the soul is the starting-point of our consideration, complete relation can be understood only in a bipolar way, only as the *coincidentia oppositorum*, as the coincidence of oppositions of feeling. Of course, the one pole— suppressed by the person's basic religious attitude—often disappears from the reflective consciousness, and can only be recalled in the purest and most ingenuous consideration of the depths of the being.

Yes; in pure relation you have felt yourself to be simply dependent, as you are able to feel in no other relation—and simply free, too, as in no other time or place: you have felt yourself to be both creaturely and creative. You had the one feeling then no longer limited by the other, but you had both of them limitlessly and together.

You know always in your heart that you need God more than every-thing; but do you not know too that God needs you—in the fulness of His eternity needs you? How would man be, how would you be, if God did not need him, did not need you? You need God, in order to be—and God needs you, for the very meaning of your life. In instruction and in poems men are at pains to say more, and they say too much—what turgid and presump-tuous talk that is about the "God who becomes"; but we know unshakably in our hearts that there is a becoming of the God that is. The world is not divine sport, it is divine destiny. There is divine meaning in the life of the world, of man, of human persons, of you and of me.

Creation happens to us, burns itself into us, recasts us in burning—we tremble and are faint, we submit. We take part in creation, meet the Creator, reach out to Him, helpers and companions.

Two great servants pace through the ages, prayer and sacrifice. The man who prays pours himself out in unrestrained dependence, and knows that he has—in an incomprehensible way—an effect upon God, even though he obtains nothing from God; for when he no longer desires anything for himself he sees the flame of his effect burning at its highest.—And the man who makes sacrifice? —I cannot despise him, this upright servant of former times, who believed that God yearned for the scent of his burnt-offering. In a foolish but powerful way he knew that we can and ought to give to God. This is known by him, too, who offers up his little will to God and meets Him in the grand will. "Thy will be done," he says, and says no more; but truth adds for him, "through me whom Thou needest."

What distinguishes sacrifice and prayer from all magic? —Magic de-sires to obtain its effects without entering into relation, and practises its tricks in the void. But sacrifice and prayer are set "before the Face," in the consum-mation of the holy primary word that means mutual action: they speak the *Thou*, and then they hear.

To wish to understand pure relation as dependence is to wish to empty one of the bearers of the relation, and hence the relation itself, of reality. . . .

✳ ST. JOHN OF THE CROSS

16. *The Mystical Ascent*

St. John of the Cross (1542–1591) was a Spanish Carmelite. He is representative of the recurring form of Christian mysticism (and classical mysticism in general) which attempts to ascend to an ecstatic and ineffable union with God by emptying the soul of sense-impressions and ideas—the state which St. John of the Cross called "the dark night of the soul."

From *The Dark Night of the Soul*

PART I

The main theme and final goal: the soul's union with God

This treatise deals with the manner in which a soul may prepare itself to attain to union with God. It gives useful advice and instruction, both to beginners and to those more advanced in the spiritual life, so that they may learn how to free themselves from all that is temporal and not weigh themselves down with the spiritual, and remain in that complete nakedness and freedom of the spirit which are necessary for union with God.

The entire doctrine which I intend to discuss in the Ascent to Mount Carmel[1] is contained in the following stanzas, and they describe also the manner of ascending to the peak of the mountain, that is, that high state of perfection which we here designate as the union of the soul with God. The poem reads as follows:

1
In a dark night,
My longing heart, aglow with love,
—Oh, blessed lot!—
I went forth unseen
From my house that was at last in deepest rest.

2
Secure and protected by darkness,
I climbed the secret ladder, in disguise,
—Oh, blessed lot!—
In darkness, veiled and concealed I went
Leaving behind my house in deepest rest.

St. John of the Cross, *The Dark Night of the Soul,* tr. and ed. Kurt F. Reinhardt (New York: Ungar, 1957). Reprinted by permission of Frederick Ungar Publishing Co.
[1][I.e. Part I of *The Dark Night of the Soul.*]

3

Oh, blissful night!
Oh, secret night, when I remained unseeing and unseen,
When the flame burning in my heart
Was my only light and guide.

4

This inward light,
A safer guide than noonday's brightness,
Showed me the place where He awaited me
—My soul's Beloved—
A place of solitude.

5

Oh, night that guided me!
Oh, night more lovely than the rosy dawn!
Oh, night whose darkness guided me
To that sweet union,
In which the lover and Beloved are made one.

6

Upon the flower of my breast,
Kept undefiled for Him alone,
He fell asleep,
While I was waking
Caressing Him with gentle cedars' breeze.

7

And when Aurora's breath
Began to spread His curled hair,
His gentle hand
He placed upon my neck.
And all my senses were in bliss suspended.

8

Forgetful of myself,
My head reclined on my Beloved,
The world was gone
And all my cares at rest,
Forgotten all my grief among the lilies.

Book II

Chapter 5: The union of the soul with God is a union of love and of likeness, not division of substance

To understand, then, the nature of this union, it must be known that God dwells or is present substantially in every soul, even in the soul of the greatest sinner. This kind of union between God and all His creatures is never lacking, since it is in and by this union that He sustains their being; and if it were ever lacking, these creatures would immediately cease to be and would fall back into nothingness. Thus, if we here speak of the union of the soul with God, we do not have in mind this ever-present substantial union, but we do mean that union of the soul with God which is consummated in the soul's transformation in God—a union which can come about only when the soul attains to a likeness with God by virtue of love. We shall therefore call this the union of likeness, to distinguish it from the union of substance or essence. The former is supernatural, the latter natural. And the supernatural union comes about when the two wills—that of the soul and that of God—are conformed in one, so that there is nothing in the one that is repugnant to the other. Thus, when the soul rids itself totally of that which is repugnant to and not in conformity with the Divine will, it is transformed in God through love. This applies not only to whatever is repugnant to God in human action, but also in habit, so that the soul must not only desist from all voluntary acts of imperfection but must also completely overcome the acquired habits of these imperfections. And since no creature nor the actions or capabilities of any creature can ever measure up or attain to that which is God, the soul must be stripped of all creaturely attachments as well as of its own activities and capabilities—that is to say, of its understanding, its likings, and its feelings—so that, when all that which is unlike God and unconformed to Him is cast out, the soul may then receive the likeness of God.

Supernatural being is communicated only by love and grace. Not all souls, however, abide in God's love and grace, and those who do not possess them in the same degree; for some attain higher degrees of love than others. And thus, God communicates Himself most to that soul which has progressed farthest in love and has most conformed its will to God's will. And that soul which has attained to a total conformity and likeness of its will and God's will is totally united with Him and supernaturally transformed in Him.

Let me clarify [the nature of this union][2] by a simile. Picture a ray of sunlight that is striking a window. Now if the window is coated with stains or vapors, the ray will be unable to illumine it and transform it into its own light; this it could do only if the window were stainless and pure. And the greater or lesser degree of illumination will be strictly in proportion to the window's greater or lesser purity; and this will be so, not because of the ray of sunlight but because of the condition of the window. Thus, if the window were entirely clean and pure, the ray would transform and illumine it in such a way that it would become almost undistinguishable from the brightness of the ray and would diffuse the same light as the ray. And yet, however much the window may resemble the ray of sunlight, it actually retains its own distinct nature. But this does not prevent us from saying that this window is luminous as a ray of the sun or is sunlight by participation. Now the soul is like this window: the Divine light of the Being of God is unceasingly

---

[2][Translator's bracketing here and following.]

beating upon it, or, to use a better expression, the Divine light is ever dwelling in it.

When the soul thus allows God to work in it, it will soon be transformed and transfigured in God, and God will communicate to it His supernatural Being in such a way that the soul appears to be God Himself, and it will indeed be God by participation. Yet it remains true nevertheless that the soul's natural being—notwithstanding the soul's supernatural transformation—remains as distinct from the Being of God as it was before, even as the window has and retains a nature of its own, distinct from the nature of the ray, although it owes its luminosity to the light of the sun.

This consideration should make it clearer why a soul cannot dispose itself for this union by either understanding, or sensory apperception, or inner feelings and imaginings, or by any other experiences relating either to God or to anything else, but only by purity and love, that is, by perfect resignation and total detachment from all things for the sake of God alone. And as there can be no perfect transformation unless there be perfect purity, the soul will not be perfect unless it be totally cleansed and wholly pure.

Those souls [who attain to Divine union] do so according to their greater or smaller capacity and thus not in the same degree; and the degree of union depends also on what the Lord wishes to grant to each soul. And it is similar in the beatific vision: though some souls will have a more perfect vision of God in Heaven than others, they all see God, and all are content, since their capacity is satisfied. And in this life, too, all souls [who have attained to the state of perfection] will be equally satisfied, each one according to its knowledge of God and thus according to its capacity. A soul, on the other hand, that does not attain to a degree of purity corresponding to its capacity, will never find true peace and contentment.

Chapter 6: The three theological virtues perfect the three faculties of the soul

We shall now endeavor to show how the three faculties of the soul— understanding, memory, and will—are brought into this spiritual night, which is the means leading to the end of Divine union. To do this, it is necessary first of all to explain in this chapter how the three theological virtues—faith, hope, and love—by means of which the soul is united with God according to its faculties, produce an identical emptiness and darkness, each one with respect to its corresponding faculty. Thus, faith produces darkness in the understanding; hope, in the memory; love, in the will. Subsequently, we shall describe how the understanding is perfected in the darkness of faith, and memory in the emptiness of hope; and we shall then show how the will must be voided and stripped of all affection in order to move toward God. For, as we have pointed out, the soul is united with God in this life not through the understanding, nor through joyous feelings, nor through imagination, nor through any other sensory experience; but only through faith, which perfects the understanding; through hope, which perfects the memory; and through love, which perfects the will.

Faith, then, tells us what cannot be comprehended with the [natural] *understanding.* According to St. Paul, "Faith is the substance of our hopes; it convinces us of things we cannot see" [Heb. 11:1]. Although the understanding may give its consent with a firm and perfect assurance, the things of faith are not revealed to the understanding; for, if they were revealed to it, there would be no need for faith. Wherefore, though faith gives certainty to the understanding, it does not illumine it, but leaves it in darkness.

As to *hope,* there is no doubt that it in its turn plunges the *memory* into emptiness and darkness with respect to both things here below and things above. For hope has always to do with that which is not yet in our possession, since, if we already possessed it, there would no longer be room for hope. This is what St. Paul means when he says: "Hope would no longer be hope if its object were in plain view; for how could a man still hope for something that is fully seen [that is, fully possessed]?" [Rom. 8:24].

And, similarly, *love* empties the *will* of all things, since it obliges us to love God above them all; this, however, we cannot do unless we detach our affection from all of them in order to attach it wholly to God. Wherefore, Christ tells us through the mouth of St. Luke: "No one can be My disciple who does not detach himself from all that he [wilfully] possesses" [Luke 14:33]. All three of these virtues, then, plunge the soul into darkness and emptiness with respect to all things.

This, then, is the spiritual night which we have called *active*; for all the soul is able to do to enter into this night, it does by its own power. And as, when we were speaking of the night of sense, we described a method of emptying the faculties of sense of all the objects of sense—so that the soul might advance from its point of departure to the intermediate state of faith—so also, in this spiritual night, we shall, with Divine aid, describe a method whereby the spiritual faculties are emptied and purified of all that is not God. As a result, the spiritual faculties will then be placed in the darkness of the three [theological] virtues, which, as we have seen, are the means that dispose the soul for its unon with God. And it should be noted that I am now speaking in particular to those who have begun to enter the state of contemplation.

Chapter 7: The narrow road; detachment of the understanding; spiritual poverty

Speaking of the road [that leads to eternal life], Our Saviour said: "How small is the gate and how narrow the road that leads to Life; and there are few who find it" [Matt. 7:14]. Now what Christ says of the small gate, we may understand in relation to the sensual part of man; and what He says of the narrow road, may be understood in relation to the spiritual or rational part. And the reason for His saying that "there are few who find it" is that there are few who know how to enter and who actually desire to enter into this total nakedness and emptiness of the spirit. For this path that leads to the high mountain of perfection is steep and narrow and therefore requires travellers who are not weighed down and encumbered by any cares for either the lower things of sense or the higher things of the spirit. Since this is an undertaking in which the prize of our search is God alone, He alone must be the object of our striving and our victory.

Hence we can see clearly that the soul which travels on this road must not only be free from all creaturely attachments but must also be spiritually poor and as dead to its own self. This is why Our Lord taught us through the mouth of St. Mark that priceless doctrine which, because of its great importance and because it specifically applies to our purpose, I shall quote here in full and then explain in its true spiritual meaning.

Our Lord says: "If any man wishes to go My way, let him deny his own self, and take up his cross, and follow Me. He who tries to save his life will lose it; but he who loses his life for My sake will save it" [Mark 8:34–35].

I wish someone would properly teach us how to understand, practise, and inwardly grasp the true meaning and significance of this counsel, so that spiritual persons would see how different is the method they should employ on this road from what many of them regard as proper. While some believe that any kind of withdrawal from the world and any external reform suffice, others are content with practising the virtues and continuing in prayer and penance; but neither attain to that nakedness, self-denial, and spiritual poverty which the Lord here commends to us; for they prefer feeding and clothing their natural selves with spiritual feelings and consolations to emptying themselves of all things and renouncing their natural selves for God's sake. Or they think that it suffices to strip their natural selves of worldly things, without purifying themselves by the total renunciation also of spiritual attachments. Thus, when they get a glimpse of this concrete and perfect life of the spirit— which manifests itself in the complete absence of all sweetness, in aridity, distaste, and in the many trials that are the true spiritual cross—they flee from it as from death. What they seek in their communion with God is sweet and delectable feelings; but this is a sort of spiritual gluttony rather than self-denial and spiritual poverty. As far as their spirituality is concerned, they become enemies of Christ. They seek themselves in God, which is the very opposite of love; for to seek oneself in God is to seek the favors and refreshing delights of God, whereas to seek God in oneself is to incline oneself to choose, for Christ's sake, all that is most distasteful; and this is love of God.

And when Our Lord said that he who tries to save his life will lose it, He meant that he who desires to possess anything for himself will lose it; whereas he who for Christ's sake renounces all that his will can desire and enjoy, and chooses that which is most like to the Cross, will save his life. This is precisely what His Majesty taught to those two disciples [the sons of Zebedee] who asked that they be allowed a place on His right and on His left. He answered their request for such glory by offering them the cup of which He had to drink, as a thing more precious and more secure on this earth than any joy of possession. [cf. Mark 10:35–45].

To drink of this cup, however, is to die to the natural self by detachment and self-annihilation, so that the soul may be able to travel by this narrow path unimpeded, since there remains to it nothing but self-denial and the Cross. And this Cross is the pilgrim's staff on which the soul may lean on its way to God and which greatly eases its burden and travail. Wherefore Our Lord said through the mouth of St. Matthew: "My yoke is easy, and My burden is light" [Matt. 11:30]. For if a man resolves to carry this cross willingly, that is, if he is truly determined to undergo and bear hardships and trials for God's Sake, he will find in them great solace and sweetness. If, on the other hand, he desires to possess anything or remains attached to anything whatsoever, his self is not totally stripped and emptied of all things, and he will not be able to continue his upward journey on this narrow path. For progress [in the spiritual life] can be made only by imitating Christ, Who is the Way, the Truth, and the Life; and no one can come to the Father, except through Christ [cf. John 14:6].

Christ, then, is the Way, and this way is death to the natural self in both sense and spirit. And I shall now try to explain how we must die [to our natural selves], following the example of Christ, Who is our guiding light.

First, it is certain that, as far as the senses are concerned, He died (spiritually) in His life and (naturally) in His death. For, as He said, He had not in His life where to lay His head [cf. Matt. 8:20], and in His death He had even less.

Second, it is equally certain that in the hour of His death He felt annihilated and abandoned also in His soul, deprived of all consolation and help, since His Father left His humanity in a state of such complete aridity that the cry "My God, My God, why hast Thou forsaken Me?" [Matt. 27:46] forced itself upon His lips. This was, with respect to His sensory nature, the greatest desolation He had suffered in His life. And yet, it was then that he wrought the greatest work of His entire life, greater than any of His miracles and other mighty deeds—the reconciliation and union of the human race with God, through grace.

The words of David, "I was reduced to nothingness and unknowing" [Ps. 72:22], point to the mystery of the small gate and the narrow way, so that the truly spiritual man may learn to understand the way of Christ, the way of union with God. He will learn from these words that the more he becomes as nothing, the more intimately he is united with God and the greater is the work that he accomplishes. This union, then, consists not in delights, consolations, and sweet spiritual feelings, but in a living sensual and spiritual, internal and external, death of the cross.

Chapter 8: No creature nor any knowledge that can be comprehended by the understanding can serve as proximate means of union with God

Before we enter into a discussion of faith—the appropriate means of union with God—it seems necessary to demonstrate that no created thing, whether it be real or a product of our imagination, can serve the understanding as a proper means of union with God; and that everything that falls within the reach of the understanding is an impediment rather than a means, if the understanding desires to cling to it. In this present chapter we are offering a general demonstration, but subsequently we shall discuss this matter in greater detail.

It is one of the principal rules of philosophy that all means must be proportioned to the end; that is, they must have some proportionate relation to and some similarity with the end. If, for example, fire is to be joined with wood, it is necessary that heat, which is the means, first prepare the wood, by transmitting to it such an intensity of heat that the wood will acquire a high degree of similarity or a proportionate assimilation to fire. Similarly, if the understanding is to be united with God—as far as this is possible in this life—it is necessary that the understanding employ that means which bears the closest resemblance to Him.

Here it should be pointed out that no creature—high or low—approximates God or bears any resemblance to His Being. For, though it is true that all creatures have, as the theologians tell us, a certain relation to God and bear a Divine impress—some more and others less, according to the greater or lesser amount of being of their natures—yet there is no essential similarity between them and God. On the contrary, the distance between their being and His Divine Being is infinite. And therefore it is impossible for the understanding to attain to God by means of creatures—whether they be celestial or earthly—since there is no proportionate similitude between God and creatures. No creature, then, can serve the understanding as a proportionate means to attain to God. Nor can anything that the imagination is able to imagine or that the understanding is capable of receiving and comprehending in this life be a proximate means of union with God. Neither can the understanding with its insight comprehend anything that is like Him, nor can the will taste any delight and sweetness comparable to that which is God, nor can the memory inject into the imagination any representations and images that mirror Him. It is clear, then, that none of these kinds of knowledge can lead the understanding straightway to God. In order to reach Him, the soul must go forward by not-understanding rather than by desiring to understand, by rendering itself blind and by entering into darkness rather than by opening its eyes.

Contemplation is a secret wisdom concerning God and is therefore called mystical theology

And thus *contemplation*—by which the understanding is given the most sublime knowledge of God—is called *mystical theology*, because it is a secret wisdom concerning God: it is a secret even to the very understanding that receives it. And this is why Dionysius [the Areopagite] calls this wisdom a ray of darkness.[3] Aristotle tells us that, as the eyes of the bat are in total darkness with respect to the sun, so is our understanding in total darkness to that which is brightest in God. And he adds that the more sublime and

[3][Cf. Pseudo-Dionysius, *On Mystical Theology*, I, 1.]

luminous the things of God are in themselves, the more obscure and unknown they are to us.[4] And the Apostle Paul confirms this when he says: The most sublime things of God are the least known to men [cf. I Cor. 2].

Chapter 12: Natural imaginary apprehensions cannot be a proportionate means to attain to union with God

What must first be discussed now is that internal bodily sense known as imagination and fancy. This internal sense must likewise be emptied of all those imaginative forms and apprehensions with which it may be naturally occupied; and we must show here how impossible it is for the soul to attain to union with God until it ceases to be actively preoccupied with them.

It must be known, then, that the sense of which we are here speaking in particular consists really of two internal bodily senses—imagination and fancy—which are subservient one to the other in due order. For the one thinks, as it were, by imagining, while the other uses the power of fancy to give form to the imagination (or to that which is imagined). All the things, then, which these senses can receive and construe are called imaginations and fantasies [or phantasms], that is, forms which are represented in these senses by means of corporeal images and figures. These can be of two kinds: they are supernatural if they can be and are represented in these senses *passively*; and these we call supernaturally induced imaginary visions. Others are natural, which means that the soul can produce them within itself *actively*, by its own operative ability, in the shape of forms, figures, and images. And thus to these two faculties pertains *meditation*, which is a discursive mental activity by means of images, forms, and figures that are produced imaginatively by these two senses; as happens, for example, when we picture in our imagination Christ crucified, or bound to the pillar, or at one of the other stations [of the Cross]. Or our imagination may envision God seated upon a throne with great majesty; or we may mediate imaginatively on the radiant beauty of the light of Glory, and so on. Now the soul must be emptied of all these imagined forms, figures, and images, and it must remain in darkness with respect to these [internal] senses if it is to attain to Divine union; for these [contents of the imagination] cannot serve as proportionate means of union with God any more than can the corporeal objects of the five external senses.

The reason of this is that the imagination cannot fashion or imagine anything beyond that which it has experienced by means of the external senses—that is, beyond that which it has seen with the eyes, heard with the ears, and so on. The most it can do is to compound likenesses of the things which it has seen, or heard, or felt; and these composites do not even possess as much substantial reality as the apprehensions that have been received by the external senses. For, though one may envision with the imagination palaces made of pearls and mountains of gold—because the sight of pearls and of gold is familiar to sense experience—all this is actually less than the essence

[4][Cf. Aristotle, *Metaphysics*, II, 1 (993b 9).]

of one small piece of gold or one single pearl, although to the imagination the composite appears greater in quantity and ideal splendor.

Those, therefore, who imagine they can find God beneath any of these figures, are very far indeed from approaching Him. For, though these forms and modes of meditation are necessary for beginners, so that by means of sensory perceptions they may feed and enkindle their souls with love—thus using them as remote means to union with God and spiritual repose—yet they must merely pass through them and never allow themselves to be detained by them. Just so the stairs of a staircase are merely the means to reach the top of the staircase and the room to which it leads. And if the person who climbs the stairs would want to stay on any one of them, he would never arrive at the top. Similarly, the soul which is to attain in this life to the union of that supreme repose and bliss must pass through and leave behind all the steps of these meditations, forms, and apprehensions; for they bear no resemblance or proportion to the goal to which they lead, which is God.

Many spiritual persons commit this grave error: they have started out—as it befits beginners—by trying to approach God by means of certain images, forms, and meditations; but now God wishes to use their collected spiritual strength to lead them further on to more spiritual—internal and invisible—treasures, by depriving them of all taste for the delights of discursive meditation; and they do not possess the required ability, courage, and knowledge that would enable them to detach themselves from those more tangible methods to which they have grown accustomed. And so they continually labor to retain them, finding, however, little or no sweetness in their efforts but rather experience an increasing aridity and weariness of soul. For, as we have pointed out, the soul enjoys no longer that food of sense but needs another kind of food, more delicate, more internal and less of the nature of sense, a food which imparts to the soul deep spiritual quietude and repose. And the more the soul learns to abide in the spiritual, the more comes to a halt the operation of its faculties in particular acts, since the soul becomes more and more collected in one undivided and pure act. And thus the faculties cease to work, even as the feet cease to move and come to a halt when the journey is ended. For if the movement of going were forever to continue, one would never arrive; and if there were nothing but end-less means, it is hard to see when and where there could ever be a fruition of the end and the goal.

As these souls, however, are unfamiliar with the mystery of this novel experience, they are apt to believe that they are idle and are doing nothing at all [in this state]; and they allow themselves no rest, but endeavor to continue their meditating and reasoning. The result is that they are filled with desolation and aridity, since they are trying to find sweetness where none can any longer be found. We may even say that the greater their endeavor, the smaller their progress, for the more they persist in the pursuit [of this method], the worse becomes their state of mind, because their soul is drawn farther and farther away from spiritual peace. By trying to retrace their steps and to do all over again what has already been done, they give up the greater for the less. To such persons, therefore, we must give the advice to learn how to abide in the quietude of the presence of God, attentively, patiently, and lovingly, paying no heed to the work of the imagination. For, as we have previously stated, here the faculties [of the soul] are at rest, or rather, they are working not actively, but passively, by receiving that which God works in them.

Part II, Book II

Chapter 9: This night darkens the spirit, but only in order to illuminate it. The mystical union

This blissful night darkens the spirit, but only in order to illuminate it afterwards with respect to all things; it humbles the spirit and makes it miserable, but only in order to raise it up and exalt it; it impoverishes the spirit and deprives it of every natural possession and affection, but only to enable it to rise, divinely, in unfettered spiritual freedom, to a perfect fruition of all things in Heaven and on earth. And, owing to its purity, the spirit tastes the sweetness of all things in a preeminently sublime manner.

We know that the children of Israel could not relish, in the desert, the sweetness of the manna—the bread of angels—solely because they had retained a single affectionate remembrance of the fleshpots and meals which they had tasted in Egypt. Similarly, the spirit cannot attain to the delights of the supernatural as long as it remains attached to any actual or habitual desire or to any particular object or apprehension of the understanding.

The light which is here imparted to the soul is truly a most sublime Divine light, which transcends every natural light, and which cannot be grasped by the understanding in a natural manner. If, then, the understanding is to be united with this light and is to become Divine in the state of perfection, it must first be purged and annihilated with respect to its natural light and led into darkness by means of this dark contemplation. When this has been done, the Divine light and illumination will take the place of the natural mode and manner of the soul's understanding.

Moreover, in order to attain to the union to which this dark night is leading it, the soul must be filled with a certain glorious splendor, to become disposed for its communion with God. Included herein are innumerable blessings and delights which far exceed all the abundance which the soul can naturally possess. For, as Isaiah says: "No eye has seen, and no ear has heard, nor has it ever entered into a human heart, what God has prepared for those who love Him" [Isa. 64:4]. And this is the reason why the soul must first become empty and poor in spirit and purged from all natural support, so that, in total poverty of spirit and liberated from the old man, it may be able to live that new and blessed life which is attained by means of this night, and which is the state of union with God. . . .

❀ *THE BHAGAVAD-GITA*

17. *The Way of Renunciation*

Among the most important of the Hindu Sacred Scriptures are the *Vedas*, the *Epics*, the *Puranas*, and the *Yoga-* and *Brahma-Sutras*. The *Bhagavad-Gita*, or "Song of the Lord" (contained in the epic *Mahabharata*) is surely the most celebrated text of Hinduism. Probably composed between 600 B.C. and 300 B.C., the *Gita* concerns the renunciation of the illusory world of the senses and the soul's return to the primordial Unity.

From *The Bhagavad-Gita*

CHAPTER 2: THE YOGA OF KNOWLEDGE

SANJAYA:

Then his eyes filled with tears, and his heart grieved and was bewildered with pity. And Sri Krishna spoke to him, saying:

SRI KRISHNA:

Arjuna, is this hour of battle the time for scruples and fancies? Are they worthy of you, who seek enlightenment? Any brave man who merely hopes for fame or heaven would despise them.

What is this weakness? It is beneath you. Is it for nothing men call you the foe-consumer? Shake off this cowardice, Arjuna. Stand up.

ARJUNA:

Bhisma and Drona are noble and ancient, worthy of the deepest reverence. How can I greet them with arrows, in battle? If I kill them, how can I ever enjoy my wealth, or any other pleasure? It will be cursed with blood-guilt. I would much rather spare them, and eat the bread of a beggar.

Which will be worse, to win this war, or to lose it? I scarcely know. Even the sons of Dhritarashtra stand in the enemy ranks. If we kill them, none of us will wish to live.

Is this real compassion that I feel, or only a delusion? My mind gropes about in darkness. I cannot see where my duty lies. Krishna, I beg you, tell me frankly and clearly what I ought to do. I am your disciple. I put myself into your hands. Show me the way.

> Not this world's kingdom,
> Supreme, unchallenged,
> No, nor the throne
> Of the gods in heaven,
> Could ease this sorrow
> That numbs my senses!

The Song of God: Bhagavad-Gita, tr. Swami Prabhavananda and Christopher Isherwood (New York: New American Library Inc., 1951). Reprinted by permission of Vedanta Society of Southern California, copyright holder. Also reprinted by permission of Laurence Pollinger, Ltd.

SANJAYA:

When Arjuna, the foe-consuming, the never-slothful, had spoken thus to Govinda, ruler of the senses, he added: 'I will not fight,' and was silent.

Then to him who thus sorrowed between the two armies, the ruler of the senses spoke, smiling:

SRI KRISHNA:

Your words are wise, Arjuna, but your sorrow is for nothing. The truly wise mourn neither for the living nor for the dead.

There was never a time when I did not exist, nor you, nor any of these kings. Nor is there any future in which we shall cease to be.

Just as the dweller in this body passes through childhood, youth and old age, so at death he merely passes into another kind of body. The wise are not deceived by that.

Feelings of heat and cold, pleasure and pain, are caused by the contact of the senses with their objects. They come and they go, never lasting long. You must accept them.

A serene spirit accepts pleasure and pain with an even mind, and is unmoved by either. He alone is worthy of immortality.

That which is non-existent can never come into being, and that which is can never cease to be. Those who have known the inmost Reality know also the nature of *is* and *is not*.

That Reality which pervades the universe is indestructible. No one has power to change the Changeless.

Bodies are said to die, but That which possesses the body is eternal. It cannot be limited, or destroyed. Therefore you must fight.

> Some say this Atman[1]
> Is slain, and others
> Call It the slayer:
> They know nothing.
> How can It slay
> Or who shall slay It?

> Know this Atman
> Unborn, undying,
> Never ceasing,
> Never beginning,
> Deathless, birthless,
> Unchanging for ever.
> How can It die
> The death of the body?

> Knowing It birthless,
> Knowing It deathless,
> Knowing It endless,

[1][Atman: "Self," known after enlightenment to be identical with Brahman, the supreme, impersonal principle of all things (according to Advaita, the best-known school of interpretation).]

For ever unchanging,
Dream not you do
The deed of the killer,
Dream not the power
Is yours to command it.

Worn-out garments
Are shed by the body:
Worn-out bodies
Are shed by the dweller
Within the body.
New bodies are donned
By the dweller, like garments.

Not wounded by weapons,
Not burned by fire,
Not dried by the wind,
Not wetted by water:
Such is the Atman,
Not dried, not wetted,
Not burned, not wounded,
Innermost element,
Everywhere, always,
Being of beings,
Changeless, eternal,
For ever and ever.

This Atman cannot be manifested to the senses, or thought about by the mind. It is not subject to modification. Since you know this, you should not grieve.

But if you should suppose this Atman to be subject to constant birth and death, even then you ought not to be sorry.

Death is certain for the born. Rebirth is certain for the dead. You should not grieve for what is unavoidable.

Before birth, beings are not manifest to our human senses. In the interim between birth and death, they are manifest. At death they return to the unmanifest again. What is there in all this to grieve over?

There are some who have actually looked upon the Atman, and understood It, in all Its wonder. Others can only speak of It as wonderful beyond their understanding. Others know of Its wonder by hearsay. And there are others who are told about It and do not understand a word.

He Who dwells within all living bodies remains for ever indestructible. Therefore, you should never mourn for any one.

Even if you consider this from the standpoint of your own caste-duty, you ought not to hesitate; for, to a warrior, there is nothing nobler than a righteous war. Happy are the warriors to whom a battle such as this comes: it opens a door to heaven.

But if you refuse to fight this righteous war, you will be turning aside from your duty. You will be a sinner, and disgraced. People will speak ill of you throughout the ages. To a man who values his honour, that is surely worse than death. The warrior-chiefs will believe it was fear that drove you from the battle; you will be despised by those who have admired you so long. Your enemies, also, will slander your courage. They will use the words which should never be spoken. What could be harder to bear than that?

Die, and you win heaven. Conquer, and you enjoy the earth. Stand up now, son of Kunti, and resolve to fight. Realize that pleasure and pain, gain and loss, victory and defeat, are all one and the same: then go into battle. Do this and you cannot commit any sin.

I have explained to you the true nature of the Atman. Now listen to the method of Karma Yoga.[2] If you can understand and follow it, you will be able to break the chains of desire which bind you to your actions.

In this yoga, even the abortive attempt is not wasted. Nor can it produce a contrary result. Even a little practise of this yoga will save you from the terrible wheel of rebirth and death.

In this yoga, the will is directed singly toward one ideal. When a man lacks this discrimination, his will wanders in all directions, after innumerable aims. Those who lack discrimination may quote the letter of the scripture, but they are really denying its inner truth. They are full of worldly desires, and hungry for the rewards of heaven. They use beautiful figures of speech. They teach elaborate rituals which are supposed to obtain pleasure and power for those who perform them. But, actually, they understand nothing except the law of Karma,[3] that chains men to rebirth.

Those whose discrimination is stolen away by such talk grow deeply attached to pleasure and power. And so they are unable to develop that concentration of the will which leads a man to absorption in God.

The Vedas teach us about the three gunas[4] and their functions. You, Arjuna, must overcome the three gunas. You must be free from the pairs of opposites. Poise your mind in tranquility. Take care neither to acquire nor to hoard. Be established in the consciousness of the Atman, always.

When the whole country is flooded, the reservoir becomes superfluous. So, to the illumined seer, the Vedas are all superfluous.

You have the right to work, but for the work's sake only. You have no right to the fruits of work. Desire for the fruits of work must never be your motive in working. Never give way to laziness, either.

Perform every action with your heart fixed on the Supreme Lord. Renounce attachment to the fruits. Be even-tempered in success and failure; for it is this evenness of temper which is meant by yoga.

[2][Karma Yoga: Way or path of selfless action.]
[3][Law of Karma: the law by which every deed or action (karma) eventually produces its effects, either in this life or a future one.]
[4][The three gunas: strands or qualities of life (intelligence, emotion, and insensibility) more or less present in all men.]

Work done with anxiety about results is far inferior to work done without such anxiety, in the calm of self-surrender. Seek refuge in the knowledge of Brahman. They who work selfishly for results are miserable.

In the calm of self-surrender you can free yourself from the bondage of virtue and vice during this very life. Devote yourself, therefore, to reaching union with Brahman. To unite the heart with Brahman and then to act: that is the secret of non-attached work. In the calm of self-surrender, the seers renounce the fruits of their actions, and so reach enlightenment. Then they are free from the bondage of rebirth, and pass to that state which is beyond all evil.

When your intellect has cleared itself of its delusions, you will become indifferent to the results of all action, present or future. At present, your intellect is bewildered by conflicting interpretations of the scriptures. When it can rest, steady and undistracted, in contemplation of the Atman, then you will reach union with the Atman.

ARJUNA:

Krishna, how can one identify a man who is firmly established and absorbed in Brahman? In what manner does an illumined soul speak? How does he sit? How does he walk?

SRI KRISHNA:
He knows bliss in the Atman
And wants nothing else.
Cravings torment the heart:
He renounces cravings.
I call him illumined.

Not shaken by adversity,
Not hankering after happiness:
Free from fear, free from anger,
Free from the things of desire.
I call him a seer, and illumined.
The bonds of his flesh are broken.
He is lucky, and does not rejoice:
He is unlucky, and does not weep.
I call him illumined.

The tortoise can draw in his legs:
The seer can draw in his senses.
I call him illumined.

The abstinent run away from what they desire
But carry their desires with them:
When a man enters Reality,
He leaves his desires behind him.

Even a mind that knows the path
Can be dragged from the path:
The senses are so unruly.
But he controls the senses
And recollects the mind
And fixes it on me.
I call him illumined.

Thinking about sense-objects
Will attach you to sense-objects;
Grow attached, and you become addicted;
Thwart your addiction, it turns to anger;
Be angry, and you confuse your mind;
Confuse your mind, you forget the lesson of experience;
Forget experience, you lose discrimination;
Lose discrimination, and you miss life's only purpose.

When he has no lust, no hatred,
A man walks safely among the things of lust and hatred.
To obey the Atman
Is his peaceful joy:
Sorrow melts
Into that clear peace:
His quiet mind
Is soon established in peace.

The uncontrolled mind
Does not guess that the Atman is present:
How can it meditate?
Without meditation, where is peace?
Without peace, where is happiness?

The wind turns a ship
From its course upon the waters:
The wandering winds of the senses
Cast man's mind adrift
And turn his better judgment from its course.
When a man can still the senses
I call him illumined.
The recollected mind is awake
In the knowledge of the Atman
Which is dark night to the ignorant:
The ignorant are awake in their sense-life
Which they think is daylight:
To the seer it is darkness.

Water flows continually into the ocean
But the ocean is never disturbed:
Desire flows into the mind of the seer
But he is never disturbed.
The seer knows peace:
The man who stirs up his own lusts
Can never know peace.
He knows peace who has forgotten desire.
He lives without craving:
Free from ego, free from pride.

This is the state of enlightenment in Brahman:
A man does not fall back from it
Into delusion.
Even at the moment of death
He is alive in that enlightenment:
Brahman and he are one.

CHAPTER 3: KARMA YOGA

ARJUNA:
But, Krishna, if you consider knowledge of Brahman superior to any
sort of action, why are you telling me to do these terrible deeds?

Your statements seem to contradict each other. They confuse my mind.
Tell me one definite way of reaching the highest good.

SRI KRISHNA:
I have already told you that, in this world, aspirants may find enlightenment by two different paths. For the contemplative is the path of knowledge:
for the active is the path of selfless action.

Freedom from activity is never achieved by abstaining from action.
Nobody can become perfect by merely ceasing to act. In fact, nobody can
ever rest from his activity even for a moment. All are helplessly forced to
act, by the gunas.

A man who renounces certain physical actions but still lets his mind
dwell on the objects of his sensual desire, is deceiving himself. He can only
be called a hypocrite. The truly admirable man controls his senses by the
power of his will. All his actions are disinterested. All are directed along
the path to union with Brahman.

Activity is better than inertia. Act, but with self-control. If you are
lazy, you cannot even sustain your own body.

The world is imprisoned in its own activity, except when actions are
performed as worship of God. Therefore you must perform every action sacra-
mentally, and be free from all attachments to results.

In the beginning
The Lord of beings
Created all men,
To each his duty.
'Do this,' He said,
'And you shall prosper.
Duty well done
Fulfils desire
Like Kamadhenu[5]
The wish-fulfiller.'
'Doing of duty
Honours the devas[6]:
To you the devas
In turn will be gracious:
Each honouring other,
Man reaches the Highest.
Please the devas:
Your prayer will be granted.'
But he who enjoys the devas' bounty
Showing no thanks,
He thieves from the devas.

Pious men eat
What the gods leave over
After the offering:
Thus they are sinless.
But those ungodly
Cooking good food
For the greed of their stomachs
Sin as they eat it.
Food quickens the life-sperm:
Food grows from the rainfall
Called down out of heaven
By sacrifice offered:
Sacrifice speaks
Through the act of the ritual.
This is the ritual
Taught by the sacred
Scriptures that spring
From the lips of the Changeless:
Know therefore that Brahman
The all-pervading
Is dwelling for ever
Within this ritual.

[5][Kamadhenu: a legendary cow.]
[6][Devas: inhabitants of heaven, gods.]

If a man plays no part
In the acts thus appointed
His living is evil
His joy is in lusting.
Know this, O Prince:
His life is for nothing.

But when a man has found delight and satisfaction and peace in the Atman, then he is no longer obliged to perform any kind of action. He has nothing to gain in this world by action, and nothing to lose by refraining from action. He is independent of everybody and everything. Do your duty, always; but without attachment. That is how a man reaches the ultimate Truth; by working without anxiety about results. In fact, Janaka[7] and many others reached enlightenment, simply because they did their duty in this spirit. Your motive in working should be to set others, by your example, on the path of duty.

Whatever a great man does, ordinary people will imitate; they follow his example. Consider me: I am not bound by any sort of duty. There is nothing, in all the three worlds, which I do not already possess; nothing I have yet to acquire. But I go on working, nevertheless. If I did not continue to work untiringly as I do, mankind would still follow me, no matter where I led them. Suppose I were to stop? They would all be lost. The result would be caste-mixture and universal destruction.

The ignorant work
For the fruit of their action:
The wise must work also
Without desire
Pointing man's feet
To the path of his duty.

Let the wise beware
Lest they bewilder
The minds of the ignorant
Hungry for action:
Let them show by example
How work is holy
When the heart of the worker
Is fixed on the Highest.

Every action is really performed by the gunas. Man, deluded by his egoism, thinks: 'I am the doer.' But he who has the true insight into the operations of the gunas and their various functions, knows that when senses attach themselves to objects, gunas are merely attaching themselves to gunas. Knowing this, he does not become attached to his actions.

[7][A Hindu saint.]

The illumined soul must not create confusion in the minds of the ignorant by refraining from work. The ignorant, in their delusion, identify the Atman with the gunas. They become tied to the senses and the action of the senses.

Shake off this fever of ignorance. Stop hoping for worldly rewards. Fix your mind on the Atman. Be free from the sense of ego. Dedicate all your actions to me. Then go forward and fight.

If a man keeps following my teaching with faith in his heart, and does not make mental reservations, he will be released from the bondage of his karma. But those who scorn my teaching, and do not follow it, are lost. They are without spiritual discrimination. All their knowledge is a delusion.

Even a wise man acts according to the tendencies of his own nature. All living creatures follow their tendencies. What use is any external restraint? The attraction and aversion which the senses feel for different objects are natural. But you must not give way to such feelings; they are obstacles.

It is better to do your own duty, however imperfectly, than to assume the duties of another person, however successfully. Prefer to die doing your own duty: the duty of another will bring you into great spiritual danger.

ARJUNA:

Krishna, what is it that makes a man do evil, even against his own will; under compulsion, as it were?

SRI KRISHNA:

The rajo-guna[8] has two faces,
Rage and lust: the ravenous, the deadly:
Recognize these: they are your enemies.
Smoke hides fire,
Dust hides a mirror,
The womb hides the embryo:
By lust the Atman is hidden.
Lust hides the Atman in its hungry flames,
The wise man's faithful foe.
Intellect, senses and mind
Are fuel to its fire:
Thus it deludes
The dweller in the body,
Bewildering his judgment.

Therefore, Arjuna, you must first control your senses, then kill this evil thing which obstructs discriminative knowledge and realization of the Atman.

The senses are said to be higher than the sense-objects. The intelligent will is higher than the mind. What is higher than the intelligent will? The Atman Itself.

[8][Rajo-guna: guna of passion.]

You must know Him who is above the intelligent will. Get control of the mind through spiritual discrimination. Then destroy your elusive enemy, who wears the form of lust.

CHAPTER 11: THE VISION OF GOD IN HIS UNIVERSAL FORM

ARJUNA:

By your grace, you have taught me the truth about the Atman. Your words are mystic and sublime. They have dispelled my ignorance.

From you, whose eyes are like the lotus-flowers, I have learnt in detail of the origin and dissolution of creatures, and of your own infinite glory.

O Supreme Lord, you are as you describe yourself to be: I do not doubt that. Nevertheless, I long to behold your divine Form.

If you find me worthy of that vision, then reveal to me, O Master of yogis, your changeless Atman.

SRI KRISHNA:

Behold, O Prince, my divine forms, hundreds upon thousands, various in kind, various in colour and in shape.

Behold the Adityas, and the Vasus, and the Rudras, and the Aswins, and the Maruts.[9] Behold many wonders, O Descendant of Bharata, that no man has seen before.

O conqueror of sloth, this very day you shall behold the whole universe with all things animate and inert made one within this body of mine. And whatever else you desire to see, that you shall see also.

But you cannot see me thus with those human eyes. Therefore, I give you divine sight. Behold—this is my yoga power.

SANJAYA:

Then, O King, when he had spoken these words, Sri Krishna, Master of all yogis, revealed to Arjuna his transcendent, divine Form, speaking from innumerable mouths, seeing with a myriad eyes, of many marvellous aspects, adorned with countless divine ornaments, brandishing all kinds of heavenly weapons, wearing celestial garlands and the raiment of paradise, anointed with perfumes of heavenly fragrance, full of revelations, resplendent, boundless, of ubiquitous regard.

Suppose a thousand suns should rise together into the sky: such is the glory of the Shape of Infinite God.

Then the son of Pandu beheld the entire universe, in all its multitudinous diversity, lodged as one being within the body of the God of gods.

Then was Arjuna, that lord of mighty riches, overcome with wonder. His hair stood erect. He bowed low before God in adoration, and clasped his hands, and spoke:

[9][A group of lesser gods.]

ARJUNA:

Ah, my God, I see all gods within your body;
Each in his degree, the multitude of creatures;
See Lord Brahma[10] throned upon the lotus;
See all the sages, and the holy serpents.

Universal Form, I see you without limit,
Infinite of arms, eyes, mouths and bellies—
See, and find no end, midst, or beginning.

Crowned with diadems, you wield the mace and
    discus,
Shining every way—the eyes shrink from your
    splendour
Brilliant like the sun; like fire, blazing, boundless.

You are all we know, supreme, beyond man's
    measure,
This world's sure-set plinth and refuge never shaken,
Guardian of eternal law, life's Soul undying.
Birthless, deathless; yours the strength titanic,
Million-armed, the sun and moon your eyeballs,
Fiery-faced, you blast the world to ashes,

Fill the sky's four corners, span the chasm
Sundering heaven from earth. Superb and awful
Is your Form that makes the three worlds tremble.

Into you, the companies of devas
Enter with clasped hands, in dread and wonder.
Crying 'Peace,' the Rishis and the Siddhas
Sing your praise with hymns of adoration.

Adityas and Rudras, Sadhyas, Viswas, Aswins,
Maruts and Vasus, the hosts of the Gandharvas,
Yakshas, Asuras, Ushmapas and Siddhas—
All of them gaze upon you in amazement.

At the sight of this, your Shape stupendous
Full of mouths and eyes, feet, thighs and bellies,
Terrible with fangs, O mighty master,
All the worlds are fear-struck, even as I am.

---

[10][Brahma: the Creator; in later Hinduism the first person of the Trimurti or Hindu
Trinity, including also Vishnu the Preserver and Shiva the Destroyer.]

When I see you, Vishnu, omnipresent,
Shouldering the sky, in hues of rainbow,
With your mouths agape and flame-eyes staring—
All my peace is gone; my heart is troubled.

Now with frightful tusks your mouths are gnashing,
Flaring like the fires of Doomsday morning—
North, south, east and west seem all confounded—
Lord of devas, world's abode, have mercy!

Dhritarashtra's offspring, many a monarch,
Bhisma, Drona, and the son of Karna,
There they go—with our own warriors also—
Hurrying to your jaws, wide-fanged and hideous—
See where mangled heads lie crushed between them!

Swift as many rivers streaming to the ocean,
Rush the heroes to your fiery gullets:
Mothlike, to meet the flame of their destruction,
Headlong these plunge into you, and perish.

Licking with your burning tongues, devouring
All the worlds, you probe the heights of heaven
With intolerable beams, O Vishnu.

Tell me who you are, and were from the beginning,
You of aspect grim, O God of gods, be gracious.
Take my homage, Lord. From me your ways are
        hidden.
> SRI KRISHNA:
>   I am come as Time, the waster of the peoples,
> Ready for that hour that ripens to their ruin.
> All these hosts must die; strike, stay your hand—no
>   matter.

Therefore, strike. Win kingdom, wealth and glory.
Arjuna, arise, O ambidextrous bowman.
Seem to slay. By me these men are slain already.

You but smite the dead, the doom-devoted heroes,
Jayadratha, Drona, Bhisma, Karna.
Fight, and have no fear. The foe is yours to conquer.

> SANJAYA:
>   After Arjuna had heard these words of the Lord Krishna, he folded
> his palms and bowed down, trembling. Prostrating himself, with great fear,
> he addressed Krishna once more in a choking voice:

ARJUNA:

Well it is the world delights to do you honour!
At the sight of you, O master of the senses,
Demons scatter every way in terror,
And the hosts of Siddhas bow adoring.

Mightiest, how should they indeed withhold their
  homage?
O Prime Cause of all, even Brahma the Beginner—
Deathless, world's abode, the Lord of devas,
You are what is not, what is, and what transcends
  them.

You are first and highest in heaven, O ancient Spirit.
It is within you the cosmos rests in safety.
You are known and knower, goal of all our striving.
Endless in your change, you body forth creation.

Lord of fire and death, of wind and moon and
  waters,
Father of the born, and this world's father's Father.
Hail, all hail to you—a thousand salutations.

Take our salutations, Lord, from every quarter,
Infinite of might and boundless in your glory,
You are all that is, since everywhere we find you.

Carelessly I called you 'Krishna' and 'my comrade,'
Took undying God for friend and fellow-mortal,
Overbold with love, unconscious of your greatness.

Often I would jest, familiar, as we feasted
Midst the throng, or walked, or lay at rest together:
Did my words offend? Forgive me, Lord Eternal.

Author of this world, the unmoved and the moving,
You alone are fit for worship, you the highest.
Where in the three worlds shall any find your equal?

Therefore I bow down, prostrate and ask for pardon:
Now forgive me, God, as friend forgives his
  comrade,
Father forgives son, and man his dearest lover.

I have seen what no man ever saw before me:
Deep is my delight, but still my dread is greater.
Show me now your other Form, O Lord, be gracious.

Thousand-membered, Universal Being,
Show me now the Shape I knew of old, the four-
    armed,
With your diadem and mace, the discus-bearer.

SRI KRISHNA:

This my Form of fire, world-wide, supreme,
    primeval,
Manifest by yoga power, alone of all men,
Arjuna, I showed to you because I love you.

Neither through sacrifice, nor study of the Vedas,
Nor strict austerities, nor alms, nor rituals,
Shall this my Shape be viewed by any mortal,
Other than you, O hero of the Pandus.

Now you need fear no more, nor be bewildered,
Seeing me so terrible. Be glad, take courage.
Look, here am I, transformed, as first you knew me.

SANJAYA:

Having spoken thus to Arjuna, Krishna appeared in his own shape.
The Great-Souled One, assuming once more his mild and pleasing form,
brought peace to him in his terror.

ARJUNA:

O Krishna, now I see your pleasant human form, I am myself again.

SRI KRISHNA:

That Shape of mine which you may have seen is very difficult to
behold. Even the devas themselves are always longing to see it. Neither by
study of the Vedas, nor by austerities, nor by alms-giving, nor by rituals
can I be seen as you have seen me. But by single-minded and intense devotion,
that Form of mine may be completely known, and seen, and entered into,
O Consumer of the foe.

Whosoever works for me alone, makes me his only goal and is devoted
to me, free from attachment, and without hatred toward any creature—that
man, O Prince, shall enter into me.

CHAPTER 12: THE YOGA OF DEVOTION

ARJUNA:

Some worship you with steadfast love. Others worship God the unmanifest and changeless. Which kind of devotee has the greater understanding
of yoga?

SRI KRISHNA:

Those whose minds are fixed on me in steadfast love, worshipping
me with absolute faith. I consider them to have the greater understanding
of yoga.

As for those others, the devotees of God the unmanifest, indefinable and changeless, they worship that which is omnipresent, constant, eternal, beyond thought's compass, never to be moved. They hold all the senses in check. They are tranquil-minded, and devoted to the welfare of humanity. They see the Atman in every creature. They also will certainly come to me.

But the devotees of the unmanifest have a harder task, because the unmanifest is very difficult for embodied souls to realize.

> Quickly I come
> To those who offer me
> Every action,
> Worship me only,
> Their dearest delight,
> With devotion undaunted.

> Because they love me
> These are my bondsmen
> And I shall save them
> From mortal sorrow
> And all the waves
> Of Life's deathly ocean.

> Be absorbed in me,
> Lodge your mind in me:
> Thus you shall dwell in me,
> Do not doubt it,
> Here and hereafter.

If you cannot become absorbed in me, then try to reach me by repeated concentration. If you lack the strength to concentrate, then devote yourself to works which will please me. For, by working for my sake only, you will achieve perfection. If you cannot even do this, then surrender yourself to me altogether. Control the lusts of your heart, and renounce the fruits of every action.

Concentration which is practised with discernment is certainly better than the mechanical repetition of a ritual or a prayer. Absorption in God—to live with Him and be one with Him always—is even better than concentration. But renunciation brings instant peace to the spirit.

A man should not hate any living creature. Let him be friendly and compassionate to all. He must free himself from the delusion of 'I' and 'mine.' He must accept pleasure and pain with equal tranquillity. He must be forgiving, ever-contented, self-controlled, united constantly with me in his meditation. His resolve must be unshakable. He must be dedicated to me in intellect and in mind. Such a devotee is dear to me.

He neither molests his fellow men, nor allows himself to become disturbed by the world. He is no longer swayed by joy and envy, anxiety and fear. Therefore he is dear to me.

He is pure, and independent of the body's desire. He is able to deal with the unexpected: prepared for everything, unperturbed by anything. He is neither vain nor anxious about the results of his actions. Such a devotee is dear to me.

He does not desire or rejoice in what is pleasant. He does not dread what is unpleasant, or grieve over it. He remains unmoved by good or evil fortune. Such a devotee is dear to me.

His attitude is the same toward friend and foe. He is indifferent to honour and insult, heat and cold, pleasure and pain. He is free from attachment. He values praise and blame equally. He can control his speech. He is content with whatever he gets. His home is everywhere and nowhere. His mind is fixed upon me, and his heart is full of devotion. He is dear to me.

This true wisdom I have taught will lead you to immortality. The faithful practise it with devotion, taking me for their highest aim. To me they surrender heart and mind. They are exceedingly dear to me.

✳ C. D. BROAD

18. *Religious Experience: An Analysis*

C. D. Broad (born 1887) was Knightbridge Professor of Moral Philosophy at Cambridge University from 1933 to 1953. Though Broad does not have a philosophical "system," his contributions lie in a variety of fields including theory of knowledge, ethics, philosophy of science, and psychical research. Among his most important works are *Scientific Thought*, *Five Types of Ethical Theory*, and *The Mind and Its Place in Nature*.

From *Religion, Philosophy and Psychical Research*

Section II: Religion

Arguments for the Existence of God

. . . I shall confine myself to specifically religious experience and the argument for the existence of God which has been based on it.

This argument differs in the following important respect from the other two empirical types of argument. The Argument from Design and the arguments from ethical premises start from facts which are common to every one. But some people seem to be almost wholly devoid of any specifically religious experience; and among those who have it the differences of kind

C. D. Broad, *Religion, Philosophy and Psychical Research* (London: Routledge & Kegan Paul, 1953). Reprinted by permission of Routledge & Kegan Paul, Ltd., and Humanities Press, Inc., New York.

and degree are enormous. Founders of religions and saints, e.g., often claim to have been in direct contact with God, to have seen and spoken with Him, and so on. An ordinary religious man would certainly not make any such claim, though he might say that he had had experiences which assured him of the existence and presence of God. So the first thing that we have to notice is that capacity for religious experience is in certain respects like an ear for music. There are a few people who are unable to recognize and distinguish the simplest tune. But they are in a minority, like the people who have absolutely no kind of religious experience. Most people have some slight appreciation of music. But the differences of degree in this respect are enormous, and those who have not much gift for music have to take the statements of accomplished musicians very largely on trust. Let us, then, compare tone-deaf persons to those who have no recognizable religious experience at all; the ordinary followers of a religion to men who have some taste for music but can neither appreciate the more difficult kinds nor compose; highly religious men and saints to persons with an exceptionally fine ear for music who may yet be unable to compose it; and the founders of religions to great musical composers, such as Bach and Beethoven.

This analogy is, of course, incomplete in certain important respects. Religious experience raises three problems, which are different though closely interconnected. (i) What is the *psychological analysis* of religious experience? Does it contain factors which are present also in certain experiences which are not religious? Does it contain any factor which never occurs in any other kind of experience? If it contains no such factor, but is a blend of elements each of which can occur separately or in non-religious experiences, its psychological peculiarity must consist in the characteristic way in which these elements are blended in it. Can this peculiar structural feature of religious experience be indicated and described? (ii) What are the *genetic and causal conditions* of the existence of religious experience? Can we trace the origin and development of the disposition to have religious experiences (*a*) in the human race, and (*b*) in each individual? Granted that the disposition is present in nearly all individuals at the present time, can we discover and state the variable conditions which call it into activity on certain occasions and leave it in abeyance on others? (iii) Part of the content of religious experience is alleged knowledge or well-founded belief about the nature of reality, e.g., that we are dependent on a being who loves us and whom we ought to worship, that values are somehow conserved in spite of the chances and changes of the material world at the mercy of which they seem *prima facie* to be, and so on. Therefore there is a third problem. Granted that religious experience exists, that it has such-and-such a history and conditions, that it seems vitally important to those who have it, and that it produces all kinds of effects which would not otherwise happen, is it *veridical*? Are the claims to knowledge or well-founded belief about the nature of reality, which are an integral part of the experience, *true or probable*? Now in the case of musical experience, there are analogies to the psychological problem and to the genetic or causal problem, but there is no analogy to the epistemological problem of validity. For, so far as I am aware, no part of the content of musical experience is alleged knowledge about the nature of reality; and therefore no question of its being veridical or delusive can arise.

Since both musical experience and religious experience certainly exist, any theory of the universe which was incompatible with their existence would be false, and any theory which failed to show the connexion between their existence and the other facts about reality would be inadequate. So far the two kinds of experience are in exactly the same position. But a theory which answers to the condition that it allows of the *existence* of religious experience and indicates the *connexion* between its existence and other facts about reality may leave the question as to its *validity* quite unanswered. Or, alternatively, it may throw grave doubt on its cognitive claims, or else it may tend to support them. Suppose, e.g., that it could be shown that religious experience contains no elements which are not factors in other kinds of experience. Suppose further it could be shown that this particular combination of factors tends to originate and to be activated only under certain conditions which are known to be very commonly productive of false beliefs held with strong conviction. Then a satisfactory answer to the question of psychological analysis and causal antecedents would have tended to answer the epistemological question of validity in the negative. On the other hand, it might be that the only theory which would satisfactorily account for the origin of the religious disposition and for the occurrence of actual religious experiences under certain conditions was a theory which allowed some of the cognitive claims made by religious experience to be true or probable. Thus the three problems, though entirely distinct from each other, may be very closely connected; and it is the existence of the third problem in connexion with religious experience which puts it, for the present purpose, in a different category from musical experience.

In spite of this essential difference the analogy is not to be despised, for it brings out at least one important point. If a man who had no ear for music were to give himself airs on that account, and were to talk *de haut en bas* about those who can appreciate music and think it highly important, we should regard him, not as an advanced thinker, but as a self-satisfied Philistine. And, even if he did not do this but only propounded theories about the nature and causation of musical experience, we might think it reasonable to feel very doubtful whether his theories would be adequate or correct. In the same way, when persons without religious experience regard themselves as being *on that ground* superior to those who have it, their attitude must be treated as merely silly and offensive. Similarly, any theories about religious experience constructed by persons who have little or none of their own should be regarded with grave suspicion. (For that reason it would be unwise to attach very much weight to anything that the present writer may say on this subject.)

On the other hand, we must remember that the possession of a great capacity for religious experience, like the possession of a great capacity for musical appreciation and composition, is no guarantee of high general intelligence. A man may be a saint or a magnificent musician and yet have very little common sense, very little power of accurate introspection or of seeing causal connexions, and scarcely any capacity for logical criticism. He may also be almost as ignorant about other aspects of reality as the non-musical or non-religious man is about musical or religious experience. If such a man starts to theorize about music or religion, his theories may be quite as absurd, though in a different way, as those made by persons who are devoid of musical or religious experience. Fortunately it happens that some religious mystics of a high order have been extremely good at introspecting and describing their own experiences. And some highly religious persons have had very great critical and philosophical abilities. St. Teresa is an example of the first, and St. Thomas Aquinas of the second.

Now I think it must be admitted that, if we compare and contrast the statements made by religious mystics of various times, races, and religions, we find a common nucleus combined with very great differences of detail. Of course the interpretations which they have put on their experiences are much more varied than the experiences themselves. It is obvious that the interpretations will depend in a large measure on the traditional religious beliefs in which various mystics have been brought up. I think that such traditions probably act in two different ways.

(i) The tradition no doubt affects the theoretical interpretation of experiences which would have taken place even if the mystic had been brought up in a different tradition. A feeling of unity with the rest of the universe will be interpreted very differently by a Christian who has been brought up to believe in a personal God and by a Hindu mystic who has been trained in a quite different metaphysical tradition.

(ii) The traditional beliefs, on the other hand, probably determine many of the details of the experience itself. A Roman Catholic mystic may have visions of the Virgin and the saints, whilst a Protestant mystic pretty certainly will not.

Thus the relations between the experiences and the traditional beliefs are highly complex. Presumably the outlines of the belief are determined by the experience. Then the details of the belief are fixed for a certain place and period by the special peculiarities of the experiences had by the founder of a certain religion. These beliefs then become traditional in that religion. Thenceforth they in part determine the details of the experiences had by subsequent mystics of that religion, and still more do they determine the interpretations which these mystics will put upon their experiences. Therefore, when a set of religious beliefs has once been established, it no doubt tends to produce experiences which can plausibly be taken as evidence for it. If it is a tradition in a certain religion that one can communicate with saints, mystics of that religion will seem to see and to talk with saints in their mystical visions; and this fact will be taken as further evidence for the belief that one can communicate with saints.

Much the same double process of causation takes place in sense-perception. On the one hand, the beliefs and expectations which we have at any moment largely determine what *interpretation* we shall put on a certain sensation which we should in any case have had then. On the other hand, our beliefs and expectations do to some extent determine and modify some of the sensible characteristics of the *sensa themselves*. When I am thinking only of diagrams a certain visual stimulus may produce a sensation of a sensibly flat sensum; but a precisely similar stimulus may produce a sensation of a sensibly solid sensum when I am thinking of solid objects.

Such explanations, however, plainly do not account for the first origin of religious beliefs, or for the features which are common to the religious experiences of persons of widely different times, races, and traditions.

Now, when we find that there are certain experiences which, though never very frequent in a high degree of intensity, have happened in a high degree among a few men at all times and places; and when we find that, in spite of differences in detail which we can explain, they involve certain fundamental conditions which are common and peculiar to them; two alternatives are open to us. (i) We may suppose that these men are in contact with an aspect of reality which is not revealed to ordinary persons in their everyday experience. And we may suppose that the characteristics which they agree in ascribing to reality on the basis of these experiences probably do belong to it. Or (ii) we may suppose that they are all subject to a delusion from which other men are free. In order to illustrate these alternatives it will be useful to consider three partly analogous cases, two of which are real and the third imaginary.

(*a*) Most of the detailed facts which biologists tell us about the minute structure and changes in cells can be perceived only by persons who have had a long training in the use of the microscope. In this case we believe that the agreement among trained microscopists really does correspond to facts which untrained persons cannot perceive. (*b*) Persons of all races who habitually drink alcohol to excess eventually have perceptual experiences in which they seem to themselves to see snakes or rats crawling about their rooms or beds. In this case we believe that this agreement among drunkards is merely a uniform hallucination. (*c*) Let us now imagine a race of beings who can walk about and touch things but cannot see. Suppose that eventually a few of them developed the power of sight. All that they might tell their still blind friends about colour would be wholly unintelligible to and unverifiable by the latter. But they would also be able to tell their blind friends a great deal about what the latter would feel if they were to walk in certain directions. These statements would be verified. This would not, of course, *prove* to the blind ones that the unintelligible statements about colour correspond to certain aspects of the world which they cannot perceive. But it would show that the seeing persons had a source of additional information about matters which the blind ones could understand and test for themselves. It would not be unreasonable then for the blind ones to believe that probably the seeing ones are also able to perceive other aspects of reality which they are describing correctly when they make their unintelligible statements containing colour-names. The question then is whether it is reasonable to regard the agreement between the experiences of religious mystics as more like the agreement among trained microscopists about the minute structure of cells, or as more like the agreement among habitual drunkards about the infestation of their rooms by pink rats or snakes, or as more like the agreement about colours which the seeing men would express in their statements to the blind men.

Why do we commonly believe that habitual excess of alcohol is a cause of a uniform delusion and not a source of additional information? The main reason is as follows. The things which drunkards claim to perceive are not fundamentally different in kind from the things that other people perceive. We have all seen rats and snakes, though the rats have generally been grey or brown and not pink. Moreover the drunkard claims that the rats and snakes which he sees are literally present in his room and on his bed, in the same sense in which his bed is in his room and his quilt is on his bed. Now we may fairly argue as follows. Since these are the sort of things which we could see if they were there, the fact that we cannot see them makes it highly probable that they are not there. Again, we know what kinds of perceptible effect would generally follow from the presence in a room of such things as rats or snakes. We should expect fox-terriers or mongooses to show traces of excitement, and cheese to be nibbled, corn to disappear from bins, and so on. We find that no such effects are observed in the bedrooms of persons suffering from *delirium tremens.* It therefore seems reasonable to conclude that the agreement among drunkards is a sign, not of a revelation, but of a delusion.

Now the assertions in which religious mystics agree are not such that they conflict with what we can perceive with our senses. They are about the structure and organization of the world as a whole and about the relations of men to the rest of it. And they have so little in common with the facts of daily life that there is not much chance of direct collision. I think that there is only one important point on which there is conflict. Nearly all mystics seem to be agreed that time and change and unchanging duration are unreal or extremely superficial, whilst these seem to plain men to be the most fundamental features of the world. But we must admit, on the one hand, that these temporal characteristics present very great philosophical difficulties and puzzles when we reflect upon them. On the other hand, we may well suppose that the mystic finds it impossible to state clearly in ordinary language what it is that he experiences about the facts which underlie the appearance of time and change and duration. Therefore it is not difficult to allow that what we experience as the temporal aspect of reality corresponds in some sense to certain facts, and yet that these facts appear to us in so distorted a form in our ordinary experience that a person who sees them more accurately and directly might refuse to apply temporal names to them.

Let us next consider why we feel fairly certain that the agreement among trained microscopists about the minute structure of cells expresses an objective fact, although we cannot get similar experiences. One reason is that we have learned enough, from simpler cases of visual perception, about the laws of optics to know that the arrangement of lenses in a microscope is such that it will reveal minute structure, which is otherwise invisible, and will not simply create optical delusions. Another reason is that we know of other cases in which trained persons can detect things which untrained people will overlook, and that in many cases the existence of these things can be verified by indirect methods. Probably most of us have experienced such results of training in our own lives.

Now religious experience is not in nearly such a strong position as this. We do not know much about the laws which govern its occurrence and determine its variations. No doubt there are certain standard methods of training and meditation which tend to produce mystical experiences. These have been elaborated to some extent by certain Western mystics and to a very much greater extent by Eastern Yogis. But I do not think that we can see here, as we can in the case of microscopes and the training which is required to make the best use of them, any conclusive reason why these methods should produce veridical rather than delusive experiences. Uniform methods of training and meditation would be likely to produce more or less similar experiences, whether these experiences were largely veridical or wholly delusive.

Is there any analogy between the facts about religious experience and the fable about the blind men some of whom gained the power of sight? It might be said that many ideals of conduct and ways of life, which we can all recognize now to be good and useful, have been introduced into human history by the founders of religions. These persons have made actual ethical discoveries which others can afterwards recognize to be true. It might be said that this is at least roughly analogous to the case of the seeing men telling the still blind men of facts which the latter could and did verify for themselves. And it might be said that this makes it reasonable for us to attach some weight to what founders of religions tells us about things which we cannot understand or verify for ourselves; just as it would have been reasonable for the blind men to attach some weight to the unintelligible statements which the seeing man made to them about colours.

I think that this argument deserves a certain amount of respect, though I should find it hard to estimate how much weight to attach to it. I should be inclined to sum up as follows. When there is a nucleus of agreement between the experiences of men in different places, times, and traditions, and when they all tend to put much the same kind of interpretation on the cognitive content of these experiences, it is reasonable to ascribe this agreement to their all being in contact with a certain objective aspect of reality *unless* there be some positive reason to think otherwise. The practical postulate which we go upon everywhere else is to treat cognitive claims as veridical unless there be some positive reason to think them delusive. This, after all, is our only guarantee for believing that ordinary sense-perception is veridical. We cannot *prove* that what people agree in perceiving really exists independently of them; but we do always assume that ordinary waking sense-perception is veridical unless we can produce some positive ground for thinking that it is delusive in any given case. I think it would be inconsistent to treat the experiences of religious mystics on different principles. So far as they agree they should be provisionally accepted as veridical unless there be some positive ground for thinking that they are not. So the next question is whether there is any positive ground for holding that they are delusive.

There are two circumstances which have been commonly held to cast doubt on the cognitive claims of religious and mystical experience. (i) It is alleged that founders of religions and saints have nearly always had certain neuropathic symptoms or certain bodily weaknesses, and that these would be likely to produce delusions. Even if we accept the premises, I do not think that this is a very strong argument. (a) It is equally true that many founders of religions and saints have exhibited great endurance and great power of organization and business capacity which would have made them extremely successful and competent in secular affairs. There are very few offices in the cabinet or in the highest branches of the civil service which St. Thomas Aquinas could not have held with conspicuous success. I do not, of course, regard this as a positive reason *for* accepting the metaphysical doctrines which saints and founders of religions have based on their experiences; but it is relevant as a *rebuttal* of the argument which we are considering. (b) Probably very few people of extreme genius in science or art are perfectly normal mentally or physically, and some of them are very crazy and eccentric indeed. Therefore it would be rather surprising if persons of religious genius were completely normal, whether their experiences be veridical or delusive. (c) Suppose, for the sake of argument, that there is an aspect of the world which remains altogether outside the ken of ordinary persons in their daily life. Then it seems very likely that some degree of mental and physical abnormality would be a necessary condition for getting sufficiently loosened from the objects of ordinary sense-perception to come into cognitive contact with this aspect of reality. Therefore the fact that those persons who claim to have this peculiar kind of cognition generally exhibit certain mental and physical abnormalities is rather what might be anticipated if their claims were true. One might need to be slightly 'cracked' in order to have some peep-holes into the supersensible world. (d) If mystical experience were veridical, it seems quite likely that it would *produce* abnormalities of behaviour in those who had it strongly. Let us suppose, for the sake of argument, that those who have religious experience are in frequent contact with an aspect of reality of which most men get only rare and faint glimpses. Then such persons are, as it were, living in two worlds, while the ordinary man is living in only one of them. Or, again, they might be compared to a man who has to conduct his life with one ordinary eye and another of a telescopic kind. Their behaviour may be appropriate to the aspect of reality which they alone perceive and think all-important; but, for that very reason, it may be inappropriate to those other aspects of reality which are all that most men perceive or judge to be important and on which all our social institutions and conventions are built.

(ii) A second reason which is commonly alleged for doubt about the claims of religious experience is the following. It is said that such experience always originates from and remains mixed with certain other factors, e.g., sexual emotion, which are such that experiences and beliefs that arise from them are very likely to be delusive. I think that there are a good many confusions on this point, and it will be worth while to begin by indicating some of them.

When people say that B 'originated from' A, they are liable to confuse at least three different kinds of connexion between A and B. (i) It might be that A is a necessary but insufficient condition of the existence of B. (ii) It might be that A is a necessary and sufficient condition of the existence of B. Or (iii) it might be that B simply *is* A in a more complex and disguised form. Now, when there is in fact evidence only for the first kind of connexion, people are very liable to jump to the conclusion that there is the third kind of connexion. It may well be the case, e.g., that no one who was incapable of strong sexual desires and emotions could have anything worth calling religious experience. But it is plain that the possession of a strong capacity for sexual experience is not a *sufficient* condition of having religious experience; for we know that the former quite often exists in persons who show hardly any trace of the latter. But, even if it could be shown that a strong capacity for sexual desire and emotion is *both* necessary and sufficient to produce religious experience, it would not follow that the latter is just the former in disguise. In the first place, it is not at all easy to discover the exact meaning of this metaphorical phrase when it is applied to psychological topics. And, if we make use of physical analogies, we are not much helped. A mixture of oxygen and hydrogen in presence of a spark is necessary and sufficient to produce water accompanied by an explosion. But water accompanied by an explosion is not a mixture of oxygen and hydrogen and a spark 'in a disguised form,' whatever that may mean.

Now I think that the present rather vaguely formulated objection to the validity of the claims of religious experience might be stated somewhat as follows. 'In the individual religious experience originates from, and always remains mixed with, sexual desires and emotions. The other generative factor of it is the religious tradition of the society in which he lives, the teachings of his parents, nurses, schoolmasters, etc. In the race religious experience originated from a mixture of false beliefs about nature and man, irrational fears, sexual and other impulses, and so on. Thus the religious tradition arose from beliefs which we now recognize to have been false and from emotions which we now recognize to have been irrelevant and misleading. It is now drilled into children by those who are in authority over them at a time of life when they are intellectually and emotionally at much the same stage as the primitive savages among whom it originated. It is, therefore, readily accepted, and it determines beliefs and emotional dispositions which persist long after the child has grown up and acquired more adequate knowledge of nature and of himself.'

Persons who use this argument might admit that it does not definitely *prove* that religious beliefs are false and groundless. False beliefs and irrational fears in our remote ancestors might conceivably be the origin of true beliefs and of an appropriate feeling of awe and reverence in ourselves. And, if sexual desires and emotions be an essential condition and constituent of religious experience, the experience *may* nevertheless be veridical in important respects. We might merely have to rewrite one of the beatitudes and say 'Blessed are the *impure* in heart, for they shall see God.' But, although it is logically possible that such causes should produce such effects, it would be said that they are most unlikely to do so. They seem much more likely to produce false beliefs and misplaced emotions.

It is plain that this argument has considerable plausibility. But it is worth while to remember that modern science has almost as humble an ancestry as contemporary religion. If the primitive witch-smeller is the spiritual progenitor of the Archbishop of Canterbury, the primitive rain-maker is equally the spiritual progenitor of the Cavendish Professor of Physics. There has obviously been a gradual refinement and purification of religious beliefs and concepts in the course of history, just as there has been in the beliefs and concepts of science. Certain persons of religious genius, such as some of the Hebrew prophets and the founders of Christianity and of Buddhism, do seem to have introduced new ethico-religious concepts and beliefs which have won wide acceptance, just as certain men of scientific genius, such as Galileo, Newton, and Einstein, have done in the sphere of science. It seems somewhat arbitrary to count this process as continual approximation to true knowledge of the material aspect of the world in the case of science; and to refuse to regard it as at all similar in the case of religion. Lastly, we must remember that all of us have accepted the current common-sense and scientific view of the material world on the authority of our parents, nurses, masters, and companions at a time when we had neither the power nor the inclination to criticize it. And most of us accept, without even understanding, the more recondite doctrines of contemporary physics simply on the authority of those whom we have been taught to regard as experts.

On the whole, then, I do not think that what we know of the conditions under which religious beliefs and emotions have arisen in the life of the individual and the race makes it reasonable to think that they are *specially* likely to be delusive or misdirected. At any rate any argument which starts from that basis and claims to reach such a conclusion will need to be very carefully handled if its destructive effects are to be confined within the range contemplated by its users. It is reasonable to think that the concepts and beliefs of even the most perfect religions known to us are extremely inadequate to the facts which they express, that they are highly confused and are mixed up with a great deal of positive error and sheer nonsense; and that, if the human race goes on and continues to have religious experiences and to reflect on them, they will be altered and improved almost out of recognition. But all this could be said, *mutatis mutandis*, of scientific concepts and theories. The claim of any particular religion or sect to have complete or final truth on these subjects seems to me to be too ridiculous to be worth a moment's consideration. But the opposite extreme of holding that the whole religious experience of mankind is a gigantic system of pure delusion seems to me to be almost (though not quite) as far-fetched.

❋ SELECTED BIBLIOGRAPHY
FOR SECTION 4

No doubt the most influential general treatment of religious experience is William James' collection of lectures in *The Varieties of Religious Experience* (New York: Longmans, Green & Co., 1902), containing discussions of conversion, the "medical" and freudian critiques, asceticism, the sense of the divine, and the like. Two useful works (also general in their scope) by James Bissett Pratt include his exhaustive analysis in *The Religious Consciousness* (New York: Macmillan, 1920) and the briefer and more recent discussion in *Eternal Values in Religion* (New York: Macmillan, 1950). Expositions of religious experience from a specifically Christian point of view may be found in John Baillie, *The Sense of the Presence of God* (London: Oxford University Press, 1962); John Oman, *The Natural and the Supernatural* (Cambridge, England: Cambridge University Press, 1931); and H. D. Lewis, *Our Experience of God* (New York: Macmillan, 1959).

Recent and critical approaches are reflected in C. B. Martin, *Religious Belief*, Ch. 5 (Ithaca, N. Y.: Cornell University Press, 1959) and Ronald Hepburn, *Christianity and Paradox*, Chs. 3 and 4 (London: Watts, 1958) who provides a critique of the specifically I-Thou version of religious experience. Contemporary approaches are further represented by Thomas McPherson, "Religion as the Inexpressible" and Alasdair MacIntyre, "Visions," both contained in *New Essays in Philosophical Theology*, ed. Antony Flew and Alasdair MacIntyre (London: Student Christian Movement Press, 1955).

Selections from the various mystics may be found in the following: W. T. Stace (ed.) *The Teachings of the Mystics* (New York: New American Library, 1960); F. C. Happold (ed.) *Mysticism: A Study and an Anthology* (Baltimore: Penguin Books, 1963); and Anne Fremantle (ed.), *The Protestant Mystics* (New York: New American Library, 1964). Stace's anthology is especially useful; the selections range from pagan to Christian mystics and from Eastern to Western, and the editor's introduction is succinct and lucid, excellent for the beginner.

Four general, and rather classic, treatments of mysticism include James' famous discussion in *The Varieties of Religious Experience*, Lectures 16 and 17; W. R. Inge, *Christian Mysticism*, seventh ed. (London: Methuen, 1899); Evelyn Underhill, *Mysticism* (London: Methuen, 1911); and Baron F. von Hügel, *The Mystical Element of Religion*, second ed. (London: J. M. Dent, 1923). In addition one should consult Rudolf Otto, *Mysticism East and West*, tr. Bertha L. Bracey and Richenda C. Payne (New York: Macmillan, 1932); W. T. Stace *Mysticism and Philosophy* (Philadelphia: Lippencott, 1960); R. C. Zaehner, *Mysticism: Sacred and Profane* (Oxford, England: Clarendon Press, 1957); and Sidney Spencer, *Mysticism in World Religions* (New York: Barnes, 1963). For a psychological criticism of mysticism, see J. H. Leuba, *The Psychology of Religious Mysticism* (New York: Harcourt, Brace & World, 1925). Logical problems for the mystic are raised by Paul Henle, "Mysticism and Semantics," *Philosophy and Phenomenological Research*, IX (March, 1949) and W. P. Alston, "Ineffability," *The Philosophical Review*, LXV (October, 1956).

On the relation of mysticism to hallucinogenic experiences (and related topics), see Aldous Huxley, *The Doors of Perception* (London: Chatto & Windus, 1954) ; R. C. Zaehner, *Mysticism: Sacred and Profane*, Ch. 1 and Appendices A and B, *op. cit.*; and Huston Smith, "Do Drugs Have Religious Import?" *Journal of Philosophy*, LXI (October 1, 1964). Zaehner answers Huxley, who defends the religious significance of drugs, and Smith answers Zaehner. One might also consult R. E. L. Masters, *The Varieties of Psychedelic Experience* (New York: Holt, Rinehart and Winston, 1966).

For a study of Martin Buber, see Maurice S. Friedman, *Martin Buber: The Life of Dialogue* (New York: Harper & Row, 1960). A standard exposition of St. John of the Cross is provided in E. Allison Peers, *Studies of the Spanish Mystics*, Vol. I, Ch. 5 (London: Sheldon Press, 1927–30). Thomas Merton's *The Ascent to Truth* (New

York: Harcourt, Brace & Co., 1951) provides a readable and thorough treatment. Merton was himself a modern day example of Christian mysticism as is evident in many of his works including the autobiographical *Seven Storey Mountain* (New York: Harcourt, Brace & World, 1948) and *The New Seeds of Contemplation* (New York: New Directions, 1949). On the *Bhagavad-Gita*, see Sri Aurobindo, *Essays on the Gita* (Calcutta: Arya, 1950) and S. Radhakrishnan's *The Bhagavadgītā* (London: George Allen & Unwin, 1948) which contains a series of essays on the *Gita* and a commentary on the translation.

The Zen scholar D. T. Suzuki has done more than anyone to familiarize westerners with the mystical thought of the East, especially Zen Buddhism. Among his several useful works is *Studies in Zen* (New York: Philosophical Library, 1955) and his edition of Zen Buddhist sources, *Manual of Zen Buddhism* (New York: Evergreen, 1960).

BELIEF AND MEANING

Faith and Reason

❋ INTRODUCTION

The question of God's existence may be in some ways the central question of philosophical theology, but it is obviously not the only question, and it is perhaps not even the most fundamental one. It is true that St. Thomas Aquinas said that all theologizing depends on the existence of God, but even St. Thomas, in both his *Summa Theologica* and *Summa Contra Gentiles*, considers the problem of faith and reason before he considers God. The reason is that one cannot pursue a knowledge of God (and related matters) unless some judgment has been made as to the possibility and nature of such knowledge. In that sense, at least, the question of faith and reason may be foundational to all the others.

But what, more exactly, is the problem of faith and reason? The answer depends on what one means by "faith," an ambiguous word indeed. Kierkegaard's notion of faith as subjective appropriation, for example, will be seen to be a very different one from St. Thomas' view that faith is essentially a matter of intellectual assent to divine truths. Depending on one's conception of faith, it may further be wondered whether the problem must necessarily to restricted to the religious or theological sphere: Is it not possible for the scientist and poet, as well as the religious man or theologian, to have difficulty reconciling faith and reason? Be that as it may, it is no accident that this problem is usually construed and understood as a theological one, for, more often than not, faith is taken to mean allegiance to divine authority either in the form of revealed scripture, a divine person, an inner experience, or the like. And the question becomes this: In view of the acceptance of divine authority, what is the relevance and contribution of natural reason? This question (or some version of it) has been the cause of important rifts and very different theological styles throughout the history of religious thought. And, as was suggested above, all theologizing presupposes some answer to it.

St. Thomas Aquinas, then, establishes at the very beginning of his philosophical-theological system the necessary roles to be played by reason and revelation. Aquinas adhered to the Augustinian dictum *Credo ut intelligam*, "I believe in order that I may understand," and emphasized repeatedly the absolute necessity of special revelation, without which "the human race would remain in the blackest shadows of ignorance." On the other hand, the reasons why the natural intellect should be exercised and enjoyed reduce, essentially, to two. First, and again reflecting the influence of Aristotle, man's highest and noblest activity lies in knowing, and he thereby realizes his nature and happiness as a rational being; second, it is required of Christians to meet the pagans (who do not acknowledge the Christian revelation) on the common ground of reason and philosophy if the unbelieving pagan is to be persuaded of the truth of Christianity. Both reason and revelation thus make their important contributions.

It will be noticed that for Thomas the acceptance of revelation both is and is not a rational affair. Insofar as the divinely disclosed truths of revelation exceed our natural reason (and are usually first accepted on faith anyway), revelation does not commend itself to us on rational grounds. Nonetheless, Thomas suggests that there is a certain reasonableness in the acceptance of Christian revelation, and he appeals primarily to the supernatural signs and wonders that have accompanied it. It might be objected that this is a circular move inasmuch as we can hardly be confronted with the supernatural attestations of revelation (for example, the voice that spoke to Moses out of a burning bush) unless we already accept the authority of the Bible. Perhaps, though, revelation should be distinguished from the miracles that attend it, the latter being matters of historical fact which are to be believed or not believed on grounds independent of revelation. Aside from the possibility of thus separating the concept of the miraculous from that of revelation, miracles themselves remain for many (as we will see from Hume in the next selection) no less a problem than before. In the meantime, it must constantly be borne in mind that the full significance of the many statements in this volume can often be appreciated only if every care has been exercised to situate them in the religious and cultural contexts for which they were articulated.

The British thinker John Locke, who antedated David Hume by a philosophical generation, had attempted to delineate a rational principle by which we may be enabled to identify a false from a genuine revelation: ". . . whether it be a *divine* revelation or no reason must judge; which can never permit the mind to reject a greater evidence to embrace what is less evident, nor allow it to entertain probability in opposition to knowledge and certainty."[1] Locke did not suspect that Hume would base his famous (infamous) attack on miracles virtually on this very rule. Carrying the principle to the opposite conclusion, Hume announces that (among other things) established custom, the whole weight of experience, the knavery and credulity of men, plus the intrinsic incredibility of miracles renders their acceptance by reasonable and enlightened men impossible. Indeed, "Upon the whole . . . it appears that no testimony for any kind of miracle has ever amounted to a probability, much less to a proof."

One might ask, however, whether Hume's criteria for the establishment of the truth of miracle-testimony are practicable. What, for example, constitutes a "sufficient number" of witnesses? how does one certify their "unquestioned good-sense"? their "reputation in the eyes of mankind"? Further, Hume suggests (or does he?) that miracles *by their nature* are impossible, but this *a priori* and dogmatic intrusion would seem to contradict his interest in proceeding in a purely empirical manner, generalizing from experience.

[1]John Locke, *An Essay Concerning Human Understanding,* ed. Alexander Campbell Fraser (Oxford, England: Clarendon Press, 1894), II, 425.

At any rate, it is important to notice that with his rejection of miracles Hume destroyed—to his satisfaction—the miraculous witness to the truth of religion, thereby destroying also what many (including St. Thomas) regarded as the supernatural foundation and authority of Christianity.

Of course, Hume's conclusion concerning the impossibility of miracles would hardly bother the Church Father Tertullian, who said in reference to the death and resurrection of Christ, "It is by all means to be believed, because it is absurd. . . . the fact is certain because it is impossible."[2] Nor would it bother any of a number of thinkers comprising a kind of "fideist" tradition (from the Latin *Fides*, "faith") which, contrary to the rationalist tradition that includes St. Thomas, affirms the complete sufficiency of faith and rejects emphatically any contribution of natural reason to spiritual truth and understanding.

To such a strain of thinkers belongs Sören Kierkegaard, who represents at once a profound influence on all subsequent theology and the fountainhead of contemporary existential philosophy. Kierkegaard's attack was directed primarily at the philosophical system of Hegel with its indifference towards the concretely existing individual, and also at the easy, indifferent faith of Christendom in which everyone going through the motions freely acclaimed himself a "Christian." Kierkegaard rejects the "objective" approach to Christianity for the "subjective." Christianity, for Kierkegaard, is not a doctrine or theological system, nor is it an objective truth awaiting demonstration through historical research or speculative reason. Rather, Christianity is a Person, Jesus Christ, the God-Man, the Paradox, an offence to the reason. And faith is not therefore a matter of intellectual assents to certain dogmas, but rather a matter of individual or subjective appropriation, an inward passion involving an existential leap; intellectually, it is an "objective uncertainty" and a "risk." Kierkegaard hoped thus to recover for the existing individual the fully personal, urgent, and existential character of genuine Christian faith.

William James, in his celebrated essay "The Will To Believe," agrees that we may be driven, finally, to a belief in God rather than an intellectual knowledge, but the motivation for this position is quite different from Kierkegaard's. For James it is not an existential matter but a practical or pragmatic one. The question of God and religion is, for example, a legitimate and even urgent one; unfortunately it is also one of those questions concerning which the evidence on both sides often appears insufficient, preventing a decision on intellectual grounds alone. What can one intelligently do in such a situation, James asks, but be willing to make a decision on the basis of desire. The ideal of complete intellectual objectivity and suspension of judgment when the evidence is incomplete possesses a *prima facie* attractiveness. James argues, however, that we are most interested in being *right*, and that this is exactly what we might miss out on if we follow the advice of intellectual objectivists. Better to heed the advice of the French thinker Pascal: "Let us weigh the gain and loss in wagering that God is. Let us estimate these two chances.

---

[2]Tertullian, *On the Flesh of Christ*, 5, tr. Peter Holmes, *Ante-Nicene Christian Library*, XV (Edinburgh: T. & T. Clark, 1884).

If you gain, you gain all; if you lose, you lose nothing. Wager, then, without hesitation that He is."[3]

Before one indicts James with the inevitable charge that God could hardly take pleasure in faith thus selfishly motivated, he will want to be certain that he has appreciated the full implications of James' concept of a "living, forced, and momentous option." He may also wish to consider the role of self-interest as it manifests itself (quite legitimately) in other spheres of belief and conduct. More interesting, perhaps, is the question whether one can believe without really believing.

✳ ST. THOMAS AQUINAS

19. *The Twofold Truth*

St. Thomas Aquinas (1225–1274) was a Dominican friar and the most influential thinker of the scholastic period. His most important works, the *Summa Theologica* and the *Summa Contra Gentiles*, were intended to demonstrate that belief in revelation is not incompatible with a philosophical theology that proceeds by the light of natural reason and draws its concepts from the created order. Thomism continues to be the dominating philosophy of the Roman Catholic Church.

From *Summa Contra Gentiles*

BOOK I

Chapter 2: The Author's Intention in the Present Work

[1] Among all human pursuits, the pursuit of wisdom is more perfect, more noble, more useful, and more full of joy.

It is more perfect because, in so far as a man gives himself to the pursuit of wisdom, so far does he even now have some share in true beatitude. And so a wise man has said: "Blessed is the man that shall continue in wisdom" [Ecclus. 14:20].

It is more noble because through this pursuit man especially approaches to a likeness to God Who "made all things in wisdom" [Ps. 104:24]. And since likeness is the cause of love, the pursuit of wisdom especially joins man to God in friendship. That is why it is said of wisdom that "she is an infinite treasure to men! which they that use become the friends of God" [Wis. 7:14].

St. Thomas Aquinas, *Summa Contra Gentiles*, tr. Anton C. Pegis (Garden City, N. Y.: Image Books, 1955). Copyright © 1955 by Doubleday & Company, Inc. Reprinted by permission of the publisher.

[3]Blaise Pascal, *Pensées*, no. 233, in *Pensées and The Provincial Letters*, tr. W. F. Trotter and Thomas M'Crie (New York: Modern Library, 1941).

It is more useful because through wisdom we arrive at the kingdom of immortality. For "the desire of wisdom bringeth to the everlasting kingdom" [Wis. 6:20].

It is more full of joy because "her conversation hath no bitterness, nor her company any tediousness, but joy and gladness" [Wis. 8:16].

[2] And so, in the name of the divine Mercy, I have the confidence to embark upon the work of a wise man, even though this may surpass my powers, and I have set myself the task of making known, as far as my limited powers will allow, the truth that the Catholic faith professes, and of setting aside the errors that are opposed to it. To use the words of Hilary: "I am aware that I owe this to God as the chief duty of my life, that my every word and sense may speak of Him."[1]

[3] To proceed against individual errors, however, is a difficult business, and this for two reasons. In the first place, it is difficult because the sacrilegious remarks of individual men who have erred are not so well known to us so that we may use what they say as the basis of proceeding to a refutation of their errors. This is, indeed, the method that the ancient Doctors of the Church used in the refutation of the errors of the Gentiles. For they could know the positions taken by the Gentiles since they themselves had been Gentiles, or at least had lived among the Gentiles and had been instructed in their teaching. In the second place, it is difficult because some of them, such as the Mohammedans and the pagans, do not agree with us in accepting the authority of any Scripture, by which they may be convinced of their error. Thus, against the Jews we are able to argue by means of the Old Testament, while against heretics we are able to argue by means of the New Testament. But the Mohammedans and the pagans accept neither the one nor the other. We must, therefore, have recourse to the natural reason, to which all men are forced to give their assent. However, it is true, in divine matters the natural reason has its failings.

[4] Now, while we are investigating some given truth, we shall also show what errors are set aside by it; and we shall likewise show the truth that we come to know by demonstration is in accord with the Christian religion.

Chapter 3: On the Way in which Divine Truth Is to Be Made Known

[1] The way of making truth known is not always the same, and, as the Philosopher has very well said, "it belongs to an educated man to seek such certitude in each thing as the nature of that thing allows."[2] The remark is also introduced by Boethius.[3] But, since such is the case, we must first show what way is open to us in order that we may make known the truth which is our object.

[1][St. Hilary, *On the Trinity*, I, 37.]
[2][Aristotle, *Nicomachean Ethics*, I, 3 (1094b 24).]
[3][Cf. Boethius, *On the Trinity*, II.]

[2] There is a twofold mode of truth in what we profess about God. Some truths about God exceed all the ability of the human reason. Such is the truth that God is triune. But there are some truths which the natural reason also is able to reach. Such are that God exists, that He is one, and the like. In fact, such truths about God have been proved demonstratively by the philosophers, guided by the light of the natural reason.

[3] That there are certain truths about God that totally surpass man's ability appears with the greatest evidence. Since, indeed, the principle of all knowledge that the reason perceives about one thing is the understanding of the very substance of that being (for according to Aristotle "what a thing is" is the principle of demonstration),[4] it is necessary that the way in which we understand the substance of a thing determines the way in which we know what belongs to it. Hence, if the human intellect comprehends the substance of some thing, for example, that of a stone or of a triangle, no intelligible characteristic belonging to that thing surpasses the grasp of the human reason. But this does not happen to us in the case of God. For the human intellect is not able to reach a comprehension of the divine substance through its natural power. For, according to its manner of knowing in the present life, the intellect depends on the sense for the origin of knowledge; and so those things that do not fall under the senses cannot be grasped by the human intellect except in so far as the knowledge of them is gathered from sensible things. Now, sensible things cannot lead the human intellect to the point of seeing in them the nature of the divine substance; for sensible things are effects that fall short of the power of their cause. Yet, beginning with sensible things, our intellect is led to the point of knowing about God that He exists, and other such characteristics that must be attributed to the First Principle. There are, consequently, some intelligible truths about God that are open to the human reason; but there are others that absolutely surpass its power.

[4] We may easily see the same point from the gradation of intellects. Consider the case of two persons of whom one has a more penetrating grasp of a thing by his intellect than does the other. He who has the superior intellect understands many things that the other cannot grasp at all. Such is the case with a very simple person who cannot at all grasp the subtle speculations of philosophy. But the intellect of an angel surpasses the human intellect much more than the intellect of the greatest philosopher surpasses the intellect of the most uncultivated simple person; for the distance between the best philosopher and a simple person is contained within the limits of the human species, which the angelic intellect surpasses. For the angel knows God on the basis of a more noble effect than does man; and this by as much as the substance of an angel, through which the angel in his natural knowledge is led to the knowledge of God, is nobler than sensible things and even than the soul itself, through which the human intellect mounts to the knowledge of God. The divine intellect surpasses the angelic intellect much more than

4[Aristotle, *Posterior Analytics*, II, 3 (90b 31).]

the angelic surpasses the human. For the divine intellect is in its capacity equal to its substance, and therefore it understands fully what it is, including all its intelligible attributes. But by his natural knowledge the angel does not know what God is, since the substance itself of the angel, through which he is led to the knowledge of God, is an effect that is not equal to the power of its cause. Hence, the angel is not able, by means of his natural knowledge, to grasp all the things that God understands in Himself; nor is the human reason sufficient to grasp all the things that the angel understands through his own natural power. Just as, therefore, it would be the height of folly for a simple person to assert that what a philosopher proposes is false on the ground that he himself cannot understand it, so (and even more so) it is the acme of stupidity for a man to suspect as false what is divinely revealed through the ministry of the angels simply because it cannot be investigated by reason.

[5] The same thing, moreover, appears quite clearly from the defect that we experience every day in our knowledge of things. We do not know a great many of the properties of sensible things, and in most cases we are not able to discover fully the natures of those properties that we apprehend by the sense. Much more is it the case, therefore, that the human reason is not equal to the task of investigating all the intelligible characteristics of that most excellent substance.

[6] The remark of Aristotle likewise agrees with this conclusion. He says that "our intellect is related to the prime beings, which are most evident in their nature, as the eye of an owl is related to the sun."[5]

[7] Sacred Scripture also gives testimony to this truth. We read in Job: "Peradventure thou wilt comprehend the steps of God, and wilt find out the Almightty perfectly?" [11:7]. And again: "Behold, God is great, exceeding our knowledge" [Job 36:26]. And St. Paul: "We know in part" [I Cor. 13:4].

[8] We should not, therefore, immediately reject as false, following the opinion of the Manicheans and many unbelievers, everything that is said about God even though it cannot be investigated by reason.

Chapter 4: That the Truth about God to which the Natural Reason Reaches Is Fittingly Proposed to Men for Belief

[1] Since, therefore, there exists a twofold truth concerning the divine being, one to which the inquiry of the reason can reach, the other which surpasses the whole ability of the human reason, it is fitting that both of these truths be proposed to man divinely for belief. This point must first be shown concerning the truth that is open to the inquiry of the reason; otherwise, it might perhaps seem to someone that, since such a truth can be known by the reason, it was uselessly given to me through a supernatural inspiration as an object of belief.

[5][Aristotle, *Metaphysics*, II, 1 (993b 9).]

[2] Yet, if this truth were left solely as a matter of inquiry for the human reason, three awkward consequences would follow.

[3] The first is that few men would possess the knowledge of God. For there are three reasons why most men are cut off from the fruit of diligent inquiry which is the discovery of truth. Some do not have the physical disposition for such work. As a result, there are many who are naturally not fitted to pursue knowledge; and so, however much they tried, they would be unable to reach the highest level of human knowledge which consists in knowing God. Others are cut off from pursuing this truth by the necessities imposed upon them by their daily lives. For some men must devote themselves to taking care of temporal matters. Such men would not be able to give so much time to the leisure of contemplative inquiry as to reach the highest peak at which human investigation can arrive, namely, the knowledge of God. Finally, there are some who are cut off by indolence. In order to know the things that the reason can investigate concerning God, a knowledge of many things must already be possessed. For almost all of philosophy is directed towards the knowledge of God, and that is why metaphysics, which deals with divine things, is the last part of philosophy to be learned. This means that we are able to arrive at the inquiry concerning the aforementioned truth only on the basis of a great deal of labor spent in study. Now, those who wish to undergo such a labor for the mere love of knowledge are few, even though God has inserted into the minds of men a natural appetite for knowledge.

[4] The second awkward effect is that those who would come to discover the abovementioned truth would barely reach it after a great deal of time. The reasons are several. There is the profundity of this truth, which the human intellect is made capable of grasping by natural inquiry only after a long training. Then, there are many things that must be presupposed, as we have said. There is also the fact that, in youth, when the soul is swayed by the various movements of the passions, it is not in a suitable state for the knowledge of such lofty truth. On the contrary, "one becomes wise and knowing in repose," as it is said in the Physics.[6] The result is this. If the only way open to us for the knowledge of God were solely that of the reason, the human race would remain in the blackest shadows of ignorance. For then the knowledge of God, which especially renders men perfect and good, would come to be possessed only by a few, and these few would require a great deal of time in order to reach it.

[5] The third awkward effect is this. The investigation of the human reason for the most part has falsity present within it, and this is due partly to the weakness of our intellect in judgment, and partly to the admixture of images. The result is that many, remaining ignorant of the power of demonstration, would hold in doubt those things that have been most truly demonstrated. This would be particularly the case since they see that, among those who

[6][Aristotle, *Physics*, VII, 3 (247b 9).]

are reputed to be wise men, each one teaches his own brand of doctrine. Furthermore, with the many truths that are demonstrated, there sometimes is mingled something that is false, which is not demonstrated but rather asserted on the basis of some probable or sophistical argument, which yet has the credit of being a demonstration. That is why it was necessary that the unshakeable certitude and pure truth concerning divine things should be presented to men by way of faith.

[6] Beneficially, therefore, did the divine Mercy provide that it should instruct us to hold by faith even those truths that the human reason is able to investigate. In this way, all men would easily be able to have a share in the knowledge of God, and this without uncertainty and error.

[7] Hence it is written: "Henceforward you walk not as also the Gentiles walk in the vanity of their mind, having their understanding darkened" [Eph. 4:17-18]. And again: "All thy children shall be taught of the Lord" [Isa. 54:13].

Chapter 5: That the Truths the Human Reason Is Not Able to Investigate Are Fittingly Proposed to Men for Belief

[1] Now, perhaps some will think that men should not be asked to believe what the reason is not adequate to investigate, since the divine Wisdom provides in the case of each thing according to the mode of its nature. We must therefore prove that it is necessary for man to receive from God as objects of belief even those truths that are above the human reason.

[2] No one tends with desire and zeal towards something that is not already known to him. But, as we shall examine later on in this work, men are ordained by the divine Providence towards a higher good than human fragility can experience in the present life. That is why it was necessary for the human mind to be called to something higher than the human reason here and now can reach, so that it would thus learn to desire something and with zeal tend towards something that surpasses the whole state of the present life. This belongs especially to the Christian religion, which in a unique way promises spiritual and eternal goods. And so there are many things proposed to men in it that transcend human sense. The Old Law, on the other hand, whose promises were of a temporal character, contained very few proposals that transcended the inquiry of the human reason. Following this same direction, the philosophers themselves, in order that they might lead men from the pleasure of sensible things to virtue, were concerned to show that there were in existence other goods of a higher nature than these things of sense, and that those who gave themselves to the active or contemplative virtues would find much sweeter enjoyment in the taste of these higher goods.

[3] It is also necessary that such truth be proposed to men for belief so that they may have a truer knowledge of God. For then only do we know God truly when we believe Him to be above everything that it is possible for man to think about Him; for, as we have shown, the divine substance surpasses the natural knowledge of which man is capable. Hence, by the

fact that some things about God are proposed to man that surpass his reason, there is strengthened in man the view that God is something above what he can think.

[4] Another benefit that comes from the revelation to men of truths that exceed the reason is the curbing of presumption, which is the mother of error. For there are some who have such a presumptuous opinion of their own ability that they deem themselves able to measure the nature of everything; I mean to say that, in their estimation, everything is true that seems to them so, and everything is false that does not. So that the human mind, therefore, might be freed from this presumption and come to a humble inquiry after truth, it was necessary that some things should be proposed to man by God that would completely surpass his intellect.

[5] A still further benefit may also be seen in what Aristotle says in the *Ethics*. There was a certain Simonides who exhorted people to put aside the knowledge of divine things and to apply their talents to human occupations. He said that "he who is a man should know human things, and he who is mortal, things that are mortal." Against Simonides Aristotle says that "man should draw himself towards what is immortal and divine as much as he can."[7] And so he says in the *De animalibus* that, although what we know of the higher substances is very little, yet that little is loved and desired more than all the knowledge that we have about less noble substances.[8] He also says in the *De caelo et mundo* that when questions about the heavenly bodies can be given even a modest and merely plausible solution, he who hears this experiences intense joy.[9] From all these considerations it is clear that even the most imperfect knowledge about the most noble realities brings the greatest perfection to the soul. Therefore, although the human reason cannot grasp fully the truths that are above it, yet, if it somehow holds these truths at least by faith, it acquires great perfection for itself.

[6] Therefore it is written: "For many things are shown to thee above the understanding of men" [Ecclus. 3:23]. Again: "So the things that are of God no man knoweth but the Spirit of God. But to us God hath revealed them by His Spirit" [I Cor. 2:11, 10].

Chapter 6: That to Give Assent to the Truths of Faith Is Not Foolishness Even Though They Are above Reason

[1] Those who place their faith in this truth, however, "for which the human reason offers no experimental evidence,"[10] do not believe foolishly, as though "following artificial fables" [II Peter 1:16]. For these "secrets of divine Wisdom" [Job 11:6] the divine Wisdom itself, which knows all things to the full, has deigned to reveal to men. It reveals its own presence, as well as

---

[7][Aristotle, *Nicomachean Ethics*, X, 7 (1177b 31).]
[8][Cf. Aristotle, *On the Parts of Animals*, I, 5 (644b 32).]
[9][Cf. Aristotle, *On the Heavens*, II, 12 (291b 26).]
[10][St. Gregory, *Homilies on the Gospels*, II, 26, 1.]

the truth of its teaching and inspiration, by fitting arguments; and in order to confirm those truths that exceed natural knowledge, it gives visible manifestation to works that surpass the ability of all nature. Thus, there are the wonderful cures of illnesses, there is the raising of the dead, and the wonderful immutation in the heavenly bodies; and what is more wonderful, there is the inspiration given to human minds, so that simple and untutored persons, filled with the gift of the Holy Spirit, come to possess instantaneously the highest wisdom and the readiest eloquence. When these arguments were examined, through the efficacy of the abovementioned proof, and not the violent assault of arms or the promise of pleasures, and (what is most wonderful of all) in the midst of the tyranny of the persecutors, an innumerable throng of people, both simple and most learned, flocked to the Christian faith. In this faith there are truths preached that surpass every human intellect; the pleasures of the flesh are curbed; it is taught that the things of the world should be spurned. Now, for the minds of mortal men to assent to these things is the greatest of miracles, just as it is a manifest work of divine inspiration that, spurning visible things, men should seek only what is invisible. Now, that this has happened neither without preparation nor by chance, but as a result of the disposition of God, is clear from the fact that through many pronouncements of the ancient prophets God had foretold that He would do this. The books of these prophets are held in veneration among us Christians, since they give witness to our faith.

[2]   The manner of this confirmation is touched on by St. Paul: "Which," that is, human salvation, "having begun to be declared by the Lord, was confirmed unto us by them that hear Him: God also bearing them witness of signs, and wonders, and divers miracles, and distributions of the Holy Ghost" [Heb. 2:3-4].

[3]   This wonderful conversion of the world to the Christian faith is the clearest witness of the signs given in the past; so that it is not necessary that they should be further repeated, since they appear most clearly in their effect. For it would be truly more wonderful than all signs if the world had been led by simple and humble men to believe such lofty truths, to accomplish such difficult actions, and to have such high hopes. Yet it is also a fact that, even in our own time, God does not cease to work miracles through His saints for the confirmation of the faith.

[4]   On the other hand, those who founded sects committed to erroneous doctrines proceeded in a way that is opposite to this. The point is clear in the case of Mohammed. He seduced the people by promises of carnal pleasure to which the concupiscence of the flesh goads us. His teaching also contained precepts that were in conformity with his promises, and he gave free rein to carnal pleasure. In all this, as is not unexpected, he was obeyed by carnal men. As for proofs of the truth of his doctrine, he brought forward only such as could be grasped by the natural ability of anyone with a very modest wisdom. Indeed, the truths that he taught he mingled with many fables and with doctrines of the greatest falsity. He did not bring forth any signs produced

in a supernatural way, which alone fittingly gives witness to divine inspiration; for a visible action that can be only divine reveals an invisibly inspired teacher of truth. On the contrary, Mohammed said that he was sent in the power of his arms—which are signs not lacking even to robbers and tyrants. What is more, no wise men, men trained in things divine and human, believed in him from the beginning. Those who believed in him were brutal men and desert wanderers, utterly ignorant of all divine teaching, through whose numbers Mohammed forced others to become his followers by the violence of his arms. Nor do divine pronouncements on the part of preceding prophets offer him any witness. On the contrary, he perverts almost all the testimonies of the Old and New Testaments by making them into fabrications of his own, as can be seen by anyone who examines his law. It was, therefore, a shrewd decision on his part to forbid his followers to read the Old and New Testaments, lest these books convict him of falsity. It is thus clear that those who place any faith in his words believe foolishly.

Chapter 7: That the Truth of Reason Is Not Opposed to the Truth of the Christian Faith

[1]   Now, although the truth of the Christian faith which we have discussed surpasses the capacity of the reason, nevertheless that truth that the human reason is naturally endowed to know cannot be opposed to the truth of the Christian faith. For that with which the human reason is naturally endowed is clearly most true; so much so, that it is impossible for us to think of such truths as false. Nor is it permissible to believe as false that which we hold by faith, since this is confirmed in a way that is so clearly divine. Since, therefore, only the false is opposed to the true, as is clearly evident from an examination of their definitions, it is impossible that the truth of faith should be opposed to those principles that the human reason knows naturally.

[2]   Furthermore, that which is introduced into the soul of the student by the teacher is contained in the knowledge of the teacher—unless his teaching is fictitious, which it is improper to say of God. Now, the knowledge of the principles that are known to us naturally has been implanted in us by God; for God is the Author of our nature. These principles, therefore, are also contained by the divine Wisdom. Hence, whatever is opposed to them is opposed to the divine Wisdom, and, therefore, cannot come from God. That which we hold by faith as divinely revealed, therefore, cannot be contrary to our natural knowledge.

[3]   Again. In the presence of contrary arguments our intellect is chained, so that it cannot proceed to the knowledge of the truth. If, therefore, contrary knowledges were implanted in us by God, our intellect would be hindered from knowing truth by this very fact. Now, such an effect cannot come from God.

[4]   And again. What is natural cannot change as long as nature does not. Now, it is impossible that contrary opinions should exist in the same knowing subject at the same time. No opinion or belief, therefore, is implanted in

man by God which is contrary to man's natural knowledge.

[5] Therefore, the Apostle says: "The word is nigh thee, even in thy mouth and in thy heart. This is the word of faith, which we preach" [Rom. 10:8]. But because it overcomes reason, there are some who think that it is opposed to it: which is impossible.

[6] The authority of St. Augustine also agrees with this. He writes as follows: "That which truth will reveal cannot in any way be opposed to the sacred books of the Old and the New Testament."[11]

[7] From this we evidently gather the following conclusion: whatever arguments are brought forward against the doctrines of faith are conclusions incorrectly derived from the first and self-evident principles imbedded in nature. Such conclusions do not have the force of demonstration; they are arguments that are either probable or sophistical. And so, there exists the possibility to answer them.

Chapter 8: How the Human Reason Is Related to the Truth of Faith

[1] There is also a further consideration. Sensible things, from which the human reason takes the origin of its knowledge, retain within themselves some sort of trace of a likeness to God. This is so imperfect, however, that it is absolutely inadequate to manifest the substance of God. For effects bear within themselves, in their own way, the likeness of their causes, since an agent produces its like; yet an effect does not always reach to the full likeness of its cause. Now, the human reason is related to the knowledge of the truth of faith (a truth which can be most evident only to those who see the divine substance) in such a way that it can gather certain likenesses of it, which are yet not sufficient so that the truth of faith may be comprehended as being understood demonstratively or through itself. Yet it is useful for the human reason to exercise itself in such arguments, however weak they may be, provided only that there be present no presumption to comprehend or to demonstrate. For to be able to see something of the loftiest realities, however thin and weak the sight may be, is, as our previous remarks indicate, a cause of the greatest joy.

[2] The testimony of Hilary agrees with this. Speaking of this same truth, he writes as follows in his *De Trinitate*: "Enter these truths by believing, press forward, persevere. And though I may know that you will not arrive at an end, yet I will congratulate you in your progress. For, though he who purues the infinite with reverence will never finally reach the end, yet he will always progress by pressing onward. But do not intrude yourself into the divine secret, do not, presuming to comprehend the sum total of intelligence, plunge yourself into the mystery of the unending nativity; rather, understand that these things are incomprehensible."[12]

---

[11][St. Augustine, *Literal Commentary on Genesis*, II, 18.]
[12][St. Hilary, *On the Trinity*, II, 10, 2.]

✳ DAVID HUME

20. *Against Miracles*

David Hume (1711–1776) is often regarded as the greatest thinker of the British empiricist tradition. His skeptical philosophy is worked out in *A Treatise of Human Nature,* and his critiques of religion and theology are contained in his *Dialogues Concerning Natural Religion* (a classic indictment of the attempt to demonstrate God's attributes from his so-called effects in nature), *Natural History of Religion,* and his essay "On Miracles."

From *An Enquiry Concerning Human Understanding*

SECTION X: OF MIRACLES

Part I

There is, in Dr. Tillotson's writings, an argument against the *real presence,* which is as concise, and elegant, and strong as any argument can possibly be supposed against a doctrine, so little worthy of a serious refutation. It is acknowledged on all hands, says that learned prelate, that the authority, either of the scripture or of tradition, is founded merely in the testimony of the apostles, who were eye-witnesses to those miracles of our Saviour, by which he proved his divine mission. Our evidence, then, for the truth of the *Christian* religion is less than the evidence for the truth of our senses; because, even in the first authors of our religion, it was no greater; and it is evident it must diminish in passing from them to their disciples; nor can any one rest such confidence in their testimony, as in the immediate object of his senses. But a weaker evidence can never destroy a stronger; and therefore, were the doctrine of the real presence ever so clearly revealed in scripture, it were directly contrary to the rules of just reasoning to give our assent to it. It contradicts sense, though both the scripture and tradition, on which it is supposed to be built, carry not such evidence with them as sense; when they are considered merely as external evidences, and are not brought home to every one's breast, by the immediate operation of the Holy Spirit.

Nothing is so convenient as a decisive argument of this kind, which must at least *silence* the most arrogant bigotry and superstition, and free us from their impertinent solicitations. I flatter myself, that I have discovered an argument of a like nature, which, if just, will, with the wise and learned, be an everlasting check to all kinds of superstitious delusion, and consequently, will be useful as long as the world endures. For so long, I presume, will the accounts of miracles and prodigies be found in all history, sacred and profane.

David Hume, *An Enquiry Concerning Human Understanding,* ed. L. A. Selby-Bigge, second ed. (Oxford, England: Clarendon Press, 1902).

Though experience be our only guide in reasoning concerning matters of fact; it must be acknowledged, that this guide is not altogether infallible, but in some cases is apt to lead us into errors. One, who in our climate, should expect better weather in any week of June than in one of December, would reason justly, and conformably to experience; but it is certain, that he may happen, in the event, to find himself mistaken. However, we may observe, that, in such a case, he would have no cause to complain of experience; because it commonly informs us beforehand of the uncertainty, by that contrariety of events, which we may learn from a diligent observation. All effects follow not with like certainty from their supposed causes. Some events are found, in all countries and all ages, to have been constantly conjoined together: Others are found to have been more variable, and sometimes to disappoint our expectations; so that, in our reasonings concerning matter of fact, there are all imaginable degrees of assurance, from the highest certainty to the lowest species of moral evidence.

A wise man, therefore, proportions his belief to the evidence. In such conclusions as are founded on an infallible experience, he expects the event with the last degree of assurance, and regards his past experience as a full *proof* of the future existence of that event. In other cases, he proceeds with more caution: He weighs the opposite experiments: He considers which side is supported by the greater number of experiments: to that side he inclines, with doubt and hesitation; and when at last he fixes his judgement, the evidence exceeds not what we properly call *probability*. All probability, then, supposes an opposition of experiments and observations, where the one side is found to overbalance the other, and to produce a degree of evidence, proportioned to the superiority. A hundred instances or experiments on one side, and fifty on another, afford a doubtful expectation of any event; though a hundred uniform experiments, with only one that is contradictory, reasonably beget a pretty strong degree of assurance. In all cases, we must balance the opposite experiments, where they are opposite, and deduct the smaller number from the greater, in order to know the exact force of the superior evidence.

To apply these principles to a particular instance; we may observe, that there is no species of reasoning more common, more useful, and even necessary to human life, than that which is derived from the testimony of men, and the reports of eye-witnesses and spectators. This species of reasoning, perhaps, one may deny to be founded on the relation of cause and effect. I shall not dispute about a word. It will be sufficient to observe that our assurance in any argument of this kind is derived from no other principle than our observation of the veracity of human testimony, and of the usual conformity of facts to the reports of witnesses. It being a general maxim, that no objects have any discoverable connexion together, and that all the inferences, which we can draw from one to another, are founded merely on our experience of their constant and regular conjunction; it is evident, that we ought not to make an exception to this maxim in favour of human testimony, whose connexion with any event seems, in itself, as little necessary as any other. Were not the memory tenacious to a certain degree, had not men commonly an inclination to truth and a principle of probity; were they not sensible to shame, when detected in a falsehood: Were not these, I say, discovered by *experience* to be qualities, inherent in human nature, we should never repose the least confidence in human testimony. A man delirious, or noted for falsehood and villany, has no manner of authority with us.

And as the evidence, derived from witnesses and human testimony, is founded on past experience, so it varies with the experience, and is regarded either as a *proof* or a *probability*, according as the conjunction between any particular kind of report and any kind of object has been found to be constant or variable. There are a number of circumstances to be taken into consideration in all judgements of this kind; and the ultimate standard, by which we determine all disputes, that may arise concerning them, is always derived from experience and observation. Where this experience is not entirely uniform on any side, it is attended with an unavoidable contrariety in our judgements, and with the same opposition and mutual destruction of argument as in every other kind of evidence. We frequently hesitate concerning the reports of others. We balance the opposite circumstances, which cause any doubt or uncertainty; and when we discover a superiority on any side, we incline to it; but still with a diminution of assurance, in proportion to the force of its antagonist.

This contrariety of evidence, in the present case, may be derived from several different causes; from the opposition of contrary testimony; from the character or number of the witnesses; from the manner of their delivering their testimony; or from the union of all these circumstances. We entertain a suspicion concerning any matter of fact, when the witnesses contradict each other; when they are but few, or of a doubtful character; when they have an interest in what they affirm; when they deliver their testimony with hesitation, or on the contrary, with too violent asseverations. There are many other particulars of the same kind, which may diminish or destroy the force of any argument, derived from human testimony.

Suppose, for instance, that the fact, which the testimony endeavours to establish, partakes of the extraordinary and the marvellous; in that case, the evidence, resulting from the testimony, admits of a diminution, greater or less, in proportion as the fact is more or less unusual. The reason why we place any credit in witnesses and historians, is not derived from any *connexion*, which we perceive *a priori*, between testimony and reality, but because we are accustomed to find a conformity between them. But when the fact attested is such a one as has seldom fallen under our observation, here is a contest of two opposite experiences; of which the one destroys the other, as far as its force goes, and the superior can only operate on the mind by the force, which remains. The very same principle of experience, which gives us a certain degree of assurance in the testimony of witnesses, gives us also, in this case, another degree of assurance against the fact, which they endeavour to establish; from which contradition there necessarily arises a counterpoize, and mutual destruction of belief and authority.

I should not believe such a story were it told me by Cato, was a proverbial saying in Rome, even during the lifetime of that philosophical patriot.[1] The incredibility of a fact, it was allowed, might invalidate so great an authority.

The Indian prince, who refused to believe the first relations concerning the effects of frost, reasoned justly; and it naturally required very strong testimony to engage his assent to facts, that arose from a state of nature, with which he was unacquainted, and which bore so little analogy to those events, of which he had had constant and uniform experience. Though they were not contrary to his experience, they were not conformable to it.[2]

But in order to encrease the probability against the testimony of witnesses, let us suppose, that the fact, which they affirm, instead of being only marvellous, is really miraculous; and suppose also, that the testimony considered apart and in itself, amounts to an entire proof; in that case, there is proof against proof, of which the strongest must prevail, but still with a diminution of its force, in proportion to that of its antagonist.

A miracle is a violation of the laws of nature; and as a firm and unalterable experience has established these laws, the proof against a miracle, from the very nature of the fact, is as entire as any argument from experience can possibly be imagined. Why is it more than probable, that all men must die; that lead cannot, of itself, remain suspended in the air; that fire consumes wood, and is extinguished by water; unless it be, that these events are found agreeable to the laws of nature, and there is required a violation of these laws, or in other words, a miracle to prevent them? Nothing is esteemed a miracle, if it ever happen in the common course of nature. It is no miracle that a man, seemingly in good health, should die on a sudden: because such a kind of death, though more unusual than any other, has yet been frequently observed to happen. But it is a miracle, that a dead man should come to life; because that has never been observed in any age or country. There must, therefore, be a uniform experience against every miraculous event, otherwise the event would not merit that appellation. And as a uniform experience amounts to a proof, there is here a direct and full *proof*, from the nature of the fact, against the existence of any miracle; nor can such a proof be

---

[1]Plutarch, in *Vita Catonis*.

[2]No Indian, it is evident, could have experience that water did not freeze in cold climates. This is placing nature in a situation quite unknown to him; and it is impossible for him to tell *a priori* what will result from it. It is making a new experiment, the consequence of which is always uncertain. One may sometimes conjecture from analogy what will follow; but still this is but conjecture. And it must be confessed, that, in the present case of freezing, the event follows contrary to the rules of analogy, and is such as a rational Indian would not look for. The operations of cold upon water are not gradual, according to the degrees of cold; but whenever it comes to the freezing point, the water passes in a moment, from the utmost liquidity to perfect hardness. Such an event, therefore, may be denominated *extraordinary*, and requires a pretty strong testimony, to render it credible to people in a warm climate: But still it is not *miraculous*, nor contrary to uniform experience of the course of nature in cases where all the circumstances are the same. The inhabitants of Sumatra have always seen water fluid in their own climate, and the freezing of their rivers ought to be deemed a prodigy: But they never saw water in Muscovy during the winter; and therefore they cannot reasonably be positive what would there be the consequence.

destroyed, or the miracle rendered credible, but by an opposite proof, which is superior.[3]

The plain consequence is (and it is a general maxim worthy of our attention), 'That no testimony is sufficient to establish a miracle, unless the testimony be of such a kind, that its falsehood would be more miraculous, than the fact, which it endeavours to establish; and even in that case there is a mutual destruction of arguments, and the superior only gives us an assurance suitable to that degree of force, which remains, after deducting the inferior.' When anyone tells me, that he saw a dead man restored to life, I immediately consider with myself, whether it be more probable, that this person should either deceive or be deceived, or that the fact, which he relates, should really have happened. I weigh the one miracle against the other; and according to the superiority, which I discover, I pronounce my decision, and always reject the greater miracle. If the falsehood of his testimony would be more miraculous, than the event which he relates; then, and not till then, can he pretend to command my belief or opinion.

Part II

In the foregoing reasoning we have supposed, that the testimony, upon which a miracle is founded, may possibly amount to an entire proof, and that the falsehood of that testimony would be a real prodigy: But it is easy to shew, that we have been a great deal too liberal in our concession, and that there never was a miraculous event established on so full an evidence.

For *first*, there is not to be found, in all history, any miracle attested by a sufficient number of men, of such unquestioned good-sense, education, and learning, as to secure us against all delusion in themselves; of such undoubted integrity, as to place them beyond all suspicion of any design to deceive others; of such credit and reputation in the eyes of mankind, as to have a great deal to lose in case of their being detected in any falsehood; and at the same time, attesting facts performed in such a public manner and in so celebrated a part of the world, as to render the detection unavoidable: All which circumstances are requisite to give us a full assurance in the testimony of men.

[3]Sometimes an event may not, *in itself, seem* to be contrary to the laws of nature, and yet, if it were real, it might, by reason of some circumstances, be denominated a miracle; because, in *fact*, it is contrary to these laws. Thus if a person, claiming a divine authority, should command a sick person to be well, a healthful man to fall down dead, the clouds to pour rain, the winds to blow, in short, should order many natural events, which immediately follow upon his command; these might justly be esteemed miracles, because they are really, in this case, contrary to the laws of nature. For if any suspicion remain, that the event and command concurred by accident, there is no miracle and no transgression of the laws of nature. If this suspicion be removed, there is evidently a miracle, and a transgression of these laws; because nothing can be more contrary to nature than that the voice or command of a man should have such an influence. A miracle may be accurately defined, *a transgression of a law of nature by a particular volition of the Deity, or by the interposition of some invisible agent.* A miracle may either be discoverable by men or not. This alters not its nature and essence. The raising of a house or ship into the air is a visible miracle. The raising of a feather, when the wind wants ever so little of a force requisite for that purpose, is as real a miracle, though not so sensible with regard to us.

Secondly. We may observe in human nature a principle which, if strictly examined, will be found to diminish extremely the assurance, which we might, from human testimony, have, in any kind of prodigy. The maxim, by which we commonly conduct ourselves in our reasonings, is, that the objects, of which we have no experience, resembles those, of which we have; that what we have found to be most usual is always most probable; and that where there is an opposition of arguments, we ought to give the preference to such as are founded on the greatest number of past observations. But though, in proceeding by this rule, we readily reject any fact which is unusual and incredible in an ordinary degree; yet in advancing farther, the mind observes not always the same rule; but when anything is affirmed utterly absurd and miraculous, it rather the more readily admits of such a fact, upon account of that very circumstance, which ought to destroy all its authority. The passion of *surprise* and *wonder*, arising from miracles, being an agreeable emotion, gives a sensible tendency towards the belief of those events, from which it is derived. And this goes so far, that even those who cannot enjoy this pleasure immediately, nor can believe those miraculous events, of which they are informed, yet love to partake of the satisfaction at second-hand or by rebound, and place a pride and delight in exciting the admiration of others.

With what greediness are the miraculous accounts of travellers received, their descriptions of sea and land monsters, their relations of wonderful adventures, strange men, and uncouth manners? But if the spirit of religion join itself to the love of wonder, there is an end of common sense; and human testimony, in these circumstances, loses all pretensions to authority. A religionist may be an enthusiast, and imagine he sees what has no reality: he may know his narrative to be false, and yet persevere in it, with the best intentions in the world, for the sake of promoting so holy a cause: or even where this delusion has not place, vanity, excited by so strong a temptation, operates on him more powerfully than on the rest of mankind in any other circumstances; and self-interest with equal force. His auditors may not have, and commonly have not sufficient judgement to canvass his evidence: what judgement they have, they renounce by principle, in these sublime and mysterious subjects: or if they were ever so willing to employ it, passion and a heated imagination disturb the regularity of its operations. Their credulity increases his impudence: and his impudence overpowers their credulity.

Eloquence, when at its highest pitch, leaves little room for reason or reflection; but addressing itself entirely to the fancy or the affections, captivates the willing hearers, and subdues their understanding. Happily, this pitch it seldom attains. But what a Tully or a Demosthenes could scarcely effect over a Roman or Athenian audience, every *Capuchin*, every itinerant or stationary teacher can perform over the generality of mankind, and in a higher degree, by touching such gross and vulgar passions.

The many instances of forged miracles, and prophecies, and supernatural events, which, in all ages, have either been detected by contrary evidence, or which detect themselves by their absurdity, prove sufficiently the strong propensity of mankind to the extraordinary and the marvellous, and ought reasonably to beget a suspicion against all relations of this kind. This is our natural way of thinking, even with regard to the most common and most credible events. For instance: There is no kind of report which rises so easily, and spreads so quickly, especially in country places and provincial towns, as those concerning marriages; insomuch that two young persons of equal condition never see each other twice, but the whole neighbourhood immediately join them together. The pleasure of telling a piece of news so interesting, of propagating it, and of being the first reporters of it, spreads the intelligence. And this is so well known, that no man of sense gives attention to these reports, till he find them confirmed by some greater evidence. Do not the same passions, and others still stronger, incline the generality of mankind to believe and report, with the greatest vehemence and assurance, all religious miracles?

Thirdly. It forms a strong presumption against all supernatural and miraculous relations, that they are observed chiefly to abound among ignorant and barbarous nations; or if a civilized people has ever given admission to any of them, that people will be found to have received them from ignorant and barbarous ancestors, who transmitted them with the inviolable sanction and authority, which always attend received opinions. When we peruse the first histories of all nations, we are apt to imagine ourselves transported into some new world; where the whole frame of nature is disjointed, and every element performs its operations in a different manner, from what it does at present. Battles, revolutions, pestilence, famine and death, are never the effect of those natural causes, which we experience. Prodigies, omens, oracles, judgements, quite obscure the few natural events, that are intermingled with them. But as the former grow thinner every page, in proportion as we advance nearer the enlightened ages, we soon learn, that there is nothing mysterious or supernatural in the case, but that all proceeds from the usual propensity of mankind towards the marvellous, and that, though this inclination may at intervals receive a check from sense and learning, it can never be thoroughly extirpated from human nature.

It is strange, a judicious reader is apt to say, upon the perusal of these wonderful historians, *that such prodigious events never happen in our days.* But it is nothing strange, I hope, that men should lie in all ages. You must surely have seen instances enough of that frailty. You have yourself heard many such marvellous relations started, which, being treated with scorn by all the wise and judicious, have at last been abandoned even by the vulgar. Be assured, that those renowned lies, which have spread and flourished to such a monstrous height, arose from like beginnings; but being sown in a more proper soil, shot up at last into prodigies almost equal to those which they relate.

It was a wise policy in that false prophet, Alexander, who though now forgotten, was once so famous, to lay the first scene of his impostures in Paphlagonia, where, as Lucian tells us, the people were extremely ignorant and stupid, and ready to swallow even the grossest delusion. People at a distance, who are weak enough to think the matter at all worth enquiry, have no opportunity of receiving better information. The stories came magnified to them by a hundred circumstances. Fools are industrious in propagating the imposture; while the wise and learned are contented, in general, to deride its absurdity, without informing themselves of the particular facts, by which it may be distinctly refuted. And thus the imposter above mentioned was enabled to proceed, from his ignorant Paphlagonians, to the enlisting of votaries, even among the Grecian philosophers, and men of the most eminent rank and distinction in Rome: nay, could engage the attention of that sage emperor Marcus Aurelius; so far as to make him trust the success of a military expedition to his delusive prophecies.

The advantages are so great, of starting an imposture among an ignorant people, that, even though the delusion should be too gross to impose on the generality of them (*which, though seldom, is sometimes the case*) it has a much better chance for succeeding in remote countries, than if the first scene had been laid in a city renowned for arts and knowledge. The most ignorant and barbarous of these barbarians carry the report abroad. None of their countrymen have a large correspondence, or sufficient credit and authority to contradict and beat down the delusion. Men's inclination to the marvellous has full opportunity to display itself. And thus a story, which is universally exploded in the place where it was first started, shall pass for certain at a thousand miles distance. But had Alexander fixed his residence at Athens, the philosophers of that renowned mart of learning had immediately spread, throughout the whole Roman empire, their sense of the matter; which, being supported by so great authority, and displayed by all the force of reason and eloquence, had entirely opened the eyes of mankind. It is true; Lucian, passing by chance through Paphlagonia, had an opportunity of performing this good office. But, though much to be wished, it does not always happen, that every Alexander meets with a Lucian, ready to expose and detect his impostures.

I may add as a *fourth* reason, which diminishes the authority of prodigies, that there is no testimony for any, even those which have not been expressly detected, that is not opposed by an infinite number of witnesses; so that not only the miracle destroys the credit of testimony, but the testimony destroys itself. To make this the better understood, let us consider, that, in matters of religion, whatever is different is contrary; and that it is impossible the religions of ancient Rome, of Turkey, of Siam, and of China should, all of them, be established on any solid foundation. Every miracle, therefore, pretended to have been wrought in any of these religions (and all of them abound in miracles), as its direct scope is to establish the particular system to which it is attributed; so has it the same force, though more indirectly, to overthrow every other system. In destroying a rival system, it likewise destroys the credit of those miracles, on which that system was established; so that all the prodigies of different religions are to be regarded as contrary facts, and the evidences of these prodigies, whether weak or strong, as opposite to each other. According to this method of reasoning, when we believe any miracle of Mahomet or his successors, we have for our warrant the testimony of a few barbarous Arabians: And on the other hand, we are to regard the authority of Titus Livius, Plutarch, Tacitus, and, in short, of all the authors and witnesses, Grecian, Chinese, and Roman Catholic, who have related any miracle in their particular religion; I say, we are to regard their testimony in the same light as if they had mentioned that Mahometan miracle, and had in express terms contradicted it, with the same certainty as they have for the miracle they relate. This argument may appear over subtile and refined; but is not in reality different from the reasoning of a judge, who supposes, that the credit of two witnesses, maintaining a crime against any one, is destroyed by the testimony of two others, who affirm him to have been two hundred leagues distant, at the same instant when the crime is said to have been committed.

One of the best attested miracles in all profane history, is that which Tacitus reports of Vespasian, who cured a blind man in Alexandria, by means of his spittle, and a lame man by the mere touch of his foot; in obedience to a vision of the god Serapis, who had enjoined them to have recourse to the Emperor, for these miraculous cures. The story may be seen in that fine historian[4]; where every circumstance seems to add weight to the testimony, and might be displayed at large with all the force of argument and eloquence, if any one were now concerned to enforce the evidence of that exploded and idolatrous superstition. The gravity, solidity, age, and probity of so great an emperor, who, through the whole course of his life, conversed in a familiar manner with his friends and courtiers, and never affected those extraordinary airs of divinity assumed by Alexander and Demetrius. The historian, a contemporary writer, noted for candour and veracity, and withal, the greatest and most penetrating genius, perhaps, of all antiquity; and so free from any tendency to credulity, that he even lies under the contrary imputation, of atheism and profaneness: The persons, from whose authority he related the miracle, of established character for judgment and veracity, as we may well presume; eye-witness of the fact, and confirming their testimony, after the Flavian family was despoiled of the empire, and could no longer give any reward, as the price of a lie. *Utrumque qui interfuere, nunc quoque memorant, postquan nullum mendacio pretium.*[5] To which if we add the public nature of the facts, as related, it will appear, that no evidence can well be supposed stronger for so gross and so palpable a falsehood.

There is also a memorable story related by Cardinal de Retz, which may well deserve our consideration. When that intriguing politician fled into Spain, to avoid the persecution of his enemies, he passed through Saragossa, the capital of Arragon, where he was shewn, in the cathedral, a man, who had served seven years as a doorkeeper, and was well known to every body in town, that had ever paid his devotions at that church. He had been seen, for so long a time, wanting a leg; but recovered that limb by the rubbing of holy oil upon the stump; and the cardinal assures us that he saw him with two legs. This miracle was vouched by all the canons of the church; and the whole company in town were appealed to for a confirmation of the fact; whom the cardinal found, by their zealous devotion, to be thorough believers of the miracle. Here the relater was also contemporary to the sup-

---

[4]*Hist.* lib iv. cap. 81. Suetonius gives nearly the same account in *Vita Vesp.*
[5]["Both eyewitnesses report it, even now when there is no reward for lying"—Tacitus.]

posed prodigy, of an incredulous and libertine character, as well as of great genius; the miracle of so *singular* a nature as could scarcely admit of a counterfeit, and the witnesses very numerous, and all of them, in a manner, spectators of the fact to which they gave their testimony. And what adds mightily to the force of the evidence, and may double our surprise on this occasion, is, that the cardinal himself, who relates the story, seems not to give any credit to it, and consequently cannot be suspected of any concurrence in the holy fraud. He considered justly, that it was not requisite, in order to reject a fact of this nature, to be able accurately to disprove the testimony, and to trace its falsehood, through all the circumstances of knavery and credulity which produced it. He knew, that, as this was commonly altogether impossible at any small distance of time and place; so was it extremely difficult, even where one was immediately present, by reason of the bigotry, ignorance, cunning, and roguery of a great part of mankind. He therefore concluded, like a just reasoner, that such an evidence carried falsehood upon the very face of it, and that a miracle, supported by any human testimony, was more properly a subject of derision than of argument.

There surely never was a greater number of miracles ascribed to one person, than those, which were lately said to have been wrought in France upon the tomb of Abbé Paris, the famous Jansenist, with whose sanctity the people were so long deluded. The curing of the sick, giving hearing to the deaf, and sight to the blind, were every where talked of as the usual effects of that holy sepulchre. But what is more extraordinary; many of the miracles were immediately proved upon the spot, before judges of unquestioned integrity, attested by witnesses of credit and distinction, in a learned age, and on the most eminent theatre that is now in the world. Nor is this all: a relation of them was published and dispersed everywhere; nor were the *Jesuits*, though a learned body, supported by the civil magistrate, and determined enemies to those opinions, in whose favour the miracles were said to have been wrought, ever able distinctly to refute or detect them. Where shall we find such a number of circumstances, agreeing to the corroboration of one fact? And what have we to oppose to such a cloud of witnesses, but the absolute impossibility or miraculous nature of the events, which they relate? And this surely, in the eyes of all reasonable people, will alone be regarded as a sufficient refutation.

Is the consequence just, because some human testimony has the utmost force and authority in some cases, when it relates the battle of Philippi or Pharsalia for instance; that therefore all kinds of testimony must, in all cases, have equal force and authority? Suppose that the Cæsarean and Pompeian factions had, each of them, claimed the victory in these battles, and that the historians of each party had uniformly ascribed the advantage to their own side; how could mankind, at this distance, have been able to determine between them? The contrariety is equally strong between the miracles related by Herodotus or Plutarch, and those delivered by Mariana, Bede, or any monkish historian.

The wise lend a very academic faith to every report which favours the passion of the reporter; whether it magnifies his country, his family, or himself, or in any other way strikes in with his natural inclinations and propensities. But what greater temptation than to appear a missionary, a prophet, and ambassador from heaven? Who would not encounter many dangers and difficulties, in order to attain so sublime a character? Or if, by the help of vanity and a heated imagination, a man has first made a convert of himself, and entered seriously into the delusion; who ever scruples to make use of pious frauds, in support of so holy and meritorious a cause?

The smallest spark may here kindle into the greatest flame; because the materials are always prepared for it. The *avidum genus auricularum*,[6] the gazing populace, receive greedily, without examination, whatever sooths superstition, and promotes wonder.

How many stories of this nature have, in all ages, been detected and exploded in their infancy? How many more have been celebrated for a time, and have afterwards sunk into neglect and oblivion? Where such reports, therefore, fly about, the solution of the phenomenon is obvious; and we judge in conformity to regular experience and observation, when we account for it by the known and natural principles of credulity and delusion. And shall we, rather than have a recourse to so natural a solution, allow of a miraculous violation of the most established laws of nature?

I need not mention the difficulty of detecting a falsehood in any private or even public history, at the place, where it is said to happen; much more when the scene is removed to ever so small a distance. Even a court of judicature, with all the authority, accuracy, and judgement, which they can employ, find themselves often at a loss to distinguish between truth and falsehood in the most recent actions. But the matter never comes to any issue, if trusted to the common method of altercations and debate and flying rumours; especially when men's passions have taken part on either side.

In the infancy of new religions, the wise and learned commonly esteem the matter too inconsiderable to deserve their attention or regard. And when afterwards they would willingly detect the cheat, in order to undeceive the deluded multitude, the season is now past, and the records and witnesses, which might clear up the matter, have perished beyond recovery.

No means of detection remain, but those which must be drawn from the very testimony itself of the reporters: and these, though always sufficient with the judicious and knowing, are commonly too fine to fall under the comprehension of the vulgar.

Upon the whole, then, it appears, that no testimony for any kind of miracle has ever amounted to a probability, much less to a proof; and that, even supposing it amounted to a proof, it would be opposed by another proof; derived from the very nature of the fact, which it would endeavour to establish. It is experience only, which gives authority to human testimony;

[6]["sort of people with eager ears"—Lucretius.]

and it is the same experience, which assures us of the laws of nature. When, therefore, these two kinds of experience are contrary, we have nothing to do but substract the one from the other, and embrace an opinion, either on one side or the other, with that assurance which arises from the remainder. But according to the principle here explained, this substraction, with regard to all popular religions, amounts to an entire annihilation; and therefore we may establish it as a maxim, that no human testimony can have such force as to prove a miracle, and make it a just foundation for any such system of religion.

I beg the limitations here made may be remarked, when I say, that a miracle can never be proved, so as to be the foundation of a system of religion. For I own, that otherwise, there may possibly be miracles, or violations of the usual course of nature, of such a kind as to admit of proof from human testimony; though, perhaps, it will be impossible to find any such in all the records of history. Thus, suppose, all authors, in all languages, agree, that, from the first of January 1600, there was a total darkness over the whole earth for eight days: suppose that the tradition of this extraordinary event is still strong and lively among the people: that all travellers, who return from foreign countries, bring us accounts of the same tradition, without the least variation or contradiction: it is evident, that our present philosophers, instead of doubting the fact, ought to receive it as certain, and ought to search for the causes whence it might be derived. The decay, corruption, and dissolution of nature, is an event rendered probable by so many analogies, that any phenomenon, which seems to have a tendency towards that catastrophe, comes within the reach of human testimony, if that testimony be very extensive and uniform.

But suppose, that all the historians who treat of England, should agree, that, on the first of January 1600, Queen Elizabeth died; that both before and after her death she was seen by her physicians and the whole court, as is usual with persons of her rank; that her successor was acknowledged and proclaimed by the parliament; and that, after being interred a month, she again appeared, resumed the throne, and governed England for three years: I must confess that I should be surprised at the concurrence of so many odd circumstances, but should not have the least inclination to believe so miraculous an event. I should not doubt of her pretended death, and of those other public circumstances that followed it: I should only assert it to have been pretended, and that it neither was, nor possibly could be real. You would in vain object to me the difficulty, and almost impossibility of deceiving the world in an affair of such consequence; the wisdom and solid judgement of that renowned queen; with the little or no advantage which she could reap from so poor an artifice: All this might astonish me; but I would still reply, that the knavery and folly of men are such common phenomena, that I should rather believe the most extraordinary events to arise from their concurrence, than admit of so signal a violation of the laws of nature.

But should this miracle be ascribed to any new system of religion; men, in all ages, have been so much imposed on by ridiculous stories of that kind, that this very circumstance would be a full proof of a cheat, and sufficient, with all men of sense, not only to make them reject the fact, but even reject it without farther examination. Though the Being to whom the miracle is ascribed, be, in this case, Almighty, it does not, upon that account, become a whit more probable; since it is impossible for us to know the attributes or actions of such a Being, otherwise than from the experience which we have of his productions, in the usual course of nature. This still reduces us to past observation, and obliges us to compare the instances of the violation of truth in the testimony of men, with those of the violation of the laws of nature by miracles, in order to judge which of them is most likely and probable. As the violations of truth are more common in the testimony concerning religious miracles, than in that concerning any other matter of fact; this must diminish very much the authority of the former testimony, and make us form a general resolution, never to lend any attention to it, with whatever specious pretence it may be covered.

Lord Bacon seems to have embraced the same principles of reasoning. 'We ought,' says he, 'to make a collection or particular history of all monsters and prodigious births or productions, and in a word of every thing new, rare, and extraordinary in nature. But this must be done with the most severe scrutiny, lest we depart from truth. Above all, every relation must be considered as suspicious, which depends in any degree upon religion, as the prodigies of Livy: And no less so, every thing that is to be found in the writers of natural magic or alchemy, or such authors, who seem, all of them, to have an unconquerable appetite for falsehood and fable.'[7]

I am the better pleased with the method of reasoning here delivered, as I think it may serve to confound those dangerous friends or disguised enemies to the *Christian Religion*, who have undertaken to defend it by the principles of human reason. Our most holy religion is founded on *Faith*, not on reason; and it is a sure method of exposing it to put it to such a trial as it is, by no means, fitted to endure. To make this more evident, let us examine those miracles, related in scripture; and not to lose ourselves in too wide a field, let us confine ourselves to such as we find in the *Pentateuch*, which we shall examine, according to the principles of these pretended Christians, not as the word or testimony of God himself, but as the production of a mere human writer and historian. Here then we are first to consider a book, presented to us by a barbarous and ignorant people, written in an age when they were still more barbarous, and in all probability long after the facts which it relates, corroborated by no concurring testimony, and resembling those fabulous accounts, which every nation gives of its origin. Upon reading this book, we find it full of prodigies and miracles. It gives an account of a state of the world and of human nature entirely different from the present: Of our fall from that state: Of the age of man, extended to near a thousand years: Of the destruction of the world by a deluge: Of the arbitrary choice of one people, as the favourites of heaven; and that people the countrymen

---

[7]*Nov. Org.* lib. ii. aph. 29.

of the author: Of their deliverance from bondage by prodigies the most astonishing imaginable: I desire any one to lay his hand upon his heart, and after a serious consideration declare, whether he thinks that the falsehood of such a book, supported by such a testimony, would be more extraordinary and miraculous than all the miracles it relates; which is, however, necessary to make it be received, according to the measures of probability above established.

What we have said of miracles may be applied, without any variation, to prophecies; and indeed, all prophecies are real miracles, and as such only, can be admitted as proofs of any revelation. If it did not exceed the capacity of human nature to foretell future events, it would be absurd to employ any prophecy as an argument for a divine mission or authority from heaven. So that, upon the whole, we may conclude, that the *Christian Religion* not only was at first attended with miracles, but even at this day cannot be believed by any reasonable person without one. Mere reason is insufficient to convince us of its veracity: And whoever is moved by *Faith* to assent to it, is conscious of a continued miracle in his own person, which subverts all the principles of his understanding, and gives him a determination to believe what is most contrary to custom and experience.

�֍ SÖREN KIERKEGAARD

21. *Truth and Subjectivity*

Sören Kierkegaard (1813–1855), "the melancholy Dane," is usually considered the father of modern existentialism. Revolting against both the speculative philosophy of Hegel with its interest in the evolving universal, and his own state church with its superficial commitment, he sought to make Christian faith a matter of individual passion and appropriation. In addition to the *Postscript*, his works include *Philosophical Fragments*, *Fear and Trembling*, *Either/Or*, and *Sickness unto Death*, all of which are studied by literary stylists as well as philosophers and theologians.

From *Concluding Unscientific Postscript*

BOOK I

Introductory Remarks concerning the Objective Problem

From an objective standpoint Christianity is a *res in facto posita*,[1] whose truth it is proposed to investigate in a purely objective manner, for the accom-

From Sören Kierkegaard, *Concluding Unscientific Postscript*, tr. David F. Swenson and Walter Lowrie (Princeton: Princeton University Press, 1941). Reprinted by permission of Princeton University Press and The American Scandinavian Foundation.
    [1]["thing posited in fact."]

modating subject is much too objective not to leave himself out; or perhaps he even unhesitatingly counts himself in, as one who possesses faith as a matter of course. The truth in this objective sense may mean, first, the historical truth; second, the philosophical truth. Viewed as historical, the truth of Christianity must be determined through a critical examination of the various sources, and so forth; in short, in the same manner that historical truth generally is determined. When the question of the philosophical truth is raised, the object is to determine the relationship of the doctrine thus historically given and verified, to the eternal truth.

The inquiring, speculating, and knowing subject thus raises a question of truth. But he does not raise the question of a subjective truth, the truth of appropriation and assimilation. The inquiring subject is indeed interested; but he is not infinitely and personally and passionately interested on behalf of his own eternal happiness for his relationship to this truth. Far be it from the objective subject to display such presumption, such vanity of spirit.

The inquiring subject must be in one or the other of two situations. *Either* he is in faith convinced of the truth of Christianity, and in faith assured of his own relationship to it; in which case he cannot be infinitely interested in all the rest, since faith itself is the infinite interest in Christianity, and since every other interest may readily come to constitute a temptation. *Or* the inquirer is, on the other hand, not in an attitude of faith, but objectively in an attitude of contemplation, and hence not infinitely interested in the determination of the question.

So much here at the outset, by way of calling attention to a consideration to be developed in Part II, namely, that the problem cannot in this manner decisively arise; which means that it does not arise at all, since decisiveness is of the essence of the problem. Let the inquiring scholar labor with incessant zeal, even to the extent of shortening his life in the enthusiastic service of science; let the speculative philosopher be sparing neither of time nor of diligence; they are none the less not interested infinitely, personally and passionately, nor could they wish to be. On the contrary, they will seek to cultivate an attitude of objectivity and disinterestedness. And as for the relationship of the subject to the truth when he comes to know it, the assumption is that if only the truth is brought to light, its appropriation is a relatively unimportant matter, something which follows as a matter of course. And in any case, what happens to the individual is in the last analysis a matter of indifference. Herein lies the lofty equanimity of the scholar, and the comic thoughtlessness of his parrot-like echo.

Book I, Part II

Chapter 2: The Subjective Truth, Inwardness; Truth Is Subjectivity

. . . In an attempt to make clear the difference of way that exists between an objective and a subjective reflection, I shall now proceed to show how a subjective reflection makes its way inwardly in inwardness. Inwardness in an existing subject culminates in passion; corresponding to passion in the subject the truth becomes a paradox; and the fact that the truth becomes a paradox is rooted precisely in its having a relationship to an existing subject. Thus the one corresponds to the other. By forgetting that one is an existing subject, passion goes by the board and the truth is no longer a paradox; the knowing subject becomes a fantastic entity rather than a human being, and the truth becomes a fantastic object for the knowledge of this fantastic entity.

When the question of truth is raised in an objective manner, reflection is directed objectively to the truth, as an object to which the knower is related. Reflection is not focussed upon the relationship, however, but upon the question of whether it is the truth to which the knower is related. If only the object to which he is related is the truth, the subject is accounted to be in the truth. When the question of the truth is raised subjectively, reflection is directed subjectively to the nature of the individual's relationship; if only the mode of this relationship is in the truth, the individual is in the truth even if he should happen to be thus related to what is not true.[2] Let us take as an example the knowledge of God. Objectively, reflection is directed to the problem of whether this object is the true God; subjectively, reflection is directed to the question whether the individual is related to a something *in such a manner* that his relationship is in truth a God-relationship. On which side is the truth now to be found? Ah, may we not here resort to a mediation, and say: It is on neither side, but in the mediation of both?[3] Excellently well said, provided we might have it explained how an existing individual manages to be in a state of mediation. For to be in a state of mediation is to be finished, while to exist is to become. Nor can an existing individual be in two places at the same time—he cannot be an identity of subject and object. When he is nearest to being in two places at the same time he is in passion; but passion is momentary, and passion is also the highest expression of subjectivity.

The existing individual who chooses to pursue the objective way enters upon the entire approximation-process by which it is proposed to bring God to light objectively. But this is in all eternity impossible, because God is a subject, and therefore exists only for subjectivity in inwardness. The existing individual who chooses the subjective way apprehends instantly the entire dialectical difficulty involved in having to use some time, perhaps a long time, in finding God objectively; and he feels this dialectical difficulty in all its painfulness, because every moment is wasted in which he does not have God.[4] That very instant he has God, not by virtue of any objective deliberation, but by virtue of the infinite passion of inwardness. The objective

[2]The reader will observe that the question here is about essential truth, or about the truth which is essentially related to existence, and that it is precisely for the sake of clarifying it as inwardness or as subjectivity that this contrast is drawn.

[3][Kierkegaard's recurring reference to "mediation" is an allusion to the Hegelian doctrine that reality is the synthesis of opposites, including the knowing subject and its object.]

[4]In this manner God certainly becomes a postulate, but not in the otiose manner in which this word is commonly understood. It becomes clear rather that the only way in which an existing individual comes into relation with God, is when the dialectical contradiction brings his passion to the point of despair, and helps him to embrace God with the "category of despair"

inquirer, on the other hand, is not embarrassed by such dialectical difficulties as are involved in devoting an entire period of investigation to finding God— since it is possible that the inquirer may die tomorrow; and if he lives he can scarcely regard God as something to be taken along if convenient, since God is precisely that which one takes *a tout prix*, which in the understanding of passion constitutes the true inward relationship to God.

It is at this point, so difficult dialectically, that the way swings off for everyone who knows what it means to think, and to think existentially; which is something very different from sitting at a desk and writing about what one has never done, something very different from writing *de omnibus dubitandum*[5] and at the same time being as credulous existentially as the most sensuous of men. Here is where the way swings off, and the change is marked by the fact that while objective knowledge rambles comfortably on by way of the long road of approximation without being impelled by the urge of passion, subjective knowledge counts every delay a deadly peril, and the decision so infinitely important and so instantly pressing that it is as if the opportunity had already passed.

Now when the problem is to reckon up on which side there is most truth, whether on the side of one who seeks the true God objectively, and pursues the approximate truth of the God-idea; or on the side of one who, driven by the infinite passion of his need of God, feels an infinite concern for his own relationship to God in truth (and to be at one and the same time on both sides equally, is as we have noted not possible for an existing individual, but is merely the happy delusion of an imaginary I-am-I): the answer cannot be in doubt for anyone who has not been demoralized with the aid of science. If one who lives in the midst of Christendom goes up to the house of God, the house of the true God, with the true conception of God in his knowledge, and prays, but prays in a false spirit; and one who lives in an idolatrous community prays with the entire passion of the infinite, although his eyes rest upon the image of an idol: where is there most truth? The one prays in truth to God though he worships an idol; the other prays falsely to the true God, and hence worships in fact an idol.

When one man investigates objectively the problem of immortality, and another embraces an uncertainty with the passion of the infinite: where is there most truth, and who has the greater certainty? The one has entered upon a never-ending approximation, for the certainty of immortality lies precisely in the subjectivity of the individual; the other is immortal, and fights for his immortality by struggling with the uncertainty. Let us consider Socrates. Nowadays everyone dabbles in a few proofs; some have several such proofs, others fewer. But Socrates! He puts the question objectively in a problematic manner: *if* there is an immortality.[6] He must therefore be accounted a doubter

---

(faith). Then the postulate is so far from being arbitrary that it is precisely a life-necessity. It is then not so much that God is a postulate, as that the existing individual's postulation of God is a necessity.

[5]["all things are to be doubted."]

[6][Cf. Plato, *Apology*, 40c ff.; *Phaedo*, 114c f.]

in comparison with one of our modern thinkers with the three proofs? By no means. On this "if" he risks his entire life, he has the courage to meet death, and he has with the passion of the infinite so determined the pattern of his life that it must be found acceptable—*if* there is an immortality. Is any better proof capable of being given for the immortality of the soul? But those who have the three proofs do not at all determine their lives in conformity therewith; if there is an immortality it must feel disgust over their manner of life: can any better refutation be given of the three proofs? The bit of uncertainty that Socrates had, helped him because he himself contributed the passion of the infinite; the three proofs that the others have do not profit them at all, because they are dead to spirit and enthusiasm, and their three proofs, in lieu of proving anything else, prove just this. A young girl may enjoy all the sweetness of love on the basis of what is merely a weak hope that she is beloved, because she rests everything on this weak hope; but many a wedded matron more than once subjected to the strongest expressions of love, has in so far indeed had proofs, but strangely enough has not enjoyed *quod erat demonstrandum.*[7] The Socratic ignorance, which Socrates held fast with the entire passion of his inwardness, was thus an expression for the principle that the eternal truth is related to an existing individual, and that this truth must therefore be a paradox for him as long as he exists; and yet it is possible that there was more truth in the Socratic ignorance as it was in him, than in the entire objective truth of the System,[8] which flirts with what the times demand and accommodates itself to *Privatdocents.*

The objective accent falls on WHAT is said, the subjective accent on HOW it is said. This distinction holds even in the aesthetic realm, and receives definite expression in the principle that what is in itself true may in the mouth of such and such a person become untrue. In these times this distinction is particularly worthy of notice, for if we wish to express in a single sentence the difference between ancient times and our own, we should doubtless have to say: "In ancient times only an individual here and there knew the truth; now all know it, except that the inwardness of its appropriation stands in an inverse relationship to the extent of its dissemination."[9] Aesthetically the contradiction that truth becomes untruth in this or that person's mouth, is

---

[7]["that which was to be demonstrated."]

[8][I.e. Hegel's philosophy.]

[9]*Stages on Life's Way*, Note on p. 426. Though ordinarily not wishing an expression of opinion on the part of reviewers, I might at this point almost desire it, provided such opinions, so far from flattering me, amounted to an assertion of the daring truth that what I say is something that everybody knows, even every child, and that the cultured know infinitely much better. If it only stands fast that everyone knows it, my standpoint is in order, and I shall doubtless make shift to manage with the unity of the comic and the tragic. If there were anyone who did not know it I might perhaps be in danger of being dislodged from my position of equilibrium by the thought that I might be in a position to communicate to someone the needful preliminary knowledge. It is just this which engages my interest so much, this that the cultured are accustomed to say: that everyone knows what the highest is. This was not the case in paganism, nor in Judaism, nor in the seventeen centuries of Christianity. Hail to the nineteenth century! Everyone knows it. What progress has been made since the time when only a few knew it. To make up for this, perhaps, we must assume that no one nowadays does it.

best construed comically: In the ethico-religious sphere, accent is again on the "how." But this is not to be understood as referring to demeanor, expression, or the like; rather it refers to the relationship sustained by the existing individual, in his own existence, to the content of his utterance. Objectively the interest is focussed merely on the thought-content, subjectively on the inwardness. At its maximum this inward "how" is the passion of the infinite, and the passion of the infinite is the truth. But the passion of the infinite is precisely subjectivity, and thus subjectivity becomes the truth. Objectively there is no infinite decisiveness, and hence it is objectively in order to annul the difference between good and evil, together with the principle of contradiction, and therewith also the infinite difference between the true and the false. Only in subjectivity is there decisiveness, to seek objectivity is to be in error. It is the passion of the infinite that is the decisive factor and not its content, for its content is precisely itself. In this manner subjectivity and the subjective "how" constitute the truth.

But the "how" which is thus subjectively accentuated precisely because the subject is an existing individual, is also subject to a dialectic with respect to time. In the passionate moment of decision, where the road swings away from objective knowledge, it seems as if the infinite decision were thereby realized. But in the same moment the existing individual finds himself in the temporal order, and the subjective "how" is transformed into a striving, a striving which receives indeed its impulse and a repeated renewal from the decisive passion of the infinite, but is nevertheless a striving.

When subjectivity is the truth, the conceptual determination of the truth must include an expression for the antithesis to objectivity, a momento of the fork in the road where the way swings off; this expression will at the same time serve as an indication of the tension of the subjective inwardness. Here is such a definition of truth: *An objective uncertainty held fast in an appropriation-process of the most passionate inwardness is the truth*, the highest truth attainable for an *existing* individual. At the point where the way swings off (and where this is cannot be specified objectively, since it is a matter of subjectivity), there objective knowledge is placed in abeyance. Thus the subject merely has, objectively, the uncertainty; but it is this which precisely increases the tension of that infinite passion which constitutes his inwardness. The truth is precisely the venture which chooses an objective uncertainty with the passion of the infinite. I contemplate the order of nature in the hope of finding God, and I see omnipotence and wisdom; but I also see much else that disturbs my mind and excites anxiety. The sum of all this is an objective uncertainty. But it is for this very reason that the inwardness becomes as intense as it is, for it embraces this objective uncertainty with the entire passion of the infinite. In the case of a mathematical proposition the objectivity is given, but for this reason the truth of such a proposition is also a indifferent truth.

But the above definition of truth is an equivalent expression for faith. Without risk there is no faith. Faith is precisely the contradiction between the infinite passion of the individual's inwardness and the objective uncertainty. If I am capable of grasping God objectively, I do not believe, but precisely because I cannot do this I must believe. If I wish to preserve myself in faith I must constantly be intent upon holding fast the objective uncertainty, so as to remain out upon the deep, over seventy thousand fathoms of water, still preserving my faith.

In the principle that subjectivity, inwardness, is the truth, there is comprehended the Socratic wisdom, whose everlasting merit it was to have become aware of the essential significance of existence, of the fact that the knower is an existing individual. For this reason Socrates was in the truth by virtue of his ignorance, in the highest sense in which this was possible within paganism. To attain to an understanding of this, to comprehend that the misfortune of speculative philosophy is again and again to have forgotten that the knower is an existing individual, is in our objective age difficult enough. But to have made an advance upon Socrates without even having understood what he understood, is at any rate not "Socratic." Compare the "Moral" of the *Fragments*.

Let us now start from this point, and as was attempted in the *Fragments*, seek a determination of thought which will really carry us further. I have nothing here to do with the question of whether this proposed thought-determination is true or not, since I am merely experimenting; but it must at any rate be clearly mainfest that the Socratic thought is understood within the new proposal, so that at least I do not come out behind Socrates.

When subjectivity, inwardness, is the truth, the truth becomes objectively a paradox; and the fact that the truth is objectively a paradox shows in its turn that subjectivity is the truth. For the objective situation is repellent; and the expression for the objective repulsion constitutes the tension and the measure of the corresponding inwardness. The paradoxical character of the truth is its objective uncertainty; this uncertainty is an expression for the passionate inwardness, and this passion is precisely the truth. So far the Socratic principle. The eternal and essential truth, the truth which has an essential relationship to an existing individual because it pertains essentially to existence (all other knowledge being from the Socratic point of view accidental, its scope and degree a matter of indifference), is a paradox. But the eternal essential truth is by no means in itself a paradox; but it becomes paradoxical by virtue of its relationship to an existing individual. The Socratic ignorance gives expression to the objective uncertainty attaching to the truth, while his inwardness in existing is the truth. To anticipate here what will be developed later, let me make the following remark. The Socratic ignorance is an analogue to the category of the absurd, only that there is still less of objective certainty in the absurd, and in the repellent effect that the absurd exercises. It is certain only that it is absurd, and precisely on that account it incites to an infinitely greater tension in the corresponding inwardness. The Socratic inwardness in existing is an analogue to faith; only that the inwardness of faith, corresponding as it does, not to the repulsion of the Socratic ignorance, but to the repulsion exerted by the absurd, is infinitely more profound. . . .

What now is the absurd? The absurd is—that the eternal truth has come into being in time, that God has come into being, has been born, has grown up, and so forth, precisely like any other individual human being, quite indistinguishable from other individuals. For every assumption of immediate recognizability is pre-Socratic paganism, and from the Jewish point of view, idolatry; and every determination of what really makes an advance beyond the Socratic must essentially bear the stamp of having a relationship to God's having come into being; for faith *sensu strictissimo*, as was developed in the *Fragments*,[10] refers to becoming. When Socrates believed that there was a God, he saw very well that where the way swings off there is also an objective way of approximation, for example by the contemplation of nature and human history, and so forth. His merit was precisely to shun this way, where the quantitative siren song enchants the mind and deceives the existing individual.

In relation to the absurd, the objective approximation-process is like the comedy, *Misunderstanding upon Misunderstanding*, which is generally played by *Privatdocents* and speculative philosophers. The absurd is precisely by its objective repulsion the measure of the intensity of faith in inwardness. Suppose a man who wishes to acquire faith; let the comedy begin. He wishes to have faith, but he wishes also to safeguard himself by means of an objective inquiry and its approximation-process. What happens? With the help of the approximation-process the absurd becomes something different; it becomes probable, it becomes increasingly probable, it becomes extremely and emphatically probable. Now he is ready to believe it, and he ventures to claim for himself that he does not believe as shoemakers and tailors and simple fold believe, but only after long deliberation. Now he is ready to believe it; and lo, now it has become precisely impossible to believe it. Anything that is almost probable, or probable, or extremely and emphatically probable, is something he can almost know, or as good as know, or extremely and emphatically almost *know*—but it is impossible to *believe*. For the absurd is the object of faith, and the only object that can be believed.

Or suppose a man who says that he has faith, but desires to make his faith clear to himself, so as to understand himself in his faith. Now the comedy again begins. The object of faith becomes almost probable, as good as probable, extremely and emphatically probable. He has completed his investigations, and he ventures to claim for himself that he does not believe as shoemakers and tailors and other simple fold believe, but that he has also understood himself in his believing. Strange understanding! On the contrary, he has in fact learned something else about faith than when he believed; and he has learned that he no longer believes, since he almost knows, or as good as knows, or extremely and emphatically almost knows.

In so far as the absurd comprehends within itself the factor of becoming, one way of approximation will be that which confuses the absurd fact of such a becoming (which is the object of faith) with a simple historical fact, and hence seeks historical certainty for that which is absurd, because

---

[10][Cf. Sören Kierkegaard, *Philosophical Fragments*, "The Interlude," sect. 4.]

it involves the contradiction that something which can become historical only in direct opposition to all human reason, has become historical. It is this contradiction which constitutes the absurd, and which can only be believed. If historical certainty with respect to it is assumed, the certainty attained is merely that the something which is thus assumed as certain is not the thing in question. A witness can testify that he has believed it, and hence that so far from being an historical certainty it is directly contrary to his own reason; but such a witness thrusts the individual away in precisely the same sense that the absurd itself does. And a witness who does not so repel is *eo ipso* a deceiver, or a man who talks about something quite different, and can help only to obtain certainty about something quite different. A hundred thousand individual witnesses, who are individual witnesses precisely on account of the peculiar character of their testimony (that they have believed the absurd), cannot *en masse* become anything else, so as to make the absurd less absurd—and why less absurd? Because a hundred thousand human beings have separately, each one for himself, believed that it was absurd? On the contrary, these hundred thousand witnesses again exercise a repellent influence in nearly the same way that the absurd itself exercises it.

But this I need not here expound in greater detail. In the *Fragments* (especially where the distinction between the disciple at first-hand and at second-hand is shown to be illusory),[11] and in the first part of this book, I have already carefully enough expounded the thesis that all approximation is useless, since on the contrary it behooves us to get rid of introductory guarantees of security, proofs from consequences, and the whole mob of public pawnbrokers and guarantors, so as to permit the absurd to stand out in all its clarity—in order that the individual may believe if he wills it; I merely say that it must be strenuous in the highest degree so to believe.

If speculative philosophy wishes to take cognizance of this, and say as always, that there is no paradox when the matter is viewed eternally, divinely, theocentrically—then I admit that I am not in a position to determine whether the speculative philosopher is right, for I am only a poor existing human being, not competent to contemplate the eternal either eternally or divinely or theocentrically, but compelled to content myself with existing. So much is certain, however, that speculative philosophy carries everything back, back past the Socratic position, which at least comprehended that for an existing individual existence is essential; to say nothing of the failure of speculative philosophy to take time to grasp what it means to be so critically situated in existence as the existing individual in the experiment.

The difference between the Socratic position as here described and the position which goes beyond it is clear enough, and essentially the same as in the *Fragments*. For nothing is altered in the latter, and the former is made only a little more difficult, though not more difficult than it is. The difficulty has also been a little increased by the fact that while in the *Fragments* I merely brought out the thought-determinations of the paradox experi-

[11][Cf. *Ibid.*, Ch. 5.]

mentally, I have here at the same time subjoined an attempt latently to make the necessity of the paradox evident. Even if this attempt is somewhat weak, it is at any rate rather different from the speculative annulment of the paradox.

Christianity has declared itself to be the eternal essential truth which has come into being in time. It has proclaimed itself as the *Paradox*, and it has required of the individual the inwardness of faith in relation to that which stamps itself as an offense to the Jews and a folly to the Greeks—and an absurdity to the understanding [cf. I Cor. 1:18 ff.]. It is impossible more strongly to express the fact that subjectivity is truth, and that the objectivity is repellent, repellent even by virtue of its absurdity. And indeed it would seem very strange that Christianity should have come into the world merely to receive an explanation; as if it had been somewhat bewildered about itself, and hence entered the world to consult that wise man, the speculative philosopher, who can come to its assistance by furnishing the explanation. It is impossible to express with more intensive inwardness the principle that subjectivity is truth, than when subjectivity is in the first instance untruth, and yet subjectivity is the truth.

Suppose Christianity to be a mystery and intentionally so, a genuine and not a theatrical mystery, which is revealed in the fifth act of the drama, while a clever spectator sees through it in the course of the exposition. Suppose that a revelation *sensu strictissimo* must be a mystery, and that its sole and sufficient mark is precisely that it is a mystery; while a revelation *sensu laxiori*, the withdrawl by way of recollection into the eternal, is a revelation in the direct sense. Suppose that the degree of intellectual talent in relation to the misunderstanding was marked by the varying ability of the individual to make it seem more and more deceptively plausible that he had understood the mystery. Suppose it were after all a blessed thing, critically situated in the extreme press of existence, to sustain a relation to this mystery without understanding it, merely as a believer. Suppose Christianity never intended to be understood; suppose that, in order to express this, and to prevent anyone from misguidedly entering upon the objective way, it has declared itself to be the paradox. Suppose it wished to have significance only for existing individuals, and essentially for existing individuals in inwardness, in the inwardness of faith; which cannot be expressed more definitely than in the proposition that Christianity is the absurd, held fast in the passion of the infinite. Suppose it refuses to be understood, and that the maximum of understanding which could come in question is to understand that it cannot be understood. Suppose it therefore accentuates existence so decisively that the individual becomes a sinner, Christianity the paradox, existence the period of decision. Suppose that speculation were a temptation, the most dubious of all. Suppose that the speculative philosopher is, not indeed the prodigal son, for so the anxious divinity would characterize only the offended individual whom he nevertheless continues to love, but is the naughty child who refuses to remain where existing individuals belong, namely, in the existential training school where one becomes mature only through inwardness in existing, but instead demands a place in the divine council chamber, constantly shouting that viewed eternally, divinely, theocentrically, there is no paradox. Suppose the speculative philosopher were the restless tenant, who though it is notorious that he is merely a tenant, in view of the abstract truth that all property is from the standpoint of the eternal and the divine, in common, insists on playing the owner, so that there is nothing else to do than to send for an officer to say to him what the policemen said to Geert Westphaler: "It hurts us to have to come on such an errand."[12]

Has the thing of being human now become somewhat different from what it was in older times, are the conditions not still the same, namely, to be a particular existing being, for whom existing is essential as long as he continues in existence? But men have now so much more knowledge than formerly. Quite true, but suppose Christianity is not a matter of knowledge, so that the increased knowledge is of no avail, except to make it easier to fall into the confusion of considering Christianity as a matter of knowledge. And if men do have more knowledge, and we are not speaking about the knowledge of railroads, machines, and kaleidoscopes, but knowledge about the religious, how have they acquired it? Surely with the aid of Christianity. So this is the way men show their gratitude. They learn something from Christianity, misunderstand it, and by way of additional misunderstanding use it against Christianity. If in olden times the fearful thing was that one might be offended, now the fearful thing is that there is nothing fearful any more, that in a trice, before the individual has time to look around, he becomes a philosopher who speculates over faith. And over what faith does he speculate? Is it over the faith that he has, and especially over whether he has it or not? Ah, no, such a subject is too trifling for an objective speculative philosopher. What he speculates about is the objective faith. The objective faith, what does that mean? It means a sum of doctrinal propositions. But suppose Christianity were nothing of the kind; suppose on the contrary it were inwardness, and hence also the paradox, so as to thrust the individual away objectively, in order to obtain significance for the existing individual in the inwardness of his existence, in order to place him as decisively as no judge can place an accused person, between time and eternity in time, between heaven and hell in the time of salvation. The objective faith—it is as if Christianity also had been promulgated as a letter system, if not quite so good as the Hegelian; it is as if Christ—aye, I speak without offense—it is as if Christ were a professor, and as if the Apostles had formed a little scientific society. Verily, if it was once difficult to become a Christian, now I believe it becomes increasingly difficult year by year, because it has now become so easy that the only ambition which stirs any competition is that of becoming a speculative philosopher. And yet the speculative philosopher is perhaps at the farthest possible remove from Christianity, and it is perhaps far preferable to an offended individual who nevertheless sustains a relation to Christianity than a speculative philosopher who assumes to have understood it. In so far there is hope that there will be some resemblance left between

[12][From Ludwig Holberg's comedy, *Mester Geert Westphaler*.]

a Christian now and in the earliest days, so that it will again be regarded as folly for anyone to entertain the notion of becoming a Christian. In the earliest days the Christian was a fool in the eyes of the world, and to Jews and pagans alike it seemed folly for anyone to seek to become one. Now we are Christians as a matter of course, but if anyone desires to be a Christian with infinite passion he is judged to be a fool, just as it is always folly to put forth an infinite passionate exertion for the sake of becoming what one already is; as if a man were to sacrifice all his wealth to buy a jewel—which he already owned. Formerly a Christian was a fool in the eyes of the world, and now that all men are Christians he nevertheless becomes a fool—in the eyes of Christians. . . .

Chapter 3: Real or Ethical Subjectivity—The Subjective Thinker

. . . When the different spheres are not decisively distinguished from one another, confusion reigns everywhere. When people are curious about a thinker's reality and find it interesting to know something about it, and so forth, this interest is intellectually reprehensible. The maximum of attainment in the sphere of the intellectual is to become altogether indifferent to the thinker's reality. But by being thus muddle-headed in the intellectual sphere, one acquires a certain resemblance to a believer. A believer is one who is infinitely interested in another's reality. This is a decisive criterion for faith, and the interest in question is not just a little curiosity, but an absolute dependence upon faith's object.

The object of faith is the reality of another, and the relationship is one of infinite interest. The object of faith is not a doctrine, for then the relationship would be intellectual, and it would be of importance not to botch it, but to realize the maximum intellectual relationship. The object of faith is not a teacher with a doctrine; for when a teacher has a doctrine, the doctrine is *eo ipso* more important than the teacher, and the relationship is again intellectual, and it again becomes important not to botch it, but to realize the maximum intellectual relationship. The object of faith is the reality of the teacher, that the teacher really exists. The answer of faith is therefore unconditionally yes or no. For it does not concern a doctrine, as to whether the doctrine is true or not; it is the answer to a question concerning a fact: "Do you or do you not suppose that he has really existed?" And the answer, it must be noted, is with infinite passion. In the case of a human being, it is thoughtlessness to lay so great and infinite a stress on the question whether he has existed or not. If the object of faith is a human being, therefore, the whole proposal is the vagary of a stupid person, who has not even understood the spirit of the intellectual and the aesthetic. The object of faith is hence the reality of the God-man in the sense of his existence. But existence involves first and foremost particularity, and this is why thought must abstract from existence, because the particular cannot be thought, but only the universal. The object of faith is thus God's reality in existence as a particular individual, the fact that God has existed as an individual human being.

Christianity is no doctrine concerning the unity of the divine and the human, or concerning the identity of subject and object; nor is it any other of the logical transcriptions of Christianity. If Christianity were a doctrine, the relationship to it would not be one of faith, for only an intellectual type of relationship can correspond to a doctrine. Christianity is therefore not a doctrine, but the fact that God has existed.

The realm of faith is thus not a class for numskulls in the sphere of the intellectual, or an asylum for the feeble-minded. Faith constitutes a sphere all by itself, and every misunderstanding of Christianity may at once be recognized by its transforming it into a doctrine, transferring it to the sphere of the intellectual. The maximum of attainment within the sphere of the intellectual, namely, to realize an entire indifference as to the reality of the teacher, is in the sphere of faith at the opposite end of the scale. The maximum of attainment within the sphere of faith is to become infinitely interested in the reality of the teacher. . . .

✳ WILLIAM JAMES

22. *In Justification of Faith*

William James (1842–1910) was one of the founders of the American philosophy known as Pragmatism. In his well-known essay "The Will to Believe" (first presented as a lecture to the philosophy clubs of Yale and Brown Universities), James argues on behalf of the pragmatic or practical advantage of certain kinds of beliefs. James' *Varieties of Religious Experience*, a classic study in the psychology of religion, reflects still another side of his contribution to the study of religious conviction.

From *The Will to Believe and Other Essays*

THE WILL TO BELIEVE

In the recently published *Life* by Leslie Stephen of his brother, Fitz-James, there is an account of a school to which the latter went when he was a boy. The teacher, a certain Mr. Guest, used to converse with his pupils in this wise: "Gurney, what is the difference between justification and sanctification?—Stephen, prove the omnipotence of God!" etc. In the midst of our Harvard freethinking and indifference we are prone to imagine that here at your good old orthodox College conversation continues to be somewhat upon this order; and to show you that we at Harvard have not lost all interest in these vital subjects, I have brought with me to-night something like a sermon on justification by faith to read to you,—I mean an essay in justification *of* faith, a defence of our right to adopt a believing attitude in religious matters,

William James, *The Will to Believe and Other Essays* (New York: Longmans Green & Co., 1896).

in spite of the fact that our merely logical intellect may not have been coerced. 'The Will to Believe,' accordingly, is the title of my paper.

I have long defended to my own students the lawfulness of voluntarily adopted faith; but as soon as they have got well imbued with the logical spirit, they have as a rule refused to admit my contention to be lawful philosophically, even though in point of fact they were personally all the time chock-full of some faith or other themselves. I am all the while, however, so profoundly convinced that my own position is correct, that your invitation has seemed to me a good occasion to make my statements more clear. Perhaps your minds will be more open than those with which I have hitherto had to deal. I will be as little technical as I can, though I must begin by setting up some technical distinctions that will help us in the end.

I

Let us give the name of *hypothesis* to anything that may be proposed to our belief; and just as the electricians speak of live and dead wires, let us speak of any hypothesis as either *live* or *dead*. A live hypothesis is one which appeals as a real possibility to him to whom it is proposed. If I ask you to believe in the Mahdi, the notion makes no electric connection with your nature,—it refuses to scintillate with any credibility at all. As an hypothesis it is completely dead. To an Arab, however (even if he be not one of the Mahdi's followers), the hypothesis is among the mind's possibilities: it is alive. This shows that deadness and liveness in an hypothesis are not intrinsic properties, but relations to the individual thinker. They are measured by his willingness to act. The maximum of liveness in an hypothesis means willingness to act irrevocably. Practically, that means belief; but there is some believing tendency wherever there is willingness to act at all.

Next, let us call the decision between two hypotheses an *option*. Options may be of several kinds. They may be—1, *living* or *dead*; 2, *forced* or *avoidable*; 3, *momentous* or *trivial*; and for our purposes we may call an option a *genuine* option when it is of the forced, living, and momentous kind.

1. A living option is one in which both hypotheses are live ones. If I say to you: "Be a theosophist or be a Mohammedan," it is probably a dead option, because for you neither hypothesis is likely to be alive. But if I say: "Be an agnostic or be a Christian," it is otherwise: trained as you are, each hypothesis makes some appeal, however small, to your belief.

2. Next, if I say to you: "Choose between going out with your umbrella or without it," I do not offer you a genuine option, for it is not forced. You can easily avoid it by not going out at all. Similarly, if I say, "Either love me or hate me," "Either call my theory true or call it false," your option is avoidable. You may remain indifferent to me, neither loving nor hating, and you may decline to offer any judgment as to my theory. But if I say, "Either accept this truth or go without it," I put on you a forced option, for there is no standing place outside of the alternative. Every dilemma based on a complete logical disjunction, with no possibility of not choosing, is an option of this forced kind.

3. Finally, if I were Dr. Nansen and proposed to you to join my North Pole expedition, your option would be momentous; for this would probably be your only similar opportunity, and your choice now would either exclude you from the North Pole sort of immortality altogether or put at least the chance of it into your hands. He who refuses to embrace a unique opportunity loses the prize as surely as if he tried and failed. *Per contra*, the option is trivial when the opportunity is not unique, when the stake is insignificant, or when the decision is reversible if it later prove unwise. Such trivial options abound in the scientific life. A chemist finds an hypothesis live enough to spend a year in its verification: he believes in it to that extent. But if his experiments prove inconclusive either way, he is quit for his loss of time, no vital harm being done.

It will facilitate our discussion if we keep all these distinctions well in mind.

II

The next matter to consider is the actual psychology of human opinion. When we look at certain facts, it seems as if our passional and volitional nature lay at the root of all our convictions. When we look at others, it seems as if they could do nothing when the intellect had once said its say. Let us take the latter facts up first.

Does it not seem preposterous on the very face of it to talk of our opinions being modifiable at will? Can our will either help or hinder our intellect in its perceptions of truth? Can we, by just willing it, believe that Abraham Lincoln's existence is a myth, and that the portraits of him in *McClure's Magazine* are all of some one else? Can we, by any effort of our will, or by any strength of wish that it were true, believe ourselves well and about when we are roaring with rheumatism in bed, or feel certain that the sum of the two one-dollar bills in our pocket must be a hundred dollars? We can *say* any of these things, but we are absolutely impotent to believe them; and of just such things is the whole fabric of the truths that we do believe in made up,—matters of fact, immediate or remote, as Hume said, and relations between ideas, which are either there or not there for us if we see them so, and which if not there cannot be put there by any action of our own.

In Pascal's *Thoughts*[1] there is a celebrated passage known in literature as Pascal's wager. In it he tries to force us into Christianity by reasoning as if our concern with truth resembled our concern with the stakes in a game of chance. Translated freely his words are these: You must either believe or not believe that God is—which will you do? Your human reason cannot say. A game is going on between you and the nature of things which at the day of judgment will bring out either heads or tails. Weigh what your gains and your losses would be if you should stake all you have on heads,

[1][Blaise Pascal, *Pensées*, no. 233.]

or God's existence: if you win in such case, you gain eternal beatitude; if you lose, you lose nothing at all. If there were an infinity of chances, and only one for God in this wager, still you ought to stake your all on God; for though you surely risk a finite loss by this procedure, any finite loss is reasonable, even a certain one is reasonable, if there is but the possibility of infinite gain. Go, then, and take holy water, and have masses said; belief will come and stupefy your scruples,—*Cela vous fera croire et vous abêtira.* Why should you not? At bottom, what have you to lose?

You probably feel that when religious faith expresses itself thus, in the language of the gaming-table, it is put to its last trumps. Surely Pascal's own personal belief in masses and holy water had far other springs; and this celebrated page of his is but an argument for others, a last desperate snatch at a weapon against the hardness of the unbelieving heart. We feel that a faith in masses and holy water adopted wilfully from such a mechanical calculation would lack the inner soul of faith's reality; and if we were ourselves in the place of the Deity, we should probably take particular pleasure in cutting off believers of this pattern from their infinite reward. It is evident that unless there be some pre-existing tendency to believe in masses and holy water, the option offered to the will by Pascal is not a living option. Certainly no Turk ever took to masses and holy water on its account; and even to us Protestants these means of salvation seem such foregone impossibilities that Pascal's logic, invoked for them specifically, leaves us unmoved. As well might the Mahdi write to us, saying, "I am the Expected One whom God has created in his effulgence. You shall be infinitely happy if you confess me; otherwise you shall be cut off from the light of the sun. Weigh, then, your infinite gain if I am genuine against your finite sacrifice if I am not!" His logic would be that of Pascal; but he would vainly use it on us, for the hypothesis he offers us is dead. No tendency to act on it exists in us to any degree.

The talk of believing by our volition seems, then, from one point of view, simply silly. From another point of view it is worse than silly, it is vile. When one turns to the magnificent edifice of the physical sciences, and sees how it was reared; what thousands of disinterested moral lives of men lie buried in its mere foundations; what patience and postponement, what choking down of preference, what submission to the icy laws of outer fact are wrought into its very stones and mortar; how absolutely impersonal it stands in its vast augustness,—then how besotted and contemptible seems every little sentimentalist who comes blowing his voluntary smoke-wreaths, and pretending to decide things from out of his private dream! Can we wonder if those bred in the rugged and manly school of science should feel like spewing such subjectivism out of their mouths? The whole system of loyalties which grow up in the schools of science go dead against its toleration; so that it is only natural that those who have caught the scientific fever should pass over to the opposite extreme, and write sometimes as if the incorruptibly truthful intellect ought positively to prefer bitterness and unacceptableness to the heart in its cup.

> It fortifies my soul to know
> That, though I perish, Truth is so—

sings Clough, while Huxley exclaims: "My only consolation lies in the reflection that, however bad our posterity may become, so far as they hold by the plain rule of not pretending to believe what they have no reason to believe, because it may be to their advantage so to pretend [the word 'pretend' is surely here redundant],[2] they will not have reached the lowest depth of immorality." And that delicious *enfant terrible* Clifford writes: "Belief is desecrated when given to unproved and unquestioned statements for the solace and private pleasure of the believer. . . . Whoso would deserve well of his fellows in this matter will guard the purity of his belief with a very fanaticism of jealous care, lest at any time it should rest on an unworthy object, and catch a stain which can never be wiped away. . . . If [a] belief has been accepted on insufficient evidence [even though the belief be true, as Clifford on the same page explains] the pleasure is a stolen one. . . . It is sinful because it is stolen in defiance of our duty to mankind. That duty is to guard ourselves from such beliefs as from a pestilence which may shortly master our own body and then spread to the rest of the town. . . . It is wrong always, everywhere, and for every one, to believe anything upon insufficient evidence."[3]

III

All this strikes one as healthy, even when expressed, as by Clifford, with somewhat too much of robustious pathos in the voice. Free-will and simple wishing do seem, in the matter of our credences, to be only fifth wheels to the coach. Yet if any one should thereupon assume that intellectual insight is what remains after wish and will and sentimental preference have taken wing, or that pure reason is what then settles our opinions, he would fly quite as directly in the teeth of the facts.

It is only our already dead hypotheses that our willing nature is unable to bring to life again. But what has made them dead for us is for the most part a previous action of our willing nature of an antagonistic kind. When I say 'willing nature,' I do not mean only such deliberate volitions as may have set up habits of belief that we cannot now escape from,—I mean all such factors of belief as fear and hope, prejudice and passion, imitation and partisanship, the circumpressure of our caste and set. As a matter of fact we find ourselves believing, we hardly know how or why. Mr. Balfour gives the name of 'authority' to all those influences, born of the intellectual climate, that make hypotheses possible or impossible for us, alive or dead. Here in this room, we all of us believe in molecules and the conservation of energy, in democracy and necessary progress, in Protestant Christianity and the duty of fighting for 'the doctrine of the immortal Monroe,' all for no reasons worthy of the name. We see into these matters with no more inner clearness, and

---

[2][James' bracketing here and following.]

[3][William Kingdon Clifford, *Lectures and Essays*, ed. Leslie Stephen and Frederick Pollock (London: Macmillan, 1886), pp. 343 ff.]

probably with much less, than any disbeliever in them might possess. His unconventionality would probably have some grounds to show for its conclusions; but for us, not insight, but the *prestige* of the opinions, is what makes the spark shoot from them and light up our sleeping magazines of faith. Our reason is quite satisfied, in nine hundred and ninety-nine cases out of every thousand of us, if it can find a few arguments that will do to recite in case our credulity is criticised by some one else. Our faith is faith in some one else's faith, and in the greatest matters this is most the case. Our belief in truth itself, for instance, that there is a truth, and that our minds and it are made for each other,—what is it but a passionate affirmation of desire, in which our social system backs us up? We want to have a truth; we want to believe that our experiments and studies and discussions must put us in a continually better and better position towards it; and on this line we agree to fight out our thinking lives. But if a pyrrhonistic sceptic asks us *how we know* all this, can our logic find a reply? No! certainly it cannot. It is just one volition against another,—we willing to go in for life upon a trust or assumption which he, for his part, does not care to make.[4]

As a rule we disbelieve all facts and theories for which we have no use. Clifford's cosmic emotions find no use for Christian feelings. Huxley belabors the bishops because there is no use for sacerdotalism in his scheme of life. Newman, on the contrary, goes over to Romanism, and finds all sorts of reasons good for staying there, because a priestly system is for him an organic need and delight. Why do so few 'scientists' even look at the evidence for telepathy, so called? Because they think, as a leading biologist, now dead, once said to me, that even if such a thing were true, scientists ought to band together to keep it suppressed and concealed. It would undo the uniformity of Nature and all sorts of other things without which scientists cannot carry on their pursuits. But if this very man had been shown something which as a scientist he might *do* with telepathy, he might not only have examined the evidence, but even have found it good enough. This very law which the logicians would impose upon us—if I may give the name of logicians to those who would rule out our willing nature here—is based on nothing but their own natural wish to exclude all elements for which they, in their professional quality of logicians, can find no use.

Evidently, then, our non-intellectual nature does influence our convictions. There are passional tendencies and volitions which run before and others which come after belief, and it is only the latter that are too late for the fair; and they are not too late when the previous passional work has been already in their own direction. Pascal's argument, instead of being powerless, then seems a regular clincher, and is the last stroke needed to make our faith in masses and holy water complete. The state of things is evidently far from simple; and pure insight and logic, whatever they might do ideally, are not the only things that really do produce our creeds.

---

[4]Compare the admirable page 310 in S. H. Hodgson's *Time and Space*, London, 1865.

IV

Our next duty, having recognized this mixed-up state of affairs, is to ask whether it be simply reprehensible and pathological, or whether, on the contrary, we must treat it as a normal element in making up our minds. The thesis I defend is, briefly stated, this: *Our passional nature not only lawfully may, but must, decide an option between propositions, whenever it is a genuine option that cannot by its nature be decided on intellectual grounds; for to say, under such circumstances, "Do not decide, but leave the question open," is itself a passional decision,—just like deciding yes or no,—and is attended with the same risk of losing the truth.* The thesis thus abstractly expressed will, I trust, soon become quite clear. But I must first indulge in a bit more of preliminary work.

V

It will be observed that for the purposes of this discussion we are on 'dogmatic' ground,—ground, I mean, which leaves systematic philosophical scepticism altogether out of account. The postulate that there is truth, and that it is the destiny of our minds to attain it, we are deliberately resolving to make, though the sceptic will not make it. We part company with him, therefore, absolutely, at this point. But the faith that truth exists, and that our minds can find it, may be held in two ways. We may talk of the *empiricist* way and of the *absolutist* way of believing in truth. The absolutists in this matter say that we not only can attain to knowing truth, but we can *know when* we have attained to knowing it; while the empiricists think that although we may attain it, we cannot infallibly know when. To *know* is one thing, and to know for certain *that* we know is another. One may hold to the first being possible without the second; hence the empiricists and the absolutists, although neither of them is a sceptic in the usual philosophic sense of the term, show very different degrees of dogmatism in their lives.

If we look at the history of opinions, we see that the empiricist tendency has largely prevailed in science, while in philosophy the absolutist tendency has had everything its own way. The characteristic sort of happiness, indeed, which philosophies yield has mainly consisted in the conviction felt by each successive school or system that by it bottom-certitude had been attained. "Other philosophies are collections of opinions, mostly false; *my* philosophy gives standing-ground forever,"—who does not recognize in this the key-note of every system worthy of the name? A system, to be a system at all, must come as a *closed* system, reversible in this or that detail, perchance, but in its essential features never!

Scholastic orthodoxy, to which one must always go when one wishes to find perfectly clear statement, has beautifully elaborated this absolutist conviction in a doctrine which it calls that of "objective evidence." If, for example, I am unable to doubt that I now exist before you, that two is less than three, or that if all men are mortal then I am mortal too, it is because these things illumine my intellect irresistibly. The final ground of this objective evidence possessed by certain propositions is the *adæquatio intellectûs nostri cum rê.*[5] The certitude it brings involves an *aptitudinem ad extorquendum certum assensum*[6] on the part of the truth envisaged, and on the side of the subject a *quietem in cognitione,*[7] when once the object is mentally received, that leaves no possibility of doubt behind; and in the whole transaction nothing operates but the *entitas ipsa*[8] of the object and the *entitas ipsa* of the mind. We slouchy modern thinkers dislike to talk in Latin,—indeed, we dislike to talk in set terms at all; but at bottom our own state of mind is very much like this whenever we uncritically abandon ourselves: You believe in objective evidence, and I do. Of some things we feel that we are certain: we know, and we know that we do know. There is something that gives a click inside of us, a bell that strikes twelve, when the hands of our mental clock have swept the dial and meet over the meridian hour. The greatest empiricists among us are only empiricists on reflection: when left to their instincts, they dogmatize like infallible popes. When the Cliffords tell us how sinful it is to be Christians on such 'insufficient evidence,' insufficiency is really the last thing they have in mind. For them the evidence is absolutely sufficient, only it makes the other way. They believe so completely in an anti-christian order of the universe that there is no living option: Christianity is a dead hypothesis from the start.

VI

But now, since we are all such absolutists by instinct, what in our quality of students of philosophy ought we to do about the fact? Shall we espouse and indorse it? Or shall we treat it as a weakness of our nature from which we must free ourselves, if we can?

I sincerely believe that the latter course is the only one we can follow as reflective men. Objective evidence we can follow as reflective men. Objective evidence and certitude are doubtless very fine ideals to play with, but where on this moonlit and dream-visited planet are they found? I am, therefore, myself a complete empiricist so far as my theory of human knowledge goes. I live, to be sure, by the practical faith that we must go on experiencing and thinking over our experience, for only thus can our opinions grow more true; but to hold any one of them—I absolutely do not care which—as if it never could be reinterpretable or corrigible, I believe to be a tremendously mistaken attitude, and I think that the whole history of philosophy will bear me out. There is but one indefectibly certain truth, and that is the truth that pyrrhonistic scepticism itself leaves standing,—the truth that the present phenomenon of consciousness exists. That, however, is the bare starting-point of knowledge, that mere admission of a stuff to be philosophized about. The various philosophies are but so many attempts at expressing what this stuff really is. And if we repair to our libraries what disagreement do we discover! Where is a certainly true answer found? Apart from abstract propositions of comparison (such as two and two are the same as four), propositions which

[5]["conforming of our mind with the thing."]
[6]["aptitude for compelling certain assent."]
[7]["rest in knowledge."]
[8]["entity itself."]

tell us nothing by themselves about concrete reality, we find no proposition ever regarded by any one as evidently certain that has not either been called a falsehood, or at least had its truth sincerely questioned by some one else. The transcending of the axioms of geometry, not in play but in earnest, by certain of our contemporaries (as Zöllner and Charles H. Hinton), and the rejection of the whole Aristotelian logic by the Hegelians, are striking instances in point.

No concrete test of what is really true has ever been agreed upon. Some make the criterion external to the moment of perception, putting it either in revelation, the *consensus gentium*, the instincts of the heart, or the systematized experience of the race. Others make the perceptive moment its own test,—Descartes, for instance, with his clear and distinct ideas guaranteed by the veracity of God; Reid with his 'common-sense;' and Kant with his forms of synthetic judgment *a priori*. The inconceivability of the opposite; the capacity to be verified by sense; the possession of complete organic unity or self-relation, realized when a thing is its own other,—are standards which, in turn, have been used. The much lauded objective evidence is never triumphantly there; it is a mere aspiration or *Grenzbegriff*,[9] marking the infinitely remote ideal of our thinking life. To claim that certain truths now possess it, is simply to say that when you think them true and they *are* true, then their evidence is objective, otherwise it is not. But practically one's conviction that the evidence one goes by is of the real objective brand, is only one more subjective opinion added to the lot. For what a contradictory array of opinions have objective evidence and absolute certitude been claimed! The world is rational through and through,—its existence is an ultimate brute fact; there is a personal God,—a personal God is inconceivable; there is an extra-mental physical world immediately known,—the mind can only know its own ideas; a moral imperative exists,—obligation is only the resultant of desires; a permanent spiritual principle is in every one,—there are only shifting states of mind; there is an endless chain of causes,—there is an absolute first cause; an eternal necessity,—a freedom; a purpose,—no purpose; a primal One,—a primal Many; a universal continuity,—an essential discontinuity in things; an infinity,—no infinity. There is this,—there is that; there is indeed nothing which some one has not thought absolutely true, while his neighbor deemed it absolutely false; and not an absolutist among them seems ever to have considered that the trouble may all the time be essential, and that the intellect, even with truth directly in its grasp, may have no infallible signal for knowing whether it be truth or no. When, indeed, one remembers that the most striking practical application to life of the doctrine of objective certitude has been the conscientious labors of the Holy Office of the Inquisition, one feels less tempted than ever to lend the doctrine a respectful ear.

But please observe, now, that when as empiricists we give up the doctrine of objective certitude, we do not thereby give up the quest or hope of truth itself. We still pin our faith on its existence, and still believe that we gain an ever better position towards it by systematically continuing to

[9]["limiting concept."]

roll up experiences and think. Our great difference from the scholastic lies in the way we face. The strength of his system lies in the principles, the origin, the *terminus a quo* of his thought; for us the strength is in the outcome, the upshot, the *terminus ad quem*. Not where it comes from but what it leads to is to decide. It matters not to an empiricist from what quarter an hypothesis may come to him: he may have acquired it by fair means or by foul; passion may have whispered or accident suggested it; but if the total drift of thinking continues to confirm it, that is what he means by its being true.

VII

One more point, small but important, and our preliminaries are done. There are two ways of looking at our duty in the matter of opinion,—ways entirely different, and yet ways about whose difference the theory of knowledge seems hitherto to have shown very little concern. *We must know the truth;* and *we must avoid error,*—these are our first and great commandments as would-be knowers; but they are not two ways of stating an identical commandment, they are two separable laws. Although it may indeed happen that when we believe the truth *A*, we escape as an incidental consequence from believing the falsehood *B*, it hardly ever happens that by merely disbelieving *B* we necessarily believe *A*. We may in escaping *B* fall into believing other falsehoods, *C* or *D*, just as bad as *B*; or we may escape *B* by not believing anything at all, not even *A* .

Believe truth! Shun error!—these, we see, are two materially different laws; and by choosing between them we may end by coloring differently our whole intellectual life. We may regard the chase for truth as paramount, and the avoidance of error as secondary; or we may, on the other hand, treat the avoidance of error as more imperative, and let truth take its chance. Clifford, in the instructive passage which I have quoted, exhorts us to the latter course. Believe nothing, he tells us, keep your mind in suspense forever, rather than by closing it on insufficient evidence incur the awful risk of believing lies. You, on the other hand, may think that the risk of being in error is a very small matter when compared with the blessings of real knowledge, and be ready to be duped many times in your investigation rather than postpone indefinitely the chance of guessing true. I myself find it impossible to go with Clifford. We must remember that these feelings of our duty about either truth or error are in any case only expressions of our passional life. Biologically considered, our minds are as ready to grind out falsehood as veracity, and he who says, "Better go without belief forever than believe a lie!" merely shows his own preponderant private horror of becoming a dupe. He may be critical of many of his desires and fears, but this fear he slavishly obeys. He cannot imagine any one questioning its binding force. For my own part, I have also a horror of being duped; but I can believe that worse things than being duped may happen to a man in this world: so Clifford's exhortation has to my ears a thoroughly fantastic sound. It is like a general informing his soldiers that it is better to keep out of battle forever than to risk a single wound. Not so are victories either over enemies or over nature gained. Our errors are surely not such awfully solemn things. In a world where we are so certain to incur them in spite of all our caution, a certain lightness of heart seems healthier than this excessive nervousness on their behalf. At any rate, it seems the fittest thing for the empiricist philosopher.

VIII

And now, after all this introduction, let us go straight at our question. I have said, and now repeat it, that not only as a matter of fact do we find our passional nature influencing us in our opinions, but that there are some options between opinions in which this influence must be regarded both as an inevitable and as a lawful determinant of our choice.

I fear here that some of you my hearers will begin to scent danger, and lend an inhospitable ear. Two first steps of passion you have indeed had to admit as necessary,—we must think so as to avoid dupery, and we must think so as to gain truth; but the surest path to those ideal consummations, you will probably consider, is from now onwards to take no further passional step.

Well, of course, I agree as far as the facts will allow. Wherever the option between losing truth and gaining it is not momentous, we can throw the chance of *gaining truth* away, and at any rate save ourselves from any chance of *believing falsehood*, by not making up our minds at all till objective evidence has come. In scientific questions, this is almost always the case; and even in human affairs in general, the need of acting is seldom so urgent that a false belief to act on is better than no belief at all. Law courts, indeed, have to decide on the best evidence attainable for the moment, because a judge's duty is to make law as well as to ascertain it, and (as a learned judge once said to me) few cases are worth spending much time over: the great thing is to have them decided on *any* acceptable principle, and got out of the way. But in our dealings with objective nature we obviously are recorders, not makers, of the truth; and decisions for the mere sake of deciding promptly and getting on to the next business would be wholly out of place. Throughout the breadth of physical nature facts are what they are quite independently of us, and seldom is there any such hurry about them that the risks of being duped by believing a premature theory need be faced. The questions here are always trivial options, the hypotheses are hardly living (at any rate not living for us spectators), the choice between believing truth or falsehood is seldom forced. The attitude of sceptical balance is therefore the absolutely wise one if we would escape mistakes. What difference, indeed, does it make to most of us whether we have or have not a theory of the Röntgen rays, whether we believe or not in mind-stuff, or have a conviction about the causality of conscious states? It makes no difference. Such options are not forced on us. On every account it is better not to make them, but still keep weighing reasons *pro et contra* with an indifferent hand.

I speak, of course, here of the purely judging mind. For purposes of discovery such indifference is to be less highly recommended, and science would be far less advanced than she is if the passionate desires of individuals to get their own faiths confirmed had been kept out of the game. See for example the sagacity which Spencer and Weismann now display. On the other hand, if you want an absolute duffer in an investigation, you must, after all, take the man who has no interest whatever in its results: he is the warranted incapable, the positive fool. The most useful investigator, because the most sensitive observer, is always he whose eager interest in one side of the question is balanced by an equally keen nervousness lest he become deceived.[10] Science has organized this nervousness into a regular *technique,* her so-called method of verification; and she has fallen so deeply in love with the method that one may even say she has ceased to care for truth by itself at all. It is only truth as technically verified that interests her. The truth of truths might come in merely affirmative form, and she would decline to touch it. Such truth as that, she might repeat with Clifford, would be stolen in defiance of her duty to mankind. Human passions, however, are stronger than technical rules. *"Le cœur a ses raisons,"* as Pascal says, *"que la raison ne connaît pas;"*[11] and however indifferent to all but the bare rules of the game the umpire, the abstract intellect, may be, the concrete players who furnish him the materials to judge of are usually, each one of them, in love with some pet 'live hypothesis' of his own. Let us agree, however, that wherever there is no forced option, the dispassionately judicial intellect with no pet hypothesis, saving us, as it does, from dupery at any rate, ought to be our ideal.

The question next arises: Are there not somewhere forced options in our speculative questions, and can we (as men who may be interested at least as much in positively gaining truth as in merely escaping dupery) always wait with impunity till the coercive evidence shall have arrived? It seems *a priori* improbable that the truth should be so nicely adjusted to our needs and powers as that. In the great boarding-house of nature, the cakes and butter and the syrup seldom come out so even and leave the plates so clean. Indeed, we should view them with scientific suspicion if they did.

IX

Moral questions immediately present themselves as questions whose solution cannot wait for sensible proof. A moral question is a question not of what sensibly exists, but of what is good, or would be good if it did exist. Science can tell us what exists; but to compare the *worths,* both of what exists and of what does not exist, we must consult not science, but what Pascal calls our heart. Science herself consults her heart when she lays it down that the infinite ascertainment of fact and correction of false belief are the supreme goods for man. Challenge the statement, and science can only repeat it oracularly, or else prove it by showing that such ascertainment and correction bring man all sorts of other goods which man's heart in turn declares. The question of having moral beliefs at all or not having them is decided by our will. Are our moral preferences true or false, or are they only odd biological phe-

[10]Compare Wilfrid Ward's Essay, "The Wish to Believe," in his *Witnesses to the Unseen,* Macmillan & Co., 1893.

[11]["The heart has its reasons, which reason does not know" (*Pensées,* no. 277).]

nomena, making things good or bad for *us*, but in themselves indifferent? How can your pure intellect decide? If your heart does not *want* a world of moral reality, your head will assuredly never make you believe in one. Mephistophelian scepticism, indeed, will satisfy the head's play-instincts much better than any rigorous idealism can. Some men (even at the student age) are so naturally cool-hearted that the moralistic hypothesis never has for them any pungent life, and in their supercilious presence the hot young moralist always feels strangely ill at ease. The appearance of knowingness is on their side, of *naiveté* and gullibility on his. Yet, in the inarticulate heart of him, he clings to it that he is not a dupe, and that there is a realm in which (as Emerson says) all their wit and intellectual superiority is no better than the cunning of a fox. Moral scepticism can no more be refuted or proved by logic than intellectual scepticism can. When we stick to it that there *is* truth (be it of either kind), we do so with our whole nature, and resolve to stand or fall by the results. The sceptic with his whole nature adopts the doubting attitude; but which of us is the wiser, Omniscience only knows.

Turn now from these wide questions of good to a certain class of questions of fact, questions concerning personal relations, states of mind between one man and another. *Do you like me or not?*—for example. Whether you do or not depends, in countless instances, on whether I meet you half-way, am willing to assume that you must like me, and show you trust and expectation. The previous faith on my part in your liking's existence is in such cases what makes your liking come. But if I stand aloof, and refuse to budge an inch until I have objective evidence, until you shall have done something apt, as the absolutists say, *ad extroquendum assensum meum*,[12] ten to one your liking never comes. How many women's hearts are vanquished by the mere sanguine insistence of some man that they *must* love him! he will not consent to the hypothesis that they cannot. The desire for a certain kind of truth here brings about that special truth's existence; and so it is in innumerable cases of other sorts. Who gains promotions, boons, appointments, but the man in whose life they are seen to play the part of live hypotheses, who discounts them, sacrifices other things for their sake before they have come, and takes risks for them in advance? His faith acts on the powers above him as a claim, and creates its own verification.

A social organism of any sort whatever, large or small, is what it is because each member proceeds to his own duty with a trust that the other members will simultaneously do theirs. Wherever a desired result is achieved by the co-operation of many independent persons, its existence as a fact is a pure consequence of the precursive faith in one another of those immediately concerned. A government, an army, a commercial system, a ship, a college, an athletic team, all exist on this condition, without which not only is nothing achieved, but nothing is even attempted. A whole train of passengers (individually brave enough) will be looted by a few highwaymen, simply because the latter can count on one another, while each passenger fears that if he

---

[12]["for compelling my assent."]

makes a movement of resistence, he will be shot before any one else backs him up. If we believed that the whole car-full would rise at once with us, we should each severally rise, and train-robbing would never even be attempted. There are, then, cases where a fact cannot come at all unless a preliminary faith exists in its coming. *And where faith in a fact can help create the fact,* that would be an insane logic which should say that faith running ahead of scientific evidence is the 'lowest kind of immorality' into which a thinking being can fall. Yet such is the logic by which our scientific absolutists pretend to regulate our lives!

X

In truths dependent on our personal action, then, faith based on desire is certainly a lawful and possibly an indispensable thing.

But now, it will be said, these are all childish human cases, and have nothing to do with great cosmical matters, like the question of religious faith. Let us then pass on to that. Religions differ so much in their accidents that in discussing the religious question we must make it very generic and broad. What then do we now mean by the religious hypothesis? Science says things are; morality says some things are better than other things; and religion says essentially two things.

First, she says that the best things are the more eternal things, the overlapping things, the things in the universe that throw the last stone, so to speak, and say the final word. "Perfection is eternal,"—this phrase of Charles Secrétan seems a good way of putting this first affirmation of religion, an affirmation which obviously cannot yet be verified scientifically at all.

The second affirmation of religion is that we are better off even now if we believe her first affirmation to be true.

Now, let us consider what the logical elements of this situation are *in case the religious hypothesis in both its branches be really true.* (Of course, we must admit that possibility at the outset. If we are to discuss the question at all, it must involve a living option. If for any of you religion be a hypothesis that cannot, by any living possibility be true, then you need go no farther. I speak to the 'saving remnant' alone.) So proceeding, we see, first, that religion offers itself as a *momentous* option. We are supposed to gain, even now, by our belief, and to lose by our non-belief, a certain vital good. Secondly, religion is a *forced* option, so far as that good goes. We cannot escape the issue by remaining sceptical and waiting for more light, because, although we do avoid error in that way *if religion be untrue,* we lose the good, *if it be true,* just as certainly as if we positively chose to disbelieve. It is as if a man should hesitate indefinitely to ask a certain woman to marry him because he was not perfectly sure that she would prove an angel after he brought her home. Would he not cut himself off from that particular angel-possibility as decisively as if he went and married some one else? Scepticism, then, is not avoidance of option; it is option of a certain particular kind of risk. *Better risk loss of truth than chance of error,*—that is your faith-vetoer's exact position. He is actively playing his stake as much as the believer is; he is backing the field against the religious hypothesis, just as the believer is backing the religious hypothesis against the field. To preach scepticism to us as a duty until 'sufficient evidence' for religion be found, is tantamount therefore to telling us, when in presence of the religious hypothesis, that to yield to our fear of its being error is wiser and better than to yield to our hope that it may be true. It is not intellect against all passions, then; it is only intellect with one passion laying down its law. And by what, forsooth, is the supreme wisdom of this passion warranted? Dupery for dupery, what proof is there that dupery through hope is so much worse than dupery through fear? I, for one, can see no proof; and I simply refuse obedience to the scientist's command to imitate his kind of option, in a case where my own stake is important enough to give me the right to choose my own form of risk. If religion be true and the evidence for it be still insufficient, I do not wish, by putting your extinguisher upon my nature (which feels to me as if it had after all some business in this matter), to forfeit my sole chance in life of getting upon the winning side,—that chance depending, of course, on my willingness to run the risk of acting as if my passional need of taking the world religiously might be prophetic and right.

All this is on the supposition that it really may be prophetic and right, and that, even to us who are discussing the matter, religion is a live hypothesis which may be true. Now, to most of us religion comes in a still further way that makes a veto on our active faith even more illogical. The more perfect and more eternal aspect of the universe is represented in our religions as having personal form. The universe is no longer a mere *It* to us, but a *Thou*, if we are religious; and any relation that may be possible from person to person might be possible here. For instance, although in one sense we are passive portions of the universe, in another we show a curious autonomy, as if we were small active centres on our own account. We feel, too, as if the appeal of religion to us were made to our own active good-will, as if evidence might be forever withheld from us unless we met the hypothesis half-way. To take a trivial illustration: just as a man who in a company of gentlemen made no advances, asked a warrant for every concession, and believed no one's word without proof, would cut himself off by such churlishness from all the social rewards that a more trusting spirit would earn,—so here, one who should shut himself up in snarling logicality and try to make the gods extort his recognition willy-nilly, or not get it at all, might cut himself off forever from his only opportunity of making the gods' acquaintance. This feeling, forced on us we know not whence, that by obstinately believing that there are gods (although not to do so would be so easy both for our logic and our life) we are doing the universe the deepest service we can, seems part of the living essence of the religious hypothesis. If the hypothesis *were* true in all its parts, including this one, then pure intellectualism, with its veto on our making willing advances, would be an absurdity; and some participation of our sympathetic nature would be logically required. I, therefore, for one, cannot see my way to accepting the agnostic rules for truth-seeking, or wilfully agree to keep my willing nature out of the game. I cannot do so for this plain reason, that *a rule of thinking which would absolutely prevent me from acknowledging certain kinds of truth if those kinds of truth were really there, would be an irrational rule.* That for me is the long and short of the formal logic of the situation, no matter what the kinds of truth might materially be.

I confess I do not see how this logic can be escaped. But sad experience makes me fear that some of you may still shrink from radically saying with me, *in abstracto*, that we have the right to believe at our own risk any hypothesis that is live enough to tempt our will. I suspect, however, that if this is so, it is because you have got away from the abstract logical point of view altogether, and are thinking (perhaps without realizing it) of some particular religious hypothesis which for you is dead. The freedom to 'believe what we will' you apply to the case of some patent superstition; and the faith you think of is the faith defined by the schoolboy when he said, "Faith is when you believe something that you know ain't true." I can only repeat that this is misapprehension. *In concreto*, the freedom to believe can only cover living options which the intellect of the individual cannot by itself resolve; and living options never seem absurdities to him who has them to consider. When I look at the religious question as it really puts itself to concrete men, and when I think of all the possibilities which both practically and theoretically it involves, then this command that we shall put a stopper on our heart, instincts, and courage, and *wait*—acting of course meanwhile more or less as if religion were *not* true[13]—till doomsday, or till such time as our intellect and senses working together may have raked in evidence enough,—this command, I say, seems to me the queerest idol ever manufactured in the philosophic cave. Were we scholastic absolutists, there might be more excuse. If we had an infallible intellect with its objective certitudes, we might feel ourselves disloyal to such a perfect organ of knowledge in not trusting to it exclusively, in not waiting for its releasing word. But if we are empiricists, if we believe that no bell in us tolls to let us know for certain when truth is in our grasp, then it seems a piece of idle fantasticality to preach so solemnly our duty of waiting for the bell. Indeed we *may* wait if we will,—I hope you do not think that I am denying that,—but if we do so, we do so at our peril as much as if we believed. In either case we *act*, taking our life in our hands. No one of us ought to issue vetoes to the other, nor should we bandy words of abuse. We ought, on the contrary, delicately and profoundly to respect one another's mental freedom: then only shall we bring about the intellectual republic; then only shall we have that spirit of inner

---

[13]Since belief is measured by action, he who forbids us to believe religion to be true, necessarily also forbids us to act as we should if we did believe it to be true. The whole defence of religious faith hinges upon action. If the action required or inspired by the religious hypothesis is in no way different from that dictated by the naturalistic hypothesis, then religious faith is a pure superfluity, better pruned away, and controversy about its legitimacy is a piece of idle trifling, unworthy of serious minds. I myself believe, of course, that the religious hypothesis gives to the world an expression which specifically determines our reactions, and makes them in a large part unlike what they might be on a purely naturalistic scheme of belief.

tolerance without which all our outer tolerance is soulless, and which is empiricism's glory; then only shall we live and let live, in speculative as well as in practical things.

I began by a reference to Fitz-James Stephen; let me end by a quotation from him. "What do you think of yourself? What do you think of the world? . . . These are questions with which all must deal as it seems good to them. They are riddles of the Sphinx, and in some way or other we must deal with them. . . . In all important transactions of life we have to take a leap in the dark. . . . If we decide to leave the riddles unanswered, that is a choice; if we waver in our answer, that, too, is a choice: but whatever choice we make, we make it at our peril. If a man chooses to turn his back altogether on God and the future, no one can prevent him; no one can show beyond reasonable doubt that he is mistaken. If a man thinks otherwise and acts as he thinks, I do not see that any one can prove that *he* is mistaken. Each must act as he thinks best; and if he is wrong, so much the worse for him. We stand on a mountain pass in the midst of whirling snow and blinding mist, through which we get glimpses now and then of paths which may be deceptive. If we stand still we shall be frozen to death. If we take the wrong road we shall be dashed to pieces. We do not certainly know whether there is any right one. What must we do? 'Be strong and of a good courage.' Act for the best, hope for the best, and take what comes. . . . If death ends all, we cannot meet death better."[14]

✻ SELECTED BIBLIOGRAPHY
FOR SECTION 5

Fifteen selections on faith and reason, drawn from both classical and modern periods and representing a full spectrum of positions on the problem, are reproduced in Ed. L. Miller (ed.), *Classical Statements on Faith and Reason* (New York: Macmillan, 1972); the editor's introduction provides a brief analysis of the problem, introducing relevant distinctions and concepts.

A complete history of the problem is to be found in three volumes by Richard Kroner: *Speculation in Pre-Christian Philosophy* (Philadelphia: Westminster Press, 1956); *Speculation and Revelation in the Age of Christian Philosophy* (Philadelphia: Westminster Press, 1959); and *Speculation and Revelation in Modern Philosophy* (Philadelphia: Westminster Press, 1961). In addition to these, one should consult also Kroner's earlier work, *The Primacy of Faith* (New York: Macmillan, 1943). Further treatment of the medieval-scholastic version of the problem is provided in Étienne Gilson, *Reason and Revelation in the Middle Ages* (New York: Scribner, 1938) and *The Spirit of Medieval Philosophy*, Chs. 1 and 2 (New York: Scribner, 1940). Gilson's exposition of the specifically Thomistic position may be found in *The Christian Philosophy of St. Thomas Aquinas* (New York: Random House, 1956) and *The Elements of Christian Philosophy*, Part I (Garden City, N. Y.: Doubleday, 1960). An additional Thomistic analysis is provided by Jacques Maritain, *The Degrees of Knowledge*, Part II, tr. Gerald B. Phelan (New York: Scribner, 1959).

Approaches to the problem of religious knowledge from differing religious standpoints are reflected in John Baillie, *Our Knowledge of God* (New York: Scribner,

---

[14]*Liberty, Equality, Fraternity*, p. 353, 2d edition. London, 1874.

1939); F. R. Tennant, *Philosophical Theology,* Vol II, Ch. 8 (Cambridge, England: University Press, 1928–30); John Oman, *The Natural and the Supernatural* (Cambridge, England: University Press, 1931); John Hick, *Faith and Knowledge,* second ed. (Ithaca, N. Y.: Cornell University Press, 1966); and Austin Farrer, *Faith and Speculation* (New York: New York University Press, 1967). In addition to the last two works, analyses by contemporary language-philosophers (and others) may be found also in the discussions contained in John Hick (ed.), *Faith and the Philosophers* (London: Macmillan, 1964); Alvin Plantinga (ed.), *Faith and Philosophy* (Grand Rapids, Mich.: Eerdman, 1964); and a collection of more general scope edited by Sidney Hook, *Religious Experience and Truth* (New York: New York University Press, 1961).

For a consideration of the problem from a conservative theological perspective, see Benjamin Breckenridge Warfield, *The Inspiration and Authority of the Bible,* ed. Cornelius Van Til (Philadelphia: Presbyterian and Reformed Publishing Co., 1948) and J. G. Machen, *What is Faith?* (New York: Macmillan, 1925). A whole collection of essays on relevant topics, written from the evangelical standpoint, is provided in Carl F. Henry (ed.), *Revelation and the Bible* (Grand Rapids, Mich.: Baker, 1958). Expressions of the two most influential neo-orthodox approaches may be found in a lively interchange of essays by Emil Brunner and Karl Barth reproduced as *Natural Theology,* tr. Peter Fraenkel (London: Bles, 1946). Brunner's full exposition of the problem is published as *Revelation and Reason,* tr. Olive Wyon (Philadelphia: Westminster Press, 1946). For an additional statement by Barth, see *The Doctrine of the Word of God,* tr. G. T. Thomson (Edinburgh: T. & T. Clark, 1936). The conception of revelation as *Heilsgeschichte,* that is, as God acting in history rather than a body of propositions contained in a book, is reflected in Barth and Brunner, but is developed further in H. Richard Niebuhr, *The Meaning of Revelation* (New York: Macmillan, 1941) and John Baillie, *The Idea of Revelation in Recent thought* (New York: Columbia University Press, 1956). C. H. Dodd's *The Authority of the Bible* (New York: Harper & Row, 1929) has been for many years an esteemed general discussion of the whole area.

The selection from Kierkegaard's *Concluding Unscientific Postscript* should be supplemented with his *Philosophical Fragments,* tr. David F. Swenson, rev. Howard V. Hong (Princeton, N. J.: Princeton University Press, 1962). The introduction to the latter work, by Niels Thulstrup, is substantive and helpful. For a general introduction and interpretation of Kierkegaard, see David F. Swenson, *Something About Kierkegaard,* ed. Lillian Marvin Swenson, revised ed. (Minneapolis, Minn.: Augsburg, 1945), especially Chapter 5, "The Anti-Intellectualism of Kierkegaard." See also the several articles comprising Part Two of *Essays on Kierkegaard,* ed. Jerry H. Gill, (Minneapolis, Minn.: Burgess, 1969) and the discussions in *A Kierkegaard Critique,* ed. Howard A. Johnson and Niels Thulstrup (New York: Harper & Row, 1962).

Additional existentialist treatments are to be found in Karl Jaspers, *Philosophical Faith and Revelation,* tr. E. B. Ashton (New York: Harper & Row, 1957); Nicolai A. Berdyaev, *Truth and Revelation,* tr. R. M. French (London: Bles, 1953); and Paul Tillich, *Systematic Theology,* Vol. I, Part I (Chicago: University of Chicago Press, 1951–63). A rich treatment of the problem from a Jewish-existentialist point of view is provided by Lev Shestov, *Athens and Jerusalem,* tr. Bernard Martin (New York: Simon & Schuster, 1966).

A succinct expression of the unyielding rationalist position (which James attacked in "The Will to Believe") is William Kingdon Clifford's forceful essay "The Ethics of Belief" in *Lectures and Essays,* ed. Leslie Stephen and Frederick Pollock (London: Macmillan, 1886). Both James' and Clifford's theses are considered in George Mavrodes' "James and Clifford on 'The Will to Believe,' " *The Personalist,* XLIV (Spring, 1963). One might note, further, William J. MacLeod, "James's 'Will to Believe': Revisited," *The Personalist,* XLVIII (Spring, 1967). On voluntarism in general, see John Hick, *Faith and Knowledge,* Ch. 2.

On Hume's rejection of the miraculous, see Antony Flew, *Hume's Philosophy of Belief,* Ch. 8 (London: Routledge & Kegan Paul, 1961). For a rebuttal of Hume, see A. E. Taylor, *Philosophical Studies*, Ch. 9 (London: Macmillan, 1934). Miracles are defended in various ways in the following: F. R. Tennant, *Miracle and Its Philosophical Presuppositions* (Cambridge, England: University Press, 1925); H. H. Farmer, *The World and God*, Chs. 9 and 10 (London: Nisbet, 1935); and C. S. Lewis, *Miracles* (London: Centenary Press, 1947). One should consult also the distinctions and points raised by Patrick Nowell-Smith in his article "Miracles," in *New Essays in Philosophical Theology*, ed. Antony Flew and Alasdair MacIntyre (London: Student Christian Movement Press, 1955). For a consideration of the miraculous by a Biblical theologian, see Helmut Thielicke, *Man in God's World*, Chs. 7 and 8 tr. and ed. John W. Doberstein (New York: Harper & Row, 1963) .

The Meaning of Evil

❋ INTRODUCTION

It is doubtful whether any issue in philosophy and theology has generated as much passionate argument and intellectual despair as the problem of reconciling evil (in the form of both innocent suffering and moral perversity) with a belief in an omnipotent and loving God. This problem has been called, appropriately, the *crux* of theism.

In view of the skeptical and critical role played thus far by Hume, it should be no surprise that he is now found, in the first selection, cataloguing evils and miseries in order to heap them as a grotesque and monstrous burden on the head of the theist. From these pages also comes what is perhaps the most familiar (certainly one of the simplest) statements of the problem. Philo (who no doubt represents Hume) quotes the ancient Greek Epicurus: "Is God willing to prevent evil, but not able? then is He impotent. Is He able, but not willing? then is He malevolent. Is He both able and willing? whence then is evil?"

Philosophers and theologians have attempted to come to grips with this dilemma in a number of ways. One classical theodicy (literally, "justification of God") is that of the ancient Stoics who believed, quite simply, that there is no evil, at least not *sub specie aeternitatis*, "from the standpoint of eternity." Of course we judge some things to be evil, but that merely reflects our inability to grasp at once the whole of things. Were we able to view all things from the standpoint of God, then we could appreciate the beauty, unity, harmony, in a word, the rationality of the whole. Cleanthes' *Hymn to Zeus* is an excellent witness to the Stoic conviction that *Logos*, "Reason," rules all: Everything unfolds according to a divine and all-pervasive reason and purpose. It follows that a man ought not protest and whimper over the things that lie not in his power; rather, let him joyfully embrace his lot and cooperate with the divine purpose. In every age many have found at least some truth (and much comfort) in a Stoic-type optimism concerning the whole. At the very least, Cleanthes raises two crucial questions: Do we or do we not believe that the world and history are possessed of Reason? And if we do, why?

St. Augustine's answer, too, has been regarded by many as forceful and cogent. Augustine held also to the "aesthetic" conception of nature, believing, as the Apostle Paul says, that "everything works together for good . . ." (Rom. 8:24). More important, though, is his analysis of evil as a privation of good. Operating within a Platonic understanding of reality, Augustine believed that some things possess more being than others by virtue of their greater unity and immutability. The created order, though God pronounced it "good," cannot possess the absolute being of God himself (for then there would be two absolute beings, which is self-contradictory) and is therefore characterized by a degree of multiplicity and mutability reflected in natural processes and laws, and resulting in the vicissitudes of nature and suffering for man. On the other hand, man suffers only as a just judgment for his sin, a turning aside from God, a failure to do the good. Evil, then, is not a *substance*. It results, rather, from man's defection from his own proper being and good and represents therefore a corruption or *privation* of that being and good. Since evil is not a substance it is not something created by God, and God is thus not responsible for it. God is responsible for what *is*, not what *is not*.

It may appear, on the surface, that Augustine is denying that evil exists, but it is extremely important to see that this is not so. Clearly, there is a difference between saying that evil does not exist, and saying that evil, as to its nature, does not exist as a substance or a *thing*. It is not possible to read the selection from Augustine and not be impressed by the seriousness with which he took sin and suffering. Indeed, Augustine's most famous work, *The Confessions*, is an extended prayer of thanksgiving to God for his gracious deliverance from the awful reality of evil. It is, then, not the reality, but the substantial nature of evil that Augustine denies. It is also important to notice that there occurs explicitly in Augustine the important distinction between natural and moral evil, that is, the evil or suffering that results from natural occurrences, and the evil or wickedness that is the product of the human will, and how Augustine resolves both of these through his theory of evil as the privation of good.

Not so optimistic is John Stuart Mill, who rejects absolutely all attempts to reconcile the fact of evil with an omnipotent Deity. It should be noticed that Mill, who found the Cosmological Argument wanting but the Teleological Argument compelling, clearly distinguishes between the *origin* of nature and the origin of nature's *order* (it is important to note that Mill employs the word "Kosmos" in its fundamental sense of "*ordered*-universe"), and turns his attention to the implications of the latter for the divine nature. Mill's simple, and for many brash, conclusion is that though God must exist as the intelligent cause of nature's contrivance, he is certainly not omnipotent but, rather, limited by the intractable materials with which he must work: God "had to adapt himself to a set of conditions which he did not make," and the result was less than perfect. His reasoning revolves, in part, around the observation that the apparent necessity laid upon God to design and contrive the order of the cosmos by various means—the adaptation of means to ends and other manipulations of the properties of matter and force—witnesses to the limitation of his power; surely a being who was able to impose order on nature unhindered by the use of secondary and instrumental causes would be a more powerful being. By an interesting twist, then, Mill infers the limitation of God from the very thing from which others infer his omnipotence, namely, the design of the comsos. Mill's general position on God, insofar as he may be known philosophically, is summarized in the following statement which occurs a few pages beyond the end of the present selection:

These, then, are the net results of Natural Theology on the question of the divine attributes. A Being of great but limited power, how or by what limited we cannot even conjecture; of great, and perhaps unlimited intelligence, but perhaps, also, more narrowly limited than his power: who desires, and pays some regard to, the happiness of his creatures, but who seems to have other motives of action which he cares more for, and who can hardly be supposed to have created the universe for that purpose alone. Such is the Deity whom Natural Religion points to; and any idea of God more captivating than this comes only from human wishes, or from the teaching of either real or imaginary Revelation.[1]

It would appear simple enough to reject, in this way, one half of the dilemma proposed by Hume; whether it raises more problems than it solves is another question. It may be asked, for instance, whether Mill's position poses any logical difficulties. Such a God could hardly be, as St. Anselm insisted he is, "that than which no greater can be conceived," which may cause us to wonder whether Mill is still talking about *God*. Or at least whose God? We might justly suspect that many (especially those belonging to the Judeo-Christian tradition) will find the notion of a God who, so to say, "did the best he could" as anthropomorphic in more ways than one, and as somehow falling short of the object of their religious worship! In short, we may ask, as Mill himself suggests in the quotation above, whether this conception of God is compatible with the Biblical picture—the problem of faith and reason again.

All of these thinkers, including even Hume, at least share the belief that it is possible to bring to bear our critical faculties and make a rational judgment on the nature of evil, its relation to God, and so on. Modern existentialism, however, in most of its forms, has abandoned such an intellectual confidence and especially all hope of comprehending evil. For existentialist thinkers like Sartre and Camus, evil and suffering are the most striking manifestations of the ultimate absurdity of existence.

At this point Albert Camus represents somewhat of a variation on the Sartrean position encountered in an earlier section. According to Camus, the fundamental question of philosophy concerns suicide, that is, whether or not one ought to take his own life in view of his hopelessness in the presence of the absurd. But Camus' answer is an emphatic *No*: "It is essential to die unreconciled and not of one's own free will." Suicide signals a resignation, and therefore a victory for the absurd. Our dignity lies, rather, in our revolt, our challenge, our struggle, as in the case of the mythological Sisyphus, Camus' hero, who transcends his absurd fate and negates the gods by struggling endlessly toward the heights: ". . . the point is to live." Camus' position represents, of course, the opposite extreme from the position of the Stoics. It springs from a radically different view of existence, one that despairs of ultimate meaning and hope, and it leads us to ask a question quite opposite

[1]John Stuart Mill, *Three Essays on Religion*, third ed. (New York: Longman's, Green & Co., 1875), pp. 194 f.

to the one we asked earlier: We may be unable to believe that all things manifest a universal rationality and purpose, but can we by any means bring ourselves to believe that existence is wholly devoid of reason and that authentic living derives merely from an outburst of subjective indignation?

The selection from Camus reminds us that there are, after all, fundamentally different approaches to philosophical and religious issues, different philosophical styles, different ways of feeling and interpreting such issues. (Not the least of these is the difference between the existentialist approach and the more academic-scientific approach, both of which appear recurringly in the present volume.) But should this surprise us? The direction of our thought is determined by many things, including our particular experiences, differing perspectives, and philosophical moods. While it matters very much how we see the world, no two people can ever see it in the same way.

❀ DAVID HUME

23. *A Statement of the Problem*

David Hume (1711–1776) is often regarded as the greatest thinker of the British empiricist tradition. His skeptical philosophy is worked out in *A Treatise of Human Nature,* and his critiques of religion and theology are contained in his *Dialogues Concerning Natural Religion* (a classic indictment of the attempt to demonstrate God's attributes from his so-called effects in nature), *Natural History of Religion,* and his essay "On Miracles."

From *Dialogues Concerning Natural Religion*

PART X

It is my opinion, I own, replied Demea, that each man feels, in a manner, the truth of religion within his own breast, and, from a consciousness of his imbecility and misery rather than from any reasoning, is led to seek protection from that Being on whom he and all nature is dependent. So anxious or so tedious are even the best scenes of life that futurity is still the object of all our hopes and fears. We incessantly look forward and endeavour, by prayers, adoration, and sacrifice, to appease those unknown powers whom we find, by experience, so able to afflict and oppress us. Wretched creatures that we are! What resource for us amidst the innumerable ills of life did not religion suggest some methods of atonement, and appease those terrors with which we are incessantly agitated and tormented?

I am indeed persuaded, said Philo, that the best and indeed the only method of bringing everyone to a due sense of religion is by just repre-

David Hume, *Dialogues Concerning Natural Religion,* ed. Henry D. Aiken (New York: Hafner, 1948). Reprinted by permission of the publisher.

sentations of the misery and wickedness of men. And for that purpose a talent of eloquence and strong imagery is more requisite than that of reasoning and argument. For is it necessary to prove what everyone feels within himself? It is only necessary to make us feel it, if possible, more intimately and sensibly.

The people, indeed, replied Demea, are sufficiently convinced of this great and melancholy truth. The miseries of life, the unhappiness of man, and general corruptions of our nature, the unsatisfactory enjoyment of pleasures, riches, honours—these phrases have become almost proverbial in all languages. And who can doubt of what all men declare from their own immediate feeling and experience?

In this point, said Philo, the learned are perfectly agreed with the vulgar; and in all letters, *sacred* and *profane*, the topic of human misery has been insisted on with the most pathetic eloquence that sorrow and melancholy could inspire. The poets, who speak from sentiment, without a system, and whose testimony has therefore the more authority, abound in images of this nature. From Homer down to Dr. Young, the whole inspired tribe have ever been sensible that no other representation of things would suit the feeling and observation of each individual.

As to authorities, replied Demea, you need not seek them. Look round this library of Cleanthes. I shall venture to affirm that, except authors of particular sciences, such as chemistry or botany, who have no occasion to treat of human life, there is scarce one of those innumerable writers from whom the sense of human misery has not, in some passage or other, extorted a complaint and confession of it. At least, the chance is entirely on that side; and no one author has ever, so far as I can recollect, been so extravagant as to deny it.

There you must excuse me, said Philo: Leibniz has denied it, and is perhaps the first[1] who ventured upon so bold and paradoxical an opinion; at least, the first who made it essential to his philosophical system.

And by being the first, replied Demea, might he not have been sensible of his error? For is this a subject in which philosophers can propose to make discoveries especially in so late an age? And can any man hope by a simple denial (for the subject scarcely admits of reasoning) to bear down the united testimony of mankind, founded on sense and consciousness?

And why should man, added he, pretend to an exemption from the lot of all other animals? The whole earth, believe me, Philo, is cursed and polluted. A perpetual war is kindled amongst all living creatures. Necessity, hunger, want stimulate the strong and courageous; fear, anxiety, terror agitate the weak and infirm. The first entrance into life gives anguish to the new-born infant and to its wretched parent; weakness, impotence, distress attend each stage of that life, and it is, at last, finished in agony and horror.

Observe, too, says Philo, the curious artifices of nature in order to embitter the life of every living being. The stronger prey upon the weaker and keep them in perpetual terror and anxiety. The weaker, too, in their

[1]That sentiment had been maintained by Dr. King and some few others before Leibniz, though by none of so great fame as that German philosopher.

turn, often prey upon the stronger, and vex and molest them without relaxation. Consider that innumerable race of insects, which either are bred on the body of each animal or, flying about, infix their stings in him. These insects have others still less than themselves which torment them. And thus on each hand, before and behind, above and below, every animal is surrounded with enemies which incessantly seek his misery and destruction.

Man alone, said Demea, seems to be, in part, an exception to this rule. For by combination in society he can easily master lions, tigers, and bears, whose greater strength and agility naturally enable them to prey upon him.

On the contrary, it is here chiefly, cried Philo, that the uniform and equal maxims of nature are most apparent. Man, it is true, can, by combination, surmount all his *real* enemies and become master of the whole animal creation; but does he not immediately raise up to himself *imaginary* enemies, the demons of his fancy, who haunt him with superstitious terrors and blast every enjoyment of life? His pleasure, as he imagines, becomes in their eyes a crime; his food and repose give them umbrage and offence; his very sleep and dreams furnish new materials to anxious fear; and even death, his refuge from every other ill, presents only the dread of endless and innumerable woes. Nor does the wolf molest more the timid flock than superstition does the anxious breast of wretched mortals.

Besides, consider, Demea: This very society by which we surmount those wild beasts, our natural enemies, what new enemies does it not raise to us? What woe and misery does it not occasion? Man is the greatest enemy of man. Oppression, injustice, contempt, contumely, violence, sedition, war, calumny, treachery, fraud—by these they mutually torment each other, and they would soon dissolve that society which they had formed were it not for the dread of still greater ills which must attend their separation.

But though these external insults, said Demea, from animals, from men, from all the elements, which assault us form a frightful catalogue of woes, they are nothing in comparison of those which arise within ourselves, from the distempered condition of our mind and body. How many lie under the lingering torment of diseases? Hear the pathetic enumeration of the great poet.

> Intestine stone and ulcer, colic-pangs,
> Demoniac frenzy, moping melancholy,
> And moon-struck madness, pining atrophy,
> Marasmus, and wide-wasting pestilence.
> Dire was the tossing, deep the groans: *Despair*
> Tended the sick, busiest from couch to couch.
> And over them triumphant *Death* his dart
> Shook: but delay'd to strike, though oft invok'd
> With vows, as their chief good and final hope.

The disorders of the mind, continued Demea, though more secret, are not perhaps less dismal and vexatious. Remorse, shame, anguish, rage, disappointment, anxiety, fear, dejection, despair—who has ever passed through life without cruel inroads from these tormentors? How many have scarcely ever felt any better sensations? Labour and poverty, so abhorred by everyone, are the certain lot of the far greater number; and those few privileged persons who enjoy ease and opulence never reach contentment or true felicity. All the goods of life united would not make a very happy man, but all the ills united would make a wretch indeed; and any one of them almost (and who can be free from every one?), nay, often the absence of one good (and who can possess all?) is sufficient to render life ineligible.

Were a stranger to drop on a sudden into this world, I would show him, as a specimen of its ills, an hospital full of diseases, a prison crowded with malefactors and debtors, a field of battle strewed with carcases, a fleet foundering in the ocean, a nation languishing under tyranny, famine, or pestilence. To turn the gay side of life to him and give him a notion of its pleasures—whether should I conduct him? To a ball, to an opera, to court? He might justly think that I was only showing him a diversity of distress and sorrow.

There is no evading such striking instances, said Philo, but by apologies which still further aggravate the charge. Why have all men, I ask, in all ages, complained incessantly of the miseries of life? . . . They have no just reason, says one: these complaints proceed only from their discontented, repining, anxious disposition. . . . And can there possibly, I reply, be a more certain foundation of misery than such a wretched temper?

But if they were really as unhappy as they pretend, says my antagonist, why do they remain in life? . . .

Not satisfied with life, afraid of death—

this is the secret chain, say I, that holds us. We are terrified, not bribed to the continuance of our existence.

It is only a false delicacy, he may insist, which a few refined spirits indulge, and which has spread these complaints among the whole race of mankind. . . . And what is this delicacy, I ask, which you blame? Is it anything but a greater sensibility to all the pleasures and pains of life? And if the man of a delicate, refined temper, by being so much more alive than the rest of the world, is only so much more unhappy, what judgment must we form in general of human life?

Let men remain at rest, says our adversary, and they will be easy. They are willing artificers of their own misery. . . . No! reply I: an anxious languor follows their repose; disappointment, vexation, trouble, their activity and ambition.

I can observe something like what you mention in some others, replied Cleanthes, but I confess I feel little or nothing of it in myself, and hope that it is not so common as you represent it.

If you feel not human misery yourself, cried Demea, I congratulate you on so happy a singularity. Others, seemingly the most prosperous, have not been ashamed to vent their complaints in the most melancholy strains. Let us attend to the great, the fortunate emperor, Charles V, when, tired with human grandeur, he resigned all his extensive dominions into the hands of his son. In the last harangue which he made on that memorable occasion, he publicly avowed *that the greatest prosperities which he had ever enjoyed had been mixed with so many adversities that he might truly say he had never enjoyed any satisfaction or contentment.* But did the retired life in which he sought for shelter afford him any greater happiness? If we may credit his son's account, his repentance commenced the very day of his resignation.

Cicero's fortune, from small beginnings, rose to the greatest lustre and renown; yet what pathetic complaints of the ills of life do his familiar letters, as well as philosophical discourses, contain? And suitably to his own experience, he introduces Cato, the great, the fortunate Cato protesting in his old age that had he a new life in his offer he would reject the present.

Ask yourself, ask any of your acquaintance, whether they would live over again the last ten or twenty years of their life. No! but the next twenty, they say, will be better:

> And from the dregs of life, hope to receive
> What the first sprightly running could not give.

Thus, at last, they find (such is the greatness of human misery, it reconciles even contradictions) that they complain at once of the shortness of life and of its vanity and sorrow.

And is it possible, Cleanthes, said Philo, that after all these reflections, and infinitely more which might be suggested, you can still persevere in your anthropomorphism, and assert the moral attributes of the Deity, his justice, benevolence, mercy, and rectitude, to be of the same nature with these virtues in human creatures? His power, we allow, is infinite; whatever he wills is executed; but neither man nor any other animal is happy; therefore, he does not will their happiness. His wisdom is infinite; he is never mistaken in choosing the means to any end; but the course of nature tends not to human or animal felicity; therefore, it is not established for that purpose. Through the whole compass of human knowledge there are no inferences more certain and infallible than these. In what respect, then, do his benevolence and mercy resemble the benevolence and mercy of men?

Epicurus' old questions are yet unanswered.

Is he willing to prevent evil, but not able? then is he impotent. Is he able, but not willing? then is he malevolent. Is he both able and willing? whence then is evil?

You ascribe, Cleanthes, (and I believe justly) a purpose and intention to nature. But what, I beseech you, is the object of that curious artifice and machinery which she has displayed in all animals—the preservation alone of individuals, and propagation of the species? It seems enough for her purpose, if such a rank be barely upheld in the universe, without any care or concern for the happiness of the members that compose it. No resource for this purpose: no machinery in order merely to give pleasure or ease; no fund of pure joy and contentment; no indulgence without some want or necessity accompanying it. At least, the few phenomena of this nature are overbalanced by opposite phenomena of still greater importance.

Our sense of music, harmony, and indeed beauty of all kinds, gives satisfaction, without being absolutely necessary to the preservation and propagation of the species. But what racking pains, on the other hand, arise from gouts, gravels, megrims, toothaches, rheumatisms, where the injury to the animal machinery is either small or incurable? Mirth, laughter, play, frolic seem gratuitous satisfactions which have no further tendency; spleen, melancholy, discontent, superstitions are pains of the same nature. How then does the Divine benevolence display itself, in the sense of you anthropomorphites? None but we mystics, as you were pleased to call us, can account for this strange mixture of phenomena, by deriving it from attributes infinitely perfect but incomprehensible.

And have you, at last, said Cleanthes smiling, betrayed your intentions, Philo? Your long agreement with Demea did indeed a little surprise me, but I find you were all the while erecting a concealed battery against me. And I must confess that you have now fallen upon a subject worthy of your noble spirit of opposition and controversy. If you can make out the present point, and prove mankind to be unhappy or corrupted, there is an end at once of all religion. For to what purpose establish the natural attributes of the Deity, while the moral are still doubtful and uncertain?

You take umbrage very easily, replied Demea, at opinions the most innocent and the most generally received, even amongst the religious and devout themselves; and nothing can be more surprising than to find a topic like this—concerning the wickedness and misery of man—charged with no less than atheism and profaneness. Have not all pious divines and preachers who have indulged their rhetoric on so fertile a subject, have they not easily, I say, given a solution of any difficulties which may attend it? This world is but a point in comparison of the universe; this life but a moment in comparison of eternity. The present evil phenomena, therefore, are rectified in other regions, and in some future period of existence. And the eyes of men, being then opened to larger views of things, see the whole connection of general laws, and trace, with adoration, the benevolence and rectitude of the Deity through all the mazes and intricacies of his providence.

No! replied Cleanthes, no! These arbitrary suppositions can never be admitted, contrary to matter of fact, visible and uncontroverted. Whence can any cause be known but from its known effects? Whence can any hypothesis be proved but from the apparent phenomena? To establish one hypothesis upon another is building entirely in the air; and the utmost we ever attain by these conjectures and fictions is to ascertain the bare possibility of our opinion, but never can we, upon such terms, establish its reality.

The only method of supporting Divine benevolence—and it is what I willingly embrace—is to deny absolutely the misery and wickedness of man. Your representations are exaggerated; your melancholy views mostly fictitious;

your inferences contrary to fact and experience. Health is more common than sickness; pleasure than pain; happiness than misery. And for one vexation which we meet with, we attain, upon computation, a hundred enjoyments.

Admitting your position, replied Philo, which yet is extremely doubtful, you must at the same time allow that, if pain be less frequent than pleasure, it is infinitely more violent and durable. One hour of it is often able to outweigh a day, a week, a month of our common insipid enjoyments; and how many days, weeks, and months are passed by several in the most acute torments? Pleasure, scarcely in one instance, is ever able to reach ecstasy and rapture; and in no one instance can it continue for any time at its highest pitch and altitude. The spirits evaporate, the nerves relax, the fabric is disordered, and the enjoyment quickly degenerates into fatigue and uneasiness. But pain often, good God, how often! rises to torture and agony; and the longer it continues, it becomes still more genuine agony and torture. Patience is exhausted, courage languishes, melancholy seizes us, and nothing terminates our misery but the removal of its cause or another event which is the sole cure of all evil, but which, from our natural folly, we regard with still greater horror and consternation.

But not to insist upon these topics, continued Philo, though most obvious, certain, and important, I must use the freedom to admonish you, Cleanthes, that you have put the controversy upon a most dangerous issue, and are unawares introducing a total scepticism into the most essential articles of natural and revealed theology. What! no method of fixing a just foundation for religion unless we allow the happiness of human life, and maintain a continued existence even in this world, with all our present pains, infirmities, vexations, and follies, to be eligible and desirable! But this is contrary to everyone's feeling and experience; it is contrary to an authority so established as nothing can subvert. No decisive proofs can ever be produced against this authority; nor is it possible for you to compute, estimate, and compare all the pains and all the pleasures in the lives of all men and of all animals; and thus, by your resting the whole system of religion on a point which, from its very nature, must for ever be uncertain, you tacitly confess that that system is equally uncertain.

But allowing you what never will be believed, at least, what you never possibly can prove, that animal or, at least, human happiness in this life exceeds its misery, you have yet done nothing; for this is not, by any means, what we expect from infinite power, infinite wisdom, and infinite goodness. Why is there any misery at all in the world? Not by chance, surely. From some cause then. Is it from the intention of the Deity? But he is perfectly benevolent. Is it contrary to his intention? But he is almighty. Nothing can shake the solidity of this reasoning, so short, so clear, so decisive, except we assert that these subjects exceed all human capacity, and that our common measures of truth and falsehood are not applicable to them—a topic which I have all along insisted on, but which you have, from the beginning, rejected with scorn and indignation.

But I will be contented to retire still from this intrenchment, for I deny that you can ever force me in it. I will allow that pain or misery in man is *compatible* with infinite power and goodness in the Deity, even in your sense of these attributes: what are you advanced by all these concessions? A mere possible compatibility is not sufficient. You must *prove* these pure, unmixt, and uncontrollable attributes from the present mixed and confused phenomena, and from these alone. A hopeful undertaking! Were the phenomena ever so pure and unmixed, yet, being finite, they would be insufficient for that purpose. How much more, where they are also so jarring and discordant!

Here, Cleanthes, I find myself at ease in my argument. Here I triumph. Formerly, when we argued concerning the natural attributes of intelligence and design, I needed all my sceptical and metaphysical subtilty to elude your grasp. In many views of the universe and of its parts, particularly the latter, the beauty and fitness of final causes strike us with such irresistible force that all objections appear (what I believe they really are) mere cavils and sophisms; nor can we then imagine how it was ever possible for us to repose any weight on them. But there is no view of human life or of the condition of mankind from which, without the greatest violence, we can infer the moral attributes or learn that infinite benevolence, conjoined with infinite power and infinite wisdom, which we must discover by the eyes of faith alone. It is your turn now to tug the labouring oar, and to support your philosophical subtilties against the dictates of plain reason and experience.

✳ CLEANTHES

24. *The Goodness of the Whole*

Cleanthes succeeded Zeno as head of the Stoic school (founded in Athens about 300 B.C.) and remained in that position from 301 to 232 B.C. Cleanthes contributed to Stoicism much of its religious element. His *Hymn to Zeus* is a remarkable summary of the central ideas of Stoicism, most notably its teaching that all things unfold in strict accordance with a divine-cosmic *Logos* ("Reason").

Hymn to Zeus

Most glorious of immortals, many-named, omnipotent ever,
King of Nature, Zeus, who steer all things by Law,
Hail! for it is right that all mortals too address thee.
For we are sprung from thee, allotted the image of God,
We alone of mortal things that live and creep upon the earth.
Thus shall I praise thee and sing thy power always.

Cleanthes, *Hymn to Zeus*, tr. Ed. L. Miller, in *God and Reason* (New York: Macmillan, 1972) , Ch. 8. Reprinted by permission of The Macmillan Company.

By thee the whole of heaven, spinning 'round the earth,
Is guided where you lead, and willingly is ruled by thee.
In thine hand invincible you wield the aweful tool:
The forked and fiery everliving thunderbolt.
For Nature's every work advances by that blow
By which you guide the universal Reason, ranging over all,
Mingling with celestial lights both great and small. . . .

[How greatly born, thou King supreme forever!]
No deed is wrought upon the earth apart from thee, O God,
Nor down the divine aetherial sky, nor in the sea,
Save what the wicked do in their own unthinking.
But you know how to set excess aright,
To order things disordered, and the not-fair are fair to you.
Thus have you harmonized all into one, the evil with the good:
And the Reason of all is made one, eternal.

But this the wicked of mortals abandon, fleeing.
Ill-fated, these, ever bent on possession of goods,
Perceive not nor obey God's universal Law,
Which wisely trusting in they'd find a noble life.
But they, fools, rush each one to a different evil:
Some with contentious zeal for glory,
Some in reckless pursuit of profit,
Others to license and delights of the body.
. . . borne along from one to another,
In search of a goal opposite their end.

But Zeus! all-giving cloud-wrapt thunderer,
Deliver men from ruinous ignorance.
Dispel it from their souls and grant them, Father, to find
Knowledge, wherein trusting you steer all things with justice.
That honored thus by thee we may honor thee in turn,
Singing ever of thy works, a fitting thing for a mortal.
For greater blessing there is not, for mortals or for gods,
Than justly to sing the ever universal Law.

✵ ST. AUGUSTINE

25. *Evil as the Privation of Good*

St. Augustine (354–430), Bishop of Hippo, was perhaps the most influential theologian of the Christian tradition. Augustine's youthful encounter with Platonism, with its conception of an incorporeal truth and reality, prepared the way for his conversion to Christianity, and his voluminous writings articulate the first systematic-philosophical exposition of Christian doctrine. The most famous of Augustine's writing include his *Confessions* (the first autobiography) and *The City of God* (the first philosophy of history).

From *The Enchiridion on Faith, Hope and Love*

Chapter 10: The Supremely Good Creator Made All Things Good

By the Trinity, thus supremely and equally and unchangeably good, all things were created; and these are not supremely and equally and unchangeably good, but yet they are good, even taken separately. Taken as a whole, however, they are very good, because their *ensemble* constitutes the universe in all its wonderful order and beauty.

Chapter 11: What Is Called Evil in the Universe Is but the Absence of Good

And in the universe, even that which is called evil, when it is regulated and put in its own place, only enhances our admiration of the good; for we enjoy and value the good more when we compare it with the evil. For the Almighty God, who, as even the heathen acknowledge, has supreme power over all things, being Himself supremely good, would never permit the existence of anything evil among His works, if He were not so omnipotent and good that He can bring good even out of evil. For what is that which we call evil but the absence of good? In the bodies of animals, disease and wounds mean nothing but the absence of health; for when a cure is effected, that does not mean that the evils which were present—namely, the diseases and wounds—go away from the body and dwell elsewhere: they altogether cease to exist; for the wound or disease is not a substance, but a defect in the fleshly substance—the flesh itself being a substance, and therefore something good, of which those evils—that is, privations of the good which we call health—are accidents. Just in the same way, what are called vices in the soul are nothing but privations of natural good. And when they are cured, they are not transferred elsewhere: when they cease to exist in the healthy soul, they cannot exist anywhere else.

St. Augustine, *The Enchiridion on Faith, Hope, and Love*, tr. J. F. Shaw, ed. Henry Paolucci (Chicago: Henry Regnery, 1961). Reprinted by permission of the publisher.

Chapter 12: All Beings Were Made Good, but Not Being Made Perfectly Good, Are Liable to Corruption

All things that exist, therefore, seeing that the Creator of them all is supremely good, are themselves good. But because they are not, like their Creator, supremely and unchangeably good, their good may be diminished and increased. But for good to be diminished is an evil, although, however much it may be diminished, it is necessary, if the being is to continue, that some good should remain to constitute the being. For however small or of whatever kind the being may be, the good which makes it a being cannot be destroyed without destroying the being itself. An uncorrupted nature is justly held in esteem. But if, still further, it be incorruptible, it is undoubtedly considered of still higher value. When it is corrupted, however, its corruption is an evil, because it is deprived of some sort of good. For if it be deprived of no good, it receives no injury; but it does receive injury, therefore it is deprived of good. Therefore, so long as a being is in process of corruption, there is in it some good of which it is being deprived; and if a part of the being should remain which cannot be corrupted, this will certainly be an incorruptible being, and accordingly the process of corruption will result in the manifestation of this great good. But if it do not cease to be corrupted, neither can it cease to possess good of which corruption may deprive it. But if it should be thoroughly and completely consumed by corruption, there will then be no good left, because there will be no being. Wherefore corruption can consume the good only by consuming the being. Every being, therefore, is a good; a great good, if it cannot be corrupted; a little good, if it can: but in any case, only the foolish or ignorant will deny that it is a good. And if it be wholly consumed by corruption, then the corruption itself must cease to exist, as there is no being left in which it can dwell.

Chapter 13: There Can Be No Evil Where There Is No Good; and an Evil Man Is an Evil Good

Accordingly, there is nothing of what we call evil, if there be nothing good. But a good which is wholly without evil is a perfect good. A good, on the other hand, which contains evil is a faulty or imperfect good; and there can be no evil where there is no good. From all this we arrive at the curious result: that since every being, so far as it is a being, is good, when we say that a faulty being is an evil being, we just seem to say that what is good is evil, and that nothing but what is good can be evil, seeing that every being is good, and that no evil can exist except in a being. Nothing, then, can be evil except something which is good. And although this, when stated, seems to be a contradiction, yet the strictness of reasoning leaves us no escape from the conclusion. We must, however, beware of incurring the prophetic condemnation: "Woe unto them that call evil good, and good evil: that put darkness for light, and light for darkness: that put bitter for sweet, and sweet for bitter" [Isa. 5:20]. And yet our Lord says: "An evil man out of the evil treasure of his heart bringeth forth that which is evil" [Luke 6:45].

Now, what is an evil man but an evil being? for a man is a being. Now, if a man is a good thing because he is a being, what is an evil man but an evil good? Yet, when we accurately distinguish these two things, we find that it is not because he is a man that he is an evil, or, because he is wicked that he is a good; but that he is a good because he is a man, and an evil because he is wicked. Whoever, then, says, "To be a man is an evil," or "To be wicked is a good," falls under the prophetic denunciation: "Woe unto them that call evil good, and good evil!" For he condemns the work of God, which is the man, and praises the defect of man, which is the wickedness. Therefore every being, even if it be a defective one, in so far as it is a being is good, and in so far as it is defective is evil.

Chapter 14: Good and Evil Are an Exception to the Rule That Contrary Attributes Cannot Be Predicated of the Same Subject. Evil Springs Up in What Is Good, and Cannot Exist Except in What Is Good

Accordingly, in the case of these contraries which we call good and evil, the rule of the logicians, that two contraries cannot be predicated at the same time of the same thing, does not hold. No weather is at the same time dark and bright: no food or drink is at the same time sweet and bitter: no body is at the same time and in the same place black and white: none is at the same time and in the same place deformed and beautiful. And this rule is found to hold in regard to many, indeed nearly all, contraries, that they cannot exist at the same time in any one thing. But although no one can doubt that good and evil are contraries, not only can they exist at the same time, but evil cannot exist without good, or in anything that is not good. Good, however, can exist without evil. For a man or an angel can exist without being wicked; but nothing can be wicked except a man or an angel: and so far as he is a man or an angel, he is good; so far as he is wicked, he is an evil. And these two contraries are so far co-existent, that if good did not exist in what is evil, neither could evil exist; because corruption could not have either a place to dwell in, or a source to spring from, if there were nothing that could be corrupted; and nothing can be corrupted except what is good, for corruption is nothing else but the destruction of good. From what is good, then, evils arose, and except in what is good they do not exist; nor was there any other source from which any evil nature could arise. For if there were, then, in so far as this was a being, it was certainly a good: and a being which was incorruptible would be a great good; and even one which was corruptible must be to some extent a good, for only by corrupting what was good in it could corruption do it harm.

Chapter 15: The Preceding Argument Is in No Wise Inconsistent With the Saying of Our Lord: "A Good Tree Cannot Bring Forth Evil Fruit"

But when we say that evil springs out of good, let it not be thought that this contradicts our Lord's saying: "A good tree cannot bring forth evil fruit" [Matt. 7:18]. For, as the Truth says, you cannot gather grapes of thorns [cf. Matt. 7:16], because grapes do not grow on thorns. But we see that on good soil both vines and thorns may be grown. And in the same way, just as an evil tree cannot bring forth good fruit, so an evil will cannot produce good works. But from the nature of man, which is good, may spring either a good or an evil will. And certainty there was at first no source from which an evil will could spring, except the nature of angel or of man which was good. And our Lord Himself clearly shows this in the very same place where He speaks about the tree and its fruit. For He says: "Either make the tree good, and his fruit good; or else make the tree corrupt, and his fruit corrupt" [Matt. 12:33]—clearly enough warning us that evil fruits do not grow on a good tree, nor good fruits on an evil tree; but that nevertheless the ground itself, by which He meant those whom He was then addressing, might grow either kind of trees.

Chapter 16: It Is Not Essential to Man's Happiness That He Should Know the Causes of Physical Convulsions; but It Is, That He should Know the Causes of Good and Evil

Now, in view of these considerations, when we are pleased with that line of Maro, "Happy the man who has attained to the knowledge of the causes of things," we should not suppose that it is necessary to happiness to know the causes of the great physical convulsions, causes which lie hid in the most secret recesses of nature's kingdom, "whence comes the earthquake whose force makes the deep seas to swell and burst their barriers, and again to return upon themselves and settle down." But we ought to know the causes of good and evil as far as man may in this life know them, in order to avoid the mistakes and troubles of which this life is so full. For our aim must always be to reach that state of happiness in which no trouble shall distress us, and no error mislead us. If we must know the causes of physical convulsions, there are none which it concerns us more to know than those which affect our own health. But seeing that, in our ignorance of these, we are fain to resort to physicians, it would seem that we might bear with considerable patience our ignorance of the secrets that lie hid in the earth and heavens.

From *On Free Choice of the Will*

Book II

Chapter 18: Freedom of the Will, though It May Be Abused, Is Good and Divinely Given, since without It No One Could Live Rightly

Evodius. I admit that I am quite convinced—insofar as it can be proved in this life among such as we—that God exists and that all goods are from God, since all things that exist are from God, whether they under-

St. Augustine, *On Free Choice of the Will*, tr. Anna S. Benjamin and L. H. Hackstaff (Indianapolis, Ind.: Library of Liberal Arts, 1964). Copyright 1964 by The Bobbs-Merrill Company, Inc. Reprinted by permission of the Liberal Arts Press Division of The Bobbs-Merrill Company, Inc.

stand, live, and exist, or whether they live and exist only, or whether they merely exist. Now let us turn to a third question: whether we can establish that free will is to be numbered among the goods. When this has been proven, I will grant without hesitation that God gave us free will, and that He was right to have given it.

Augustine. You have remembered well the points we proposed to discuss, and have seen clearly that the second question has already been answered. But you should also have seen that the third question, too, is already solved.

You said you thought that free choice of the will ought not to have been given because through it man sins. To this opinion I replied that no righteous act could be performed except by free choice of the will, and I asserted that God gave it for this reason. You replied that free will ought to have been given as justice was given, so that no one could make evil use of it. This answer of yours forced us to go into a long circuitous course of argument, by which we proved that both greater and lesser goods came only from God. This could not be proved conclusively until we had met the wicked and foolish objections of the fool who "hath said in his heart, 'There is no God'" [Ps. 14:1]. Whatever reasoning we performed, within our limited means, concerning such a great question was directed toward what was obvious, with God Himself assisting us in so perilous a course. These two facts, nevertheless, that God exists and that all goods come from Him, were thus discussed—even though we previously believed them in firm faith—in such a way that this third question, that free will is to be numbered among the goods, might also appear in the clearest light.

In the previous argument, we proved and established that the nature of the body is on a lower plane than that of the spirit, and because of this, the spirit is a greater good than the body. If, therefore, we find among the goods of the body some that a man can use wrongly, but that we cannot say ought not to have been given to man, since we have agreed that they are goods, why should we wonder if there are in the spirit certain goods, of which we can make wrong use, but which, because they are goods, could not have been given by anyone but Him from whom all good things proceed?

Indeed, you see how great a good is wanting to anybody that has no hands; yet he who works cruel or shameful deeds with his hands uses them for evil. Should you see someone without feet, you would acknowledge what an important good was lacking to make his body complete. Yet you would not deny that the man who made evil use of his feet, either for injuring another or for dishonoring himself, was using his feet wrongfully.

With our eyes we see light and distinguish the forms of bodies. The faculty of sight is the fairest in our body, and therefore the eyes are placed, as it were, in the highest position, the place of honor. We use our eyes for keeping safe and for serving life in many other ways. Yet many men commit many shameful deeds by means of their eyes, and force their eyes into the service of lust. You see what a great good the face would lack if there were no eyes; but when we possess them, who gave them but God, the Giver of all good things?

Just as you approve those goods of the body and, disregarding the people who make evil use of them, you praise Him who gave them, so you should admit that free will, without which no one can live rightly, is good and divinely given; and you should grant that those who make evil use of free will ought to be condemned, rather than saying that He who gave it ought not to have given it.

E. First, however, I wish that you would prove to me that free will is a good. Then I will grant that God gave it to us, since I acknowledge that all goods proceed from God.

A. Did I not prove this to you in the great toils of our earlier discussion, when you agreed that every type and form of body is derived from the Form which is supreme over all things, that is, from Truth, and when you acknowledged also that it is a good? For the Truth itself speaks out in the Gospel that even the hairs of our head are numbered [cf. Matt. 10:30]. Have you forgotten what we said about the supremacy of number and its power which extends for ever and ever? What perversity that is! To count the hairs of our head, however scant and useless they may be, among the goods and to find that they can be attributed to no other cause than to God, the Cause of all goods, since the greatest and the least come from Him; yet to hesitate on the question of free will, without which even men who lead the most evil lives agree that they cannot live rightly!

Tell me now, please, which you think is better in us: that without which we can live rightly or that without which we cannot live rightly?

E. Please excuse me; I am ashamed of my blindness. Who would doubt that the more excellent thing by far is that without which there is no righteous life?

A. You will not deny then that a blind man can live rightly?

E. May I never be so foolish!

A. Since, then, you admit that the eye in the body is a good although its loss will not prevent us from living rightly, will you think that free will is not a good when no one can live rightly without it?

Look at justice, which no one uses wrongly. This is numbered among the highest goods of the mind and among all the virtues of the soul, upon which an upright and righteous life depends. No one uses wisdom, courage, or temperance for evil; for in these as in justice, which you have just mentioned, right reason prevails, and without it virtues cannot exist. No one can use right reason for evil.

Chapter 19: Of the Three Classes of Goods, Great, Intermediate, and Lowest, Freedom of the Will Is an Intermediate Good

A. These are great goods. Yet remember that not only the great goods but also the least ones can be from no one other than Him from whom all goods proceed, namely from God. Our previous argument proved that, and you have already gladly given your assent to it.

Therefore the virtues, by which men live rightly, are great goods, while all kinds of physical beauty, without which men can live rightly, are the lowest goods. The powers of the spirit, without which no one can live rightly, are the intermediate goods between these two. No one uses the virtues for evil. However the other goods, the lowest and the intermediate ones, can be used not only for good, but also for evil. No one uses virtues for evil because the very action of a virtue is the good use of those things that we can also use for evil. Moreover, no one can make wrong use of using a thing rightly. Therefore, the abundant generosity of God's goodness is responsible not only for the great goods, but for the intermediate and lowest goods as well. His goodness ought to be praised more in the case of the greatest goods than in that of the intermediate ones, and more in the case of the intermediate goods than the lowest; but more in all goods than if He had not bestowed all.

E. I agree. But the following troubles me, since it involves free will, and we see that free will uses some things for good and some for evil: how is free will to be counted among those goods which we use?

A. In the same way as we know by reason everything that we know, and nevertheless even reason itself is numbered among the things that we know by reason. Have you forgotten that when we asked what is known by reason, you admitted that reason was known by reason? Do not wonder, then, that we can use the free will by means of itself, if we use other things through our free will. As reason, knowing other things, also knows itself, so the free will, which makes use of other things, also makes use of itself. So also memory grasps not only all the other things which we remember, but also retains itself in us, because we do not forget that we have a memory. It remembers not only other things, but also itself; through memory, in other words, we remember ourselves, other things, and memory itself.

When the will, which is an intermediate good, clings to immutable good, and this good is not private but is common to all (like truth, about which we have said much, though nothing really worthy of it), then man leads a happy life. The happy life—that disposition of the spirit which clings to immutable goods—is man's proper and primary good. In this good lie all the virtues that man cannot use for evil. For although these goods are great and most important in man, it is known that they belong to each man, and are not common. But it is by clinging to truth and wisdom, which are common to all, that all men may become wise and happy.

Moreover, one man does not become happy because of another man's happiness. This is because even when he seeks to be happy by imitating another, he desires to become happy through that by which he saw the other man made happy, that is, by immutable truth, which is common to all.

No one becomes prudent through another's prudence, or brave through another's courage, or temperate through another's temperance. So too, no one becomes just through the justice of another. Instead, man obtains virtues by adapting his spirit to the immutable rules and lights of those virtues which dwell incorruptible in truth itself and in common wisdom, to which the virtuous man has adapted himself and fitted his spirit. The man seeking virtue has determined to imitate this spirit, because it is endowed with virtue. Therefore the will, clinging to common and immutable goods, obtains the first and great goods of man, although it is itself only an intermediate good. The will, however, commits sin when it turns away from immutable and common goods, toward its private good, either something external to itself or lower than itself. It turns to its own private good when it desires to be its own master; it turns to external goods when it busies itself with the private affairs of others or with whatever is none of its concern; it turns to goods lower than itself when it loves the pleasures of the body. Thus a man becomes proud, meddlesome, and lustful; he is caught up in another life which, when compared to the higher one, is death. Yet he is ruled by the administration of divine providence, which places everything in its proper order and gives to each what is his own. So it follows that [1] neither the goods desired by sinners, nor the free will itself which we found to have been numbered among certain intermediate goods, are evil in any way, and that [2] evil is a turning away from immutable goods and a turning toward changeable goods. This turning away and turning toward result in the just punishment of unhappiness, because they are committed, not under compulsion, but voluntarily.

Chapter 20: The Movement of the Will from Immutable to Transient Goods, since It Is Evil, Is Not from God

A. Because the will is moved when it turns from an immutable good to a changeable one, you may perhaps ask how this movement arises. For the movement itself is certainly evil, although the free will must be numbered among the goods, because without it no one can live rightly. Even if this movement, that is, the turning of the will from the Lord God, is without doubt a sin, we cannot say, can we, that God is the cause of sin? This movement will not be from God, but what then is its origin? If I should answer your question by saying that I do not know, you would perhaps be disappointed; yet that would be the truth, for that which is nothing cannot be known. Only hold to your firm faith, since no good thing comes to your perception, understanding, or thought which is not from God. Nothing of any kind can be discovered which is not from God. Wherever you see measure, number, and order, you cannot hesitate to attribute all these to God, their Maker. When you remove measure, number, and order, nothing at all remains. Even if the beginning of some form were to remain, where you do not find order or measure or number (since wherever these exist, form is complete), you must remove even that very beginning of form which seems to be the artisan's raw material. If the completion of form is a good, there is some good even in the rudimentary beginning of form. Thus, if all good is completely removed, no vestige of reality persists; indeed, nothing remains. Every good is from God. There is nothing of any kind that is not from God. Therefore, since the movement of turning away from good, which we admit to be sin, is a defective movement and since, moreover, every defect comes from nothing, see where this movement belongs: you may be sure that it does not belong to God.

Yet since this defect is voluntary, it lies within our power. You must not be willing to fear this defect, for if you do not desire it, it will not exist. What greater security can there be than to live a life where what you do not will cannot happen to you? Since a man cannot rise of his own will as he fell by his own will, let us hold with firm faith the right hand of God, Jesus Christ our Lord, which is stretched out to us. Let us wait for Him with steadfast hope; let us love Him with burning love.

If, however—though I myself do not think it necessary—you think that we ought to examine the question of the origin of sin more carefully, let us put it off for some other discussion.

E. I follow your will gladly. Let us postpone to some other time the points suggested in this discussion. I will not, however, grant to you that enough has been said on the subject.

Book III

Chapter 15: Not All Imperfections in Creatures are Worthy of Blame

A. If, therefore, by blaming imperfections we suggest the beauty and worth of the very natures which possess imperfections, how much more should we praise God, the Creator of all natures even in their imperfections! For to God they owe the fact that they are natures. Their imperfection is as great as the distance they have gone from the design by which God made them. When we blame them, we do so in terms of the design by which we see they were made; thus, we blame them for what we do not see in them. And if the very design through which all things were made (namely, the highest and immutable Wisdom of God) truly exists in the highest degree—and indeed it does—see what may become of whatever departs from the design.

Nevertheless, this defect would not deserve blame if it were not voluntary. Listen then, please: are you right to blame what is as it ought to be? I think not. Yet you are right to blame what is not as it ought to be. No one owes what he has not received. And to whom does the debtor owe, if not to him from whom he has received? The debts which are returned in a bequest are returned to the man who made the bequest. Any credit returned to the rightful heirs is paid to those who succeed by that right; otherwise it would not be a payment but only a release or surrender, or something of the sort. Therefore, it is foolish for us to say that temporal objects ought not to pass away. They have been placed in the order of the universe in such a way that, unless they do pass away, future objects cannot succeed to past ones, and only thus can the whole beauty of times past, present, and future be accomplished in their own kind. They use what they have received and return it to Him to whom they owe their existence and greatness. The man who grieves that these things pass away ought to listen to his own speech, to see if he thinks the complaint that he makes is just and proceeds from prudence. If someone likes the least bit of the complaint that comes to his ears and does not want it to pass on and yield its place, so that the whole complaint may be made by passing and succeeding parts, he will be judged quite mad!

Therefore, in the case of objects which pass away because they have been granted only a limited existence in order that everything may be accomplished in its time, no one is right to blame this deficiency. No one can say, "It ought to remain," when it cannot pass the accepted limits. Moreover, in the case of rational creatures (in whom, whether they sin or not, the beauty of the universe finds its fullest expression), either there are no sins—which is a most foolish thing to say, for he sins who condemns things as sins which are not sins; or else sins are not to be blamed—which is no less foolish. For then, either things wrongly made will begin to receive praise, and the whole attention of the human mind will be disturbed and will upset life; or else the deed which has been done as it ought to have been done will be blamed, and accursed madness will result—or, to speak more mildly, a wretched error. If truest reason forces us to blame sins, and whatever is rightly blamed is blamed because it is not as it ought to be, ask what a sinful nature owes and you will find the answer, "right action." Ask to whom it owes this and you will find the answer, "to God." For from God the rational nature received the possibility of acting rightly when it so willed; from God, too, comes the fact that it is unhappy if it has not acted rightly, and happy if it has acted rightly.

Since no one is above the laws of the omnipotent Creator, the soul is not allowed not to repay what it owes. Either it repays what it received by using it rightly, or else it repays the debt by forfeiting what it is not willing to use well. If the soul does not pay its debt by doing justice, it will pay its debt by enduring unhappiness—the word "debt" is applicable in either case. We can express what we have said in the following way: If a man does not pay his debt by doing what he ought, he pays it by suffering what he ought. These are not separated by any interval of time, however, so that a man at one time does not do what he ought and at some other time suffer what he ought. The universal beauty is not marred by time. Thus, the ugliness of sin is never without the beauty of punishment. But all that is now secretly punished will be disclosed, with all its bitter unhappiness, in the judgment to come. Just as anyone who is not awake is asleep, so anyone who does not do what he ought suffers at once what he ought, because there is such great beauty in justice that no one can escape from it, except into unhappiness. In every case of deficiency, therefore, either the natures have not received what they lack and thus there is no sin (just as while they exist there is no sin since they have not received more than they are); or they are unwilling to be what, if they were willing, they could be, and because the nature that they received is good, they are punished if they are unwilling to fulfill that nature.

Chapter 16: God Is Not Responsible for Human Sin

A. But God owes nothing to anyone, for He freely maintains the universe. Even if someone should say that God owes him something for his merits, surely God is under no obligation for having given the man existence; it is not to the man that something is owing. Besides, what is the merit in turning to God, from whom you have your existence, since you do so to better yourself through Him who gave you your existence? What then do you ask—as if you were demanding payment of a debt? If you do not will to turn to Him, what loss is it to God? It is your loss, for you would be nothing without Him who made you something. Unless you turn to Him and repay the existence that He gave you, you won't be "nothing"; you will be wretched. All things owe to God, first of all, what they are insofar as they are natures. Then, those who have received a will owe to Him whatever better thing they can will to be, and whatever they ought to be. No man is ever blamed for what he has not been given, but he is justly blamed if he has not done what he should have done; and if he has received free will and sufficient power, he stands under obligation. When a man does not do what he ought, God the Creator is not at fault. It is to His glory that a man suffers justly; and by blaming a man for not doing what he should have done, you are praising what he ought to do. You are praised for seeing what you ought to do, even though you see this only through God, who is immutable Truth; how much more, then, should God be praised, since He has taught you to will, has given you the power to will, and has not allowed unwillingness to go unpunished! If every man owes what he has received, and if man was made so that he must necessarily sin, then he is obliged to sin. Therefore, when he sins, he does what he ought. But if it is wicked to say this, then no one is forced to sin by his own nature; nor is he forced to sin by any other nature. Indeed, no one sins when he suffers what he has not willed. If he suffers justly, his sin lies, not in the fact that he suffers unwillingly, but in the fact that he willingly acted in such a way as to suffer justly what he did not will. If he suffers unjustly, how does he sin? For to sin is not to suffer something unjustly, but to do something unjust. But if no one is forced to sin, either by his own nature or by that of another, it follows that he sins of his own will. If you wish to attribute his sin to the Creator, you will acquit the sinner of his sin. If the sinner is rightly defended, he has not sinned, and there is nothing to be imputed to the Creator. Let us, therefore, praise the Creator if the sinner can be defended, and let us praise Him if he cannot. For if he is justly defended, he is not a sinner—therefore, praise the Creator. If he cannot be defended, he is a sinner insofar as he has turned away from his Creator—therefore, praise the Creator.

I cannot find, and I assert that there cannot be found, any way in which to attribute our sins to God the Creator. I find that He is to be praised in these very sins, because He punishes them and because they occur when we turn from His truth.

E. I willingly accept and approve, and I agree that our sins cannot properly be attributed to our Creator.

✳ JOHN STUART MILL

26. *A Limited God*

John Stuart Mill (1806–1873) received a strict education from his father, beginning the study of Greek at the age of three. He was schooled in Bentham's ethical philosophy and, pursuing his own version of this position, published the little work *Utilitarianism* which stands as its classic expression. In addition to moral philosophy, Mill's interests included logic, politics, economy, and the critical analysis of religion.

From *Three Essays on Religion*

THEISM

Part II: Attributes

The question of the existence of a Deity, in its purely scientific aspect, standing as is shown in the First Part, it is next to be considered, given the indications of a Deity, what *sort* of a Deity do they point to? What attributes are we warranted, by the evidence which Nature affords of a creative mind, in assigning to that mind?

It needs no showing that the power if not the intelligence, must be so far superior to that of Man, as to surpass all human estimate. But from this to Omnipotence and Omniscience there is a wide interval. And the distinction is of immense practical importance.

It is not too much to say that every indication of Design in the Kosmos is so much evidence against the Omnipotence of the Designer. For what is meant by Design? Contrivance: the adaptation of means to an end. But the necessity for contrivance—the need of employing means—is a consequence of the limitation of power. Who would have recourse to means if to attain his end his mere word was sufficient? The very idea of means implies that the means have an efficacy which the direct action of the being who employs them has not. Otherwise they are not means, but an incumbrance. A man does not use machinery to move his arms. If he did, it could only be when paralysis had deprived him of the power of moving them by volition. But if the employment of contrivance is in itself a sign of limited power, how much more so is the careful and skilful choice of contrivances? Can any wisdom be shown in the selection of means, when the means have no efficacy but

John Stuart Mill, *Three Essays on Religion*, third ed. (London: Longmans, Green & Co., 1875).

what is given them by the will of him who employs them, and when his will could have bestowed the same efficacy on any other means? Wisdom and contrivance are shown in overcoming difficulties, and there is no room for them in a Being for whom no difficulties exist. The evidences, therefore, of Natural Theology distinctly imply that the author of the Kosmos worked under limitations; that he was obliged to adapt himself to conditions independent of his will, and to attain his ends by such arrangements as those conditions admitted of.

And this hypothesis agrees with what we have seen to be the tendency of the evidences in another respect. We found that the appearances in Nature point indeed to an origin of the Kosmos, or order in Nature, and indicate that origin to be Design but do not point to any commencement, still less creation, of the two great active elements of the Universe, the passive element and the active element, Matter and Force. There is in Nature no reason whatever to suppose that either Matter or Force, or any of their properties, were made by the Being who was the author of the collocations by which the world is adapted to what we consider as its purposes; or that he has power to alter any of those properties. It is only when we consent to entertain this negative supposition that there arises a need for wisdom and contrivance in the order of the universe. The Deity had on this hypothesis to work out his ends by combining materials of a given nature and properties. Out of these materials he had to construct a world in which his designs should be carried into effect through given properties of Matter and Force, working together and fitting into one another. This did require skill and contrivance, and the means by which it is effected are often such as justly excite our wonder and admiration: but exactly because it requires wisdom, it implies limitation of power, or rather the two phrases express different sides of the same fact.

If it be said, that an Omnipotent Creator, though under no necessity of employing contrivances such as man must use, thought fit to do so in order to leave traces by which man might recognize his creative hand, the answer is that this equally supposes a limit to his omnipotence. For if it was his will that men should know that they themselves and the world are his work, he, being omnipotent, had only to will that they should be aware of it. Ingenious men have sought for reasons why God might choose to leave his existence so far a matter of doubt that men should not be under an absolute necessity of knowing it, as they are of knowing that three and two make five. These imagined reasons are very unfortunate specimens of casuitry; but even did we admit their validity they are of no avail on the supposition of omnipotence, since if it did not please God to implant in man a complete conviction of his existence, nothing hindered him from making the conviction fall short of completeness by any margin he chose to leave. It is usual to dispose of arguments of this description by the easy answer, that we do not know what wise reasons the Omniscient may have had for leaving undone things which he had the power to do. It is not perceived that this plea itself implies a limit to Omnipotence. When a thing is obviously good and obviously in accordance with what all the evidences of creation imply to have been the Creator's design, and we say we do not know what good reason he may have had for not doing it, we mean that we do not know to what other, still better object—to what object still more completely in the line of his purposes, he may have seen fit to postpone it. But the necessity of postponing one thing to another belongs only to limited power. Omnipotence could have made the objects compatible. Omnipotence does not need to weigh one consideration against another. If the Creator, like a human ruler, had to adapt himself to a set of conditions which he did not make, it is as unphilosophical as presumptuous in us to call him to account for any imperfections in his work; to complain that he left anything in it contrary to what, if the indications of design prove anything, he must have intended. He must at least know more than we know, and we cannot judge what greater good would have had to be sacrificed, or what greater evil incurred, if he had decided to remove this particular blot. Not so if he be omnipotent. If he be that, he must himself have willed that the two desirable objects should be incompatible; he must himself have willed that the obstacle to his supposed design should be insuperable. It cannot therefore *be* his design. It will not do to say that it was, but that he had other designs which interfered with it; for no one purpose imposes necessary limitations on another in the case of a Being not restricted by conditions of possibility.

Omnipotence, therefore, cannot be predicated of the Creator on grounds of natural theology. The fundamental principles of natural religion as deduced from the facts of universe, negative his omnipotence. They do not, in the same manner, exclude omniscience: if we suppose limitation of power, there is nothing to contradict the supposition of perfect knowledge and absolute wisdom. But neither is there anything to prove it. The knowledge of the powers and properties of things necessary for planning and executing the arrangements of the Kosmos, is no doubt as much in excess of human knowledge as the power implied in creation is in excess of human power. And the skill, the subtlety of contrivance, the ingenuity as it would be called in the case of a human work, is often marvellous. But nothing obliges us to suppose that either the knowledge or the skill is infinite. We are not even compelled to suppose that the contrivances were always the best possible. If we venture to judge them as we judge the works of human artificers, we find abundant defects. The human body, for example, is one of the most striking instances of artful and ingenious contrivance which nature offers, but we may well ask whether so complicated a machine could not have been made to last longer, and not to get so easily and frequently out of order. We may ask why the human race should have been so constituted as to grovel in wretchedness and degradation for countless ages before a small portion of it was enabled to lift itself into the very imperfect state of intelligence, goodness and happiness which we enjoy. The divine power may not have been equal to doing more; the obstacles to a better arrangement of things may have been insuperable. But it is also possible that they were not. The skill of the Demiourgos[1] was sufficient to produce what we see; but we cannot tell that this skill reached the extreme limit of perfection compatible with the material it employed and the forces it had to work with. I know not how we can even satisfy ourselves on grounds of natural theology, that the Creator forsees all the future; that he foreknows all the effects that will issue from his own contrivances. There may be great wisdom without the power of forseeing and calculating everything: and human workmanship teaches us the possibility that the workman's knowledge of the properties of the things he works on may enable him to make arrangements admirably fitted to produce a given result, while he may have very little power of forseeing the agencies of another kind which may modify or counteract the operation of the machinery he has made. Perhaps a knowledge of the laws of nature on which organic life depends, not much more perfect than the knowledge which man even now possesses of some other natural laws, would enable man, if he had the same power over the materials and the forces concerned which he has over some of those of inanimate nature, to create organized beings not less wonderful nor less adapted to their conditions of existence than those in Nature.

Assuming then that while we confine ourselves to Natural Religion we must rest content with a Creator less than Almighty; the question presents itself, of what nature is the limitation of his power? Does the obstacle at which the power of the Creator stops, which says to it: Thus far shalt thou go and no further, lie in the power of other Intelligent Beings; or in the insufficiency and refractoriness of the materials of the universe; or must we resign ourselves to admitting the hypothesis that the author of the Kosmos, though wise and knowing, was not all-wise and all-knowing, and may not always have done the best that was possible under the conditions of the problem?

The first of these suppositions has until a very recent period been and in many quarters still is, the prevalent theory even of Christianity. Though attributing, and in a certain sense sincerely, omnipotence to the Creator, the received religion represents him as for some inscrutable reason tolerating the perpetual counteraction of his purposes by the will of another Being of opposite character and of great though inferior power, the Devil. The only difference on this matter between popular Christianity and the religion of Ormuzd and Ahriman,[2] is that the former pays its good Creator the bad compliment of having been the maker of the Devil and of being at all times able to crush and annihilate him and his evil deeds and counsels, which nevertheless he does not do. But, as I have already remarked, all forms of polytheism, and this among the rest, are with difficulty reconcileable with an universe governed by general laws. Obedience to law is the note of a settled government, and not of a conflict always going on. When powers are at war with one another

[1][Demiourgos: from a Greek word meaning "craftsman."]

[2][Ormuzd and Ahriman: Zoroastrian personifications of the co-eternal principles of Good (Ormuzd) and Evil (Ahriman), locked in unending struggle for supremecy.]

for the rule of the world, the boundary between them is not fixed but constantly fluctuating. This may seem to be the case on our planet as between the powers of good and evil when we look only at the results; but when we consider the inner springs, we find that both the good and evil take place in the common course of nature, by virtue of the same general laws originally impressed—the same machinery turning out now good, now evil things, and oftener still, the two combined. The division of power is only apparently variable, but really so regular that, were we speaking of human potentates, we should declare without hesitation that the share of each must have been fixed by previous consent. Upon that supposition indeed, the result of the combination of antagonist forces might be much the same as on that of a single creator with divided purposes.

But when we come to consider, not what hypothesis may be conceived, and possibly reconciled with known facts, but what supposition is pointed to by the evidences of natural religion; the case is different. The indications of design point strongly in one direction, the preservation of the creatures in whose structure the indications are found. Along with the preserving agencies there are destroying agencies, which we might be tempted to ascribe to the will of a diffferent Creator: but there are rarely appearances of the recondite contrivance of means of destruction, except when the destruction of one creature is the means of preservation to others. Nor can it be supposed that the preserving agencies are wielded by one Being, the destroying agencies by another. The destroying agencies are a necessary part of the preserving agencies: the chemical compositions by which life is carried on could not take place without a parallel series of decompositions. The great agent of decay in both organic and inorganic substances is oxidation, and it is only by oxidation that life is continued for even the length of a minute. The imperfections in the attainment of the purposes which the appearances indicate, have not the air of having been designed. They are like the unintended results of accidents insufficiently guarded against, or of a little excess or deficiency in the quantity of some of the agencies by which the good purpose is carried on, or else they are consequences of the wearing out of a machinery not made to last for ever: they point either to short comings in the workmanhip as regards its intended purpose, or to external forces not under the control of the workman, but which forces bear no mark of being wielded and aimed by any other rival Intelligence.

We may conclude, then, that there is no ground in Natural Theology for attributing intelligence or personality to the obstacles which partially thwart what seem the purposes of the Creator. The limitation of his power more probably results either from the qualities of the material—the substances and forces of which the universe is composed not admitting of any arrangements by which his purposes could be more completely fulfilled: or else, the purposes might have been more fully attained, but the Creator did not know how to do it; creative skill, wonderful as it is, was not sufficiently perfect to accomplish his purposes more thoroughly. . . .

✽ ALBERT CAMUS

27. *Philosophical Revolt*

Albert Camus (1913–1960) was, with Jean-Paul Sartre, one of the foremost existentialist thinkers. Camus describes his philosophy as an "invitation to live and to create" even in the face of death and ultimate meaninglessness. During World War II he was active in the French Resistance and produced the underground paper *Combat*. Camus wrote essays, plays, and novels (including *The Rebel, Caligula, The Plague,* and *The Stranger*) , and in 1957 was awarded the Nobel prize for literature.

From *The Myth of Sisyphus and Other Essays*

An Absurd Reasoning

Absurdity and Suicide

There is but one truly serious philosophical problem, and that is suicide. Judging whether life is or is not worth living amounts to answering the fundamental question of philosophy. All the rest—whether or not the world has three dimensions, whether the mind has nine or twelve categories—comes afterwards. These are games; one must first answer. And if it is true, as Nietzsche claims, that a philosopher, to deserve our respect, must preach by example, you can appreciate the importance of that reply, for it will precede the definitive act. These are facts the heart can feel; yet they call for careful study before they become clear to the intellect.

If I ask myself how to judge that this question is more urgent than that, I reply that one judges by the actions it entails. I have never seen anyone die for the ontological argument. Galileo, who held a scientific truth of great importance, abjured it with the greatest ease as soon as it endangered his life. In a certain sense, he did right.[1] That truth was not worth the stake. Whether the earth or the sun revolves around the other is a matter of profound indifference. To tell the truth, it is a futile question. On the other hand, I see many people die because they judge that life is not worth living. I see others paradoxically getting killed for the ideas or illusions that give them a reason for living (what is called a reason for living is also an excellent reason for dying). I therefore conclude that the meaning of life is the most urgent of questions. How to answer it? On all essential problems (I mean

Albert Camus, *The Myth of Sisyphus and Other Essays*, tr. Justin O'Brien (New York: Vintage Books, 1955). Copyright © 1955 by Alfred A. Knopf, Inc. Copyright © by Albert Camus 1942, 1955 (Hamish Hamilton, London). Reprinted by permission of the publisher.

[1]From the point of view of the relative value of truth. On the other hand, from the point of view of virile behavior, this scholar's fragility may well make us smile.

thereby those that run the risk of leading to death or those that intensify the passion of living) there are probably but two methods of thought: the method of La Palisse and the method of Don Quixote. Solely the balance between evidence and lyricism can allow us to achieve simultaneously emotion and lucidity. In a subject at once so humble and so heavy with emotion, the learned and classical dialectic must yield, one can see, to a more modest attitude of mind deriving at one and the same time from common sense and understanding.

Suicide has never been dealt with except as a social phenomenon. On the contrary, we are concerned here, at the outset, with the relationship between individual thought and suicide. An act like this is prepared within the silence of the heart, as is a great work of art. The man himself is ignorant of it. One evening he pulls the trigger or jumps. Of an apartment-building manager who had killed himself I was told that he had lost his daughter five years before, that he had changed greatly since, and that that experience had "undermined" him. A more exact word cannot be imagined. Beginning to think is beginning to be undermined. Society has but little connection with such beginnings. The worm is in man's heart. That is where it must be sought. One must follow and understand this fatal game that leads from lucidity in the face of existence to flight from light.

There are many causes for a suicide, and generally the most obvious ones were not the most powerful. Rarely is suicide committed (yet the hypothesis is not excluded) through reflection. What sets off the crisis is almost always unverifiable. Newspapers often speak of "personal sorrows" or of "incurable illness." These explanations are plausible. But one would have to know whether a friend of the desperate man had not that very day addressed him indifferently. He is the guilty one. For that is enough to precipitate all the rancors and all the boredom still in suspension.[2]

But if it is hard to fix the precise instant, the subtle step when the mind opted for death, it is easier to deduce from the act itself the consequences it implies. In a sense, and as in melodrama, killing yourself amounts to confessing. It is confessing that life is too much for you or that you do not understand it. Let's not go too far in such analogies, however, but rather return to everyday words. It is merely confessing that that "is not worth the trouble." Living, naturally, is never easy. You continue making the gestures commanded by existence for many reasons, the first of which is habit. Dying voluntarily implies that you have recognized, even instinctively, the ridiculous character of that habit, the absence of any profound reason for living, the insane character of that daily agitation, and the uselessness of suffering.

What, then, is that incalculable feeling that deprives the mind of the sleep necessary to life? A world that can be explained even with bad reasons is a familiar world. But, on the other hand, in a universe suddenly divested of illusions and lights, man feels an alien, a stranger. His exile is without

[2]Let us not miss this opportunity to point out the relative character of this essay. Suicide may indeed be related to much more honorable considerations—for example, the political suicides of protest, as they were called, during the Chinese revolution.

remedy since he is deprived of the memory of a lost home or the hope of a promised land. This divorce between man and his life, the actor and his setting, is properly the feeling of absurdity. All healthy men having thought of their own suicide, it can be seen, without further explanation, that there is a direct connection between this feeling and the longing for death.

The subject of this essay is precisely this relationship between the absurd and suicide, the exact degree to which suicide is a solution to the absurd. The principle can be established that for a man who does not cheat, what he believes to be true must determine his action. Belief in the absurdity of existence must then dictate his conduct. It is legitimate to wonder, clearly and without false pathos, whether a conclusion of this importance requires forsaking as rapidly as possible an incomprehensible condition. I am speaking, of course, of men inclined to be in harmony with themselves. . . .

Absurd Freedom

. . . Now I can broach the notion of suicide. It has already been felt what solution might be given. At this point the problem is reversed. It was previously a question of finding out whether or not life had to have a meaning to be lived. It now becomes clear, on the contrary, that it will be lived all the better if it has no meaning. Living an experience, a particular fate, is accepting it fully. Now, no one will live this fate, knowing it to be absurd, unless he does everything to keep before him that absurd brought to light by consciousness. Negating one of the terms of the opposition on which he lives amounts to escaping it. To abolish conscious revolt is to elude the problem. The theme of permanent revolution is thus carried into individual experience. Living is keeping the absurd alive. Keeping it alive is, above all, contemplating it. Unlike Eurydice, the absurd dies only when we turn away from it. One of the only coherent philosophical positions is thus revolt. It is a constant confrontation between man and his own obscurity. It is an insistence upon an impossible transparency. It challenges the world anew every second. Just as danger provided man the unique opportunity of seizing awareness, so metaphysical revolt extends awareness to the whole of experience. It is that constant presence of man in his own eyes. It is not aspiration, for it is devoid of hope. That revolt is the certainty of a crushing fate, without the resignation that ought to accompany it.

This is where it is seen to what a degree absurd experience is remote from suicide. It may be thought that suicide follows revolt—but wrongly. For it does not represent the logical outcome of revolt. It is just the contrary by the consent it presupposes. Suicide, like the leap, is acceptance at its extreme. Everything is over and man returns to his essential history. His future, his unique and dreadful future—he sees and rushes toward it. In its way, suicide settles the absurd. It engulfs the absurd in the same death. But I know that in order to keep alive, the absurd cannot be settled. It escapes suicide to the extent that it is simultaneously awareness and rejection of death. It is, at the extreme limit of the condemned man's last thought, that shoelace that despite everything he sees a few yards away, on the very brink of his dizzying fall. The contrary of suicide, in fact, is the man condemned to death.

That revolt gives life its value. Spread out over the whole length of a life, it restores its majesty to that life. To a man devoid of blinders, there is no finer sight than that of the intelligence at grips with a reality that transcends it. The sight of human pride is unequaled. No disparagement is of any use. That discipline that the mind imposes on itself, that will conjured up out of nothing, that face-to-face struggle have something exceptional about them. To impoverish that reality whose inhumanity constitutes man's majesty is tantamount to impoverishing him himself. I understand then why the doctrines that explain everything to me also debilitate me at the same time. They relieve me of the weight of my own life, and yet I must carry it alone. At this juncture, I cannot conceive that a skeptical metaphysics can be joined to an ethics of renunciation.

Consciousness and revolt, these rejections are the contrary of renunciation. Everything that is indomitable and passionate in a human heart quickens them, on the contrary, with its own life. It is essential to die unreconciled and not of one's own free will. Suicide is a repudiation. The absurd man can only drain everything to the bitter end, and deplete himself. The absurd is his extreme tension, which he maintains constantly by solitary effort, for he knows that in that consciousness and in that day-to-day revolt he gives proof of his only truth, which is defiance. This is a first consequence.

If I remain in that prearranged position which consists in drawing all the conclusions (and nothing else) involved in a newly discovered notion, I am faced with a second paradox. In order to remain faithful to that method, I have nothing to do with the problem of metaphysical liberty. Knowing whether or not man is free doesn't interest me. I can experience only my own freedom. As to it, I can have no general notions, but merely a few clear insights. The problem of "freedom as such" has no meaning. For it is linked in quite a different way with the problem of God. Knowing whether or not man is free involves knowing whether he can have a master. The absurdity peculiar to this problem comes from the fact that the very notion that makes the problem of freedom possible also takes away all its meaning. For in the presence of God there is less a problem of freedom than a problem of evil. You know the alternative: either we are not free and God the all-powerful is responsible for evil. Or we are free and responsible but God is not all-powerful. All the scholastic subtleties have neither added anything to nor subtracted anything from the acuteness of this paradox.

This is why I cannot get lost in the glorification or the mere definition of a notion which eludes me and loses its meaning as soon as it goes beyond the frame of reference of my individual experience. I cannot understand what kind of freedom would be given me by a higher being. I have lost the sense of hierarchy. The only conception of freedom I can have is that of the prisoner or the individual in the midst of the State. The only one I know is freedom of thought and action. Now if the absurd cancels all my chances of eternal freedom, it restores and magnifies, on the other hand, my freedom of action.

That privation of hope and future means an increase in man's availability.

Before encountering the absurd, the everyday man lives with aims, a concern for the future or for justification (with regard to whom or what is not the question). He weighs his chances, he counts on "someday," his retirement or the labor of his sons. He still thinks that something in his life can be directed. In truth, he acts as if he were free, even if all the facts make a point of contradicting that liberty. But after the absurd, everything is upset. That idea that "I am," my way of acting as if everything has a meaning (even if, on occasion, I said that nothing has)—all that is given the lie in vertiginous fashion by the absurdity of a possible death. Thinking of the future, establishing aims for oneself, having preferences—all this presupposes a belief in freedom, even if one occasionally ascertains that one doesn't feel it. But at that moment I am well aware that that higher liberty, that freedom to *be*, which alone can serve as basis for a truth, does not exist. Death is there as the only reality. After death the chips are down. I am not even free, either, to perpetuate myself, but a slave, and, above all, a slave without hope of an eternal revolution, without recourse to contempt. And who without revolution and without contempt can remain a slave? What freedom can exist in the fullest sense without assurance of eternity?

But at the same time the absurd man realizes that hitherto he was bound to that postulate of freedom on the illusion of which he was living. In a certain sense, that hampered him. To the extent to which he imagined a purpose to his life, he adapted himself to the demands of a purpose to be achieved and became the slave of his liberty. Thus I could not act otherwise than as the father (or the engineer or the leader of a nation, or the post-office sub-clerk) that I am preparing to be. I think I can choose to be that rather than something else. I think so unconsciously, to be sure. But at the same time I strengthen my postulate with the beliefs of those around me, with the presumptions of my human environment (others are so sure of being free, and that cheerful mood is so contagious!). However far one may remain from any presumption, moral or social, one is partly influenced by them and even, for the best among them (there are good and bad presumptions), one adapts one's life to them. Thus the absurd man realizes that he was not really free. To speak clearly, to the extent to which I hope, to which I worry about a truth that might be individual to me, about a way of being or creating, to the extent to which I arrange my life and prove thereby that I accept its having a meaning, I create for myself barriers between which I confine my life. I do like so many bureaucrats of the mind and heart who only fill me with disgust and whose only vice, I now see clearly, is to take man's freedom seriously.

The absurd enlightens me on this point: there is no future. Henceforth this is the reason for my inner freedom. I shall use two comparisons here. Mystics, to begin with, find freedom in giving themselves. By losing themselves in their god, by accepting his rules, they become secretly free. In spontaneously accepted slavery they recover a deeper independence. But what does that freedom mean? It may be said, above all, that they *feel* free with regard to themselves, and not so much free as liberated. Likewise, completely turned toward death (taken here as the most obvious absurdity), the absurd man feels released from everything outside that passionate attention crystallizing in him. He enjoys a freedom with regard to common rules. It can be seen at this point that the initial themes of existential philosophy keep their entire value. The return to consciousness, the escape from everyday sleep represent the first steps of absurd freedom. But it is existential *preaching* that is alluded to, and with it that spiritual leap which basically escapes consciousness. In the same way (this is my second comparison) the slaves of antiquity did not belong to themselves. But they knew that freedom which consists in not feeling responsible.[3] Death, too, has patrician hands which, while crushing, also liberate.

Losing oneself in that bottomless certainty, feeling henceforth sufficiently remote from one's own life to increase it and take a broad view of it—this involves the principle of a liberation. Such new independence has a definite time limit, like any freedom of action. It does not write a check on eternity. But it takes the place of the illusions of *freedom*, which all stopped with death. The divine availability of the condemned man before whom the prison doors open in a certain early dawn, that unbelievable disinterestedness with regard to everything except for the pure flame of life—it is clear that death and the absurd are here the principles of the only reasonable freedom: that which a human heart can experience and live. This is a second consequence. The absurd man thus catches sight of a burning and frigid, transparent and limited universe in which nothing is possible but everything is given, and beyond which all is collapse and nothingness. He can then decide to accept such a universe and draw from it his strength, his refusal to hope, and the unyielding evidence of a life without consolation.

But what does life mean in such a universe? Nothing else for the moment but indifference to the future and a desire to use up everything that is given. Belief in the meaning of life always implies a scale of values, a choice, our preferences. Belief in the absurd, according to our definitions, teaches the contrary. But this is worth examining.

Knowing whether or not one can live *without appeal* is all that interests me. I do not want to get out of my depth. This aspect of life being given me, can I adapt myself to it? Now, faced with this particular concern, belief in the absurd is tantamount to substituting the quantity of experiences for the quality. If I convince myself that this life has no other aspect than that of the absurd, if I feel that its whole equilibrium depends on that perpetual opposition between my conscious revolt and the darkness in which it struggles, if I admit that my freedom has no meaning except in relation to its limited fate, then I must say that what counts is not the best living but the most living. It is not up to me to wonder if this is vulgar or revolting, elegant or deplorable. Once and for all, value judgments are discarded here in favor

---

[3] I am concerned here with a factual comparison, not with an apology of humility. The absurd man is the contrary of the reconciled man.

of factual judgments. I have merely to draw the conclusions from what I can see and to risk nothing that is hypothetical. Supposing that living in this way were not honorable, then true propriety would command me to be dishonorable.

The most living; in the broadest sense, that rule means nothing. It calls for definition. It seems to begin with the fact that the notion of quantity has not been sufficiently explored. For it can account for a large share of human experience. A man's rule of conduct and his scale of values have no meaning except through the quantity and variety of experiences he has been in a position to accumulate. Now, the conditions of modern life impose on the majority of men the same quantity of experiences and consequently the same profound experience. To be sure, there must also be taken into consideration the individual's spontaneous contribution, the "given" element in him. But I cannot judge of that, and let me repeat that my rule here is to get along with the immediate evidence. I see, then, that the individual character of a common code of ethics lies not so much in the ideal importance of its basic principles as in the norm of an experience that it is possible to measure. To stretch a point somewhat, the Greeks had the code of their leisure just as we have the code of our eight-hour day. But already many men among the most tragic cause us to foresee that a longer experience changes this table of values. They make us imagine that adventurer of the everyday who through mere quantity of experiences would break all records (I am purposely using this sports expression) and would thus win his own code of ethics.[4] Yet let's avoid romanticism and just ask ourselves what such an attitude may mean to a man with his mind made up to take up his bet and to observe strictly what he takes to be the rules of the game.

Breaking all the records is first and foremost being faced with the world as often as possible. How can that be done without contradictions and without playing on words? For on the one hand the absurd teaches that all experiences are unimportant, and on the other it urges toward the greatest quantity of experiences. How, then, can one fail to do as so many of those men I was speaking of earlier—choose the form of life that brings us the most possible of that human matter, thereby introducing a scale of values that on the other hand one claims to reject?

But again it is the absurd and its contradictory life that teaches us. For the mistake is thinking that that quantity of experiences depends on the circumstances of our life when it depends solely on us. Here we have to be over-simple. To two men living the same number of years, the world always provides the same sum of experiences. It is up to us to be conscious of them. Being aware of one's life, one's revolt, one's freedom, and to the maximum, is living, and to the maximum. Where lucidity dominates, the scale of values becomes useless. Let's be even more simple. Let us say that

[4]Quantity sometimes constitutes quality. If I can believe the latest restatements of scientific theory, all matter is constituted by centers of energy. Their greater or lesser quantity makes its specificity more or less remarkable. A billion ions and one ion differ not only in quantity but also in quality. It is easy to find an analogy in human experience.

the sole obstacle, the sole deficiency to be made good, is constituted by premature death. Thus it is that no depth, no emotion, no passion, and no sacrifice could render equal in the eyes of the absurd man (even if he wished it so) a conscious life of forty years and a lucidity spread over sixty years.[5] Madness and death are his irreparables. Man does not choose. The absurd and the extra life it involves *therefore do not depend on man's will*, but on its contrary, which is death.[6] Weighing words carefully, it is altogether a question of luck. One just has to be able to consent to this. There will never be any substitute for twenty years of life and experience.

By what is an odd inconsistency in such an alert race, the Greeks claimed that those who died young were beloved of the gods. And that is true only if you are willing to believe that entering the ridiculous world of the gods is forever losing the purest of joys, which is feeling, and feeling on this earth. The present and the succession of presents before a constantly conscious soul is the ideal of the absurd man. But the word "ideal" rings false in this connection. It is not even his vocation, but merely the third consequence of his reasoning. Having started from an anguished awareness of the inhuman, the meditation on the absurd returns at the end of its itinerary to the very heart of the passionate flames of human revolt.[7]

Thus I draw from the absurd three consequences, which are my revolt, my freedom, and my passion. By the mere activity of consciousness I transform into a rule of life what was an invitation to death—and I refuse suicide. I know, to be sure, the dull resonance that vibrates throughout these days. Yet I have but a word to say: that it is necessary. When Nietzsche writes: "It clearly seems that the chief thing in heaven and on earth is to *obey* at length and in a single direction: in the long run there results something for which it is worth the trouble of living on this earth as, for example, virtue, art, music, the dance, reason, the mind—something that transfigures, something delicate, mad, or divine," he elucidates the rule of a really distinguished code of ethics. But he also points the way of the absurd man. Obeying the flame is both the easiest and the hardest thing to do. However, it is good for man to judge himself occasionally. He is alone in being able to do so.

"Prayer," says Alain, "is when night descends over thought." "But

---

[5] Same reflection on a notion as different as the idea of eternal nothingness. It neither adds anything to nor subtracts anything from reality. In psychological experience of nothingness, it is by the consideration of what will happen in two thousand years that our own nothingness truly takes on meaning. In one of its aspects, eternal nothingness is made up precisely of the sum of lives to come which will not be ours.

[6] The will is only the agent here: it tends to maintain consciousness. It provides a discipline of life, and that is appreciable.

[7] What matters is coherence. We start out here from acceptance of the world. But Oriental thought teaches that one can indulge in the same effort of logic by choosing *against* the world. That is just as legitimate and gives this essay its perspectives and its limits. But when the negation of the world is pursued just as rigorously, one often achieves (in certain Vedantic schools) similar results regarding, for instance, the indifference of works. In a book of great importance, *Le Choix*, Jean Grenier establishes in this way a veritable "philosophy of indifference."

the mind must meet the night," reply the mystics and the existentials. Yes, indeed, but not that night that is born under closed eyelids and through the mere will of man—dark, impenetrable night that the mind calls up in order to plunge into it. If it must encounter a night, let it be rather that of despair, which remains lucid—polar night, vigil of the mind, whence will arise perhaps that white and virginal brightness which outlines every object in the light of the intelligence. At that degree, equivalence encounters passionate understanding. Then it is no longer even a question of judging the existential leap. It resumes its place amid the age-old fresco of human attitudes. For the spectator, if he is conscious, that leap is still absurd. In so far as it thinks it solves the paradox, it reinstates it intact. On this score, it is stirring. On this score, everything resumes its place and the absurd world is reborn in all its splendor and diversity.

But it is bad to stop, hard to be satisfied with a single way of seeing, to go without contradiction, perhaps the most subtle of all spiritual forces. The preceding merely defines a way of thinking. But the point is to live.

THE MYTH OF SISYPHUS

The gods had condemned Sisyphus to ceaselessly rolling a rock to the top of a mountain, whence the stone would fall back of its own weight. They had thought with some reason that there is no more dreadful punishment than futile and hopeless labor.

If one believes Homer, Sisyphus was the wisest and most prudent of mortals. According to another tradition, however, he was disposed to practice the profession of highwayman. I see no contradiction in this. Opinions differ as to the reasons why he became the futile laborer of the underworld. To begin with, he is accused of a certain levity in regard to the gods. He stole their secrets. Aegina, the daughter of Aesopus, was carried off by Jupiter. The father was shocked by that disappearance and complained to Sisyphus. He, who knew of the abduction, offered to tell about it on condition that Aesopus would give water to the citadel of Corinth. To the celestial thunderbolts he preferred the benediction of water. He was punished for this in the underworld. Homer tells us also that Sisyphus had put Death in chains. Pluto could not endure the sight of his deserted, silent empire. He dispatched the god of war, who liberated Death from the hands of her conqueror.

It is said also that Sisyphus, being near to death, rashly wanted to test his wife's love. He ordered her to cast his unburied body into the middle of the public square. Sisyphus woke up in the underworld. And there, annoyed by an obedience so contrary to human love, he obtained from Pluto permission to return to earth in order to chastise his wife. But when he had seen again the face of this world, enjoyed water and sun, warm stones and the sea, he no longer wanted to go back to the infernal darkness. Recalls, signs of anger, warnings were of no avail. Many years more he lived facing the curve of the gulf, the sparkling sea, and the smiles of earth. A decree of the gods was necessary. Mercury came and seized the impudent man by the collar and, snatching him from his joys, led him forcibly back to the underworld, where his rock was ready for him.

You have already grasped that Sisyphus is the absurd hero. He *is*, as much through his passions as through his torture. His scorn of the gods, his hatred of death, and his passion for life won him that unspeakable penalty in which the whole being is exerted toward accomplishing nothing. This is the price that must be paid for the passions of this earth. Nothing is told us about Sisyphus in the underworld. Myths are made for the imagination to breathe life into them. As for this myth, one sees merely the whole effort of a body straining to raise the huge stone, to roll it and push it up a slope a hundred times over; one sees the face screwed up, the cheek tight against the stone, the shoulder bracing the clay-covered mass, the foot wedging it, the fresh start with arms outstretched, the wholly human security of two earth-clotted hands. At the very end of his long effort measured by skyless space and time without depth, the purpose is achieved. Then Sisyphus watches the stone rush down in a few moments toward that lower world whence he will have to push it up again toward the summit. He goes back down to the plain.

It is during that return, that pause, that Sisyphus interests me. A face that toils so close to stones is already stone itself! I see that man going back down with a heavy yet measured step toward the torment of which he will never know the end. That hour like a breathing-space which returns as surely as his suffering, that is the hour of consciousness. At each of those moments when he leaves the heights and gradually sinks toward the lairs of the gods, he is superior to his fate. He is stronger than his rock.

If this myth is tragic, that is because its hero is conscious. Where would his torture be, indeed, if at every step the hope of succeeding upheld him? The workman of today works every day in his life at the same tasks, and this fate is no less absurd. But it is tragic only at the rare moments when it becomes conscious. Sisyphus, proletarian of the gods, powerless and rebellious, knows the whole extent of his wretched condition: it is what he thinks of during his descent. The lucidity that was to constitute his torture at the same time crowns his victory. There is no fate that cannot be surmounted by scorn.

If the descent is thus sometimes performed in sorrow, it can also take place in joy. This word is not too much. Again I fancy Sisyphus returning toward his rock, and the sorrow was in the beginning. When the images of earth cling too tightly to memory, when the call of happiness becomes too insistent, it happens that melancholy rises in man's heart: this is the rock's victory, this is the rock itself. The boundless grief is too heavy to bear. These are our nights of Gethsemane. But crushing truths perish from being acknowledged. Thus, Oedipus at the outset obeys fate without knowing it. But from the moment he knows, his tragedy begins. Yet at the same moment, blind and desperate, he realizes that the only bond linking him to the world is the cool hand of a girl. Then a tremendous remark rings out: "Despite so many ordeals, my advanced age and the nobility of my soul make me conclude that all is well." Sophocles' Oedipus, like Dostoevsky's Kirilov, thus gives the recipe for the absurd victory. Ancient wisdom confirms modern heroism.

One does not discover the absurd without being tempted to write a manual of happiness. "What! by such narrow ways—?" There is but one world, however. Happiness and the absurd are two sons of the same earth. They are inseparable. It would be a mistake to say that happiness necessarily springs from the absurd discovery. It happens as well that the feeling of the absurd springs from happiness. "I conclude that all is well," says Oedipus, and that remark is sacred. It echoes in the wild and limited universe of man. It teaches that all is not, has not been, exhausted. It drives out of this world a god who had come into it with dissatisfaction and a preference for futile sufferings. It makes of fate a human matter, which must be settled among men.

All Sisyphus' silent joy is contained therein. His fate belongs to him. His rock is his thing. Likewise, the absurd man, when he contemplates his torment, silences all the idols. In the universe suddenly restored to its silence, the myriad wondering little voices of the earth rise up. Unconscious, secret calls, invitations from all the faces, they are the necessary reverse and price of victory. There is no sun without shadow, and it is essential to know the night. The absurd man says yes and his effort will henceforth be unceasing. If there is a personal fate, there is no higher destiny, or at least there is but one which he concludes is inevitable and despicable. For the rest, he knows himself to be the master of his days. At that subtle moment when man glances backward over his life, Sisyphus returning toward his rock, in that slight pivoting he contemplates that series of unrelated actions which becomes his fate, created by him, combined under his memory's eye and soon sealed by his death. Thus, convinced of the wholly human origin of all that is human, a blind man eager to see who knows that the night has no end, he is still on the go. The rock is still rolling.

I leave Sisyphus at the foot of the mountain! One always finds one's burden again. But Sisyphus teaches the higher fidelity that negates the gods and raises rocks. He too concludes that all is well. This universe henceforth without a master seems to him neither sterile nor futile. Each atom of that stone, each mineral flake of that night-filled mountain, in itself forms a world. The struggle itself toward the heights is enough to fill a man's heart. One must imagine Sisyphus happy.

�֍ SELECTED BIBLIOGRAPHY
FOR SECTION 6

St. Augustine's privation-theory of evil is further spelled out in his *City of God*, XII, tr. M. Dods, et al., and *The Confessions*, VII, 12, tr. J. G. Pilkington, both in *Basic Writings of St. Augustine*, ed. Whitney J. Oates (New York: Random House, 1946). A brief but helpful explanation of this position may be found in Étienne Gilson, *The Christian Philosophy of Saint Augustine*, Part II, sec. 3 and *passim*, tr. L. E. M. Lynch (New York: Random House, 1960). For a discussion of the Stoic position, see J. M. Rist, *Stoic Philosophy*, *passim* (Cambridge, England: University Press, 1969), and for a general treatment of the early Stoics, including a discussion of Cleanthes and his *Hymn to Zeus*, see R. D. Hicks, *Stoic and Epicurean*, Ch. 1 (New York: Russell & Russell, reprint 1962). A thorough discussion of Hume's critical position towards religion is provided in Antony Flew, *Hume's Philosophy of Belief* (London: Routledge & Kegan Paul, 1961). More specifically, one should note Nelson Pike, "Hume on Evil," *Philosophical Review*, LXXII (April, 1963). Camus' existentialist stance is further developed in *The Rebel*, tr. Anthony Bower (New York: Vintage Books, 1956) and otherwise expressed in his novel *The Plague*, tr. Stuart Gilbert (New York: Modern Library, 1948). For a study of Camus, see John Cruickshank, *Albert Camus and the Literature of Revolt* (New York: Galaxy Books, 1960).

Other traditional attempts to deal with evil from a religious perspective include that of the Jewish theologian Moses Maimonides, *Guide of the Perplexed*, Part III, tr. Shlomo Pines (Chicago: University of Chicago Press, 1963); G. W. Leibniz's *Theodicy*, tr. E. M. Huggard (London: Routledge & Kegan Paul, 1952); and Immanuel Kant's *Religion Within the Limits of Reason Alone*, tr. Theodore M. Greene and Hoyt H. Hudson, revised ed. (New York: Harper & Row, 1960). An important variation on the finite-God theme is suggested by Edgar Sheffield Brightman in *The Problem of God* (New York: Abingdon Press, 1930).

Recent Protestant approaches may be found in J. S. Whale, *The Christian Answer to the Problem of Evil*, fourth ed. (London: Student Christian Movement Press, 1957); Nels Ferré, *Evil and the Christian Faith* (New York: Harper & Row, 1947); Edwin Lewis, *The Creator and the Adversary* (New York: Abingdon-Cokesbury, 1948); C. S. Lewis, *The Problem of Pain* (New York: Macmillan, 1950); and Langdon Gilkey, *Maker of Heaven and Earth*, Ch. 7 (Garden City, N. Y.: Doubleday, 1959). Contemporary Catholic views are represented by François Petit in *The Problem of Evil*, tr. Christopher Williams (New York: Hawthorn Books, 1959) and by Charles Journet in *The Meaning of Evil* (London: Chapman, 1963).

An important treatment along specifically Augustinian lines is that of Austin Farrer, *Love Almighty and Ills Unlimited* (New York: Doubleday, 1961). For a discussion with special reference to the providence of God, see John Laird, *Mind and Deity* (New York: Philosophical Library, 1941), and for a treatment with special reference to original sin, see N. P. Williams, *The Ideas of the Fall and of Original Sin* (London: Longmans, Green & Co., 1927). A good example of an empirical-evolutionary theory of both natural and moral evil is provided by F. R. Tennant, *Philosophical Theology*, Vol. II, Ch. 7 (Cambridge, England: Cambridge University Press, 1928–30). A Thomistic-analytic approach is contained in James F. Ross, *Philosophical Theology*, Chs. 5 and 6 (Indianapolis, Ind.: Bobbs-Merrill, 1969). Special note should be made of John Hick's recent and exhaustive study, written from a Protestant standpoint, *Evil and the God of Love* (New York: Harper & Row, 1966). This work is a thorough review of theodicy in the theological tradition (the Fathers, Augustine, the reformers, Barth, etc.), concluding with a statement of Hick's own position based on the approach of Irenaeus.

For an attempt to resolve the problem of evil from a purely Biblical point of view, see John James, *Why Evil? A Biblical Approach* (Baltimore, Md.: Penguin Books, 1960). A lively, contemporary rejection of the Biblical approach may be found in Walter Kaufmann, *The Faith of a Heretic*, Ch. 6 (New York: McGraw-Hill, 1959). A point of view from reconstructionist Judaism is represented in Richard L. Rubenstein, *After Auschwitz*, Ch. 4 (Indianapolis, Ind.: Bobbs-Merrill, 1966).

In recent discussion the following interchange of articles is especially important: J. L. Mackie, "Evil and Omnipotence," *Mind*, LXIV (April, 1955); Antony Flew, "Divine Omnipotence and Human Freedom," in *New Essays in Philosophical Theology*, ed. Antony Flew and Alasdair MacIntyre (London: Student Christian Movement Press, 1955); Ninian Smart responded to these positions in his article, "Omnipotence, Evil and Supermen," *Philosophy* (April and July, 1961); and Smart in turn was replied to by Flew in the same journal (January, 1962) and Mackie (April, 1962). One should note also George Mavrodes' brief article, "Some Puzzles Concerning Omnipotence," *Philosophical Review*, LXXII (April, 1963). Much of the latest discussion of the problem is reflected in Alvin Plantinga, *God and Other Minds*, Chs. 5 and 6, and Ch. 7, Part II (Ithaca, N. Y.: Cornell University Press, 1967); Ch. 6 is a revised version of Plantinga's important article, "The Free Will Defense," in which he argues, against several contemporary critics, that God's omnipotence, omniscience, and goodness are indeed compatible with his having created persons who commit evil. A continuation of the above debate and a response to Plantinga's argument may be found in the discussions by J. E. Barnhart, Antony Flew, and Ingemar Hedenius in *The Personalist*, LII (Winter, 1971). Some of the above discussions, and others, are contained in Nelson Pike (ed.), *God and Evil* (Englewood Cliffs, N. J.: Prentice-Hall, 1964).

A complete history of the philosophical problem of evil and proposed solutions may be found in R. A. Tsanoff, *The Nature of Evil* (New York: Macmillan, 1931).

The Meaning of Death

❋ INTRODUCTION

Most people since Descartes, living under the spell of his mind-matter dualism, are inclined to think that they possess a body and a mind (or ego or soul or spirit), and that these are essentially different and independent substances, such that if the body dies the mind or soul may continue to exist. To say nothing of the mind-body problem, that is, the problem of explaining how these two essentially different substances can be causally related to one another, few have ever reflected on whether this view is *true*, and, if so, what reason there is to think that the soul does *in fact* survive death and continue in the hereafter, and, if so, how *long* it continues and in what *state.* The selections below speak, in one way or another, to such questions.

One might expect to find in the Bible, more than any other place, a conception of the immortality of the soul, and yet at least St. Paul teaches no such thing, certainly not in the sense of a separate, incorporeal entity existing everlastingly and independently of the body. What St. Paul does teach is the resurrection of the body. There can be little question that the primary interest of the New Testament is in the unity of body and soul, the whole man, as is clear from St. Paul's teaching in I Corinthians 15 that at the appointed hour every man shall be raised with an uncorruptible, glorified, "spiritual body." What this might mean, exactly, is difficult to say, and even New Testament authorities are by no means in agreement on the interpretation of St. Paul at this point (though Paul's analogies and his allusion to the Greek mystery religions should not be overlooked). One might also find interesting (and debatable) Paul's implication in vs. 31 that the hope of resurrection is the foundation of sober living. Obviously, St. Paul's doctrine is not a philosophical one in the sense of being a matter of argument and evidence. But neither is it an irrelevant one for untold numbers of worshippers who rise from their pews every Sunday and recite the Apostles' Creed, concluding with the words "I believe . . . in the resurrection of the body and the life everlasting."

The occasion of the Biblical selection leads us rather naturally to an important distinction which, though anticipated earlier, should now be spelled out, the distinction between *philosophical* and *revealed* theology. Philosophical (or rational, or natural) theology is a knowledge of God (and related matters) acquired through man's active intellectual pursuit. Many believe, though, that notwithstanding the utility and contribution of man's natural reason, we possess also a supernatural knowledge of God, a divine self-disclosure, a revealed theology. The Christian believes, of course, that such a special revelation is contained in his Scriptures, and his thinking about everything is bound to be colored by his acceptance of the authoritative Word. But what, more exactly, is meant by "revelation"? A Person? A Document? And what does the believer mean when he says that St. Paul's writings are "inspired"? Indeed, the centrality of special revelation in the Judeo-Christian tradition is such that no consideration of philosophical and religious issues can proceed far without coming to grips with its claim to authority—as here on the question of the future existence of the soul.

Very different from the Pauline is the Platonic view, according to which the soul is essentially different from and nobler than the body, bent upon the escape from the body's material and corrupting entanglements. In fact, as Socrates (Plato) relates in the *Phaedo*, the philosopher desires death because only in that state in which the soul exists in separation from the body will it be able finally to grasp truth and reality, unhampered by bodily distractions and undeceived by sense-experience. This selection witnesses further to the general Platonic theory of a separate and spiritual realm, which transcends the multiplicity and mutability of the sensible world, and which is the proper abode of the soul. The influence of this spiritual view of reality and of the soul has been profound. It may be, in fact, that in this respect it was Plato, not Paul, who captured Western thought.

The Platonic view (at least as transformed by Aristotle and Christianized by St. Thomas Aquinas) does, in fact, yet dominate some philosophical-theological circles. It will be seen, for example, that the contemporary scholastic Jacques Maritain reproduces a version of the Platonic proof showing how it has been refashioned by Thomas (the soul is the "substantial form of the body"), though it may be questioned whether this would-be Christian proof is, in fact, compatible with the Biblical doctrine of the resurrection. It will be observed that Maritain's proof (like most philosophical proofs) will hardly work apart from certain convictions concerning the nature of reality, knowledge, and the like. Those fundamental convictions must therefore be searched out and evaluated if his position is to be fully appreciated.

A different approach entirely is taken from the evidence of "physical research" which has explored experimentally all manner of psychical phenomena from telepathy to spirits, and which argues not speculatively but empirically for the soul's survival. The selection from John Hick summarizes this evidence and, though many are understandably suspicious, his over-view of the subject should be sufficient to caution one against too quick a rejection of the work of this still young science—if that is the correct word.

The statement by Bertrand Russell begins with a mild criticism of psychical research (it must be remembered that Russell was writing in 1935) but quickly shifts its attention to the nature of the soul itself, especially its relation to the body. Russell rejects the old Cartesian doctrine of an underlying "mental substance," and, echoing Hume's phenomenalism (the doctrine that reduces all our knowledge of things to their sensible appearances or phenomena), suggests that what is called "mind" is but an intimately joined organization of mental occurrences or events. Now what is it, Russell asks, that binds our mental events together but our memory and habits? Perhaps, in fact, this is all that *I* am: the continuity of my memories and habits. (How, otherwise, may I be sure that I am the same person who existed five minutes ago?) But these appear to be decidedly dependent on my body and brain, which suggests that personality could hardly survive in a *dis*embodied state. The psychological and physiological evidence, Russell concludes, converges on the probability of extinction.

Russell's position, however, gives rise to one especially urgent problem. Does the reduction of mind to physiological processes involve thinking and willing in the causal determinism of empirical phenomena? Many philosophers have argued that no genuine intellectual reflection (and thus no knowledge) or free choice (and thus no moral experience) is possible except on the assumption that there is, somehow, something in man that *transcends* the causality of physics and chemistry. On the other hand, both ways of talking may suggest false alternatives to the reader who resists them as resting on overly simplistic views of human nature. Still other problems may be profitably explored: the nature of mind, soul, and spirit; the difference between them (if there is any); their relation to one another; and their relation to the body, to the brain, to knowledge, will, personality, and the hereafter. At the very least, such questions will have the effect of lifting the lid to a Pandora's Box full of complex and elusive (but equally fascinating) ideas.

The last selection, from Ludwig Wittgenstein, is full of many distinctions and insights not always grasped through a superficial reading. Most notable perhaps is the following twofold observation concerning the question of immortality. First, immortality is not, after all, the real question, since even if the soul were immortal, its immortal existence is but part of a larger riddle: the riddle of existence itself. But, second, the answer to that riddle is that there is no riddle since there is no answer, at least not one that can be put into words, and as Wittgenstein expresses it in his well-known aphorism, "What we cannot speak about we must consign to silence." This latter, of course, raises the whole problem of religious language, the subject of Section 8.

✳ ST. PAUL

28. *The Resurrection of the Body*

St. Paul, a learned and faithful Hebrew and zealous persecutor of the early church, was converted to Christianity and became its greatest missionary as well as the author of thirteen books of the New Testament. An account of St. Paul's dramatic conversion on the Road to Damascus is found in Acts 9.

From *The First Epistle to the Corinthians*

CHAPTER 15

Now I would remind you, brethren, in what terms I preached to you the gospel, which you received, in which you stand,[2] by which you are saved, if you hold it fast—unless you believed in vain.

[3]For I delivered to you as of first importance what I also received, that Christ died for our sins in accordance with the scriptures, [4]that he was buried, that he was raised on the third day in accordance with the scriptures, [5]and that he appeared to Cephus, then to the twelve. [6]Then he appeared more than five hundred brethren at one time, most of whom are still alive, though some have fallen asleep. [7]Then he appeared to James, then to all the apostles. [8]Last of all, as to one untimely born, he appeared also to me. [9]For I am the least of the apostles, unfit to be called an apostle, because I persecuted the church of God. [10]But by the grace of God I am what I am, and his grace toward me was not in vain. On the contrary, I worked harder than any of them, though it was not I, but the grace of God which is with me. [11]Whether then it was I or they, so we preach and so you believed.

[12]Now if Christ is preached as raised from the dead, how can some of you say that there is no resurrection of the dead? [13]But if there is no resurrection of the dead, then Christ has not been raised; [14]if Christ has not been raised, then our preaching is in vain and your faith is in vain. [15]We are even found to be misrepresenting God, because we testified of God that he raised Christ, whom he did not raise if it is true that the dead are not raised. [16]For if the dead are not raised, then Christ has not been raised. [17]If Christ has not been raised, your faith is futile and you are still in your sins. [18]Then those also who have fallen asleep in Christ have perished. [19]If for this life only we have hoped in Christ, we are of all men most to be pitied.

²⁰But in fact Christ has been raised from the dead, the first fruits of those who have fallen asleep. ²¹For as by a man came death, by a man has come also the resurrection of the dead. ²²For as in Adam all die, so also in Christ shall all be made alive. ²³But each in his own order: Christ the first fruits, then at his coming those who belong to Christ. ²⁴Then comes the end, when he delivers the kingdom to God the Father after destroying every rule and every authority and power. ²⁵For he must reign until he has put all his enemies under his feet. ²⁶The last enemy to be destroyed is death. ²⁷"For God has put all things in subjection under his feet." But when it says, "All things are put in subjection under him," it is plain that he is excepted who put all things under him. ²⁸When all things are subjected to him, then the Son himself will also be subjected to him who put all things under him, that God may be everything to every one.

²⁹Otherwise, what do people mean by being baptized on behalf of the dead? If the dead are not raised at all, why are people baptized on their behalf? ³⁰Why am I in peril every hour? ³¹I protest, brethren, by my pride in you which I have in Christ Jesus our Lord, I die every day! ³²What do I gain if, humanly speaking, I fought with beasts at Ephesus? If the dead are not raised, "Let us eat and drink, for tomorrow we die." ³³Do not be deceived: "Bad company ruins good morals." ³⁴Come to your right mind and sin no more. For some have no knowledge of God. I say this to your shame.

³⁵But some one will ask, "How are the dead raised? With what kind of body do they come?" ³⁶You foolish man! What you sow does not come to life unless it dies. ³⁷And what you sow is not the body which is to be, but a bare kernel, perhaps of wheat or of some other grain. ³⁸But God gives it a body as he has chosen, and to each kind of seed its own body. ³⁹For not all flesh is alike, but there is one kind for men, another for animals, another for birds, and another for fish. ⁴⁰There are celestial bodies and there are terrestrial bodies; but the glory of the celestial is one, and the glory of the terrestrial is another. ⁴¹There is one glory of the sun, and another glory of the moon, and another glory of the stars; for star differs from star in glory.

⁴²So it is with the resurrection of the dead. What is sown is perishable, what is raised is imperishable. ⁴³It is sown in dishonor, it is raised in glory. It is sown in weakness, it is raised in power. ⁴⁴It is sown a physical body, it is raised a spiritual body. If there is a physical body, there is also a spiritual body. ⁴⁵Thus it is written, "The first man Adam became a living being"; the last Adam became a life-giving spirit. ⁴⁶But it is not the spiritual which is first but the physical, and then the spiritual. ⁴⁷The first man was from the earth, a man of dust; the second man is from heaven. ⁴⁸As was the man of dust, so are those who are of the dust; and as is the man of heaven, so are those who are of heaven. ⁴⁹Just as we have borne the image of the man of dust, we shall also bear the image of the man of heaven. ⁵⁰I tell you this, brethren: flesh and blood cannot inherit the kingdom of God, nor does the perishable inherit the imperishable.

[51]Lo! I tell you a mystery. We shall not all sleep, but we shall all be changed, [52]in a moment, in the twinkling of an eye, at the last trumpet. For the trumpet will sound, and the dead will be raised imperishable, and we shall be changed. [53]For this perishable nature must put on the imperishable, and this mortal nature must put on immortality. [54]When the perishable puts on the imperishable and the mortal puts on immortality, then shall come to pass the saying that is written:

"Death is swallowed up in victory."
[55]"O death, where is thy victory?
O death, where is thy sting?"

[56]The sting of death is sin, and the power of sin is the law. [57]But thanks be to God, who gives us the victory through our Lord Jesus Christ.

[58]Therefore, my beloved brethren, be steadfast, immovable, always abounding in the work of the Lord, knowing that in the Lord your labor is not in vain.

✳ PLATO

29. *The Liberation of the Soul*

Plato (427–347 B.C.) was born of aristocratic parents, but falling under the influence of Socrates (the "gadfly of Athens") he declined public life in favor of the philosophical pursuit of transcendent and fixed essences, the eternal objects of knowledge. Plato's philosophy is contained in a long series of polished dialogues which made him the finest writer of ancient Greece.

From *Phaedo*

. . . Do we believe death to be anything?

We do, replied Simmias.

And do we not believe it to be the separation of the soul from the body? Does not death mean that the body comes to exist by itself, separated from the soul, and that the soul exists by herself, separated from the body? What is death but that?

It is that, he said.

Now consider, my good friend, if you and I are agreed on another point which I think will help us to understand the question better. Do you

Plato, *Phaedo*, tr. F.J. Church (Indianapolis, Ind.: Library of Liberal Arts, 1951). Copyright © 1951 by The Liberal Arts Press, Inc. Reprinted by permission of the Liberal Arts Press Division of the The Bobbs-Merrill Company, Inc.

think that a philosopher will care very much about what are called pleasures, such as the pleasures of eating and drinking?

Certainly not, Socrates, said Simmias.

Or about the pleasures of sexual passion?

Indeed, no.

And, do you think that he holds the remaining cares of the body in high esteem? Will he think much of getting fine clothes, and sandals, and other bodily adornments, or will he despise them, except so far as he is absolutely forced to meddle with them?

The real philosopher, I think, will despise them, he replied.

In short, said he, you think that his studies are not concerned with the body? He stands aloof from it, as far as he can, and turns toward the soul?

I do.

Well then, in these matters, first, it is clear that the philosopher releases his soul from communion with the body, so far as he can, beyond all other men?

It is.

And does not the world think, Simmias, that if a man has no pleasure in such things, and does not take his share in them, his life is not worth living? Do not they hold that he who thinks nothing of bodily pleasures is almost as good as dead?

Indeed you are right.

But what about the actual acquisition of wisdom? If the body is taken as a companion in the search for wisdom, is it a hindrance or not? For example, do sight and hearing convey any real truth to men? Are not the very poets forever telling us that we neither hear nor see anything accurately? But if these senses of the body are not accurate or clear, the others will hardly be so, for they are all less perfect than these, are they not?

Yes, I think so, certainly, he said.

Then when does the soul attain truth? We see that, as often as she seeks to investigate anything in company with the body, the body leads her astray.

True.

Is it not by reasoning, if at all, that any real truth becomes manifest to her?

Yes.

And she reasons best, I suppose, when none of the senses, whether hearing, or sight, or pain, or pleasure, harasses her; when she has dismissed the body, and released herself as far as she can from all intercourse or contact with it, and so, coming to be as much alone with herself as is possible, strives after real truth.

That is so.

And here too the soul of the philosopher very greatly despises the body, and flies from it, and seeks to be alone by herself, does she not?

Clearly.

And what do you say to the next point, Simmias? Do we say that there is such a thing as absolute justice, or not?

Indeed we do.

And absolute beauty, and absolute good?

Of course.

Have you ever seen any of them with your eyes?

Indeed I have not, he replied.

Did you ever grasp them with any bodily sense? I am speaking of all absolutes, whether size, or health, or strength; in a word, of the essence or real being of everything. Is the very truth of things contemplated by the body? Is it not rather the case that the man who prepares himself most carefully to apprehend by his intellect the essence of each thing which he examines will come nearest to the knowledge of it?

Certainly.

And will not a man attain to this pure thought most completely if he goes to each thing, as far as he can, with his mind alone, taking neither sight nor any other sense along with his reason in the process of thought, to be an encumbrance? In every case he will pursue pure and absolute being, with his pure intellect alone. He will be set free as far as possible from the eye and the ear and, in short, from the whole body, because intercourse with the body troubles the soul, and hinders her from gaining truth and wisdom. Is it not he who will attain the knowledge of real being, if any man will?

Your words are admirably true, Socrates, said Simmias.

And, he said, must not all this cause real philosophers to reflect, and make them say to each other, It seems that there is a narrow path which will bring us safely to our journey's end, with reason as our guide. As long as we have this body, and an evil of that sort is mingled with our souls, we shall never fully gain what we desire; and that is truth. For the body is forever taking up our time with the care which it needs; and, besides, whenever diseases attack it, they hinder us in our pursuit of real being. It fills us with passions, and desires, and fears, and all manner of phantoms, and much foolishness; and so, as the saying goes, in very truth we can never think at all for it. It alone and its desires cause wars and factions and battles; for the origin of all wars is the pursuit of wealth, and we are forced to pursue wealth because we live in slavery to the cares of the body. And therefore, for all these reasons, we have no leisure for philosophy. And last of all, if we ever are free from the body for a time, and then turn to examine some matter, it falls in our way at every step of the inquiry, and causes confusion and trouble and panic, so that we cannot see the truth for it. Verily we have learned that if we are to have any pure knowledge at all, we must be freed from the body; the soul by herself must behold things as they are. Then, it seems, after we are dead, we shall gain the wisdom which we desire, and for which we say we have a passion, but not while we are alive, as the argument shows. For if it be not possible to have pure knowledge while the body is with us, one of two things must be true: either we cannot gain knowledge at all, or we can gain it only after death. For then, and not till then, will the soul exist by herself, separate from the body. And while we live, we shall come nearest to knowledge, if we have no communion or intercourse with the body beyond what is absolutely necessary, and if we are not defiled with its nature. We must live pure from it until God himself releases us. And when we are thus pure and released from its follies, we shall dwell, I suppose, with others who are pure like ourselves, and we shall of ourselves know all that is pure; and that may be the truth. For I think that the impure is not allowed to attain to the pure. Such, Simmias, I fancy must needs be the language and the reflections of the true lovers of knowledge. Do you not agree with me?

Most assuredly I do, Socrates.

And, my friend, said Socrates, if this be true, I have good hope that, when I reach the place whither I am going, I shall there, if anywhere, gain fully that which we have sought so earnestly in the past. And so I shall set forth cheerfully on the journey that is appointed me today, and so may every man who thinks that his mind is prepared and purified.

That is quite true, said Simmias.

And does not the purification consist, as we have said, in separating the soul from the body, as far as is possible, and in accustoming her to collect and rally herself together from the body on every side, and to dwell alone by herself as much as she can, both now and hereafter, released from the bondage of the body?

Yes, certainly, he said.

Is not what we call death a release and separation of the soul from the body?

Undoubtedly, he replied.

And the true philosopher, we hold, is alone in his constant desire to set his soul free? His study is simply the release and separation of the soul from the body, is it not?

Clearly.

Would it not be absurd then, as I began by saying, for a man to complain at death coming to him, when in his life he has been preparing himself to live as nearly in a state of death as he could? Would not that be absurd?

Yes, indeed.

In truth, then, Simmias, he said, the true philosopher studies to die, and to him of all men is death least terrible. Now look at the matter in this way. In everything he is at enmity with his body, and he longs to possess his soul alone. Would it not then be most unreasonable if he were to fear and complain when he has his desire, instead of rejoicing to go to the place where he hopes to gain the wisdom that he has passionately longed for all his life, and to be released from the company of his enemy? Many a man has willingly gone to the other world, when a human love or wife or son has died, in the hope of seeing there those whom he longed for, and of being with them: and will a man who has a real passion for wisdom, and a firm hope of really finding wisdom in the other world and nowhere else, grieve at death, and not depart rejoicing? Nay, my friend, you ought not to think that, if he be truly a philosopher. He will be firmly convinced that there and nowhere else will he meet with wisdom in its purity. And if this be so, would it not, I repeat, be very unreasonable for such a man to fear death?

Yes, indeed, he replied, it would.

Does not this show clearly, he said, that any man whom you see grieving at the approach of death is after all no lover of wisdom, but a lover of his body? He is also, most likely, a lover either of wealth, or of honor, or, it may be, of both.

Yes, he said, it is as you say. . . .

❋ JACQUES MARITAIN

30. *A Proof for Immortality*

Jacques Maritain was born in 1882 into a liberal Protestant family but converted, with his wife, to Catholicism in 1906. Maritain is no doubt the most influential Thomist thinker of the contemporary Catholic world. The scope of his contribution is reflected in such titles as *Approaches to God*, *Degrees of Knowledge*, *Creative Intuition in Art and Poetry*, *Man and the State*, and *On Philosophy of History*.

From *The Range of Reason*

CHAPTER 5: THE IMMORTALITY OF THE SOUL

I: The Views of Theodor Fechner

Before writing these lines,[1] I re-read the little book in which Gustav Theodor Fechner, the founder of Psychophysics, presented his thoughts on *Life After Death*. This book was published in 1836; an American edition appeared in 1904 with an Introduction by William James, and was reprinted some years ago with a Prefatory Note by John Erskine.[2]

We do not find any specific demonstration in Fechner's book, but rather a large conception of the world in which scientific concepts are subjected to philosophical extrapolation. In my opinion, this conception of the world is marred by a kind of idealist and panpsychist metaphysics; yet the views of such a great thinker on immortality are especially stimulating, and we cannot look without emotion upon this philosophical effort and personal testimony, which bear witness to the natural belief of man in immortality, and which are permeated by Christian elements transposed into a secular frame of mind. I do not believe that Mr. Erskine is right when he states that never does "Fechner make of immortality a moral problem." Rather does Fechner admit a sort of law of Karma; according to him, life after death is hampered or exalted, made unhappy, at least for a time, or happy, in accordance with our evil or good deeds.[3] But the fact remains that, in Fechner's views, man,

---

Jacques Maritain, *The Range of Reason* (New York: Scribners, 1952). Copyright 1952 by Jacques Maritain. Reprinted by permission of Charles Scribner's Sons.

[1]This essay is complementary to the essay *The Immortality of Man*, Chapter II in *Man's Destiny in Eternity*, A Symposium (The Garvin lectures), Beacon Press, Boston, 1949.

[2]New York: Pantheon Books, 1943.

[3]"According as the man has been good or bad, has behaved nobly or basely, was industrious or idle, will he find himself possessed of an organism, healthy or sick, beautiful or hateful, strong or weak, in the world to come, and his free activity in this world will determine his relation to other souls, his destiny, his capacity and talents for further progress in that world." *Op. cit.*, pp. 33–34.

in his third life (which succeeds death just as his second life—in his own body—succeeds birth, which is death with regard to uterine life), man in his life after death survives in other men by virtue of the spiritual waves he has produced in humanity and acquires a new organism in the whole universe: which supposes a strange and precarious idea of the self, and assumes that man is but a dwelling-place in which other spirits unite and intersect. I would say that Fechner, who at the same time admitted the reality of free will, self-determination, consciousness and reason, had a poor metaphysical concept of the soul as well as of God.

The Scholastics, on the contrary, were always concerned with demonstrative, apodictic rational proofs. In the late and decadent Middle Ages, they became skeptical with regard to the philosophical establishment of the soul's immortality, and considered immortality a mere datum of faith, unattainable by the natural forces of reason, precisely because they sought a perfectly demonstrable proof, and had become unable to realize it. But in the great age of Scholasticism, at the time of Thomas Aquinas, they were able to work out, understand and provide us with such a proof. Fechner's theory, compared with their logical and scientifically philosophical requirements, would have appeared to the great Scholastics as a set of harmonious metaphorical insights, a kind of Platonic myth.

II: "Subjective" Immortality

I am very far, nevertheless, from despising that kind of survival which consists in living in men's minds and hearts. Auguste Comte called it subjective immortality, and Fechner speaks of it in a much more profound manner, all the while mingling with it, and trying to superimpose upon it, a theory of genuine or "objective" immortality. To endure in human minds, and in the movement of human history is something momentous, in which each human person is interested by a deep-seated and more or less obscure aspiration.

At this point a great problem arises, one which is far from being solved—the problem of the universal intersolidarity. We have a feeling that there is a mysterious unity of the world, that the whole of mankind suffers from the iniquities which each one undergoes and is helped by the generosity and love which each one displays in his individual life. Somehow this feeling must be true.

Yet it does not mean that there exists a soul of the world, in a Stoic or Spinozistic sense. We live in time; each man is a spiritual unit engaged in the world of matter and change; it is by some external expression in this world, by some utterance, that the inner achievements or disasters of these spiritual units may exert influence, and that this influence may worm its way into human history and endure in it. Otherwise, why should each of us so ardently yearn to express or manifest what fills his mind and his heart, and to be heard by other spirits? "A Goethe, a Schiller, a Napoleon, a Luther, still live among us," as Fechner puts it—yes, but because they were able to make their thoughts or deeds resound loudly throughout the world.

What is true is that the energy of the spirit is so great, and its pressure on the material structures of life is so powerful, that it passes through the smallest interstices, it makes use of every possible means of communication, so as to penetrate into men's existence and human history by hidden, invisible channels.

It is in this way that the feeling I mentioned a moment ago, the feeling of the lasting, immaterial and secret progression of our deeds and thoughts, long after the death of each one of us, in the mysterious texture of the world, corresponds to reality. But such a survival remains precarious and exceedingly far from including the whole of what we bear in ourselves.

In the case of men whose life is immersed in time, their actions are born in time and die in time; but because they are men, their actions always involve and express something of the spirit abiding in them; this dynamic spiritual charge may be taken on by other minds; thus part—a small part indeed—of their spiritual efforts or trials may possibly survive in a more or less fragile way, especially in the memories of their descendants. In the case of men whose life is lived chiefly in the spirit and above time, their actions are able to conquer time; they can claim to survive for generations to come, but always on condition that certain external means of communication—however humble, poor, or humanly weak—be provided for them. And when they do survive, it is always in a terribly vulnerable, and often a terribly disappointing, manner. In any case, an immense part of the sufferings and ordeals, of the spiritual flame, love or heroism of the inner life of men, is irreparably lost, so far as their influence in the world and their survival in time and history are concerned.

When thousands of human beings are tortured and driven to despair in prisons and concentration camps, and die without their cries falling on any human ear or being heard by any star in the heavens, doubtless some slight waves of their agony find their way through cracks in the walls, and come to stir up or disturb the dreams of the world. Yet the frightful mass of their individual sufferings, heroic deeds or despairing deaths will simply fall into the gulf of forgetfulness, without exerting upon human history any influence comparable to what they have undergone and done. It is only through the justice of God, as Supreme Ruler of this universe, that they may hope that their silent sacrifice will be useful to their brothers, or to the human cause they wanted to serve.

What I mean is that it would be a supreme delusion to seek in time, and in history, and in the results of our deeds here below, to seek, that is, in subjective immortality, any adequate fulfilment of that irrepressible aspiration to survival which inhabits the depths of our substances.

It is true that death is but a second birth, and that our life on earth is a kind of uterine life, in the obscure womb of the griefs and dreams and passing images of this enigmatic world. "Life is changed, life is not taken away." That is why, in the liturgy of the Catholic Church, the feasts of the saints are celebrated on the anniversary of their death, that is, of their real and definite birth. But this is so only because the soul of man is an individual substance, existing by and unto itself as a perfectly defined unit; because it is destined to objective immortality, genuine personal immortality, not in time and history, but in eternity.

III: Personal Immortality

The Existence of the Soul

It is of this immortality, and of the way in which the Scholastics established its rational certainty, that I should now like to speak.

We must of course realize that we have a soul before we can discuss whether it is immortal. How does St. Thomas Aquinas proceed in this matter?

He observes first[4] that man has an activity, the activity of the intellect, which is in itself immaterial. The activity of the intellect is immaterial because the proportionate or "connatural" object of the human intellect is not, like the object of the senses, a particular and limited category of things, or rather a particular and limited category of the qualitative properties of things. The proportionate or "connatural" object of the intellect is the nature of the sense-perceivable things considered in an all-embracing manner, whatever the sense concerned may be. It is not only—as for sight—color or the colored thing (which absorbs and reflects such or such rays of light) nor—as for hearing—sound or the sound-source; it is the whole universe and texture of sense-perceivable reality which can be known by the intellect, because the intellect does not stop at qualities, but pierces beyond, and proceeds to look at essence (that which a thing *is*). This very fact is a proof of the spirituality, or complete immateriality of our intellect; for every activity in which matter plays an intrinsic part is limited to a given category of material objects, as is the case for the senses, which perceive only those properties which are able to act upon their physical organs.

There is already, in fact, a certain immateriality in sense-knowledge; knowledge, as such, is an immaterial activity, because when I am in the act of knowing, I become, or am, the very thing that I know, a thing other than myself, insofar as it is other than myself. And how can I be, or become, other than myself, if it is not in a supra-subjective or immaterial manner? Sense-knowledge is a very poor kind of knowledge; insofar as it is knowledge, it is immaterial, but it is an immaterial activity intrinsically conditioned by, and dependent upon, the material functioning of the sense-organs. Sense-knowledge is the immaterial achievement, the immaterial actuation and product of a living bodily organ; and its very object is also something half material, half immaterial, I mean a physical quality *intentionally* or immaterially present in the medium by which it acts on the sense-organ (something comparable to the manner in which a painter's idea is immaterially present in his paint-brush).

But with intellectual knowledge we have to do with an activity which is in itself completely immaterial. The human intellect is able to know whatever participates in being and truth; the whole universe can be inscribed in it; this means that, in order to be known, the object known by the intellect

[4][Cf. St. Thomas Aquinas, *Summa Theologica*, Part I, Qus. 75 ff.]

has been stripped of any existential condition of materiality. This rose, which I see, has contours; but Being, of which I am thinking, is more spacious than space. The object of the intellect is universal, for instance that universal or de-individualized object which is apprehended in the idea of man, of animal, of atom; the object of the intellect is a universal which remains what it is while being identified with an infinity of individuals. And this is only possible because things, in order to become objects of the mind, have been entirely separated from their material existence. To this it must be added that the operation of our intellect does not stop at the knowledge of the nature of sense-perceivable things; it goes further; it knows by analogy the spiritual natures; it extends to the realm of merely possible things; its field has infinite magnitude.

Thus, the objects known by the human intellect, taken not as things existing in themselves, but precisely as objects determining the intellect and united with it, are purely immaterial.

Furthermore, just as the condition of the *object* is immaterial, so is the condition of the *act* which bears upon it, and is determined or specified by it. The object of the human intellect is, as such, purely immaterial; the act of the human intellect is also purely immaterial.

And, moreover, if the act of the intellectual power is purely immaterial, that *power* itself is also purely immaterial. In man, this thinking animal, the intellect is a purely spiritual power. Doubtless it depends upon the body, upon the conditions of the brain. Its activity can be disturbed or hindered by a physical disorder, by an outburst of anger, by a drink or a narcotic. But this dependence is an *extrinsic* one. It exists because our intelligence cannot act without the joint activity of the memory and the imagination, of the internal senses and external senses, all of which are organic powers residing in some material organ, in some special part of the body. As for the intellect itself, it is not *intrinsically* dependent upon the body since its activity is immaterial; the human intellect does not reside in any special part of the body. It is not contained by the body, but rather contains it. It uses the brain, since the organs of the internal senses are in the brain; yet the brain is not an organ of the intelligence; there is no part of the organism whose act is intellectual operation. The intellect has no organ.

Finally, since intellectual power is spiritual, or purely immaterial in itself, its *first substantial root*, the subsisting principle from which this power proceeds and which acts through its instrumentality, is also spiritual.

So much for the spirituality of the intellect. Now, thought or the operation of the intellect is an act and emanation of man as a unit; and when I think, it is not only my intellect which thinks: it is *I*, my own self. And my own self is a bodily self; it involves matter; it is not a spiritual or purely immaterial subject. The body is an essential part of man. The intellect is not the whole man.

Therefore the intellect, or rather the substantial root of the intellect, which must be as immaterial as the intellect, is only a part, albeit an essential part, of man's substance.

But man is not an aggregate, a juxtaposition of two substances; man is a natural whole, a single being, a single substance.

Consequently, we must conclude that the essence or substance of man is single, but that this single substance itself is a compound, the components of which are the body and the spiritual intellect: or rather matter, of which the body is made, and the spiritual principle, one of the powers of which is the intellect. Matter—in the Aristotelian sense of prime matter, or of that root potentiality which is the common stuff of all corporeal substance—matter, substantially united with the spiritual principle of the intellect, is ontologically molded, shaped from within and in the innermost depths of being, by this spiritual principle as by a substantial and vital impulse, in order to constitute that body of ours. In this sense, Saint Thomas, after Aristotle, says that the intellect is the form, the substantial form of the human body.

That is the Scholastic notion of the human soul. The human soul, which is the root principle of the intellectual power, is the first principle of life of the human body, and the substantial form, the *entelechy*, of that body. And the human soul is not only a substantial form or entelechy, as are the souls of plants and animals according to the biological philosophy of Aristotle; the human soul is also a spirit, a spiritual substance able to exist apart from matter, since the human soul is the root principle of a spiritual power, the act of which is intrinsically independent of matter. The human soul is both a soul and a spirit, and it is its very substantiality, subsistence and existence, which are communicated to the whole human substance, in order to make human substance be what it is, and to make it subsist and exist. Each element of the human body is human, and exists as such, by virtue of the immaterial existence of the human soul. Our body, our hands, our eyes exist by virtue of the existence of our soul.

The immaterial soul is the first substantial root not only of the intellect, but of all that which, in us, is spiritual activity; and it is also the first substantial root of all our other living activities. It would be inconceivable that a non-spiritual soul, that kind of soul which is not a spirit and cannot exist without informing matter—namely, the souls of plants or animals in Aristotelian biology—should possess a power or faculty *superior* to its own degree in being, that is, immaterial, or act through a supra-material instrumentality independent of any corporeal organ and physical structure. But when it is a question of a spirit which is a soul, or of a *spiritual soul*, as the human soul is, then it is perfectly conceivable that such a soul should have, aside from immaterial or spiritual faculties, other powers and activities which are organic and material, and which, relating to the union between soul and body, pertain to a level of being *inferior* to that of the spirit.

The Spirituality of the Human Soul

Thus, the very way in which the Scholastics arrived at the existence of the human soul also established its spirituality. Just as the intellect is spiritual, that is to say intrinsically independent of matter in its operation and in its nature, so also, and for the same reason, the human soul, the substantial root of the intellect, is spiritual, that is, intrinsically independent of matter in its nature and in its existence; it does not live by the body, the body lives by it. The human soul is a spiritual substance which, by its substantial union with matter, gives existence and countenance to the body.

That is my second point. As we have seen, the Scholastics demonstrated it by a metaphysical analysis of the intellect's operation, carefully distinguished from the operation of the senses. They adduced, of course, much other evidence in support of their demonstration. In their consideration of the intellect, they observed, for instance, that the latter is capable of *perfect reflection*, that is, of coming back entirely upon itself—not in the manner of a sheet of paper, half of which can be folded on the other half, but in a complete manner, so that it can grasp its whole operation and penetrate it by knowledge, and can contain itself and its own principle, the existing self, in its own knowing activity, a perfect reflection or self-containing of which any material agent, extended in space and time, is essentially incapable. Here we are confronted with that phenomenon of self-knowledge, of *prise de conscience* or becoming aware of oneself, which is a privilege of the spirit, as Hegel (after St. Augustine) was to emphasize, and which plays so tremendous a part in the history of humanity and the development of its spiritual energies.

In the same way it is possible to show that the human will, which is rooted in the intellect, and which is able to determine itself, or to master the very motive or judgment which determines it and is made efficacious by the will itself, is spiritual in its operation and nature. Every material agent is subject to the universal determinism. Free will is the privilege, the glorious and weighty privilege, of an agent endowed with immaterial power.

We are responsible for ourselves; we choose for ourselves and decide on our own ends and our own destinies. We are capable of spiritual, supra-sensuous love, and desire and joy, which are naturally intermingled with our organic and sensuous emotions, but which are in themselves affections of the spiritual will, and are awakened through the immaterial light of intellectual insight. We delight in beauty, we desire perfection and justice, we love truth, we love God, we love all men—not only the members of our social group, or our family, our class or nation—but all men because they are human beings, and children of God. The saints, those men who are called everywhere spiritual men, experience a contemplation which establishes their souls in a peace superior to and stronger than the whole world, and they go through inner trials, crucifixions and deaths which only a life superior to and stronger than biological existence can suffer and go through—and still remain alive. And we ourselves know that we can deliberate about ourselves, judge our own actions, cling to what is good because it is good and for no other reason; all of us know more or less obscurely that we are persons, that we have rights and duties, that we preserve human dignity within ourselves. Each one of us can, at certain moments in his existence, descend into the innermost depths of the Ego, to make there some eternal pledge or gift of himself, or face some irrefutable judgment of his conscience; and each one of us, on such occasions, alone with himself, feels that he is a universe unto himself, immersed in, but not dominated by, the great star-studded universe.

Through all these convergent ways, we may realize and experience in a certain measure, and in a concrete fashion, that living reality of our spiritual roots, or of what is above time in us, which the philosophical proofs make intellectually certain, but in the abstract manner of scientific knowledge.

The Immortality of the Human Soul

The third point follows immediately from the second. The immortality of the human soul is an immediate corollary of its spirituality. A soul which is spiritual in itself, intrinsically independent of matter in its nature and existence, cannot cease existing. A spirit—that is, a "form" which needs nothing other than itself (save the influx of the Prime Cause) to exercise existence— once existing cannot cease existing. A spiritual soul cannot be corrupted, since it possesses no matter; it cannot be disintegrated, since it has no substantial parts; it cannot lose its individual unity, since it is self-subsisting, nor its internal energy, since it contains within itself all the sources of its energies. The human soul cannot die. Once it exists, it cannot disappear; it will necessarily exist forever, endure without end.

Thus, philosophic reason, put to work by a great metaphysician like Thomas Aquinas, is able to prove the immortality of the human soul in a demonstrative manner. Of course, this demonstration implies a vast and articulate network of metaphysical insights, notions and principles (relating to essence and nature, substance, act and potency, matter and form, operation, etc.) the validity of which is necessarily presupposed. We can appreciate fully the strength of the Scholastic demonstration only if we realize the significance and full validity of the metaphysical notions involved. If modern times feel at a loss in the face of metaphysical knowledge, I fancy that it is not metaphysical knowledge which is to blame, but rather modern times and the weakening of reason they have experienced.

It is not surprising, on the other hand, that the philosophical demonstration I have just summarized is an abstract and a difficult one. The great and fundamental truths which are spontaneously grasped by the natural instinct of the human mind are always the most arduous for philosophic reason to establish. With regard to the immortality of the human soul, philosophic reason must use the very refined and elaborate concept of immateriality, a concept remote from the natural understanding, not only of primitive men, but of everyone who thinks with his imagination rather than with his intellect. Were not certain monks of Asia Minor, in the early Christian centuries, indignant at the idea that God is an Immaterial Being? They did not use the English language, yet they were convinced that to be *immaterial*, or deprived of matter, actually meant to be something immaterial, or nothing at all. They surely believed in the immortality of the soul, but it is doubtful whether they would have understood the strength of the argument we have used.

Primitive men did not philosophize; but, for all that, they had their own way, an instinctive, non-conceptual way, of believing in the soul's immortality. It was a belief rooted in an obscure experience of the self, and in the natural aspirations of the spirit in us to overcome death. We need not embark on an analysis of this natural and instinctive, non-philosophical belief in immortality. I should like merely to quote a passage from a book by the late scientist Pierre Lecomte du Noüy. Speaking of prehistoric man, he said: "Not only did the Neanderthal Man, who lived in Paleolithic times, bury his dead, but sometimes he buried them in a common ground. An example of this is the Grotte des Enfants near Mentone. Because of this respect he had for his dead, we have reached an anatomical knowledge of the Neanderthal Man that is more perfect than that which we have of certain races which have recently become extinct, or which still exist, such as the Tasmanians. This is no longer a question of instinct. We are dealing already with the dawn of human thought, which reveals itself in a kind of revolt against death. And revolt against death implies love for those who have gone as well as the hope that their disappearance is not final. We see these *ideas*, the first perhaps, develop progressively alongside the first artistic feelings. Flat rocks in the shape of dolmens are placed so as to protect the faces and heads of those who are buried. Later, ornaments, weapons, food, and the colors which serve to adorn the body, are placed in the tombs. The idea of finality is unbearable. The dead man will awaken, he will be hungry, he will have to defend himself, he will want to adorn himself."[5]

The same author goes on to observe that because the primordial notions, like those of good and evil, or of immortality, were spontaneously born in the most primitive human beings, those notions would deserve for that very reason to be examined and scrutinized as possessing absolute value.

I think that these views expressed by Lecomte du Noüy are true and thought-provoking. *A priori* it is probable that the great and basic ideas, the prime ideas, which are contained in the myths of primitive man, and are handed down in the common heritage of mankind, are more sound than illusory, and deserve respect more than contempt. At the same time, we are free to prefer a genuine philosophical demonstration.

The Condition and Destiny of the Immortal Soul

What can philosophy tell us about the natural condition of the immortal soul after the death of its body? That is my fourth and last point. Philosophy can tell us very little indeed on this subject. Let us try to summarize the few indications there are. All the organic and sensuous powers of the human soul remain dormant in a separated soul, for they cannot be brought into play without the body. The separated soul is itself engulfed in a complete sleep with regard to the material world; the external senses and their perceptions have vanished; the images of memory and imagination, the impulses of instinct and passion have vanished. But this sleep is not like the sleep

[5]*L'Avenir de l'Esprit*, Gallimard, Paris, 1941, p. 188.

we know, obscure and filled with dreams; it is lucid and intelligent, alive to spiritual realities. For now light shines from within. The intellect and the spiritual powers are awake and active. From the very fact of its separation from the body, the soul now knows itself through itself; its very substance has become transparent to its intellect; it is intellectually penetrated to its innermost depths. The soul knows itself in an intuitive manner; it is dazzled by its own beauty, the beauty of a spiritual substance, and it knows other things through its own substance already known, in the measure in which other things resemble it. It knows God through that image of God which the soul itself is. And in accordance with its state of incorporeal existence, it receives from God, the sun of the spirits, certain ideas and inspirations which directly enlighten it, and help the natural light of the human intellect, of that intellect which is, as Saint Thomas Aquinas phrased it, the lowest in the hierarchy of spirits.

Saint Thomas teaches also that all that is of the intellect and the spirit, and especially the intellectual memory, which is but one with the intellect, keeps alive, in the separated soul, the whole treasure of knowledge acquired during our bodily life. The intellectual knowledge, the intellectual virtues acquired here below subsist in the separated soul. Whereas the images of the sense-memory, which had its seat in the brain, disappear, that which has penetrated into the intellectual memory is preserved. Thus, in an intellectual and spiritual manner, the separated soul ever knows those whom it loved. And it loves them spiritually. And it is able to converse with other spirits by opening to them what abides in its inner thoughts and is taken hold of by its free will.

We may thus imagine that, at the moment when it leaves the body, the soul is suddenly immersed into itself as into a shining abyss, where all that was buried within it, all its dead, rise up again in full light, insofar as all this was encompassed in the subconscious or supraconscious depths of the spiritual life of its intellect and will. Then all that is true and good in the soul becomes a blessing for it at the touch of this all-pervading revelatory light; all that is warped and evil becomes a torment for it under the effect of the very same light.

I do not believe that natural reason can go further in its understanding of the natural condition of the separated soul. What would be the life and happiness of souls if their state after death were a purely natural state? Their supreme good would consist in wisdom, untrammeled spiritual life, mutual friendship, and first and foremost in advancing constantly in their natural knowledge and love of God, Whom they would, however, never see face to face. It would be happiness in motion, never absolutely fulfilled—what Leibniz called *un chemin par des plaisirs*, "a road amidst spiritual pleasures."

But if we wish to know more, can we not go beyond philosophy? Philosophy itself will then entrust us to the guidance of a knowledge whose sources are superior to its own. Christians know that man does not live in a state of pure nature. They know that he was created in a state of grace, and that, after the first sin which wounded our race, he has been living in a state of fallen and redeemed nature; they know that he is made for super-natural blessedness. In answer to the question of the separated soul's destiny, the Scholastic doctors spoke not as philosophers, but as theologians whose knowledge rests on the data of Revelation.

Insofar as man participates in the metaphysical privileges of spirit and personality, he has aspirations which transcend human nature and its possibilities, and which consequently may be called transnatural aspirations: the longing for a state in which he would know things completely and without error, in which he would enjoy perfect communion with spirits, in which he would be free without being able to fail or to sin, in which he would inhabit a realm of unfading justice, in which he would have the intuitive knowledge of the First Cause of being.

Such a longing cannot be fulfilled by nature. It can be fulfilled by grace. The immortal soul is involved and engaged in the great drama of the Redemption. If, at the moment of its separation from the body, at the moment when its choice is immutably fixed forever, the immortal soul prefers its own will and self-love to the will and gift of God, if it prefers misery with pride to the blessing of grace, then it is granted what it has wished for. It has it, and it will never cease wanting and preferring it, for a free choice made in the condition of a *pure* spirit is an eternal choice. If the soul opens itself to the will and gift of God, Whom it loves more than its own existence, then it is granted what it has loved, it enters forever into the joy of the uncreated Being, it sees God face to face and knows Him as it is known by Him [cf. I Cor. 13:12], intuitively. Thus, it becomes God by participation, as Saint John of the Cross phrased it, and, through grace, it attains that commu-nion in divine life, that blessedness for the sake of which all things have been created. And the degree of its blessedness itself, the degree of its vision, will correspond to the degree of the inner impetus which projects it into God, in other words, to the degree of love to which it has attained in its life on earth. In the last analysis, therefore, we must say with Saint John of the Cross: It is upon our love that we shall be judged. In its state of blessedness the immortal soul will know creation in the Creator, by that kind of knowledge which Saint Augustine called "matutinal" knowledge, because it is produced in the eternal morning of Creative Ideas; the immortal soul will be equal to the angels, and will communicate freely with the whole realm of spirits; it will love God, henceforth clearly seen, with a sovereign necessity; and it will exert free will with regard to all its actions concerning creatures, but its free will shall no longer be liable to failure and sin; the soul will inhabit the realm of unfading justice, that of the three divine Persons and of the blessed spirits; it will grasp and possess the divine Essence which, infinitely clearer and more intelligible than any of our ideas, will illumine the human intellect from within and will itself be the intelligible medium, the actuating form through which it will be known. According to a line of the Psalms [36:9] which Saint Thomas loved and often quoted: "In Thy light shall we see light."

Such are the teachings of Saint Thomas, both as a philosopher and as a theologian, about the condition and destiny of the human soul. Immortality is not a more or less precarious, successful or unsuccessful survival in other men, or in the ideal waves of the universe. Immortality is a nature-given, inalienable property of the human soul as a spiritual substance. And grace makes eternal life possible to all, to the most destitute as well as to the most gifted. The eternal life of the immortal soul is its transforming union with God and His intimate life, a union which is to be accomplished inchoatively here below, by love and contemplation and, after the body's death, in a definite and perfect manner, by the beatific vision. For eternal life begins here upon earth, and the soul of man lives and breathes where it loves; and love, in living faith, has strength enough to make the soul of man experience unity with God—"two natures in a single spirit and love, *dos naturalezas en un espiritu y amor de Dios.*"

I do not believe that a philosopher can discuss the immortality of the soul without taking into consideration the complementary notions which religious thought adds to the true and inadequate answers which reason and philosophy can furnish by themselves.

�֍ JOHN HICK

31. *The Evidence of Psychical Research*

John Hick (born 1922) has taught at universities both in England and the United States. A philosopher of the contemporary analytic style, he has edited and authored numerous volumes and articles in the philosophy of religion. Especially important is his *Evil and the God of Love.*

From *Philosophy of Religion*

Chapter 4: Human Destiny

Does Parapsychology Help?

The Spiritualist movement claims that life after death has been proved by well-attested cases of communication between the living and the "dead." During the closing quarter of the nineteenth century and the decades of the present century, this claim has been made the subject of careful and prolonged study by a number of responsible and competent persons.[1] This work, which may be approximately dated from the founding in London of the Society for Psychical Research in 1882, is known either by the name adopted by that Society or in the United States by the name Parapsychology.

Approaching the subject from the standpoint of our interest in this chapter, we may initially divide the phenomena studied by the parapsychologist into two groups. There are those phenomena which involve no reference to the idea of a life after death, chief among these being psychokinesis and extra-sensory perception (ESP) in its various forms (such as telepathy, clairvoyance, and precognition). And there are those phenomena which raise the question of personal survival after death, such as the apparitions and other sensory manifestations of dead persons and the "spirit messages" received through mediums. This division is, however, only of preliminary use, for ESP has emerged as a clue to the understanding of much that occurs in the second group. We shall begin with a brief outline of the reasons which have induced the majority of workers in this field to be willing to postulate so strange an occurrence as telepathy.

Telepathy is a name for the mysterious fact that sometimes a thought in the mind of one person apparently causes a similar thought to occur to someone else when there are no normal means of communication between them, and under circumstances such that mere coincidence seems to be excluded.

For example, one person may draw a series of pictures or diagrams on paper and somehow transmit an impression of these to someone else in another room who then draws recognizable reproductions of them. This might well be a coincidence in the case of a single successful reproduction; but can a series consist entirely of coincidences?

Experiments have been devised to measure the probability of chance coincidence in supposed cases of telepathy. In the simplest of these, cards are used which are printed in turn with five different symbols. A pack of fifty, consisting of ten bearing each symbol, is then thoroughly shufffled, and the sender concentrates on the cards one at a time while the receiver (who of course can see neither sender nor cards) tries to write down the correct order of symbols. This procedure is repeated, with constant reshuffling, hundreds or thousands of times. Since there are only five different symbols, a random guess would stand one chance in five of being correct. Consequently, on the assumption that only "chance" is operating, the receiver should be right in about twenty per cent of his tries, and wrong in about eighty per cent; and the longer the series, the closer should be the approach to this proportion. However, good telepathic subjects are right in a far larger number

---

[1]The list of past Presidents of the Society for Psychical Research includes the philosophers Henri Bergson, William James, Hans Driesch, Henry Sidgwick, F. C. S. Schiller, C. D. Broad, and H. H. Price; the psychologists William McDougall, Gardner Murphy, Franklin Prince, and R. H. Thouless; the physicists Sir William Crookes, Sir Oliver Lode, Sir William Barrett, and Lord Rayleigh; and the classicist Gilbert Murray.

of cases than can be reconciled with random guessing. The deviation from chance expectation can be converted mathematically into "odds against chance" (increasing as the proportion of hits is maintained over a longer and longer series of tries). In this way, odds of over a million to one have been recorded. J. B. Rhine (Duke University) has reported results showing "anti-chance" values ranging from 7 (which equals odds against chance of 100,000 to one) to 82 (which converts the odds against chance to billions).[2] S. G. Soal (London Univeristy) has reported positive results for precognitive telepathy with odds against chance of $10^{35} \times 5$, or of billions to one.[3] Other researchers have also recorded confirming results.[4] In the light of these reports, it is difficult to deny that some positive factor, and not merely "chance," is operating. "Telepathy" is simply a name for this unknown positive factor.

How does telepathy operate? Only negative conclusions seem to be justified to date. It can, for example, be said with reasonable certainty that telepathy does not consist in any kind of physical radiation, analogous to radio waves. For, first, telepathy is not delayed or weakened in proportion to distances, as are all known forms of radiation; and, second, there is no organ in the brain or elsewhere which can plausibly be regarded as its sending or receiving center. Telepathy appears to be a purely mental occurrence.

It is not, however, a matter of transferring or transporting a thought out of one mind into another—if, indeed, such an idea makes sense at all. The telepathized thought does not leave the sender's consciousness in order to enter that of the receiver. What happens would be better described by saying that the sender's thought gives rise to a mental "echo" in the mind of the receiver. This "echo" occurs at the unconscious level, and consequently the version of it which rises into the receiver's consciousness may be only fragmentary, and may be distorted or symbolized in various ways, as in dreams.

According to one theory which has been tentatively suggested to explain telepathy, our minds are separate and mutually insulated only at the conscious (and preconscious) level. But at the deepest level of the unconscious, we are constantly influencing one another, and it is at this level that telepathy takes place.[5]

How is a telepathized thought directed to one particular receiver amongst so many? Apparently the thoughts are directed by some link of emotion or common interest. For example, two friends are sometimes telepa-

[2] J. B. Rhine, *Extra-Sensory Perception* (Boston: Society for Psychical Research, 1935), Table XLIII, p. 162. See also Rhine, *New Frontiers of the Mind* (New York: Farrar and Rinehart, Inc., 1937), pp. 69 f.

[3] S. G. Soal, *Proceedings of the Society for Psychical Research*, XLVI, 152–198 and XLVII, 21–150. See also S. G. Soal's *The Experimental Situation in Psychical Research* (London: The Society for Psychical Research, 1947).

[4] For surveys of the experimental work, see Whately Carrington, *Telepathy* (London: Methuen & Co., Ltd., 1945); G. N. M. Tyrrell, *The Personality of Man* (London: Penguin Books, 1946); S. G. Soal and F. Bateman, *Modern Experiments in Telepathy* (London: Faber & Faber, Ltd. and New Haven: Yale University Press, 1954).

[5] Whately Carrington, *Telepathy* (London: Methuen & Co., Ltd., 1945), Chaps. 6–8.

thically aware of any grave crisis or shock experienced by the other, even though they are at opposite ends of the earth.

We shall turn now to the other branch of parapsychology, which has more obvious bearing upon our subject. The *Proceedings of the Society for Psychical Research* contains a large number of carefully recorded and satisfactorily attested cases of the appearance of the figure of someone who has recently died to living people (in rare instances to more than one at a time) who were, in many cases, at a distance and unaware of the death. The S.P.R. reports also establish beyond reasonable doubt that the minds which operate in the mediumistic trance, purporting to be spirits of the departed, sometimes give personal information which the medium could not have acquired by normal means and at times even give information, later verified, which had not been known to any living person.

On the other hand, physical happenings, such as the "materializations" of spirit forms in a visible and tangible form, are much more doubtful. But even if we discount the entire range of physical phenomena, it remains true that the best cases of trance utterance are impressive and puzzling, and taken at face value are indicative of survival and communication after death. If, through a medium, one talks with an intelligence which gives a coherent impression of being an intimately known friend who has died and establishes identity by a wealth of private information and indefinable personal characteristics—as has occasionally happened—then we cannot dismiss without careful trial the theory that what is taking place is the return of a consciousness from the spirit world.

However, the advance of knowledge in the other branch of parapsychology, centering upon the study of extra-sensory perception, has thrown unexpected light upon this apparent commerce with the departed. For it suggests that unconsciousness telepathic contact between the medium and his or her client is an important and possibly a sufficient explanatory factor. This was vividly illustrated by the experience of two women who decided to test the spirits by taking into their minds, over a period of weeks, the personality and atmosphere of an entirely imaginary character in an unpublished novel which one of the women had written. After thus filling their minds with the characteristics of this fictitious person, they went to a reputable medium, who proceeded to describe accurately their imaginary friends as a visitant from beyond the grave and to deliver appropriate messages from him.

An even more striking case is that of the "direct voice" medium (i.e., a medium in whose seances the voice of the communicating "spirit" is heard apparently speaking out of the air) who produced the spirit of one "Gordon Davis" who spoke in his own recognizable voice, displayed considerable knowledge about Gordon Davis, and remembered his death. This was extremely impressive until it was discovered that Gordon Davis was still alive; he was, of all ghostly occupations, a real estate agent, and had been trying to sell a house at the time when the seance took place![6]

[6] S. G. Soal, "A Report of Some Communications Received through Mrs. Blanche Cooper," sec. 4, *Proceedings of the Society for Psychical Research*, XXXV, pp. 560–589.

Such cases suggest that genuine mediums are simply persons of exceptional telepathic sensitiveness who unconsciously derive the "spirits" from their clients' minds.

In connection with "ghosts," in the sense of apparitions of the dead, it has been established that there can be "meaningful hallucinations," the source of which is almost certainly telepathic. To quote a classic and somewhat dramatic example: a woman sitting by a lake sees the figure of a man running towards the lake and throwing himself in. A few days later a man commits suicide by throwing himself into this same lake. Presumably, the explanation of the vision is that the man's thought while he was contemplating suicide had been telepathically projected onto the scene via the woman's mind.[7]

In many of the cases recorded there is delayed action. The telepathically projected thought lingers in the recipient's unconscious mind until a suitable state of inattention to the outside world enables it to appear to his conscious mind in a dramatized form—for example, by a hallucinatory voice or vision—by means of the same mechanism which operates in dreams.

If phantoms of the living can be created by previously experienced thoughts and emotions of the person whom they represent, the parallel possibility arises that phantoms of the dead are caused by thoughts and emotions which were experienced by the person represented when he was alive. In other words, ghosts may be "psychic footprints," a kind of mental trace left behind by the dead, but not involving the presence or even the continued existence of those whom they represent.

These considerations tend away from the hopeful view that parapsychology will open a window onto another world. However, it is too early for a final verdict; and in the meantime one should be careful not to confuse absence of knowledge with knowledge of absence.

[7]F. W. H. Myers, *Human Personality and Its Survival of Bodily Death* (London: Longmans, Green, & Co., 1903), I, 270-71.

✳ BERTRAND RUSSELL

32. *Science and the Soul*

Bertrand Russell (1872–1970) was a leading figure of contemporary British philosophy. His contributions to modern thought lie in a number of areas ranging from scientific and logical treatises to critical analyses of religion, morals, and politics. Russell's many indictments against theology and organized religion are summarized in his volume of popular essays *Why I Am Not a Christian.*

From *Religion and Science*

CHAPTER 5: SOUL AND BODY

What science has to say on the subject of immortality is not very definite. There is, indeed, one line of argument in favour of survival after death, which is, at least in intention, completely scientific—I mean the line of argument associated with the phenomena investigated by psychical research. I have not myself sufficient knowledge on this subject to judge of the evidence already available, but it is clear that there could be evidence which would convince reasonable men. To this, however, certain provisos must be added. In the first place, the evidence, at the best, would only prove that we survive death, not that we survive for ever. In the second place, where strong desires are involved, it is very difficult to accept the testimony even of habitually accurate persons; of this there was much evidence during the War, and in all times of great excitement. In the third place, if, on other grounds, it seems unlikely that our personality does not die with the body, we shall require much stronger evidence of survival than we should if we thought the hypothesis antecedently probable. Not even the most ardent believer in spiritualism could pretend to have as much evidence of survival as historians can adduce to prove that witches did bodily homage to Satan, yet hardly anyone now regards the evidence of such occurrences as even worth examining.

The difficulty, for science, arises from the fact that there does not seem to be such an entity as the soul or self. As we saw, it is no longer possible to regard soul and body as two "substances," having that endurance through time which metaphysicians regarded as logically bound up with the notion of substance. Nor is there any reason, in psychology, to assume a "subject" which, in perception, is brought into contact with an "object." Until recently, it was thought that matter is immortal, but this is no longer assumed by the technique of physics. An atom is now merely a convenient way of

Bertrand Russell, *Religion and Science* (Oxford, England: Oxford University Press, 1935). Reprinted by permission of the Clarendon Press, Oxford, England.

grouping certain occurrences; it is convenient, up to a point, to think of the atom as a nucleus with attendant electrons, but the electrons at one time cannot be identified with those at another, and in any case no modern physicist thinks of them as "real." While there was still material substance which was supposed to be eternal, it was easy to argue that minds must be equally eternal; but this argument, which was never a very strong one, can now no longer be used. For sufficient reasons, physicists have reduced the atom to a series of events; for equally good reasons, psychologists find that a mind has not the identity of a single continuing "thing," but is a series of occurrences bound together by certain intimate relations. The question of immortality, therefore, has become the question whether these intimate relations exist between occurrences connected with a living body and other occurrences which take place after that body is dead.

We must first decide, before we can attempt to answer this question, what are the relations which bind certain events together in such a way as to make them the mental life of one person. Obviously the most important of these is memory: things that I can remember happened to *me*. And if I can remember a certain occasion, and on that occasion I could remember something else, then the something else also happened to me. It might be objected that two people may remember the same event, but that would be an error: no two people ever see exactly the same thing, because of differences in their positions. No more can they have precisely the same experiences of hearing or smelling or touching or tasting. My experience may closely resemble another person's, but always differs from it in a greater or less degree. Each person's experience is private to himself, and when one experience consists in recollecting another, the two are said to belong to the same "person."

There is another, less psychological, definition of personality, which derives it from the body. The definition of what makes the identity of a living body at different times would be complicated, but for the moment we will take it for granted. We will also take it for granted that every "mental" experience known to us is connected with some living body. We can then define a "person" as the series of mental occurrences connected with a given body. This is the legal definition. If John Smith's body committed a murder, and at a later time the police arrest John Smith's body, then the person inhabiting that body at the time of arrest is a murderer.

These two ways of defining a "person" conflict in cases of what is called dual personality. In such cases, what seems to outside observation to be one person is, subjectively, split into two; sometimes neither knows anything of the other, sometimes one knows the other, but not vice versa. In cases where neither knows anything of the other, there are two persons if memory is used as the definition, but only one if the body is used. There is a regular gradation to the extreme of dual personality, through absent-mindedness, hypnosis, and sleep-walking. This makes a difficulty in using memory as the definition of personality. But it appears that lost memories can be recovered by hypnotism or in the course of psycho-analysis; thus perhaps the difficulty is not insuperable.

In addition to actual recollection, various other elements, more or less analogous to memory, enter into personality—habits, for instance, which have been formed as a result of past experience. It is because, where there is life, events can form habits, that an "experience" differs from a mere occurrence. An animal, and still more a man, is formed by experiences in a way that dead matter is not. If an event is causally related to another in that peculiar way that has to do with habit-formation, then the two events belong to the same "person." This is a wider definition than that by memory alone, including all that the memory-definition included and a good deal more.

If we are to believe in the survival of a personality after the death of the body, we must suppose that there is continuity of memories or at least of habits, since otherwise there is no reason to suppose that the same person is continuing. But at this point physiology makes difficulties. Habit and memory are both due to effects on the body, especially the brain; the formation of a habit may be thought of as analogous to the formation of a water-course. Now the effects on the body, which give rise to habits and memories, are obliterated by death and decay, and it is difficult to see how, short of miracle, they can be transferred to a new body such as we may be supposed to inhabit in the next life. If we are to be disembodied spirits, the difficulty is only increased. Indeed I doubt whether, with modern views of matter, a disembodied spirit is logically possible. Matter is only a certain way of grouping events, and therefore where there are events there is matter. The continuity of a person throughout the life of his body, if, as I contend, it depends upon habit-formation, must also depend upon the continuity of the body. It would be as easy to transfer a water-course to heaven without loss of identity as it would be to transfer a person.

Personality is essentially a matter of organization. Certain events, grouped together by means of certain relations, form a person. The grouping is effected by means of causal laws—those connected with habit-formation, which includes memory—and the causal laws concerned depend upon the body. If this is true—and there are strong scientific grounds for thinking that it is—to expect a personality to survive the disintegration of the brain is like expecting a cricket club to survive when all its members are dead.

I do not pretend that this argument is conclusive. It is impossible to foresee the future of science, particularly of psychology, which is only just beginning to be scientific. It may be that psychological causation can be freed from its present dependence on the body. But in the present state of psychology and physiology, belief in immortality can, at any rate, claim no support from science, and such arguments as are possible on the subject point to the probable extinction of personality at death. We may regret the thought that we shall not survive, but it is a comfort to think that all the persecutors and Jewbaiters and humbugs will not continue to exist for all eternity. We may be told that they would improve in time, but I doubt it.

�֍ LUDWIG WITTGENSTEIN

33. *Death and Riddles*

Ludwig Wittgenstein (1889–1951), an Austrian by birth, taught at Cambridge University where he emerged as the most influential of those thinkers who seek to illuminate philosophical problems through "linguistic analysis." Wittgenstein's *Tractatus* and posthumously published *Philosophical Investigations* continue to dominate the attention of a large segment of contemporary philosophy.

From *Tractatus Logico-Philosophicus*

6.4   All propositions are of equal value.

6.41   The sense of the world must lie outside the world. In the world everything is as it is, and everything happens as it does happen: *in* it no value exists—and if it did, it would have no value.

If there is any value that does have value, it must lie outside the whole sphere of what happens and is the case. For all that happens and is the case is accidental.

What makes it non-accidental cannot lie *within* the world, since if it did it would itself be accidental.

It must lie outside the world.

6.42   And so it is impossible for there to be propositions of ethics. Propositions can express nothing of what is higher.

6.421 It is clear that ethics cannot be put into words.
Ethics is transcendental.
(Ethics and aesthetics are one and the same.)

6.422 When an ethical law of the form, 'Thou shalt . . . ,' is laid down, one's first thought is, 'And what if I do not do it?' It is clear, however, that ethics has nothing to do with punishment and reward in the usual sense of the terms. So our question about the *consequences* of an action must be unimportant.—At least those consequences should not be events. For there must be something right about the question we posed. There must indeed be some kind of ethical reward and ethical punishment, but they must reside in the action itself.

(And it is also clear that the reward must be something pleasant and the punishment something unpleasant.)

6.423 It is impossible to speak about the will in so far as it is the subject of ethical attributes.

Ludwig Wittgenstein, *Tractatus Logico-Philosophicus*, tr. D. F. Pears and B. F. McGuinness (London: Routledge & Kegan Paul, 1961). Reprinted by permission of Routledge & Kegan Paul, Ltd. and Humanities Press, Inc., New York.

And the will as a phenomenon is of interest only to psychology.

6.43   If good or bad acts of will do alter the world, it can only be the limits of the world that they alter, not the facts, not what can be expressed by means of language.

In short their effect must be that it becomes an altogether different world. It must, so to speak, wax and wane as a whole.

The world of the happy man is a different one from that of the unhappy man.

6.431   So too at death the world does not alter, but comes to an end.

6.4311   Death is not an event in life: we do not live to experience death.

If we take eternity to mean not infinite temporal duration but timelessness, then eternal life belongs to those who live in the present.

Our life has no end in just the way in which our visual field has no limits.

6.4312   Not only is there no guarantee of the temporal immortality of the human soul, that is to say of its eternal survival after death; but, in any case, this assumption completely fails to accomplish the purpose for which it has always been intended. Or is some riddle solved by my surviving for ever? Is not this eternal life itself as much of a riddle as our present life? The solution of the riddle of life in space and time lies *outside* space and time.

(It is certainly not the solution of any problems of natural science that is required.)

6.432   *How* things are in the world is a matter of complete indifference for what is higher. God does not reveal himself *in* the world.

6.4321   The facts all contribute only to setting the problem, not to its solution.

6.44   It is not *how* things are in the world that is mystical, but *that* it exists.

6.45   To view the world *sub specie aeterni*[1] is to view it as a whole—a limited whole.

Feeling the world as a limited whole—it is this that is mystical.

6.5   When the answer cannot be put into words, neither can the question be put into words.

The riddle does not exist.

If a question can be framed at all, it is also *possible* to answer it.

6.51   Scepticism is *not* irrefutable, but obviously nonsensical, when it tries to raise doubts where no questions can be asked.

---

[1]["from the standpoint of eternity."]

For doubt can exist only where a question exists, a question only where an answer exists, and an answer only where something *can be said.*

6.52   We feel that even when *all possible* scientific questions have been answered, the problems of life remain completely untouched. Of course there are then no questions left, and this itself is the answer.

6.521   The solution of the problem of life is seen in the vanishing of the problem.

(Is not this the reason why those who have found after a long period of doubt that the sense of life became clear to them have then been unable to say what constituted that sense?)

6.522   There are, indeed, things that cannot be put into words. They *make themselves manifest.* They are what is mystical.

6.53   The correct method in philosophy would really be the following: to say nothing except what can be said, i.e. propositions of natural science—i.e. something that has nothing to do with philosophy—and then, whenever someone else wanted to say something metaphysical, to demonstrate to him that he had failed to give a meaning to certain signs in his propositions. Although it would not be satisfying to the other person—he would not have the feeling that we were teaching him philosophy—*this* method would be the only strictly correct one.

6.54   My propositions serve as elucidations in the following way: anyone who understands me eventually recognizes them as nonsensical, when he has used them—as steps—to climb up beyond them. (He must, so to speak, throw away the ladder after he has climbed up it.)

He must transcend these propositions, and then he will see the world aright.

7   What we cannot speak about we must consign to silence. . . .

�֍ SELECTED BIBLIOGRAPHY
FOR SECTION 7

Oscar Cullmann's brief essay, "Immortality of the Soul or Resurrection of the Dead?" is, perhaps, the most lucid exposition of the New Testament teaching on the subject. Cullmann's essay is reproduced along with three others dealing with the question in terms of the Greeks, the Church Fathers, and Jesus, in Krister Stendhal (ed.), *Immortality and Resurrection* (New York: Macmillan, 1965).

For a discussion of Plato's doctrine of the soul and its immortality, see Paul Friedländer, *Plato,* Vol. I, *passim* (consult index for specific passages), tr. Hans Myerhoff (New York: Pantheon, 1958—) and G. M. A. Grube, *Plato's Thought,* Ch. 4 (London: Methuen, 1935). For the arguments of the *Phaedo,* one should consult R. Hackforth's translation, introduction, and commentary, in his *Plato's Phaedo* (Indianapolis, Ind.: Library of Liberal Arts, 1952). For an analytic critique of Plato's position, see I. M. Crombie, *An Examination of Plato's Doctrines,* Vol. I, Ch. 8 (New York: Humanities Press, 1962).

Classical expositions of the soul and immortality from a Christian standpoint include St. Augustine, *On the Immortality of the Soul*, tr. G. S. Leckie, in *Basic Writings of St. Augustine*, ed. Whitney J. Oates (New York: Random House, 1946); St. Thomas Aquinas, *Summa Theologica*, Part I, Qus. 75 and 76, in *Basic Writings of St. Thomas Aquinas*, ed. Anton C. Pegis (New York: Random House, 1945); and John Calvin, *Institutes of the Christian Religion*, Book III, Ch. 25, ed. John T. McNeill, tr. Ford Lewis Battles (Philadelphia: Westminster Press, 1960). Recent discussions include the following: John Baillie, *And the Life Everlasting* (London: Oxford University Press, 1934); A. E. Taylor, *The Christian Hope of Immortality* (London: Unicorn Press, 1938); Rudolf Bultmann, *The Presence of Eternity* (New York: Harper & Row, 1957); H. E. Fosdick, *The Assurance of Immortality* (New York: Macmillan, 1926).

A sympathetic approach from an empiricist standpoint may be found in F. R. Tennant, *Philosophical Theology*, Vol. II, Appendix, Note E (Cambridge, England: University Press, 1928–30). Bishop Butler, in the eighteenth century, formulated an inductive argument for immortality in *The Analogy of Religion*, Part I, Ch. 1 (New York: Ungar, 1961). Other differing but sympathetic treatments of immortality may be found in William James, *Human Immortality* (New York: Houghton Mifflin, 1898); George Santayana, *The Life of Reason: Reason in Religion*, Chs. 13 and 14 (New York: Scribner, 1905); and two works by C. J. Ducasse: *A Critical Examination of the Belief in a Life After Death* (Springfield, Ill.: Thomas, 1961) and *Nature, Mind and Death*, Chs. 20 and 21 (LaSalle, Ill.: Open Court, 1951).

Not so sympathetic are the ancient Greek Epicurus, *Letters*, tr. Russel M. Greer (Indianapolis, Ind.: Library of Liberal Arts, 1964) and the Roman Lucretius, *The Nature of the Universe*, tr. Ronald Latham (Baltimore, Md.: Penguin Books, 1951), both materialistic in their approaches. For a modern materialistic rejection, see P. H. D. d'Holbach, *The System of Nature*, Vol. I, Ch. 7, tr. H. D. Robinson (New York: Matsell, 1835). Still more recent, and critical, are the positions taken by Corliss Lamont, *The Illusion of Immortality* (London: Watts, 1953); C. Cohen, *The Other Side of Death* (London: Pioneer Press, 1922); and Roy Wood Sellars, *The Next Step in Religion*, Ch. 11 (New York: Macmillan, 1918). For a critique in a more popular style, see Clarence Darrow, *The Story of My Life* (New York: Scribner, 1932). Additional critical observations by Russell are contained in his *Why I Am Not a Christian, passim* (New York: Simon & Schuster, 1957).

A general discussion of immortality by an analytic philosopher is provided by Ian T. Ramsey, *Freedom and Immortality* (London: Student Christian Movement Press, 1960). One should note also the treatment by P. T. Geach, *God and the Soul* (New York: Schocken, 1969). A good history of the problem may be found in Baron F. von Hügel, *Eternal Life*, second ed. (Edinburgh: T. & T. Clark, 1913).

An interesting introduction to psychical research may be found in R. C. Johnson's little book, *Psychical Research* (New York: Philosophical Library, 1956). Three of J. B. Rhine's pioneering works in the field of parapsychology are *New Frontiers of the Mind* (New York: Farrar & Rinehart, 1937), *The Reach of the Mind* (New York: Sloane, 1947), and *New World of the Mind* (New York: Sloane, 1953). For further discussion of experimental investigations, see S. G. Soal and F. Bateman, *Modern Experiments in Telepathy* (London: Faber & Faber, 1954). Philosophical considerations of the psychical evidence for survival are suggested by Antony Flew, *A New Approach to Psychical Research* (London: Watts, 1953); C. D. Broad, *The Mind and Its Place in Nature*, sec. D (New York: Macmillan, 1925); and Broad's more recent *Lectures on Psychical Research* (New York: Humanities Press, 1962). An attempt to project the nature of the afterlife on the basis of psychical research is provided by H. H. Price, "Survival and the Idea of 'Another World,'" *Proceedings of the Society for Psychical Research*, L (January, 1953).

The contemporary discussion of the nature of mind, its relation to the body, and so forth, has its roots in Descartes' "mind-matter dualism" as expressed in his *Discourse on Method and Meditations*, tr. Laurence J. Lafleur (Indianapolis, Ind.: Library of Liberal Arts, 1960). Modern treatments of mind, more or less in Cartesian terms, are contained in John Laird, *Our Minds and Their Bodies* (London: Oxford University Press, 1925); C. D. Broad, *op. cit.*; and C. J. Ducasse, *Nature, Mind and Death, op. cit.* Critical of the traditional mind-body categories is Gilbert Ryle's important work, *The Concept of Mind* (London: Hutchinson, 1949) which provided an analytic point of departure for a whole new discussion of the question. Ryle's work was critically discussed in several articles in *Journal of Philosophy*, XLVII (April 26, 1950).

A survey of the positivistic approaches to the question is provided by Herbert Feigl in "The Mind-Body Problem in The Development of Logical Empiricism," in Herbert Feigl and May Broadbeck (eds.), *Readings in the Philosophy of Science* (New York: Appleton-Century-Crofts, 1953). A. J. Ayer, *The Problem of Knowledge*, Ch. 5 (London: Penguin Books, 1956) should be consulted for a contemporary version of Hume's mind-is-a-bundle-of-perceptions theory. The classic behaviorist position is stated by J. B. Watson in *Behaviorism* (New York: Norton, 1924).

For a series of articles by well-known philosophers on the mind-body problem, nature of mind, mental processes, consciousness, etc., plus an excellent bibliography on recent discussion, especially in the journals, see John O'Conner (ed.), *Modern Materialism* (New York: Harcourt, Brace & World, 1969). Similar discussions are contained in A. R. Anderson (ed.) *Minds and Machines* (Englewood Cliffs, N. J.: Prentice-Hall, 1964) and Sidney Hook (ed.) *Dimensions of Mind* (New York: New York University Press, 1960). Related to the issue raised by Russell, one should note John Knox's article, "Can the Self Survive the Death of its Mind?" *Religious Studies*, V (October, 1969).

Faith and Language

❊ INTRODUCTION

The problem of religious language, like that of faith and reason, occupies a special position among the questions of philosophical theology. For how we understand the nature of our religious or theological utterances, what we take to be their real significance, will surely determine something important about the nature of our theology and perhaps even the possibility of theology.

According to the classical view of St. Thomas Aquinas, the nature and possibility of our talking about God are grounded in the *analogia entis,* "analogy (or proportion) of being," that creatures bear to the Creator. Because God created the world, the world necessarily stands both in a certain likeness and unlikeness to God. Because God himself is the cause of the world, our concepts, such as goodness, derived as they are from nature, must bear some appropriateness to the divine being. On the other hand, since the being of the world is not the same as God's (God created the world out of nothing), no concept derived from nature can be wholly appropriate to the divine being. Thus our concepts and the language we employ when speaking about God are neither "equivocal" (used in completely different ways of both God and creatures), nor are they "univocal" (used in the exact same way), but "analogical," that is, standing in a certain proportion. We understand the goodness in God, for example, to be the goodness we creatures know, only infinitely maximized relative to God's infinite being, and likewise in the case of his wisdom, justice, power, and so on.

Thomas' understanding of "the names that can be predicated of God" is actually a working out, in epistemological terms, of his metaphysical position concerning God and the world; given Thomas' doctrine of the world's relation to God, it follows that our speaking about God must be analogical. For Ayer, it is precisely the nature of religious language that makes metaphysics—and thus theology—impossible from the beginning.

A. J. Ayer is a spokesman for Logical Positivism, a movement originating in the 1920's, which desires to make philosophy "scientific" through the adoption of a new and radically empirical criterion of meaningfulness. Ayer represents the "Verification Principle" as follows: " . . . a sentence is factually significant to any given person, if, and only if, he knows how to verify the proposition which it purports to express—that is, if he knows what observations would lead him under certain conditions, to accept the proposition as being true, or reject it as being false." On such a principle all metaphysical statements, such as "God exists," turn out to have no cognitive significance; they are neither true nor false, they are *meaningless.*

As one might guess, the logical positivist position generated a great deal of heated debate. The most obvious attack centered around the implication that all important knowledge reduces to mere probabilities of empirical gener- alization, to say nothing of the fact that the Verification Principle appears to be meaningless on its own showing! On the existentialist side, it has been argued that we should be suspicious of any principle that expurgates from philosophical inquiry the very questions that seem most interesting and urgent. Of course, this latter only shows (as we will see again in a moment) that while the existentialist is much troubled over the problem of meaning, he may not be much troubled over *cognitive* meaning.

Antony Flew, in the discussion "Theology and Falsification," delivers a challenge that reflects a decisive move in contemporary analytic-type consid- erations of religious language, as well as a source of continuing controversy: "What would have to occur or to have occurred to constitute for you a disproof of the love of, or of the existence of, God?" Thus redirecting the issue from the question of verification to falsification, Flew argues that religious assertions, such as "God loves me," cannot be genuine assertions since there appears to be no possible way to falsify them, no factual evidence that could conceiv- ably show them to be false; and a statement that is compatible with all possible empirical situations is not a statement about anything. Theological statements would therefore turn out to have no cognitive content or truth-value. R. M. Hare answers that religious statements may indeed be unverifiable and unfal- sifiable, but it does not follow that they are unimportant. It is, in fact, impossi- ble to evade such deeply-felt, non-rational convictions—"*bliks*" Hare calls them. Basil Mitchell represents still a third position. It may be that the theolo- gian will cling to his statement even in the face of evidence all to the contrary, but that is not to say that he does not recognize such evidence as at least bearing on his conviction and weighing against its truth. What believer does not recognize in evil a problem for his doctrine about a loving, omnipotent God—though he continues to believe nonetheless?

The countermoves employed by both Hare and Mitchell should be appreciated as clever and insightful answers to Flew's challenge. They may, however, suggest still further questions. For example, Hare tells us that it may make an important difference to us which *bliks* we hold to. But how are *bliks* acquired? If they are in no way arguable, does it follow that they are arbitrary or a matter of chance? How does one come to favor one *blik* over another? If, as Hare appears to suggest, the whole edifice of one's life is founded on *bliks*, it is clearly necessary to understand the implications of this concept. As for Mitchell, one might ask whether it is in fact possible (does Mitchell actually say this?) to really hold *x* to be true when the weight of the evidence argues against it, or at least whether it does not at some point become stupid to do so. Or does the concept of *faith* have some relevance here?

R. B. Braithwaite's well-known lecture "An Empiricist's View of the Nature of Religious Belief," regarded by many as one of the most important contributions to the contemporary discussion of religious language, begins, too, with the verificationist criterion of meaningfulness, but moves quickly in a new direction. According to Braithwaite, religious propositions are actually moral propositions inasmuch as they express primarily an intention of living and acting in a certain way. But, then, like moral assertions, they are neither logically necessary nor are they empirical statements. Their meaning lies, rather, in their use as *moral guides*. On the other hand, such statements are tied to certain stories (such as the Christian stories concerning Jesus) which shape and buttress them, though it is not required, says Braithwaite, that the stories correspond to empirical fact in order to serve this purpose. Neither is it required that the stories correspond to empirical *fact* to be empirical. All that is required is that they be "entertained," or thought of as having a meaning, in relation to a policy to live or act in a certain way. As Braithwaite sees it, this understanding resolves the problem of religious language in a way that is agreeable both to the religious man and to the empiricist.

But does Braithwaite underestimate, say, the Jew's or the Christian's *involvement* in (hardly a mere "entertaining" of) the factual, historical ground of his belief? And does he appreciate that if the factual foundation of religious belief is found to be untrue, then religious hope becomes, at least for many, an empty chimera? And, closely related, is Braithwaite's reduction of all the great religions to the common denominator of an exhortation to *agape*— love—perhaps a bit uninformed? Whether or not these are legitimate challenges for Braithwaite, one must constantly be on guard lest he be seduced by attractive solutions which are successful only because the problem has been inadequately posed.

Paul Tillich sees the meaningfulness (but now shifting to an *existential* interpretation of meaningfulness) of religious language as lying in its symbolic character. The meaning of religious statements lies not with questions of verification, falsification, truth, or falsity, but in their ability to represent the existential situation of man and his ultimate concern. (Tillich's preliminary discussion of existentialism as opposed to essentialism is an excellent introductory statement and should illuminate the existentialist writings encountered already, notably those of Sartre, Kierkegaard, and Camus.) The various religious symbols such as Creation, the Fall, and Redemption give profound expression to man's sense of finitude, his estrangement from his true being, and hope of reconciliation. According to Tillich, the true significance of religious language can only be "vitiated" by theological literalism; nor does he have much time for the positivists and analysts who, with their empiricist and linguistic preoccupations, are certain to miss its genuine and existential import.

Thus we find reflected once again fundamentally divergent approaches to philosophical and religious issues, in this case the problem of religious language. How it is that one finds himself viewing these issues from one or the other of these quite different perspectives is a hard question. No doubt it has something to do with *bliks*.

✳ ST. THOMAS AQUINAS

34. *The Way of Analogy*

St. Thomas Aquinas (1225–1274) was a Dominican friar and the most influential thinker of the scholastic period. His most important works, the *Summa Theologica* and the *Summa Contra Gentiles*, were intended to demonstrate that belief in revelation is not incompatible with a philosophical theology that proceeds by the light of natural reason and draws its concepts from the created order. Thomism continues to be the dominating philosophy of the Roman Catholic Church.

From *Summa Contra Gentiles*

BOOK I

Chapter 30: The Names that Can Be Predicated of God

[1] From what we have said we can further consider what it is possible to say or not to say of God, what is said of Him alone, and also what is said of Him and other things together.

[2] Since it is possible to find in God every perfection of creatures, but in another and more eminent way, whatever names unqualifiedly designate a perfection without defect are predicated of God and of other things: for example, goodness, wisdom, being, and the like. But when any name expresses such perfections along with a mode that is proper to a creature, it can be said of God only according to likeness and metaphor. According to metaphor, what belongs to one thing is transferred to another, as when we say that a man is a *stone* because of the hardness of his intellect. Such names are used to designate the species of a created thing, for example, *man* and *stone*; for to each species belongs its own mode of perfection and being. The same is true of whatever names designate the properties of things, which are caused by the proper principles of their species. Hence, they can be said of God only metaphorically. But the names that express such perfections along with the mode of supereminence with which they belong to God are said of God alone. Such names are the *highest good*, the *first being*, and the like.

[3] I have said that some of the aforementioned names signify a perfection without defect. This is true with reference to that which the name was imposed to signify; for as to the mode of signification, every name is defective. For by means of a name we express things in the way in which the intellect conceives them. For our intellect, taking the origin of its knowledge from

the senses, does not transcend the mode which is found in sensible things, in which the form and the subject of the form are not identical owing to the composition of form and matter. Now, a simple form is indeed found among such things, but one that is imperfect because it is not subsisting; on the other hand, though a subsisting subject of a form is found among sensible things, it is not simple but rather concreted. Whatever our intellect signifies as subsisting, therefore, it signifies in concretion; but what it signifies as simple, it signifies, not as *that which is*, but as *that by which something is.* As a result, with reference to the mode of signification there is in every name that we use an imperfection, which does not befit God, even though the thing signified in some eminent way does befit God. This is clear in the name *goodness* and *good.* For *goodness* has signification as something not subsisting, while *good* has signification as something concreted. And so with reference to the mode of signification no name is fittingly applied to God; this is done only with reference to that which the name has been imposed to signify. Such names, therefore, as Dionysius teaches,[1] can be both affirmed and denied of God. They can be affirmed because of the meaning of the name; they can be denied because of the mode of signification.

[4] Now, the mode of supereminence in which the above-mentioned perfections are found in God can be signified by names used by us only through negation, as when we say that God is *eternal* or *infinite*, or also through a relation of God to other things, as when He is called the first *cause* or the *highest good.* For we cannot grasp what God is, but only what He is not and how other things are related to Him, as is clear from what we said above.

Chapter 31: That the Divine Perfection and the Plurality of Divine Names Are Not Opposed to the Divine Simplicity

[1] From what has been said it can likewise be seen that the divine perfection and the plurality of names said of God are not opposed to His simplicity.

[2] We have said that all the perfections found in other things are attributed to God in the same way as effects are found in their equivocal causes. These effects are in their causes virtually, as heat is in the sun. For, unless the power of the sun belonged to some extent to the genus of heat, the sun acting through this power would not generate anything like itself. The sun, then, is said to be hot through this power not only because it produces heat, but also because the power through which it does this has some likeness to heat. But through the same power through which it produces heat, the sun produces also many other effects among sublunary bodies—for example, dryness. And thus heat and dryness, which in fire are diverse qualities, belong to the sun through one and the same power. So, too, the perfections of all things, which belong to the rest of things through diverse forms, must be attributed to God through one and the same power in Him. This power is nothing other than His essence, since, as we have proved, there can be no accident in God. Thus, therefore, God is called *wise* not only in so far as

---

[1][Cf. Pseudo-Dionysius, *On the Divine Names*, I, 5; *On the Celestial Hierarchy*, II, 3.]

He produces wisdom, but also because, in so far as we are wise, we imitate to some extent the power by which He makes us wise. On the other hand, God is not called a *stone*, even though He has made stones, because in the name *stone* there is understood a determinate mode of being according to which a stone is distinguished from God. But the stone imitates God as its cause in being and goodness, and other such characteristics, as do also the rest of creatures.

[3]   A similar situation obtains among the knowing and operative powers of man. For by its single power the intellect knows all the things that the sensitive part of the soul grasps through a diversity of powers—and many other things as well. So, too, the higher an intellect is, the more it can know more things through one likeness, while a lesser intellect manages to know many things only through many likenesses. So, too, a ruling power extends to all those things to which diverse powers under it are ordered. In this way, therefore, through His one simple being God possesses every kind of perfection that all other things come to possess, but in a much more diminished way, through diverse principles.

[4]   From this we see the necessity of giving to God many names. For, since we cannot know Him naturally except by arriving at Him from His effects, the names by which we signify His perfection must be diverse, just as the perfections belonging to things are found to be diverse. Were we able to understand the divine essence itself as it is and give to it the name that belongs to it, we would express it by only one name. This is promised to those who will see God through His essence: "In that day there shall be one Lord, and His name shall be one" [Zech. 14:9].

Chapter 32: That Nothing Is Predicated Univocally of God and Other Things

[1]   It is thereby evident that nothing can be predicated univocally of God and other things.

[2]   An effect that does not receive a form specifically the same as that through which the agent acts cannot receive according to a univocal predication the name arising from that form. Thus, the heat generated by the sun and the sun itself are not called univocally *hot*. Now, the forms of the things God has made do not measure up to a specific likeness of the divine power; for the things that God has made receive in a divided and particular way that which in Him is found in a simple and universal way. It is evident, then, that nothing can be said univocally of God and other things.

[3]   If, furthermore, an effect should measure up to the species of its cause, it will not receive the univocal predication of the name unless it receives the same specific form according to the same mode of being. For the house that is in the art of the maker is not univocally the same house that is in matter, for the form of the house does not have the same being in the two locations. Now, even though the rest of things were to receive a form that

is absolutely the same as it is in God, yet they do not receive it according to the same mode of being. For, as is clear from what we have said, there is nothing in God that is not the divine being itself, which is not the case with other things. Nothing, therefore, can be predicated of God and other things univocally.

[4] Moreover, whatever is predicated of many things univocally is either a genus, a species, a difference, an accident, or a property. But, as we have shown, nothing is predicated of God as a genus or a difference; and thus neither is anything predicated as a definition, nor likewise as a species, which is constituted of genus and difference. Nor, as we have shown, can there be any accident in God, and therefore nothing is predicated of Him either as an accident or a property, since property belongs to the genus of accidents. It remains, then, that nothing is predicated univocally of God and other things.

[5] Again, what is predicated of many things univocally is simpler than both of them, at least in concept. Now, there can be nothing simpler than God either in reality or in concept. Nothing, therefore, is predicated univocally of God and other things.

[6] Everything, likewise, that is predicated univocally of many things belongs through participation to each of the things of which it is predicated; for the species is said to participate in the genus and the individual in the species. But nothing is said of God by participation, since whatever is participated is determined to the mode of that which is participated and is thus possessed in a partial way and not according to every mode of perfection. Nothing, therefore, can be predicated univocally of God and other things.

[7] Then, too, what is predicated of some things according to priority and posteriority is certainly not predicated univocally. For the prior is included in the definition of the posterior, as *substance* is included in the definition of accident according as an accident is a being. If, then, being were said univocally of substance and accident, substance would have to be included in the definition of being in so far as being is predicated of substance. But this is clearly impossible. Now nothing is predicated of God and creatures as though they were in the same order, but, rather, according to priority and posteriority. For all things are predicated of God essentially. For God is called being as being entity itself, and He is called good as being goodness itself. But in other beings predications are made by participation, as Socrates is said to be a man, not because he is humanity itself, but because he possesses humanity. It is impossible, therefore, that anything be predicated univocally of God and other things.

Chapter 33: *That Not All Names Are Said of God and Creatures in a Purely Equivocal Way*

[1] From what we have said it likewise appears that not everything predicated of God and other things is said in a purely equivocal way, in the manner of equivocals by chance.

[2] For in equivocals by chance there is no order or reference of one to another, but it is entirely accidental that one name is applied to diverse things: the application of the name to one of them does not signify that it has an order to the other. But this is not the situation with names said of God and creatures, since we note in the community of such names the order of cause and effect, as is clear from what we have said. It is not, therefore, in the manner of pure equivocation that something is predicated of God and other things.

[3] Furthermore, where there is pure equivocation, there is no likeness in things themselves; there is only the unity of a name. But, as is clear from what we have said, there is a certain mode of likeness of things to God. It remains, then, that names are not said of God in a purely equivocal way.

[4] Moreover, when one name is predicated of several things in a purely equivocal way, we cannot from one of them be led to the knowledge of another; for the knowledge of things does not depend on words, but on the meaning of names. Now, from what we find in other things, we do arrive at a knowledge of divine things, as is evident from what we have said. Such names, then, are not said of God and other things in a purely equivocal way.

[5] Again, equivocation in a name impedes the process of reasoning. If, then, nothing was said of God and creatures except in a purely equivocal way, no reasoning proceeding from creatures to God could take place. But, the contrary is evident from all those who have spoken about God.

[6] It is also a fact that a name is predicated of some being uselessly unless through that name we understand something of the being. But, if names are said of God and creatures in a purely equivocal way, we understand nothing of God through those names; for the meanings of those names are known to us solely to the extent that they are said of creatures. In vain, therefore, would it be said or proved of God that He is a being, good, or the like.

[7] Should it be replied that through such names we know only what God is not, namely, that God is called *living* because He does not belong to the genus of lifeless things, and so with the other names, it will at least have to be the case that *living* said of God and creatures agrees in the denial of the lifeless. Thus, it will not be said in a purely equivocal way.

Chapter 34: That Names Said of God and Creatures Are Said Analogically

[1] From what we have said, therefore, it remains that the names said of God and creatures are predicated neither univocally nor equivocally but analogically, that is, according to an order or reference to something one.

[2] This can take place in two ways. In one way, according as many things have reference to something one. Thus, with reference to one *health* we say that an animal is healthy as the subject of health, medicine is healthy as its cause, food as its preserver, urine as its sign.

[3]   In another way, the analogy can obtain according as the order or reference of two things is not to something else but to one of them. Thus, *being* is said of substance and accident according as an accident has reference to a substance, and not according as substance and accident are referred to a third thing.

[4]   Now, the names said of God and things are not said analogically according to the first mode of analogy, since we should then have to posit something prior to God, but according to the second mode.

[5]   In this second mode of analogical predication the order according to the name and according to reality is sometimes found to be the same and sometimes not. For the order of the name follows the order of knowledge, because it is the sign of an intelligible conception. When, therefore, that which is prior in reality is found likewise to be prior in knowledge, the same thing is found to be prior both according to the meaning of the name and according to the nature of the thing. Thus, substance is prior to accident both in nature, in so far as substance is the cause of accident, and in knowledge, in so far as substance is included in the definition of accident. Hence, *being* is said of substance by priority over accident both according to the nature of the thing and according to the meaning of the name. But when that which is prior in nature is subsequent in our knowledge, then there is not the same order in analogicals according to reality and according to the meaning of the name. Thus, the power to heal, which is found in all health-giving things, is by nature prior to the health that is in the animal, as a cause is prior to an effect; but because we know this healing power through an effect, we likewise name it from its effect. Hence it is that the *health-giving* is prior in reality, but animal is by priority called *healthy* according to the meaning of the name.

[6]   Thus, therefore, because we come to a knowledge of God from other things, the reality in the names said of God and other things belongs by priority in God according to His mode of being, but the meaning of the name belongs to God by posteriority. And so He is said to be named from His effects.

✳ A.J. AYER

35. *Theology as Meaningless*

Alfred Jules Ayer was born in 1910, educated at Oxford, and taught at the University of London before returning to Oxford in 1959 as Professor of Logic. Ayer's *Language, Truth and Logic*, first published in 1936, gave far-reaching expression to the philosophy known as Logical Positivism, a philosophy that repudiates all metaphysical (and therefore theological) speculation as empirically non-verifiable and therefore meaningless.

From *Language, Truth and Logic*

CHAPTER 1: THE ELIMINATION OF METAPHYSICS

The traditional disputes of philosophers are, for the most part, as unwarranted as they are unfruitful. The surest way to end them is to establish beyond question what should be the purpose and method of a philosophical enquiry. And this is by no means so difficult a task as the history of philosophy would lead one to suppose. For if there are any questions which science leaves it to philosophy to answer, a straightforward process of elimination must lead to their discovery.

We may begin by criticising the metaphysical thesis that philosophy affords us knowledge of a reality transcending the world of science and common sense. Later on, when we come to define metaphysics and account for its existence, we shall find that it is possible to be a metaphysician without believing in a transcendent reality; for we shall see that many metaphysical utterances are due to the commission of logical errors, rather than to a conscious desire on the part of their authors to go beyond the limits of experience. But it is convenient for us to take the case of those who believe that it is possible to have knowledge of a transcendent reality as a starting-point for our discussion. The arguments which we use to refute them will subsequently be found to apply to the whole of metaphysics.

One way of attacking a metaphysician who claimed to have knowledge of a reality which transcended the phenomenal world would be to enquire from what premises his propositions were deduced. Must he not begin, as other men do, with the evidence of his senses? And if so, what valid process of reasoning can possibly lead him to the conception of a transcendent reality? Surely from empirical premises nothing whatsoever concerning the properties, or even the existence, of anything super-empirical can legitimately be inferred. But this objection would be met by a denial on the part of the metaphysician

Alfred Jules Ayer, *Language, Truth and Logic*, second ed. (London: Gollancz, 1946). Reprinted by permission of Dover Publications, Inc., New York. Also reprinted by permission of Victor Gollancz, Ltd.

that his assertions were ultimately based on the evidence of his senses. He would say that he was endowed with a faculty of intellectual intuition which enabled him to know facts that could not be known through sense-experience. And even if it could be shown that he was relying on empirical premises, and that his venture into a non-empirical world was therefore logically unjustified, it would not follow that the assertions which he made concerning this non-empirical world could not be true. For the fact that a conclusion does not follow from its putative premise is not sufficient to show that it is false. Consequently one cannot overthrow a system of transcendent metaphysics merely by criticising the way in which it comes into being. What is required is rather a criticism of the nature of the actual statements which comprise it. And this is the line of argument which we shall, in fact, pursue. For we shall maintain that no statement which refers to a "reality" transcending the limits of all possible sense-experience can possibly have any literal significance; from which it must follow that the labours of those who have striven to describe such a reality have all been devoted to the production of nonsense.

It may be suggested that this is a proposition which has already been proved by Kant. But although Kant also condemned transcendent metaphysics, he did so on different grounds. For he said that the human understanding was so constituted that it lost itself in contradictions when it ventured out beyond the limits of possible experience and attempted to deal with things in themselves. And thus he made the impossibility of a transcendent metaphysic not, as we do, a matter of logic, but a matter of fact. He asserted, not that our minds could not conceivably have had the power of penetrating beyond the phenomenal world, but merely that they were in fact devoid of it. And this leads the critic to ask how, if it is possible to know only what lies within the bounds of sense-experience, the author can be justified in asserting that real things do exist beyond, and how he can tell what are the boundaries beyond which the human understanding may not venture, unless he succeeds in passing them himself. As Wittgenstein says, "in order to draw a limit to thinking, we should have to think both sides of this limit,"[1] a truth to which Bradley gives a special twist in maintaining that the man who is ready to prove that metaphysics is impossible is a brother metaphysician with a rival theory of his own.[2]

Whatever force these objections may have against the Kantian doctrine, they have none whatsoever against the thesis that I am about to set forth. It cannot here be said that the author is himself overstepping the barrier he maintains to be impassable. For the fruitlessness of attempting to transcend the limits of possible sense-experience will be deduced, not from a psychological hypothesis concerning the actual constitution of the human mind, but from the rule which determines the literal significance of language. Our charge against the metaphysician is not that he attempts to employ the understanding in a field where it cannot profitably venture, but that he produces sentences which fail to conform to the conditions under which alone a sentence can

[1] *Tractatus Logico-Philosophicus*, Preface.
[2] Bradley, *Appearance and Reality*, 2nd ed., p. 1.

be literally significant. Nor are we ourselves obliged to talk nonsense in order to show that all sentences of a certain type are necessarily devoid of literal significance. We need only formulate the criterion which enables us to test whether a sentence expresses a genuine proposition about a matter of fact, and then point out that the sentences under consideration fail to satisfy it. And this we shall now proceed to do. We shall first of all formulate the criterion in somewhat vague terms, and then give the explanations which are necessary to render it precise.

The criterion which we use to test the genuineness of apparent statements of fact is the criterion of verifiability. We say that a sentence is factually significant to any given person, if, and only if, he knows how to verify the proposition which it purports to express—that is, if he knows what observations would lead him, under certain conditions, to accept the proposition as being true, or reject it as being false. If, on the other hand, the putative proposition is of such a character that the assumption of its truth, or falsehood, is consistent with any assumption whatsoever concerning the nature of his future experience, then, as far as he is concerned, it is, if not a tautology, a mere pseudo-proposition. The sentence expressing it may be emotionally significant to him; but it is not literally significant. And with regard to questions the procedure is the same. We enquire in every case what observations would lead us to answer the question, one way or the other; and, if none can be discovered, we must conclude that the sentence under consideration does not, as far as we are concerned, express a genuine question, however strongly its grammatical appearance may suggest that it does. . . .

Chapter 6: Critique of Ethics and Theology

. . . This mention of God brings us to the question of the possibility of religious knowledge. We shall see that this possibility has already been ruled out by our treatment of metaphysics. But, as this is a point of considerable interest, we may be permitted to discuss it at some length.

It is now generally admitted, at any rate by philosophers, that the existence of a being having the attributes which define the god of any non-animistic religion cannot be demonstratively proved. To see that this is so, we have only to ask ourselves what are the premises from which the existence of such a god could be deduced. If the conclusion that a god exists is to be demonstratively certain, then these premises must be certain; for, as the conclusion of a deductive argument is already contained in the premises, any uncertainty there may be about the truth of the premises is necessarily shared by it. But we know that no empirical proposition can ever be anything more than probable. It is only *a priori* propositions that are logicall certain. But we cannot deduce the existence of a god from an *a priori* proposition. For we know that the reason why *a priori* propositions are certain is that they are tautologies. And from a set of tautologies nothing but a further tautology can be validly deduced. It follows that there is no possibility of demonstrating the existence of a god.

What is not so generally recognized is that there can be no way of proving that the existence of a god, such as the God of Christianity, is even probable. Yet this also is easily shown. For if the existence of such a god were probable, then the proposition that he existed would be an empirical hypothesis. And in that case it would be possible to deduce from it, and other empirical hypotheses, certain experiential propositions which were not deducible from those other hypotheses alone. But in fact this is not possible. It is sometimes claimed, indeed, that the existence of a certain sort of regularity in nature constitutes sufficient evidence for the existence of a god. But if the sentence "God exists" entails no more than that certain types of phenomena occur in certain sequences, then to assert the existence of a god will be simply equivalent to asserting that there is the requisite regularity in nature; and no religious man would admit that this was all he intended to assert in asserting the existence of a god. He would say that in talking about God, he was talking about a transcendent being who might be known through certain empirical manifestations, but certainly could not be defined in terms of those manifestations. But in that case the term "god" is a metaphysical term. And if "god" is a metaphysical term, then it cannot be even probable that a god exists. For to say that "God exists" is to make a metaphysical utterance which cannot be either true or false. And by the same criterion, no sentence which purports to describe the nature of a transcendent god can possess any literal significance.

It is important not to confuse this view of religious assertions with the view that is adopted by atheists, or agnostics.[3] For it is characteristic of an agnostic to hold that the existence of a god is a possibility in which there is no good reason either to believe or disbelieve; and it is characteristic of an atheist to hold that it is at least probable that no god exists. And our view that all utterances about the nature of God are nonsensical, so far from being identical with, or even lending any support to, either of these familiar contentions, is actually incompatible with them. For if the assertion that there is a god is nonsensical, then the atheist's assertion that there is no god is equally nonsensical, since it is only a significant proposition that can be significantly contradicted. As for the agnostic, although he refrains from saying either that there is or that there is not a god, he does not deny that the question whether a transcendent god exists is a genuine question. He does not deny that the two sentences "There is a transcendent god" and "There is no transcendent god" express propositions one of which is actually true and the other false. All he says is that we have no means of telling which of them is true, and therefore ought not to commit ourselves to either. But we have seen that the sentences in question do not express propositions at all. And this means that agnosticism also is ruled out.

Thus we offer the theist the same confort as we gave to the moralist. His assertions cannot possibly be valid, but they cannot be invalid either. As he says nothing at all about the world, he cannot justly be accused of saying anything false, or anything for which he has insufficient grounds. It

---

[3]This point was suggested to me by Professor H. H. Price.

is only when the theist claims that in asserting the existence of a transcendent god he is expressing a genuine proposition that we are entitled to disagree with him.

It is to be remarked that in cases where deities are identified with natural objects, assertions concerning them may be allowed to be significant. If, for example, a man tells me that the occurrence of thunder is alone both necessary and sufficient to establish the truth of the proposition that Jehovah is angry, I may conclude that, in his usage of words, the sentence "Jehovah is angry" is equivalent to "It is thundering." But in sophisticated religions, though they may be to some extent based on men's awe of natural process which they cannot sufficiently understand, the "person" who is supposed to control the empirical world is not himself located in it; he is held to be superior to the empirical world, and so outside it; and he is endowed with super-empirical attributes. But the notion of a person whose essential attributes are non-empirical is not an intelligible notion at all. We may have a word which is used as if it named this "person," but, unless the sentences in which it occurs express propositions which are empirically verifiable, it cannot be said to symbolize anything. And this is the case with regard to the word "god," in the usage in which it is intended to refer to a transcendent object. The mere existence of the noun is enough to foster the illusion that there is a real, or at any rate a possible entity corresponding to it. It is only when we enquire what God's attributes are that we discover that "God," in this usage, is not a genuine name.

It is common to find belief in a transcendent god conjoined with belief in an after-life. But, in the form which it usually takes, the content of this belief is not a genuine hypothesis. To say that men do not ever die, or that the state of death is merely a state of prolonged insensibility, is indeed to express a significant proposition, though all the available evidence goes to show that it is false. But to say that there is something imperceptible inside a man, which is his soul or his real self, and that it goes on living after he is dead, is to make a metaphysical assertion which has no more factual content than the assertion that there is a transcendent god.

It is worth mentioning that, according to the account which we have given of religious assertions, there is no logical ground for antagonism between religion and natural science. As far as the question of truth or falsehood is concerned, there is no opposition between the natural scientist and the theist who believes in a transcendent god. For since the religious utterances of the theist are not genuine propositions at all, they cannot stand in any logical relation to the propositions of science. Such antagonism as there is between religion and science appears to consist in the fact that science takes away one of the motives which make men religious. For it is acknowledged that one of the ultimate sources of religious feeling lies in the inability of men to determine their own destiny; and science tends to destroy the feeling of awe with which men regard an alien world, by making them believe that they can understand and anticipate the course of natural phenomena, and even to some extent control it. The fact that it has recently become fashionable for physicists themselves to be sympathetic towards religion is a point in favour of this hypothesis. For this sympathy towards religion marks the physicists' own lack of confidence in the validity of their hypotheses, which is a reaction on their part from the anti-religious dogmatism of nine-teenth-century scientists, and a natural outcome of the crisis through which physics has just passed.

It is not within the scope of this enquiry to enter more deeply into the causes of religious feeling, or to discuss the probability of the continuance of religious belief. We are concerned only to answer those questions which arise out of our discussion of the possibility of religious knowledge. The point which we wish to establish is that there cannot be any transcendent truths of religion. For the sentences which the theist uses to express such "truths" are not literally significant.

An interesting feature of this conclusion is that it accords with what many theists are accustomed to say themselves. For we are often told that the nature of God is a mystery which transcends the human understanding. But to say that something transcends the human understanding is to say that it is unintelligible. And what is unintelligible cannot significantly be described. Again, we are told that God is not an object of reason but an object of faith. This may be nothing more than an admission that the existence of God must be taken on trust, since it cannot be proved. But it may also be an assertion that God is the object of a purely mystical intuition, and cannot therefore be defined in terms which are intelligible to the reason. And I think there are many theists who would assert this. But if one allows that it is impossible to define God in intelligible terms, then one is allowing that it is impossible for a sentence both to be significant and to be about God. If a mystic admits that the object of his vision is something which cannot be described, then he must also admit that he is bound to talk nonsense when he describes it.

For his part, the mystic may protest that his intuition does reveal truths to him, even though he cannot explain to others what these truths are; and that we who do not possess this faculty of intuition can have no ground for denying that it is a cognitive faculty. For we can hardly maintain *a priori* that there are no ways of discovering true propositions except those which we ourselves employ. The answer is that we set no limit to the number of ways in which one may come to formulate a true proposition. We do not in any way deny that a synthetic truth may be discovered by purely intuitive methods as well as by the rational method of induction. But we do say that every synthetic proposition, however it may have been arrived at, must be subject to the test of actual experience. We do not deny *a priori* that the mystic is able to discover truths by his own special methods. We wait to hear what are the propositions which embody his discoveries, in order to see whether they are verified or confuted by our empirical observations. But the mystic, so far from producing propositions which are empirically verified, is unable to produce any intelligible propositions at all. And therefore we say that his intuition has not revealed to him any facts. It is no use his saying that he has apprehended facts but is unable to express them. For we know that if he really had acquired any information, he would be able to express it. He would be able to indicate in some way or other how the genuineness of his discovery might be empirically determined. The fact that he cannot reveal what he "knows," or even himself devise an empirical test to validate his "knowledge," shows that his state of mystical intuition is not a genuinely cognitive state. So that in describing his vision the mystic does not give us any information about the external world; he merely gives us indirect information about the condition of his own mind.

These considerations dispose of the argument from religious experience, which many philosophers still regard as a valid argument in favour of the existence of a god. They say that it is logically possible for men to be immediately acquainted with God, as they are immediately acquainted with a sense-content, and that there is no reason why one should be prepared to believe a man when he says that he is seeing a yellow patch, and refuse to believe him when he says that he is seeing God. The answer to this is that if the man who asserts that he is seeing God is merely asserting that he is experiencing a peculiar kind of sense-content, then we do not for a moment deny that his assertion may be true. But, ordinarily, the man who says that he is seeing God is saying not merely that he is experiencing a religious emotion, but also that there exists a transcendent being who is the object of this emotion; just as the man who says that he sees a yellow patch is ordinarily saying not merely that his visual sense-field contains a yellow sense-content, but also that there exists a yellow object to which the sense-content belongs. And it is not irrational to be prepared to believe a man when he asserts the existence of a yellow object, and to refuse to believe him when he asserts the existence of a transcendent god. For whereas the sentence "There exists here a yellow-coloured material thing" expresses a genuine synthetic proposition which could be empirically verified, the sentence "There exists a transcendent god" has, as we have seen, no literal significance.

We conclude, therefore, that the argument from religious experience is altogether fallacious. The fact that people have religious experiences is interesting from the psychological point of view, but it does not in any way imply that there is such a thing as religious knowledge, any more than our having moral experiences implies that there is such a thing as moral knowledge. The theist, like the moralist, may believe that his experiences are cognitive experiences, but, unless he can formulate his "knowledge" in propositions that are empirically verifiable, we may be sure that he is deceiving himself. It follows that those philsoophers who fill their books with assertions that they intuitively "know" this or that moral or religious "truth" are merely providing material for the psycho-analyst. For no act of intuition can be said to reveal a truth about any matter of fact unless it issues in verifiable propositions. And all such propositions are to be incorporated in the system of empirical propositions which constitutes science.

✳ ANTONY FLEW, R. M. HARE, and BASIL MITCHELL

36. *Three Parables on Falsification*

Antony Flew (author of *Hume's Philosophy of Belief*), R. M. Hare (author of *The Language of Morals*), and Basil Mitchell (editor of *Faith and Logic*) are three representatives of post-war British analytic philosophy. Their symposium, "Theology and Falsification," is an influential treatment of religious language, marking a stage in the continuing verification-falsification debate.

From "Theology and Falsification"

ANTONY FLEW:

Let us begin with a parable. It is a parable developed from a tale told by John Wisdom in his haunting and revelatory article 'Gods.'[1] Once upon a time two explorers came upon a clearing in the jungle. In the clearing were growing many flowers and many weeds. One explorer says, 'Some gardener must tend this plot.' The other disagrees, 'There is no gardener.' So they pitch their tents and set a watch. No gardener is ever seen. 'But perhaps he is an invisible gardener.' So they set up a barbed-wire fence. They electrify it. They patrol with bloodhounds. (For they remember how H. G. Wells's *The Invisible Man* could be both smelt and touched though he could not be seen.) But no shrieks ever suggest that some intruder has received a shock. No movements of the wire ever betray an invisible climber. The bloodhounds never give cry. Yet still the Believer is not convinced. 'But there is a gardener, invisible, intangible, insensible to electric shocks, a gardener who has no scent and makes no sound, a gardener who comes secretly to look after the garden which he loves.' At last the Sceptic despairs, 'But what remains of your original assertion? Just how does what you call an invisible, intangible, eternally elusive gardener differ from an imaginary gardener or even from no gardener at all?'

In this parable we can see how what starts as an assertion, that something exists or that there is some analogy between certain complexes of phenomena, may be reduced step by step to an altogether different status, to an expression perhaps of a 'picture preference.'[2] The Sceptic says there is no gardener. The Believer says there is a gardener (but invisible, etc.). One

Antony Flew, et al., "Theology and Falsification," in *New Essays in Philosophical Theology*, ed. Antony Flew and Alasdair MacIntyre (London: SCM Press, 1955). Reprinted by permission of The Macmillan Company. Also reprinted by permission of SCM Press, Ltd., publishers. First published in 1953.

[1]*Proceedings of the Aristotelian Society*, 1944–5, reprinted as Ch. X of *Logic and Language*, Vol. I (Blackwell, 1951), and in his *Philosophy and Psychoanalysis* (Blackwell, 1953).

[2]Cf. J. Wisdom, 'Other Minds,' *Mind*, 1940; reprinted in his *Other Minds* (Blackwell, 1952).

man talks about sexual behaviour. Another man prefers to talk of Aphrodite (but knows that there is not really a superhuman person additional to, and somehow responsible for, all sexual phenomena).[3] The process of qualification may be checked at any point before the original assertion is completely withdrawn and something of that first assertion will remain (Tautology). Mr. Wells's invisible man could not, admittedly, be seen, but in all other respects he was a man like the rest of us. But though the process of qualification may be, and of course usually is, checked in time, it is not always judiciously so halted. Someone may dissipate his assertion completely without noticing that he has done so. A fine brash hypothesis may thus be killed by inches, the death by a thousand qualifications.

And in this, it seems to me, lies the peculiar danger, the endemic evil, of theological utterance. Take such utterances as 'God has a plan,' 'God created the world,' 'God loves us as a father loves his children.' They look at first sight very much like assertions, vast cosmological assertions. Of course, this is no sure sign that they either are, or are intended to be, assertions. But let us confine ourselves to the cases where those who utter such sentences intend them to express assertions. (Merely remarking parenthetically that those who intend or interpret such utterances as crypto-commands, expressions of wishes, disguised ejaculations, concealed ethics, or as anything else but assertions, are unlikely to succeed in making them either properly orthodox or practically effective).

Now to assert that such and such is the case is necessarily equivalent to denying that such and such is not the case.[4] Suppose then that we are in doubt as to what someone who gives vent to an utterance is asserting, or suppose that, more radically, we are sceptical as to whether he is really asserting anything at all, one way of trying to understand (or perhaps it will be to expose) his utterance is to attempt to find what he would regard as counting against, or as being incompatible with, its truth. For if the utterance is indeed an assertion, it will necessarily be equivalent to a denial of the negation of that assertion. And anything which would count against the assertion, or which would induce the speaker to withdraw it and to admit that it had been mistaken, must be part of (or the whole of) the meaning of the negation of that assertion. And to know the meaning of the negation of an assertion, is as near as makes no matter, to know the meaning of that assertion.[5]

[3]Cf. Lucretius, *De Rerum Natura*, II, 655–60,
Hic siquis mare Neptunum Ceremque vocare
Constituet fruges et Bacchi nomine abuti
Mavolat quam laticis proprium proferre vocamen
Concedamus ut hic terrarum dictitet orbem
Esse deum matrem dum verra re tamen ipse
Religione animum turpi contingere parcat.
["If, here, someone determines to call the sea Neptune and to call grain Ceres and prefers to use the name of Bacchus rather than to speak the proper name of wine, let us concede that this one would say that the world is the Mother of the gods just as long as in truth he forbears to taint his mind with foul superstition."]
[4]For those who prefer symbolism: $p \equiv \sim \sim p$.
[5]For by simply negating $\sim p$ we get $p:\sim \sim p \equiv p$.

And if there is nothing which a putative assertion denies then there is nothing which it asserts either: and so it is not really an assertion. When the Sceptic in the parable asked the Believer, 'Just how does what you call an invisible, intangible, eternally elusive gardener differ from an imaginary gardener or even from no gardener at all?' he was suggesting that the Believer's earlier statement had been so eroded by qualification that it was no longer an assertion at all.

Now it often seems to people who are not religious as if there was no conceivable event or series of events the occurrence of which would be admitted by sophisticated religious people to be a sufficient reason for conceding 'There wasn't a God after all' or 'God does not really love us then.' Someone tells us that God loves us as a father loves his children. We are assured. But then we see a child dying of inoperable cancer of the throat. His earthly father is driven frantic in his efforts to help, but his Heavenly Father reveals no obvious sign of concern. Some qualification is made—God's love is 'not a merely human love' or it is 'an inscrutable love,' perhaps—and we realize that such sufferings are quite compatible with the truth of the assertion that 'God loves us as a father (but, of course, . . .).' We are reassured again. But then perhaps we ask: what is this assurance of God's (appropriately qualified) love worth, what is this apparent guarantee really a guarantee against? Just what would have to happen not merely (morally and wrongly) to tempt but also (logically and rightly) to entitle us to say 'God does not love us' or even 'God does not exist'? I therefore put to the succeeding symposiasts the simple central questions, 'What would have to occur or to have occurred to constitute for you a disproof of the love of, or of the existence of, God?'

R. M. HARE:

I wish to make it clear that I shall not try to defend Christianity in particular, but religion in general—not because I do not believe in Christianity, but because you cannot understand what Christianity is, until you have understood what religion is.

I must begin by confessing that, on the ground marked out by Flew, he seems to me to be completely victorious. I therefore shift my ground by relating another parable. A certain lunatic is convinced that all dons want to murder him. His friends introduce him to all the mildest and most respectable dons that they can find, and after each of them has retired, they say, 'You see, he doesn't really want to murder you; he spoke to you in a most cordial manner; surely you are convinced now?' But the lunatic replies 'Yes, but that was only his diabolical cunning; he's really plotting against me the whole time, like the rest of them; I know it I tell you.' However many kindly dons are produced, the reaction is still the same.

Now we say that such a person is deluded. But what is he deluded about? About the truth or falsity of an assertion? Let us apply Flew's test to him. There is no behaviour of dons that can be enacted which he will accept as counting against his theory; and therefore his theory, on this test, asserts nothing. But it does not follow that there is no difference between what he thinks about dons and what most of us think about them—otherwise we should not call him a lunatic and ourselves sane, and dons would have no reason to feel uneasy about his presence in Oxford.

Let us call that in which we differ from this lunatic, our respective *bliks*. He has an insane *blik* about dons; we have a sane one. It is important to realize that we have a sane one, not no *blik* at all; for there must be two sides to any argument—if he has a wrong *blik*, then those who are right about dons must have a right one. Flew has shown that a *blik* does not consist in an assertion or system of them; but nevertheless it is very important to have the right *blik*.

Let us try to imagine what it would be like to have different *bliks* about other things than dons. When I am driving my car, it sometimes occurs to me to wonder whether my movements of the steering-wheel will always continue to be followed by corresponding alterations in the direction of the car. I have never had a steering failure, though I have had skids, which must be similar. Moreover, I know enough about how the steering of my car is made, to know the sort of thing that would have to go wrong for the steering to fail—steel joints would have to part, or steel rods break, or something—but how do I know that this won't happen? The truth is, I don't know; I just have a *blik* about steel and its properties, so that normally I trust the steering of my car; but I find it not at all difficult to imagine what it would be like to lose this *blik* and acquire the opposite one. People would say I was silly about steel; but there would be no mistaking the reality of the difference between our respective *bliks*—for example, I should never go in a motor-car. Yet I should hesitate to say that the difference between us was the difference between contradictory assertions. No amount of safe arrivals or bench-tests will remove my *blik* and restore the normal one; for my *blik* is compatible with any finite number of such tests.

It was Hume who taught us that our whole commerce with the world depends upon our *blik* about the world; and that difference between *bliks* about the world cannot be settled by observation of what happens in the world. That was why, having performed the interesting experiment of doubting the ordinary man's *blik* about the world, and showing that no proof could be given to make us adopt one *blik* rather than another, he turned to backgammon to take his mind off the problem. It seems, indeed, to be impossible even to formulate as an assertion the normal *blik* about the world which makes me put my confidence in the future reliability of steel joints, in the continued ability of the road to support my car, and not gape beneath it revealing nothing below; in the general non-homicidal tendencies of dons; in my own continued well-being (in some sense of that word that I may not now fully understand) if I continue to do what is right according to my lights; in the general likelihood of people like Hitler coming to a bad end. But perhaps a formulation less adequate than most is to be found in the Psalms [75:3]: 'The earth is weak and all the inhabiters thereof: I bear up the pillars of it.'

The mistake of the position which Flew selects for attack is to regard this kind of talk as some sort of *explanation*, as scientists are accustomed to use the word. As such, it would obviously be ludicrous. We no longer believe in God as an Atlas—*nous n'avons pas besoin de cette hypothèse.*[6] But it is nevertheless true to say that, as Hume saw, without a *blik* there can be no explanation; for it is by our *bliks* that we decide what is and what is not an explanation. Suppose we believed that everything that happened, happened by pure chance. This would not of course be an assertion; for it is compatible with anything happening or not happening, and so, incidentally, is its contradictory. But if we had this belief, we should not be able to explain or predict or plan anything. Thus, although we should not be *asserting* anything different from those of a more normal belief, there would be a great difference between us; and this is the sort of difference that there is between those who really believe in God and those who really disbelieve in him.

The word 'really' is important, and may excite suspicion. I put it in, because when people have had a good Christian upbringing, as have most of those who now profess not to believe in any sort of religion, it is very hard to discover what they really believe. The reason why they find it so easy to think that they are not religious, is that they have never got into the frame of mind of one who suffers from the doubts to which religion is the answer. Not for them the terrors of the primitive jungle. Having abandoned some of the more picturesque fringes of religion, they think that they have abandoned the whole thing—whereas in fact they still have got, and could not live without, a religion of a comfortably substantial, albeit highly sophisticated, kind, which differs from that of many 'religious people' in little more than this, that 'religious people' like to sing Psalms about theirs—a very natural and proper thing to do. But nevertheless there may be a big difference lying behind—the difference between two people who, though side by side, are walking in different directions. I do not know in what direction Flew is walking; perhaps he does not know either. But we have had some examples recently of various ways in which one can walk away from Christianity, and there are any number of possibilities. After all, man has not changed biologically since primitive times; it is his religion that has changed, and it can easily change again. And if you do not think that such changes make a difference, get acquainted with some Sikhs and some Mussulmans of the same Punjabi stock; you will find them quite different sorts of people.

There is an important difference between Flew's parable and my own which we have not yet noticed. The explorers do not *mind* about their garden; they discuss it with interest, but not with concern. But my lunatic, poor fellow, minds about dons; and I mind about the steering of my car; it often has people in it that I care for. It is because I mind very much about what goes on in the garden in which I find myself, that I am unable to share the explorers' detachment.

[6]["we have no need of that hypothesis"—Laplace's reply to Napoleon's question about God.]

Basil Mitchell:

Flew's article is searching and perceptive, but there is, I think, something odd about his conduct of the theologian's case. The theologian surely would not deny that the fact of pain counts against the assertion that God loves men. This very incompatibility generates the most intractable of theological problems—the problem of evil. So the theologian *does* recognize the fact of pain as counting against Christian doctrine. But it is true that he will not allow it—or anything—to count decisively against it; for he is committed by his faith to trust in God. His attitude is not that of the detached observer, but of the believer.

Perhaps this can be brought out by yet another parable. In time of war in an occupied country, a member of the resistance meets one night a stranger who deeply impresses him. They spend that night together in conversation. The Stranger tells the partisan that he himself is on the side of the resistance—indeed that he is in command of it, and urges the partisan to have faith in him no matter what happens. The partisan is utterly convinced at that meeting of the Stranger's sincerity and constancy and undertakes to trust him.

They never meet in conditions of intimacy again. But sometimes the Stranger is seen helping members of the resistance, and the partisan is grateful and says to his friends, 'He is on our side.'

Sometimes he is seen in the uniform of the police handing over patriots to the occupying power. On these occasions his friends murmur against him: but the partisan still says, 'He is on our side.' He still believes that, in spite of appearances, the Stranger did not deceive him. Sometimes he asks the Stranger for help and receives it. He is then thankful. Sometimes he asks and does not receive it. Then he says, 'The Stranger knows best.' Sometimes his friends, in exasperation, say 'Well, what *would* he have to do for you to admit that you were wrong and that he is not on our side?' But the partisan refuses to answer. He will not consent to put the Stranger to the test. And sometimes his friends complain, 'Well, if *that's* what you mean by his being on our side, the sooner he goes over to the other side the better.'

The partisan of the parable does not allow anything to count decisively against the proposition 'The Stranger is on our side.' This is because he has committed himself to trust the Stranger. But he of course recognizes that the Stranger's ambiguous behaviour *does* count against what he believes about him. It is precisely this situation which constitutes the trial of his faith.

When the partisan asks for help and doesn't get it, what can he do? He can (*a*) conclude that the stranger is not on our side or; (*b*) maintain that he is on our side, but that he has reasons for withholding help.

The first he will refuse to do. How long can he uphold the second position without its becoming just silly?

I don't think one can say in advance. It will depend on the nature of the impression created by the Stranger in the first place. It will depend, too, on the manner in which he takes the Stranger's behaviour. If he blandly dismisses it as of no consequence, as having no bearing upon his belief, it will be assumed that he is thoughtless or insane. And it quite obviously won't do for him to say easily, 'Oh, when used of the Stranger the phrase "is on our side" *means* ambiguous behavior of this sort.' In that case he would be like the religious man who says blandly of a terrible disaster 'It is God's will.' No, he will only be regarded as sane and reasonable in his belief, if he experiences in himself the full force of the conflict.

It is here that my parable differs from Hare's. The partisan admits that many things may and do count against his belief: whereas Hare's lunatic who has a *blik* about dons doesn't admit that anything counts against his *blik*. Nothing *can* count against *bliks*. Also the partisan has a reason for having in the first instance committed himself, *viz.* the character of the Stranger; whereas the lunatic has no reason for his *blik* about dons—because, of course, you can't have reasons for *bliks*.

This means that I agree with Flew that theological utterances must be assertions. The partisan is making an assertion when he says, 'The Stranger is on our side.'

Do I want to say that the partisan's belief about the Stranger is, in any sense, an explanation? I think I do. It explains and makes sense of the Stranger's behaviour: it helps to explain also the resistance movement in the context of which he appears. In each case it differs from the interpretation which the others put upon the same facts.

'God loves men' resembles 'the Stranger is on our side' (and many other significant statements, e.g. historical ones) in not being conclusively falsifiable. They can both be treated in at least three different ways: (1) As provisional hypotheses to be discarded if experience tells against them; (2) As significant articles of faith; (3) As vacuous formulae (expressing, perhaps, a desire for reassurance) to which experience makes no difference and which make no difference to life.

The Christian, once he has committed himself, is precluded by his faith from taking up the first attitude: 'Thou shalt not tempt the Lord thy God.' He is in constant danger, as Flew has observed, of slipping into the third. But he need not; and, if he does, it is a failure in faith as well as in logic.

ANTONY FLEW:

It has been a good discussion: and I am glad to have helped to provoke it. But now—at least in *University*—it must come to an end: and the Editors of *University* have asked me to make some concluding remarks. Since it is impossible to deal with all the issues raised or to comment separately upon each contribution, I will concentrate on Mitchell and Hare, as representative of two very different kinds of response to the challenge made in 'Theology and Falsification.'

The challenge, it will be remembered, ran like this. Some theological

utterances seem to, and are intended to, provide explanations or express assertions. Now an assertion, to be an assertion at all, must claim that things
stand thus and thus; *and not otherwise.* Similarly an explanation, to be an explanation at all, must explain why this particular thing occurs; *and not something
else.* Those last clauses are crucial. And yet sophisticated religious people—or
so it seemed to me—are apt to overlook this, and tend to refuse to allow,
not merely that anything actually does occur, but that anything conceivably
could occur, which would count against their theological assertions and explanations. But in so far as they do this their supposed explanations are actually
bogus, and their seeming assertions are really vacuous.

Mitchell's response to this challenge is admirably direct, straightforward, and understanding. He agrees 'that theological utterances must be assertions.' He agrees that if they are to be assertions, there must be something
that would count against their truth. He agrees, too, that believers are in
constant danger of transforming their would-be assertions into 'vacuous formulae.' But he takes me to task for an oddity in my 'conduct of the theologian's
case. The theologian surely would not deny that the fact of pain counts
against the assertion that God loves men. This very incompatibility generates
the most intractable of theological problems, the problem of evil.' I think
he is right. I should have made a distinction between two very different ways
of dealing with what looks like evidence against the love of God: the way
I stressed was the expedient of qualifying the original assertion; the way the
theologian usually takes, at first, is to admit that it looks bad but to insist
that there is—there must be—some explanation which will show that, in spite
of appearances, there really is a God who loves us. His difficulty, it seems
to me, is that he has given God attributes which rule out all possible saving
explanations. In Mitchell's parable of the Stranger it is easy for the believer
to find plausible excuses for ambiguous behaviour: for the Stranger is a man.
But suppose the Stranger is God. We cannot say that he would like to help
but cannot: God is omnipotent. We cannot say that he would help if he
only knew: God is omniscient. We cannot say that he is not responsible for
the wickedness of others: God creates those others. Indeed an omnipotent,
omniscient God must be an accessory before (and during) the fact to every
human misdeed; as well as being responsible for every non-moral defect in
the universe. So, though I entirely concede that Mitchell was absolutely right
to insist against me that the theologian's first move is to look for an *explanation*,
I still think that in the end, if relentlessly pursued, he will have to resort
to the avoiding action of *qualification.* And there lies the danger of that death
by a thousand qualifications, which would, I agree, constitute 'a failure in
faith as well as in logic.'

Hare's approach is fresh and bold. He confesses that 'on the ground
marked out by Flew, he seems to me to be completely victorious.' He therefore
introduces the concept of *blik.* But while I think that there is room for some
such concept in philosophy, and that philosophers should be grateful to Hare
for his invention, I nevertheless want to insist that any attempt to analyse
Christian religious utterances as expressions or affirmations of a *blik* rather

than as (at least would-be) assertions about the cosmos is fundamentally misguided. *First*, because thus interpreted they would be entirely unorthodox. If Hare's religion really is a *blik*, involving no cosmological assertions about the nature and activities of a supposed personal creator, then surely he is not a Christian at all? *Second*, because thus interpreted, they could scarcely do the job they do. If they were not even intended as assertions then many religious activities would become fradulent, or merely silly. If 'You ought *because* it is God's will' asserts no more than 'You ought,' then the person who prefers the former phraseology is not really giving a reason, but a fraudulent substitute for one, a dialectical dud cheque. If 'My soul must be immortal *because* God loves his children, etc.' asserts no more than 'My soul must be immortal,' then the man who reassures himself with theological arguments for immortality is being as silly as the man who tries to clear his overdraft by writing his bank a cheque on the same account. (Of course neither of these utterances would be distinctively Christian: but this discussion never pretended to be so confined.) Religious utterances may indeed express false or even bogus assertions: but I simply do not believe that they are not both intended and interpreted to be or at any rate to presuppose assertions, at least in the context of religious practice; whatever shifts may be demanded, in another context, by the exigencies of theological apologetic.

One final suggestion. The philosophers of religion might well draw upon George Orwell's last appalling nightmare *1984* for the concept of *doublethink*. '*Doublethink* means the power of holding two contradictory beliefs simultaneously, and accepting both of them. The party intellectual knows that he is playing tricks with reality, but by the exercise of *doublethink* he also satisfies himself that reality is not violated' (*1984*, p. 220).[7] Perhaps religious intellectuals too are sometimes driven to doublethink in order to retain their faith in a loving God in face of the reality of a heartless and indifferent world. But of this more another time, perhaps.

---

[7][In the American edition (New York: Harcourt, Brace & World, 1949), p. 215.]

✤ R. B. BRAITHWAITE

37. *The Significance of Religious Stories*

R. B. Braithwaite (born in 1900) was professor of Moral Philosophy at Cambridge University and is the author of *Scientific Explanation*. He is well-known for his Eddington Memorial Lecture entitled "An Empiricist's View of the Nature of Religious Belief" in which he formulates an answer to the verificationists who desire to relegate religious statements to the realm of meaninglessness.

From *An Empiricist's View of the Nature of Religious Belief*

. . . The meaning of any statement, then, will be taken as being given by the way it is used. The kernel for an empiricist of the problem of the nature of religious belief is to explain, in empirical terms, how a religious statement is used by a man who asserts it in order to express his religious conviction.

Since I shall argue that the primary element in this use is that the religious assertion is used as a moral assertion, I must first consider how moral assertions are used. According to the view developed by various moral philosophers since the impossibility of regarding moral statements as verifiable propositions was recognized, a moral assertion is used to express an *attitude* of the man making the assertion. It is not used to assert the proposition that he has the attitude—a verifiable psychological proposition; it is used to show forth or evince his attitude. The attitude is concerned with the action which he asserts to be right or to be his duty, or the state of affairs which he asserts to be good; it is a highly complex state, and contains elements to which various degrees of importance have been attached by moral philosophers who have tried to work out an "ethics without propositions." One element in the attitude is a feeling of approval towards the action; this element was taken as the fundamental one in the first attempts, and views of ethics without propositions are frequently lumped together as "emotive" theories of ethics. But discussion of the subject during the last twenty years has made it clear, I think, that no emotion or feeling of approval is fundamental to the use of moral assertions; it may be the case that the moral asserter has some specific feeling directed on to the course of action said to be right, but this is not the most important element in his "pro-attitude" towards the course of action: what is primary is his intention to perform the action when the occasion for it arises.

The form of ethics without propositions which I shall adopt is therefore a conative rather than an emotive theory: it makes the primary use of a moral assertion that of expressing the intention of the asserter to act in a particular

R. B. Braithwaite, *An Empiricist's View of the Nature of Religious Belief* (Cambridge, England: University Press, 1955). Reprinted by permission of the publisher.

sort of way specified in the assertion. A utilitarian, for example, in asserting that he ought to act so as to maximize happiness, is thereby declaring his intention to act, to the best of his ability, in accordance with the policy of utilitarianism: he is not asserting any proposition, or necessarily evincing any feeling of approval; he is subscribing to a policy of action. There will doubtless be empirical propositions which he may give as reasons for his adherence to the policy (e.g., that happiness is what all, or what most people, desire), and his having the intention will include his understanding what is meant by pursuing the policy, another empirically verifiable proposition. But there will be no specifically moral proposition which he will be asserting when he declares his intention to pursue the policy. This account is fully in accord with the spirit of empiricism, for whether or not a man has the intention of pursuing a particular behaviour policy can be empirically tested, both by observing what he does and by hearing what he replies when he is questioned about his intentions.

Not all expressions of intentions will be moral assertions: for the notion of morality to be applicable it is necessary either that the policy of action intended by the asserter should be a general policy (e.g., the policy of utilitarianism) or that it should be subsumable under a general policy which the asserter intends to follow and which he would give as the reason for his more specific intention. There are difficulties and vaguenesses in the notion of a general policy of action, but these need not concern us here. All that we require is that, when a man asserts that he ought to do so-and-so, he is using the assertion to declare that he resolves, to the best of his ability, to do so-and-so. And he will not necessarily be insincere in his assertion if he suspects, at the time of making it, that he will not have the strength of character to carry out his resolution.

The advantage this account of moral assertions has over all others, emotive non-propositional ones as well as cognitive propositional ones, is that it alone enables a satisfactory answer to be given to the question: What is the reason for my doing what I think I ought to do? The answer it gives is that, since my thinking that I ought to do the action is my intention to do it if possible, the reason why I do the action is simply that I intend to do it, if possible. On every other ethical view there will be a mysterious gap to be filled somehow between the moral judgment and the intention to act in accordance with it: there is no such gap if the primary use of a moral assertion is to declare such an intention.

Let us now consider what light this way of regarding moral assertions throws upon assertions of religious conviction. The idealist philosopher McTaggart described religion as "an emotion resting on a conviction of a harmony between ourselves and the universe at large"[1] and many educated people at the present time would agree with him. If religion is essentially concerned with emotion, it is natural to explain the use of religious assertions on the lines of the original emotive theory of ethics and to regard them as primarily

[1] J. M. E. McTaggart, *Some Dogmas of Religion* (London, 1906), p. 3.

evincing religious feelings or emotions. The assertion, for example, that God is our Heavenly Father will be taken to express the asserter's feeling secure in the same way as he would feel secure in his father's presence. But explanations of religion in terms of feeling, and of religious assertions as expressions of such feelings, are usually propounded by people who stand outside any religious system; they rarely satisfy those who speak from inside. Few religious men would be prepared to admit that their religion was a matter merely of feeling: feelings—of joy, of consolation, of being at one with the universe—may enter into their religion, but to evince such feelings is certainly not the primary use of their religious assertions.

This objection, however, does not seem to me to apply to treating religious assertions in the conative way in which recent moral philosophers have treated moral statements—as being primarily declarations of adherence to a policy of action, declarations of commitment to a way of life. That the way of life led by the believer is highly relevant to the sincerity of his religious conviction has been insisted upon by all the moral religions, above all, perhaps, by Christianity. "By their fruits ye shall know them." The view which I put forward for your consideration is that the intention of a Christian to follow a Christian way of life is not only the criterion for the sincerity of his belief in the assertions of Christianity; it is the criterion for the meaningfulness of his assertions. Just as the meaning of a moral assertion is given by its use in expressing the asserter's intention to act, so far as in him lies, in accordance with the moral principle involved, so the meaning of a religious assertion is given by its use in expressing the asserter's intention to follow a specified policy of behaviour. To say that it is belief in the dogmas of religion which is the cause of the believer's intending to behave as he does is to put the cart before the horse: it is the intention to behave which constitutes what is known as religious conviction.

But this assimilation of religious to moral assertions lays itself open to an immediate objection. When a moral assertion is taken as declaring the intention of following a policy, the form of the assertion itself makes it clear what the policy is with which the assertion is concerned. For a man to assert that a certain policy ought to be pursued, which on this view is for him to declare his intention of pursuing the policy, presupposes his understanding what it would be like for him to pursue the policy in question. I cannot resolve not to tell a lie without knowing what a lie is. But if a religious assertion is the declaration of an intention to carry out a certain policy, what policy does it specify? The religious statement itself will not explicitly refer to a policy, as does a moral statement; how then can the asserter of the statement know what is the policy concerned, and how can he intend to carry out a policy if he does not know what the policy is? I cannot intend to do something I know not what.

The reply to this criticism is that, if a religious assertion is regarded as representative of a large number of assertions of the same religious system, the body of assertions of which the particular one is a representative specimen is taken by the asserter as implicitly specifying a particular way of life. It is no more necessary for an empiricist philosopher to explain the use of a religious statement taken in isolation from other religious statements than it is for him to give a meaning to a scientific hypothesis in isolation from other scientific hypotheses. We understand scientific hypotheses, and the terms that occur in them, by virtue of the relation of the whole system of hypotheses to empirically observable facts; and it is the whole system of hypotheses, not one hypothesis in isolation, that is tested for its truth-value against experience. So there are good precedents, in the empiricist way of thinking, for considering a system of religious assertions as a whole, and for examining the way in which the whole system is used.

If we do this, the fact that a system of religious assertions has a moral function can hardly be denied. For to deny it would require any passage from the assertion of a religious system to a policy of action to be mediated by a moral assertion. I cannot pass from asserting a fact, of whatever sort, to intending to perform an action, without having the hypothetical intention to intend to do the action if I assert the fact. This holds however widely fact is understood—whether as an empirical fact or as a non-empirical fact about goodness or reality. Just as the intention-to-act view of moral assertions is the only view that requires no reason for my doing what I assert to be my duty, so the similar view of religious assertions is the only one which connects them to ways of life without requiring an additional premise. Unless a Christian's assertion that God is love (*agape*)—which I take to epitomize the assertions of the Christian religion—be taken to declare his intention to follow an agapeistic way of life, he could be asked what is the connection between the assertion and the intention, between Christian belief and Christian practice. And this question can always be asked if religious assertions are separated from conduct. Unless religious principles are moral principles, it makes no sense to speak of putting them into practice.

The way to find out what are the intentions embodied in a set of religious assertions, and hence what is the meaning of the assertions, is by discovering what principles of conduct the asserter takes the assertions to involve. These may be ascertained both by asking him questions and by seeing how he behaves, each test being supplemental to the other. If what is wanted is not the meaning of the religious assertions made by a particular man but what the set of assertions would mean were they to be made by anyone of the same religion (which I will call their *typical* meaning), all that can be done is to specify the form of behavior which is in accordance with what one takes to be the fundamental moral principles of the religion in question. Since different people will take different views as to what these fundamental moral principles are, the typical meaning of religious assertions will be different for different people. I myself take the typical meaning of the body of Christian assertions as being given by their proclaiming intentions to follow an agapeistic way of life, and for a description of this way of life—a description in general and metaphorical terms, but an empirical description nevertheless—I should quote most of the Thirteenth Chapter of I Corinthians. Others may think that the Christian way of life should be described somewhat differently, and will therefore take the typical meaning of the assertions of Christianity to correspond to their different view of its fundamental moral teaching.

My contention then is that the primary use of religious assertions is to announce allegiance to a set of moral principles: without such allegiance there is no "true religion." This is borne out by all the accounts of what happens when an unbeliever becomes converted to a religion. The conversion is not only a change in the propositions believed—indeed there may be no specifically intellectual change at all; it is a change in the state of will. An excellent instance is C. S. Lewis's . . . account of his conversion from an idealist metaphysic—"a religion [as he says] that cost nothing"—to a theism where he faced (and he quotes George MacDonald's phrase) "something to be neither more nor less nor other than *done*." There was no intellectual change, for (as he says) "there had long been an ethic (theoretically) attached to my Idealism": it was the recognition that he had to do something about it, that "an attempt at complete virtue must be made."[2] His conversion was a reorientation of the will.

In assimilating religious assertions to moral assertions I do not wish to deny that there are any important differences. One is the fact already noticed that usually the behaviour policy intended is not specified by one religious assertion in isolation. Another difference is that the fundamental moral teaching of the religion is frequently given, not in abstract terms, but by means of concrete examples—of how to behave, for instance, if one meets a man set upon by thieves on the road to Jericho. A resolution to behave like the good Samaritan does not, in itself, specify the behavior to be resolved upon in quite different circumstances. However, absence of explicitly recognized general principles does not prevent a man from acting in accordance with such principles; it only makes it more difficult for a questioner to discover upon what principles he is acting. And the difficulty is not only one way round. If moral principles are stated in the most general form, as most moral philosophers have wished to state them, they tend to become so far removed from particular courses of conduct that it is difficult, if not impossible, to give them any precise content. It may be hard to find out what exactly is involved in the imitation of Christ; but it is not very easy to discover what exactly is meant by the pursuit of Aristotle's *eudaemonia* or of Mill's *happiness*. The tests for what it is to live agapeistically are as empirical as are those for living in quest of happiness; but in each case the tests can best be expounded in terms of examples of particular situations.

A more important difference between religious and purely moral principles is that, in the higher religions at least, the conduct preached by the religion concerns not only external but also internal behaviour. The conversion involved in accepting a religion is a conversion, not only of the will, but of the heart. Christianity requires not only that you should behave towards your neighbour as if you loved him as yourself: it requires that you should love him as yourself. And though I have no doubt that the Christian concept of *agape* refers partly to external behaviour—the agapeistic behaviour for which

[2]C. S. Lewis, *Surprised by Joy* (London, 1955), pp. 198, 212–213.

there are external criteria—yet being filled with *agape* includes more than behaving agapeistically externally: it also includes an agapeistic frame of mind. I have said that I cannot regard the expression of a feeling of any sort as the primary element in religious assertion; but this does not imply that intention to feel in a certain way is not a primary element, nor that it cannot be used to discriminate religious declarations of policy from declarations which are merely moral. Those who say that Confucianism is a code of morals and not, properly speaking, a religion are, I think, making this discrimination.

The resolution proclaimed by a religious assertion may then be taken as referring to inner life as well as to outward conduct. And the superiority of religious conviction over the mere adoption of a moral code in securing conformity to the code arises from a religious conviction changing what the religious man wants. It may be hard enough to love your enemy, but once you have succeeded in doing so it is easy to behave lovingly towards him. But if you continue to hate him, it requires a heroic perseverance continually to behave as if you loved him. Resolutions to feel, even if they are only partly fulfilled, are powerful reinforcements of resolutions to act.

But though these qualifications may be adequate for distinguishing religious assertions from purely moral ones, they are not sufficient to discriminate between assertions belonging to one religious system and those belonging to another system in the case in which the behaviour policies, both of inner life and of outward conduct, inculcated by the two systems are identical. For instance, I have said that I take the fundamental moral teaching of Christianity to be the preaching of an agapeistic way of life. But a Jew or a Buddhist may, with considerable plausibility, maintain that the fundamental moral teaching of his religion is to recommend exactly the same way of life. How then can religious assertions be distinguished into those which are Christian, those which are Jewish, those which are Buddhist, by the policies of life which they respectively recommend if, on examination, these policies turn out to be the same?

Many Christians will, no doubt, behave in a specifically Christian manner in that they will follow ritual practices which are Christian and neither Jewish nor Buddhist. But though following certain practices may well be the proper test for membership of a particular religious society, a church, not even the most ecclesiastically minded Christian will regard participation in a ritual as the fundamental characteristic of a Christian way of life. There must be some more important difference between an agapeistically policied Christian and an agapeistically policied Jew than that the former attends a church and the latter a synagogue.

The really important difference, I think, is to be found in the fact that the intentions to pursue the behaviour policies, which may be the same for different religions, are associated with thinking of different *stories* (or sets of stories). By a story I shall here mean a proposition or set of propositions which are straightforwardly empirical propositions capable of empirical test and which are thought of by the religious man in connection with his resolution to follow the way of life advocated by his religion. On the assumption that the ways of life advocated by Christianity and by Buddhism are essentially the same, it will be the fact that the intention to follow this way of life is associated in the mind of a Christian with thinking of one set of stories (the Christian stories) while it is associated in the mind of a Buddhist with thinking of another set of stories (the Buddhist stories) which enables a Christian assertion to be distinguished from a Buddhist one.

A religious assertion will, therefore, have a propositional element which is lacking in a purely moral assertion, in that it will refer to a story as well as to an intention. The reference to the story is not an assertion of the story taken as a matter of empirical fact: it is a telling of the story, or an alluding to the story, in the way in which one can tell, or allude to, the story of a novel with which one is acquainted. To assert the whole set of assertions of the Christian religion is both to tell the Christian doctrinal story and to confess allegiance to the Christian way of life.

The story, I have said, is a set of empirical propositions, and the language expressing the story is given a meaning by the standard method of understanding how the story-statements can be verified. The empirical story-statements will vary from Christian to Christian; the doctrines of Christianity are capable of different empirical interpretations, and Christians will differ in the interpretations they put upon the doctrines. But the interpretations will all be in terms of empirical propositions. Take, for example, the doctrine of Justification by means of the Atonement. Matthew Arnold imagined it in terms of

. . . a sort of infinitely magnified and improved Lord Shaftesbury, with a race of vile offenders to deal with, whom his natural goodness would incline him to let off, only his sense of justice will not allow it; then a younger Lord Shaftesbury, on the scale of his father and very dear to him, who might live in grandeur and splendour if he liked, but who prefers to leave his home, to go and live among the race of offenders, and to be put to an ignominious death, on condition that his merits shall be counted against their demerits, and that his father's goodness shall be restrained no longer from taking effect, but any offender shall be admitted to the benefit of it on simply pleading the satisfaction made by the son—and then, finally, a third Lord Shaftesbury, still on the same high scale, who keeps very much in the background, and works in a very occult manner, but very efficaciously nevertheless, and who is busy in applying everywhere the benefits of the son's satisfaction and the father's goodness.[3]

Arnold's "parable of the three Lord Shaftesburys" got him into a lot of trouble: he was "indignantly censured" (as he says) for wounding "the feelings of the religious community by turning into ridicule an august doctrine, the object of their solemn faith."[4] But there is no other account of the Anselmian doctrine of the Atonement that I have read which puts it in so morally favourable a light. Be that as it may, the only way in which the doctrine can be understood verificationally is in terms of human beings—mythological beings, it may be, who never existed, but who nevertheless would have been empirically observable had they existed.

[3]Matthew Arnold, *Literature and Dogma* (1873), pp. 306–307.
[4]Matthew Arnold, *God and the Bible* (1875), pp. 18–19.

For it is not necessary, on my view, for the asserter of a religious assertion to believe in the truth of the story involved in the assertions: what is necessary is that the story should be entertained in thought, i.e., that the statement of the story should be understood as having a meaning. I have secured this by requiring that the story should consist of empirical propositions. Educated Christians of the present day who attach importance to the doctrine of the Atonement certainly do not believe an empirically testable story in Matthew Arnold's or any other form. But it is the fact that entertainment in thought of this and other Christian stories forms the context in which Christian resolutions are made which serves to distinguish Christian assertions from those made by adherents of another religion, or of no religion.

What I am calling a *story* Matthew Arnold called a *parable* and a *fairytale.* Other terms which might be used are *allegory, fable, tale, myth.* I have chosen the word "story" as being the most neutral term, implying neither that the story is believed nor that it is disbelieved. The Christian stories include straightforward historical statements about the life and death of Jesus of Nazareth; a Christian (unless he accepts the unplausible Christ-myth theory) will naturally believe some or all of these. Stories about the beginning of the world and of the Last Judgment as facts of past or of future history are believed by many unsophisticated Christians. But my contention is that belief in the truth of the Christian stories is not the proper criterion for deciding whether or not an assertion is a Christian one. A man is not, I think, a professing Christian unless he both proposes to live according to Christian moral principles and associates his intention with thinking of Christian stories; but he need not believe that the empirical propositions presented by the stories correspond to empirical fact.

But if the religious stories need not be believed, what function do they fulfil in the complex state of mind and behaviour known as having a religious belief? How is entertaining the story related to resolving to pursue a certain way of life? My answer is that the relation is a psychological and causal one. It is an empirical psychological fact that many people find it easier to resolve upon and to carry through a course of action which is contrary to their natural inclinations if this policy is associated in their minds with certain stories. And in many people the psychological link is not appreciably weakened by the fact that the story associated with the behaviour policy is not believed. Next to the Bible and the Prayer Book the most influential work in English Christian religious life has been a book whose stories are frankly recognized as fictitious—Bunyan's *Pilgrim's Progress*; and some of the most influential works in setting the moral tone of my generation were the novels of Dostoievsky. It is completely untrue, as a matter of psychological fact, to think that the only intellectual considerations which affect action are beliefs: it is *all* the thoughts of a man that determine his behaviour; and these include his phantasies, imaginations, ideas of what he would wish to be and do, as well as the propositions which he believes to be true. . . .

There is one story common to all the moral theistic religions which has proved of great psychological value in enabling religious men to persevere in carrying out their religious behaviour policies—the story that in so doing they are doing the will of God. And here it may look as if there is an intrinsic connection between the story and the policy of conduct. But even when the story is literally believed, when it is believed that there is a magnified Lord Shaftesbury who commands or desires the carrying out of the behaviour policy, that in itself is no reason for carrying out the policy: it is necessary also to have the intention of doing what the magnified Lord Shaftesbury commands or desires. But the intention to do what a person commands or desires, irrespective of what this command or desire may be, is no part of a higher religion; it is when the religious man finds that what the magnified Lord Shaftesbury commands or desires accords with his own moral judgement that he decides to obey or to accede to it. But this is no new decision, for his own moral judgement is a decision to carry out a behaviour policy; all that is happening is that he is describing his old decision in a new way. In religious conviction the resolution to follow a way of life is primary; it is not derived from believing, still less from thinking of, any empirical story. The story may psychologically support the resolution, but it does not logically justify it.

In this lecture I have been sparing in my use of the term "religious belief" (although it occurs in the title), preferring instead to speak of religious assertions and of religious conviction. This was because for me the fundamental problem is that of the meaning of statements used to make religious assertions, and I have accordingly taken my task to be that of explaining the use of such assertions, in accordance with the principle that meaning is to be found by ascertaining use. In disentangling the elements of this use I have discovered nothing which can be called "belief" in the senses of this word applicable either to an empirical or to a logically necessary proposition. A religious assertion, for me, is the assertion of an intention to carry out a certain behaviour policy, subsumable under a sufficiently general principle to be a moral one, together with the implicit or explicit statement, but not the assertion, of certain stories. Neither the assertion of the intention nor the reference to the stories includes belief in its ordinary senses. But in avoiding the term "belief" I have had to widen the term "assertion," since I do not pretend that either the behaviour policy intended or the stories entertained are adequately specified by the sentences used in making isolated religious assertions. So assertion has been extended to include elements not explicitly expressed in the verbal form of the assertion. If we drop the linguistic expression of the assertion altogether the remainder is what may be called religious belief. Like moral belief, it is not a species of ordinary belief, of belief in a proposition. A moral belief is an intention to behave in a certain way: a religious belief is an intention to behave in a certain way (a moral belief) together with the entertainment of certain stories associated with the intention in the mind of the believer. This solution of the problem of religious belief seems to me to do justice both to the empiricist's demand that meaning must be tied to empirical use and to the religious man's claim for his religious beliefs to be taken seriously.

Seriously, it will be retorted, but not objectively. If a man's religion is all a matter of following the way of life he sets before himself and of strengthening his determination to follow it by imagining exemplary fairytales, it is purely subjective: his religion is all in terms of his own private ideals and of his own private imaginations. How can he even try to convert others to his religion if there is nothing objective to convert them to? How can he argue in its defence if there is no religious proposition which he believes, nothing which he takes to be the fundamental truth about the universe? And is it of any public interest what mental techniques he uses to bolster up his will? Discussion about religion must be more than the exchange of autobiographies.

But we are all social animals; we are all members one of another. What is profitable to one man in helping him to persevere in the way of life he has decided upon may well be profitable to another man who is trying to follow a similar way of life; and to pass on information that might prove useful would be approved by almost every morality. The autobiography of one man may well have an influence upon the life of another, if their basic wants are similar.

But suppose that these are dissimilar, and that the two men propose to conduct their lives on quite different fundamental principles. Can there be any reasonable discussion between them? This is the problem that has faced the many moral philosophers recently who have been forced, by their examination of the nature of thinking, into holding non-propositional theories of ethics. All I will here say is that to hold that the adoption of a set of moral principles is a matter of the personal decision to live according to these principles does not imply that beliefs as to what are the practical consequences of following such principles are not relevant to the decision. An intention, it is true, cannot be logically based upon anything except another intention. But in considering what conduct to intend to practice, it is highly relevant whether or not the consequences of practicing that conduct are such as one would intend to secure. As R. M. Hare has well said, an ultimate decision to accept a way of life, "far from being arbitrary, . . . would be the most well-founded of decisions, because it would be based upon a consideration of everything upon which it could possibly be founded."[5] And in this consideration there is a place for every kind of rational argument.

Whatever may be the case with other religions, Christianity has always been a personal religion demanding personal commitment to a personal way of life. In the words of another Oxford philosopher, "the questions 'What shall I do?' and 'What moral principles should I adopt?' must be answered by each man for himself."[6] Nowell-Smith takes this as part of the meaning of morality: whether or not this is so, I am certain that it is of the very essence of the Christian religion.

[5] R. M. Hare, *The Language of Morals* (Oxford, 1952), p. 69.
[6] P. H. Nowell-Smith, *Ethics* (1954), p. 320.

✳ PAUL TILLICH

38. *Religious Symbols and Human Existence*

Paul Tillich (1886–1965) was born and educated in Germany. In 1933 he was forced by the Nazis to immigrate to the United States where he taught at Union Theological Seminary, Harvard, and the University of Chicago. His influential translation of traditional theology into an existential-symbolic one is contained in a plethora of works including *Dynamics of Faith, The Courage To Be, Theology of Culture,* and, most notably, his three-volume *Systematic Theology.*

EXISTENTIAL ANALYSES AND RELIGIOUS SYMBOLS

Existential analyses are older than existential philosophy. It is a familiar event in the history of philosophy that a special philosophy opens one's eyes to a special problem which was not unknown to former philosophers but which was not the center of their attention. If they or their followers then assert that this problem is nothing new for them, they are both right and wrong. They are right because most problems and perhaps even most types of solutions are as old as man's asking of the philosophical question. They are wrong because the movement of human thought is driven by the intensity with which old problems are seen in a new light and brought out of a peripheral significance into a central one. This is just what has happened to the existential problems. They were pushed into the background after the Renaissance and Reformation, definitely so following the victory of Cartesianism and theological rationalism. It was the function of the Existentialist movement to rediscover the significance of the existentialist questions and to reformulate them in the light of present day experiences and insights.

The thesis of this paper is that in the period during which the existential questions were pushed aside or forgotten, the cognitive approach to religious symbolism was largely blocked, and that the turning of many representatives of twentieth-century philosophy, literature and art to existential questions has once again opened the approach to religious symbols. For religious symbols are partly a way of stating the same situation with which existential analyses are concerned; partly they are answers to the questions implied in the situation. They are the former when they speak of man and his predicament. They are the latter when they speak of God and his reaction to this predicament. In both cases, existential analysis makes the religious symbols understandable and a matter of possible concern for our contemporaries, including contemporary philosophers.

Reprinted from Paul Tillich, "Existential Analyses and Religious Symbols," in Harold A. Basilius, ed., *Contemporary Problems in Religion* (Detroit: Wayne University Press, 1956) by permission of the Wayne State University Press. Copyright 1956.

In order to define the nature of an existential analysis we must distinguish it from an essential analysis. The terms "existential" and "essential" analyses shall be used here as grammatical abbreviations for analyses of existential structures and analyses of essential structures, while the terms "essentialist" and "existentialist" shall be used for the movements and attitudes of the one or the other character.

Since the analysis of existential structures is predominantly an analysis of the human predicament, the best way of distinguishing existential and essential analyses is to do so with respect to their doctrines of man. There is a large group of problems concerning man which have been investigated and discussed throughout the history of philosophy in purely essentialist terms. They all deal with the question, What is the "nature" of man? What is his *ousia*,[1] that which makes him what he is, in every exemplar who deserves the name man? Neither nominalism nor process philosophy, neither philosophical empiricism nor even existentialism can escape this question. Attempts to describe human nature in its essential structures, be it in more static or in more dynamic terms, can never cease to be a task of human thought.

The existentialist philosopher, for example, asks the question of the *differentia specifica* between man and nonhuman nature. If he answers the question with Aristotle, that man is *animal rationale*, this may not be specific enough, or the nature of the rational may not have been defined sufficiently, but the method itself is correct and clearly essentialist. There are theologians who react violently against the Aristotelian definition, not in order to amend it in this or that direction, but in order to deny the method in the name of an assumedly existentialist analysis of man's nature. They point to man's existential relation to God and consider this relation as the nature of man, misinterpreting for their purpose the Biblical phrase that man is the image of God. In the Biblical view, man is and always remains the image of God because of his bodily and spiritual qualities which give him control over nature in spite of his estrangement from his essential being. This is an important point because its negation was one of the ways by which neo-orthodox theology cut off all relations with essentialist philosophy and surrendered all rational criteria for theological thought.

The question of man's essential nature leads by itself to the mind-body problem. If we discuss the several monistic and dualistic answers given to this ever-present question and try to find a solution to it, we do an essentialist analysis. And we should reject theologians who interfere in this discussion out of an existential interest. They are aware of man's finitude and the question of the infinite which is implicit in his finitude. And they try to give an answer in terms of an essentialist psychology which includes an immortal part of man. This is the key to the failure of Thomas Aquinas when he tried to combine the essentialist Aristotelian doctrine of the soul as a form of the body with the Platonic-Christian dualism of the immortal soul and the mortal body. By this attempted combination, Aquinas injected existentialist analysis.

---

[1]["essential being."]

A third problem discussed in essentialist analyses of human nature is the relation of man as individuality and man as community. Again, the Aristotelian definition of man as a political animal is truly essentialist and remains valid, however it is enlarged upon or refined. Today the discussion of the problem is presented in Martin Buber's famous phrase, "the I-Thou relationship." This phrase *can* be understood in essentialist terms and can be used as a descriptive feature, showing how the ego becomes an ego only in the encounter with another ego in which it finds its limit and is thrown back upon itself. Therefore, man's ethical and cultural life is possible only in the community in which language is created. In this sense the ego-thou interdependence is a piece of essential analysis. Yet is was an existentialist invasion when Buber tried to remove the universals from the encounter between ego and thou, and to make both speechless, because there are no words for the absolute particular, the other ego. And it was a distortion of communal being when Heidegger referred to the problem as an escape into the non-authentic form of being, the being as a *"man"* (German), as an *"on"* (French), as a general "one." The political body of which Aristotle speaks is not the result of an escape into unauthentic being. Essentialism is right in rejecting this as an invasion.

A last example is man's ethical structure. Essentialist analysis has described it either in terms of the formal categories which constitute the ethical realm, as, for example, Kant did, or in terms of the ethical character and its virtues, as, for example, in the manner of Aquinas, or in terms of the embracing social structures, as, for example, according to Hegel. Kierkegaard has accused Hegel of neglecting man's ethical situation, namely, that of the individual who has to make the ethical decision. But although Hegel obviously neglects the structures which make the singular person as such a moral subject, he cannot be accused of excluding in his essentialist analyses the existentialist question, the question of the anxiety of decision to which Kierkegaard refers. If neo-orthodox theologians deny that the Bible has essentialist ethical material in the manner of Aristotle and the Stoics, they can be refuted not only by the partly Stoic elements of the Pauline letters, but also by the fact that the content of the ethical law never has been denied in the New Testament. Only its character as law is denied for those who are reconciled unto themselves. There can be no ethics without an essentialist analysis of man's ethical nature and its structures.

We have given examples of essentialist analyses of man's nature as they have been performed in all periods of philosophical thought. At the same time, we have drawn attention to existentialist attacks on this kind of philosophizing and to the necessity on our part of rejecting these attacks. In doing so, we have given first indications of what an existentialist analysis is, namely, a description of man's anti-essential or estranged predicament. We have also indicated that the existentialist attacks to which we have referred have continuously interfered with the essentialist task.

If we now turn to a more direct characterization of existential analyses, we find that in contrast to essentialism they concentrate on the human situation and that their point of departure is the immediate awareness man has of his situation. Both characteristics follow from what an existential analysis is supposed to do, namely, to describe those elements within experience which express being in contrast to what it essentially is. This experience is not a matter of objectifying observation from outside the situation. It can be understood only as an immediate awareness from inside the situation. It has, for example, the character of finitude itself in contrast to a finitude which I see objectively if something comes to an end. One may think here of the difference between the observed death of someone else and the anticipation of one's own death. In the first experience, the material of an essential analysis is given; in the second experience, one's existential situation is manifested in anxiety. Another example is the experience of guilt. It is an essentialist analysis if types of law-breakers are described or the degree of guilt in a criminal action is discussed. But guilt becomes an existentialist concept if it is the expression of one's own deviation from what one essentially is and therefore ought to be. Guilt in this sense is connected with the anxiety of losing one's true being.

A third example is provided by the experience of meaninglessness. We often have the more or less adequate impression that somebody lives an empty and meaningless life, without being fully aware of his doing so. Quite different from such an essential description is the experience of feeling oneself cut off from any meaning of life, of being lost in a desert of meaninglessness and of feeling the anxiety implicit in this situation.

In each of these examples, to which others will be added later on, I alluded to what I suggest calling "existential anxiety." This points to the fact that the concept of anxiety has played a decisive role in all existentialist thinking since Augustine and Pascal. I assume that the frequently discussed distinction between anxiety and fear is known and largely accepted. The main point is that fear has a definite object and is, as such, an object of essentialist philosophy, while anxiety has no definite object and is a matter of existential analysis. With this thought in mind, I want to draw your attention to some symbols of anxiety in literature. Dante's descriptions of the Inferno must be understood as structures of destruction in man's existential experience of estrangement, guilt and despair. They symbolize modes of despair as external punishments. Taken literally, they are absurd as are the symbols in Kafka's novels *The Castle* and *The Trial*. In the first instance, symbols of the anxiety of meaninglessness are given; in the second case, symbols of the anxiety of guilt. Conceptualized or symbolized, the description of anxiety is central for the existential attitude.

In order to give further examples of existential analyses, I want to reverse the procedure which I first used: that is, I shall cite essentialist criticisms of existential analyses and then the existential defense against the criticisms.

Essentialism criticizes the existentialist emphasis on anxiety and related concepts by denying that there is a qualitative difference between them and other internal experiences. The so-called existential analyses, are, so it is said, essential analyses of a predominantly psychological character. Experienced anxiety is like experienced anger or sadness or joy, an object of the psychology of emotions, a part of the general description of human nature. It is claimed that nothing verifiable in existential analyses is included in any essentialist description. If these arguments are valid, the existentialist claim has been refuted. But they are not valid. For there is a sharp qualitative difference between two kinds of affections (in the Cartesian-Spinozistic sense of affections). The one kind belongs to man's essential nature and embraces the totality of those affections which respond to stimuli coming from the universe of objects in the temporal-spatial continuum. Most of the affections discussed in ancient and modern philosophy have this character. They are objects of essentialist psychological descriptions.

But there is another kind, namely, those which respond to man's existence as existence and not to any stimuli coming from the contents man encounters within existence. Being aware of existence, experiencing it as existence, means being in anxiety. For existence includes finitude, and anxiety is the awareness of one's own finitude.

I have already pointed to the difference between fear and anxiety, the first having an object, the second not having one. But we must go one step further. Anxiety is the more fundamental affection because the fear of something special is ultimately rooted in the fact that as finite beings we are exposed to annihilation, to the victory of non-being in us. In this sense, anxiety is the foundation of fear. Their ontological relation is different; for anxiety has an ontological precedence; it reveals the human predicament in its fundamental quality, as finitude.

The relation of anxiety to fear is representative of similar relations in which two partly synonymous concepts point to something qualitatively different, the one to an essential structure, the other to an existential characteristic.

Since a comprehensive treatment of existential analysis is obviously impossible on this occasion, I shall restrict myself to those aspects of it which are especially useful as keys to the meaning of religious symbols.

Man in his existential anxiety feels estranged from that to which he properly belongs. Although created by Hegel in order to make the fact of nature understandable from the point of view of the absolute mind, the term soon acquired an existentialist meaning and has, since then, been used against Hegel. Man feels estranged from what he essentially is; he experiences a permanent conflict within himself and a hostility towards the world. This must be distinguished, though not separated, from the feeling of strangeness which every living being, animal as well as man, has for most of the other beings and often for himself. The motions of strangeness and its opposite, familiarity, belong to the realm of essential relationships between finite beings. But estrangement is a negation of essential belongingness. It has an existential character.

Existential estrangement expresses itself in loneliness, which should be clearly distinguished from essential solitude, the correlate of which is essential community. Loneliness is an expression of anti-essential separation from that to which one belongs. This loneliness can express itself in the flight from solitude into the *"on,"* the *"man."*

Finitude includes insecurity. There is essential insecurity, the correlate to essential security, in the biological, social, and psychological realm. In all these spheres risk and chance are at work, but also law and certainty. The contrast to that is the ultimate insecurity of existence which is experienced in anxiety and described as being homeless and lost in one's world, and as being anxious about tomorrow, in German, *sorgen*. The distinction between being anxious and taking care, between *Sorge* and *Vorsorge*, is again linguistic support for the distinction between an essentialist and an existentialist concept. Essential insecurity may provoke the feeling of ultimate insecurity; but conversely, in an externally secure situation, existential insecurity may come as a sudden shock as it breaks into the world of finite relations.

The anxiety of estrangement has the color of existential guilt. We have already spoken of "guilt" as an example of the difference between an essential and an existential analysis. This distinction must be carried through in several directions. The first is the establishment of the existentialist concept of risk or of daring decision. In every decision a risk is implied; the risk to win or to lose something or someone. This belongs to man's essential character or finite freedom. He deliberates and then risks a decision. He may even risk his life. But there is another risk which belongs to man which is the cause of guilt and estrangement, namely, the risk of actualizing or non-actualizing himself, and in doing so to lose himself, namely, his essential being. This situation can be observed in every moment in which innocence is put before the decision either to remain in a state of non-actualized potentialities or to trespass the state of innocence and to actualize them. In both cases, something is lost; in the first, a fully actualized humanity; in the second, the innocent resting in mere potentiality. The classical example is the sexual anxiety of the adolescent.

As myth and experience tell, mankind as a whole risks its self-actualization and is consequently in the state of universal, existential estrangement. This produces the situation of tragic guilt in which everyone, in spite of his personal responsibility, participates. An early philosophical expression of this experience of being involved by destiny in a universal situation for which one is at the same time responsible seems to be the fragment of Anaximander, which, however, one interprets particulars, combines separation, finitude, and guilt in a cosmic vision. This certainty transcends an essentialist analysis of responsible or irresponsible actions between persons. It judges the predicament of man and his world as such.

The last confrontation of an essentialist and an existentialist concept concerns man's cognitive estrangement from his essential being, as it is manifest in the situation of doubt. Doubt in the form of finite freedom is an essential element in the cognitive task of man. Essential doubt is the condition of all knowledge. The methodological doubt of Descartes was the entering door for the modern scientific consciousness. Quite different from it is the existential doubt, the doubt about the meaning of one's being in man's existential situation. Essential doubt is an expression of courage; existential doubt is a cause and an expression of despair. It is doubt neither of special assertions nor of all possible assertions, but it is the doubt about the meaning of being. It is the doubt concerning the being of him who doubts. It turns against itself and against the doubter and his world. And since it wrestles with the threat of meaninglessness, it cannot be answered by any of those assertions which have methodological certainty, probability, or improbability.

These are examples of existential analyses which seem to me sufficient to show the qualitative difference and independent standing of existential concepts and which may also be used as keys for the interpretation of religious symbols.

The examples we have given to show the difference between existential and essential analyses have provided us with the material necessary to interpret the basic religious symbols. It is almost a truism to assert that religious language is symbolic. But it is less of a truism to assert that for this reason religious language expresses the truth, the truth which cannot be expressed and communicated in any other language. And it is far from a truism to say that most errors in religion and most attacks on religion are due to the confusion between symbolic and literal language. This confusion, which must remain a chief concern of everyone who takes religion seriously, is not only a failure of the intellect, but also a symptom of the idolatrous distortion which is found in all religions and which makes the divine an object amongst objects to be handled by man as subject, cognitively and practically.

Once this fact is understood, one can easily see the relation between existential analyses and religious symbols. Existential analyses express conceptually what the religious myth has always said about the human predicament. And in doing so they make all of those symbols understandable in which the answer to the question implied in the human predicament is given: the symbols and myths which center around the idea of God.

Existential analysis deals with man's finitude as it is experienced in anxiety. The mythological symbol for this experience is man as a creature. Man and his world are creatures. Some forms of this symbol can be found in every religion. Man is not by himself. He has not what God has in classical theology, *aseitas*.[2] He is a mixture of contrasting elements, divine and demonic, spiritual and material, heavenly and earthly, being and non-being. This is true of Eastern as well as Western religions, although the difference between the two appears immediately if one asks for the meaning of creaturely existence. The answer given in the East is negative and non-historical. Creaturely existence is something which should not be and from which one desires to be saved. In the West, the answer is positive and historical. There should be creaturely existence, but it must be saved not from itself as creature, but from its self-estrangement.

The consequence of the Western attitude is that creation has a positive

[2]["self-existence."]

side, answering the question implied in the experience of creatureliness. The answer is not a story according to which once upon a time a divine or half-divine being decided to produce other things. But creation expresses symbolically the participation of the finite in its own infinite ground; or, more existentially expressed, the symbol of creation shows the source of the courage to affirm one's own being in terms of power and meaning in spite of the ever present threat of non-being. In this courage, the anxiety of creatureliness is not removed but taken into the courage. And in it, the loneliness of the estranged individual is taken into a unity which does not remove the threat of loneliness and its correlate, the flight into the *"man,"* the *"on,"* but which instead is able to create genuine solitude and genuine communion. And in the symbol of creation, existential insecurity is taken into a certitude which does not remove the insecurity of having no definite time and no definite space but which instead gives the security of participation in the ultimate power of being. Symbols like omnipotence, omnipresence, and providence corroborate this meaning. They become absurdities and contradictions if taken literally. They radiate existential truth if opened up with the key of existential analysis.

In the center of the symbolism of many religions we find the contrast of the fall and salvation together with a large group of corroborating symbols. The key to existential analysis is able to open them up even for those who have a special strong resistance against this kind of symbolism.

The symbolism of temptation has already been mentioned in connection with the analysis of the anxiety of existential decisions. Temptation is possibility, and the anxiety of having to decide is the awareness of possibility. There are many myths and legends of temptation of which probably the most profound is the Biblical story in which the situation of man, symbolized by Adam and Eve, is clearly the decision between remaining in the dreaming innocence of Paradise and achieving self-realization in knowledge, power, and sex. Man chooses self-realization and falls into the state of estrangement, and with him his world also falls. Understood in this way, the myth of the fall, for which there are analogies in most religions, represents a very particular case of the transition from the innocence of potentiality to the tragic guilt of self-actualization. It is a genuine description of man's predicament here and now and should not be vitiated by the absurdities of literalism.

The traditional term for man's status of estrangement is "sin," a term whose meaning has undergone more distortions and has consequently been the object of more protest than almost any other religious notion. Sin, in the light of existential analysis, is man's estrangement from his essential being, an estrangement which is both tragic necessity and personal guilt. The extremely questionable terms "original sin" and "hereditary sin" express the tragic and actual sin, the personal element. I suggest that we drop the terms "original sin" and "hereditary sin" completely. They seem to be beyond salvation. And certainly some words, especially theological and philosophical ones, need salvation. The term "original sin" should be replaced by existential descriptions of the universal and tragic character of man's estrangement. But the term can and should be saved by being reinterpreted as the stage of estrangement for which, in spite of its tragic character, we are personally responsible and out of which the concrete acts of estrangement from ourselves, from others, and from the meaning of our being, follow. If we use the term "sin," it should not be used in the plural but in the singular, without the article, as Paul does: sin, the power of estrangement.

The state of estrangement is the state in which the anxiety of guilt is amalgamated with the anxiety of finitude. The predominant religious symbols of this anxiety are, as already indicated in relation to Dante's poem, judgment, condemnation, punishment, and hell. They usually appear in a dramatic framework with a divine being as judge, demonic powers as executors, and a special place reserved for long-lasting or everlasting punishment. Although this imagery is largely recognized as such even in the average membership of the Christian churches, it is good to apply here also the keys of existential and depth-psychological analyses. It seems that in people like Peter Brueghel this was already a conscious situation. His highly existential pictures of the demonic realm are understandable only in the light of an existential analysis of the anxiety of guilt. Seen in this light, the divine law, according to which judgment is executed, is obviously the law of one's essential being, judging us because of the estrangement from ourselves. Only because of this situation has the law as law an unconditional character, however the content of the law may change. Seen in this light, condemnation and punishment are obviously not things which judge us from above, but symbols of the judgment we inescapably make against ourselves, of the painful split within ourselves, of the moments of despair in which we want to get rid of ourselves without being able to, of the feeling of being possessed by structures of self-destruction, in short, of all of that which the myth calls demonic.

The question and perhaps the passionate quest included in this situation is mythologically expressed in symbols such as salvation, redemption, regeneration, and justification, or in personal symbols such as savior, mediator, Messiah, Christ. Such symbols are common to most of the great religions, although the description of the way of salvation is immensely different.

Existential analyses have given decisive keys for the understanding of this symbolism, the dramatic frame of which corresponds to the dramatic frame of the symbols of estrangement. Some of these keys merit special mention. The first is connected with a semantic reflection by means of which salvation makes a whole of something which is split. *Salvus* and *saos* mean whole and healed. Salvation is the act in which the cleavage between man's essential being and his existential situation is overcome. It is the religious answer to the innumerable analyses which can be summed up in the title of Menninger's book *Man Against Himself.* The second key is equally prepared by existential analysis, namely, the insight that the situation of existence cannot be overcome in the power of this situation. Every attempt to do so strengthens this situation, which can be summed up in the title of Sartre's play, *No Exit.* That is how the religious symbols which point to saving powers in non-personal and personal embodiments must be understood. The tragic bondage of estranged existence produces the quest for that which transcends existence although it appears within it, creating a new being. This and this alone is the religious paradox and not simply a logically "nonsense-ical" statement. The third key which has been successfully used is the understanding of reconciliation in the light of the experience of methodological as well as poetic-intuitive psychology. It is the idea that the most difficult thing for a human being is to accept himself and that the basic step in the process of healing is to give man the feeling that he *is* accepted and therefore can accept himself. Nobody understands today what justification by faith means. Everyone understands what it means to accept oneself as accepted.

In the analysis of existential doubt, in contrast to essential doubt, we touched on the concept of despair, literally, of hopelessness. Existentialist thinking, especially at one period of its development, devoted a great deal of work to the problem of nihilism, meaninglessness, nothingness, etc. The wide spread of this feeling is confirmed by many witnesses in this country as well as in Europe. Its analysis gives a key to a long neglected part of religious symbolism, the symbols of hope. Most religions are full of mythological, usually very fanciful, images of hope. Taken literally in any sense, they appear as pale but beautified images of our daily experienced world. Taken as highly symbolical, they express the conviction that in the realities of our daily experience, in spite of their seemingly meaningless transitoriness and ultimate emptiness, there is a dimension of meaning which points to an ultimate or external meaning in which they participate here and now. This is the key to the symbol of eternal life which can be more easily used in such an interpretation because it is less open to literalism than more dramatic but dangerously inadequate symbols such as life after death, immortality, reincarnation, heaven. Eternal life means that the joy of today has a dimension which gives it trans-temporal meaning.

In each of our attempts to open up a religious symbol with the help of an existential analysis, we open up implicitly the basic and all-embracing symbol of religion, namely the symbol of God. In relation to creation, He is creator; in relation to salvation, He is savior; in relation to fulfillment, He is the eternal. We lead from different points and with different keys to the central symbol. But we do not start with it. This is an implication of the existential method, which, I believe, is adequate to religion, because religion is a matter of man's existential situation. We must start from below and not from above. We must start with man's experienced predicament and the questions implied in it; and we must proceed to the symbols which claim to contain the answer. But we must not start with the question of the being of God, which, if discussed in terms of the existence or non-existence of God, is in itself a lapse into a disastrous literalism.

Following the method which goes from below to above, we reach an idea of God which avoids literalism and which, just for this reason, establishes the reality of that which answers the questions implied in human existence. God, in the light of this question, is the power of being itself, prevailing over against non-being, overcrowding estrangement, providing us the courage to take the anxiety of finitude, guilt, and doubt upon ourselves.

This experience is expressed in innumerable largely personal symbols describing the idea of God. Symbols are not signs. They participate in the power of what they symbolize. They are not true or false in the sense of cognitive judgments. But they are authentic or inauthentic with respect to their rise; they are adequate or inadequate with respect to their expressive power; they are divine or demonic with respect to their relation to the ultimate power of being.

The vast problem of symbols, however, lies beyond the scope of the present discussion. My task was to show that existential analysis has made it more difficult for the modern mind to dispose of religious symbols by first taking them literally and then properly rejecting them as absurd. Any attack on symbolism must be conducted on a much deeper level, namely that of symbolism itself. Genuine symbols can be overcome only by other genuine symbols, not by criticism of their literalistic distortions.

✳ SELECTED BIBLIOGRAPHY
FOR SECTION 8

Two important and standard works on the Thomistic doctrine of analogy may be mentioned: E. L. Mascall's *Existence and Analogy* (London: Longmans, Green & Co., 1949) and George P. Klubertanz, *St. Thomas Aquinas on Analogy* (Chicago: Loyola University Press, 1960). The latter is an exhuastive historical and textual analysis and provides complete bibliographical information. A summary account may be found in F. C. Copleston, *Aquinas* (London: Penguin, 1955), pp. 126 ff., and an extended "semantical analysis" in James F. Ross, "Analogy as a Rule of Meaning for Religious Language," in *Aquinas: A Collection of Critical Essays*, ed. Anthony Kenny (Garden City, N.Y.: Anchor Books, 1969).

Ayer's logical positivist epistemology is more recently elaborated in *The Problem of Knowledge* (Baltimore, Md.: Penguin Books, 1956), and a series of essays by other thinkers of more or less the same persuasion is provided in A. J. Ayer (ed.), *Logical Positivism* (Glencoe, Ill.: Free Press, 1959). Specifically on the verification question, as it is represented in Ayer, one should note the first in a long string of discussions that soon filled the philosophical journals: A. C. Ewing, "Meaninglessness," *Mind*, XLVI (July, 1937). Also of interest is a debate between Ayer and Father Copleston, originally broadcast over the BBC and now reproduced in Geddes MacGregor and J. Wesley Robb (eds.), *Readings in Religious Philosophy* (Boston: Houghton Mifflin, 1962), pp. 328 ff. David Cox brings the question directly to God in his article, "The Significance of Christianity," *Mind*, LIX (April, 1950) which should be read with Thomas McPherson's reply in the same volume (October, 1950). For a general discussion of the logical positivist position from a Catholic standpoint, see Frederick Copleston. *Contemporary Philosophy*. Chs. 1–7 (Westminster, Md.: Newman Press, 1956). A history of the verificationist position is recorded in Carl Hempel's essay, "Problems and Changes in the Empiricist Criterion of Meaning," in Leonard Lensky (ed.), *Semantics and the Philosophy of Language* (Urbana, Ill.: University of Illinois Press, 1952). For an evaluation, see C. E. M. Joad, *A Critique of Logical Positivism* (Chicago: University of Chicago Press, 1950) .

Discussions of Braithwaite's position are contained in the following: A. C. Ewing, "Religious Assertions in the Light of Contemporary Philosophy," *Philosophy*, XXXII (July, 1957); J. A. Passmore, "Christianity and Positivism," *Australasian Journal of Philosophy*, XXXV (August, 1957); and H. J. N. Horsburgh, "Professor Braithwaite and Billy Brown," *Australasian Journal of Philosophy*, XXXVI (December, 1958)

Several useful anthologies may be consulted, containing more or less analytic discussions of religious language, often with a view towards the verification-falsification issue. These include: John Hick (ed.), *Faith and the Philosophers* (London: Macmillan, 1964); Alvin Plantinga (ed.) *Faith and Philosophy* (Grand Rapids, Mich.: Eerdman, 1964); and Dallas M. High (ed.), *New Essays on Religious Language* (New York: Oxford University Press, 1969). Insightful and helpful articles may also be found in the very influential *New Essays in Philosophical Theology*, ed. Antony Flew and Alasdair MacIntyre (London: Student Christian Movement Press, 1955).

Individual works (in the same style as the above) include Ian T. Ramsey's important *Religious Language* (New York: Macmillan, 1957); Ian T. Ramsey, *Christian Discourse* (London: Oxford University Press, 1965); Frederick Ferré, *Language, Logic and God* (New York: Harper & Row, 1961); William Hordern, *Speaking of God* (New York: Macmillan, 1964); John Hick, *Faith and Knowledge*, second ed. (Ithaca, N. Y.: Cornell University Press, 1966); T. R. Miles, *Religion and the Scientific Outlook* (London: George Allen & Unwin, 1959); John Macquarrie, *God-Talk* (New York: Harper & Row, 1967); John A. Hutchison, *Language and Faith* (Philadelphia: Westminster Press, 1963); and John Wilson, *Language and Christian Belief* (London: Macmillan, 1958). Of course, all language philosophers acknowledge their indebtedness to Ludwig Wittgenstein whose works include *Philosophical Investigations*, tr. G. E. M. Anscombe (New York: Macmillan, 1953); *Tractatus Logico-Philosophicus*, tr. D. F. Pears and B. F. McGuinness (London: Routledge & Kegan Paul, 1961); and *Lectures and Conversations on Aesthetics, Psychology, and Religious Belief*, ed. Cyril Barrett (Berkeley, Calif.: University of California Press, 1966).

The specifically Flew-Hare-Mitchell strain of the discussion has its roots in John Wisdom's important article, "Gods," reprinted in his *Philosophy and Psycho-Analysis* (Oxford, England: Blackwell, 1953). One should note especially John Hick's extension of the debate (and the introduction of his concept of "eschatological verification") in his article "Religious Statements as Factually Significant," revised and reproduced as Ch. 8 in his *Faith and Knowledge, op. cit.* Hick's position in turn spawned a number of replies, for example, Kai Nielsen, "Eschatological Verification," *Canadian Journal of Theology*, IX (October, 1963). One should consider also George Mavrodes' reply to Nielsen's reply to Hick, in "God and Verification," *Canadian Journal of Theology*, X (July, 1964). The falsification question has again been renewed in a series of four articles by John F. Miller, J. Kellenberger, Antony Flew, and Thomas McPherson, all in *Religious Studies*, V (October, 1969). For forceful reply to Flew's original challenge (and verificationism in general), see Alvin Plantinga, *God and Other Minds*, Ch. 7, Part I (Ithaca, N. Y.: Cornell University Press, 1967).

E. L. Mascall's *Words and Images* (London: Longmans, Green, & Co., 1958) represents a reaction to the above approaches. William T. Blackstone's *The Problem of Religious Language* (Englewood Cliffs, N.J.: Prentice-Hall, 1963) provides a complete survey of the recent discussions on the cognitive or non-cognitive status of religious discourse. An altogether different approach is suggested in Sten H. Stenson, *Sense and Nonsense* (Nashville, Tenn.: Abingdon Press, 1969).

Paul Tillich's existential-symbolic interpretation of religious language may be found also in his *Dynamics of Faith* (New York: Harper & Row, 1957); *Theology of Culture*, Ch. 3, ed. Robert C. Kimball (New York: Oxford University Press, 1959); and *Systematic Theology*, (consult index for specific passages) (Chicago: University of Chicago Press, 1951–1963). For a discussion of Tillich's understanding of religious symbols, see William L. Rowe, *Religious Symbols and God* (Chicago: University of Chicago Press, 1968) and the relevant passages (consult index) in Alexander J. McKelway, *The Systematic Theology of Paul Tillich* (Richmond, Va.: John Knox Press, 1964). Note also Tillich's contribution to *Religious Experience and Truth*, ed. Sidney Hook (New York: New York University Press, 1961) and William Alston's philosophical critique, "Tillich's Conception of a Religious Symbol," in the same volume. The whole first part of this volume is devoted to articles written from a variety of standpoints on the topic of religious symbols.

PART THREE

THE NEW THEOLOGIES

God and the Modern World

❈ INTRODUCTION

As stated in the Preface, it seems no longer an easy matter to distinguish philosophical from theological endeavors. This is largely the case because theologians have found themselves newly motivated by both positivistic-analytic and existential strains of contemporary philosophy and have, in turn, advanced from their theological perspectives the frontiers of philosophical thought. Whatever the causes, it appears to be impossible to appreciate the full reach of philosophical theology apart from the recent contributions of professional theologians. It is perhaps in the present section more than any other that it is most difficult to represent a meaningful spectrum of positions in the course of a few selections. A full presentation of the important theological positions, personalities, innovations, and movements of even the last several years could easily fill a book. Nonetheless, the thinkers represented below may be taken as an indication of the ways in which a few of the most consequential theological positions have unfolded from the thirties to the present.

There is a sense in which the beginning of the modern theologies must be traced to Karl Barth, whose theology, often referred to as Neo-orthodoxy, took shape as a reaction to the liberalizing trend of the nineteenth and early twentieth centuries. Barth sought to recover for modern man a true estimation of his situation before God. For Barth this was the Biblical estimation with its picture of man as a fallen creature, his intellect darkened, his will weakened, stripped of his supernatural gifts, and unable in his own power to approach God. This idea is fundamental to Barth's theology and is apparent at every stage of its development from the early *Epistle to the Romans* to the last volume of the uncompleted *Church Dogmatics*. Two consequences of this position, namely, Barth's rejection of natural theology and his emphasis on the centrality of special revelation, are quite evident in Barth's lectures (first delivered at Bonn in 1946) on the Apostles' Creed. The lecture reproduced below underlines the typically Barthian judgment that there is no salvation but what God himself has provided, no authentic knowledge of God apart from his "mighty acts" in history and epitomized in the revelation of Jesus Christ.

Rudolf Bultmann, too, represents an attempt to confront the contemporary world with the genuine message of the Gospel. He is not willing, however, to impose upon modern technological man the pre-scientific world-view and mythological trappings of the New Testament which can only be a hindrance to a contemporary appreciation of the Gospel. Thus, in 1941, in a little pamphlet from which the selection below is taken, there entered a concept that stood the theological world on its head: the *demythologization of the New Testament*. Let us, says Bultmann, eliminate from the New Testament (or better, reinterpret) its mythological elements, so that its genuine and always valid *kerygma* ("proclamation") may speak to all men, providing them with authentic self-understanding and challenging them to genuine existential decision.

Whereas Barth and Bultmann are Biblical theologians, Paul Tillich is a systematic and philosophical theologian, though the Biblical revelation continues as the focal point of his thought. We have already encountered something of Tillich's existential theology in his discussion of religious symbols. The present selection will suggest more emphatically his conception of God, or more accurately, the Ground of Being of which "God" is a symbol. Tillich indicts both traditional supernaturalism and naturalism as idolatrous distortions. According to Tillich, God is not a thing or even a person existing alongside or above the world. Such a supernaturalistic conception denies the immanent depth at which God, the Ground of Being, exists in all things. On the other hand, naturalism denies the infinite distance between the Ground of Being and that of which it is the ground. This God, who is something above and beyond the traditional conceptions, who is Being Itself, has appeared in the "New Being" of Christ, and confronted man with salvation, that is, healing of man's existential estrangement from his essential being.

Both Bultmann and Tillich provide an occasion for raising the important question concerning the relation of theology to history. The first problem is to determine in what way and to what extent they seek to dehistoricize the Christ "event," and then to ask, *a la* St. Paul, whether they have thrown out the baby with the bath water: ". . . if Christ be not raised, your faith is vain . . ." (I Cor. 15:17). For many, indeed, the decisive question at this point is: What truth and real significance (the problem of religious language again) can the Christian message possess apart from something that really happened?

With Dietrich Bonhoeffer "secular" theology received, no doubt, its strongest impetus. This kind of theology, though variously represented by numerous thinkers, affirms, as Harvey Cox has expressed it, ". . . the liberation of man from religious and metaphysical tutelage, the turning of his attention away from other worlds toward this one."[1] It would appear that Bonhoeffer would have agreed with that much. There is much in Bonhoeffer's writings to support such an interpretation. Certainly in the *Ethics* he rejects as ill-conceived the distinction between sacred and secular, and in the *Letters* says that man has "come of age" and can now do quite well without religion and without God. On the other hand, one must be careful to understand what Bonhoeffer means and does not mean by "religion" and "God." Certainly there is a positive kind of piety and a certain theological orthodoxy that is sustained from the early *Cost of Discipleship* to the very last of his *Letters*, and any legitimate interpretation of Bonhoeffer will have to do justice also to

[1]Harvey Cox, *The Secular City* (New York: Macmillan, 1965), p. 17.

these aspects of his position as well as the more radical-sounding aspects. At any rate, this is a time, say many, for a "religionless" Christianity. Bonhoeffer said it first. But what he meant is another question, and the incomplete character of his writings does not help.

Paul M. van Buren, unlike Bultmann and Tillich, is concerned not with the existential meaning of the Gospel but its *cognitive* meaning. He represents, then, a return to the problem of religious language. Very much influenced by analytic and empirical philosophy, and especially by Braithwaite, van Buren seeks to provide a statement of the Gospel that would be meaningful to the secular man who is imbued, usually, with a thoroughly empirical outlook. For van Buren "God"—the word—must be discarded and theological statements must henceforth ground themselves in the concrete, historical figure of Christ and the empirically "contagious" love generated by him. Van Buren's analysis thus updates the language and expression of the Gospel in terms of contemporary empiricist demands, while reaffirming the centrality of Christology. Indeed, van Buren represents an interesting synthesis of diverse and important philosophical and religious strains confronted throughout the present volume, as well as a decisive alternative on the theology-history issue mentioned above.

For van Buren the word "God" may be dead, but for William Hamilton God himself is dead. The exact interpretation of the phrase "death of god" is not a simple thing, but one might be cautioned that he is in greater danger of underinterpreting than of overinterpreting. Of course many others have declared the death of God, for example Nietzsche, but none has meant quite what Hamilton and Thomas J. J. Altizer (the most influential of these theologians) appear to mean. As Hamilton himself emphasizes, the death-of-God theologians must not be taken to be speaking symbolic rhetoric: "There really is a sense of non-having, of not-believing, of having lost, not just the idols or the gods of religion, but God himself." This is not, however, as dismal a situation as it might seem. For these thinkers, the death (or transformation?) of God is for us a liberating event, allowing us to concentrate our energies upon this world and the concrete realities of suffering and love.

It is already popular to observe that the Death of God movement itself is dead and to look upon it, perhaps, as a cultural curiosity or a fad having passed. It is doubtful that the same judgment will be made concerning the Theology of Hope. The theologians of hope (including, among others, Jürgen Moltmann, Leslie Dewart, and Carl E. Braaten) seek to return us to a more Biblical understanding of our human situation, shifting the object of Christian faith to the future and recovering what they perceive to be the genuinely eschatological (eschatology: the study of the future or the end-times) character of Christianity. For Braaten (whose *The Future of God* did much to bring this German-sponsored theology to the attention of American readers, and whose discussion sweeps back over Barth, Bultmann, Tillich, the Death of God theologians, and others), Christian faith is a matter of living in anticipation and openness to God's future as Jesus did; it is a matter of being involved and active in the Church's effort to realize the coming Kingdom;

and it is a matter of living in the hope of resurrection and newness of life, confirmed to us through the historical resurrection of Jesus Christ—which, in a way, brings us back to the beginning.

✳ KARL BARTH

39. *God's Mighty Acts*

Karl Barth (1886-1968) was a professor at German universities until he was ousted by the Nazis in 1935. Returning to the city of his birth, he became Professor of Theology at the University of Basel, Switzerland, and Protestantism's outstanding spokesman against liberal theology. Barth's prolific writings include the monumental *Commentary on the Epistle to the Romans* and his vast *Church Dogmatics* on which he was working at the time of his death.

From *Dogmatics in Outline*

CHAPTER 5: GOD IN THE HIGHEST

The Confession which we have made the basis of these lectures begins with the words, 'I believe in God.' In them we have pronounced the mighty word whose unfolding is the Christian Creed. God is the *Object* of the faith of which we have been speaking in the last lectures. God: that is, comprehensively regarded and expressed, the content of the proclamation of the Christian congregation. But now we are faced with the fact that this word 'God,' that the concept of God, the idea of God seems to be a reality which is familiar in one way or another to all history of religion and philosophy. And before we go any further, we must stop a moment and ask ourselves how this word 'God,' in the sense in which Christian faith utters it, is related to what has been so termed at all times and in all nations in the history of religion and philosophy. Let us be clear about what is usually meant by 'God' outside the Christian faith. When man speaks of God, of the divine nature, of the divine essence, or of God simply, then he means the object of the universally present and active longing, the object of man's homesickness and man's hope for a unity, a basis, a meaning to his existence, and the meaning of the world; he means thereby the existence and the nature of a Being who, whether in this or that connexion with the realities other than Himself, is to be regarded as the Supreme Being that determines and dominates all that exists. And if we glance at the history of human desire, human assertion about this Being, the first and strongest impression we receive is that of a human skill in invention, active on all sides and taking the most various routes; but also of human waywardness and human violence with this concept, this idea of God. Hence the picture of an infinite variety of possibilities, the picture of a great uncertainty, of great contradictions.

We must be clear that when we are speaking of God in the sense of Christian faith, He who is called God is not to be regarded as a continuation and enrichment of the concepts and ideas which usually constitute religious thought in general about God. In the sense of Christian faith, God is not to be found in the series of gods. He is not to be found in the pantheon of human piety and religious inventive skill. So it is not that there is in humanity something like a universal natural disposition, a general concept of the divine, which at some particular point involves the thing which we Christians call God and as such believe in and confess; so that Christian faith would be one among many, an instance within a general rule. A Christian Father once rightly said that *Deus non est in genere*, 'God is not a particular instance within a class.' When we Christians speak of 'God,' we may and must be clear that this word signifies *a priori* the fundamentally Other, the fundamental deliverance from that whole world of man's seeking, conjecturing, illusion, imagining and speculating. It is not that on the long road of human seeking and longing for the divine a definite stopping-place has in the end been reached in the form of the Christian Confession. The God of the Christian Confession is, in distinction from all gods, not a found or invented God or one at last and at the end discovered by man; He is not a fulfilment, perhaps the last, supreme and best fulfilment, of what man was in course of seeking and finding. But we Christians speak of Him who completely takes the place of everything that elsewhere is usually called 'God,' and therefore suppresses and excludes it all, and claims to be alone the truth. Where that is not realised, it is still not realised what is involved when the Christian Church confesses, 'I believe in God.' What is involved is man's meeting with the Reality which he has never of himself sought out or first of all discovered. 'What no eye hath seen nor ear heard, what hath not entered into the heart of any man, God hath given to those who love Him' [I Cor. 2:9], is St. Paul's way of speaking of this matter. And there is no other way in which we can speak of it. God in the sense of the Christian Confession is and exists in a completely different way from that which we can speak of it. God in the sense of the Christian Confession is and exists in a completely different way from that which is elsewhere called divine. And so His nature, His being is different from the nature and being of all alleged gods. We summarise all that is to be said of God, in the sense of the Christian Confession, in the words 'God in the Highest.' You all know where I take this idea from. It is in Luke 2. 14: 'Glory to God in the highest'; therefore our song is, 'Glory to God alone in the highest.' This 'in the highest,' *in excelsis*, I shall now try to expound.

In view of what has been said so far, this 'in the highest' means quite simply that He is the One who stands *above* us and also above our highest and deepest feelings, strivings, intuitions, above the products, even the most sublime, of the human spirit. God in the highest means first of all—recalling what was said earlier—He who is in no way established in us, in no way corresponds to a human disposition and possibility, but who is in every sense established simply in Himself and is real in that way; and who is manifest and made manifest to us men, not because of our seeking and finding, feeling and thinking, but again and again only through Himself. It is this God in the highest who has turned as such to man, given Himself to man, made Himself knowable to him. God in the highest does not mean someone quite other, who has nothing to do with us, who does not concern us, who is eternally alien to us; God in the highest, in the sense of the Christian Confession, means He who from on high has condescended to us, has come to us, has become ours. God in the highest is the God who shows Himself to be the real God, and so the One who is in no way in our control and who none the less and just because of that has taken us to Himself. God is He who alone deserves to be called God, as distinct from all gods, different from all that exists otherwise, and yet the One who has united Himself to us. If we say with the Christian Confession, 'I believe in God' or 'I believe on God,' we have to do with *this God*.

Let us attempt to describe more closely, in a few concrete sketches, what I have been outlining. I said that God is He who, according to Holy Scripture, exists, lives and acts, and makes Himself known. By this definition something fundamentally different is taking place from what would happen, if I should try and set before you conceptually arranged ideas of an infinite, supreme Being. In such a case I would be speculating. But I am not inviting you to speculate. I maintain that this is a radically wrong road which can never lead to God, but to a reality called so only in a false sense. God is He who is to be found in the book of the Old and New Testaments, which speaks of Him. And the Christian definition of God consists simply in the statement, 'He is spoken of there, so let us listen to what is said of Him there.' He who is to be seen and heard there is God. Note well: in the whole Bible of the Old and New Testaments not the slightest attempt is ever made to *prove* God. This attempt has always been made only outside the biblical view of God, and only where it has been forgotten with whom we have to do, when we speak of God. What sort of attempts were they, after all, where the attempt was made to *prove* a perfect Being alongside imperfect ones? Or from the existence of the world to prove its ultimate and supreme cause, God? Or from the alleged order of the world to prove the ordering Power? Or the moral proof of God from the face of man's conscience? I will not enter into these 'proofs' of God. I don't know whether you can at once see the humour and the fragility of these proofs. These proofs may avail for the alleged gods; if it were my task to make you acquainted with these allegedly supreme beings, I would occupy myself with the five famous proofs of God. In the Bible there is no such argumentation; the Bible speaks of God simply as of One who needs no proof. It speaks of a God who *proves Himself* on every hand: Here am I, and since I am and live and act it is superfluous that I should be proved. On the basis of this divine self-proof the prophets and apostles speak. In the Christian Church there can be no speaking about God in any other way. God has not the slightest need for our proofs. He who is called God in Holy Scripture is unsearchable—that is, He has not been discovered by any man. But when our talk is of Him and we speak of Him as about a familiar entity, who is more familiar and real than any other reality and who is nearer us than we are to ourselves, it is not because there may have been particularly pious people who were successful in investigating this Being, but because He who was hidden from us has disclosed Himself.

And it is part of this, that God is not only unprovable and unsearchable, but also *inconceivable*. No attempt is made in the Bible to define God—that is, to grasp God in our concepts. In the Bible God's name is named, not as philosophers do it, as the name of a timeless Being, surpassing the world, alien and supreme, but as the name of the living, acting, working Subject who makes Himself known. The Bible tells the story of God; it narrates His deeds and the history of this God in the highest, as it takes place on earth in the human sphere. The Bible proclaims the significance and the importance of this working and acting, this story of God, and in this way it proves God's existence, describes His being and His nature. Knowledge of God in the sense of Holy Scripture and the Confession is knowledge of His existence, His life, His action, His revelation in His work. And so the Bible is not a philosophical book, but a history book, the book of God's mighty acts, in which God becomes knowable by us.

Holy Scripture describes a work, and first the work of Creation. Alongside Himself God puts something else, something different from Himself—namely, the creature, without having need of it, in the power of His Almightiness, in His holy, overflowing love. Secondly, a covenant is set up between God and one of His creatures, between God and man. Once more an inconceivable fact: why precisely between God and *man*, of whom from the beginning it is narrated that he is unthankful to God, that he is a sinner? In spite of this sin, sovereignly overlooking it, reserving for Himself its amendment, God surrenders Himself. He lends Himself to become the God of a tiny, despised people in Asia Minor, Israel. He lends Himself to become a member of this people, a little child, and then to die. And thirdly—but the whole thing is one—there is the work of redemption, the unveiling of the purpose of God's free love for man and the world, the annihilation of all that would hinder this purpose; there is the revelation and the manifestation of the new heaven and the new earth. All this is a way, under the sign of the name of Jesus Christ, the man Jesus Christ, in whom God Himself has become visible and active on earth, who is at once the goal of the history of the nation Israel, and the beginning and starting-point of the Church, and at the same time the revelation of the redemption, of the completion, of the whole. The whole work of God lives and moves in this one Person. He who says God in the sense of Holy Scripture will necessarily have to say Jesus Christ over and over again.

This work of creation, of the covenant and of redemption is the reality in which God exists, lives and acts and makes Himself known. From this work we must make no abstractions, if we would know God's nature and existence. Here, in this work, God is the Person who expounds Himself, and is thus the subject of this work. It is the work of God's free love. We may venture to describe the reality which the work expounds, the nature and the essence of God, by these two concepts of freedom and love. But we must be careful, lest we tumble back again out of the concrete into the abstract, out of history into the realm of ideas. I would not say that God is freedom or that God is love—even though the second pronouncement is a biblical one [cf. I John 4:8]. We do not know what love is and we do not know what freedom is; but *God* is love and *God* is freedom. What freedom is and what love is, we have to learn from Him. As predicate to this subject it may be said that He is the God of free love. In His work of creation, covenant and redemption, He proves Himself to be this God. It is there that we experience what love is, this desire of the other for his own sake, so that the one is no longer alone, but completely together with the other. This is love, this is God's *free* love. God is not lonely, not even without the world. He does not need the other and nevertheless He loves. This love cannot be understood apart from the majesty of His freedom. It is God's love, that He, the Father, loves the Son, who Himself is God. What in His work becomes visible is an uncovering of this mystery of His inner Being, where all is freedom and all is love.

And now perhaps the title of this lecture, 'God in the highest,' becomes comprehensible. By being the Father, the Son and the Holy Ghost in His work in Jesus Christ, God is in the highest. He whose nature and essence consist, whose existence is proved, in His descending into the depths, He the Merciful, who gives Himself up for His creature to the utter depths of the existence of His creature—He is God in the highest. Not in spite of this, not in remarkable paradoxical opposition, but the highness of God consists in His thus descending. This is His exalted nature, this His free love. Anyone who wants to look up to some other height has not understood the utter otherness in God, he would still be in the tracks of the heathen, who look for God in an endlessness. But He is utterly other than we think our gods. It is He who calls Abraham and who led that wretched nation through the desert, who never swerves through the centuries-long disloyalty and disobedience of this nation, who causes Himself to be born in the stable at Bethlehem as a little child and who dies on Golgotha. He is the glorious Lord, He is divine. Do you understand what monotheism in Christian faith means? God knows, not the foolish delight in the number 'one.' It has nothing to do with the number 'one,' but with this subject in His sheer uniqueness and otherness over against all others, different from all the ridiculous deities whom man invents. Once we have realised this, we can only laugh, and there is a laugh running through the Bible at these figures. Once the true God has been seen, the gods collapse into dust, and He remains the only One. 'I am the Lord thy God . . . thou shalt have no other gods before Me' [Ex. 20:2-3]. This 'thou shalt not' has the force of 'thou canst not.' He who calls himself 'god alongside Him becomes the mere shadow of man's extravagant longing, which has its ill results. And the Second Commandment also becomes quite clear then: 'Thou shalt not make unto thee any image nor any sort of likeness. Thou shalt not bow down to them nor worship them' [Ex. 20:4]. That too is not a sign of Israelite ways of thinking and there is no philosophical concept of invisibility in the background. But God has Himself done everything in order to present Himself. How should man make an image of Him after He has presented His likeness Himself? A well-intentioned business, this entire 'spectacle' of Christian art, well-intentioned but impotent, since God Himself has made His own image. Once a man has understood 'God in the highest,' it becomes impossible for him to want any imagery in thought, or any other kind of imagery.

❊ RUDOLF BULTMANN

40. *Faith, Existence, and Mythology*

Rudolf Bultmann (born 1884) studied philosophy and theology at the University of Marburg, Tübingen, and Berlin. In 1921 he returned to Marburg to become Professor of New Testament as well as a leading Biblical theologian. The result of Bultmann's demythologizing and existential reinterpretation of the Bible may be found in numerous works including *Theology of the New Testament, The Gospel of John, Jesus and the Word,* and the 1941 pamphlet *New Testament and Mythology.*

From "New Testament and Mythology"

A: The Problem

I: The Mythical View of the World and the Mythical Event of Redemption

The cosmology of the New Testament is essentially mythical in character. The world is viewed as a three-storied structure, with the earth in the centre, the heaven above, and the underworld beneath. Heaven is the abode of God and of celestial beings—the angels. The underworld is hell, the place of torment. Even the earth is more than the scene of natural, everyday events, of the trivial round and common task. It is the scene of the supernatural activity of God and his angels on the one hand, and of Satan and his daemons on the other. These supernatural forces intervene in the course of nature and in all that men think and will and do. Miracles are by no means rare. Man is not in control of his own life. Evil spirits may take possession of him. Satan may inspire him with evil thoughts. Alternatively, God may inspire

Rudolf Bultmann, "New Testament and Mythology," in *Kerygma and Myth*, ed. Hans Werner Bartsch, tr. Reginald H. Fuller (New York: Harper & Row, 1961). Reprinted by permission of S. P. C. K., Holy Trinity Church, London.

his thought and guide his purposes. He may grant him heavenly visions. He may allow him to hear his word of succour or demand. He may give him the supernatural power of his Spirit. History does not follow a smooth unbroken course; it is set in motion and controlled by these supernatural powers. This aeon is held in bondage by Satan, sin, and death (for "powers" is precisely what they are), and hastens towards its end. That end will come very soon, and will take the form of a cosmic catastrophe. It will be inaugurated by the "woes" of the last time. Then the Judge will come from heaven, the dead will rise, the last judgment will take place, and men will enter into eternal salvation or damnation.

This then is the mythical view of the world which the New Testament presupposes when it presents the event of redemption which is the subject of its preaching. It proclaims in the language of mythology that the last time has now come. "In the fulness of time" God sent forth his Son, a pre-existent divine Being, who appears on earth as a man.[1] He dies the death of a sinner[2] on the cross and makes atonement for the sins of men.[3] His resurrection marks the beginning of the cosmic catastrophe. Death, the consequence of Adam's sin, is abolished,[4] and the daemonic forces are deprived of their power.[5] The risen Christ is exalted to the right hand of God in heaven[6] and made "Lord" and "King."[7] He will come again on the clouds of heaven to complete the work of redemption, and the resurrection and judgement of men will follow.[8] Sin, suffering and death will then be finally abolished.[9] All this is to happen very soon; indeed, St Paul thinks that he himself will live to see it.[10]

All who belong to Christ's Church and are joined to the Lord by Baptism and the Eucharist are certain of resurrection to salvation,[11] unless they forfeit it by unworthy behaviour. Christian believers already enjoy the first instalment of salvation, for the Spirit[12] is at work within them, bearing witness to their adoption as sons of God,[13] and guaranteeing their final resurrection.[14]

2: The Mythological View of the World Obsolete

All this is the language of mythology, and the origin of the various themes can be easily traced in the contemporary mythology of Jewish Apocalyptic and in the redemption myths of Gnosticism. To this extent *the kerygma*

---

[1]Gal. 4. 4; Phil. 2. 6ff.; 2 Cor. 8. 9; John 1. 14, etc.
[2]2 Cor. 5. 21; Rom. 8. 3.
[3]Rom. 3. 23–26; 4. 25; 8. 3; 2 Cor. 5. 14, 19; John 1. 29; 1 John 2. 2, etc.
[4]1 Cor. 15. 21f.; Rom. 5. 12ff.
[5]1 Cor. 2. 6; Col. 2. 15; Rev. 12. 7ff., etc.
[6]Acts 1. 6f.; 2. 33; Rom. 8. 34, etc.
[7]Phil. 2. 9–11; 1 Cor. 15. 25.
[8]I Cor. 15. 23f., 50ff., etc.
[9]Rev. 21. 4, etc.
[10]I Thess. 4. 15ff.; I Cor. 15. 51f.; cf. Mark 9. 1.
[11]Rom. 5. 12ff.; I Cor. 15. 21ff., 44b, ff.
[12]Ἀπαρχή: Rom. 8. 23, ἀρραβών: 2 Cor. 1 22; 5. 5.
[13]Rom. 8. 15; Gal. 4. 6.
[14]Rom. 8. 11.

is incredible to modern man, for he is convinced that the mythical view of the world is obsolete. We are therefore bound to ask whether, when we preach the Gospel to-day, we expect our converts to accept not only the Gospel message, but also the mythical view of the world in which it is set. If not, does the New Testament embody a truth which is quite independent of its mythical setting? If it does, theology must undertake the task of stripping the Kerygma from its mythical framework, of "demythologizing" it.

Can Christian preaching expect modern man *to accept the mythical view of the world as true?* To do so would be both senseless and impossible. It would be senseless, because there is nothing specifically Christian in the mythical view of the world as such. It is simply the cosmology of a pre-scientific age. Again, it would be impossible, because no man can adopt a view of the world by his own volition—it is already determined for him by his place in history. Of course such a view is not absolutely unalterable, and the individual may even contribute to its change. But he can do so only when he is faced by a new set of facts so compelling as to make his previous view of the world untenable. He has then no alternative but to modify his view of the world or produce a new one. The discoveries of Copernicus and the atomic theory are instances of this, and so was romanticism, with its discovery that the human subject is richer and more complex than enlightenment or idealism had allowed, and nationalism, with its new realization of the importance of history and the tradition of peoples.

It may equally well happen that truths which a shallow enlightenment had failed to perceive are later rediscovered in ancient myths. Theologians are perfectly justified in asking whether this is not exactly what has happened with the New Testament. At the same time it is impossible to revive an obsolete view of the world by a mere fiat, and certainly not a mythical view. For all our thinking to-day is shaped irrevocably by modern science. A blind acceptance of the New Testament mythology would be arbitrary, and to press for its acceptance as an article of faith would be to reduce faith to works. Wilhelm Herrmann pointed this out, and one would have thought that his demonstration was conclusive. It would involve a sacrifice of the intellect which could have only one result—a curious form of schizophrenia and insincerity. It would mean accepting a view of the world in our faith and religion which we should deny in our everyday life. Modern thought as we have inherited it brings with it criticism of *the New Testament view of the world.*

Man's knowledge and mastery of the world have advanced to such an extent through science and technology that it is no longer possible for anyone seriously to hold the New Testament view of the world—in fact, there is no one who does. What meaning, for instance, can we attach to such phrases in the creed as "decended into hell" or "ascended into heaven"? We no longer believe in the three-storied universe which the creeds take for granted. The only honest way of reciting the creeds is to strip the mythological framework from the truth they enshrine—that is, assuming that they contain any truth at all, which is just the question that theology has to ask. No one who is old enough to think for himself supposes that God lives in a local heaven.

There is no longer any heaven in the traditional sense of the word. The same applies to hell in the sense of a mythical underworld beneath our feet. And if this is so, the story of Christ's descent into hell and of his Ascension into heaven is done with. We can no longer look for the return of the Son of Man on the clouds of heaven or hope that the faithful will meet him in the air (I Thess. 4. 15ff.).

Now that the forces and the laws of nature have been discovered, we can no longer believe in *spirits, whether good or evil*. We know that the stars are physical bodies whose motions are controlled by the laws of the universe, and not daemonic beings which enslave mankind to their service. Any influence they may have over human life must be explicable in terms of the ordinary laws of nature; it cannot in any way be attributed to their malevolence. Sickness and the cure of disease are likewise attributable to natural causation; they are not the result of daemonic activity or of evil spells.[15] The *miracles of the New Testament* have ceased to be miraculous, and to defend their historicity by recourse to nervous disorders or hypnotic effects only serves to underline the fact. And if we are still left with certain physiological and psychological phenomena which we can only assign to mysterious and enigmatic causes, we are still assigning them to causes, and thus far are trying to make them scientifically intelligible. Even occultism pretends to be a science.

It is impossible to use electric light and the wireless and to avail ourselves of modern medical and surgical discoveries, and at the same time to believe in the New Testament world of spirits and miracles.[16] We may think we can manage it in our own lives, but to expect others to do so is to make the Christian faith unintelligible and unacceptable to the modern world.

The mythical eschatology is untenable for the simple reason that the parousia of Christ never took place as the New Testament expected. History did not come to an end, and, as every schoolboy knows, it will continue to run its course. Even if we believe that the world as we know it will come to an end in time, we expect the end to take the form of a natural catastrophe, not of a mythical event such as the New Testament expects. And if we explain the parousia in terms of modern scientific theory, we are applying criticism to the New Testament, albeit unconsciously.

[15]It may of course be argued that there are people alive to-day whose confidence in the traditional scientific view of the world has been shaken, and others who are primitive enough to qualify for an age of mythical thought. And there are also many varieties of superstition. But when belief in spirits and miracles has degenerated into superstition, it has become something entirely different from what it was when it was genuine faith. The various impressions and speculations which influence credulous people here and there are of little importance, nor does it matter to what extent cheap slogans have spread an atmosphere inimical to science. What matters is the world view which men imbibe from their environment, and it is science which determines that view of the world through the school, the press, the wireless, the cinema, and all the other fruits of technical progresss.

[16]Cp. the observations of Paul Schütz on the decay of mythical religion in the East through the introduction of modern hygiene and medicine.

But natural science is not the only challenge which the mythology of the New Testament has to face. There is the still more serious challenge presented by *modern man's understanding of himself.*

Modern man is confronted by a curious dilemma. He may regard himself as pure nature, or as pure spirit. In the latter case he distinguishes the essential part of his being from nature. In either case, however, *man is essentially a unity.* He bears the sole responsibility for his own feeling, thinking, and willing.[17] He is not, as the New Testament regards him, the victim of a strange dichotomy which exposes him to the interference of powers outside himself. If his exterior behaviour and his interior condition are in perfect harmony, it is something he has achieved himself, and if other people think their interior unity is torn asunder by daemonic or divine interference, he calls it schizophrenia.

Although biology and psychology recognize that man is a highly dependent being, that does not mean that he has been handed over to powers outside of and distinct from himself. This dependence is inseparable from human nature, and he needs only to understand it in order to recover his self-mastery and organize his life on a rational basis. If he regards himself as spirit, he knows that he is permanently conditioned by the physical, bodily part of his being, but he distinguishes his true self from it, and knows that he is independent and responsible for his mastery over nature.

In either case he finds *what the New Testament has to say about the "Spirit"* ($\pi\nu\varepsilon\tilde{\nu}\mu\alpha$) *and the sacraments utterly strange and incomprehensible.* Biological man cannot see how a supernatural entity like the $\pi\nu\varepsilon\tilde{\nu}\mu\alpha$ can penetrate within the close texture of his natural powers and set to work within him. Nor can the idealist understand how a $\pi\nu\varepsilon\tilde{\nu}\mu\alpha$ working like a natural power can touch and influence his mind and spirit. Conscious as he is of his own moral responsibility, he cannot conceive how baptism in water can convey a mysterious something which is henceforth the agent of all his decisions and actions. He cannot see how physical food can convey spiritual strength, and how the unworthy receiving of the Eucharist can result in physical sickness and death (I Cor. 11. 30). The only possible explanation is that it is due to suggestion. He cannot understand how anyone can be baptized for the dead (I Cor. 15. 29).

We need not examine in detail the various forms of modern *Weltanschauung,* whether idealist or naturalist. For the only criticism of the New Testament which is theologically relevant is that which arises *necessarily* out of the situation of modern man. The biological *Weltanschauung* does not, for instance, arise necessarily out of the contemporary situation. We are still free to adopt it or not as we choose. The only relevant question for the theologian is the basic assumption on which the adoption of a biological as of every other *Weltanschauung* rests, and that assumption is the view of the world which has been moulded by modern science and the modern conception of human

---

[17]Cp. Gerhardt Krüger, *Einsicht und Leidenschaft, Das Wesen des platonischen Denkens,* Frankfort, 1939, p. 11f.

nature as a self-subsistent unity immune from the interference of supernatural powers.

Again, the biblical doctrine that *death is the punishment of sin* is equally abhorrent to naturalism and idealism, since both regard death as a simple and necessary process of nature. To the naturalist death is no problem at all, and to the idealist it is a problem for that very reason, for so far from arising out of man's essential spiritual being it actually destroys it. The idealist is faced with a paradox. On the one hand man is a spiritual being, and therefore essentially different from plants and animals, and on the other hand he is the prisoner of nature, whose birth, life, and death are just the same as those of the animals. Death may present him with a problem, but he cannot see how it can be a punishment for sin. Human beings are subject to death even before they have committed any sin. And to attribute human mortality to the fall of Adam is sheer nonsense, for guilt implies personal responsibility, and the idea of original sin as an inherited infection is sub-ethical, irrational, and absurd.

The same objections apply to *the doctrine of the atonement.* How can the guilt of one man be expiated by the death of another who is sinless—if indeed one may speak of a sinless man at all? What primitive notions of guilt and righteousness does this imply? And what primitive idea of God? The rationale of sacrifice in general may of course throw some light on the theory of the atonement, but even so, what a primitive mythology it is, that a divine Being should become incarnate, and atone for the sins of men through his own blood! Or again, one might adopt an analogy from the law courts, and explain the death of Christ as a transaction between God and man through which God's claims on man were satisfied. But that would make sin a juridical matter; it would be no more than an external transgression of a commandment, and it would make nonsense of all our ethical standards. Moreover, if the Christ who died such a death was the pre-existent Son of God, what could death mean for him? Obviously very little, if he knew that he would rise again in three days!

The *resurrection of Jesus* is just as difficult for modern man, if it means an event whereby a living supernatural power is released which can henceforth be appropriated through the sacraments. To the biologist such language is meaningless, for he does not regard death as a problem at all. The idealist would not object to the idea of a life immune from death, but he could not believe that such a life is made available by the resuscitation of a dead person. If that is the way God makes life available for man, his action is inextricably involved in a nature miracle. Such a notion he finds incomprehensible, for he can see God at work only in the reality of his personal life and in his transformation. But, quite apart from the incredibility of such a miracle, he cannot see how an event like this could be the act of God, or how it could affect his own life.

Gnostic influence suggests that this Christ, who died and rose again, was not a mere human being but a God-man. His death and resurrection were not isolated facts which concerned him alone, but a cosmic event in which we are all involved.[18] It is only with effort that modern man can think himself back into such an intellectual atmosphere, and even then he could never accept it himself, because it regards man's essential being as nature and redemption as a process of nature. And as for the pre-existence of Christ, with its corollary of man's translation into a celestial realm of light, and the clothing of the human personality in heavenly robes and a spiritual body—all this is not only irrational but utterly meaningless. Why should salvation take this particular form? Why should this be the fulfilment of human life and the realization of man's true being?

B: The Task before Us

1: Not Selection or Subtraction

Does this drastic criticism of the New Testament mythology mean the complete elimination of the kerygma?

Whatever else may be true, we cannot save the kerygma by selecting some of its features and subtracting others, and thus reduce the amount of mythology in it. For instance, it is impossible to dismiss St Paul's teaching about the unworthy reception of Holy Communion or about baptism for the dead, and yet cling to the belief that physical eating and drinking can have a spiritual effect. If we accept *one* idea, we must accept everything which the New Testament has to say about Baptism and Holy Communion, and it is just this one idea which we cannot accept.

It may of course be argued that some features of the New Testament mythology are given greater prominence than others: not all of them appear with the same regularity in the various books. There is for example only one occurrence of the legends of the Virgin birth and the Ascension; St Paul and St John appear to be totally unaware of them. But, even if we take them to be later accretions, it does not affect the mythical character of the event of redemption as a whole. And if we once start subtracting from the kerygma, where are we to draw the line? The mythical view of the world must be accepted or rejected in its entirety.

At this point absolute clarity and ruthless honesty are essential both for the academic theologian and for the parish priest. It is a duty they owe to themselves, to the Church they serve, and to those whom they seek to win for the Church. They must make it quite clear what their hearers are expected to accept and what they are not. At all costs the preacher must not leave his people in the dark about what he secretly eliminates, nor must he be in the dark about it himself. In Karl Barth's book *The Resurrection of the Dead* the cosmic eschatology in the sense of "chronologically final history" is eliminated in favour of what he intends to be a non-mythological "ultimate history." He is able to delude himself into thinking that this is exegesis of St Paul and of the New Testament generally only because he gets rid of

[18]Rom. 5. 12ff.; I Cor. 15. 21ff., 44b.

everything mythological in I Corinthians by subjecting it to an interpretation which does violence to its meaning. But that is an impossible procedure.

If the truth of the New Testament proclamation is to be preserved, the only way is to demythologize it. But our motive in so doing must not be to make the New Testament relevant to the modern world at all costs. The question is simply whether the New Testament message consists exclusively of mythology, or whether it actually demands the elimination of myth if it is to be understood as it is meant to be. This question is forced upon us from two sides. First there is the nature of myth in general, and then there is the New Testament itself.

2: The Nature of Myth

The real purpose of myth is not to present an objective picture of the world as it is, but to express man's understanding of himself in the world in which he lives. Myth should be interpreted not cosmologically, but anthropologically, or better still, existentially.[19] Myth speaks of the power or the powers which man supposes he experiences as the ground and limit of his world and of his own activity and suffering. He describes these powers in terms derived from the visible world, with its tangible objects and forces, and from human life, with its feelings, motives, and potentialities. He may, for instance, explain the origin of the world by speaking of a world egg or a world tree. Similarly he may account for the present state and order of the world by speaking of a primeval war between the gods. He speaks of the other world in terms of this world, and of the gods in terms derived from human life.[20]

Myth is an expression of man's conviction that the origin and purpose of the world in which he lives are to be sought not within it but beyond it—that is, beyond the realm of known and tangible reality and that this realm is perpetually dominated and menaced by those mysterious powers which are its source and limit. Myth is also an expression of man's awareness that he is not lord of his own being. It expresses his sense of dependence not only within the visible world, but more especially on those forces which hold sway beyond the confines of the known. Finally, myth expresses man's belief that in this state of dependence he can be delivered from the forces within the visible world.

Thus myth contains elements which demand its own criticism—namely, its imagery with its apparent claim to objective validity. The real purpose of myth is to speak of a transcendent power which controls the world and man, but that purpose is impeded and obscured by the terms in which it is expressed.

[19]Cp. Gerhardt Krüger, *Einsicht und Leidenschaft*, esp. p. 17f., 56f.

[20]Myth is here used in the sense popularized by the 'History of Religions' school. Mythology is the use of imagery to express the other worldly in terms of this world and the divine in terms of human life, the other side in terms of this side. For instance, divine transcendence is expressed as spatial distance. It is a mode of expression which makes it easy to understand the cultus as an action in which material means are used to convey immaterial power. Myth is not used in that modern sense, according to which it is practically equivalent to ideology.

Hence the importance of the New Testament mythology lies not in its imagery but in the understanding of existence which it enshrines. The real question is whether this understanding of existence is true. Faith claims that it is, and faith ought not to be tied down to the imagery of New Testament mythology.

3: *The New Testament Itself*

The New Testament itself invites this kind of criticism. Not only are there rough edges in its mythology, but some of its features are actually contradictory. For example, the death of Christ is sometimes a sacrifice and sometimes a cosmic event. Sometimes his person is interpreted as the Messiah and sometimes as the Second Adam. The kenosis of the pre-existent Son (Phil. 2. 6ff.) is incompatible with the miracle narratives as proofs of his messianic claims. The Virgin birth is inconsistent with the assertion of his pre-existence. The doctrine of the Creation is incompatible with the conception of the "rulers of this world" (I Cor. 2. 6ff.), the "god of this world" (2 Cor. 4. 4) and the "elements of this world" στοιχεῖα τοῦ κόσμου, Gal. 4. 3). It is impossible to square the belief that the law was given by God with the theory that it comes from the angels (Gal. 3. 19f.).

But the principal demand for the criticism of mythology comes from a curious contradiction which runs right through the New Testament. Sometimes we are told that human life is determined by cosmic forces, at others we are challenged to a decision. Side by side with the Pauline indicative stands the Pauline imperative. In short, man is sometimes regarded as a cosmic being, sometimes as an independent "I" for whom decision is a matter of life or death. Incidentally, this explains why so many sayings in the New Testament speak directly to modern man's condition while others remain enigmatic and obscure. Finally, attempts at demythologization are sometimes made even within the New Testament itself. But more will be said on this point later.

4: *Previous Attempts at Demythologizing*

How then is the mythology of the New Testament to be re-interpreted? This is not the first time that theologians have approached this task. Indeed, all we have said so far might have been said in much the same way thirty or forty years ago, and it is a sign of the bankruptcy of contemporary theology that it has been necessary to go all over the same ground again. The reason for this is not far to seek. The liberal theologians of the last century were working on the wrong lines. They threw away not only the mythology but also the kerygma itself. Were they right? Is that the treatment the New Testament itself required? That is the question we must face to-day. The last twenty years have witnessed a movement away from criticism and a return to a naïve acceptance of the kerygma. The danger both for theological scholarship and for the Church is that this uncritical resuscitation of the New Testament mythology may make the Gospel message unintelligible to the modern world. We cannot dismiss the critical labours of earlier generations without further ado. We must take them up and put them to constructive use. Failure to do so will mean that the old battles between orthodoxy and liberalism will have to be fought out all over again, that is assuming that there will be any Church or any theologians to fight them at all! Perhaps we may put it schematically like this: whereas the older liberals used criticism to *eliminate* the mythology of the New Testament, our task to-day is to use criticism to *interpret* it. Of course it may still be necessary to eliminate mythology here and there. But the criterion adopted must be taken not from modern thought, but from the understanding of human existence which the New Testament itself enshrines.[21]

To begin with, let us review some of these earlier attempts at demythologizing. We need only mention briefly the allegorical interpretation of the New Testament which has dogged the Church throughout its history. This method spiritualizes the mythical events so that they become symbols of processes going on in the soul. This is certainly the most comfortable way of avoiding the critical question. The literal meaning is allowed to stand and is dispensed with only for the individual believer, who can escape into the realm of the soul.

It was characteristic of the older liberal theologians that they regarded mythology as relative and temporary. Hence they thought they could safely eliminate it altogether, and retain only the broad, basic principles of religion and ethics. They distinguished between what they took to be the essence of religion and the temporary garb which it assumed. Listen to what Harnack has to say about the essence of Jesus' preaching of the Kingdom of God and its coming: "The kingdom has a triple meaning. Firstly, it is something supernatural, a gift from above, not a product of ordinary life. Secondly, it is a purely religious blessing, the inner link with the living God; thirdly, it is the most important experience that a man can have, that on which everything else depends; it permeates and dominates his whole existence, because sin is forgiven and misery banished." Note how completely the mythology is eliminated: "The kingdom of God comes by coming to the individual, by entering into his *soul* and laying hold of it."[22]

It will be noticed how Harnack reduces the kerygma to a few basic principles of religion and ethics. Unfortunately this means that *the kerygma has ceased to be kerygma:* it is no longer the proclamation of the decisive act of God in Christ. For the liberals the great truths of religion and ethics are timeless and eternal, though it is only within human history that they are realized, and only in concrete historical processes that they are given clear expression. But the apprehension and acceptance of these principles does not depend on the knowledge and acceptance of the age in which they first took shape, or of the historical persons who first discovered them. We are all capable of verifying them in our own experience at whatever period we happen to live. History may be of academic interest, but never of paramount importance for religion.

[21]As an illustration of this critical re-interpretation of myth cf. Hans Jonas, *Augustin und das paulinische Freiheitsproblem*, 1930, pp. 66–76.

[22]*What is Christianity?* Williams and Norgate, 1904, pp. 63–4 and 57.

But the New Testament speaks of an *event* through which God has wrought man's redemption. For it, Jesus is not primarily the teacher, who certainly had extremely important things to say and will always be honoured for saying them, but whose person in the last analysis is immaterial for those who have assimilated his teaching. On the contrary, his person is just what the New Testament proclaims as the decisive event of redemption. It speaks of this person in mythological terms, but does this mean that we can reject the kerygma altogether on the ground that it is nothing more than mythology? That is the question.

Next came the History of Religions school. Its representatives were the first to discover the extent to which the New Testament is permeated by mythology. The importance of the New Testament, they saw, lay not in its teaching about religion and ethics but in its actual religion and piety; in comparison with that all the dogma it contains, and therefore all the mythological imagery with its apparent objectivity, was of secondary importance or completely negligible. The essence of the New Testament lay in the religious life it portrayed; its high-watermark was the experience of mystical union with Christ, in whom God took symbolic form.

These critics grasped one important truth. Christian faith is not the same as religious idealism; the Christian life does not consist in developing the individual personality, in the improvement of society, or in making the world a better place. The Christian life means a turning away from the world, a detachment from it. But the critics of the History of Religions school failed to see that in the New Testament this detachment is essentially eschatological and not mystical. Religion for them was an expression of the human yearning to rise above the world and transcend it: it was the discovery of a supramundane sphere where the soul could detach itself from all earthly care and find its rest. Hence the supreme manifestation of religion was to be found not in personal ethics or in social idealism but in the cultus regarded as an end in itself. This was just the kind of religious life portrayed in the New Testament, not only as a model and pattern, but as a challenge and inspiration. The New Testament was thus the abiding source of power which enabled man to realize the true life of religion, and Christ was the eternal symbol for the cultus of the Christian Church.[23] It will be noticed how the Church is here defined exclusively as a worshipping community, and this represents a great advance on the older liberalism. The school rediscovered the Church as a *religious* institution. For the idealist there was really no place for the Church at all. But did they succeed in recovering the meaning of the Ecclesia in the full, New Testament sense of the word? For in the New Testament the Ecclesia is invariably a phenomenon of salvation history and eschatology.

Moreover, if the History of Religions school is right, the kerygma has once more ceased to be kerygma. Like the liberals, they are silent about a decisive act of God in Christ proclaimed as the event of redemption. So we are still left with the question whether this event and the person of Jesus,

[23]Cp. e.g. Troeltsch, *Die Bedeutung der Geschichtlichkeit Jesu Für den Glauben*, Tübingen, 1911.

both of which are described in the New Testament in mythological terms, are nothing more than mythology. Can the kerygma be interpreted apart from mythology? Can we recover the truth of the kerygma for men who do not think in mythological terms without forfeiting its character as kerygma?

5: An Existentialist Interpretation the Only Solution

The theological work which such an interpretation involves can be sketched only in the broadest outline and with only a few examples. We must avoid the impression that this is a light and easy task, as if all we have to do is to discover the right formula and finish the job on the spot. It is much more formidable than that. It cannot be done single-handed. It will tax the time and strength of a whole theological generation.

The mythology of the New Testament is in essence that of Jewish apocalyptic and the Gnostic redemption myths. A common feature of them both is their basic dualism, according to which the present world and its human inhabitants are under the control of daemonic, satanic powers, and stand in need of redemption. Man cannot achieve this redemption by his own efforts; it must come as a gift through a divine intervention. Both types of mythology speak of such an intervention: Jewish apocalyptic of an imminent world crisis in which this present aeon will be brought to an end and the new aeon ushered in by the coming of the Messiah, and Gnosticism of a Son of God sent down from the realm of light, entering into this world in the guise of a man, and by his fate and teaching delivering the elect and opening up the way for their return to their heavenly home.

The meaning of these two types of mythology lies once more not in their imagery with its apparent objectivity but in the understanding of human existence which both are trying to express. In other words, they need to be interpreted existentially. A good example of such treatment is to be found in Hans Jonas's book on Gnosticism.[24]

Our task is to produce an existentialist interpretation of the dualistic mythology of the New Testament along similar lines. When, for instance, we read of daemonic powers ruling the world and holding mankind in bondage, does the understanding of human existence which underlies such language offer a solution to the riddle of human life which will be acceptable even to the non-mythological mind of to-day? Of course we must not take this to imply that the New Testament presents us with an anthropology like that which modern science can give us. It cannot be proved by logic or demonstrated by an appeal to factual evidence. Scientific anthropologies always take for granted a definite understanding of existence, which is invariably the consequence of a deliberate decision of the scientist, whether he makes it consciously or not. And that is why we have to discover whether the New Testament offers man an understanding of himself which will challenge him to a genuine existential decision.

---

[24]*Gnosis und spätantiker Geist. I. Die mythologische Gnosis,* 1934.

✳ PAUL TILLICH

41. *The God above God*

Paul Tillich (1886–1965) was born and educated in Germany. In 1933 he was forced by the Nazis to immigrate to the United States where he taught at Union Theological Seminary, Harvard, and the University of Chicago. His influential translation of traditional theology into an existential-symbolic one is contained in a plethora of works such as *Dynamics of Faith, The Courage To Be, Theology of Culture,* and, most notably, his three-volume *Systematic Theology.*

From *The Courage To Be*

Chapter 6: Courage and Transcendence

Theism Transcended

The courage to take meaninglessness into itself presupposes a relation to the ground of being which we have called "absolute faith." It is without a *special* content, yet it is not without content. The content of absolute faith is the "God above God." Absolute faith and its consequence, the courage that takes the radical doubt, the doubt about God, into itself, transcends the theistic idea of God.

Theism can mean the unspecified affirmation of God. Theism in this sense does not say what it means if it uses the name of God. Because of the traditional and psychological connotations of the word God such an empty theism can produce a reverent mood if it speaks of God. Politicians, dictators, and other people who wish to use rhetoric to make an impression on their audience like to use the word God in this sense. It produces the feeling in their listeners that the speaker is serious and morally trustworthy. This is especially successful if they can brand their foes as atheistic. On a higher level people without a definite religious commitment like to call themselves theistic, not for special purposes but because they cannot stand a world without God, whatever this God may be. They need some of the connotations of the word God and they are afraid of what they call atheism. On the highest level of this kind of theism the name of God is used as a poetic or practical symbol, expressing a profound emotional state or the highest ethical idea. It is a theism which stands on the boundary line between the second type of theism and what we call "theism transcended." But it is still too indefinite to cross this boundary line. The atheistic negation of this whole type of theism is as vague as the theism itself. It may produce an irreverent mood and angry reaction of those who take their theistic affirmation seriously. It may even be felt as justified against the rhetorical-political abuse of the name God, but it is ultimately as irrelevant as the theism which it negates. It cannot reach the state of despair any more than the theism against which it fights can reach the state of faith.

Theism can have another meaning, quite contrary to the first one: it can be the name of what we have called the divine-human encounter. In this case it points to those elements in the Jewish-Christian tradition which emphasize the person-to-person relationship with God. Theism in this sense emphasizes the personalistic passages in the Bible and the Protestant creeds, the personalistic image of God, the word as the tool of creation and revelation, the ethical and social character of the kingdom of God, the personal nature of human faith and divine forgiveness, the historical vision of the universe, the idea of a divine purpose, the infinite distance between creator and creature, the absolute separation between God and the world, the conflict between holy God and sinful man, the person-to-person character of prayer and practical devotion. Theism in this sense is the nonmystical side of biblical religion and historical Christianity. Atheism from the point of view of this theism is the human attempt to escape the divine-human encounter. It is an existential—not a theoretical—problem.

Theism has a third meaning, a strictly theological one. Theological theism is, like every theology, dependent on the religious substance which is conceptualizes. It is dependent on theism in the first sense insofar as it tries to prove the necessity of affirming God in some way; it usually develops the so-called arguments for the "existence" of God. But it is more dependent on theism in the second sense insofar as it tries to establish a doctrine of God which transforms the person-to-person encounter with God into a doctrine about two persons who may or may not meet but who have a reality independent of each other.

Now theism in the first sense must be transcended because it is irrelevant, and theism in the second sense must be transcended because it is one-sided. But theism in the third sense must be transcended because it is wrong. It is bad theology. This can be shown by a more penetrating analysis. The God of theological theism is a being beside others and as such a part of the whole of reality. He certainly is considered its most important part, but as a part and therefore as subjected to the structure of the whole. He is supposed to be beyond the ontological elements and categories which constitute reality. But every statement subjects him to them. He is seen as a self which has a world, as an ego which is related to a thou, as a cause which is separated from its effect, as having a definite space and an endless time. He is a being, not being-itself. As such he is bound to the subject-object structure of reality, he is an object for us as subjects. At the same time we are objects for him as a subject. And this is decisive for the necessity of transcending theological theism. For God as a subject makes me into an object which is nothing more than an object. He deprives me of my subjectivity because he is all-powerful and all-knowing. I revolt and try to make *him* into an object, but the revolt fails and becomes desperate. God appears as the invincible tyrant, the being in contrast with whom all other beings are without freedom and subjectivity. He is equated with the recent tyrants who with the help of terror try to transform everything into a mere object, a thing among things, a cog in the machine they control. He becomes the model of everything against which Existentialism revolted. This is the God Nietzsche said had to be killed because nobody can tolerate being made into a mere object of absolute knowledge and absolute control. This is the deepest root of atheism. It is an atheism which is justified as the reaction against theological theism and its disturbing implications. It is also the deepest root of the Existentialist despair and the widespread anxiety of meaninglessness in our period.

Theism in all its forms is transcended in the experience we have called absolute faith. It is the accepting of the acceptance without somebody or something that accepts. It is the power of being-itself that accepts and gives the courage to be. This is the highest point to which our analysis has brought us. It cannot be described in the way the God of all forms of theism can be described. It cannot be described in mystical terms either. It transcends both mysticism and personal encounter, as it transcends both the courage to be as a part and the courage to be as oneself.

The God above God and the Courage to Be

The ultimate source of the courage to be is the "God above God"; this is the result of our demand to transcend theism. Only if the God of theism is transcended can the anxiety of doubt and meaninglessness be taken into the courage to be. The God above God is the object of all mystical longing, but mysticism also must be transcended in order to reach him. Mysticism does not take seriously the concrete and the doubt concerning the concrete. It plunges directly into the ground of being and meaning, and leaves the concrete, the world of finite values and meanings, behind. Therefore it does not solve the problem of meaninglessness. In terms of the present religious situation this means that Eastern mysticism is not the solution of the problems of Western Existentialism, although many people attempt this solution. The God above the God of theism is not the devaluation of the meanings which doubt has thrown into the abyss of meaninglessness; he is their potential restitution. Nevertheless absolute faith agrees with the faith implied in mysticism in that both transcend the theistic objectivation of a God who is a being. For mysticism such a God is not more real than any finite being, for the courage to be such a God has disappeared in the abyss of meaninglessness with every other value and meaning.

The God above the God of theism is present, although hidden, in every divine-human encounter. Biblical religion as well as Protestant theology are aware of the paradoxical character of this encounter. They are aware that if God encounters man God is neither object nor subject and is therefore above the scheme into which theism has forced him. They are aware that personalism with respect to God is balanced by a transpersonal presence of the divine. They are aware that forgiveness can be accepted only if the power of acceptance is effective in man—biblically speaking, if the power of grace is effective in man. They are aware of the paradoxical character of every prayer, of speaking to somebody to whom you cannot speak because he is not "somebody," of asking somebody of whom you cannot ask anything because he gives or gives not before you ask, of saying "thou" to somebody who is nearer to the I than the I is to itself. Each of these paradoxes drives the religious consciousness toward a God above the God of theism.

The courage to be which is rooted in the experience of the God above the God of theism unites and transcends the courage to be as a part and the courage to be as oneself. It avoids both the loss of oneself by participation and the loss of one's world by individualization. The acceptance of the God above the God of theism makes us a part of that which is not also a part but is the ground of the whole. Therefore our self is not lost in a larger whole, which submerges it in the life of a limited group. If the self participates in the power of being-itself it receives itself back. For the power of being acts through the power of the individual selves. It does not swallow them as every limited whole, every collectivism, and every conformism does. This is why the Church, which stands for the power of being-itself or for the God who transcends the God of the religions, claims to be the mediator of the courage to be. A church which is based on the authority of the God of theism cannot make such a claim. It inescapably develops into a collectivist or semicollectivist system itself.

But a church which raises itself in its message and its devotion to the God above the God of theism without sacrificing its concrete symbols can mediate a courage which takes doubt and meaninglessness into itself. It is the Church under the Cross which alone can do this, the Church which preaches the Crucified who cried to God who remained his God after the God of confidence had left him in the darkness of doubt and meaninglessness. To be as a part in such a church is to receive a courage to be in which one cannot lose one's self and in which one receives one's world.

Absolute faith, or the state of being grasped by the God beyond God, is not a state which appears beside other states of the mind. It never is something separated and definite, an event which could be isolated and described. It is always a movement in, with, and under other states of the mind. It is the situation on the boundary of man's possibilities. It *is* this boundary. Therefore it is both the courage of despair and the courage in and above every courage. It is not a place where one can live, it is without the safety of words and concepts, it is without a name, a church, a cult, a theology. But it is moving in the depth of all of them. It is the power of being, in which they participate and of which they are fragmentary expressions.

One can become aware of it in the anxiety of fate and death when the traditional symbols, which enable men to stand the vicissitudes of fate and the horror of death have lost their power. When "providence" has become a superstition and "immortality" something imaginary that which once was the power in these symbols can still be present and create the courage to be in spite of the experience of a chaotic world and a finite existence. The Stoic courage returns but not as the faith in universal reason. It returns as the absolute faith which says Yes to being without seeing anything concrete which could conquer the nonbeing in fate and death.

And one can become aware of the God above the God of theism in the anxiety of guilt and condemnation when the traditional symbols that enable men to withstand the anxiety of guilt and condemnation have lost their power. When "divine judgment" is interpreted as a psychological complex and forgiveness as a remnant of the "father-image," what once was the power in those symbols can still be present and create the courage to be in spite of the experience of an infinite gap between what we are and what we ought to be. The Lutheran courage returns but not supported by the faith in a judging and forgiving God. It returns in terms of the absolute faith which says Yes although there is no special power that conquers guilt. The courage to take the anxiety of meaninglessness upon oneself is the boundary line up to which the courage to be can go. Beyond it is mere non-being. Within it all forms of courage are re-established in the power of the God above the God of theism. *The courage to be is rooted in the God who appears when God has disappeared in the anxiety of doubt.*

From *Systematic Theology*, Volume II

INTRODUCTION, B: RESTATEMENTS OF ANSWERS GIVEN IN VOLUME I

1: Beyond Naturalism and Supranaturalism

. . . Much criticism has been made concerning the doctrine of God as developed in the second part of the system, "Being and God." Since the idea of God is the foundation and the center of every theological thought, this criticism is most important and welcome. For many, the stumbling block was the use of the term "Being" in relation to God, especially in the statement that the first thing we must say about God is that he is being-itself or being as being. Before speaking directly on this issue, I want to explain in a different terminology the basic intention of my doctrine of God. This is more simply expressed in the title of this section: "Beyond Naturalism and Supranaturalism." An idea of God which overcomes the conflict of naturalism and supranaturalism could be called "self-transcendent" or "ecstatic." In order to make this (tentative and preliminary) choice of words understandable, we may distinguish three ways of interpreting the meaning of the term "God." The first one separates God as a being, the highest being, from all other beings, alongside and above which he has his existence. In this position he has brought

Paul Tillich, *Systematic Theology* (Chicago: University of Chicago Press, 1952-63), II. Copyright ©1952, 1957, 1963. First published 1952, 1957, 1963. Reprinted by permission of The University of Chicago Press.

the universe into being at a certain moment (five thousand or five billion years ago), governs it according to a plan, directs it toward an end, interferes with its ordinary processes in order to overcome resistance to fulfil his purpose, and will bring it to consummation in a final catastrophe. Within this framework the whole divine-human drama is to be seen. Certainly this is a primitive form of supranaturalism, but a form which is more decisive for the religious life and its symbolic expression than any theological refinement of this position.

The main argument against it is that it transforms the infinity of God into a finiteness which is merely an extension of the categories of finitude. This is done in respect to space by establishing a supranatural divine world alongside the natural human world; in respect to time by determining a beginning and an end of God's creativity; in respect to causality by making God a cause alongside other causes; in respect to substance by attributing individual substance to him. Against this kind of supranaturalism the arguments of naturalism are valid and, as such, represent the true concern of religion, the infinity of the infinite, and the inviolability of the created structures of the finite. Theology must accept the antisupranatural criticism of naturalism.

The second way of interpreting the meaning of the term "God" identifies God with the universe, with its essence or with special powers within it. God is the name for the power and meaning of reality. He is not identified with the totality of things. No myth or philosophy has ever asserted such an absurdity. But he is a symbol of the unity, harmony, and power of being; he is the dynamic and creative center of reality. The phrase *deus sive natura*,[1] used by people like Scotus Erigena and Spinoza, does not say that God is identical with nature but that he is identical with the *natura naturans*,[2] the creative nature, the creative ground of all natural objects. In modern naturalism the religious quality of these affirmations has almost disappeared, especially among philosophizing scientists who understand nature in terms of materialism and mechanism. In philosophy proper, in so far as it became positivistic and pragmatistic, such assertions about nature as a whole were required. In so far as a whole philosophy of life involving dynamic processes developed, it again approached the religious forms of naturalism.

The main argument against naturalism in whatever form is that it denies the infinite distance between the whole of finite things and their infinite ground, with the consequence that the term "God" becomes interchangeable with the term "universe" and therefore is semantically superfluous. This semantic situation reveals the failure of naturalism to understand a decisive element in the experience of the holy, namely, the distance between finite man, on the one hand, and the holy in its numerous manifestations, on the other hand. For this, naturalism cannot account.

This criticism of the supranaturalistic and the naturalistic interpretations of the meaning of "God" calls for a third way which will liberate the

---

[1] ["God or nature."]
[2] [Literally, "nature naturing."]

discussion from the oscillation between two insufficient and religiously dangerous solutions. Such a third way is not new.

Theologians like Augustine, Thomas, Luther, Zwingli, Calvin, and Schleiermacher have grasped it, although in a restricted form. It agrees with the naturalistic view by asserting that God would not be God if he were not the creative ground of everything that has being, that, in fact, he is the infinite and unconditional power of being or, in the most radical abstraction, that he is being-itself. In this respect God is neither alongside things nor even "above" them; he is nearer to them than they are to themselves. He is their creative ground, here and now, always and everywhere.

Up to this point, the third view could be accepted by some forms of naturalism. But then the ways part. At this point the terms "self-transcendent" and "ecstatic," which I use for the third way of understanding the term "God," become meaningful. The term "self-transcendent" has two elements: "transcending" and "self." God as the ground of being infinitely transcends that of which he is the ground. He stands *against* the world, in so far as the world stands against him, and he stands *for* the world, thereby causing it to stand for him. This mutual freedom from each other and for each other is the only meaningful sense in which the "supra" in "supranaturalism" can be used. Only in this sense can we speak of "transcendent" with respect to the relation of God and the world. To call God transcendent in this sense does not mean that one must establish a "superworld" of divine objects. It does mean that, within itself, the finite world points beyond itself. In other words, it is self-transcendent.

Now the need for the syllable "self" in "self-transcendent" has also become understandable: the one reality which we encounter is experienced in different dimensions which point to one another. The finitude of the finite points to the infinity of the infinite. It goes beyond itself in order to return to itself in a new dimension. This is what "self-transcendence" means. In terms of immediate experience it is the encounter with the holy, an encounter which has an ecstatic character. The term "ecstatic" in the phrase "ecstatic idea of God" points to the experience of the holy as transcending ordinary experience without removing it. Ecstasy as a state of mind is the exact correlate to self-transcendence as the state of reality. Such an understanding of the idea of God is neither naturalistic nor supranaturalistic. It underlies the whole of the present theological system.

If, on the basis of this idea of God, we ask: "What does it mean that God, the ground of everything that is, can stand against the world and for the world?" we must refer to that quality of the world which expresses itself in finite freedom, the quality we experience within ourselves. The traditional discussion between the naturalistic and the supranaturalistic ideas of God uses the prepositions "in" and "above," respectively. Both are taken from the spatial realm and therefore are unable to express the true relation between God and the world—which certainly is not spatial. The self-transcendent idea of God replaces the spatial imagery—at least for theological thought—by the concept of finite freedom. The divine transcendence is identical with the freedom of the created to turn away from the essential unity with the creative ground of its being. Such freedom presupposes two qualities of the created: first, that it is substantially independent of the divine ground; second, that it remains in substantial unity with it. Without the latter unity, the creature would be without the power of being. It is the quality of finite freedom within the created which makes pantheism impossible and not the notion of a highest being alongside the world, whether his relation to the world is described in deistic or theistic terms.

The consequences of the self-transcendent idea of God for concepts like revelation and miracle (which are decisive for the christological problem) have been fully developed in the part entitled "Reason and Revelation." These do not need restatement, but they do show the far-reaching significance of the ecstatic interpretation of the relation between God and the world.

However, there is one problem which has moved into the center of the philosophical interest in religion since the appearance of the first volume. This is the problem of the symbolic knowledge of God. If God as the ground of being infinitely transcends everything that is, two consequences follow: first, whatever one knows about a finite thing one knows about God, because it is rooted in him as its ground; second, anything one knows about a finite thing cannot be applied to God, because he is, as has been said, "quite other" or, as could be said, "ecstatically transcendent." The unity of these two divergent consequences is the analogous or symbolic knowledge of God. A religious symbol uses the material of ordinary experience in speaking of God, but in such a way that the ordinary meaning of the material used is both affirmed and denied. Every religious symbol negates itself in its literal meaning, but it affirms itself in its self-transcending meaning. It is not a sign pointing to something with which it has no inner relationship. It represents the power and meaning of what is symbolized through participation. The symbol participates in the reality which is symbolized. Therefore, one should never say "only a symbol." This is to confuse symbol with sign. Thus it follows that everything religion has to say about God, including his qualities, actions, and manifestations, has a symbolic character and that meaning of "God" is completely missed if one takes the symbolic language literally.

But, after this has been stated, the question arises (and has arisen in public discussion) as to whether there is a point at which a non-symbolic assertion about God must be made. There is such a point, namely, the statement that everything we say about God is symbolic. Such a statement is an assertion about God which itself is not symbolic. Otherwise we would fall into a circular argument. On the other hand, if we make *one* non-symbolic assertion about God, his ecstatic-transcendent character seems to be endangered. This dialectical difficulty is a mirror of the human situation with respect to the divine ground of being. Although man is actually separated from the infinite, he could not be aware of it if he did not participate in it potentially. This is expressed in the state of being ultimately concerned, a state which is universally human, whatever the content of the concern may be. This is the point at which we must speak non-symbolically about God, but in terms of a quest for him. In the moment, however, in which we describe the character of this point or in which we try to formulate that for which we ask, a combination of symbolic with non-symbolic elements occurs. If we say that God is the infinite, or the unconditional, or being-itself, we speak rationally and ecstatically at the same time. These terms precisely designate the boundary line at which both the symbolic and the non-symbolic coincide. Up to this point every statement is non-symbolic (in the sense of religious symbol). Beyond this point every statement is symbolic (in the sense of religious symbol). The point itself is both non-symbolic and symbolic. This dialectical situation is the conceptual expression of man's existential situation. It is the condition for man's religious existence and for his ability to receive revelation. It is another side of the self-transcendent or ecstatic idea of God, beyond naturalism and supranaturalism.

2: The Use of the Concept of Being in Systematic Theology

When a doctrine of God is initiated by defining God as being-itself, the philosophical concept of being is introduced into systematic theology. This was so in the earliest period of Christian theology and has been so in the whole history of Christian thought. It appears in the present system in three places: in the doctrine of God, where God is called being as being or the ground and the power of being; in the doctrine of man, where the distinction is carried through between man's essential and his existential being; and, finally, in the doctrine of the Christ, where he is called the manifestation of the New Being, the actualization of which is the work of the divine Spirit.

In spite of the fact that classical theology has always used the concept of "being," the term has been criticized from the standpoint of nominalistic philosophy and that of personalistic theology. Considering the prominent role which the concept plays in the system, it is necessary to reply to the criticisms and at the same time to clarify the way in which the term is used in its different applications.

The criticism of the nominalists and their positivistic descendants to the present day is based on the assumption that the concept of being represents the highest possible abstraction. It is understood as the genus to which all other genera are subordinated with respect to universality and with respect to the degree of abstraction. If this were the way in which the concept of being is reached, nominalism could interpret it as it interprets all universals, namely, as communicative notions which point to particulars but have no reality of their own. Only the completely particular, the thing here and now, has reality. Universals are means of communication without any power of being. Being as such, therefore, does not designate anything real. God, if he exists, exists as a particular and could be called the most individual of all beings.

The answer to this argument is that the concept of being does not have the character that nominalism attributed to it. It is not the highest abstraction, although it demands the ability of radical abstraction. It is the expression of the experience of being over against non-being. Therefore, it can be described as the power of being which resists non-being. For this reason, the medieval philosophers called being the basic *transcendentale*, beyond the universal and the particular. In this sense the notion of being was understood alike by such people as Parmenides in Greece and Shankara in India. In this sense its significance has been rediscovered by contemporary existentialists, such as Heidegger and Marcel. This idea of being lies beyond the conflict of nominalism and realism. The same word, the emptiest of all concepts when taken as an abstraction, becomes the most meaningful of all concepts when it is understood as the power of being in everything that has being.

No philosophy can suppress the notion of being in this latter sense. It can be hidden under presuppositions and reductive formulas, but it nevertheless underlies the basic concepts of philosophizing. For "being" remains the content, the mystery, and the eternal *aporia*[3] of thinking. No theology can suppress the notion of being as the power of being. One cannot separate them. In the moment in which one says that God *is* or that he has being, the question arises as to how his relation to being is understood. The only possible answer seems to be that God is being-itself, in the sense of the power of being or the power to conquer non-being.

The main argument of personalistic theology against the use of the concept of being is derived from the personalism of man's experience of the holy as expressed in the personal figures of the gods and the person-to-person relation of man to God in living piety. This personalism is most pronounced in biblical religion. In contrast to many Asiatic religions and to Christian mysticism, the question of being is not asked. For an extensive discussion of this problem I refer to my little book *Biblical Religion and the Search for Ultimate Reality* (Chicago: University of Chicago Press, 1955). The radical contrast of biblical personalism and philosophical ontology is elaborated without compromise. And it is emphasized that no ontological search can be found in the biblical literature. At the same time, the necessity to ask the ontological question is taken with equal seriousness. There is no ontological thought in biblical religion; but there is no symbol or no theological concept in it which does not have ontological implications. Only artificial barriers can stop the searching mind from asking the question of the being of God, of the gap between man's essential and existential being, of the New Being in the Christ.

For some, it is mostly the impersonal sound of the word "being" which produces concern. But suprapersonal is not impersonal; and I would ask those who are afraid to transcend the personalistic symbolism of the religious language to think, even if only for a short moment, of the words of Jesus about the hairs on our head being counted—and, we could add, the atoms and electrons constituting the universe. In such a statement there is at least as much potential ontology as there is actual ontology in the whole system of Spinoza. To prohibit the transformation of the potential into an

[3]["impasse."]

actual ontology—of course, within the theological circle—would reduce theology to a repetition and organization of biblical passages. It would be impossible to call the Christ "the Logos."

In the last chapter of my book *The Courage to Be* (New Haven: Yale University Press, 1952) I have written of the God above the God of theism. This has been misunderstood as a dogmatic statement of a pantheistic or mystical character. First of all, it is not a dogmatic, but an apologetic, statement. It takes seriously the radical doubt experienced by many people. It gives one the courage of self-affirmation even in the extreme state of radical doubt. In such a state the God of both religious and theological language disappears. But something remains, namely, the seriousness of that doubt in which meaning within meaninglessness is affirmed. The source of this affirmation of meaning within meaninglessness, of certitude within doubt, is not the God of traditional theism but the "God above God," the power of being, which works through those who have no name for it, not even the name God. This is the answer to those who ask for a message in the nothingness of their situation and at the end of their courage to be. But such an extreme point is not a space within which one can live. The dialectics of an extreme situation are a criterion of truth but not the basis on which a whole structure of truth can be built.

II, E: THE NEW BEING IN JESUS AS THE CHRIST AS THE POWER OF SALVATION

1: The Meaning of Salvation

The universal significance of Jesus as the Christ, which is expressed in the symbols of subjection to existence and of victory over existence, can also be expressed in the term "salvation." He himself is called the Savior . . .

The term "salvation" has as many connotations as there are negativities from which salvation is needed. But one can distinguish salvation from ultimate negativity and from that which leads to ultimate negativity. Ultimate negativity is called condemnation or eternal death, the loss of the inner *telos*[4] of one's being, the exclusion from the universal unity of the Kingdom of God, and the exclusion from eternal life. In the overwhelming majority of occasions in which the word "salvation" or the phrase "being saved" is used, it refers to salvation from this ultimate negativity. The tremendous weight of the question of salvation is rooted in this understanding of the term. It becomes the question of "to be or not to be."

The way in which the ultimate aim—eternal life—can be gained or lost decides about the more limited meaning of "salvation." Therefore, for the early Greek church death and error were the things from which one needed and wanted to be saved. In the Roman Catholic church salvation is from guilt and its consequences in this and the next life (in purgatory and hell). In classical Protestantism salvation is from the law, its anxiety-producing and

---

[4]['fulfillment.'']

its condemning power. In pietism and revivalism salvation is the conquest of the godless state through conversion and transformation for those who are converted. In ascetic and liberal Protestantism salvation is the conquest of special sins and progress toward moral perfection. The question of life and death in the ultimate sense has not disappaered in the latter groups (except in some forms of so-called theological humanism), but it has been pushed into the background.

With respect to both the original meaning of salvation (from *salvus*, "healed") and our present situation, it may be adequate to interpret salvation as "healing." It corresponds to the state of estrangement as the main characteristic of existence. In this sense, healing means reuniting that which is estranged, giving a center to what is split, overcoming the split between God and man, man and his world, man and himself. Out of this interpretation of salvation, the concept of the New Being has grown. Salvation is reclaiming from the old and transferring into the New Being. This understanding includes the elements of salvation which were emphasized in other periods; it includes, above all, the fulfilment of the ultimate meaning of one's existence, but it sees this in a special perspective, that of making *salvus*, of "healing."

If Christianity derives salvation from the appearance of Jesus as the Christ, it does not separate salvation through the Christ from the processes of salvation, i.e., of healing, which occur throughout all history. We have discussed the problem of "healing" universally in the section on revelation. There is a history of concrete revelatory events in all periods in which man exists as man. It would be wrong to call that history itself the history of revelation (with some theological humanists). But it would be equally wrong to deny that revelatory events occur anywhere besides the appearance of Jesus as the Christ. There is a history of revelation, the center of which is the event Jesus the Christ; but the center is not without a line which leads to it (preparatory revelation) and a line which leads from it (receiving revelation). Further, we have asserted that where there is revelation, there is salvation. Revelation is not information about divine things; it is the ecstatic manifestation of the Ground of Being in events, persons, and things. Such manifestations have shaking, transforming, and healing power. They are saving events in which the power of the New Being is present. It is present in a preparatory way, fragmentarily, and is open to demonic distortion. But it is present and heals where it is seriously accepted. On these healing forces the life of mankind always depends; they prevent the self-destructive structures of existence from plunging mankind into complete annihilation. This is true of individuals as well as of groups and is the basis for a positive evolution of the religions and cultures of mankind. However, the idea of a universal history of salvation can be developed fully only in the parts of *Systematic Theology* which deal with "Life and the Spirit" and with "History and the Kingdom of God" (Vol. III).

This view of the history of salvation excludes an unbiblical but nevertheless ecclesiastical view of salvation. It is the belief that salvation is either total or non-existent. Total salvation, in this view, is identical with being

taken into the state of ultimate blessedness and is the opposite of total condemnation to everlasting pain or eternal death. If, then, the salvation to eternal
life is made dependent upon the encounter with Jesus as the Christ and the
acceptance of his saving power, only a small number of human beings will
ever reach salvation. The others, either through a divine decree or through
the destiny which came upon them from Adam's Fall or through their own
guilt, are condemned to exclusion from eternal life. Theologies of universalism
always tried to escape this absurd and demonic idea, but it is difficult to
do so, once the absolute alternative between salvation and condemnation is
presupposed. Only if salvation is understood as healing and saving power
through the New Being in all history is the problem put on another level.
In some degree all men participate in the healing power of the New Being.
Otherwise, they would have no being. The self-destructive consequences of
estrangement would have destroyed them. But no men are totally healed,
not even those who have encountered the healing power as it appears in
Jesus as the Christ. Here the concept of salvation drives us to the eschatological
symbolism and its interpretation. It drives us to the symbol of cosmic healing
and to the question of the relation of the eternal to the temporal with respect
to the future.

What, then, is the peculiar character of the healing through the New
Being in Jesus as the Christ? If he is accepted as the Savior, what does salvation
through him mean? The answer cannot be that there is no saving power apart
from him but that he is the ultimate criterion of every healing and saving
process. We said before that even those who have encountered him are only
fragmentarily healed. But now we must say that in him the healing quality
is complete and unlimited. The Christian remains in the state of relativity
with respect to salvation; the New Being in the Christ transcends every relativity in its quality and power of healing. It is just this that makes him the
Christ. Therefore, wherever there is saving power in mankind, it must be
judged by the saving power in Jesus as the Christ.

❈ DIETRICH BONHOEFFER

42. *Religionless Christianity*

Dietrich Bonhoeffer (born 1906) was for a time a professor of theology at
the University of Berlin, then a pastor of several congregations, and
eventually a worker for the German "Confessing Church" which opposed
the Nazis. He became involved in the plot to assassinate Hitler, was
imprisoned, and executed on April 9, 1945. The evolution of Bonhoeffer's
"non-religious" interpretation of Christianity is discernible in his *The Cost
of Discipleship*, *Ethics*, and *Letters and Papers from Prison*.

From *Letters and Papers from Prison*

16 July 1944

. . . Now for a few more thoughts on our theme. I am only gradually working my way to the non-religious interpretation of biblical concepts; the job is too big for me to finish just yet.

On the historical side: There is one great development that leads to the world's autonomy. In theology one sees it first in Lord Herbert of Cherbury, who maintains that reason is sufficient for religious knowledge. In ethics it appears in Montaigne and Bodin with their substitution of rules of life for the commandments. In politics Machiavelli detaches politics from morality in general and founds the doctrine of "reasons of State." Later, and very differently from Machiavelli, but tending like him towards the autonomy of human society, comes Grotius, setting up his natural law as international law, which is valid *etsi deus non daretur*, "even if there were no God." The philosophers provide the finishing touches: on the one hand we have the deism of Descartes, who holds that the world is a mechanism, running by itself with no interference from God; and on the other hand the pantheism of Spinoza, who says that God is nature. In the last resort, Kant is a deist, and Fichte and Hegel are pantheists. Everywhere the thinking is directed towards the autonomy of man and the world.

(It seems that in the natural sciences the process begins with Nicolas of Cusa and Giordano Bruno and their "heretical" doctrine of the infinity of the universe. The classical *cosmos* was finite, like the created world of the Middle Ages. An infinite universe, however it may be conceived, is self-subsisting, *etsi deus non daretur*. It is true that modern physics is not as sure as it was about the infinity of the universe, but it has not gone back to the earlier conceptions of its finitude.)

God as a working hypothesis in morals, politics, or science, has been surmounted and abolished; and the same thing has happened in philosophy and religion (Feuerbach!). For the sake of intellectual honesty, that working hypothesis should be dropped, or as far as possible eliminated. A scientist or physician who sets out to edify is a hybrid.

Anxious souls will ask what room there is left for God now; and as they know of no answer to the question, they condemn the whole development that has brought them to such straits. I wrote to you before about the various emergency exits that have been contrived; and we ought to add to them the *salto mortale* (death-leap) back into the Middle Ages. But the principle of the Middle Ages is heteronomy in the form of clericalism; a return to that can only be a counsel of despair, and it would be at the cost of intellectual honesty. It is a dream that reminds one of the song *O wüsst ich doch den*

Dietrich Bonhoeffer, *Letters and Papers from Prison*, ed. Eberhard Bethge, tr. Reginald Fuller, revised ed. (New York: Macmillan, 1967). Reprinted by permission of The Macmillan Company. Copyright by the Macmillan Company, 1953. Also reprinted by permission of SCM Press, Ltd., publishers. © SCM Press, Ltd., 1967.

Weg zurück, den weiten Weg ins Kinderland.[1] There is no such way—at any rate not if it means deliberately abandoning our mental integrity; the only way is that of Matt. 18.3, i.e. through repentance, through *ultimate* honesty.

And we cannot be honest unless we recognize that we have to live in the world *etsi deus non daretur*. And this is just what we do recognize—before God! God himself compels us to recognize it. So our coming of age leads us to a true recognition of our situation before God. God would have us know that we must live as men who manage our lives without him. The God who is with us is the God who forsakes us (Mark 15.34). The God who lets us live in the world without the working hypothesis of God is the God before whom we stand continually. Before God and with God we live without God. God lets himself be pushed out of the world on to the cross. He is weak and powerless in the world, and that is precisely the way, the only way, in which he is with us and helps us. Matt. 8.17 makes it quite clear that Christ helps us, not by virtue of his omnipotence, but by virtue of his weakness and suffering.

Here is the decisive difference between Christianity and all religions. Man's religiosity makes him look in his distress to the power of God in the world: God is the *deus ex machina*. The Bible directs man to God's powerlessness and suffering; only the suffering God can help. To that extent we may say that the development towards the world's coming of age outlined above, which has done away with a false conception of God, opens up a way of seeing the God of the Bible, who wins power and space in the world by his weakness. This will probably be the starting-point for our "secular interpretation."

Who Am I?

Who am I? They often tell me
I step from my cell's confinement
calmly, cheerfully, firmly,
like a squire from his country-house.
Who am I? They often tell me
I talk to my warders
freely and friendly and clearly,
as though it were mine to command.
Who am I? They also tell me
I bear the days of misfortune
equably, smilingly, proudly,
like one accustomed to win.

Am I then really all that which other men tell of?
Or am I only what I know of myself,
restless and longing and sick, like a bird in a cage,
struggling for breath, as though hands were compressing
　　my throat,

---

[1]["Oh if only I knew the way back, the long way back to the land of childhood."]

yearning for colours, for flowers, for the voices of birds,
thirsting for words of kindness, for neighbourliness,
tossing in expectation of great events,
powerlessly trembling for friends at an infinite distance,
weary and empty at praying, at thinking, at making,
faint, and ready to say farewell to it all?
Who am I? This or the other?
Am I one person today, and tomorrow another?
Am I both at once? A hypocrite before others,
and before myself a contemptibly woebegone weakling?
Or is something within me still like a beaten army,
fleeing in disorder from victory already achieved?

Who am I? They mock me, these lonely questions of mine.
Whoever I am, thou knowest, O God, I am thine.

18 July 1944

I wonder whether any letters have been lost in the raids on Munich. Did you get the one with the two poems? It was just sent off that evening, and it also contained a few introductory remarks on our theological theme. The poem about Christians and pagans contains an idea that you will recognize: "Christians stand by God in his hour of grieving"; that is what distinguishes Christians from pagans. Jesus asked in Gethsemane, "Could you not watch with me one hour?" [Matt. 26:40]. That is a reversal of what the religious man expects from God. Man is summoned to share in God's sufferings at the hands of a godless world.

He must therefore really live in the godless world, without attempting to gloss over or explain its ungodliness in some religious way or other. He must live a "secular" life, and thereby share in God's sufferings. He *may* live a "secular" life: i.e. he is freed (as one who has been liberated from false religious obligation inhibitions). To be a Christian does not mean to be religious in a particular way, to make something of oneself (a sinner, a penitent, or a saint) on the basis of some method or other, but to be a man—not a type of man, but the man that Christ creates in us. It is not the religious act that makes the Christian, but participation in the sufferings of God in the secular life.

That is *metanoia*[2]: not in the first place thinking about one's own needs, problems, sins, and fears, but allowing oneself to be caught up into the way of Jesus Christ, into the messianic event, thus fulfilling Isa. 53. Therefore "believe in the gospel" [Mark 1:15], or, in the words of John the Baptist, "Behold, the Lamb of God, who takes away the sin of the world" (John 1.29). (By the way, Jeremias has recently asserted that the Aramaic word for "lamb" may also be translated "servant"; this is very appropriate in view of Isa. 53.)

[2]["repentance."]

This being caught up into the messianic suffering of God in Jesus Christ takes a variety of forms in the New Testament. It appears in the call to discipleship, in Jesus' table-fellowship with sinners, in "conversions" in the narrower sense of the word (e.g. Zacchaeus), in the act of the woman who was a sinner (Luke 7)—an act that she performed without any confession of sin, in the healing of the sick (Matt. 8.17; see above), in Jesus' acceptance of children. The shepherds, like the wise men from the East, stand at the crib, not as "converted sinners," but simply because they are drawn to the crib by the star just as they are. The centurion of Capernaum (who makes no confession of sin) is held up as a model of faith [cf. Matt. 8] (cf. Jairus [cf. Mark 5]). Jesus "loved" the rich young man [cf. Mark 10]. The eunuch (Acts 8) and Cornelius (Acts 10) are not standing at the edge of an abyss. Nathaniel is "an Israelite indeed, in whom there is no guile" (John 1.47). Finally, Joseph of Arimathea and the women at the tomb [cf. Mark 15–16]. The only thing that is common to all these is their sharing in the suffering of God in Christ. That is their "faith."

There is nothing of religious method here. The "religious act" is always something partial; "faith" is something whole, involving the whole of one's life. Jesus calls men, not to a new religion, but to life. But what does this life look like, this participation in the powerlessness of God in the world? I will write about that next time, I hope.

Just one more point for today. When we speak of God in a "non-religious" way, we must speak of him in such a way that the godlessness of the world is not in some way concealed but for that very reason revealed rather in, and thus exposed to, an unexpected light. The world that has come of age is more godless, and perhaps its coming of age is nearer to God than before.

Forgive me for still putting it all so terribly clumsily and badly, as I really feel I am. . . . We are getting up at 1.30 almost every night here; it is a bad time, and it handicaps mental work.

CHRISTIANS AND PAGANS

Men go to God when they are sore bestead,
Pray to him for succour, for his peace, for bread,
For mercy for them sick, sinning, or dead;
All men do so, Christian and unbelieving.

Men go to God when he is sore bestead,
Find him poor and scorned, without shelter or bread,
Whelmed under weight of the wicked, the weak, the dead;
Christians stand by God in his hour of grieving.

God goeth to every man when sore bestead,
Feedeth body and spirit with his bread;
For Christians, pagans alike he hangeth dead,
And both alike forgiving.

21 July 1944

All I want to do today is to send you a short greeting. I expect you are often with us here in your thoughts and are always glad of any sign of life, even if the theological discussion stops for a moment. These theological thoughts are, in fact, always occupying my mind; but there are times when I am just content to live the life of faith without worrying about its problems. At those times I simply take pleasure in the day's *Losungen*—in particular those of yesterday and today; and I am always glad to go back to Paul Gerhardt's beautiful hymns.

During the last year or so I have come to know and understand more and more the profound this-worldliness of Christianity. The Christian is not a *homo religiosus*, but simply a man, as Jesus was a man—in contrast, shall we say, to John the Baptist. I don't mean the shallow and banal this-worldliness of the enlightened, the busy, the comfortable, or the lascivious, but the profound this worldliness, characterized by discipline and the constant knowledge of death and resurrection. I think Luther lived a this-worldly life in this sense.

I remember a conversation that I had in A.[3] thirteen years ago with a young French pastor. We were asking ourselves quite simply what we wanted to do with our lives. He said he would like to become a saint (and I think it is quite likely that he did become one). At the time I was very impressed, but I disagreed with him, and said, in effect, that I should like to learn to have faith. For a long time I did not realize the depth of the contrast. I thought I could acquire faith by trying to live a holy life, or something like it. I suppose I wrote *The Cost of Discipleship* as the end of that path. Today I can see the dangers of that book, though I still stand by what I wrote.

I discovered later, and I am still discovering right up to this moment, that it is only by living completely in this world that one learns to have faith. One must completely abandon any attempt to make something of oneself, whether it be a saint, or a converted sinner, or a churchman (a so-called priestly type!), a righteous man or an unrighteous one, a sick man or a healthy one. By this-worldliness I mean living unreservedly in life's duties, problems, successes and failures, experiences and perplexities. In so doing we throw ourselves completely into the arms of God, taking seriously, not our own sufferings, but those of God in the world—watching with Christ in Gethsemane. That I think is faith, that is *metanoia*; and that is how one becomes a man and a Christian (cf. Jer. 45!). How can success make us arrogant, or failure lead us astray, when we share in God's sufferings through a life of this kind?

I think you see what I mean, even though I put it so briefly. I am glad to have been able to learn this, and I know I have been able to do so only along the road that I have travelled. So I am grateful for the past and present, and content with them. You may be surprised at such a personal letter; but if for once I want to say this kind of thing, whom should I say

[3][America.]

it to? May God in his mercy lead us through these times; but above all may he lead us to himself.

I was delighted to hear from you, and am glad you are not finding it too hot. There must be a good many letters from me on the way. Didn't we go more or less along that way in 1936?

Good-bye. Keep well, and don't lose hope that we shall all meet again soon.

STATIONS ON THE ROAD TO FREEDOM

Discipline

If you set out to seek freedom, then learn above all things
to govern your soul and your senses, for fear that your passions
and longings may lead you away from the path you should follow.
Chaste be your mind and your body, and both in subjection,
obediently, steadfastly seeking the aim set before them;
only through discipline may a man learn to be free.

Action

Daring to do what is right, not what fancy may tell you,
valiantly grasping occasions, not cravenly doubting—
freedom comes only through deeds, not through thoughts taking wing.
Faint not nor fear, but go out to the storm and the action,
trusting in God whose commandment you faithfully follow;
freedom, exultant, will welcome your spirit with joy.

Suffering

A change has come indeed. Your hands, so strong and active,
are bound in helplessness now you see your action ended; you sigh in
relief, your cause committing
to stronger hands; so you now may rest contented.
Only for one blissful moment could you draw near to touch freedom;
then, that it might be perfect in glory, you gave it to God.

Death

Come now, thou greatest of feasts on the journey to freedom eternal;
death, cast aside all the burdensome chains, and demolish
the walls of our temporal body, the walls of our souls that are blinded,
so that at last we may see that which here remains hidden.
Freedom, how long we have sought thee in discipline, action, and
suffering;
dying, we now may behold thee revealed in the Lord.

I wrote these lines in a few hours this evening. They are quite unpolished, but they may perhaps please you and be something of a birthday present for you.

I can see this morning that I shall again have to revise these lines completely. Still, I am sending them to you as they are, in the rough. I am certainly no poet!

3 August 1944

. . . I wonder whether you will be moved again soon, and if so, where to. I should like to know whether you have read my poems. You must read the very long one (in rhyme), *Nächtliche Stimmen in Tegel,* some time later. I am enclosing the outline of a book that I have planned. I don't know whether you can get anything from it, but I think you more or less understand what I am driving at. I hope I shall be given the peace and strength to finish it. The Church must come out of its stagnation. We must move out again into the open air of intellectual discussion with the world, and risk saying controversial things, if we are to get down to the serious problems of life. I feel obliged to tackle these questions as one who, although a "modern" theologian, is still aware of the debt that he owes to liberal theology. There will not be many of the younger men in whom these two trends are combined. How very useful your help would be! But even if we are prevented from clarifying our minds by talking things over, we can still pray, and it is only in the spirit of prayer that any such work can be begun and carried through.

I have been reading about "tropical heat" in Italy. Is it very bad? . . . There is nothing to report about the family; I am always glad when I can write that. Good-bye.

Outline for a Book

I should like to write a book of not more than 100 pages, divided into three chapters:

1. A Stocktaking of Christianity.
2. The Real Meaning of Christian Faith.
3. Conclusions.

Chapter 1 to deal with:

(*a*) The coming of age of mankind (as already indicated). The safeguarding of life against "accidents" and "blows of fate"; even if these cannot be eliminated, the danger can be reduced. Insurance (which, although it lives on "accidents," seeks to mitigate their effects) as a western phenomenon. The aim: to be independent of nature. Nature was formerly conquered by spiritual means, with us by technical organization of all kinds. Our immediate environment is not nature, as formerly, but organization. But with this protection from nature's menace there arises a new one—through organization itself.

But the spiritual force is lacking. The question is: What protects us against the menace of organization? Man is again thrown back on himself. He has managed to deal with everything, only not with himself. He can insure against everything, only not against man. In the last resort it all turns on man.

(*b*) The religionlessness of man who has come of age. "God" as a working hypothesis, as a stop-gap for our embarrassments, has become superfluous (as already indicated).

(c) The Protestant Church: Pietism as a last attempt to maintain evangelical Christianity as a religion; Lutheran orthodoxy, the attempt to rescue the Church as an institution for salvation; the Confessing Church: the theology of revelation; a δὸς μοὶ ποῦ στῶ[4] over against the world, involving a "factual" interest in Christianity; art and science searching for their origin. Generally in the Confessing Church: standing up for the Church's "cause," but little personal faith in Christ. "Jesus" is disappearing from sight. Sociologically: no effect on the masses—interest confined to the upper and lower middle classes. A heavy incubus of difficult traditional ideas. The decisive factor: the Church on the defensive. No taking risks for others.

(d) Public morals—as shown by sexual behaviour.

Chapter 2.

(a) God and the secular.

(b) Who is God? Not in the first place an abstract belief in God, in his omnipotence, etc. This is not a genuine experience of God, but a partial extension of the world. Encounter with Jesus Christ. The experience that a transformation of all human life is given in the fact that "Jesus is there only for others." His "being there for others" is the experience of transcendence. It is only this "being there for others," maintained till death, that is the ground of his omnipotence, omniscience, and omnipresence. Faith is participation in this being of Jesus (incarnation, cross, and resurrection). Our relation to God is not a "religious" relationship to the highest, most powerful, and best Being imaginable—that is not authentic transcendence—but our relation to God is a new life in "existence for others," through participation in the being of Jesus. The transcendental is not infinite and unattainable tasks, but the neighbour who is within reach in any given situation. God in human form—not, as in oriental religions, in animal form, monstrous, chaotic, remote, and terrifying, nor in the conceptual forms of the absolute, metaphysical, infinite, etc., nor yet in the Greek divine-human form of "man in himself," but "the man for others," and therefore the Crucified, the man who lives out of the transcendent.

(c) Interpretation of biblical concepts on this basis. (Creation, fall, atonement, repentance, faith, the new life, the last things.)

(d) Cultus. (Details to follow later, in particular on cultus and "religion.")

(e) What do we really believe? I mean, believe in such a way that we stake our lives on it? The problem of the Apostles' Creed? "What *must* I believe?" is the wrong question; antiquated controversies, especially those between the different sects; the Lutheran versus Reformed, and to some extent the Roman Catholic versus Protestant, are now unreal. They may at anytime be revived with passion, but they no longer carry conviction. There is no proof of this, and we must simply take it that it is so. All that we can prove is that the faith of the Bible and Christianity does not stand or fall by these issues. Karl Barth and the Confessing Church have encouraged us to entrench

---

[4]["Give me a place to stand (and I will move the world)"—Archimedes.]

ourselves persistently behind the "faith of the Church," and evade the honest question as to what we ourselves really believe. That is why the air is not quite fresh, even in the Confessing Church. To say that it is the Church's business, not mine, may be a clerical evasion, and outsiders always regard it as such. It is much the same with the dialectical assertion that I do not control my own faith, and that it is therefore not for me to say what my faith is. There may be a place for all these considerations, but they do not absolve us from the duty of being honest with ourselves. We cannot, like the Roman Catholics, simply identify ourselves with the Church. (This, incidentally, explains the popular opinion about Roman Catholics' insincerity.) Well then, what do we really believe? Answer: see (*b*), (*c*), and (*d*) .

Chapter 3.

Conclusions:

The Church is the Church only when it exists for others. To make a start, it should give away all its property to those in need. The clergy must live solely on the free-will offerings of their congregations, or possibly engage in some secular calling. The Church must share in the secular problems of ordinary human life, not dominating, but helping and serving. It must tell men of every calling what it means to live in Christ, to exist for others. In particular, our own Church will have to take the field against the vices of *hubris*, power-worship, envy, and humbug, as the roots of all evil. It will have to speak of moderation, purity, trust, loyalty, constancy, patience, discipline, humility, contentment, and modesty. It must not underestimate the importance of human example (which has its origin in the humanity of Jesus and is so important in Paul's teaching); it is not abstract argument, but example, that gives its word emphasis and power. (I hope to take up later this subject of "example" and its place in the New Testament; it is something that we have almost entirely forgotten). Further: the question of revising the creeds (the Apostles' Creed); revision of Christian apologetics; reform of the training for the ministry and the pattern of clerical life.

All this is very crude and condensed, but there are certain things that I am anxious to say simply and clearly—things that we so often like to shirk. Whether I shall succeed is another matter, especially if I cannot discuss it with you. I hope it may be of some help for the Church's future.

23 AUGUST 1944

. . . Please don't ever get anxious or worried about me, but don't forget to pray for me—I'm sure you don't! I am so sure of God's guiding hand that I hope I shall always be kept in that certainty. You must never doubt that I am travelling with gratitude and cheerfulness along the road where I am being led. My past life is brim-full of God's goodness, and my sins are covered by the forgiving love of Christ crucified. I am most thankful for the people I have met, and I only hope that they never have to grieve about me, but that they, too, will always be certain of, and thankful for,

God's mercy and forgiveness. Forgive my writing this. Don't let it grieve or upset you for a moment, but let it make you happy. But I did want to say it for once, and I could not think of anyone else who I could be sure would take it aright.

Did you get the poem on freedom? It was very unpolished, but it is a subject about which I feel deeply.

I am now working at the chapter on "A Stocktaking of Christianity." Unfortunately my output of work has come to depend increasingly on smoking, but I am lucky enough to have a good supply from the most varied sources, so that I am getting on more or less. Sometimes I am quite shocked at what I say, especially in the first part, which is mainly critical; and so I am looking forward to getting to the more constructive part. But the whole thing has been so little discussed that it often sounds too clumsy. In any case, it can't be printed yet, and it will have to go through the "purifier" later on. I find it hard work to have to write everything by hand, and it seems hardly legible. (Amusingly enough, I have to use German script, and then there are the corrections!). We shall see; perhaps I shall write out a fair copy. . . .

I do so hope you will have a quiet time in body and mind. May God take care of you and all of us, and grant us the joy of meeting again soon. I am praying for you every day.

Your true and grateful friend,
D.

❋ PAUL VAN BUREN

43. *Christ and the Secular Man*

Paul van Buren received his B.A. degree (in government) from Harvard University, his B.D. from the Episcopal Theological School, and his doctorate (in theology) from the University of Basel, Switzerland, where he studied with Karl Barth. Van Buren, who has served as a parish minister and is presently a professor of theology at Temple University, attempts to synthesize classical Christology with the empirical outlook of contemporary secular man.

From *The Secular Meaning of the Gospel*

CHAPTER 6: THE MEANING OF THE GOSPEL

The Gospel as the Expression of a Historical Perspective

The Gospel, the "good news" of the apostles concerning Jesus of Nazareth and what happened on Easter, was proclaimed as news of an event

Paul M. van Buren, *The Secular Meaning of the Gospel* (New York: Macmillan, 1963). © by Paul van Buren, 1963. Reprinted by permission of The Macmillan Company. Also reprinted with permission of SCM Press, Ltd., publishers.

which it was good for men to hear. The result of its proclamation was that many responded with joy and became "Christians." They shared the way of life of the apostles and the apostles' conviction that the history of Jesus and the event of Easter had universal significance. We shall introduce our analysis of the language of this Gospel by comparing the positions of those who first preached it on the basis of the Easter experience, and of those who became believers later. After a discussion of particularity and universality in the language of the kerygma, we shall analyze the content of the kerygma itself in its basic form, comparing our result with other analyses of the language of faith. Our result will then be compared with some typical, central christological assertions of the Gospel and with the "call and response" Christology developed in Chapter 2. Although our analysis cannot cover every detail of the language of the Gospel, we intend to give careful attention to the central assertions of the kerygma, so that the logic of its language will be clear.

In the last chapter, we analyzed the language of those who experienced the appearances of Easter described in I Cor. 15:3 ff.[1] Faith in the Gospel of the resurrection was not confined, however, to those who had been "eye witnesses" of the Easter event. The apostles proclaimed the Gospel to others, and some of their hearers responded positively. Those who became Christians in this way understood themselves as sharing with the apostles in a freedom defined by the freedom of Jesus of Nazareth and in a new perspective upon life and the world. This experience has been traditionally called conversion.

A man who has been converted to Christian faith does not ordinarily go about saying, "I have seen the Lord." He may say, "I have seen the light," however, and this suggests how his experience at once resembles and differs from that of the apostles on Easter. Theology has traditionally accounted for his conversion not by referring to an appearance of Jesus, as in the case of the apostles, but by referring to the work of the Holy Spirit. It should not be necessary at this stage of our argument to explain why saying that a man was brought to faith and freedom "by the operation of the Holy Spirit" is not an empirical assertion, in any unsophisticated sense of the word "empirical." If a man says this, he may indeed intend to call our attention to certain aspects of how things are in the world, and if we see things as he does, we may also attend to these aspects, which would provide some empirical grounding for his statement. The divine reference ("Holy Spirit") does indicate, for instance, that the new freedom and perspective are received as gifts by the believer and that they are of fundamental importance to him. The divine reference is also at least an indirect reference to Jesus.[2] Christian theology, especially in the classical Protestant tradition, has underscored this reference to Jesus by saying that such an "operation of the Holy Spirit" does not take place apart from the "proclamation of the Word."[3] The story of the man who was free for others even to the point of death, and whose freedom has been contagious, is held up to the listener, who is invited to share in this event.[4] In the context of hearing the Gospel proclaimed, the listener may

---

[1]Cf. also I Cor. 9:1.
[2]John 15:26; 16:14.
[3]Typically, Calvin *Institutes*, I, ix, 1–3.
[4]Gal. 3:1; Heb. 2:8–9.

have an experience of discernment. He may "see" Jesus in a new way and acquire a new perspective upon himself and the whole of life. A long tradition of Christian devotional literature has emphasized the act of historical imagination in which the reader is invited to be "present" at the events of which the Gospel speaks, and this imaginative act has also played its part in much of Christian worship. Although the language of conversion differs from the language of those involved in the Easter event, they function in a remarkably similar manner. The difference between the two lies in the fact that the believers' expression of faith depends logically and historically upon that of the apostles.

The language of faith, whether that of the first apostles or of a modern believer, contains an exclusive element: it claims the universal significance of a particular, historical individual, Jesus of Nazareth. In our interpretation of the history of Jesus and of Easter, we emphasized the freedom of Jesus. It is evident, however, that there have been other free men in history. We have already suggested some of the dynamics of interpersonal relations which may result from an encounter with a free man. If our reaction is positive, we may feel attracted to him and we may be encouraged to be more free ourselves, or at least challenged to be more free. Our fears may be calmed simply by the presence of one who is unafraid and free from the fears and anxieties which bind us. On the other hand, our reaction may be negative: we may be threatened by a free person; we may feel judged in our insecurity and bondage. This is an odd experience and if we speak of it at all, we will do so with odd words. We might say that there is a certain mystery about it, a mystery of the depths of human personality and relationships.

Jesus of Nazareth may be distinguished, however, from other men who might have a liberating effect upon men. We must grant a "family resemblance" between the language with which we speak of Jesus and the language used to speak of other free men, of course, in order to be able to describe him at all. Nevertheless, we may use a number of the same words in describing two men without denying that the men are actually quite different. When we compare Socrates as portrayed in Plato's *Dialogues*, for example, and Jesus as portrayed in the Gospels, we may say that both men were "free," but we can also see subtle differences. Two different words for "love," *philia* (the attraction of like to like) and *agape* (a love which makes no distinctions and seeks no return on its investment), may serve to indicate something of the difference which we detect between the two descriptions.

The Gospel, however, is not merely about a free man; it is the good news of a free man who has set other men free, first proclaimed by those to whom this had happened. And it has happened again and again during nineteen centuries that, in the context of hearing this apostolic proclamation, men have been liberated. Their response, which the New Testament calls "faith," consists in acknowledging that this has happened by accepting the liberator, Jesus of Nazareth, as the man who defines for them what it means to be a man and as the point of orientation for their lives. They are "in Christ," which is to say that their understanding of themselves and their lives and all things is determined by their understanding of Jesus. They are a "new creation" in that this orientation to the whole world is new for them.

There is no empirical ground, however, for the Christian's saying that something of this sort could not happen to a disciple of Socrates. Reading the history of Socrates might conceivably have a liberating effect on a person, who might say that he shared in the freedom of the philosopher. If this were to happen, the Socratic's freedom, presumably, would be defined by the peculiar character of Socrates' freedom. He would acknowledge Socrates as his norm. He would be "in Socrates," let us say, not "in Christ." Perhaps the Socratic, like the Christian, would claim that his was the only valid norm. The exclusiveness of such a claim, as we saw in Chapter 3, would express the firmness of his conviction. Understanding the claim of exclusiveness in this way, we take this to be its meaning.

The language of the Gospel contains not only exclusive claims; it has a universal aspect also. It claims that in the history of Jesus of Nazareth something universal, eternal, absolute, something it calls "God," was manifested. We discussed the difficulties of such language in Chapter 3, but a further consideration is in order. Whether formulated in terms of eternity in time, the divine in human form, or the transcendent in the historical, the Gospel is expressed traditionally in language which has its roots in that of the New Testament and which reflects the patristic doctrine of incarnation. Its earliest and most basic form is the confession "Jesus is Lord."[5] This confession is held to be valid regardless of circumstances,[6] but a believer might say that if he never saw any love among men, he would find it almost impossible to make this confession. In that case, part of the meaning of the confession would be to call our attention to the experience of human love. If we grant that human love or its absence is a part of how things are in the world, we can say that the confession has, in this sense, an "empirical" grounding. Our impression from the New Testament, however, is that this confession implies that the believer is saying, "Even if I saw any love in others, I have nevertheless seen it in the man Jesus and I recognize the claim of love on me." In this case, the empirical anchorage of the confession is in the history of Jesus and in the actions of the believer. The logic of this confession is at least implied by the traditional assertion that there are practical consequences for the man who confesses the Lordship of Jesus, that Christian faith involves a way of life.

Those who first said, "Jesus is Lord," expressed a particular perspective upon life and history.[7] This confession, ascribing universality to a particular man, indicated that faith constituted a certin understanding of self, man, history, and the whole world, and that this universal perspective had its norm in the history of Jesus of Nazareth and Easter. This perspective upon life and the world was understood not as a point of view selected by the believer,

---

[5]I Cor. 12:3; Phil. 2:11; O. Cullmann, *Die ersten christlichen Glaubensbekenntnisse* (Zollikon-Zürich: Evangelischer Verlag, 1943).

[6]Rom. 8:35–39.

[7]Acts 2:36–42; cf. Phil. 2:1–11.

but as a "blik" by which the believer was "grasped" and "held." The perspective of faith was spoken of as a response "drawn from" the believer. The language of the Gospel implies consistently that faith is "given," that the believer cannot and does not want to take any credit for it. By its very nature, faith excludes all boasting.[8]

The issue between those whose perspective on life and history is defined by the history of Jesus and those whose perspective is defined by another reference is notoriously one that cannot be settled by argument. This shows that the function of the Gospel is to indicate not only the norm of the Christian's perspective but also the character of the perspective itself. This perspective cannot be held as one point of view among many. It is not a logical conclusion to a chain of reasoning. Of either of these, a man might say, "This is the position which I chose." The language of faith says, "I did not choose; I was chosen. I did not take this piece of history as the clue to my life and understanding of all history; it took me." The language of faith, by referring to a transcendent element, indicates that something has happened to the believer, rather than that he has done something.

On the other hand, if in response to the proclamation of the free man who has set men free the hearer finds himself to some extent set free, if Jesus of Nazareth has in fact become the historical point of orientation for his own perspective upon history, then this response is certainly his own act also. It is a historical perspective which *he* holds. This paradox finds classic expression in the words of Paul: "I worked harder than any of them, though it was not I, but the grace of God which is with me."[9] This paradox is related linguistically to the pecularities we have noted in speaking of the effect of a liberated man upon men who are not free. It points to the fact that the new discernment and its accompanying commitment to a way of life is experienced as a response. This perspective arises in connection with hearing the Gospel concerning Jesus of Nazareth and it looks back to him continually as its historical point of orientation. To affirm the Gospel is to express this historical perspective.

The man who says, "Jesus is Lord," is saying that the history of Jesus and of what happened on Easter has exercised a liberating effect upon him, and that he has been so grasped by it that it has become the historical norm of his perspective upon life. His confession is a notification of this perspective and a recommendation to his listener to see Jesus, the world, and himself in this same way and to act accordingly. It is an important perspective and it can be distinguished from other points of view. We may illustrate the difference by comparing the perspective of Christian faith and the point of view of the man whose perspective upon life is founded on the life of his nation. The nationalist understands himself first of all as a patriot and he defines his freedom in the context of loyalty to his country. He can understand the Gospel only as making a relative claim at most. He may allow that there is some freedom to be found in Jesus and in loyalty to him, but it is secondary

[8]Rom. 3:27; I Cor. 1:27–29; Gal. 6:14.
[9]I Cor. 15:10.

to his freedom as a citizen. For the Christian, however, the situation will be reversed. His assertion, "Jesus is Lord," expresses the fact that Jesus has become his point of orientation, with the consequence that he is freed from acknowledging final loyalty to his nation, family, church, or any other person and is liberated for service to these other centers of relative loyalty. Because he sees not only his own history but the history of all men in the light of the one history of Jesus of Nazareth and Easter, he will not rest content when his nation, family, or church seek to live only for themselves; he will try to set them in the service of others.

He who says, "Jesus is Lord," says that Jesus' freedom has been contagious and has become the criterion for his life, public and private. As Jesus was led, because of his freedom, into the midst of social and political conflict, so it is with one who shares his freedom. The Gospel asserts that Jesus is Lord of the whole world.[10] This means that the freedom for which the Christian has been set free allows him to see the whole world in its light. When the Christian says that Jesus' Lordship is not limited to the church, he is saying that he understands all free men, regardless of where they may say they have found their freedom, as having "caught" their freedom from the same source as he. He will regard them as the ten cleansed lepers of Luke 17:11 ff., who were all set free from their burden, although only one acknowledged Jesus as his liberator. If someone were to object that Jesus is the Lord and Saviour only of believers, he would be saying that he does not see the freedom of unbelievers with the perspective arising from his discernment and commitment as a Christian. The difference is more than a case of theological hair-splitting. It is empirically significant and it has led to serious human consequences in history.

This interpretation of Christian faith is related to Hare's concept of "blik." The language of faith expressed in the Gospel may be understood if it is seen to express, define, or commend a basic presupposition by which a man lives and acts in the world of men. That is why we call it a historical perspective. As Hare has pointed out, a "blik" is not an explanation of the world or of anything else, but without a "blik" there can be no explanations.[11] He appeals to Hume in support of his conclusion that "the difference between *bliks* about the world cannot be settled by observation of what happens in the world." Although the assertions of the Gospel are meaningless if they are taken empirically, they do have a use. As Hare suggests, "The earth is weak and all the inhabitants thereof: I bear up the pillars of it" [Ps. 75:3], has a meaning, if it is taken as the formulation of a "blik." As an explanation it would "obviously be ludicrous. We no longer believe in God as an Atlas— *nous n'avons pas besoin de cette hypothèse.*"[12] The "blik" of the Christian finds its adequate expression in the Gospel, however, and it is related always, if

[10]Matt. 28:18; Eph. 1:20–22; Phil. 2:9–11.

[11]R. M. Hare, *New Essays in Philosophical Theology*, A. Flew and A. MacIntyre, eds. (London: SCM Press, 1955) , p. 101.

[12]*Ibid.* ["we have no need of that hypothesis"—Laplace's reply to Napoleon's question about God.]

sometimes indirectly, to the history of Jesus of Nazareth. This is why we call this perspective *historical*.

Ramsey has suggested how a "blik" arises. It comes out of what he calls a situation of discernment or disclosure, or situation which is seen suddenly in a new way demanding a commitment of the viewer.[13] The languages of revelation, Easter, the "illumination of the Holy Spirit," and conversion reflect just such a situation. The decisive discernment situation for Christianity is Easter and the Easter proclamation concerning Jesus of Nazareth. Men may come to Christian faith in all sorts of ways, of course. A man may have begun to be a Christian from reading the book of Genesis, or he may have come through a more distant point of entry. When he has "arrived," however, when he has heard and accepted the whole of what the Gospel has to say, the norm of his perspective will always be the history of Jesus and Easter. Because the sources for this history present Jesus as fulfilling the destiny of his people in his own life, his history receives illumination from that of the people from which he came, but in the last analysis, the Christian will read Genesis, Exodus, and all the rest of biblical history in the light of the history of the Gospels.

Our interpretation has underscored an element in Christian faith not immediately evident when it is considered as a "blik" or the consequence of a disclosure situation. We pointed out that on Easter the disciples came to see Jesus in a *new* way. That implies that they *had* seen Jesus in an *old* way. Their new perspective depended upon prior acquaintance with Jesus as a free man. Even Paul had some prior knowledge concerning Jesus. Conversion to the Christian historical perspective depends in part upon some acquaintance with the history of Jesus. To speak of a sheer discernment, whatever that would be, resting on no prior acquaintance with at least some elements of the situation in which it arose, would be like speaking of a sheer experience concerning which we could not say what was experienced. The various illustrations which we have used along the way make the same point. Lincoln's Gettsyburg Address presupposed some awareness of the Civil War and the American Revolution. Hamlet's recognition of his father's ghost rested on prior acquaintance with his father. So Easter faith depended on the disciples' memory of Jesus, and Christian faith requires minimal acquaintance with the Gospel narratives.

Miles has spoken of faith as the way of silence qualified by parables.[14] Certainly the Christian possesses no special sources for the scientific description of the universe. Before such questions as whether there is some absolute being, even "Being itself," which is "behind" or "beyond" all we know and are, some final "ground and end of all created things," he will be wise to remain silent. He may qualify his silence, however, by telling something beside a parable. What he has to tell is the history of Jesus and the strange story of how his freedom became contagious on Easter.

[13] I. T. Ramsey, *Religious Language* (London: SCM Press, 1957).

[14] T. R. Miles, *Religion and the Scientific Outlook* (London: Allen & Unwin, 1959), pp. 161 ff.

Finally, Braithwaite has taken religious statements to be assertions of an intention to act in a certain way, together with the entertainment of certain stories.[15] As far as it goes, this analysis agrees with our interpretation. We would clarify the "intention" with such words as "discernment" and "commitment," and we would define the "certain way" as a response to and a reflection of the way of Jesus of Nazareth. It is a way characterized by a freedom "caught" from him. We would go further than this, however. In order to live in the "freedom for which Christ has set us free," we need indeed to "entertain" again and again that piece of history, for it does not just provide an encouragement to walk in the way of freedom; it is the context in which the light dawns anew and in which that freedom proves again to be contagious for us. Braithwaite's presentation of the relationship between "entertaining" the story and the "intention to behave" is not adequate to the language of the Gospel of Easter, helpful as it has been in indicating of what sort that language is, because he has not done justice to the historical aspect of the Gospel and has completely neglected the peculiar "story" of Easter.

The Language of New Testament Christology

The foregoing interpretation of the history of Jesus, Easter, and of the Gospel provides a logical account of the language of Christian faith without resort to a misleading use of words. The word "God" has been avoided because it equivocates and misleads. It seems to be a proper name, calling up the image of a divine entity, but it refuses to function as any other proper name does. Circumlocutions such as "transcendence," "being," and "absolute" only evade but do not overcome the difficulty. An interpretation of the language of the Gospel which does not necessitate assertions concerning "the nature and activities of a supposed personal creator," in Flew's phrase, involves discarding some of the traditional language of Christianity, no matter how much other ages have revered this language. When Flew assumes that this language is of the essence of Christianity, he passes judgment on cherished traditions, not on every expression of faith. Nevertheless the question that Flew asks applies: Is this interpretation "Christian at all"? The interpretation must therefore be measured against the assertions of the Christology of the New Testament and of the Christology of "call and response" which summarizes the concerns of the theological "right."

To what extent do biblical-christological statements and our interpretation's statements about Jesus and Easter function in the same way? An important New Testament statement about Jesus is that made by the Gospel of John, claiming that he who has seen Jesus has seen the Father,[16] an assertion which summarizes the New Testament witness to Jesus as the full and adequate revelation of God. This saying occurs in the context of a discussion with his disciples on the night in which he was arrested. One of the disciples

---

[15]R. B. Braithwaite, *An Empiricist's View of Religious Belief* (Cambridge: Cambridge University Press, 1955).
[16]John 14:9.

has asked Jesus to "show" them the Father, as though something were still lacking in what Jesus has "shown" them until that time. Jesus answers, "Have I been with you so long, and yet you do not know me, Philip? He who has seen me has seen the Father; how can you say, 'Show us the Father'? Do you not believe that I am in the Father and the Father in me?"[17]

"Father" is the word which Jesus apparently used frequently in cases where his contemporaries might have used the word "God." It presents all the problems which arise when we try to analyze the word "God." The further explication of this word, however, is not the only, and not even the best, way to understand this passage, for the passage itself suggests a *via negativa* of an odd sort. The author asks us to stop "looking for the 'Father,'" for we shall not find him and the quest is beside the point in any case. Silence is the first and best answer to questions concerning the "Father." There are "many 'gods' and many 'lords'"[18] but for those for whom the freedom of Jesus is contagious, who have been so touched and claimed by him that he has become the criterion of their understanding of themselves, other men, and the world, there is but one "Lord": Jesus of Nazareth. Since there is no "Father" to be found apart from him, and since his "Father" can only be found in him, the New Testament (and this passage specifically) gives its answer to the question about "God" by pointing to the man Jesus. Whatever men were looking for in looking for "God" is to be found by finding Jesus of Nazareth.

The assertion that Jesus is "in" the Father and the Father "in" Jesus suggests just this transposition of the question concerning "God," which lies deep in the Christology of the New Testament. Whatever can be known concerning "God" has been answered by the knowledge of Jesus made available in the event of Easter. Whatever "God" means—as the goal of human existence, as the truth about man and the world, or as the key to the meaning of life—"he" is to be found in Jesus, the "way, the truth, and the life."

We have no idea what would count for or against the assertion that in seeing Jesus one had seen the Father. Unless we knew already the meaning of the word "Father," how could we verify or falsify this claim? The New Testament, and the Gospel of John especially, insist, moreover, that apart from Jesus we can have only false conceptions of "God."[19] But if this passage is understood as a recommendation to turn away from asking about the Father and to ask about Jesus of Nazareth instead, its meaning becomes clear. We *can* say what would tend to verify a man's saying that Jesus is the key to his understanding and living of life. One could ask him questions and examine his actions. One could compare his words and actions with the teachings of the New Testament to see what correlation there was. This would be a subtle business, certainly, but it is not in principle beyond the realm of human investigation. In fact it is exactly what the church has been doing, under the name of "pastoral care" or "the cure of souls," throughout its history.

[17] John 14:9–10.
[18] I Cor. 8:5–6.
[19] Matt. 11:27 (Luke 10:22); I Cor. 1:21; John 1:18; 8:19; 17:25. Conversely, "with" Jesus, one has no need to seek a conception of God, a point argued by Luther. Cf. B. A. Gerrish, *Grace and Reason* (London: Oxford University Press, 1962), pp. 76 ff.

The passage at which we have been looking is followed by a sentence which deserves attention in this context: "The words that I say to you I do not speak on my own authority; but the Father who dwells in me does his works."[20] This has many parallels in the Gospel of John, for in spite of the author's many assertions of the functional equivalent of "Jesus" and "God," there is also a strong emphasis on the submission of Jesus to the "Father." In the later Christology of the church, this became the basis of the problem of the "subordination" of the Son to the Father.

The verification principle precludes taking this assertion of cosmological obedience as a straightforward empirical proposition. Its function is to say something about Jesus which we have already noticed in speaking of his freedom to make no claims for himself. We called attention to the characteristics of humility, service, and living for other men. Undoubtedly Jesus believed he was obeying some "one," whom he called "Father," but the Gospel of John, as well as the logic of language, forces us to silence before all questions concerning that "one." We can only follow the recommendation of the evangelist to look at Jesus himself; questions about "God" will receive their only useful answer in the form of the history of that man.

A second important aspect of the New Testament witness to Jesus is seen in the assertion that he is not only the revelation of God, but also the act of God: his history is God's decisive act of love for this world. This idea may be summed up typically in Paul's words: "in Christ God was reconciling the world to himself."[21] This is a more difficult passage to understand than the one from the Gospel of John because it is so largely a "God"-statement. Its verification would depend upon knowing what to do with the word "God," and that is just the problem. The statement may be taken in another way, however. Does it not suggest that the history of Jesus, including the event of Easter, is the history of a reconciliation of a peculiar sort? Jesus was the cause of division as well as reconciliation among men. As we pointed out, a free man can antagonize as well as attract men, and this was certainly the case with Jesus. He who asserts that the history of Jesus was a normative history of reconciliation means that he is committed to the *sort* of reconciliation revealed in that history. Reconciliation, for the Christian, will always have something to do with the freedom for which Christ has set men free, with being free for one's neighbor. To accept and live such a conception of reconciliation will tend to have serious personal, social, and political consequences, for the Pauline passage has a wide range: the world. The Christian understanding of reconciliation has no limit to its application. it will bear upon all areas of human life, personal and public, local and foreign. It will bear upon the way in which the Christian thinks and acts concerning the relations between nations, peoples, and political groups, as well as upon relationships in his own family. Wherever he sees at work in the world any reconciliation at

[20]John 14:10.

[21]II Cor. 5:19. An alternative translation, asserting first that "God was in Christ" and then saying that he was "reconciling the world to himself," breaks the temporal emphasis in the verb form. If this alternative reading were followed, the first assertion would be parallel to the "in me" of John 14:10, which we have already analyzed. Only the second assertion would speak of what was accomplished in the history of Jesus of Nazareth.

all like that which characterized the history of Jesus of Nazareth, he will support it, and he will rejoice over signs of such reconciliation accomplished, however partially, as much as he rejoices over the reconciliation with his neighbor which has been made possible by his having been set free for that neighbor.

This verse from chapter 5 of II Corinthians is in the past tense. Then and there, in the history of Jesus, in his life, death, and resurrection, the world was being reconciled to "God." According to the words which immediately follow in Paul's letter, this means that "God . . . did not count men's trespasses against them and entrusted [to the apostles] the word of reconciliation." What can this mean? It cannot be a straighforward empirical assertion, for who can say how the world would be different if men had not been pardoned? We can say, however, how we should treat men if we regarded them as pardoned and accepted in some "final" sense which qualifies all human judging and forgiving. Would it not make a difference in our attitude toward a man who had been found guilty of a crime if we were convinced that his guilt was "born by another," that he was pardoned in some "final" sense? This is another way of expressing the Christian's historical perspective, which leads him to take sides with reconciliation, mercy, and forgiveness and to oppose enmity, retribution, and revenge. Jesus' parable of the unforgiving servant[22] helps us to see the meaning of this perspective and its ethical consequences. The "word of reconciliation" expresses a perspective which leads the Christian to understand and act in the world under the criterion of the freedom of Jesus for his neighbor.

The New Testament frequently speaks of that which "God accomplished" in the history of Jesus by saying that Jesus died for our sins.[23] This has been influential in a theological tradition which says that Jesus became the representative of sinful men by the will of God and suffered the "wages of sin" in their place. Paul said of Jesus that God had made him to be sin who knew no sin,[24] and that in that one died for all, "all have died."[25] The same theme is developed in the Epistle to the Hebrews around the image of Jesus as the perfect and eternal high priest who became also a sacrificial offering.[26] This strain of the tradition has been important in Western theology, especially since Augustine; it received a particularly clear expression in the theology of Calvin and, in our time, in that of Karl Barth.[27] How are we to understand this language?

We have seen that Jesus' freedom was freedom for his neighbor, that he was free from self-concern and therefore open to the concerns of others. We might speak of his solidarity with men: he "put himself in their shoes";

[22]Matt. 18:23–34.
[23]I Cor. 15:3.
[24]II Cor. 5:21.
[25]II Cor. 5:14.
[26]Heb. 5:1 ff.; 8:1 ff.; 9:11 ff.
[27]Calvin, *op. cit.*, II, xvi, 5 ff.; Paul M. van Buren, *Christ in Our Place* (Edinburgh: Oliver & Boyd, 1957), Part II, *passim*; Barth, *Kirkliche Dogmatik* (Zollikon-Zürich: Evangelischer Verlag, 1952 f.), IV/1, §59, 2 *passim*.

he carried their burdens. In addition, by daring to regard men classed as "sinners" as forgiven and by proclaiming their forgiveness, he convinced them that they were released from the burden of guilt and the consequences of their acts.[28] But what can it mean to say, "He *died* for our sins"? The emphasis is on his death, but we need to remember that theology, as well as the New Testament, speaks of the "cross" or the death of Jesus as the consequence of his life. "The cross" and other references to Jesus' death became summary ways of speaking of his whole history, as indeed his end seemed to his disciples, after the fact, to have been foreshadowed in all of his life. Since his life was one of solidarity with men, compassion for them, mercy toward their weakness and wrong, it is not surprising that his death, which was the consequence of his freedom to be related to men in this way, was spoken of as a death "for us." His death (which could so easily have been avoided if he had taken the way of caution, calculation, and self-interest) was regarded as the measure of the freedom for which he set other men free. The man for whom the history of Jesus and of his liberation of his disciples on Easter is a discernment situation of prime importance will say, "He died for me, for my forgiveness and freedom." When the New Testament says that he died not only for "our" sins, "but also for the sins of the whole world,"[29] it reflects the fact that Jesus was free for every man, those who did not acknowledge him as well as those that did, and it articulates a perspective by which all men, not just believers, are seen.

On the basis of these considerations, we can clarify the dilemma posed by Bultmann: "Does he [Jesus] help me because he is God's Son, or is he the Son of God because he helps me?"[30] The question as it stands only invites confusion. We may say that Jesus helps me because of "what" he is ("Son of God"), and we may also say that such titles as "Son of God" were given to him because of the help he provided. When we say both of these, however, we are using the words "Son of God" in two different ways and are also playing tricks with the slippery word "is." The problem is more clearly expressed if we ask: Does the Gospel speak of a "saving" event which has happened already and which is reported to the listener, who is invited to acknowledge and give thanks for it (a so-called "objective" atonement), or does it announce the possibility of a "saving" event which takes place in the act of acknowledging it (a so-called "subjective" atonement)? Does the Gospel announce a reality accomplished, or a possibility to be actualized by the hearer? This way of phrasing the question makes it clear that we are speaking about *words* (the Gospel) spoken presumably by a believer.

Now of what precisely does the believer speak? He speaks in part of a piece of history, which is certainly in the past. It is the history of a free man and the peculiar character of his freedom. But the Gospel goes on

---

[28]*E.g.* the story of the woman taken in adultery, usually found in John 8:3–11.

[29]I John 2:2.

[30]Rudolf Bultmann, *Glauben and Verstehen* (Tübingen: Mohr, 1952), Vol. II, p. 252; English translation by. J. C. G. Grieg, *Essays Philosophical and Theological* (London: SCM Press, 1955), p. 280 [van Buren's bracketing].

to speak of the moment in which this freedom became contagious in the Easter event, and the speaker, by his very speaking and by the way in which he does it, indicates that this contagious freedom has also touched him. All this constitutes an invitation to the listener to share this discernment and commitment. Perhaps (but also perhaps not) the listener will "see" for the first time, or he will see again, or he will see more clearly than he has in the past. The light will dawn; he will be possessed of a new way of seeing himself, the world, and all things, and he will "catch" something of the contagious freedom of Jesus.

Now, when was he liberated? Or rather, when will he say he was liberated? He will surely say that he became free at the time he acquired his new perspective. But he will be even readier to point to his liberator. It belongs to the language of a discernment situation that we speak of that situation as containing already ("objectively"), prior to its becoming the occasion of a discernment, what was only "seen" at a later time. As the lover might say to his beloved, "I must have passed you a thousand times and spoken to you a hundred, and there you were, the most beautiful girl in the world, and I did not see you. And then, that night, all of a sudden I realized. . . ." She did not become the most beautiful girl in the world for him only "that night." He will insist that she always was that, and that he, poor fool, woke up only later to the fact.[31] Such is the language of the "objective" liberation of mankind in the death and resurrection of Jesus. To insist that this is incorrect and that the actual liberation takes place in the moment of believing, which is perfectly true in a psychological sense, is to misunderstand the language appropriate to a situation of discernment which leads one to a commitment embracing all of life.

An analysis of the language of the Christology of "call and response" presented in Chapter 2 confirms our conclusions about the function of biblical-christological statements. The statements that Jesus was "called by God" to be the one man who was free to be for all the others, that he "bore the divine election" of Israel to be a light for the Gentiles, that his history "was the enactment of God's eternal plan and purpose," if taken to be cosmological assertions, are meaningless in the terms of the empirical attitudes in which this study is grounded. These statements, however, belong after the words "I believe," and the word "I" is important. The statements, in the form of a confession of faith, reflect or suggest a situation in which the history of Jesus has been or might be seen in a new way. They also express the commitment of the speaker to what he has now "seen." To speak of Jesus' "call" or "election" is to speak of Jesus as one with a history which is different from that of any other man, and of Jesus as one who is "set apart" from all the others and for all the others. As the language of one who, in seeing Jesus as the free man who has set others free, has also been set free himself,

[31]The case of "love at first sight" is a compressed variation. The "prior acquaintance," which we have already discussed, would in this case be prior acquaintance with other people and prior knowledge of the fact of "falling in love," together with at least the first impression of the beloved as a person distinct from these other people.

the statement is appropriate and logically meaningful. This clarifies also the statements concerning Jesus' "response," for his response was only the other side of the coin. To speak of Jesus' "response" is another way of speaking of his history as a free man. Since according to the New Testament his response of obedience was authenticated as perfect obedience by the event of Easter, we may say that it is the contagious aspect of his freedom which authenticates the language which the believer uses of Jesus. To say that Jesus embodies the plan of God and that he was perfectly faithful to this election is to make the sort of final statement which Ramsey says takes the form "I'm I." In this case, however, the "I" is what "I" have become as a result of the liberation arising from hearing the story of Jesus, his life, his death, and Easter.

Finally, the "eschatological" hope, in this interpretation of the language of the Gospel, is the conviction that the freedom which the believer has seen in Jesus and which has become contagious for him, and the reconciliation which he sees to be associated with this freedom, will prevail on this earth among all men. That is his conviction, not a prediction. To say that this hope is "eschatological" is to say that one would die rather than abandon it. It indicates the unqualified, undebatable aspect of the Christian's historical perspective.

As Hare points out, there is no arguing about "bliks." Another man may find some other piece of history to be his key to the understanding of life and history: that of the Buddha or Mary Baker Eddy. Or his perspective might be informed by some idea or ideology. It might be a dialectic of history and the Communist Manifesto, an eighteenth-century Declaration of Independence, or the economic theory of Adam Smith. He who has his freedom from Jesus will not agree, however, with those who would say that all sources of freedom are the same. The fact remains that the history of Jesus is not the same as the history of the Buddha, the Communist Revolution, or Henry Ford. It is one thing to say that Christians have always taken the history of Jesus to be indispensable and definitive for their faith, but it is quite another to think that this "uniqueness" can somehow be proved. Christians have never been able, however (and when they were at their best have not tried), to *prove* the "superiority" of their historical perspective over other perspectives. Claims of "finality" are simply the language appropriate to articulating a historical perspective. The logic of these claims can be illuminated by setting them alongside the statement "I'm I."

The meaning of the Gospel is its use on the lips of those who proclaim it. The Christian has seen a man of remarkable and particular freedom, and this freedom has become contagious for him, as it was for the apostles on Easter. The history of this man and of Easter has become a situation of discernment, reorienting his perspective upon the world. If he should have occasion to tell that story, therefore, he can only do so to express, define, or commend this historical perspective, for this is the secular meaning of that Gospel.

That assertion is itself, of course, a recommendation to the reader to see the language of faith in the way expressed, on the assumption that there is a possibility of his holding empirical attitudes similar to those in the light of which this interpretation has been made. This commendation may also be made in the form of two principles which sum up what we have done:

(1) *Statements of faith are to be interpreted, by means of the modified verification principle, as statements which express, describe, or commend a particular way of seeing the world, other men, and oneself, and the way of life appropriate to such a perspective.* A restatement of the Gospel should allow the logical structure of its language to become clear. With this first principle we indicate that we share certain of the empirical attitudes reflected in the "revolution" in modern philosophy. This principle more than meets the concern of the theological "left" to accept the modern criticism of ancient ways of thinking.

(2) *The norm of the Christian perspective is the series of events to which the New Testament documents testify, centering in the life, death, and resurrection of Jesus of Nazareth.* We have approached the problem of Christology by way of an investigation of the peculiar way in which Christians talked from the first about the man Jesus of Nazareth. Following our first principle, we explored the logic of the language of the New Testament authors concerning Jesus. Our aim has been to discover the *meaning* of their words and to find appropriate and clear words with which to express that meaning today, asking after a functional equivalence between a contemporary Christology and the language of the New Testament. With our second principle, we acknowledge the concern of the theological right wing that Christology be central, and that the norm of Christology be Jesus of Nazareth as the subject of the apostolic witness. These two principles have guided us in the constructive task of interpreting the Gospel in a way which may be understood by a Christian whose empirical attitudes are such as to lead us to call him a secular man.

✳ WILLIAM HAMILTON

44. *The Death of God*

William Hamilton, an ordained Baptist minister and Professor of Religion at New College, Sarasota, Florida, is (with Thomas J. J. Altizer) the best known of the "Death of God" theologians. He is author of *Radical Theology and the Death of God* (with Altizer) and *The New Essence of Christianity*. His essay "The Death of God" may be one of the clearest statements of this (to many) enigmatic position.

The Death of God

Have you ever heard of the madman who on a bright morning lighted a lantern and ran to the market place calling out unceasingly: "I seek God! I seek

William Hamilton, "The Death of God," *Playboy*, XIII (August 1966). Copyright 1966 by HMH Publishing Co. Inc. Reprinted by permission of the author and the publisher.

God!"—As there were many people standing about who did not believe in God, he caused a great deal of amusement. Why! is he lost? said one. Has he strayed away like a child? said another. Or does he keep himself hidden? Is he afraid of us? Has he taken a sea-voyage? Has he emigrated?—the people cried out laughingly, all in a hubbub. The insane man jumped into their midst and transfixed them with his glances. "Where is God gone?" he called out. "I mean to tell you! *We have killed him*—you and I! We are all his murderers! . . .

"Do we not smell the divine putrefaction?—for even Gods putrefy! God is dead! God remains dead! And we have killed him! How shall we console ourselves, the most murderous of all murderers? . . . Is not the magnitude of this deed too great for us? Shall we not ourselves have to become Gods, merely to seem worthy of it? There never was a greater event—and on account of it, all who are born after us belong to a higher history than any history hitherto!"—Here the madman was silent and looked again at his hearers: they also were silent and looked at him in surprise. At last he threw his lantern on the ground, so that it broke in pieces and was extinguished. "I come too early," he then said, "I am not yet at the right time. This prodigious event is still on its way, and is traveling—it has not yet reached men's ears . . ."[1]

These wild and lovely words, written by Friedrich Nietzsche toward the close of the last century, have recently broken loose from the obscurity of lecture, textbook and monograph, into the incomprehending world of cocktail party, newsmagazine with intellectual pretensions and television. Why? What has happened? Is there really an event properly called "the death of God"? Or is the current chatter enveloping the phrase simply another of the many non-events afflicting our time?

No. The death of God *has* happened. To those of us with gods, and to those without. To the indifferent, the cynical and the fanatical. God is dead, whatever that means. To some, this is an event of terror, warranting tears and the writing of requiems. In the above passage, Nietzsche seems to reflect some of this cosmic horror. But to others, the event is one of great liberation and joy; an event not keeping one from something, but making something newly possible, in this case the Christian faith. In another connection, Nietzsche knew this joy as well.

In fact, we . . . feel ourselves irradiated as by a new dawn by the report that the "old God is dead"; our hearts overflow with gratitude, astonishment, presentiment and expectation. At last the horizon seems open once more, granting even that it is not bright; our ships can at last put out to sea in face of every danger; every hazard is again permitted to the discerner; the sea, our sea, again lies open before us; perhaps never before did such an "open sea" exist.[2]

I am a Christian theologian by profession; I have recently been involved in the death-of-God fuss, and I am, as well, committed to the death of God as a theological and human event.

It is hard to know just exactly why the furor started last fall. I had been defending the death of God, off and on for years, on C.B.S. television

[1][Friedrich Nietzsche, *Joyful Wisdom*, no. 125, tr. Thomas Common (New York: Ungar, 1960).]

[2][*Ibid.*, no. 343.]

programs, coast to coast, as the saying goes. But this was in the decent obscurity of the Sunday-morning cultural ghetto, and no one really listens to the words people say on television anyhow. What matters is if you are sincere, like Hugh Downs. A book or two came out in 1963, and in 1964 and 1965 a few articles began to appear indicating a common interest in doing Christianity without God. Three or four of us seemed to be working similar lines, and critics—both fearful and interested—began to call us a movement, and we looked around and decided that perhaps they were right. This was the first decisive alteration in Protestant theology to take place since the communications explosion of the early Fifties, and no one was prepared for the rapidity of information passing when the snowball really started to pick up momentum. A handful of articles, commissioned by a bland weekly Protestant journal (which in turn is earnestly monitored by the religion editors of the weekly newsmagazines), provided perhaps the real trigger last fall. An excellent analysis by a young *New York Times* reporter was syndicated quite widely, and a rather ineffectual and tired piece in *Time* made the kind of mark that ineffectual and tired pieces in *Time* often do. A confused *New Yorker* series on the "new theology" added words without sense to the scene, and, at last, the religion-desk people in wire services, local chains and papers moved in and rewrote the rewritten work of others. By about Christmas, the non-events and the events were thoroughly mixed together; hostile reactions were being recorded to words never uttered, institutions were upset, trustees perplexed, colleagues bewildered and hostile, and in general the reaction to the news and publicity was becoming part of the news and publicity, which in turn engendered more reaction, and so on. For a while it looked as if the reaction had become the event, and otherwise sensible Christian critics decided to reject the death-of-God theology on the grounds that it was faddish and beginning to turn up at cocktail parties. As time went on, and cooler heads prevailed, it was appraently decided that mention at cocktail parties is evidence for neither the truth nor falsity of an idea.

One of the consequences of the mishmash character of the intellectual life of our day is that it makes clarity and precision difficult to obtain. "Death of God" is a difficult, complex, rather mysterious idea, and I'd like to set down some of the meanings that it seems to me to have today.

There is no question about it: "death of God" is a striking, rhetorical and offensive phrase. We death-of-God theologians do not call ourselves that in order to give offense. We mean "death." Traditional religious thought has spoken about the "disappearance" or "absence" or "eclipse" or "silence" of God. It means, by these words, that men do not permanently enjoy the experience of faith or the presence of God. The presence is, from time to time, withdrawn, and men cannot count on the timing or character of its return. This is a common enough religious affirmation in our time, but it is not what we death-of-God people are talking about. We are talking about a real loss, a real doing without, and—whatever we do expect of the future—we do not expect the return of the Christian God, open or disguised.

"Death of God" sounds not only offensive, it sounds arrogant. It seems to suggest not only that this experience has happened to us, but that it has, or ought to have, happened to everybody. "Death" seems to legislate for you as well as to illuminate for me. This is, however, not as great a problem as first appears. We death-of-God theologians, along with a good many others today, accept without reservation the relativistic intellectual and spiritual climate of our time. We may fight passionately for what we hold. But we have given up believing that there is something about Christians that makes our views inevitable or necessary or (by definition) better than alternatives. We merely represent one of the possible intellectual options today. We expect to be listened to, if we say anything honest and clear, and we expect to listen. Given this relativism, the arrogant sound to the declaration of God's death is partly overcome.

There is, incidentally, a practical advantage in the shocking character of the phrase "death of God." It is just not something that conventional religious people or bishops or officials can pick up and use in their own way, saying, "Why, we've been saying that all along." There are those who feature this kind of complacency, but it is tough to do it with "death of God." The phrase is, you might say, nonsoluble in holy water, even when uttered with extreme unction.

The affirmation of the death of God is Christian in two senses. It is, for the most part, made by Christian theologians. (Not entirely, however, and a dialog between Christians and Jews around this idea is coming into being that seems most promising and exciting.) And it is made by us in order to affirm the possibility of thinking and living as Christians, To say "death of God," then, is somehow to move toward and not away from Christianity. Thus it should be clear that we theologians are not trying to reduce the Christian faith to a bland and noncontroversial minimum so that it can be accepted by scientists, rationalists and freethinkers. We are not particularly anxious about relevance of communication. It is not because we long to slip something into the mind of "modern man" that we do what we do. It is because something has happened to us, and because we suspect that it may have happened to others, that we are talking about the death of God.

But let's move beyond introductory matters. Just what does the phrase "death of God" mean as we "radical" theologians use it? And how is this related to other possible and historical uses of the phrase? The best way to start this answer is to indicate that there are perhaps ten possible meanings for the phrase "death of God" in use today:

1. It might mean that there is no God and that there never has been. This position is traditional atheism of the old-fashioned kind, and it does seem hard to see how it could be combined, except very unstably, with Christianity or any of the Western religions.

2. It might mean that there once was a God to whom adoration, praise and trust were appropriate, possible and even necessary, but that there is now no such God. This is the position of the death-of-God or radical theology. It is an atheist position, but with a difference. If there was a God, and if there now isn't, it should be possible to indicate why this change took place,

when it took place and who was responsible for it. I will be returning to questions like this.

3. It might mean that the idea of God and the word God itself both are in need of radical reformulation. Perhaps totally new words are needed; perhaps a decent silence about God should be observed; but ultimately, a new treatment of the idea and the word can be expected, however unexpected and surprising it may turn out to be.

4. It might mean that our traditional liturgical and theological language needs a thorough overhaul; the reality abides, but classical modes of thought and forms of language may well have had it.

5. It might mean that the Christian story is no longer a saving or healing story. It may manage to stay on as merely illuminating or instructing or guiding, but it no longer performs its classical functions of salvation or redemption. In this new form, it might help us cope with the demons, but it cannot abolish them.

6. It might mean that certain concepts of God, often in the past confused with the classical Christian doctrine of God, must be destroyed: for example, God as problem solver, absolute power, necessary being, the object of ultimate concern.

7. It might mean that men do not today experience God except as hidden, absent, silent. We live, so to speak, in the time of the death of God, though that time will doubtless pass.

8. It might mean that the gods men make, in their thought and action (false gods or idols, in other words), must always die so that the true object of thought and action, the true God, might emerge, come to life, be born anew.

9. It might have a mystical meaning: God must die in the word so that he can be born in us. In many forms of mysticism the death of Jesus on the cross is the time of that worldly death. This is a medieval idea that influenced Martin Luther, and it is probably this complex of ideas that lies behind the German chorale *God Himself Is Dead* that may well be the historical source for our modern use of "death of God."

10. Finally, it might mean that our language about God is always inadequate and imperfect.

I want to go back to the second meaning of the phrase. If there was once a God and there is now not one, when did this change take place? There are a number of paths toward an answer. In one sense, God is always dying, giving himself to the world and to men, as in the fall of the primitive sky gods into animism. In a more decisive sense for Christians, the coming and the death of Jesus (the Incarnation, to use the technical term) stand for a kind of death of God. Here God, Christians have always said, takes on sin and suffering. Can it not also be said that God takes on mortality, that the coming of Jesus is the beginning of the death of God, and that because of this coming, men no longer need gods in the old religious sense? The New Testament perhaps comes closest to this in the saying, "He who abides in love abides in God" [I John 4:16].

But the "when" question has to be answered not only in terms of Jesus, but in terms of the nineteenth century. If Jesus makes the death of God a possible experience for men, the nineteenth century lives that reality and instructs us to do the same. A whole series of themes in the nineteenth century deals, directly or indirectly, with the collapse of God into the world, and thus with the death of God. Goethe and the roman-Protestants were invited by some of their spokesmen at the beginning of the century to fling themselves on the bosom of nature in order to recapture a lost divinity. William Blake is singing mysteriously of the death of the transcendent God at the close of the eighteenth century, and in the French Revolution itself we can perceive the close connection between regicide and deicide. Hegel, as early as 1807, speaks elliptically of God's death, and the left-wing Hegelians like Strauss and Feuerbach make it much clearer—the attributes of God must be transmuted into concrete human values. Karl Marx's own Marxism is in one sense an attempt to recover for the human community the values previously ascribed to God.

Ibsen and Strindberg knew the death of God, as did Victorian England. George Eliot found God and immortality impossible, duty alone irresistible, while the young Matthew Arnold's *Dover Beach* sang a song for a whole generation.

> The Sea of Faith
> Was, once, too, at the full, and round earth's shore
> Lay like the folds of a bright girdle furl'd.
> But now I only hear
> Its melancholy, long, withdrawing roar,
> Retreating, to the breath
> Of the night-wind, down the vast edges drear
> And naked shingles of the world.

And on our side of the Atlantic, Hawthorne rather quietly, and Melville with unforgettable force, laid the God of the Puritan tradition to rest. Perhaps the most unforgettable image of the dying God in our language is that of Ahab finally fixing his harpoon in Moby Dick's side, as the two of them sink together, both of them God, both of them evil.

Cryptically, but not entirely falsely, in Europe and America between the French Revolution and the start of World War One, the Christian God is dying. The coming and death of Jesus makes God's death possible; the nineteenth century makes it real. And today, it is our turn to understand and to accept.

Thus, "When did it happen?" gets a three-part answer. In one sense with Jesus and the cross. In another sense in the Europe and America of the last century. In a final sense, today, just now. Just what is there about our time that has led us to see and to grasp this event?

Every man must answer for himself the question "What is the special quality of your experience of the death of God?" In one sense, I don't think one can or should try to persuade anyone else of the reality of the death of God. When I talk or write about it, I don't try to place a new thing into

another's head, I try to remind him of what he already knows. If there is
no answer, no recognition, I can be of no further use to him except as an
example of the way he should not go. For me, the death of God is not a
consequence of a simple experience like the discovery of, say, the scientific
method that automatically rules out God. It is an emotional event, in the
guts. It is made up of a number of things, modest in themselves, but overwhelming when taken together. It is for me partly the disappearance of the
idea of God as a meeter of needs and a solver of problems. For much of
its history, classical Christianity felt that while men, by their own hands,
could solve many of the problems of life, there was always a dimension where
man was powerless and which had to be ascribed to God. In this sense the
longing for God was said to be common to all. Our hearts are restless, Saint
Augustine said, until they come to rest in God. Today we must say some
hearts are and some hearts aren't. Men may not need God, just as they may
not need a single ultimate loyalty. Needs and problems are for the world
to meet, and if it cannot meet them, nothing else can. This is one stand
in the experience of the death of God for me.

Another has to do with the problem of suffering. If for you there
is nothing special about the twentieth century's experience of suffering, then
this line of argument will not persuade. There has always been unmerited
suffering in the world, and it has always been a problem for the heart and
the head to hold to the reality of suffering and to the goodness and power
of God at the same time. It has always been hard, I am saying, and now
it is impossible; for the terrible burden of suffering our time has witnessed
can be ascribed to God only by turning him into a monster. The problem
of Job, of Ivan Karamazov, of Albert Camus has fallen on our heads. It was
Christians who did the work at Auschwitz, and their God became impossible
after they had finished. Ernest Hemingway, whom we do not ordinarily think
of as having been moved by these problems, has a touching scene on this
point in *For Whom the Bell Tolls:* Anselmo is speaking to Jordan about his
hopes when the war is over.

"But if I live later, I will try to live in such a way, doing no harm to any
one, that it will be forgiven."

"By whom?"

"Who knows? Since we do not have God here any more, neither His Son
nor the Holy Ghost, who forgives? I do not know."

"You have not God any more?"

"No. Man. Certainly not. If there were God, never would He have permitted
what I have seen with my eyes. Let *them* have God."

"They claim Him."

"Clearly I miss Him, having been brought up in religion. But now a man
must be responsible to himself."

"Then it is thyself who will forgive thee for killing."

"I believe so," Anselmo said.

Let me put this in another way. The death of God means two closely
related things: that some of the human experiences to which men have tradi-

tionally given the name of God must be redescribed and renamed, and also that some of those experiences are no longer ours. For example, religious men have often pointed to experiences of dependence, awe, reverence, wonder, mystery, tragedy as signs of the incalculable and mysterious character of life, saying of these experiences taken together, "Something like this is what we mean by God." There are, of course, such things about us, and the only point I wish to make here is that one needn't give any of them the name of God. They are real facts of our life, we have human sciences and arts to clarify them, and they point to mystery and wonder, but not to God.

But a second thing is just as true. There are experiences that men have had in the past and which they have traditionally understood as pointing to God that are simply not available to us in the same way today. Take the experiences of dependence, especially in the presence of nature. Listen to a research biologist or a doctor or a physicist or a space scientist talk about his work. He is talking about mastery, control and power; not about a sense of his smallness before the universe. This is true of our kids as well. The other night I was out in the back yard with one of my children, who had to identify some constellations for his science homework. When I was young and used to stand under the starry sky, I recall being filled with all the things you were supposed to be filled with: awe, a sense of my own smallness, dependence. But my son is a full citizen of the modern world, and said to me, after he had located the required constellations, "Which are the ones we put up there, Dad?" He was more interested in what he could do up there than in what he could feel down here. He had become a technological man, and this means something religiously. Are there other traditional religious experiences that we're losing touch with? The death of God lives in this kind of world.

It is quite foolish to say that the death-of-God theology wants to reduce life to the scientifically knowable or the immediately relevant. It has no special interest in relevance or in being acceptable to that non-existent chimera, "modern man." In no sense does it wish to turn its back on the mysterious, the sacred, the holy or the transcendent. It simply will not call such things by the name of God. As a matter of fact, it might be very interesting to work out a way of talking about godless forms of the sacred—ideas and experiences of the sacred that need not include the experience of God. It is doubtless true that some roads to the sacred are ruled out for many of us in our rationalized and technological culture. There probably cannot be, for example, any way to the sacred via holy men, holy books or holy gestures in the usual sense. But even if our way to God is cut off, need it be the case for our experience of the sacred? Can the experience of sex become a way to the sacred for some? Not just sex as intercourse, but as total affirmation of one's sexuality in the midst of the human community. What would it mean to say that sex can become a new kind of sacred space? What would sacred mean in such a statement?

Perhaps death can also become a sacred event in our time of the death of God. Not, of course, our experience of our own death, but at least the experience of its coming, of mortality, and a facing up to death, our own and others, so as to befriend it and deprive it of its ability to hurt and surprise us. What meaning would "sacred" have if we tried to say that death may become a way to a godless form of the sacred today?

Some examples might make this point a bit less bewildering. In the Gettysburg Address, Lincoln was offering what seems to me a moving example of death as a human, godless form of the sacred. He said, you'll recall, that they had met to dedicate a portion of the battlefield. Then he went on:

But, in a larger sense, we cannot dedicate—we cannot consecrate—we cannot hallow—this ground.

You might have expected him to make the pious point here and to say that we mortals cannot consecrate anything because that is God's prerogative alone. But he didn't say that:

The brave men, living and dead, who struggled here, have consecrated it, far above our poor power to add or detract.

Not just the "right" side, but all those who fought, are the consecrators. Suffering and dying men, he suggests, have the power to make holy or sacred what was ordinary and profane before.

It would be easy to find a contemporary example of sex as a sacred event. Such a view is common rhetoric in our modern sentimental panegyrics to sex, both Christian and secular. So I would rather turn to another source, to Puritan New England, as a matter of fact. This is from Nathaniel Hawthorne's *The Scarlet Letter*, and Dimmesdale is speaking to Hester about their adulterous love.

"We are not, Hester, the worst sinners in the world. There is one worse than even the polluted priest! That old man's revenge has been blacker than my sin. [He is referring to Chillingworth's diabolical attack on him.][3] He has violated, in cold blood, the sanctity of a human heart. Thou and I, Hester, never did so!"

"Never, never," whispered she. "What we did had a consecration of its own. We felt it so! We said so to each other! Hast thou forgotten it?"

Here is not only sex, but nonmarital sex, and in the heart of Puritanism, affirmed as a form of the sacred. Along such lines as these, I think, a conception of the sacred without God might be worked out.

I want to raise one final question about the idea of the death of God. If God is dead, as we say, what do we put in his place? What does the work in this godless Christian vision that God used to do in the classical tradition? Have we, it might be asked, taken the full measure of the terrible cry of Ivan Karamazov, If there is no God, then everything is permitted? Are people really strong enough to lose not only the fear of hell and the consolations of the next life, but also the reality of God?

There are two answers, or two forms of the same answer, to the question about the replacement of God. In one sense the answer must be "the human community" and in another sense it must be "Jesus." Let us distinguish between two kinds of meaning or function classically ascribed

[3][Hamilton's bracketing.]

to God. If by God you mean the means by which forgiveness is mediated, or consolation in time of sorrow or despair, or judge of my arrogance and my idolatry—then we say that these functions, as central for us as they ever were in classical Christianity, must be taken over by the human community. We must learn to forgive each other with the radical unconditioned grace men used to ascribe to God. (Recall the touching words between Anselmo and Jordan quoted above.) We must learn to comfort each other, and we must learn to judge, check and rebuke one another in the communities within which we are wounded and in which we are healed. If these things cannot now be done by the human communities in the world, then these communities must be altered until they can perform these tasks and whatever others, once ascribed to God, that need to be done in this new context. In this sense the death of God leads to politics, to social change, and even to the foolishness of utopias.

But it would be misleading to pass over to what we are calling the human community every task once given to God. There is another kind of meaning attached to the classical idea of God that needs another kind of surrogate. If by God you mean the focus of obedience, the object of trust and loyalty, the meaning I give to love, my center, my meaning—then these meanings are given not to men in general but to Jesus, the *man*, in his life, his way with others and his death. We death-of-God theologians thus stake out a claim to be able to make it as Christians not merely because we speak of the death of the Christian God, but because we see as the center of the Christian faith a relation of obedience and trust directed to Jesus. Something like this is placed on the lips of Uncle Nikolai by Boris Pasternak in *Doctor Zhivago*:

"As I was saying, one must be true to Christ. I'll explain. What you don't understand is that it is possible to be an atheist, it is possible not to know whether God exists, or why, and yet believe that man does not live in a state of nature but in history, and that history as we know it now began with Christ, and that Christ's Gospel is its foundation. Now what is history? It is the centuries of systematic explorations of the riddle of death, with a view to overcoming death. That's why people discover mathematical infinity and electromagnetic waves, that's why they write symphonies. Now, you can't advance in this direction without a certain faith. you can't make such discoveries without spiritual equipment. And the basic elements of this equipment are in the Gospels. Why are they? To begin with, love of one's neighbor, which is the supreme form of vital energy. Once it fills the heart of man it has to overflow and spend itself. And then the two basic ideals of modern man—without them he is unthinkable—the idea of free personality and the idea of life as sacrifice.

The human community in general—not as it is, but as it might be altered to become—and that particular instance of the human community, Jesus of Nazareth, thus take over the work, the action, the deeds, once ascribed to the Christian God. Thus the death of God is the least abstract event one can imagine. It moves straight into politics, revolutionary change, and the tragedies and delights of this world.

At the start of this article, the question was posed whether the death

of God might be a non-event, fashioned by nothing more substantial than
the eager and empty publicity mills of our day. We radical theologians have
found, I think, that it is something more. It is a real event; it is a joyous
event; it is a liberating event, removing everything that might stand between
man and the relief of suffering, man and the love of his neighbor. It is a
real event making possible a Christian form of faith for many today. It is
even making possible church and ministry in our world.

✳ CARL E. BRAATEN

45. *The Theology of Hope*

Carl E. Braaten, Professor of Systematic Theology at Chicago's Lutheran
School of Theology, is one of the leading American spokesmen for the
Theology of Hope which espouses a radical reinterpretation of Biblical
eschatology. He is the author of *The Future of God* and *History and
Hermeneutics*.

From *The Future of God*

Preface

In the long run it may become evident that radical theology has been
having a cathartic effect on the church and its theology. The "death of God"
phase may have helped to force theology to find a new beginning. I am partisan
in this quest for a new way to start theology. Therefore, while I am unable
to count myself, and few others would wish to number me, among the radical
theologians, I feel myself closer to them than this book, or any of my other
writings, can adequately indicate. Their questions are always in my mind.
Their answers are always challenging those I prefer. I share with them some
of the shock at witnessing the collapse of the going systems. Whether one
cut his theological eyeteeth more on Barth, Bultmann, or Tillich, the feeling
is quite general that we can hardly go on the way we have been going. But
how do we begin again? Where do we go from here?

This book on the concept of the future works in alliance with a new
movement in modern theology which grasps the gravity of the issues which
confront the church and its theology today. The new place to start in theology
is at the end—eschatology. The rediscovery of the role of eschatology in the
preaching of Jesus and of early Christianity has been one of the most important
events of recent theological history. The findings of biblical theologians, however, have not always been taken seriously by systematic theologians. The

main response of systematic theology to the rediscovery of eschatology has been so to redefine the eschatology in question that it loses its futurity. Eschatology has been predominantly understood as the dimension of the eternal shining through the temporal in rather Platonic fashion. This is true not only of the Continentals who have operated under some version of dialectical or existentialist theology but also of the Anglo-Saxons who, following C. H. Dodd, have accepted some form of realized eschatology. Both in exegetical and in systematic circles the dimension of the future in biblical eschatology has been a source of embarrassment. This horror of the future is perhaps best understood as a sign of the degree to which modern theology as a function of the church has succumbed to the establishmentarian mentality that has crippled the Christian movement in modern times, and set it in opposition to the revolutionary forces at work to change the world. Revolutionary thinking is always oriented to the future; it does not accept the past or the status quo as the picture of the "homeland" and "happy days" which all men seek in one way or another. It has been good form for future-less Christians to deride utopianism. Little did they realize—or did they—that in chucking utopianism altogether they lost their own eschatology which looks to the future of God's final and fulfilling coming. It is this loss of eschatology which has precipitated that mood in theology which feels it has lost God. Hope-lessness is God-lessness, because both are future-lessness.

Hope is a word whose correlate is the future. As a questioning being, man is oriented in hope toward the future. The categories of "hope" and "future" are crucial in the new theology which begins with eschatology. For this reason it is variously referred to as a "theology of hope" or a "theology of the future," but sometimes also as a "theology of promise" or a "theology of revolution." What one cares to call it matters very little, except that every new movement finds its own slogans, its own alluring rhetoric. A theology that addresses the "whole man" should not be faulted for using rhetoric, provided that that does not blur the rationality of its vision. Especially when one's vision orients to the future, there is admittedly a need for reason to apply the brakes and to give an account of the logic of the language of hope that prospects the future. We do not claim to have offered more than a start toward such an account. But had we achieved even more, it would not be convincing enough to many of our contemporaries who conform to the image Herbert Marcuse has so skillfully drawn in his *One-Dimensional Man.*

"One-dimensional man" is given to a preference for ordinary language that deals with the ordinary world of "words and things." We have instead turned to extraordinary language, the visionary language of hope, the utopian language of revolutionaries, and the apocalyptic language of the future. This is language which transgresses against the ready-made world. It gives us some resources from which to contradict and violate the established universe of discourse. The aim of our interest in the extraordinary language of future-oriented thinkers is manifestly revolutionary. That is a Christian prejudice we share with the early Christians whose hope was pulled forward by the future of God's coming kingdom.

The story of the idea of the future in modern theology is one that unfolds in at least three steps. First, the giants of the older generation—Barth, Bultmann, and Tillich—let the dimension of the future slip into an eternal present, with the result that the transcendence of God could only be viewed in vertical terms as "above us" or, as the case may be, "below us." Second, the "death of God" stage in theology, following so quickly on the heels of the older generation of dialectical theologians, was no accident. The "God above us" died as the retribution exacted from theology for the sterility of its future-less eschatology. We are now in a third stage that began with theologians like Pannenberg and Moltmann who seized upon the occasion to take up the theme of eschatology as a new point of departure for a total recasting of the Christian message. A number of factors contributed to the ripening of the moment—the futurological tendencies in modern culture, the stimulus of Ernst Bloch's philosophy of hope, the rediscovery of apocalypticism in earliest Christian circles and in the historical Jesus, besides the exposure of critical weaknesses within the reigning systems of theology. . . .

Chapter 2: The Power of the Future—God

1. Natural Theology and the Question of God

Jesus of Nazareth is the person in whom the promises of the God of Israel and the hopes of men for fulfillment are joined. The question "Who is God?" arises out of man's concern for his future. It is simply a human question, as natural to man as the air he breathes and the bread he eats. There are as many answers to this question as there are religions. Christianity confesses God as Yahweh, the God of Israel, whom Jesus identified as his Father and whose coming kingdom he announced. The question "What is God?" is answered in terms of the promises of Yahweh to Israel. These promises were compressed and summed up in Jesus and his message of the kingdom of God. The identity of God is made known through the history of the promises of Yahweh to Israel, as they reach their point of concentration and fulfillment in Jesus of Nazareth. According to the preaching of the early church, the fulfillment of these promises in Jesus is for all men. They are universally true and meaningful for all nations, for all individuals, for all time to come. This means that the genuine hopes of mankind, through which the future of man's essence is expressed, are grounded in the promises of God. The hopes of men, and therefore their religious concerns, are gathered up and given a share in the realization of the eschatological promises of God in the Messiah of Israel.

The joining of the promises of God and the hopes of men in Jesus of Nazareth has become problematic in our time. It is not so much whether they should be joined in Jesus of Nazareth rather than elsewhere which seems to cause the difficulty, but whether there is anything to be joined at all. Who is this God? What are these hopes? Is not God an illusion? Are not hopes an escape? And if man has hope for the future, is it not a future which he himself must forge without God? The barometer of man's hopes seems to go up and down, from an opulent optimism to a pathetic pessimism, even among Christians, without any connection with their belief in God. It is our contention that where men seek a God without hope or their future without God, not only the foundation of Christianity but the very structure of human existence is being assailed. For religion as hope is the human quest for meaningful fulfillment beyond the present experiences of alienation and destruction within each individual and the whole gamut of life. Religion as hope is the question about the possibility of man's becoming truly fulfilled beyond the deformities of his past and present, and especially beyond the inevitability of his having to die. Man's hopes burst open his present, driving him beyond existing frontiers, searching the horizions for new reality. Man's hopes arouse his memories of reality that is no more, that has faded away into the stillness of the past. They give rise to the question whether the power of the future can reach also the past and connect it in wholeness with our present. If, as Ernst Bloch says, the key to human existence is to be found in the hopes which man holds for the future state of humanity and the world, then we ought to use this key to reopen the door to the message of Jesus. For Jesus' Father was the God of hope, who was about to keep his promises, to fulfill the hopes of mankind, by coming with his kingdom in the immediate future. If Christians today are to speak of God in any meaningful way, they must do it at the point where the promises of the God of history are revealed in Jesus as the answer to the truest and deepest hopes of mankind for fulfillment.

The question of the identity of God must become liberated today from all the counterfeit answers in the Christian tradition. When the word "God" falls on our ears like a big thud, it is primarily not because of a shift in world-views, not because man has come of age, with his science and technology maturing him beyond the need for God, not because of the empirical outlook of the secular man, not because of the horrific brutalities of the twentieth century, as much as all of these must be a challenge to any contemporary belief in God. There are two other reasons: first, the loss of the eschatological irradiation of meaning in the use of the word "God," and second, the collapse of the whole enterprise of natural theology. For centuries natural theology had been assigned the task of establishing the identity of God, prior to and apart from his self-revelation in Jesus of Nazareth. One could perhaps add a third reason. In compensation for the loss of natural theology, modern theology advanced with Karl Barth to a new christocentric definition of God. This was an important step; it gave back to theology its *norm* in christology. Yet it did so without reaching a new understanding of its eschatological *form.* It sidestepped the rediscovery of the eschatological shape of christology in Jesus' proclamation of the kingdom. The question of who and what and where God is was rightly answered by his self-revelation in Jesus Christ. Nevertheless, the word "God" was lacking its eschatological orientation and its definite connection with the question of man's hope for the future. Karl Barth rejected every form of natural theology, even in the restricted sense of raising the question of God out of man's awareness of his own radical questionability.

The eschatological frame of God's self-definition in Jesus of Nazareth was replaced already in the ancient church by Hellenistic ontology. In this framework God revealed himself everywhere through the Logos in the world and in human existence. In Jesus of Nazareth he revealed himself more particularly as the Logos in the flesh. The basic pattern prevailed in the church's thinking in some form or other until modern times. The identity of God could be known apart from Jesus, apart from the history of Israel, by some form of natural theology. Classical Christian theology made a great investment in natural theology. This Hellenized form of natural theology, which can tell us who and what God is in advance of his own self-definition in the eschatological history of the Messiah Jesus, has collapsed. The "death of God" theology is, in one respect, only drawing out the more painful implications of this collapse.

What does the collapse of natural theology mean? It does not mean merely that the classical proofs of the existence of God have lost their argumentative force. It means rather that the classical media of general revelation, apart from God's self-definition in Jesus of Nazareth, are no longer felt to mediate knowledge of God. Ever since Kant, the media of a general revelation of God through the Logos in the world and in man have been getting less and less numenous and luminous. Even the question of the existence of God, let alone his divine attributes, is not clearly answered through the traditional channels of natural theology. Take nature, for instance. If once it communicated something stirringly suggestive to man about God, now it is quite exclusively the field for the experimental and controlling techniques of natural science. The heavens may still declare the glory of God, but the God whose glory they declare is not first identified by looking into a telescope. Theology at first resisted the prospect of losing access to God from the world of nature but then gave up in face of the overwhelming success of science. With nature gone, theology turned hopefully to history, as if there it could find, so to speak, the footprints of God in the sands of the past. History fell victim to the science of historiography under the aegis of a positivism which disencumbered itself of any God-hypothesis to explain historical causality and historical contingency. In its hands the facts of history become as dumb—Godward—as the phenomena of nature. The historian did not see God or the slightest trace of a God acting in history. God was no longer the real bearer of history; man was! Historical events, movements, and epochs can be understood, if at all, only as stories about man.

If theology loses history as a medium of the knowledge of God, along with the loss of nature, then the route of knowledge from the world to God is totally blocked. But there remains another way, from the inner experience of the self to God. God may be known immediately in the self, in the depths of subjective feeling. For some time this seemed to be an invulnerable arena. The word "God" was explicated by man's feeling of absolute dependence, to use Schleiermacher's term, or man's sense of the numinous, in the nonrational feelings of awe, dread, and fascination (Rudolf Otto). But soon the science of psychology placed its web of interpretation over these feelings and proceeded to explain every response without reference to the stimulus of

God. When such feelings become overactive, the common opinion is that they should be taken to the psychoanalyst and that a healthy man ought to be cured of them.

By the same token, the moral dimension of human subjectivity need not be a medium of the knowledge of God. For a while it was hoped that the undeniable datum of conscience, the immediacy of the moral imperative, of the experience of oughtness or thou-shaltness, would be the divine *carte d'identité.*[1] But we know what happened. As cultural anthropology analyzed the moral systems of mankind, it proceeded without the assumption of an unconditioned element underlying the relativities of experience. A Kantian moral proof of God would be no more successful than the classical and ontological and cosmological proofs, so far as these proofs are expected to establish the existence of God and therewith his identity prior to his self-revelation in Jesus of Nazareth. The death of natural theology signifies that its traditional channels of communication are no longer giving us knowledge of who and what God is—or even if he exists for sure.

The collapse of natural theology, however, does not mean that none of its classical functions can survive. A "new style natural theology" is needed as a dimension within any Christian theology that bases itself on the self-revelation of God in Jesus of Nazareth. To be sure, it ought not create an image of God alongside of the history of God in Jesus the Messiah. That would after all be an idol worthy of destruction. Such a god would be an extension of the world or of the self. Such a god is always a boring succedaneum for the living God in whose name the first work of demythologization was done by the prophets of Yahweh. In spite of all that, however, natural theology is not irrelevant so far as it deals with the conditions in man and his word which give rise to the question of God. Nature, history, moral conscience, and numinous experience mediate an awareness of their own lack and their openness to a power which can promise unity, wholeness, and fulfillment beyond negativity. Natural theology today is a doctrine not of God, of his being and nature, but of man in quest of his own identity and meaning, of the future of humanity and of the world. Man cannot cease asking the question of God. It is not natural for man to be an atheist! Christian theology must not stiffen to the point that its own premises place it at odds with the promises of God which have the needs and hopes of man in view. In asking the question of God, man will continually project images of reality, dream dreams, or make myths which purport to give an ultimate answer. Not these answers, but the conditions which give rise to the question, are of interest to a Christian natural theology.[2] Without an awareness of these

---

[1] ["identification card."]

[2] It is an open question for me how to take the measure of John B. Cobb's book *A Christian Natural Theology* (Westminster Press, 1965), with respect to the task of systematic theology today. What is not yet clear to me is the character and the content of the theology in the light of which Cobb's own construction of Whiteheadian natural theology might be called "Christian." What makes it "Christian"? It might even seem that this "Christian natural theology" could stand by itself, without need of any supplementation, and therefore be taken, contrary to Cobb's intention, as a substitute for a genuinely Christian theology based on the revelatory history of God in the person of Jesus of Nazareth. Can it not be said of Whitehead as surely as of Heidegger

conditions, the promises of God are spoken into a void. If man does not hope or need to hope for the coming of God, then what sense does it make for anyone to speak of God? Natural theology cannot tell us who and what God is, but it can trace out the contexts and conditions in human existence and in the world which correlate to the meaning of the word "God" when it is used. By way of natural theology we can establish the necessity, that is, the fundamental humanness, of the question of God, even though there is no longer any way of demonstrating the existence and nature of God apart from his self-revelation in Jesus of Nazareth.

If there are no needs in man and his world which still cry out to be filled, or if all needs can adequately be filled by man, then either God has become obsolete or the promised kingdom of total fulfillment has already arrived. Then not even the question of God will arise. The meaning of asking a question presupposes the need for an answer, that is, an awareness of a lack that needs to be filled. There are some theologians today who are trying to continue to talk about God while at the same time alleging that their God-talk is unrelated to any *needs* in man and his world. They have been frightened away from speaking of needs by Bonhoeffer's warning against the "God of the gaps." Any God who is invoked as the answer to human need is irrelevant in a world come of age. So they say. But is that really so? Presumably man no longer has any needs which he cannot handle. But while it is easy to say that, to the accompaniment of a loud chorus of voices chanting the slogans of the later Bonhoeffer, these same theologians have not made any headway at all in showing what sense it makes to speak of God. They may continue to speak of God for a while out of force of habit, but when the habit wears thin and they become inflated with the sense of having no longer any need for God, they will land, in effect, in the same camp with those who say "God is dead" or call the word literally non-sense.

In our view, the classical proofs of God may continue to stand as exemplary evidence of the power of the question of God. The media through which a general knowledge of God was once derived may thus still mediate the question of God in the form of the questionableness of all reality and of human existence. Does this mean that apart from Jesus there is no knowledge of God? There are, of course, many *claims* to the knowledge of God apart from his self-definition in Jesus of Nazareth, as the God "who gives life to the dead and calls into existence the things that do not exist."[3] But there is no knowledge of God, and no acceptable claim to the knowledge of God, derived from natural theology or other religions, on the foundations of which Christian theology can build its own doctrine of God. The Christian

---

that what we have is as much a "secularized Christian theology" as a "Christian natural theology"? Is the Whiteheadian scheme, furthermore, one in which the *eschatological* dimension of reality as history and the future-oriented character of man as a hoping creature can adequately be brought to expression? In principle I agree with the need for something that could be called "a Christian natural theology," though the phrase itself does not enchant me; however, I am not yet in fact able to recognize that what Cobb has found in Whitehead is what we need.

[3]Rom. 4:17.

doctrine of God stands or falls with God's self-identification in Jesus of Nazareth. This does not place the knowledge of God in strange isolation from all other reality. The *question* of God is not first mediated through an encounter with Christ. What is claimed, however, is that he is the sole medium through which God reveals himself as the finally valid *answer*. Jesus the Messiah is the exclusive medium of the divine self-revelation as the eschatological event of salvation. As the eschatological event he is the One in whom the final destiny of each individual and the ultimate future of all reality are represented. The meaning of inquiring after God and an understanding of what it means to speak of God can be reached by searching the human condition. But if Jesus of Nazareth is the *self*-revelation of God, then this is the eschatological event after which there need not be another such revelation of God. Jesus the Messiah is our hope because he is our future; he is our future as the eschatological event.

When Christians speak of God, they do not expect to be understood only by those who already believe. That would render preaching and verbal witness completely pointless. They expect others to be able to *understand* what they mean by the word "God," even though an *acceptance* of the truth of their assertions might come only later—coinciding with the act of faith. The task of natural theology is to enlarge the sphere of understanding so that when Christians proclaim God's identity in Jesus of Nazareth, the word "God" might carry some meaning between persons who do not yet share the same faith. By pointing out the phenomenon of hope in human existence, and by locating the essence of religion in the human question of the future of hope, we have achieved a possible starting point for a new type of natural theology. The great hopes of mankind may be embraced by the promises of the God of Israel, as they converge on Jesus' announcement of the impending future of God's kingdom. A person moved by the question of hope for the future may discover that biblical faith in God speaks that same language. This is the language of promise and future, of hope and fulfillment. As long as man has something to hope for, the message of the promise of fulfillment will get a hearing. Only when the kingdom has fully come, bringing the fullness of life, peace, and righteousness, will the agonizing question of God be silenced in the heart of man.

2. Jesus and the Power of the Future

The Christian who can no longer identify God through the means of natural theology must come to the Father through Jesus of Nazareth. Jesus' God will be his God, or he will have no God. He will still be agitated by the question of God in the form of a quest for newness and wholeness, hoping for a future of identity in fulfillment. Thus, the God of natural theology is not dead; he is hiddenly active in the form of an unanswered question, anonymously present in the awareness of a new, fulfilling reality that does not yet exist. We can no longer proceed in the old way from "back there" or "deep inside," whether the highest being, universal essence, or first cause. These gods of natural theology have lured believing Christians into a posture of atheism. These gods cannot promise or bring the fulfillment that man as man needs and hopes for. We do not already know who God is, and then puzzle ourselves over the question how so big a God can indwell or unite with so puny a thing as man. We do not have the same problem as the ancient christologists who wondered how the Infinite could become finite in the incarnation. For their Infinite Being was the God of Greek metaphysics who, of course, had to suffer a kind of ontological collapse to bring off a real incarnation.

If we bring our question of God to Jesus of Nazareth, we may let him show us his Father. "He that hath seen me hath seen the Father."[4] This is the favorite text of so-called radical theology, by which it claims biblical warrant to dispense with God, while keeping Jesus only. The text, of course, does not mean that we can have Jesus instead of his God. Rather it means that God has identified himself in Jesus. Jesus represents God to us. God the Father is united with Jesus as One who is different. There is not a unity of *dead* identity but a unity in difference. "Jesus" is not the name of a substitute for God. It is the essence of heathenism to make divine substitutes. The "God is dead" theology is a revival of heathenism on Christian soil, only blessing itself with the unction of a few Jesus-phrases. If we wish to refer our hopes to Jesus, we must see how he referred them to the approaching kingdom of God. Jesus did not draw attention to himself for his own sake. The claims he made about himself were entirely based on the authority of the kingdom of God. Jesus can define God for us, only because he first let himself be defined wholly by the future of God's coming kingdom. If we delete the reference to God and his kingdom in the appearance of Jesus of Nazareth, there is nothing left in Jesus to which we can refer our own hopes. And if Jesus can no longer define and mobilize our hopes, he is irrelevant to our future. Then "Jesus" is but an empty name, in no way exalted above all others.

Jesus defined God for us in terms of the imminent future of his kingdom. Jesus' God was Yahweh; he knew of the promises that had been given to Israel. He shared the horizon of hopes in Jewish apocalypticism. All of these promises and hopes he packed into his preaching of the kingdom of God. The kingdom of God was the power of the future pressing in upon him, and through him upon his hearers. How can we today understand what Jesus meant by the kingdom of God? Do we have a contemporary translation of this term? Ours is an age in which kings have been dethroned. Kingdom-language is, therefore, bound to suffer from this general cultural shift away from monarchism. And who would wish to revive it? Modern exegesis has shown us, however, that the primary meaning in Jesus' idea of the kingdom of God was *power*, not realm. The age of monarchy was unable to understand this eschatological language of the New Testament. The most disastrous error was made when the church identified itself with the kingdom, as the territory ruled by a divinely established hierarchy. The empire-building notions in

[4]John 14:9 (KJV).

Christianity to date stem from this confusion, even when, as in Protestantism, its *de facto* hierarchy cannot claim to act by divine right.

The kingdom of God, as Jesus announced it, was awaited as the power of the future. Is this an adequate translation? We have already stated that the main motif in *basileia*[5] was power. God's kingdom comes *en dunamei*—in power. But it was the power of God which Jesus anticipated from the future. In late Judaism and in the New Testament the word "God" was often replaced by "heaven." The kingdom of God and the kingdom of heaven meant the same thing. Power was something that came into our world from heaven above. But heaven for us today is a poor equivalent for God. As an attempt to symbolize the transcendence of God, it no longer irradiates much meaning. For us the heavens are not filled with the mystery and majesty of God, and we do not expect deliverance from above. The power which was then expected from heaven we await from the future. God's transcendence can be conceived today as the absolute power of the future. He comes to us not "from above" but "from ahead." And this accords better with the futurity of Jesus' own eschatological expectation.

When the Jews of the intertestamental period became reticent in using the name of God, they chose the symbol "heaven" as a translation of the divine name. We are in a similar position today of having to find a translation, not because the divine name is so charged with holy meaning but for the opposite reason. The tradition of natural theology affected a deeschatologization of the name of God. Its meaning faded with the loss of the futurity of its power. In addition to this, the Christian God gained a foul reputation by the established Christendom of our immediate imperial and colonial past. The name of God became part of "the cult of the absolute,"[6] invoked to guarantee the prevailing forces in society. The God whom Jesus proclaimed is not the guarantor of the status quo. He is the power of the future pressing for a radical conversion of the present.

Jesus did not offer a definition of God to which he later affixed an eschatological attribute. God is not a king in search of a kingdom. The being of God is his eschatological power. Futurity is essential to his very being. When Jesus said, "Seek ye first the kingdom of God," he fused the reality of God's kingdom into his being. God's kingdom is not something additional to himself, else we would have no business seeking it first. What God brings when he brings his kingdom is himself, in the power of judgment and salvation. The God who comes, who is anticipated, is the God of the Old Testament whose promises are fulfilled in the future of God himself. God is not other than his promises. That is to say, God is the reality of his Word, first in the form of promise, finally as fulfillment. The ancient church fought fiercely for the essential identity of God with his Word. Unfortunately, however, the dominant notion of the Word at that time was the apophantic Logos of Stoic

[5]["kingdom."]
[6]Jürgen Moltmann, *Theology of Hope*, tr. by James W. Leitch (Harper & Row, 1967), p. 304.

and Platonic philosophy rather than the Word of promise in the history of Israel and the message of Jesus. If God is identical with his Word, this involves an eschatological unity between the content of the Word and the author,[7] so that the Word is not misunderstood as an eternal self-manifestation of a stationary God, but as the Word of promise through which a future fulfillment is anticipated. In this unity of the divine mode of being as promise in history and the divine mode of being as fulfillment from the future there lies the root of an eschatological conception of the Trinity. We will say more on this later.

As a symbol for God we prefer "the power of the future" over some others recently attempted, for example, Tillich's "ground of being" or "power of being." The reason is simply that "the power of the future" is a phrase deliberately chosen to reactivate the eschatological orientation of Jesus' preaching of the kingdom of God, in which the being of God is identified with the power and glory of his rule, now pressing in from the immediate future, whereas a term like the "ground of being" owes its life to the very mystical ontology (Neo-Platonism) which replaced the eschatological framework of early Christianity.

The power of the future became present in Jesus' ministry in a unique way. This sounds like an incautious assertion, in view of the unending debate in the New Testament field whether in Jesus' preaching the kingdom of God was expected in the future or was something already present. Sayings can be found in the earliest strata to support both sides. Some scholars attempt to reduce all the futurist passages to the present, to turn them in support of a realized eschatology, or simply to remove the more stubborn ones as editorial retouchment. We cannot here recap the debate we have summarized elsewhere.[8] In general, however, one cannot escape the conclusion that the facts are better known than loved. Hermeneutical interests more than exegetical findings are often at work to absorb the eschatological future into an existential present in Jesus' ministry. It seems hopeless and disingenuous to try to switch all the tenses onto one track or another. On the other hand, the counsel of *Heilsgeschichte* theologians,[9] which has virtually crystallized into a new orthodoxy among moderate and conservative biblical scholars, that we must place the references to the present and the future of the kingdom of God side by side or one after the other, forming thereby a time line running from the present into the future, is not the only way of solving the problem of the juxtaposed sayings in a systematic conception. Agreed: it is not a question of either a present-tense or a future-tense eschatology. It will not do to overcome an eschatology that projects everything into the future leaving a vacuum in the present of Jesus' own ministry, by a realized eschatology

[7]Wolfhart Pannenberg, "Der Gott der Hoffnung," *Grundfragen systematischer Theologie* (Göttingen: Vandenhoek und Ruprecht, 1967), p. 397.

[8]In my book *History and Hermeneutics*, Chapter VII, "Eschatology and History," pp. 160-79.

[9][*Heilsgeschichte:* "Salvation-history." Heilsgeschichte theology locates within history the revelation of God's redemptive purposes.]

that assimilates everything to the present, making the future a dead end. The systematic question is this, as Moltmann has formulated it: "Does the present determine the future in extrapolations, or does the future determine the present in anticipations?"[10] It is, therefore, not enough to settle for a both/and formula, which retains the "already" of the present and the "not yet" of the future side by side in Jesus' message of the kingdom of God. A decision has to be made on how to understand the connection between the present and the future. There is a commonsense element in the standard *Heilsgeschichte* scheme, according to which, just as the power of the past has determined the present, so the power of the present will determine the future. But common sense can deceive. In the ministry of Jesus the power that determines all reality was awaited from the future of God's coming kingdom. The power of the future pressed for an unconditional obedience, radical receptivity to the new conditions of eschatological existence, and above all, freedom from bondage to the past. "No one who puts his hand to the plow and looks back is fit for the kingdom of God."[11]

The power of the future was present in Jesus of Nazareth without ceasing to be future. The kingdom was present through advance symptoms and premonitory signs of its futurity. Jesus did not go before his hearers with the information that there is such a thing as the kingdom of God; that would have been no news to them. What he announced was that the kingdom was drawing so near that its impact was already being impressed upon them through him. The eschatological day is dawning; its glimmerings are already breaking out in Jesus' works and words. It invokes judgment. A person will be judged by his attitude to Jesus who is the fulcrum of the future, the place where the old is phasing out to make room for the new. Disciples of Jesus become partisans of the future, advocates of freedom and forerunners of newness. For to be free is to have a future. To believe in Jesus is to let him keep our future open for new things which the power of the future aims to release into our present. A man will be justified, therefore, through his relation to Jesus, if Jesus' claim to authority is not mistaken. The justification of sinners and the godless is linked to the eschatological judgment already proleptically enacted in Jesus' ministry. The Messiah Jesus is the believer's hope because through faith in him he, so to speak, pockets in advance a merciful verdict which he can anticipate *propter Christum*.[12]

The effusion and efficacy of the power of the future in the person, acts, and sayings of Jesus constitute a real presence and union of God with him. This is a confession of the Godhood of Jesus that can only be made, as indeed it first came to be made, retrospectively in the light of Easter. None of the contemporaries of the historical Jesus called him God, not even his closest disciples. The power that was operative in Jesus was not even self-evidently God's. Some thought that Jesus was in league with Beelzebub, the

---

[10]Moltmann, *Diskussion über die "Theologie der Hoffnung,"* ed. by Wolf-Dieter Marsch (München: Chr. Kaiser Verlag, 1967), p. 209.

[11]Luke 9:62.

[12]["on account of Christ."]

prince of demons, and others demanded a sign from heaven, real proof of his authorization. Jesus refused to give a sign—"except the sign of the prophet Jonah. For as Jonah was three days and three nights in the belly of the whale, so will the Son of man be three days and three nights in the heart of the earth."[13] According to Matthew's account, then, the full eschatological certification of Jesus' pre-Easter ministry was bound up with the resurrection. The resurrection of Jesus acted like a magnet, drawing the exalted christological titles from numerous religious sources, giving the evangelists the means to discern retrospectively the swaying power of the eschatological future in Jesus' earthly ministry.

3. God's Self-Definition in Jesus' Resurrection

Christian hope is grounded in the resurrection of Jesus of Nazareth because through it God defined himself as the power of the future beyond the finality of death. Jesus' earthly claim to authority was not in itself adequate as the basis of Christian faith. The crucifixion of Jesus dashed the hopes which his announcement of the coming kingdom had aroused. A new event was needed to confirm Jesus' claim to stand for God. Though laying no claim to titles that placed himself directly on the line with God, Jesus had spoken and acted as though he were on the inside of God's will for the world. His encroachment on the authority of God, as the Jewish leaders felt so keenly, was a blasphemy unless his claim were legitimated, as Jesus himself expected, from the inrushing future of God's kingdom. Jesus was making claims and promises which he himself did not and could not fully keep in his lifetime. To be sure, he was already bringing eschatological foretokens of salvation in the concrete present. But in no sense was salvation realized by the poor and the meek, by the sick and the blind, by traitors and sinners, as though they had nothing further to await from the future of God's coming kingdom. Rather, Jesus' offer of salvation was a sample now, not an imitation but the real thing, of a future fulfillment of life in peace and joy, in freedom and righteousness. . . .

✳ SELECTED BIBLIOGRAPHY
FOR SECTION 9

A broader range of positions than is represented in the present volume is contained in William Robert Miller (ed.), *The New Christianity* (New York: Delacorte Press, 1967). Also useful is the collection of essays edited by Philip Edgcumbe Hughes, *Creative Minds in Contemporary Theology* (Grand Rapids, Mich.: Eerdman, 1966). Articles suggestive of more recent approaches are contained in Dean Peerman (ed.) *Frontline Theology* (Richmond, Va.: John Knox Press, 1967) and Thomas F. O'Meara and Donald M. Weisser (eds.), *Projections* (Garden City, N.Y.: Image Books, 1971). Special mention should be made of the continuing series edited by Martin E. Marty and Dean G. Peerman, *New Theology No. 1*—(New York: Macmillan, 1964–); these volumes, published periodically, represent the new approaches and interests as they emerge.

[13]Matt. 12:39–40; Luke 11:29.

An excellent beginner's introduction to contemporary Protestant thought is William E. Hordern's *A Layman's Guide to Protestant Theology*, revised ed. (New York: Macmillan, 1968). A small but extremely influential volume is John A. T. Robinson's *Honest to God* (Philadelphia: Westminster Press, 1963), which brought the several strands of the new theologies (for example, Bultmann, Tillich, and Bonhoeffer) within reach of a popular reading audience. One should note also the sequel to Robinson's book, David L. Edwards (ed.) *The Honest to God Debate* (Philadelphia: Westminster Press, 1963) with reviews, responses, and critiques of Robinson. Another introductory treatment, written from a more theologically conservative standpoint, is Alan Richardson's *Religion in Contemporary Debate* (Philadelphia: Westminster Press, 1966). More advanced and scholarly is John Macquarrie's *Twentieth Century Religious Thought* (New York: Harper & Row, 1963), a complete and authoritative survey, extending beyond the obvious figures. A useful (and often fascinating) guide to conservative and radical European thought on more specifically Biblical issues may be found in the essays and interviews in Werner Harenberg, *Der Spiegel on the New Testament*, tr. James H. Burtness (New York: Macmillan, 1970).

Among Barth's enormous literary output, two works stand as monumental. *The Epistle to the Romans*, tr. Edwyn C. Hoskyns, sixth ed. (London: Oxford University Press, 1933), first German edition published in 1919, marked the beginning of a new theological era, and his multi-volume *Church Dogmatics*, ed. G. W. Bromiley and T. F. Torrance (Edinburgh: T. & T. Clark, 1963—) contains the exhaustive statement of his Biblical theology. Selections from this latter work may be found in the useful *Church Dogmatics: A selection with Introduction*, tr. and ed. G. W. Bromiley (Edinburgh: T. & T. Clark, 1961), and for a brief introduction and summary, see Barth's *Dogmatics in Outline*, tr. G. T. Thomson (London: Student Christian Movement Press, 1949). Barth's other important works include *Anselm: Fides Quarens Intellectum*, tr. Ian W. Robertson, second ed. (Richmond, Va.: John Knox Press, 1960); *The Word of God and the Word of Man*, tr. Douglas Horton (Boston: Pilgrim Press, 1928); *Evangelical Theology: An Introduction*, tr. Grover Foley (New York: Holt, Rinehart & Winston, 1963); and *Against the Stream*, ed. Ronald Gregor Smith, tr. E. M. Delacour and Stanley Godman (London: Student Christian Movement Press, 1954).

Three important and readable essays by Barth reflecting his late reflections on the unfolding of his own theology may be found in *The Humanity of God*, tr. Thomas Wieser and John Newton Thomas (Richmond, Va.: John Knox Press, 1960). Of similar interest is Barth's *How I Changed My Mind*, ed. John Godsey (Richmond, Va.: John Knox Press, 1966) which contains three essays that appeared over three decades in *The Christian Century* and chronicling the movement of Barth's thought and activity during the years 1928–38, 1938–48, 1948–58.

Some helpful and not too difficult introductions to the thought of Barth include the following: George Casalis, *Portrait of Karl Barth*, tr. Robert McAfee Brown (Garden City, N.Y.: Doubleday, 1963); Thomas C. Oden, *The Promise of Barth* (Philadelphia: Lippencott, 1969). A full treatment of the theological movements and trends setting the stage for Barthianism is provided in Hugh Ross MacKintosh, *Types of Modern Theology: Schleiermacher to Barth* (New York: Scribner, n.d.). Essays and discussions from the formative years of Barth's theology by Barth, Bultmann, Gogarten, Tillich, and others are collected in James M. Robinson (ed.) *The Beginnings of Dialectic Theology*, tr. Keith R. Crim and Louis De Grazia (Richmind, Va.: John Knox Press, 1968—).

Of Bultmann's more theological works, his *Theology of the New Testament* (two vols.), tr. Kendrick Grobel (New York: Scribner, 1951, 1955) stands as his magnum opus along side his commentary on the Fourth Gospel, *Das Evangelium des Johannes* (Meyer's Kritisch-exegetischer Kommentar über das Neue Testament) (Göttingen: Vandenhoeck & Ruprecht, 1941). A collection of Bultmann's theological-Biblical essays (arranged chronologically and extending from 1917 to 1957) may be found in *Existence and Faith*, ed. and tr. Schubert M. Ogden (Cleveland, Ohio: Meridian, 1960), as well as a helpful introduction by the editor and useful bibliography. Bultmann's more philosophical-existential theology is best reflected, of course, in the 1941 essay "New Testament and Mythology" which, in the English edition, is published along with responses by several other theologians in *Kerygma and Myth*, ed. Hans Werner Bartsch, tr. Reginald H. Fuller, revised ed. (New York: Harper & Row, 1961). A simpler statement of his position is provided in the small volume *Jesus Christ and Mythology* (New York: Scribner, 1958).

A non-technical introduction to Bultmann is Norman Perrin's *The Promise of Bultmann* (Philadelphia: Lippencott, 1969). A series of essays by well-known scholars on various aspects of Bultmann's thought may be found in Charles W. Kegley (ed.) *The Theology of Rudolf Bultmann* (New York: Harper & Row, 1966). More specifically on the question of demythologization, one should see John Macquarrie, *The Scope of Demythologizing* (New York: Harper & Row, 1960). James D. Smart, in *The Divided Mind of Modern Theology* (New York: Harper & Row, 1965), examines the writings of Barth and Bultmann published during the years between their university graduation and the rise of Hitler and sees therein the sources of the two directions of modern theology.

For Tillich's completed philosophical-theological system, one should consult his three-volume *Systematic Theology* (Chicago: University of Chicago Press, 1951–63). Various aspects of his thought are represented in the instructive essays in *Theology of Culture*, ed. Robert C. Kimball (New York: Oxford University Press, 1959). In this latter work, one should note especially the influential essay "The Two Types of Philosophy of Religion" as well as his discussions of existentialism, psychoanalysis, and the symbolic significance of religious language. The latter concept is developed more fully, along with the concept of faith as "ultimate concern," in *Dynamics of Faith* (New York: Harper & Row, 1957). The metaphysic of Tillich's "God above God" is further considered in his *Biblical Religion and the Search for Ultimate Reality* (Chicago: University of Chicago Press, 1955), and its existential backdrop is developed in *The Courage To Be* (New Haven, Conn.: Yale University Press, 1952). Other of Tillich's works include *The Protestant Era*, tr. James Luther Adams (Chicago: University of Chicago Press, 1948); *The Shaking of the Foundations* (New York: Scribner, 1948); *The New Being* (New York: Scribner, 1955); and, of autobiographical interest, *On the Boundary* (New York: Scribner, 1936).

For discussions of Tillich, one might consult David Hopper, *Tillich: A Theological Portrait* (Philadelphia: Lippencott, 1968); David H. Kelsey, *The Fabric of Paul Tillich's Theology* (New Haven, Conn.: Yale University Press, 1967); James Luther Adams, *Paul Tillich's Philosophy of Culture, Science, and Religion* (New York: Harper & Row, 1965); and William L. Rowe, *Religious Symbols and God* (Chicago: University of Chicago Press, 1968). Also of interest is the small volume of articles, *Paul Tillich: Retrospect and Future*, ed. T. A. Kantonen (Nashville, Tenn.: Abingdon Press, 1966), especially James C. Livingston's scholarly critique, "Tillich's Christology and Historical Research."

The three most important of Bonhoeffer's works are *The Cost of Discipleship*, tr. R. H. Fuller, second ed. (New York: Macmillan, 1959); *Ethics*, ed. Eberhard Bethge, tr. Neville Horton Smith (New York: Macmillan, 1955); and *Letters and Papers from Prison*, ed. Eberhard Bethge, tr. Reginald Fuller, revised ed. (New York: Macmillan, 1967). Most Bonhoeffer discussion is based on these works (which do in fact suggest the central development of his thought), although his other writings should not be overlooked by the student seeking a full representation of his position. These include *Act and Being*, tr. Bernard Noble (New York: Harper & Row, 1962); *Christ the Center*, tr. John Bowden (New York: Harper & Row, 1966); *Creation and Fall*, tr. John C. Fletcher (New York: Macmillan, 1959); *Temptation*, tr. Kathleen Downham (New York: Macmillan, 1955); and *Psalms: The Prayer Book of the Bible*, tr. James H. Burtness (Minneapolis, Minn.: Augsburg, 1970).

For an introduction to Bonhoeffer, see Benjamin A. Reist, *The Promise of Bonhoeffer* (Philadelphia: Lippencott, 1969). For weightier studies, one should consult

John D. Godsey, *The Theology of Dietrich Bonhoeffer* (Philadelphia: Westminster Press, 1960) and Jürgen Moltmann and Jürgen Weissbach, *Two Studies in the Theology of Bonhoeffer*, tr. Reginald H. Fuller and Ilse Fuller (New York: Scribner, 1967). Many helpful essays on many aspects of Bonhoeffer's thought are contained in Peter Vorkink, II (ed.), *Bonhoeffer In a World Come of Age* (Philadelphia: Fortress Press, 1968) and Martin E. Marty (ed.), *The Place of Bonhoeffer* (New York: Association Press, 1962). The former includes a good bibliography, especially of recent articles. On the biographical side, two works should be mentioned: Eberhard Bethge, *Dietrich Bonhoeffer*, tr. Erich Mosbacher, et al. (New York: Harper & Row, 1970), called "the definitive" biography of Bonhoeffer, and Wolf-Dieter Zimmermann and Ronald Gregor Smith, *I Knew Dietrich Bonhoeffer*, tr. Käthe Gregor Smith (New York: Harper & Row, 1966), a collection of reminiscences of Bonhoeffer's life by several of his acquaintances. Special attention should be called to James Woelfel's *Bonhoeffer's Theology: Classical and Revolutionary* (Nashville, Tenn.: Abingdon Press, 1970) .

For better or for worse, Bonhoeffer unwittingly fathered so-called "secular" theology which, in turn, is closely related to the Death of God movement. Three different and very influential versions of Christian secularity are reflected in Paul van Buren, *The Secular Meaning of the Gospel* (New York: Macmillan, 1963); Gabriel Vahanian, *The Death of God* (New York: Braziller, 1961); and Harvey Cox's best-seller, *The Secular City* (New York: Macmillan 1965). Responses and counter-moves to Cox's version may be found in Daniel Callahan (ed.), *The Secular City Debate* (New York: Macmillan, 1966), and for an ecumenical symposium, see Albert Schlitzer (ed.), *The Spirit and Power of Christian Secularity* (Notre Dame, Ind.: University of Notre Dame Press, 1969).

Though many thinkers including Tillich, van Buren, Vahanian, and even Bonhoeffer have been (erroneously) identified as Death of God theologians, the two main spokesmen are Thomas J. J. Altizer and William Hamilton. Altizer's work is *The Gospel of Christian Atheism* (Philadelphia: Westminster Press, 1966) and Hamilton's is *The New Essence of Christianity* (New York: Association Press, 1961). Both Altizer and Hamilton have published several of their essays on Death of God themes in their joint effort, *Radical Theology and The Death of God* (Indianapolis, Ind.: Bobbs-Merrill, 1966). Altizer has published a Death of God anthology, *Toward a New Christianity* (New York: Harcourt, Brace & World, 1967). The title of this book is a misnomer inasmuch as the book contains selections from thinkers such as Bultmann, Barth, and Kierkegaard; on the other hand, it contains also material from genuinely Death of God or radical or secular theologians, including a full bibliography for his approach. Reactions and interpretations of the Death of God may be found in two collections: Gabriel Vahanian (ed.), *The Death of God Debate* (New York: McGraw-Hill, 1967) and Bernard Murchland (ed.), *The Meaning of the Death of God* (New York: Vintage, 1967). For a general discussion, see Thomas W. Ogletree, *The Death of God Controversy* (Nashville, Tenn.: Abingdon Press, 1966).

A Jewish expression of radical theology may be found in Richard L. Rubenstein's *After Auschwitz* (Indianapolis, Ind.: Bobbs-Merrill, 1967). Examples of Catholic responses to recent trends are: John Courtney Murray, *The Problem of God* (New Haven, Conn.: Yale University Press, 1964), and the essays in Johannes Metz (ed.), *Fundamental Theology: Is God Dead?* (Glen Rock, N. J.: Paulist Press, 1966). For general discussion, critiques, and alternatives, see C. W. Christian and Glenn R. Wittig (eds.), *Radical Theology, Phase Two* (Philadelphia: Lippencott, 1967).

The most influential expression of German Theology of Hope is that of Jürgen Moltmann, *Theology of Hope*, tr. James W. Leitch (New York: Harper & Row, 1967). One should note the sequel to Moltmann's work, *Diskussion über die Theologie der Hoffnung*, ed. Wolf-Dieter Marsch (Munich: Kaiser, 1967). Carl Braaten's *The Future of God* (New York: Harper & Row, 1969) may be the most important American contribution. A third and extremely influential work is that of Catholic thinker Leslie Dewart, *The Future of Belief* (New York: Herder & Herder, 1966). Most of the Theology of Hope Thinkers acknowledge a debt to the Marxist philosopher Ernst Bloch and his multi-volume *Das Prinzip Hoffnung* (Frankfurt: Suhrkamp, 1959). Inevitably, there is the *The Future of Belief Debate*, ed. Gregory Baum (New York: Herder & Herder, 1967). Special attention should be called to *New Theology No. 5, op. cit.* This volume is a kind of introduction to the Theology of Hope, containing many instructive articles on differing aspects of this movement by Wolfhart Pannenberg, Johannes Metz, Leslie Dewart, Harvey Cox, and others; one should note especially Carl Braaten's article, "Toward a Theology of Hope."